A DICTIONARY OF

PASSENGER SHIP
DISASTERS

A DICTIONARY OF
PASSENGER SHIP
DISASTERS

David L. Williams

Ian Allan
PUBLISHING

First published 2009

ISBN 978 0 7110 3359 7

Published by Ian Allan Publishing

an imprint of Ian Allan Publishing Ltd, Hersham, Surrey, KT12 4RG

Printed by Ian Allan Printing Ltd, Hersham, Surrey, KT12 4RG

Code: 0911/B2

Visit the Ian Allan website at www.ianallanpublishing.com

Distributed in the United States of America and Canada by BookMasters Distribution Services.

This book is dedicated to my wonderful mother
Phyllis Margaret Williams
6 November 1920 – 23 December 2008

CONTENTS

FOREWORD

The sea is a dangerous place and barely a day goes by without the loss, somewhere in the world, of a ship.

Few things illustrate the scale of the risks faced by those who work at sea than the official UK government statistics which show that seafarers on UK merchant vessels are still 12 times more likely to die at work than members of the land-based workforce. And the fishing industry is even more dangerous — crew members are 115 times more likely to suffer a fatal accident than non-seafarers.

The position for many more of the world's 1.2 million seafarers will be even worse – with large numbers working on ships that can reasonably be described as the rotten underbelly of the maritime industry.

Around one in every 20 of the vessels visiting European ports over the past 10 years have had to be detained because checks showed them to be unseaworthy. And between 2005 and 2008 the number of deficiencies discovered in EU port state control inspections increased by an alarming 34%.

Against such a background, we can only welcome David L. Williams' new book.

It provides a stark account of more than 1,000 passenger shipping disasters and offers a welcome reminder of the need for the highest of standards to govern our industry.

Recent years have witnessed spectacular growth of passenger shipping. The international cruise shipping industry is spectacularly successful. For the past two decades it has notched up successive annual increases in the number of passengers and, based on the number of ships presently on order, is set to expand even further in the next few years.

For an industry in the public spotlight, with ships now frequently carrying more than 4,000 passengers at a time, safety is paramount. However, in recent times there have been some worrying warning signals.

The increase in size of large passenger vessels has resulted in considerable concern being expressed with respect to their watertight integrity and fire-fighting protection. Concern has also been expressed about the adequacy of life-saving appliances, and the quality and quantity of crews and their training and experience in operating these vessels and dealing with emergency situations, including evacuation.

There have also been some disturbing cases of accidents with passenger ships operating in increasingly remote areas, such as Polar waters or exotic tropical islands. The marked trend towards operations in inherently hazardous areas, often several days' sailing from major shipping routes or large ports, raises serious issues concerning the adequacy of search and rescue cover, and the additional burden of responsibility placed on masters when vessels are operating in remote areas.

There is, therefore, much we can continue to learn from the lessons served up by the incidents catalogued within this book. It is to be hoped that it serves a good purpose in focussing attention on the need for constant vigilance to protect passengers, seafarers and the marine environment.

Mark Dickinson
General Secretary
Nautilus International

INTRODUCTION

This book is not intended to provide in-depth, detailed descriptions of passenger ship disaster events. Nor does it attempt to explore the reasons why they occurred or whether, individually, any lessons were learned from them or any specific remedies subsequently applied in order to prevent repetition. It simply provides the basic facts relating to, as far as possible, a comprehensive range of open-sea and port disasters involving engine-powered passenger-carrying vessels of all types and is intended as a single source of reference on this subject.

In this Introduction, however, there is an opportunity to look at the overall picture of disasters affecting passenger ships and to give consideration to the levels of occurrence by various causes and the trends that have manifested themselves over the 175 or so years of the book's time-span. It also permits a review of the steps taken in general terms to decrease risk and, where new hazards may be emerging in the present day, to pose questions as to whether there is sufficient vigilance in the continuing quest for safety at sea.

It is evident that passenger shipping disasters have not occurred with a consistent regularity throughout the last 175 years or that there has been heavy loss of life in every case. If the overall figures for passenger ship losses for each of those years were plotted as a histogram it would reveal that more than 50 per cent were accounted for over the ten-year span of the two World Wars of the 20th century, the vast majority resulting from military action of one sort or another. Prior to that, over the 60-70 years from the mid-19th century to the outbreak of the First World War – in effect, the era that in the main preceded the introduction of electronic aids to navigation and communication – losses of passenger ships were occurring in what could only be described as epidemic proportions. Quite apart from the absence of sophisticated equipment like radar, ship-to-shore radio and electronic depth-sounding devices, the comparatively primitive vessels of those times had little or no sub-division and often lacked basic amenities now considered commonplace, such as electricity for lighting and to operate pumps and lifeboat davits or on-board telephone systems to permit communication and coordinated action between different areas of the ship during an emergency.

The causes of those passenger ship losses were manifold, arising from stranding on rocks or coastlines, foundering in deep water and collisions between ships or with floating objects such as wreckage or icebergs. One of the major causes of maritime tragedy that persisted throughout that period and which has continued largely unabated into the modern era was fire. Fire on board any type of vessel is bad news, but on a passenger ship, where the potential for loss of life is so great, it is an even more frightening prospect. The enduring dilemma of an outbreak of fire within the confines of a hull upon the open ocean is summed up succinctly in the words of Frank Rushbrook in his book *Fire Aboard*:

'Fire has not ceased to take its toll of human life with the passage of time, despite the growing pace of fire-fighting invention and technique. Indeed, so long as inflammable fuels are used, mixed cargoes carried and conventional furnishings provided, for so long must the risk of fire remain an ever-present danger to those who sail the seas.'

Today, despite all the advantages of more than a century and a half of progress in improving maritime safety standards, the risk of disaster at sea still remains. Though substantially reduced – when the numbers of ships involved in accidents today are factored against the world fleet as a whole – it most certainly has not been eradicated altogether, as will be seen. Yet, harking back to the pioneering years of powered navigation, the situation was, on the face of it, significantly worse, as revealed by the annual casualty figures for the period. Accidents happened all too frequently and loss of life and property were commonplace. The traveller at that time was to some extent gambling with his life by taking an ocean voyage, with unduly high odds against a safe arrival at his port of destination, a matter mitigated only by the fact that there was no alternative transoceanic travel option.

This situation was one of great concern to all those engaged in maritime affairs, while the wider public's intolerance of accidents at sea was also growing. Although motivated by somewhat disparate interests, shipowners, insurance underwriters and legislators alike were galvanised into action and an enormous amount of effort was generated across a broad front in a bid to tackle the various factors contributing to shipping disasters. Long before the end of the 19th century, the impetus to promote, assist and achieve better ship-borne safety standards had swiftly gathered pace. Much in the way of procedures, practices or safety facilities was either developed, placed on the statute book or agreed internationally. And those efforts to improve safety at sea have continued throughout the 20th century to the present day with an enormous amount of positive achievement.

In the face of so much progress in all aspects of maritime safety – shipping regulation, crew training, design improvements and the introduction of safety equipment, procedures and technology – it would be reasonable to have expected that disasters involving ships, and in particular passenger ships, would have been all but eradicated, notwithstanding, of course, the unpredictable nature of the elements. However, the evidence shows that this is not the case. If anything, the situation has gradually worsened. Over the past 25 to 30 years alone there have been, on average, three or more major disasters involving passenger ships every year, in some cases with extraordinarily high loss of life. Among them is one disaster that ranks as the worst ever to occur in peacetime, measured by the number of its victims.

Earlier, observations were made based on the spread of occurrence of passenger ship disasters (numbers of ships sunk) over the entire 175 years of this book by plotting total losses annually. If this data had superimposed over it the severity figures (numbers of human casualties) for each year, a rather different picture would be revealed. Ignoring for now the extraordinary wartime losses, the distribution and scale of the peacetime risk by period will be seen to have changed. Where in the early days of passenger shipping the losses were attritional – many in number but, apart from certain exceptional cases, generally limited in severity, even in the event of total loss of the entire ship – today the numbers of losses are much lower but when disasters occur they quite often have the potential to be catastrophic. So what has gone wrong?

As stated earlier, this book deals with passenger-carrying vessels of all types. Today, there are two distinct types of ship in service having that function, each of which stands out as being vulnerable to a unique set of hazards. They are the large cruise ships (both purpose-built and the residue of converted scheduled-service passenger liners) and the roll-on roll-off (ro-ro or ro-pax) vehicle/passenger ferries. A combined total of more than 80 of these vessel types have come to grief in major disasters since 1975. Collectively they have accounted for more than 18,000 deaths, a massive loss of life.

The majority of the recent losses have involved vehicle/passenger ferries, with vessels registered under certain flags, such as Greece, Indonesia and the Philippines, featuring most prominently. Nevertheless, the particular vulnerability of this type of vessel, wherever it is operated, is a major cause of concern.

While the spotlight may be on ferry-type vessels, the incidents involving cruise ships should not be ignored simply because, by comparison, they appear to have been less grave in their consequences. There have been countless near misses, and it should be noted that the figures given above relate only to total losses whereas, thus far, the majority of affected cruise ships have been recovered, repaired and returned to service. As to the causes to which these heavy losses can be attributed, three stand out above all the rest: fire, then collision, followed by foundering or capsize due to flooding.

Looking first at the ro-ro ferry, such vessels, designed for rapid loading and discharge of vehicles, have an inherent Achilles heel in their design: their open, un-partitioned vehicle decks. If flooded in an accident, rapid and dangerous loss of stability may result, as happened in the cases of the *Princess Victoria*, *Herald of Free Enterprise* and *Estonia* disasters. Classified as single-compartment vessels, the arrangement of the watertight subdivision peculiar to these ships will inherently result in them having marginal or insufficient residual stability if hull integrity is compromised. Efforts to improve this, for instance by partitioning the vehicle decks, would result in interference to routine vehicle loading and discharge procedures, delaying turn-rounds and reducing profitability, and hence would be unpopular design changes from a commercial point of view.

That said, susceptible stability is not the only safety concern where the modern, high-sided ro-ro passenger ferry is concerned. A study by shipping correspondent Dag Pike, back in August 1985, highlighted a range of additional hazards: their box-like construction, the high position of lifeboats and life rafts stowed on the topmost open deck, waterline rubbing strips that could foul lifeboats or prevent rescue ships from coming close enough alongside for a safe evacuation, the greater fire risk from the fuel in the tanks of transported vehicles, and so on. While the IMO has commissioned a study into the safety of passenger/vehicle ferries, many of the design improvements so far recommended have largely been obstructed by operators because of their impact on operating costs and profitability. Although the current generation of ferries operating in European and Japanese waters has benefited from a certain amount of design development in the wake of the *Herald of Free Enterprise* and *Estonia* disasters, notably under the amendments to the IMO's 1988

Load Lines Convention, regrettably their less safe predecessors have been sold off to Third World countries, having the effect of moving the problem elsewhere.

Turning to cruise ships, these vessels reflect the growth of a burgeoning leisure industry, which, though now targeted at a broader range of age groups, is still predominantly patronised by the upper-middle-aged, those persons who in general have retired and who, having paid off their mortgages and their children's higher-education fees, have a greater amount of disposable income left to spend as they please. Unfortunately, the passengers who fall in this category are generally not as fit or physically able as they once were, introducing one of the major concerns associated with potential cruise ship emergencies.

The modern trend towards increased size in merchant ships has probably seen its greatest manifestation in the purpose-built cruise ship, with examples in service today that are more than twice the size of the largest scheduled-service passenger liners of the past. There are even larger, mega-sized vessels on order of up to 220,000 gross tons, with projected occupancy levels of 5,000 or more guests. Until recently, conventional wisdom held that the key to passenger survivability in an emergency was rapid abandonment, a view reflected in existing regulations. But in a forced evacuation from vessels of this size, given the inevitable scale of such an exercise, the matter of passenger infirmity would only serve to exacerbate a situation already fraught with enough difficulties. It is hard to see how the currently mandated SOLAS requirement for a full emergency evacuation in 30 minutes could ever be achieved from those vessels with the highest passenger densities.

The design of the new generation of cruise ships, highly functional and focussed on their primary role, has brought with it another set of concerns, each of which individually or in combination could turn an emergency into a tragedy.

No longer needing long forward well decks with holds for cargo stowage, the bridge and wheelhouse in the modern cruise ship design are now typically placed much further forward than on a passenger liner. In this position they are vulnerable to severe heavy weather damage, with the prospect that this vital command centre of the ship could be knocked out altogether or its coordinating function in an emergency critically impaired.

While there may now be adequate lifeboats, as stipulated by the SOLAS regulations adopted in the wake of the *Titanic* disaster, if a ship takes on a severe list, half the available number could still be made effectively redundant. Besides this, on the high-sided, enclosed hulls of modern cruise ships, increasingly given over to outside stateroom balconies, the lifeboats are either stowed low down within the superstructure or high up on the topmost deck. The first location raises the issue of keeping and organising fearful passengers essentially within the hull of a sinking ship, while the alternative introduces the risk of a long fall to the sea if a lifeboat was to overturn, both likely to influence the degree of cooperation from those who can only too well see the dangers facing them, besides creating potential confusion.

In the light of this, a new cruise ship safety concept, the so-called 'Citadel Concept, has been conceived by the IMO under the Cruise Ship Safety Forum in which the ship itself would be treated as its best lifeboat and, by designing in greater damage redundancy, the procedure in an emergency would be to proceed to port rather than evacuate.

As to safety at sea during wartime, it is recognised that this was attained more through luck than by judgement. Fought out on the grey, inhospitable expanse of the oceans, maritime conflict not only exposed seafarers and their passengers, already facing enough natural hazards, to the additional dangers of torpedo, shell and bomb, but also at a time when rescue in an emergency was much less likely to be forthcoming. Dictated by factors beyond the control of shipowners, those wartime risks were taken because the situation demanded it.

In an attempt to minimise exposure to attack at sea, a range of measures (radar, sonar, camouflage, air cover, convoy practices and international conventions identifying certain protected vessels) were introduced, but it was largely impossible to eliminate the wartime dangers, and the safe transport of passengers at these times was more a matter of good fortune.

It is appreciated that during times of conflict, requisitioned passenger liners convey troop, refugee and prisoner complements in vast proportions, far higher than the occupancy levels of the new generation of giant cruise ships – Cunard Line's *Queen Elizabeth* and *Queen Mary* each carried as many as 16,000 troops on Atlantic crossings in the run-up to D-Day, and if either of them had been unfortunate enough to fall victim to a U-boat, the resulting loss of life would inevitably have dwarfed every other maritime disaster that has occurred. But today, it could be argued that there is a hint, where safety matters are concerned, of treating cruise passengers somewhat like wartime complements by leaving a great deal to chance.

The one thing that should be learned from the more extreme circumstances of certain wartime passenger ship disasters is that the dangers could and did multiply, rapidly overwhelming the available rescue resources. This may well explain why the maritime trades unions, representing experienced and qualified seafarers, hold the view that the IMO's proposed approach to future cruise ship emergency procedures is seriously flawed. So what of the future? Are there even worse passenger ship accidents waiting to happen?

Today, we are in the age of SatNav and the Global Positioning System and highly sophisticated means of communication, all of which, one would think, would have favourably tipped the balance where maritime safety is concerned. But there are new factors to consider that are aggravating the risks. Among them are greater pressures to increase competitiveness and profitability, calling for faster turn-rounds, lower crew numbers, less training and reduced levels of routine maintenance (including the inspection and test of safety equipment). Regular evacuation dry-runs have tended to become little more than token compliance with the regulatory requirements rather than serious attempts to expose areas of procedural weakness – the requisite lifeboat drill on some ocean-going passenger ships can be farcical, having little real benefit in preparing passengers for a genuine emergency. Often disgruntled with the inconvenience, there are passengers who are likely to give little more than a passing thought to their safety after lifeboat drills of this sort have taken place. On passenger ferries, of course, there are no requirements for evacuation drills.

The high levels of casualty in some recent ro-ro disasters also point at inadequate operational regulation, leading to overcrowding and an absence of proper manifests to indicate the precise number of passengers carried. The general desire of business for deregulation and the trend to globalisation are not helping. One example of the adverse consequences of these commercial inclinations is the practice of flagging out to countries with lax attitudes towards the control of shipping, or those that are known to have severe maritime safety problems of their own. Another is the recruitment of low-paid but under-trained and inexperienced crews from Third World countries.

Historically, legislation to tackle maritime safety deficiencies has been reactive, following in the wake of a disaster, as evidenced by the introduction of new regulatory measures after, rather than before, the *Titanic*, *Herald of Free Enterprise*, *Estonia* and other major disasters. At a time when the risks are once more increasing alarmingly, there is a widely held view in the industry that a different approach to safety is required, placing prevention before cure and emphasising the need for meaningful risk analyses backed up by pre-emptive corrective action.

There are evidently shipping companies who do take passenger safety seriously but, as one industry commentator has expressed it, 'There is today a need for an urgent debate about passenger ship safety that must review design, operation and response – in short, everything.' The challenge, it is suggested, must be to explore how future designs, safety procedures and response strategies should best be evolved to protect the hundreds, even thousands, of lives that are being placed, avoidably, at risk with potential ramifications that could gravely undermine a buoyant industry.

It may seem a cynical observation, but one cannot help wondering, however, whether there will need to be another wake-up call like the *Titanic* disaster before international safety authorities, governmental agencies and ship operators alike take the necessary action.

There is a dimension to many of these passenger ship losses described in the pages that follow that must essentially be mentioned here. Indeed, it is the paramount dimension, for it is the one that turns accidents and incidents into disasters and tragedies, and that is the immense loss of human life that too often has accompanied the losses of the ships, a matter which is certainly not raised here, at the end of the Introduction, as a mere afterthought. By presenting the information herein as it is – as a book of basic facts about the incidents – it is not my intention to degrade the human aspect of these shipping disasters. Throughout the course of the research and writing it was a constant cause for reflection, not just the scale of certain of these human tragedies but also the terrifying, painful and harrowing circumstances in which so many of the casualties perished. On the memorial to the officers and seamen of the Merchant Navy killed in the two World Wars, at Tower Hill in London, the inscription to those gallant seafarers contains the words 'To the honour of [those true men] who have no grave but the sea'. This is, perhaps, an equally fitting epitaph to the countless wartime and peacetime victims of all the passenger ship disasters related in this volume.

David L. Williams
February 2009

EXPLANATORY NOTES

The reader will appreciate that the compilation of a dictionary of passenger ship disasters that embraces passenger-carrying vessels of all types (ocean liners, cruise ships, ferries, excursion vessels etc) over the entire period of powered navigation is an ambitious exercise. The dictionary definition of the term 'comprehensive' is "being of wide scope" and, to that extent, this volume can be considered as being comprehensive in its coverage. However, while every effort has been made to ensure that the contents are as complete as possible – within certain necessary boundaries – there may well be cases which merited inclusion which, regrettably, have slipped through the net.

Moreover, because space is not unlimited, it was necessary to restrict the scope of the contents in accordance with certain criteria. These are set out below.

First, there is the matter of what constitutes a 'passenger ship' to ensure that the subject vessels rightly belong within these pages. For these purposes, a 'passenger ship' has been treated as a vessel that was primarily designed for and which routinely carried substantial numbers of civilian passengers or military personnel – as indicated by its passenger certificate, troopship specification or other recognised measure – in either permanent cabin or saloon accommodation or on allocated deck space. Encompassed within the scope of this definition are those ships which were lost while performing temporary wartime duties in other capacities on the assumption that, had they survived the conflict, most probably they would have reverted back to their peacetime passenger-carrying roles. In other words, the vessels described within these pages were first and foremost engaged in or intended for passenger transportation rather than fitted with a small amount of passenger space as an adjunct to another revenue-earning function.

The vessels of this description were generally of the ocean-going, short-sea and inter-island types but also included within the coverage are passenger ships lost on the Great Lakes and other large bodies of land-enclosed water of comparable area. Excluded from the dictionary, with certain minor exceptions, are those passenger vessels that operated on rivers or smaller inland lakes and waterways.

Secondly, to keep the contents within manageable dimensions, it was also necessary to impose a lower size limit of 2,500 gross tons on the subject vessels. Though arbitrary, this places the focus on larger passenger ships lost at sea.

However, as is often the case, the solution to one problem can introduce new problems. The potential hazards of ocean or sea travel, or of the operation of passenger ships, do not confine themselves to larger vessels and it is a fact that some of the worst disasters that have occurred have involved small vessels of a size below this self-imposed limit. Likewise, some of the worst wartime disasters affected vessels that had not been passenger carriers during peacetime but which, for expedience, had been pressed into transportation duties for the duration.

Thus, as a consequence of applying the criteria outlined above, there was a danger that certain major incidents involving heavy loss of life at sea, in some cases of catastrophic proportions, would have been omitted simply because the vessels concerned fell outside of those limits.

Although the Dictionary is principally intended as a source of information on passenger ship losses, it was also considered to be important to ensure that the contents reflected an appropriate interpretation of the word 'disaster' in the context of human misfortune. Therefore, to address these potential anomalies, Appendices supplement the main body of the volume, providing the details of certain vessels involved in highly-significant or exceptional losses that would otherwise have fallen outside the specified scope. There is no particular formula behind the selection of these additional entries other than their gravity in human terms.

Appendix 1 is a table giving details of smaller passenger vessels, below the lower tonnage threshold, including some which operated on rivers, all of which were involved in particularly serious loss incidents. Appendix 2 provides similar details for what were essentially passenger-cargo vessels, with limited passenger accommodation, or pure freighters that were engaged in the wartime transportation of refugees, prisoners or troops at the time when they were sunk, where again the defining factor was the extreme loss of life.

Thirdly, returning to the specification of the Dictionary's contents, a disaster or shipping casualty as applied here was any case of Actual Total Loss or Constructive Total Loss (see the Glossary of Terms) occasioned by all causes whether of a natural, accidental, deliberate or military origin. Included among the qualifying vessels are certain vessels that were judged through the extent of the damage they had sustained to be Constructive Total Losses but which were rescued from demolition for a variety of reasons, undergoing extreme, often punitively expensive reconstruction in order to perform continued service, sometimes in a quite different, non-passenger, capacity.

The format of each entry in the main section of the dictionary, as applicable and where known, is as follows:

NAME [alternative spelling] (year built) former names (years); owners, country
Temporary name bestowed in wartime
Passenger numbers (normal employment) and number of accommodation classes
Gross tonnage; length overall (loa) or length between perpendiculars (lbp) and beam in feet (metres)
Builder, shipyard location and (yard number)
Engine type, number of screws

Following the technical information for each entry is a concise description of the loss event, giving the date, cause and location of the loss with, where known, the position in degrees of latitude and longitude. Also stated, where known, are the number of persons on board at the time of the disaster and the number of survivors, either as total figures or split between passengers and crew.

With reference to the various content elements, the following points should be borne in mind:
The date of a loss can be different according to where in the world it was reported. In most cases, with few exceptions, the dates given are those recorded in British official documents.
In some cases, ships were lost through multiple causes, for instance an engine-room explosion starting a fire which gutted the ship causing it to founder. Where known, all

contributory causes have been identified, beginning with the initial cause.

For some incidents, there are discrepancies as to the numbers of victims and survivors, even between different official records. Effort has been made to try to provide definitive figures. However, where this has not been possible, the figures from conflicting sources have been provided.

With reference to the alternative spellings of ship's names – the first line of the technical block – this refers primarily to certain Japanese passenger ships lost during World War Two. As the result of the adoption of the Romaji system of phonetic transliteration (the method by which the sounds of the spoken Japanese are expressed using the letters of the Greek alphabet) during the 1930s, some names, while they retained their original pronunciation, were spelt differently on the ship's themselves, eg: *Fuji Maru* became *Huzi Maru*, *Chichibu Maru* became *Titibu Maru*, etc. In the entries in this Dictionary, in order to assist correct identification, the pre-1937 spelling has been used in all cases with, where applicable, the modified version alongside in brackets, eg: *Fuji [Huzi] Maru*. The same applies to the names of certain Russian ships where the conversion from the Cyrillic to Greek alphabets has rendered alternative spellings.

All distances stated in the descriptions of incidents are expressed in nautical miles.

It should be noted with regard to wartime losses that, due to the circumstances, reports of casualty numbers were imprecise and figures vary considerably from source to source. Those quoted have been either drawn from reliable sources or have been calculated using details extracted from contemporary reports or other published sources that themselves have drawn from original documents.

ABBREVIATIONS

ft	feet
grt	gross registered tonnage
lbp	length between perpendiculars
loa	length overall
LP	Low Pressure
m	metres

GLOSSARY OF TERMS

These definitions have been compiled by reference to the section on shipping, insurance and legal terms in the Lloyds Nautical Year Book; also to "The Oxford Companion to Ships and the Sea" by Peter Kemp (Oxford University Press, 1976)

Actual Total Loss: A marine insurance term which can relate to four situations:
(1) when the vessel is completely destroyed
(2) when the owner is irretrievably deprived of the vessel
(3) when the vessel is changed in character to such a degree that it can no longer be said to be the vessel insured by the policy
(4) when the vessel is recorded as 'Missing' at Lloyds

Beyond Economic Recovery (BER): Synonymous with 'Constructive Total Loss' (qv)

Capsize: A ship has capsized when it has upset or overturned at sea or in harbour. In general the term is normally applied to natural causes such as high winds or heavy seas but it also refers to human error in such cases as faulty stowage of cargo or during fire-fighting operations which may cause a ship to become unstable or top-heavy and thus overturn. Flooded ships that settle on the bottom on an even keel are not considered to have capsized.

Constructive Total Loss: (CTL) A marine insurance term which indicates that, in order to prevent an Actual Loss, it would be necessary to incur an expenditure which would exceed the saved value of the vessel. The term also applies to situations where
(1) the vessel is lost and recovery is unlikely
(2) an Actual Loss appears to be unavoidable

Founder: A ship has foundered when it sinks at sea by the complete flooding of its hull either through springing a leak, being overwhelmed by weather or through striking an object which has compromised hull integrity. The wreck of a foundered ship is completely submerged.

Missing: A ship is deemed to be 'Missing' when, following extensive but unfruitful inquiries as to its whereabouts, it is officially posted as 'Missing' at Lloyds of London. It is then considered to be an Actual Total Loss having no known cause or explanation.

Scuttle: A ship is scuttled when it is deliberately sunk by opening her seacocks or by blowing holes in her bottom with explosive charges so that it fills with water. A ship may be scuttled in wartime to avoid capture or to act as a block-ship obstructing a harbour entrance. A ship may also be scuttled for reasons of insurance fraud.

Strand: A ship has stranded when it is driven ashore or on to a shoal by force of the weather. A stranded ship, though flooded, is not generally completely submerged but, if it is, the wreck will be visible at the lowest level of the tide.

Wreck: A wreck is the remains of the hull of a ship which has become an Actual Total Loss through stress of weather, stranding, collision or any other cause, whether it lies on the bottom of the sea or on the shore.

The terms 'Fire' and 'Collision' have not been defined here as they are self-explanatory. Suffice to say that the former can be caused by either the accidental or deliberate ignition of flammable materials or by an onboard explosion either originating in the engines or as an act of sabotage. A ship may also be engulfed by flames from a fire that has spread from a shore installation. Collisions include incidents where a ship strikes another ship – either manned or a derelict (an abandoned ship) – or where a ship strikes some other floating object such as an iceberg or a large piece of flotsam.

ABESSINIA (1900) Hamburg Amerika Line, Germany

5,753grt; 451ft (137.8m) lbp x 52ft (15.9m) beam
Passenger numbers not known
Palmers, Jarrow (Yard No 746)
Triple-expansion steam reciprocating, single screw
The passenger steamer *Abessinia* was lost on 3 September 1921. She ran onto the Knavestone Rock in the Farne Islands, Northumberland, close to the Longstone lighthouse, and was stranded. At the time she was en route to Germany to surrender to the Allied powers, having been interned in Chile since 1917.
Casualties: not known

ABKHAZIA [ABHAZIJA] (1927) Black Sea Shipping Co (Sovtorgflot), USSR

4,727grt; 354ft (107.9m) loa x 51ft (15.5m) beam
450 passengers
Baltic Shipbuilding & Engineering Works, Leningrad
(Yard No not known)
Motor-ship, twin screws
The Soviet-flag short-sea passenger ship *Abkhazia* was bombed and sunk by German aircraft in Suharnoj Bay, at Sevastopol in the Ukraine on 10 June 1942. The wreck, lying close inshore, was later cleared.
Casualties: not known

The wreck of the Russian passenger ship *Abkhazia* [*Abhazija*] sunk in Suharnoj Bay, near Sevastopol, in the Crimea. *Infoflot*

ABOSSO (1912) Elder Dempster Line, UK

7,782grt; 426ft (129.5m) loa x 57ft (17.4m) beam
400 passengers in two classes
Harland & Wolff, Belfast (Yard No 430)
Quadruple-expansion steam reciprocating, twin screw
The German submarine U43 torpedoed the steamship *Abosso* south-west of Ireland on 24 April 1917, while she was bound from Lagos to Liverpool. She sank 180 miles west by north of the Fastnet Rock in the position 57.10N, 14.58W.
Casualties: 65

ABOSSO (1935) Elder Dempster Line, UK

11,330grt; 481ft (146.5m) loa x 65ft (19.9m) beam
550 passengers in two classes

Cammell Laird, Birkenhead (Yard No 1006)
Motor-ship, twin screw
The replacement *Abosso*, serving as a troopship, was also torpedoed, in her case by the German submarine U575 on 29 October 1942. The attack occurred while the *Abosso* was on passage from Cape Town to Liverpool carrying 189 passengers and 161 crew. She sank in the position 48.30N, 28.50W with quite heavy loss of life, for only one lifeboat managed to get away.
Casualties: 340 (173 passengers and 147 crew). There is uncertainty as to the correctness of the number of casualties, as reports from the time state that there were 31 survivors, of whom 17 were passengers.

From June 1935, when she first entered service, until the outbreak of the Second World War, the *Abosso* served on the Liverpool to Apapa route. *H. B. Christiansen Collection / Online Transport Archive*

ABYSSINIA (1870) Guion Line, UK

3,651grt; 367ft (112.0m) loa x 42ft (12.9m) beam
1,250 passengers in two classes
J. & G. Thomson Ltd, Clydebank, Glasgow (Yard No 110)
Inverted steam engines, single-screw
The transatlantic steamship *Abyssinia* was destroyed by fire in mid-Atlantic on 18 December 1891, when five days out from New York bound for Liverpool. Abandoned by her passengers and crew, all were saved by the Norddeutscher Lloyd passenger ship *Spree*.
Casualties: None

ACHILLE LAURO (1947) ex-*Willem Ruys* (1965) Star Lauro SpA, Italy

23,862grt; 631ft (192.4m) loa x 82ft (25.1m) beam
1,097 passengers in single class
'De Schelde', Vlissingen (Yard No 214)
Motor-ship, twin screw

The cruise ship *Achille Lauro* seen in her later, darker colour scheme at Piraeus in July 1994. *Frank Heine FERRIES*

The cruise ship *Achille Lauro*, formerly an emigrant carrier and passenger liner, was destroyed by a fire on 30 November 1994 while on passage in the Indian Ocean with a total complement of almost 1,000. While under tow on 2 December, still ablaze, she sank following an explosion, in the position 07.14N, 51.50E. The *Achille Lauro* had been damaged by fire on two earlier occasions, at Palermo on 29 August 1965 while under reconstruction and on 19 May 1972 during a refit at Genoa. She was also the victim of a terrorist hijacking in the eastern Mediterranean in October 1985.
Casualties: 4

ACCRA (1926) Elder Dempster Line, UK

9,337grt; 450ft (137.2m) lbp x 62ft (18.9m) beam
313 passengers in two classes
Harland & Wolff, Belfast (Yard No 616)
Motor-ship, twin screw
While sailing in convoy from Liverpool bound for Freetown and other West African ports, serving as a troopship and carrying a complement of 333 passengers and 163 crew, the *Accra* was torpedoed and sunk on 26 July 1940 by the German submarine U34. The attack took place off the west coast of Ireland and the ship went down in the position 55.40N, 16.28W. The sea was very choppy and one of her lifeboats capsized as it was being lowered, spilling its occupants who were swept away.
Casualties: 19 (11 passengers and 8 crew)

The *Accra*, with her sister *Apapa*, was constructed for the West African passenger-cargo service from Liverpool. Both were Belfast-built motor-ships. *M. R. M. Cooper*

ADDA (1922) Elder Dempster Line, UK

7,816grt; 435ft (132.7m) lbp x 57ft (17.5m) beam
331 passengers in two classes
Harland & Wolff, Greenock (Yard No 608)
Motor-ship, twin screw

The *Adda* was introduced to the England-West Africa service shortly after the First World War, as part of British India Line's post-war fleet replacement programme. *M. R. M. Cooper*

The passenger-cargo ship *Adda*, carrying 260 passengers and 159 crew, was bound from Liverpool to Freetown, Takoradi, Accra and Lagos, when she was torpedoed and sunk by the German submarine U107 on 8 June 1941. The attack took place about 80 miles west of Freetown, in the position 08.30N, 14.39W.
Casualties: 12 (2 passengers and 10 crew)

ADEN (1892) P&O Line, UK

3,935grt; 366ft (111.6m) loa x 46ft (14.0m) beam
36 passengers, plus troops
Raylton Dixon, Middlesbrough (Yard No 340)
Triple-expansion steam reciprocating, single screw
The steamship *Aden*, which carried auxiliary schooner-rigged sails, ran onto rocks and was wrecked a mile north-east of Ras Redressa on the island of East Socotra in the Gulf of Aden, on 9 June 1897, during a homeward-bound voyage for London from Yokohama and Colombo. She had experienced bad weather for much of the passage across the Indian Ocean and, just as shelter was near at hand, the conditions intensified, sweeping her well off course. The mountainous seas tore away the port-side boats and by daybreak only three starboard lifeboats remained intact. The ship was plunged into darkness upon impact and her occupants, 34 passengers and 83 crew, were mustered on deck where they remained throughout the night until morning, when evacuation of the ship could be commenced. In spite of the terrifying circumstances there was no panic. The remaining boats were then launched but lost soon after, one empty and another, with all the women and children that had been aboard, never seen again. The ship's Master and four of the officers were drowned while supervising the launching operations. Only 39 persons were left alive after these distressing occurrences, nine of whom were passengers, all trapped aboard the wreck. After surviving like this for 17 days, during which time, to keep alive, they subsisted on meagre rations sourced from the edible content of the ship's cargo, they were rescued by the Royal Indian Marine ship *Mayo* and taken to Aden.
Casualties: 78 (27 passengers and 51 crew)

ADMIRAL NAKHIMOV (1925) ex-*Berlin* (1949)
Black Sea Shipping Co (Sovtorgflot), USSR

17,053grt; 572ft (174.3m) loa x 69ft (21.1m) beam
870 passengers in single class
Bremer Vulkan, Vegesack (Yard No 614)
Triple-expansion steam reciprocating, twin screw
The former Norddeutscher Lloyd passenger ship *Admiral Nakhimov*, a war prize salvaged after the Second World War, was in collision with the cargo ship *Pyotr Vasev* in Tsemesskaya Bay, near Novorossiysk, in the Black Sea on 31 August 1986. The passenger liner, bound on a scheduled voyage from Odessa to Batumi, was carrying 888 passengers and 346 crew. The disaster occurred at night, but in bright and clear conditions, and despite repeated, but apparently ignored, warning calls transmitted from the *Admiral Nakhimov* over the preceding 45 minutes. The *Pyotr Vasev* struck the *Admiral Nakhimov*, which had held her course, with huge and devastating impact and she sank within ten minutes. In fact, she sank with such speed that there was no time to launch the boats. Her captain attempted to run her aground but was unsuccessful as her engines failed early on,

besides which she was taking water extremely fast. An extensive rescue operation involving both ships and aircraft was mounted but failed to secure the rescue of more than 836 survivors, itself an astounding number given the swiftness with which the *Admiral Nakhimov* foundered. Her loss, one of the worst shipping disasters of the past quarter-century, has been overshadowed by even worse incidents since that time.

Casualties: 398 (425 in some reports)

Rebuilt from the Norddeutscher Lloyd passenger ship *Berlin*, the *Admiral Nakhimov* is seen on shipyard trials prior to entering passenger service on the Black Sea. *Warnow Werft*

ADOLPH WOERMANN (1922) Woermann Line, Germany

8,577grt; 434ft (132.1m) lbp x 58ft (17.7m) beam
291 passengers in three classes
Blohm & Voss, Steinwerder, Hamburg (Yard No 395)
Steam turbines, single screw

The passenger-cargo ship *Adolph Woermann* was trapped in the South Atlantic by the British naval blockade imposed early in the Second World War. She embarked passengers at Mombasa for an attempted run for Hamburg, but on 21 November 1939 she was intercepted by the cruiser HMS *Neptune* near Ascension Island, following a reported sighting by a merchantman, and to avoid capture she was scuttled by her crew.

Casualties: 0

ADZHARISTAN (1927) ex-*Adzhariya* (1940) Black Sea Shipping Co (Sovtorgflot), USSR

4,727 grt; 354ft (107.7m) loa x 51ft (15.5m) beam
450 passengers
Baltic Shipbuilding & Engineering Works
(Ordzhonikidze), Leningrad (Yard No 176)
Motor-ship, twin screw

The Russian passenger ship *Adzharistan* was bombed and sunk by German aircraft at Odessa in the Ukraine on 23 July 1941. Apparently, she was salvaged after the end of the Second World War and following repairs was returned to Black Sea service but it is not known when this was or whether it was in a full passenger capacity.

Casualties: not known

AENEAS (1910) Blue Funnel Line (Alfred Holt), UK

10,058grt; 509ft (155.1m) loa x 60ft (18.4m) beam
288 passengers in single class
Workman Clark, Belfast (Yard No 294)
Triple-expansion steam reciprocating, twin screw

In the autumn of 1939, for the second time in her career, the passenger-cargo ship *Aeneas* was commandeered for auxiliary duties. German aircraft bombed and sank her on 2 July 1940, some 21 miles south-east of Start Point, as she was making her way in convoy through the English Channel, bound for London but with Glasgow as her ultimate destination. She was hit by a number of bombs, one penetrating her port-side decking and another exploding deep within her, blowing out the starboard side of the hull and killing many of her engine room crew. The *Aeneas* caught fire and the remaining 103 members of her crew abandoned her. She drifted in the Channel empty and on fire for almost 48 hours, finally foundering 11 miles from Portland Bill, in the approximate position 50.00N, 03.00W.

Casualties: 19 (all engine room crew)

AFRIC (1899) White Star Line, UK

11,999grt; 570ft (173.7m) loa x 63ft (19.3m) beam
350 passengers in single class
Harland & Wolff, Belfast (Yard No 322)
Quadruple-expansion steam reciprocating, twin screw

The *Afric* was bound from Liverpool to Devonport and Sydney with a complement of 167 persons when she was torpedoed and sunk on 12 February 1917 by the German submarine UC66. The attack took place twelve miles south-south-west of the Eddystone lighthouse, in the approximate position 50.00N, 04.25W.

Casualties: 22

Originally built for the New York to Liverpool run, the *Afric* spent most of her life in the Liverpool to Sydney, Australia, service. *H. B. Christiansen Collection / Online Transport Archive*

AFRICA MARU (1918) Osaka Shosen Kaisha, Japan

9,476grt; 475ft (144.5m) lbp x 61ft (18.6m) beam
167 passengers in two classes
Mitsubishi, Nagasaki (Yard No 270)
Triple-expansion steam reciprocating, twin screw

The Japanese passenger-cargo steamship *Africa Maru* was torpedoed and sunk in the Formosa Strait by the American submarine USS *Finback* on 20 October 1942. She sank in the position 24.26N, 120.26E.

Casualties: not known

AFRIQUE (1907) Chargeurs Réunis, France

5,404grt; 409ft (124.7m) loa x 48ft (14.8m) beam
458 passengers in four classes
Swan Hunter & Wigham Richardson, Wallsend-on-Tyne (Yard No 801)
Triple-expansion steam reciprocating, twin screw

While bound for West Africa on 11 January 1920 with a complement of 585 persons, passengers and crew, the small French steamship *Afrique* stranded on the Roche-Bonne Bank, a reef some 50 miles from La Rochelle, after developing engine trouble. The combination of rough seas and gale-force northerly winds made it impossible for rescue ships, which had answered her distress signals, to render assistance, among them the passenger vessels *Lapland* and *Anversville*, and the passenger-cargo ship *Ceylan*. All, however, stood by in the hope that the weather would moderate. Unfortunately, early on 12 January the *Afrique* hit the reef, 37 miles west-north-west of the Ile de Ré, and sank, taking the majority of her occupants with her. Only 32 persons were saved, making it the worst French maritime disaster since the *La Bourgogne* in 1898.
Casualties: 553 (234 passengers, 192 Senegalese soldiers (riflemen) and 127 crew)

France's worst peacetime passenger shipping disaster of the 20th century was the sinking of the *Afrique*, which operated in the West Africa service until her loss in January 1920. *Ian Rae*

AGAMEMNON (1953) Nomikos Lines (Dorian Cruises SA), Greece

5,557grt; 416ft (126.9m) loa x 55ft (16.8m) beam
300 passengers in single class
Cantieri del Tirreno, Riva Trigoso, Genoa (Yard No 217)
Steam turbines, twin screw
While undergoing repair at a shipyard at Piraeus on 27 March 1968, the Greek passenger steamship *Agamemnon* sprang a leak, listed to starboard and rolled over onto her beam ends. Twenty members of her crew were aboard her, together with 40 shipyard workers, all of whom escaped. The wreck of the *Agamemnon* was not raised until 1974. Declared a constructive total loss, she was broken up. The *Agamemnon* was one of a pair of vessels completed originally for the Greek government under its reparations account.
Casualties: 0

AIGAION (1958) ex-*Artevelde* (1976) Agapitos Express Ferries, Greece

2,812grt; 384ft (116.9m) loa x 52ft (16.0m) beam
794 passengers
Cockerill Ougrée, Hoboken (Yard No 794)
Motor-ship, twin screw
The *Aigaion* (also rendered as *Aegeon* but clearly not marked as such on the ship itself), originally a Belgian Marine Administration cross-Channel car ferry, was lost on 19 February 1996. She caught fire while undergoing refurbishment in the shipyard at Drapetzona, Piraeus. Towed to Atalanti, she was beached and abandoned, but heeled over and sank the same day.
Casualties: not known

The ferry *Aigaion*, formerly the Belgian *Artevelde*, at Keratsini in July 1994. *Frank Heine FERRIES*

AIKOKU MARU (1940) Osaka Shosen Kaisha, Japan

10,437grt; 537ft (163.8m) loa x 66ft (20.2m) beam
400 passengers in three classes (304 in dormitories)
Tama Shipbuilding Co, Tama (Yard No 252)
Motor-ship, twin screw
Requisitioned for conversion into an auxiliary cruiser in August 1941 and commissioned by the Imperial Japanese Navy in the following March, it was in this capacity that the *Aikoku Maru* was involved in an action in the Indian Ocean in consort with her sister ship *Hokuku Maru* (qv). Having survived that engagement, the damaged *Aikoku Maru* returned to base for repairs. A year later, in October 1943, she reverted to the role of troop transport, surviving for another three months until, on 17 February 1944, she was bombed and sunk by American carrier-based aircraft in the harbour at Truk Atoll. Her wreck lies in the position 07.22N, 151.54E.
Casualties: not known

The *Aikoku Maru* operated on the Japan to Europe service for just over twelve months before she was requisitioned for war duties. *Mitsui-OSK Lines*

AKI MARU (1942) Nippon Yusen Kaisha, Japan

11,409grt; 535ft (163.1m) loa x 66ft (20.1m) beam
296 passengers in two classes (revised design)
Mitsubishi, Nagasaki (Yard No 761)
Motor-ship, twin screw
Incomplete at the outbreak of war in the Pacific, the *Aki*

Maru entered service, in May 1942, as a naval troop transport. While performing these duties she was torpedoed and sunk by the American submarine USS *Crevalle* on 26 July 1944, in the position 18.28N, 117.59E, west of Luzon, Philippine Islands.
Casualties: 41

ALAMEDA (1883) Alaska Steamship Co, USA

3,709grt; 327ft (99.7m) loa x 41ft (12.5m) beam
324-plus passengers in three classes
William Cramp, Chester, Pennsylvania (Yard No 234)
Triple-expansion steam reciprocating, single screw
The steamship *Alameda*, owned until 1910 by the Oceanic Steamship Co, was destroyed by fire at Seattle on 28 November 1931.
Casualties: not known

ALASKA (1889) ex-*Kansas City* (1916) Alaska Steamship Co, USA

3,709 grt; 327ft (99.7m) lbp x 45ft (13.7m) beam
249 passengers in single class
Delaware River Co, Chester, Pennsylvania (Yard No 254)
Triple-expansion steam reciprocating, single screw
Built originally for service on America's eastern seaboard, the passenger-cargo steamship *Alaska* was lost on the west coast on 6 August 1921, during a scheduled voyage. She struck rocks on Blunts Reef, forty miles to the south of Eureka, California and sank.
Casualties: not known

ALAUNIA (1913) Cunard Line, UK

13,405grt; 540ft (164.6m) loa x 64ft (19.5m) beam
2,140 passengers in two classes
Scott's, Greenock (Yard No 447)
Quadruple-expansion steam reciprocating, twin screw
On 19 October 1916, while bound from New York to London carrying 180 passengers and 166 crew, the passenger steamship *Alaunia* struck a mine and sank two miles south of the Royal Sovereign lightship. At the time she was serving as a First World War troopship.
Casualties: 2 (both crew)

ALBERTVILLE (1928) Cie Maritime Belge, Belgium

11,047grt; 537ft (163.7m) loa x 62ft (18.9m) beam
358 passengers in two classes
Ateliers et Chantiers de la Loire, St Nazaire (Yard No 260)
Quadruple-expansion steam reciprocating with LP turbine, twin screw
In June 1940 the Belgian liner *Albertville*, which was at Bordeaux, was ordered to sail to Le Havre to assist in the evacuation of British and French troops retreating in the face of the German advance. After she had reached the French channel port on 11 June, she came under attack by German aircraft and was sunk in the roadstead.
Casualties: not known

ALCANTARA (1913) Royal Mail Lines, UK

15,831grt; 589ft (179.5m) loa x 67ft (20.5m) beam

1,330 passengers in three classes
Harland & Wolff, Govan (Yard No 435)
Triple-expansion steam reciprocating with LP turbine, triple screw
On 29 February 1916, just under a year after she had been commandeered as an auxiliary cruiser serving with the 10th Cruiser Squadron, the *Alcantara* intercepted the German raider *Greif* in the entrance to the Skagerrak, which was within her patrol area, extending from Scapa Flow to the Norwegian coast. The *Greif* was disguised as a Norwegian vessel named *Reno*, although her true identity was suspected and the *Alcantara*'s guns were therefore manned in readiness. Blanks were fired across the *Greif*'s bow and she was ordered to stop. The two ships had by then closed to within 3,000 yards and, just as a boat from the *Alcantara* was being lowered with a boarding party, the *Greif* ran up the German battle ensign and opened fire on the British ship, which, at that distance, was a sitting duck. The first salvo destroyed the *Alcantara*'s steering gear, her engine room telegraph and her telephone system. Nevertheless, she returned fire and, after a brief but intense exchange at such close range, with virtually every shell hitting the target, both ships were left sinking. The *Alcantara* listed heavily to port before turning over. She remained afloat, keel uppermost, for a short time before sinking beneath the surface in the position 61.48N, 01.40E. The *Greif*, ablaze from stem to stern, was finished off soon after by the *Alcantara*'s sister liner *Andes*, also serving as an auxiliary cruiser, together with the cruiser HMS *Comus* and the destroyer HMS *Munster*, all of which had arrived on the scene to render assistance. They also picked up the survivors from the ships' companies of the *Alcantara* and *Greif*.
Casualties: 69 (from the *Alcantara*, plus 80 from the *Greif*)

Sister ship to the *Andes* and *Almanzora*, the *Alcantara* operated with them on the service from Southampton to Atlantic coast ports of South America. *World Ship Society*

ALESIA (1902) ex-*Princetown* (1917) ex-*Prinz Adalbert* (1914) Cie Sud-Atlantique, France

6,030grt; 403ft (122.8m) lbp x 49ft (14.9m) beam
1,260 passengers in two classes
Bremer Vulkan, Vegesack (Yard No 450)
Quadruple-expansion steam reciprocating, twin screw
The *Alesia*, a former German passenger ship seized in 1914 and placed in Royal Navy service until 1917, was lost under the French flag on 6 September 1917. She was sunk 40 miles north-west of Ushant by the German submarine UC50 while bound from the River Tyne and Cardiff to Bordeaux, where she was to take up her new duties.
Casualties: not known

ALEUTIAN (1898) ex-*Panama* (1926) ex-*Havana* (1905) Alaska Steamship Co, USA

5,667grt; 360ft (109.7m) lbp x 50ft (15.2m) beam
334 passengers
William Cramp, Philadelphia (Yard No 294)
Triple-expansion steam reciprocating, twin screw
On 26 May 1929, during a northbound voyage from Seattle, the passenger-cargo ship *Aleutian* struck a rock in Uyak Bay, Amook Island, and sank.
Casualties: not known

ALFONSO XII (1888) Cia Trasatlantica Española, Spain

5,063grt; 439ft (133.7m) loa x 48ft (14.6m) beam
240 passengers in three classes plus 800 troops
Wigham Richardson, Walker-on-Tyne (Yard No 209)
Triple-expansion steam reciprocating, single screw

The *Alfonso XII*, a victim of the Spanish-American War, was a product of the Wigham Richardson shipyard at Walker-on-Tyne. *Ian Rae*

During the Spanish-American War, on 7 July 1898, the clipper-bowed passenger ship *Alfonso XII* attempted to outrun American warships blockading the island of Cuba. Pursued by the American patrol vessel USS *Hawk*, which she easily outpaced, the *Alfonso XII* managed to reach Port Mariel, west of Havana, only to run aground in the harbour entrance where she was helplessly exposed to gunfire. After an attempt to take the Spanish ship as a war prize, the *Hawk*, together with the USS *Castine* and USS *Prairie*, pounded the liner to a wreck. It is believed that most of her passengers, crew and troops made their escape in lifeboats.
Casualties: not known

AL-KHAFAIN (1967) ex-*La Patria* (2005) ex-*Poseidonia* (2000) ex-*Ala-Eddin* (1988) ex-*Al Kahera* (1987) ex-*Med Sea* (1986) ex-*Ulster Queen* (1982) Al-Khafain Est Contracting & Trade

4,269grt; 377ft (115.0m) loa x 54ft (16.5m) beam
428 berthed and 594 deck passengers (as built)
Cammell Laird, Birkenhead (Yard No 1323)
Motor-ship, twin screw
The career of the *Al-Khafain*, a former Irish Sea ferry that had gone through a sequence of name changes, came to an end on 1 November 2005 when she was destroyed by fire in the Red Sea, off Hurghada. Later that day, the gutted vessel capsized and foundered some four miles from Safaga while under tow, fortunately after 58 of her crew had been evacuated. It is believed that she was not carrying passengers at the time of the disaster.
Casualties: not known

The passenger ferry *Poseidonia*, the one-time *Ulster Queen* of Irish Sea service, became the *Al-Khafain* in 2005, the name under which she was lost that November. *Frank Heine FERRIES*

AL JAWAHER (1964) ex-*Hae Jon* (1988) ex-*Tsugaru Maru* (1985) Transoceanic Alliance SA, Panama

4,911grt; 436ft (133.0m) loa x 59ft (17.9m) beam
1,330 passengers (as built)
Uraga Heavy Industries, Uraga (Yard No 846)
Motor-ship, twin screw
The ro-ro passenger ferry *Al Jawaher* was gutted by fire on 20 May 1998 while lying at anchor, under arrest, in the inner harbour at Port Suez. The fire started in her passenger accommodation, rapidly spreading to the bridge area. As the fire gained hold, the fire-fighting operations being prematurely interrupted, there were explosions within the hull, which added to the devastation. The wreck was subsequently broken up locally.
Casualties: not known

The *Al Jawaher* off Suez on 18 May 1998. *Frank Heine FERRIES*

Two days later the *Al Jawaher* is seen on fire at Suez, dangerously close to an oil tanker terminal. *Frank Heine FERRIES*

ALMEDA STAR (1926) ex-*Almeda* (1929)
Blue Star Line, UK

14,935grt; 597ft (181.9m) loa x 68ft (20.8m) beam
150 passengers in single class
Cammell Laird, Birkenhead (Yard No 919)
Steam turbines, twin screw
While she was making an unescorted wartime voyage from Liverpool to the River Plate on 17 January 1941, the passenger-cargo liner *Almeda Star* was torpedoed by the German submarine U96 when she was 350 miles west of the Hebrides. The weather at the time was severe with extremely rough seas and the *Almeda Star* sustained severe damage, hit by seven torpedoes. It is reported that she remained afloat for 6 hours before sinking, which seems unlikely, but despite this there were no survivors. She sank in the position 58.16N, 13.40W, about 35 miles north of Rockall.
Casualties: 360 (194 passengers, 137 crewmen and 29 gunners)

Together with her consorts, the *Almeda Star*, the lead ship of her class, was lengthened and increased in size during 1935. She operated on the route from London to the La Plata ports, South America. *Bettina Rohbrecht*

ALNWICK CASTLE (1901) Union-Castle Line, UK

5,893grt; 400ft (122.1m) loa x 50ft (15.3m) beam
540 passengers in three classes
William Beardmore, Govan (Yard No 475)
Triple-expansion steam reciprocating, twin screw
The emigrant steamer *Alnwick Castle* was requisitioned for troopship duties in September 1914 but was later returned to her owners to resume scheduled commercial sailings. On 17 March 1917 she sailed from Plymouth bound for Cape Town with a total of 139 persons, of whom 14 were passengers, including a mother and her four-month-old baby. Two days later she was attacked and torpedoed by the German submarine U81 when she was about 310 miles west-half-south of Bishop Rock lighthouse. The *Alnwick Castle* did not remain afloat for long but six lifeboats were launched before she sank in the position 47.38N, 13.24W. However, her boats became separated as the weather deteriorated and two were never seen again. Among their occupants were the woman and her child. The remaining four boats drifted awaiting rescue, but when they were found, after five days for the first of them and after ten days for the last, some of the occupants had died and others had lost the balance of their minds. The Fabre liner *Venezia* picked up one boat in mid-ocean, while another was taken by Spanish fishermen to Carino near Cape Ortegal.
Casualties: 40, including three persons out of 25 rescued from the *Trevose*, an earlier U-boat victim

The *Alnwick Castle*, one of a group of five similar vessels, was employed on Union-Castle's intermediate services to South Africa, from Southampton. *David Reed*

AL-QAMAR EL-SAUDI EL-MISRI (1970) ex-*Al Qamar Al Saudi* (1989) ex-*Al Qamar Al Saudi II* (1988) ex-*Dana Sirena* (1983) ex-*Dana Corona* (1979) ex-*Trekroner* (1971) Khaled Ali Fouda, Egypt

7,697grt; 410ft (124.9m) loa x 63ft (19.3m) beam
622 passengers including about 250 on deck
Cantieri Navali del Tirreno e Riuniti, Riva Trigoso (Yard No 281)
Motor-ship, twin screw
The *Al-Qamar El-Saudi El-Misri*, a much-renamed Red Sea ro-ro ferry whose career had begun on trans-Baltic routes, was lost on 19 May 1994 when she caught fire following a boiler explosion, while crossing from Jeddah and Safaga to Suez. She sank the following day 30 miles north of Safaga, in the position 27.45N, 33.52E.
Casualties: 21

The Red Sea ferry *Al-Qamar El-Saudi El-Misri*, originally the DFDS-owned *Trekroner*, at Suez on 1 April 1991. *Frank Heine FERRIES*

AL SALAM BOCCACCIO 98 (1970) ex-*Boccaccio* (1999) Al Salam Maritime Transport, Egypt (registered in Panama)

11,779grt; 430ft (131.0m) loa x 77ft (23.6m) beam
506 berthed and 494 deck passengers
Italcantieri SpA, Monfalcone (Yard No 4237)
Motor-ship, twin screw

The former Tirrenia-owned ro-ro ferry *Boccaccio* was sold to Egyptian operators because she did not meet the Stockholm Rules introduced following the sinking of the *Estonia*. The incorporation of two additional upper decks had increased her vulnerability to capsize. On 3 February 2006, while bound across the Red Sea from Dhuba, Saudi Arabia, to Safada, Egypt, with 1,310 persons in total, of whom the majority were Egyptian contract workers and Muslim pilgrims, there was an outbreak of fire aboard the heavily laden vessel. Contact with the *Al Salam Boccaccio 98* was lost around 22.00 hours local time, but prior to this no distress calls had been transmitted. It was around this time that the *Al Salam Boccaccio 98* foundered. Reports claimed that 112 survivors were either rescued from the sea or from the five lifeboats that had been launched. Other reports stated that there were 350 survivors. If correct, the number of victims (see below) would have been lower, at 960, but it was still one of the most tragic maritime disasters of recent times.
Casualties: 1,198

Formerly the Italian ferry *Boccaccio*, the *Al Salam Boccaccio 98*, seen here at Genoa on 22 July 2001, was lost in one of the worst shipping disasters of recent times while carrying Hajj pilgrims from Mecca. *Frank Heine FERRIES*

ALSINA (1922) Société Générale de Transports Maritimes à Vapeur, France

8,404grt; 451ft (137.3m) lbp x 59ft (17.8m) beam
250-plus passengers in four classes
Swan Hunter & Wigham Richardson, Low Walker, Tyneside (Yard No 1110)
Steam turbines, twin screw
The passenger-cargo ship *Alsina* was bombed and sunk by Allied aircraft at Bougie, Algeria, on 13 November 1942, at the time of the Allied landings in North Africa. The wreck was raised in 1943 but it was another ten years before it was disposed of for scrap.
Casualties: not known

AMAZON (1906) Royal Mail Line, UK

10,037grt; 530ft (161.5m) loa x 60ft (18.4m) beam
870 passengers in three classes
Harland & Wolff, Belfast (Yard No 372)
Quadruple-expansion steam reciprocating, twin screw
While on a voyage from Liverpool to Buenos Aires, on 15 March 1918, the liner *Amazon* was torpedoed 30 miles north-by-west of Malin Head, near the coast of Ireland, by the German submarine U52. She sank in the position 55.49N, 08.06W.
Casualties: 0

The *Amazon* was the first of five 'A' class steamers built between 1906 and 1912 for the Royal Mail Line's service from Southampton to La Plata ports. *World Ship Society*

AMERICA (1869) Pacific Mail Steamship Co, USA

4,454grt; 363ft (110.6m) loa x 49ft (14.9m) beam
Passenger numbers not known
Henry Steers, Long Island, New York (Yard No not known)
Steam engines, paddle wheels
While lying at anchor in Yokohama harbour on 24 August 1872, the paddle steamer *America* was destroyed by fire. At the time she was carrying many hundreds of Chinese passengers, returning home from California. Despite the close proximity of safety ashore and the attempts of numerous harbour craft to render assistance, the *America* was soon burnt down to the waterline.
Casualties: 59

AMERICA (1905) ex-*Amerika* (1917) United States Lines, USA

21,114grt; 700ft (213.4m) loa x 74ft (22.7m) beam
2,662 passengers in four classes (as built)
Harland & Wolff, Belfast (Yard No 357)
Quadruple-expansion steam reciprocating, twin screw

Seen in dock at the Newport News shipyard, the United States Lines' *America* is engulfed in flames at the time of the fire on 10 March 1926. *Richard de Kerbrech collection*

The passenger liner *America* was gutted by fire on 10 March 1926 while undergoing a refit at the Newport News shipbuilding yard in Virginia. Apart from the fire devastation, the *America* developed a severe list because of the volumes of water pumped into her. Extensively damaged, with all of her passenger accommodation aft of the bridge on A, B, C and

D decks completely destroyed, it was initially concluded that she was fit only for breaking up, and this was considered. However, because her underwater hull and engines and the lower deck fittings were relatively intact, it was decided that she should be reconstructed, the extensive restoration work costing £400,000 (equivalent to around £20 million today). She returned to service on 21 March 1928, only to be laid up just four years later. Reactivated for Second World War service as the troopship *Edmund B. Alexander*, thereafter she languished in the Federal Reserve Fleet until broken up in 1958, having given only four more years' commercial service in return for the high cost of being rebuilt.
Casualties: not known

AMERICA MARU (1898) Osaka Shosen Kaisha, Japan

6,307grt; 423ft (128.9m) lbp x 51ft (15.6m) beam
644 passengers in three classes
C. S. Swan & Hunter, Wallsend-on-Tyne (Yard No 229)
Triple-expansion steam reciprocating, twin screw
While she was serving as a Japanese wartime transport, the old passenger ship *America Maru* was sunk on 6 March 1944, torpedoed by the American submarine USS *Nautilus*, when she was between Iwo Jima and the Ladrone Islands, in the Marianas Group. The position was 22.19N, 143.54E. At the time, the *America Maru* had been conveying 1,700 evacuees from Saipan, mainly the families of sugar plantation labourers. There was heavy loss of life from among this large complement.
Casualties: precise number not known

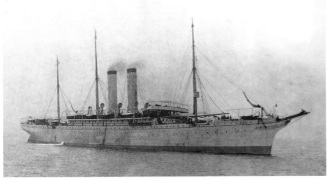

The passenger ship *America Maru* was owned originally by Toyo Kisen Kaisha. She was acquired by Osaka Shosen Kaisha in the 1920s for service on trans-Pacific routes. *Ian Rae*

AMERICAN STAR (1940) ex-*Alferdoss* (1993) ex-*Noga* (1984) ex-*Italis* (1980) ex-*America* (1978) ex-*Australis* (1978) ex-*America* (1964) ex-*West Point* (1946) ex-*America* (1941) Chaophraya Development & Transportation, Panama

26,353grt; 723ft (220.4m) loa x 93ft (28.3m) beam
2,258 passengers in single class
Newport News Shipbuilding & Drydock Co, Newport News, Virginia (Yard No 369)
Steam turbines, twin screw
After a long career, latterly characterised by many changes of name and long periods of idleness laid up in Greece, the one-time flagship of the US Merchant Marine was activated late in 1993 in preparation for conversion into a floating hotel to be based at Phuket, Thailand. Denied passage through the Suez

Canal because of concerns about her seaworthiness, the *American Star* was taken in tow at the beginning of a long voyage through the Mediterranean, around Africa and across the Indian Ocean. In the event she only made it as far as the Canary Islands, where, on 18 January 1994, in hurricane-force winds, the tow lines parted and she drifted ashore on the west coast of the island of Fuerteventura. Stranded there, pounded by Atlantic rollers, she was slowly reduced to a broken wreck, finally disappearing altogether.
Casualties: not known

The wreck of the *American Star*, the former *America* and *Australis*, at Fuerteventura. She gradually broke up over a long period, buffeted by Atlantic swells. This view of the remains of her bow section dates from August 1999. *Steven Tacey*

AMIRAL DE KERSAINT (1904) Chargeurs Réunis, France

5,533grt; 389ft (118.7m) lbp x 50ft (15.2m) beam
Passenger numbers not known
Chantiers de la Loire, St Nazaire (Yard No 70)
Triple-expansion steam reciprocating, single screw
The passenger-cargo steamer *Amiral de Kersaint* was torpedoed and sunk by the German submarine U64 on 14 September 1917 while she was bound from Le Havre and Oran to Marseilles and Indo-Chinese ports. She was attacked five miles off Cape Tortosa, about 40 miles (65 kilometres) south-west of Tarragona, Spain.
Casualties: 10

AMIRAL MAGON (1904) Chargeurs Réunis, France

5,566grt; 390ft (118.9m) lbp x 50ft (15.2m) beam
Passenger numbers not known
Chantiers de la Loire, St Nazaire (Yard No 71)
Triple-expansion steam reciprocating, single screw
On 28 January 1917 the passenger steamer *Amiral Magon* was en route to Salonica (Thessaloniki) from Marseilles carrying some 900 French troops when she was torpedoed without warning by the German submarine U39. The attack occurred 160 miles west of Antikythera Island (135 miles south-west of Cape Matapan), in the position 35.49N, 20.02E. The damage to the *Amiral Magon* was cataclysmic and she only remained afloat for ten minutes. In these circumstances, a full evacuation was impossible and many of those on board went down with her.
Casualties: 203

The *Amiral Magon*, like two other ships of her class, was lost in a First World War torpedo attack with heavy loss of life. *Musée de la Marine*

The North Sea ferry *Amsterdam*, one of a trio of LNER ships on the Harwich to Hook service before the Second World War. *Real Photos*

AMIRAL OLRY (1904) Chargeurs Réunis, France

5,566grt; 389ft (118.7m) lbp x 50ft (15.2m) beam
Passenger numbers not known
Chantiers de la Loire, St Nazaire (Yard No 72)
Triple-expansion steam reciprocating, single screw
While she was bound from Le Havre to South East Asia on 1 September 1917, the passenger-cargo ship *Amiral Olry* was lost in a submarine attack. She was torpedoed by the German submarine UC74 as she was sailing some 38 miles north-west of Cape Sidero, Crete, heading for the Suez Canal. She sank in the position 35.40N, 25.47E.
Casualties: not known

AMSTERDAM (1880) Holland America Line, The Netherlands

2,949grt; 320ft (100.6m) lbp x 39ft (11.9m) beam
694 passengers in two classes
Archibald McMillan, Dumbarton (Yard No 221)
Compound-expansion steam reciprocating, single screw
Four years after the iron-hulled passenger steamship *Amsterdam* commenced service on the North Atlantic, she was wrecked off Sable Island, Nova Scotia, on 30 July 1884. Following inspection of the wreck on 26 October 1884, it was abandoned with no hope of salvage.
Casualties: 4

AMSTERDAM (1930) London & North Eastern Railway, UK

4,220grt; 351ft (106.9m) lbp x 50ft (15.3m) beam
550 passengers in two classes
John Brown, Clydebank (Yard No 529)
Steam turbines, twin screw
While operating in the Bay of the Seine on 7 August 1944, the North Sea ferry *Amsterdam* struck a mine and sank. At the time she was engaged off the Normandy coast in the capacity of auxiliary hospital carrier during the continuing operations following the Operation 'Overlord' landings. The position was 49.26N, 00.35W. There are conflicting figures as to the number of fatalities in the disaster, the figure below being that published by Lloyd's Register.
Casualties: 33 plus 26 wounded (some reports give the number killed as 95)

ANADYR (1873) Messageries Maritimes, France

3,714grt; 398ft (121.3m) loa x 39ft (11.9m) beam
194 passengers in three classes
Messageries Maritimes, La Ciotat (Yard No not known)
Compound-expansion steam reciprocating, single screw
While in Aden Roads on 11 July 1889, engaged on the Marseilles to Far East service via Suez, the steamship *Anadyr* was in collision with her fleet-mate *Oxus* and was holed by the impact. With her hull flooding, she stranded in a partially submerged state on a sandbank. All her passengers and crew were safely taken ashore. Attempts to salvage the *Anadyr* were hampered by powerful monsoon winds and, before she could be refloated, she began to break up.
Casualties: 0

ANCHISES (1911) Blue Funnel Line (Alfred Holt & Co), UK

10,046grt; 509ft (155.1m) loa x 60ft (18.3m) beam
288 passengers in single class
Workman Clark, Belfast (Yard No 296)
Triple-expansion steam reciprocating, twin screw
As the passenger-cargo ship *Anchises* was nearing the end of a voyage in convoy from Hong Kong to Liverpool on 27 February 1941, she came under sustained attack from German aircraft off the coast of Ireland. The attacks continued through to the next day and, after repeated bomb hits, she sank in the position 55.30N, 13.17W, 140 miles west of the Bloody Foreland, County Donegal. There were 169 survivors from the 39 passengers and 146-man crew she was carrying.
Casualties: 16 (her Master, 3 passengers and 12 crew)

ANCONA (1908) Italia Soc Anon di Navigazione, Italy

8,885grt; 482ft (146.9m) lbp x 58ft (17.7m) beam
2,680 passengers in three classes
Workman Clark, Belfast (Yard No 270)
Triple-expansion steam reciprocating, twin screw
The Italian passenger ship *Ancona* left Messina on 7 November 1915, bound from Naples for New York carrying 283 passengers and 163 crew. As she passed between Cape Carbonara, Sardinia, and Maréttimo, Sicily, she was fired on by a surfaced submarine flying the Austrian ensign. In fact, as was revealed later, the attacker was the German submarine U38,

even though there was no state of war between Italy and Germany at that time. Shortly after the shelling had stopped, the submarine torpedoed and sank the *Ancona*. Her lifeboats were lowered, but because she was still moving ahead the majority capsized upon reaching the water and many lives were lost. The survivors were picked up by the French cruiser *Pluton*.

Casualties: 194, including 11 American citizens

The *Ancona*, with her sisters *Taormina* and *Verona*, worked the passenger services from Genoa, Naples, Messina and Palermo to both New York and South American ports. *World Ship Society*

ANDALUCIA STAR (1927) ex-*Andalucia* (1929) Blue Star Line, UK

14,943grt; 597ft (181.9m) loa x 68ft (20.8m) beam
150 passengers in single class
Cammell Laird, Birkenhead (Yard No 920)
Steam turbines, twin screw
While bound from Buenos Aires and Freetown to Liverpool on 6 October 1942, the passenger-cargo liner *Andalucia Star* was torpedoed by the German submarine U107. The attack took place about 400 miles west of Monrovia, Liberia, and after she had been hit by three torpedoes she sank in the position 06.38N, 15.46W. The *Andalucia Star* had been carrying 246 persons, most of whom safely abandoned the sinking ship. The survivors, who were picked up two days later by the corvette HMS *Petunia*, were taken to Freetown.

Casualties: 4 (1 passenger and 3 crew)

The *Andalucia Star* was the second of the group of five vessels constructed for Blue Star's passenger-cargo service from London to South America, the others being the *Almeda Star, Avila Star, Avelona Star* and *Arandora Star*. *World Ship Society*

ANDANIA (1913) Cunard Line, UK

13,404grt; 540ft (164.6m) loa x 64ft (19.5m) beam
2,140 passengers in two classes
Scott's, Greenock (Yard No 446)
Quadruple-expansion steam reciprocating, twin screw
After a brief period as a troopship following the outbreak of the First World War, the *Andania* resumed a reduced scheduled passenger service on the Liverpool to New York route. She was sunk on 27 January 1918 by torpedoes fired by the German submarine U46 when she was two miles north-north-east of Rathlin Island lighthouse.

Casualties: 7

ANDANIA (1922) Cunard Line, UK

13,950grt; 538ft (164.0m) loa x 65ft (19.8m) beam
1,706 passengers in two classes
Hawthorn Leslie, Hebburn-on-Tyne (Yard No 500)
Steam turbines, twin screw
Requisitioned by the Admiralty for war service as an armed merchant cruiser, the passenger liner *Andania* was lost on 16 June 1940 while on patrol in the Northern Approaches. She was torpedoed and sunk by the submarine UA70, seventy miles south-east of Reykjavik, Iceland, in the position 62.36N, 15.09W. She remained afloat long enough to permit a full evacuation.

Casualties: 0

Built for the Southampton to Montreal service, the second *Andania* was switched to the Hamburg to New York route and later still to the service from Liverpool to Montreal. *Ian Rae*

ANDREA DORIA (1953) Italia Line, Italy

29,083grt; 700ft (213.4m) loa x 90ft (27.5m) beam
1,241 passengers in three classes
Ansaldo, Sestri Ponente, Genoa (Yard No 918)
Steam turbines, twin screw
As she was approaching New York at the end of a transatlantic crossing from Genoa, the Italian passenger liner *Andrea Doria* sank 45 miles south-east of Nantucket on 26 July 1956 following a collision in dense fog, just before midnight the previous day, with the Swedish motor passenger liner *Stockholm*. Given the conditions, both vessels were proceeding at excessive speed. Despite the fact that they were both navigating with the use of radar and had made course adjustments, they nevertheless remained on a collision course. The ice-reinforced bow of the outward-bound *Stockholm* ploughed into the starboard side of the *Andrea Doria*, immediately below her navigating bridge,

with considerable impact, and she immediately began to list to starboard, rapidly flooding. The bow of the *Stockholm* was badly contracted and mangled but otherwise she was still seaworthy and able to render assistance to the passengers and crew evacuating the sinking Italian ship.

Thanks to the timely arrival of a number of ships that rushed to the scene to provide aid, a major catastrophe was averted, for the *Andrea Doria* was sinking fast and she foundered 10 hours after the collision. Among the rescue ships were the French liner *Ile de France*, the US transport *Private William H. Thomas*, the fruit ship *Cape Ann* and the US destroyer *Edward H. Allen*. Between them they rescued 1,121 from the *Andrea Doria*, which had been carrying 1,706 passengers and crew. The crippled *Stockholm*, whose Gothenburg-bound complement comprised 750 passengers and crew, also took another 538 persons with her back to New York. The loss of life could have been much higher but for the fact that so many other ships had been in the vicinity and able to answer the distress calls in good time. The *Andrea Doria* finally rolled over and sank in the position 40.29N, 69.50W.

A study into the loss of the *Andrea Doria*, published in the United States Naval Institute Proceedings, has suggested that the two vessels, rather than being on parallel courses as believed by their respective duty officers, had been on slightly converging courses, a matter that caused confusion when it came to making decisions as to the correct direction to turn to avoid a collision. Moreover, according to the evidence of the study, the situation may have been further complicated because, aboard the *Stockholm*, it appears that the calculations of course and distance were based on a 15-mile radar range setting when, in fact, the equipment was set to a 5-mile range.

Casualties: 52 (47 from the *Andrea Doria* and 5 from the *Stockholm*)

Italia Line's *Andrea Doria* and her sister-ship *Cristoforo Colombo* were considered to be among the most elegant passenger liners ever built. *Tom Rayner collection*

This painting by Carl Evers shows the moment of impact when the *Stockholm*'s bow ploughed into the *Andrea Doria*'s side. *United States Naval Institute*

Shortly before she slipped below the surface, the heavily listing *Andrea Doria* is seen off Nantucket on 26 July 1956. Her loss came as a stark reminder that, even in the modern era of radar, ocean travel had its risks. *United States Coast Guard*

ANDREI ZHDANOV (1928) ex-*Aleksey Rikov* (1937)
Baltic Shipping Co (Sovtorgflot), USSR

3,870grt; 325ft (99.1m) loa x 48ft (14.6m) beam
300 passengers in single class
Severney Shipbuilding Yard, Leningrad
(Yard No not known)
Motor-ship, single screw
Built with five sisters for the pre-Second World War service from Leningrad to London via north European ports, the *Andrei Zhdanov* sank off Hango, Finland, after striking a mine on 11 November 1941.
Casualties: not known

ANGELINA LAURO (1939) ex-*Oranje* (1964)
Achille Lauro, Italy

24,377grt; 674ft (205.5m) loa x 84ft (25.5m) beam
1,616 passengers in two classes (single-class when cruising)
Nederlandsche Schps Maats, Amsterdam (Yard No 270)
Motor-ship, twin screw
The cruise ship *Angelina Lauro* was engaged in a Caribbean cruise under charter to Costa Armatori SpA when she was lost on 30 March 1979. While berthed at Charlotte Amalie on the island of St Thomas, Virgin Islands, an outbreak of fire in her galley rapidly engulfed her and she was completely gutted. To reduce the risk of an explosion in her fuel storage tanks, she was deliberately scuttled, settling on the bottom with her hull flooded, listing away from the quay. Fortunately, her passengers were ashore and all her crew managed to escape. Later, after she had been pumped out and re-floated that June, the *Angelina Lauro* sank in the position 11.44N, 121.43W, midway between Panama and Hawaii, on 24 September 1979 while under tow to Taiwanese ship-breakers.
Casualties: 0

The *Angelina Lauro* (ex-*Oranje*) at Cape Town. *Ian Shiffman*

ANGLIA (1889) Anchor Line, UK

3,287grt; 340ft (103.6m) lbp x 43ft (13.1m) beam
485 passengers in two classes
D. & W. Henderson, Meadowside, Glasgow (Yard No 335)
Triple-expansion steam reciprocating, single screw

The passenger steamship *Anglia* ran aground in the Hooghly River, Calcutta, in the Jellingham Channel, near Sangor, during a homeward-bound voyage from India to the United Kingdom. As she was anchoring on 25 August 1892, she swung round and struck a sandbank. She immediately assumed a list and capsized. Only 47 persons, including two passengers, were aboard the vessel and it was while she lay on her beam ends that the 32 survivors were rescued by the British India vessel *Goa*. A number of men who were trapped inside the *Anglia* could not escape because of the small diameter of her portholes. During efforts to open up the ship's side to set them free, the *Anglia* suddenly slipped off the bank and sank in deep water before the rescue had been accomplished. The *Anglia* had been due to embark many additional passengers at Calcutta; had the accident occurred later there could have been a much higher death toll.
Casualties: 15

ANIWA MARU (1927) Department of Communications & Railways, Government of Japan

3,297grt; 310ft (94.4m) lbp x 45ft (13.7m) beam
754 passengers in three classes
Kobe Steel Works, Aioi (Yard No 130)
Triple-expansion steam reciprocating, twin screw

The Japanese ferry *Aniwa Maru* was bombed and sunk by United States warplanes near Moura in the Tsugaru Strait, between Hokkaido and Honshu, on 10 August 1945.
Casualties: not known

ANSELM (1935) Booth Line, UK

5,954grt; 412ft (125.6m) lbp x 55ft (16.7m) beam
150 passengers in single class
William Denny, Dumbarton (Yard No 1276)
Steam turbines, single screw

The passenger-cargo ship *Anselm* was torpedoed and sunk by the German submarine U96 on 5 July 1941, in the position 44.25N, 28.35W, some 300 nautical miles north of the Azores. Requisitioned as a wartime auxiliary transport, she was in a troop-carrying convoy bound from Gourock to Freetown,

Sierra Leone, at the time of the attack, her total complement comprising 1,210 troops and a crew of 98.
Casualties: ~254 (about 250 soldiers plus 4 crew)

The Booth liner *Anselm* operated a cargo and passenger service to South America from Liverpool. *World Ship Society*

ANTILLES (1952) Compagnie Générale Transatlantique (French Line), France

19,828grt; 600ft (182.8m) loa x 80ft (24.5m) beam
778 passengers in three classes
Arsenal de Brest, Brest (Yard No not known)
Steam turbines, twin screw

On 8 January 1971, during a winter cruise bound from La Guaira, Venezuela, to Barbados, the passenger liner *Antilles* struck an unmarked reef off North Point, Mustique, a Caribbean island near St Vincent, in the Grenadines (Windward Islands). The impact opened up the ship's hull and, while waiting to have her pulled free, it was decided to jettison fuel. It is possible that her fuel lines had also been ruptured and were leaking. Whatever its origin, the fuel ignited and the resulting fire, low inside the ship, rapidly intensified as it spread from the engine room into the dining areas. As the situation worsened it became necessary to evacuate the 635 persons, passengers and crew, aboard the *Antilles*. Escape was made in life rafts, lifeboats and the ship's own launches as well as on small boats that had raced to the scene from nearby Mustique, to where the survivors were taken. All were subsequently picked up safely by either Cunard's *Queen Elizabeth 2* or the *Suffren*, a fleet-mate of the *Antilles*. The *Antilles* herself was soon engulfed in flames and continued to burn into the following day, when she capsized. Nine days later, on 18 January, the wrecked ship broke in two, a complete loss.
Casualties: 0

Sister ship of the *Flandre*, later *Pallas Athena*, the *Antilles* operated mainly on the Central America route, although she also made North Atlantic crossings. Here she is seen alongside a quay in the West Indies. *Ian Allan Library*

ANTONINA NEZHDANOVA (1978)
Northern Shipping Co, Russia

4,254grt; 328ft (100.0m) loa x 53ft (16.2m) beam
200 berthed and 56 deck passengers
Titovo, Kraljevica, Yugoslavia (Yard No 419)
Motor-ship, twin screw

While the former Soviet passenger ship *Antonina Nezhdanova* was berthed at the Japanese port of Fushiki, on 21 October 2004, it was struck by the full force of Typhoon 'Tokage'. The ship was repeatedly and violently buffeted against the quayside until she was holed and flooded; she settled on the harbour bottom where the constant pounding in the very rough sea continued. There were only 112 persons aboard her, 44 passengers and 68 crew, all of whom were safely evacuated. When examined, after the storm had subsided, the *Antonina Nezhdanova* was declared to be a constructive total loss, so extensive was the damage that she had sustained. After salvage she was broken up.
Casualties: 0

A Russian-flag loss of recent times was the *Antonina Nezhdanova*, sunk in a typhoon at Fushiki. *Mick Lindsay*

ANTONY (1907) Booth Line, UK

6,446grt; 418ft (127.4m) lbp x 52ft (15.9m) beam
572 passengers in two classes
Hawthorn Leslie, Hebburn-on-Tyne (Yard No 413)
Triple-expansion steam reciprocating, twin screw

While bound from Para (Belém), Brazil, to Liverpool on 17 March 1917, the passenger ship *Antony* was torpedoed and sunk by the German submarine UC48. The attack occurred as she approached the British Isles, about 19 miles west-by-north of the Coningbeg light vessel, close to the Saltee Islands, to the south of County Wexford.
Casualties: 55

The *Antony* and her sisters, *Hilary* and *Lanfranc*, operated between England and South America on a route that included a 1,000-mile-long passage up the River Amazon. *World Ship Society*

ANYO MARU (1913) Nippon Yusen Kaisha, Japan

9,257grt; 460ft (140.2m) lbp x 58ft (17.7m) beam
680 passengers
Mitsubishi, Nagasaki (Yard No 229)
Steam turbines, twin screw

The passenger-cargo ship *Anyo Maru* was torpedoed by the American submarine USS *Barb* on 8 January 1945 between the Pescadores Islands and Formosa (Taiwan), in the Formosa Strait. She sank in the position 24.54N, 120.26E.
Casualties: not known

AOTEAROA (1916) Union Steamship Co of New Zealand, UK

serving under the wartime name HMS AVENGER
14,744grt; 550ft (167.6m) loa x 66ft (20.1m) beam
600 passengers in three classes (as designed)
Fairfield, Govan (Yard No 499)
Steam turbines, twin screw

Her construction having been delayed following the outbreak of the First World War, the passenger liner *Aotearoa*, intended for operation on the New Zealand and Australia to Canada route, was taken over by the Admiralty for completion as an armed merchant cruiser, and she was commissioned in 1916 as HMS *Avenger*, attached to the 9th Cruiser Squadron. In this auxiliary capacity her duties were to patrol the North Atlantic sea lanes in the approaches to the British Isles and help frustrate enemy attacks against commercial shipping. While approaching Scapa Flow on 14 June 1917, at the end of a routine patrol, the German submarine U69 torpedoed and sank HMS *Avenger*, preventing her from ever entering peacetime service. The explosion killed one of her complement but the remainder were taken off safely before she went down in the position 60.20N, 03.58W (other sources give the position as 61.03N, 03.57W).
Casualties: 1

The *Aotearoa* was laid down in 1913 for the Union Steamship Company of New Zealand but was still incomplete on the outbreak of the First World War. The Admiralty took over the ship on 21 June 1915 and had her completed as the auxiliary cruiser HMS *Avenger*. *Maritime Photo Library*

This second view of HMS *Avenger*, the former *Aotearoa*, shows her sinking following the torpedo attack in June 1917. *Maritime Photo Library*

APAPA (1914) Elder Dempster Lines, UK

7,832grt; 426ft (129.8m) lbp x 57ft (17.4m) beam
400 passengers in two classes
Harland & Wolff, Govan (Yard No 443) (completed at Belfast)
Quadruple-expansion steam reciprocating engines, twin screw

On 28 November 1917 the steamship *Apapa*, carrying 129 passengers and 120 crew, was torpedoed without warning during a voyage from Lagos and Freetown to Liverpool. The attack took place three miles north-east of Lynas Point, near Liverpool. Struck amidships on the starboard side by the torpedo, the impact immediately caused the electric light system to fail, throwing the ship into darkness. Despite great difficulty in organising the evacuation in these circumstances, most of the lifeboats were got away safely, although one boat was struck by a second torpedo when the U96 resumed the attack, killing most of its occupants. The *Apapa* sank in the position 53.26N, 04.18W.

Casualties: 77 (40 passengers and 37 crew)

The Elder Dempster steamship *Apapa*, lost in 1917, operated on the England to West Africa service. *Alex Duncan*

APAPA (1927) Elder Dempster Lines, UK

9,333grt; 451ft (137.5m) loa x 62ft (18.9m) beam
313 passengers in two classes
Harland & Wolff, Belfast (Yard No 695)
Motor-ship, twin screw

On 15 November 1940 the passenger ship *Apapa* was bound from Lagos to her home port of Liverpool with 95 passengers and a crew of 158 when she was bombed and sunk by German aircraft 200 miles west of County Mayo, Ireland. According to her Master the attack took place in the position 54.34N, 16.47W, and this is the official location given in the HMSO publication *British Merchant Vessels Lost or Damaged by Enemy Action during the Second World War*. However, the alternative positions of 54.31N, 16.34W and 53.50N, 16.23W have also been recorded.

Casualties: 24 (5 passengers and 19 crew)

Previous column, bottom: **The motor passenger liner *Apapa* joined her sister *Accra* on the Liverpool to West Africa route in January 1927.** *H. B. Christiansen Collection / Online Transport Archive*

Above: **Still ablaze, the *Apapa* sinks stern-first following the torpedo attack.** *Maritime Photo Library*

AQUILEJA (1914) ex-*Prins der Nederlanden* (1935) Lloyd Triestino, Italy

9,448grt; 498ft (151.8m) loa x 57ft (17.4m) beam
312 passengers in three classes
Nederlandsche Schps Maats, Amsterdam (Yard No 123)
Quadruple-expansion steam reciprocating, twin screw

From May 1940 the *Aquileja* was employed as a wartime hospital ship by the Italian Navy. In this role she was seized by the Germans at Spezia in September 1943 and moved to Marseilles, where, on 15 December 1943, she was attacked by Allied aircraft. The blazing and flooded ship settled on the bottom by the quayside where she remained until salvage commenced in February 1944. However, four months later, on 26 June 1944, the *Aquileja* was deliberately scuttled by the retreating German forces in a bid to deny use of the port to the advancing Allies. Raised later, the *Aquileja* was declared to be beyond restoration and was broken up.

Casualties: not known

ARABIA (1898) P&O Line, UK

7,933grt; 500ft (152.4m) loa x 54ft (16.5m) beam
524 passengers in two classes or 2,500 troops
Caird, Greenock (Yard No 286)
Triple-expansion steam reciprocating, single screw

The *Arabia* operated between England, India and Australia, together with class-mates *China*, *Egypt*, *India* and *Persia*. *Tom Rayner collection*

The *Arabia* was a sister ship of the *Egypt*, *India* and *Persia*, all of which were also lost – four out of a class of five ships – in incidents described elsewhere in this book. The *Arabia* fell victim to a German torpedo. While returning to London from Sydney on 6 November 1916 she was struck by a torpedo fired by the German submarine UB43. The attack occurred

about 112 miles west-by-south of Cape Matapan (Akra Tainaron), the southernmost point of the Greek mainland, in the approximate position 36.00N, 21.00E. The *Arabia* had a total of 732 persons aboard, 437 passengers and a crew of 295, and even though she remained afloat for only a very short time, thanks to an orderly evacuation the vast majority were saved, picked up by trawlers and the Ellerman's steamer *City of Marseilles*.
Casualties: 11 (all engine room crew)

ARABIA MARU (1936) Osaka Shosen Kaisha, Japan

9,480grt; 475ft (144.8m) loa x 61ft (18.6m) beam
167 passengers in two classes
Mitsubishi, Nagasaki (Yard No 271)
Triple-expansion steam reciprocating, twin screw
Utilised as a naval transport during the Second World War, the *Arabia Maru* was torpedoed and sunk by the American submarine USS *Bluegill* on 18 October 1944, while serving in this capacity. The position was 14.06N, 119.40E, about 100 miles east of Manila, Philippine Islands.
Casualties: not known

ARABIC (1903) White Star Line, UK

15,801grt; 616ft (187.8m) loa x 69ft (21.0m) beam
1,400 passengers in three classes
Harland & Wolff, Belfast (Yard No 340)
Quadruple-expansion steam reciprocating, twin screw
While bound for New York with passengers, including a number of American citizens, on 19 August 1915, the *Arabic* was torpedoed by the German submarine U24 off the Old Head of Kinsale, southern Ireland. Hit on her starboard side, the *Arabic* was critically damaged and she sank inside 15 minutes in the position 50.50N, 08.32W. Even in that brief period of time 390 persons were safely got off largely thanks to prompt action and good discipline.
Casualties: 44, including some of the American passengers

White Star Line's *Arabic*, laid down as the *Minnewaska* for the Atlantic Transport Line, operated on the transatlantic service from Liverpool to either Boston or New York.
H. B. Christiansen Collection / Online Transport Archive

ARAGON (1905) Royal Mail Line, UK

9,588grt; 530ft (161.5m) loa x 60ft (18.3m) beam
1,004 passengers in three classes
Harland & Wolff, Belfast (Yard No 367)
Quadruple-expansion steam reciprocating, twin screw
Taken over as a troop transport on the outbreak of the First World War, a role she maintained for more than three years, the liner *Aragon* was employed from late 1917 carrying troop reinforcements to General Allenby's army fighting the Turks

in Palestine. After departing from Marseilles in convoy, carrying 2,500 troops and a crew of 200, she arrived off Alexandria on 30 December 1917 but was ordered to an anchorage outside the harbour because of congestion in the port. As instructed, she anchored near the entrance to the swept mine channel, about 11 miles north of the GI Pass Beacon, in a position that was particularly exposed to submarine attack. As evidence of her susceptibility, the *Aragon* was hit by torpedoes from the German submarine UC34 later that very day and sank with heavy loss of life in the position 31.18N, 29.48E.
Casualties: 610, including 19 crew

A slightly smaller half-sister of the *Amazon*, *Araguaya* and *Avon*, the *Aragon* joined them on the service from Southampton to ports on the Atlantic coast of South America.
Tom Rayner collection

ARAMIS (1932) Messageries Maritimes, France

serving under the wartime name TEIA MARU
17,537grt; 566ft (172.5m) loa x 69ft (21.0m) beam
1,045 passengers in four classes
Forges et Chantiers de la Méditerranée, La Seyne
(Yard No 1206)
Motor-ship, twin screw

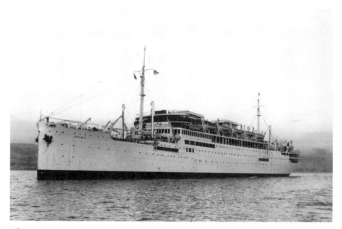

The passenger liner *Aramis* was the last of her class of unusual square-funnelled motor liners built for Messageries Maritimes' premier service from Marseilles to the Far East. The other two ships of this type were the *Felix Roussel* and the unlucky *Georges Philippar*. *Ian Allan Library*

In September 1939 the *Aramis* was converted into an auxiliary cruiser at Saigon and engaged in patrolling the China Sea and the Gulf of Siam. Laid up at Saigon on 1 August 1940, the Japanese took possession of her there on 10 April

1942 and she re-entered service on 2 June that year under the name *Teia Maru*, employed as a troop transport. She also completed a prisoner-exchange voyage to Lourenço Marques in 1943 as a diplomat ship under the auspices of the International Red Cross. The *Teia Maru* was sunk on 18 August 1944, torpedoed by the American submarine USS *Rasher* 150 miles west of Negra Point, off the north-west coast of Luzon, in the Philippines. The position was 18.18N, 120.13E.
Casualties: not known

ARANDORA STAR (1927) ex-*Arandora* (1929) Blue Star Line, UK

15,501grt; 535ft (163.1m) loa x 68ft (20.7m) beam
375 passengers in single class
Cammell Laird, Birkenhead (Yard No 921)
Steam turbines, twin screw
The *Arandora Star*, completed originally for route service from London to La Plata ports, was reconstructed in 1928 as a luxury cruise ship, continuing in this role until the outbreak of war. From December 1939 she was utilised by the Royal Navy for experimental purposes, evaluating and developing anti-torpedo nets. She was converted into a troopship in May 1940 but survived for only two more months. While bound from Liverpool to Canada on 2 July 1940, carrying 1,299 German and Italian internees and prisoners of war, a military guard of 200 men and her crew of 174, she was torpedoed by the German submarine U47 in the position 55.20N, 10.33W, some 75 miles west of the Bloody Foreland. The torpedo struck her in the region of her engine room, triggering panic among the prisoners and frustrating an orderly abandonment of the ship. There was a delay in launching the lifeboats and, with so many persons crowding uncontrolled on the boat deck, many were forced overboard and drowned. The *Arandora Star* sank an hour after the attack, in the position 56.30N, 10.38W. The survivors, in lifeboats, were sighted by a Sunderland flying boat, which directed the Canadian destroyer *St Laurent* to their aid.
Casualties: From Blue Star Line's records, 805 (243 German and 470 Italian enemy aliens, 37 military guards and 55 crew) From Lloyd's War Loss Records, 761 (143 German and 470 Italian enemy aliens, 91 military guards and 57 crew) The Lloyd's War Loss Records also differ with regard to the ship's complement, said to have comprised 1,178 enemy aliens and prisoners, 254 military guardsmen and a crew of 176.

The *Arandora Star* joined her four sisters on the London to La Plata ports service in May 1927, but in 1928 she was singled out for overhaul for a dedicated cruising role. As such, she established a fine reputation for herself between 1929 and 1939. This view shows her after the removal of her mainmast.
Maritime Photo Library

ARCADIAN (1899) ex-*Ortona* (1910) Royal Mail Line, UK

8,939grt; 500ft (152.4m) lbp x 55ft (16.8m) beam
320 passengers in single class
Vickers & Maxim, Barrow-in-Furness (Yard No 272)
Triple-expansion steam reciprocating, twin screw
On the outbreak of the First World War the passenger liner *Arcadian* was commandeered for duties as a troopship. On 15 April 1917, while transporting 1,335 troops and crew from Salonica (Thessaloniki) to Alexandria, she was torpedoed by the German submarine UC74 when she was 26 miles north-east of Milo, in the position 36.50N, 24.50E. She sank within five minutes, such was the extent of the damage caused by the torpedo. Despite this and thanks to a rapid but disciplined evacuation, 1,058 of those aboard managed to safely leave the ship before the *Arcadian* suddenly capsized and slid beneath the surface. Those who survived the ordeal held the view that more could have been saved but for the fact that the ship turned over as she sank.
Casualties: 279 (234 military personnel, comprising 19 officers and 215 lower ranks, plus 10 naval ratings and 35 crew members)

Before joining Royal Mail in 1905, the *Arcadian* sailed for the Pacific Steam Navigation Co as the *Ortona*. She also spent some time employed in the Australia service for the Orient Line.
Real Photos

The *Arcadian* sank rapidly after the torpedo attack in April 1917 but the moment was still caught on camera.
Imperial War Museum (SP813)

ARCTIC (1850) Collins Line, USA

2,860grt; 282ft (86.0m) lbp x 45ft (13.7m) beam
280 passengers in two classes
Brown & Bell, New York (Yard No not known)
Side-lever steam engines, paddles
Two years after the pioneering transatlantic steamship *Arctic* had achieved record-breaking speeds on the run, she was to figure in an incident that was to represent the turning point in the Collins Line's fortunes. While bound for New York with 246 passengers on 27 September 1854, she was in a collision

in dense fog with the French steamship *Vesta*, owned by Compagnie Générale Maritime, 65 miles south-west of Cape Race, in the approximate position 45.00N, 52.00W. The *Arctic* stood by the *Vesta* in case she needed assistance, but after the *Vesta* had satisfactorily proceeded in the direction of St John's, Newfoundland, it was realised that the *Arctic* was in fact the more seriously stricken vessel. An attempt was made to get her to Cape Race, but within half an hour the ship's furnaces were flooded and she was dead in the water. Heavy seas made the launching of boats difficult and many were smashed or swamped. Only 59 were saved from her 381 passengers and crew. Some of the survivors were picked up by the Canadian barque *Huron* and the Cunard passenger ship *Cambria*, while the occupants of two lifeboats managed to reach the Newfoundland coast.
Casualties: 322 (plus another 13 from the *Vesta*)

One of the worst shipping disasters of the early years of powered navigation was the foundering of the Collins Line transatlantic steamer *Arctic* following a collision. Her loss, together with the disappearance of her sister ship *Pacific*, combined to hasten the downfall of this pioneering American shipping line. *Merseyside County Museums*

A. REGINA (1967) ex-*Stena Germanica* (1979) Armateur SA, Panama

5,195grt; 364ft (111.0m) loa x 61ft (18.5m) beam
384 berthed and 916 deck passengers
A/S Langesunds Mek. Verks, Langesund (Yard No 54)
Motor-ship, twin screw

The roll-on roll-off ferry *A. Regina*, a stranding loss off Puerto Rico in February 1985. *Bettina Rohbrecht*

The roll-on roll-off ferry *A. Regina*, formerly a Swedish-owned Baltic ferry, ran aground south of Mona Island, west of Puerto Rico, during the night of 15 February 1985, while bound from Mayaguez, Puerto Rico, to San Pedro de Macoris, Dominican Republic. She sustained severe hull damage and began to flood through ruptured bottom plating. Her occupants, 143 passengers and 70 crew, were airlifted to safety by helicopters of the United States Navy. After attempts to refloat her failed, the *A. Regina* was abandoned as a constructive total loss.
Casualties: 0

ARGENTINA (1913) ex-*Reina Victoria Eugenia* (1931) Cia Trasatlantica Española, Spain

10,137grt; 500ft (152.4m) loa x 61ft (18.7m) beam
2,143 passengers in four classes
Swan Hunter & Wigham Richardson, Low Walker, Tyneside (Yard No 884)
Triple-expansion steam reciprocating with LP turbines, quadruple screw
After 23 years operating routes from Spain to Central and South America, the *Argentina* was laid up in 1936 following the outbreak of the Spanish Civil War. She was sunk during an air attack on Barcelona in January 1939 by bombs dropped by Spanish Nationalist warplanes. That September, the badly damaged ship was raised only to be laid up with no attempt made to rebuild her. Five years later she was sold for breaking up.
Casualties: not known

Completed as the *Reina Victoria Eugenia*, as shown here, the *Argentina*, together with her sister ship *Uruguay*, was a casualty of the Spanish Civil War. *Ian Rae*

ARGENTINA MARU (1939) Osaka Shosen Kaisha, Japan

serving under the wartime name IJNS KAIYO
12,755grt; 544ft (165.8m) loa x 68ft (20.7m) beam
901 passengers in three classes
Mitsubishi, Nagasaki (Yard No 734)
Motor-ship, twin screw
The passenger-cargo liner *Argentina Maru*, which had been requisitioned initially as a troop transport, was converted by her builders into the Japanese escort aircraft carrier *Kaiyo*, part of the work involving the substitution of her diesel engines with steam turbines. She was commissioned on 23 November 1943. The intention had been to do likewise with her sister ship *Brazil Maru* (qv), but this never transpired. The *Kaiyo* was bombed by United States naval aircraft on 19 March 1945 while she was moored at the Kure naval base, causing extensive flooding. Four months later she hit a mine. Finally, on 24 July 1945, only a few days after the mine

incident, when she was in Beppu Bay, ten miles north-west of Oita, Kyushu, she was attacked and seriously damaged during a British air raid. She was beached in the position 33.21N, 131.32E, but sustained more damage during later air strikes. The wreck was refloated and broken up locally between 1946 and 1948.

Casualties: not known

Prior to the Second World War, the *Argentina Maru* spent three years on the Japan to South America service. *Alex Duncan*

The escort carrier *Kaiyo*, the former *Argentina Maru*. *Imperial War Museum (MH5932)*

The wreck of the *Kaiyo*, half-submerged off Kyushu, photographed after the end of the Pacific War. *US Naval Historical Center (NH 85386)*

ARION (1965) ex-*Jamaican Queen* (1975) ex-*Hansa Express* (1967) ex-*Nili* (1965) Maritime Co of Lesvos, Greece

7,851grt; 450ft (137.1m) loa x 62ft (18.9m) beam
544 passengers
Fairfield, Govan (Yard No 825)
Motor-ship, twin screw

The roll-on roll-off passenger/vehicle ferry *Arion* was approaching Haifa on 20 December 1981, having arrived there from Piraeus, Rhodes and Limassol, when an explosion, caused by a Palestinian terrorist bomb, ripped through her and set her on fire. All the 250 passengers and 150 crew, apart from one who was killed by the blast, were taken off safely by small boats that rushed to the scene. The crippled and flooded vessel was beached in Haifa Bay where she remained, completely gutted, with her main deck warped and buckled,

until she was refloated on 13 January 1982. Declared a war constructive total loss, the *Arion* was towed back to Piraeus where, after a period laid up, she was scrapped.

Casualties: 1

The *Arion*, formerly the *Nili*, berthed at Piraeus in April 1978. *Frank Heine FERRIES*

Four years later the *Arion* is in the same location, showing fire damage following sabotage. *Frank Heine FERRIES*

ARIZONA MARU (1920) Osaka Shosen Kaisha, Japan

9,684grt; 475ft (144.8m) lbp x 61ft (18.6m) beam
173 passengers in two classes
Mitsubishi, Nagasaki (Yard No 280)
Triple-expansion steam reciprocating, twin screw

The *Arizona Maru* was sunk on 14 November 1942 in a bombing attack carried out by American land- and carrier-based aircraft while she was operating near the Solomon Islands. She sank in the position 08.30S, 158.45E.

Casualties: not known

The *Arizona Maru* was the last vessel of a five-ship class built for trans-Pacific operations. All five were war losses, the *Arizona Maru* in an aerial attack, the others sunk by torpedoes. *Mitsui-OSK Lines*

ARMENIA (1928) Black Sea Shipping Co (Sovtorgflot), USSR

4,727grt; 354ft (17.9m) loa x 51ft (15.5m) beam
450 passengers in single class
Baltic Shipbuilding & Engineering Works, Leningrad (Yard No not known)
Motor-ship, twin screw

The sinking of the short-sea passenger ship *Armenia* on 7 November 1941 was the worst disaster to affect a Russian or Soviet passenger ship, the loss of life amounting to as high as 7,000 according to some reports. On 8 August 1941 she was taken in hand for conversion for auxiliary service and emerged as a hospital ship, fully painted in the recognised colours of the International Red Cross. On 6 November she sailed from Sevastopol to Yalta via Tuapse, and after her arrival she embarked between 5,000 and 7,000 persons, the majority wounded servicemen but with them up to 2,000 medical staff and un-manifested civilians. Exercising caution, the Russian Naval Command ordered the ship to remain in port until after dark and for escort vessels to become available before she sailed. For some unknown reason, her Master ignored these instructions and sailed the following morning virtually unescorted (there were just two small patrol boats), her destination unknown. Between Yalta and Gurzuf she became a victim of the Luftwaffe, despite her clearly marked function, attacked by marauding Heinkel He-111H bombers, which launched torpedoes at her. Two struck, one hitting the fore section causing her to break in two. Within four minutes she had sunk to the bottom of the Black Sea off Cape Aj-Todor – there were only eight survivors! Her wreck lies in the position 44.15N, 34.17E at a depth of some 1,500 feet (455 metres).
Casualties: About 7,000

ARMONIA (1891) ex-*Santiago* (1909) ex-*Weimar* (1908) Canada Steamship Lines, Canada

4,996grt; 430ft (131.2m) loa x 48ft (14.6m) beam
1,994 passengers in three classes (as built)
Fairfield, Govan (Yard No 355)
Triple-expansion steam reciprocating, single screw

The passenger-cargo steamer *Armonia*, a former Norddeutscher Lloyd ship, was on passage from Genoa to New York in ballast on 15 March 1918 when she was torpedoed and sunk by the German submarine UC67 in the position 42.33N, 06.46E, 38 miles off Perquerolles Island, 15 miles south-east of Toulon.
Casualties: 7

ARMONIA (1966) ex-*Angamos* (1993) ex-*Puerto Montt* (1977) ex-*Presidente Aguirre Cerda* (1974) ex-*Kobenhavn* (1973) owners not known, St Vincent & Grenadines registration

3,559grt; 308ft (93.9m) loa x 53ft (16.2m) beam
800 passengers
Orenstein Koppel, Lübeck (Yard No 622)
Motor-ship, twin screw

Fire broke out on 16 February 1993 aboard the ro-ro passenger ferry *Armonia*, originally employed in the Baltic Sea, when she was some 600 miles to the west of Nouadhibou (Port Etienne), Mauritania, in the position 22.27N, 27.23W.

The fire could not be controlled and the following day she was abandoned by her 19-man crew. Other than them, she was empty, being on a repositioning voyage to Greece from Chile. It was thought that she had sunk but, after the fire had burned out, she was re-boarded, eventually arriving at Piraeus under tow on 3 June 1993 and later moved to Elefsina, where she was laid up pending decisions on her future. It would appear that the extent of her damage had been underestimated and the vessel was abandoned, beyond economic recovery.
Casualties: 0

The burned-out hulk of the *Armonia* at Elefsina on 17 July 1994. *Frank Heine FERRIES*

ARNO (1912) ex-*Cesarea* (1938) ex-*Fort St George* (1935) ex-*Wandilla* (1921) Lloyd Triestino, Italy

8,024grt; 428ft (130.5m) loa x 56ft (17.1m) beam
450 passengers
William Beardmore, Dalmuir (Yard No 506)
Quadruple-expansion steam reciprocating, twin screw

The passenger-cargo ship *Arno* was sunk by a British torpedo bomber on 10 September 1942, when she was forty miles north of Tobruk, Libya, in the position 33.14N, 23.23E. The Italian government condemned the attack, claiming that the *Arno* was in service as a hospital ship and clearly marked as such.
Casualties: 27

Seen here as the *Fort St George*, the sinking of the Lloyd Triestino passenger ship *Arno* while serving as a hospital ship, one of many such cases, aroused controversy. *Ian Allan Library*

ASAMA MARU (1929) Nippon Yusen Kaisha, Japan

16,975grt; 583ft (177.7m) loa x 72ft (21.9m) beam
822 passengers in three classes
Mitsubishi, Nagasaki (Yard No 450)
Motor-ship, quadruple screw

The passenger liner *Asama Maru* survived an incident on 2 September 1937, which could have prematurely ended her career, when she was driven ashore at Saiwan Bay, Hong Kong,

in a typhoon. Left high and dry, refloating her proved to be extremely difficult and required the removal of two of her four main engines before it could be achieved. In December 1941, three years later, she was requisitioned as a Japanese navy transport and in this capacity she was torpedoed and sunk on 1 November 1944 by the submarine USS *Atule*. The attack took place approximately 100 miles south of Pratas Island in the South China Sea, in the position 20.09N, 117.38E.
Casualties: not known

The trans-Pacific motor liner *Asama Maru* survived a stranding in a typhoon in September 1937 only to be torpedoed in the Second World War. It is believed that at the time she was engaged on a so-called 'Hell Ship' voyage, illegally transporting prisoners of war in breach of the Geneva Convention.
Mitsubishi Heavy Industries

ASCANIA (1911) ex-*Gerona* (launch name, 4 March 1911) Cunard Line, UK

9,121grt; 482ft (146.9m) loa x 56ft (17.1m) beam
1,700 passengers in two classes
Swan Hunter & Wigham Richardson, Wallsend-on-Tyne (Yard No 869)
Triple-expansion steam reciprocating, twin screw
On 13 June 1918, while the passenger-cargo ship *Ascania* was bound from Liverpool to Montreal in ballast, she was wrecked twenty miles east of Cape Bay, Newfoundland.
Casualties: 0

ASIA (1907) ex-*Alice* (1917) Fabre Line, France

6,122grt; 415ft (126.6m) lbp x 50ft (15.1m) beam
1,480 passengers
Russell, Port Glasgow (Yard No 581)
Triple-expansion steam reciprocating, twin screw
Late on 21 May 1930, while en route from Jeddah to Djibouti with 1,500 Moslem pilgrims, fire broke out in the Second-class cabins aboard the passenger ship *Asia* and she was burned out. At the height of the blaze the vessel was unapproachable, by which time she had been abandoned by her crew and passengers. Several small craft from within Jeddah harbour rushed to the scene and assisted with the evacuation throughout the night, 950 persons being taken aboard boats, and another 300 to 400 taken ashore. Because it was feared she would sink and become a danger to navigation, the listing *Asia* was eventually beached on Bahri Reef.
Casualties: 112 (all pilgrims)

ASIE (1914) Chargeurs Réunis, France

serving under the wartime name ROSSANO
8,561grt; 439ft (133.8m) lbp x 55ft (16.8m) beam
335 passengers
Ateliers et Chantiers de France, Dunkirk (Yard No 95)
Triple-expansion steam reciprocating, twin screw
The passenger-cargo liner *Asie* was seized by the Germans at Marseilles on 13 March 1943. She was not retained, however, but transferred instead on 4 May of the same year to the Italians who renamed her *Rossano*. Under this name she was bombed, burned out and sunk on 10 May 1944 during an Allied air raid on the port of Genoa.
Casualties: not known

ASKA (1939) British India Line, UK

8,323grt; 461ft (140.5m) loa x 61ft (18.6m) beam
2,634 passengers
Swan Hunter & Wigham Richardson, Low Walker, Tyneside (Yard No 1596)
Steam turbines, twin screw
The new British passenger-cargo ship *Aska* sailed from Freetown, Sierra Leone, and Bathurst (Banjul), Gambia, in early September 1940 bound for Liverpool carrying 358 French soldiers, who were to join the Free French Forces, and a crew of 186. She was not in convoy, making the voyage alone. As she entered the Irish Sea by the North Channel on 16 September she was attacked by a German bomber near Rathlin Island, in the position 55.15N, 05.55W. The German warplane scored three hits, causing severe damage in the *Aska*'s engine room and to her forecastle area, setting her on fire, and the order was given to abandon ship. The survivors, who were rescued from the lifeboats by trawlers, were taken to Greenock. The *Aska*, abandoned drifting and ablaze in a north-westerly direction, ran ashore on Cara Island the following day where she became a total wreck.
Casualties: 30 (19 troops and 11 crew)

ASTURIAS (1908) Royal Mail Line, UK

12,002grt; 535ft (163.1m) loa x 62ft (19.0m) beam
1,640 passengers in three classes
Harland & Wolff, Belfast (Yard No 388)
Quadruple-expansion steam reciprocating, twin screw

Royal Mail's first *Asturias*, a torpedo loss in the First World War, served on the run to South America from Southampton.
H. B. Christiansen Collection / Online Transport Archive

Taken over as a hospital ship in 1914, the passenger liner *Asturias* was torpedoed by the German submarine UC66 while in the English Channel on 21 March 1917 bound from Avonmouth to Southampton. Completely unmanoeuvrable, she stranded off Bolt Head, five miles from Start Point. Abandoned to underwriters and declared a total loss, she was recovered after a lengthy salvage operation undertaken by the Admiralty, which had purchased the wreck. Taken to Plymouth, she was used as a munitions hulk there until 1919 when she was sold back to her original owners. Repaired and reconstructed by her builders over a period of more than two years, the *Asturias* returned to service in 1923 as the cruise ship *Arcadian*.
Casualties: 35

ASTURIAS (1926) Royal Mail Line, UK

22,048grt; 666ft (203.0m) loa x 78ft (23.9m) beam
1,318 passengers in three classes
Harland & Wolff, Belfast (Yard No 507)
Steam turbines, twin screw
The liner *Asturias* was requisitioned by the Admiralty in October 1939 for service as an armed merchant cruiser, her forward funnel being removed during the conversion. After almost four years serving in this role, she was torpedoed by the Italian submarine *Cagni* on 25 July 1943 while she was patrolling in the South Atlantic. The severely damaged and unmanoeuvrable ship was towed to Freetown where she remained until early 1945, then only to be declared a constructive total loss. However, the Admiralty purchased the wreck, as they had done with her earlier namesake in similar circumstances, and had it towed to Belfast for repairs and fitting out as a permanent troopship. The *Asturias* re-entered service in this capacity in 1947, managed by her former owners, and she continued with both troop-carrying and emigrant voyages for the Ministry of Transport until she was broken up from September 1957.
Casualties: not known

Built as a motor-ship, the second *Asturias* was converted to turbine propulsion in 1934. She is seen in dry dock probably during conversion into an armed merchant cruiser, her forward funnel partially removed. *Author's collection*

Asturias is seen again during wartime as an armed merchant cruiser, at Freetown in 1944. *H. B. Christiansen collection / Online Transport Archive*

ATHENIA (1905) Anchor-Donaldson Line, UK

8,668grt; 478ft (145.7m) lbp x 56ft (17.1m) beam
500 passengers in two classes
Vickers & Maxim, Barrow-in-Furness (Yard No 288)
Triple-expansion steam reciprocating, twin screw
While bound from Montreal to Glasgow on 16 August 1917, the passenger ship *Athenia* was torpedoed without warning by the German submarine U53, and sank seven miles north of Inishtrahull Island, County Donegal. The position was 55.33N, 07.23W.
Casualties: 15

The ships of the Anchor-Donaldson Line operated between Glasgow and Canadian St Lawrence ports. The *Athenia* joined this service in March 1905. *World Ship Society*

ATHENIA (1923) Anchor-Donaldson Line, UK

13,581grt; 538ft (164.0m) loa x 66ft (20.1m) beam
1,552 passengers in three classes
Fairfield, Glasgow (Yard No 596)
Steam turbines, twin screw
While still engaged in peacetime business, the *Athenia*, bound from the Clyde and Liverpool for Montreal, was torpedoed by U30 on 4 September 1939, some 200 miles west of the Hebrides, and sank in the position 56.44N, 14.05W. The attack took place only a matter of hours after war had been declared, making the *Athenia* the first submarine victim of the Second World War. She was carrying 1,418 persons, of whom 1,103 were passengers, including 311 Americans, and the remainder were crew. Not only did the submarine torpedo her but, after it surfaced, it proceeded to fire shells into the liner, destroying the radio equipment and preventing the transmission of distress calls. Although the *Athenia* carried sufficient lifeboats for all aboard her, she developed a severe list, making it difficult to launch them, and three boats were lost with all their occupants.
Casualties: 112 (93 passengers and 19 crew)

The replacement *Athenia* was the first torpedo victim of the Second World War, sunk on the day that war was declared. *Ian Allan Library*

ATHINAI (1908) National Steam Navigation Co, Greece

6,742grt; 420ft loa (128.0m) lbp x 52ft (15.9m) beam
2,300 passengers in three classes
Raylton Dixon, Middlesbrough (Yard No 537)
Triple-expansion steam reciprocating, twin screw

Originally built for the Moraitis Line, the *Athinai* was transferred to her new owners in 1914 for employment on the run from Piraeus to Halifax and New York. She was destroyed by fire in mid-Atlantic on a westbound crossing on 19 September 1915. The ship was abandoned in the approximate position 41.00N, 54.00W. Fortunately all 409 of her emigrant passengers and the entire crew were rescued from the sinking ship by the Anchor liner *Tuscania*.
Casualties: 0

ATHOS (1915) Messageries Maritimes, France

12,692grt; 528ft (160.9m) loa x 61ft (18.6m) beam
384 passengers in three classes
Ateliers et Chantiers de France, Dunkirk (Yard No 93),
but towed to St Nazaire for completion because of bomb-ing at Dunkirk
Triple-expansion steam reciprocating, twin screw

After maintaining French postal services for two years, the passenger liner *Athos* was taken over in 1917 for employment as an auxiliary supporting the Allied war effort. As she was steaming through the Mediterranean escorted by the destroyers *Enseigne Henry* and *Mameluck*, bound for Marseilles from Yokohama, she was torpedoed and sunk on 17 February 1917 by the German submarine U65 when 180 miles south-west of Malta. The *Athos* had some 1,950 persons on board, among them, besides her crew, a large contingent of Senegalese troops and many Chinese passengers. The ship sank in less than fifteen minutes and there was heavy loss of life.
Casualties: 754, including 12 members of the crew

ATLANTIC (1871) White Star Line, UK

3,707grt; 432ft (131.6m) loa x 41ft (12.8m) beam
1,166 passengers in two classes
Harland & Wolff, Belfast (Yard No 74)
Compound-expansion steam reciprocating, single screw

On 1 April 1873, less than two years after she had entered service, the passenger steamship *Atlantic* was wrecked on Marrs Rock, Meagher's Island, near Halifax, Nova Scotia, during a voyage from Liverpool to New York. She had left the Mersey twelve days earlier and had made the entire crossing in the face of severe gales, carrying a total of 952 persons, of whom 811 were passengers. As the passage proceeded, the weather worsened to such an extent that the course was altered for Halifax because of diminishing fuel supplies. Owing to mistaken position reckoning, however, the *Atlantic* was steered towards the coast, hitting the rocks at full speed in the middle of the night. The impact of the crash seriously damaged the ship and left her exposed to the full fury of the seas. Listing to starboard with the waves ripping away the plates on that side and with all her lifeboats torn loose and totally destroyed, the *Atlantic* appeared to be doomed with little hope for her occupants.

Those persons who had come on deck found themselves at the mercy of both the seas crashing over the ship and from her standing gear that was breaking free. The passengers were instructed to climb the rigging to escape the relentless waves, but in the bitter cold many fell to their deaths as exhaustion overtook them. The third officer and two seamen managed to swim ashore where they secured five lines to rocks permitting a considerable number of her occupants to reach safety. Local craft did not reach the scene to offer assistance until the following morning, by which time it was too late for many.

At the official Canadian enquiry it was revealed that her Master had turned in for the night at the time of the disaster, leaving the ship in the charge of junior officers. It was also suggested that the *Atlantic*'s bunkers were insufficiently stocked with coal when she put to sea. The loss of the *Atlantic* was the worst disaster to involve a ship on the British register until the sinking of the *Titanic* in 1912.
Casualties: 585, including all the women passengers and all but one of the children. This figure is disputed in some sources and higher and lower numbers are quoted. One explanation for some of the variation may be that there was thought to be as many as fourteen stowaways aboard the *Atlantic*.

A graphic representation of the White Star liner *Atlantic* after she crashed onto the rocks in April 1873, the result, it was claimed, of the coal in her fuel bunkers being exhausted. *Mariners Museum*

ATLANTIS (1965) ex-*Adonis* (1976) Kavounides Shipping Co SA, Greece

4,504grt; 319ft (97.2m) loa x 53ft (16.1m) beam
332 passengers
Cantieri Riuniti dell'Adriatico, Monfalcone
(Yard No 1881)
Motor-ship, twin screw

The Kavounides passenger ship *Atlantis*, described as a ro-ro ferry, looks more like a small cruise ship. *Mick Lindsay*

While undergoing repairs at Piraeus on 7 March 1983, the Greek roll-on roll-off vehicle/passenger ferry *Atlantis* had an outbreak of fire in her accommodation areas, which rapidly spread throughout the ship. The blazing vessel was towed to Cape Pounta, Salamis Island, in the position 37.58N, 23.32E, where she was beached and left for the fire to burn itself out. Completely gutted, the *Atlantis* refloated herself without assistance later that month but was judged, nevertheless, to be a constructive total loss and was broken up in Greece later that year.
Casualties: not known

ATSUTA [ATUTA] MARU (1909) Nippon Yusen Kaisha, Japan

7,983grt; 473ft (144.2m) lbp x 54ft (16.5m) beam
176 passengers in three classes
Mitsubishi, Nagasaki (Yard No 197)
Triple-expansion steam reciprocating, twin screw
The *Atsuta Maru*, which had been taken over as a naval transport, was sunk in the East China Sea, in the position 26.07N, 129.06E, on 30 May 1942, torpedoed by the American submarine USS *Pompano*.
Casualties: not known

AUGUSTUS (1927) Italia Line, Italy

serving under the wartime name SPARVIERO
30,418grt; 711ft (216.7m) loa x 82ft (25.0m) beam
2,034 passengers in four classes
Ansaldo, Sestri Ponente, Genoa (Yard No 282)
Motor-ship, quadruple screw

The *Augustus* of Navigazione Generale Italiana was the largest motor-ship in the world prior to the Second World War. With her sister ship, the turbine-driven *Roma*, she served on both the North and South Atlantic routes, from January 1932 under the Italia Line house flag. Conversion to turbine propulsion to improve her speed was considered in 1939 but never took place. *Author's collection*

In May 1940 the passenger liner *Augustus* was requisitioned by the Italian government but remained laid up at Genoa until July 1942 when she was taken over by the Italian Navy for conversion into a fleet aircraft carrier, along the lines of her sister ship *Roma* (qv), at the OARN shipyard, Genoa. These plans were later 'watered down' through financial constraints and because of bomb damage inflicted in November 1942, and a revised scheme, for an escort carrier conversion, was adopted instead. By the time of the Armistice in September 1943, work on the *Sparviero*, as she had been by then

renamed, had proceeded to the point where all her upperworks had been removed, leaving her flush-decked at the level of her hull. Seized by the Germans, all conversion work was terminated and the *Sparviero* remained inactive until 25 September 1944, when she was scuttled to block the entrance to Genoa harbour. Her wreck was refloated in December 1946 to clear the shipping channel, and in July 1947 it was sold to be broken up at La Spezia, where work commenced that August.
Casualties: not known

AURANIA (1917) Cunard Line, UK

13,936grt; 540ft (164.6m) loa x 64ft (19.5m) beam
2,156 passengers in two classes (as designed)
Swan Hunter & Wigham Richardson, Wallsend-on-Tyne (Yard No 965)
Steam turbines, twin screw
Intended to enter the London to Montreal or Boston service with two sister ships, instead, because of the outbreak of war in 1914, the *Aurania* started her career as a troopship, making her first voyage in this capacity, from Newcastle to New York, on 28 March 1917. She never survived the war and was thus never engaged in commercial service. Her end came on 4 February 1918 when she was torpedoed by the German submarine UB67, when she was approximately fifteen miles north-half-west of Inishtrahull, in the position 56.36N, 06.20W, outward bound for New York from Liverpool in ballast. An attempt was made to tow the *Aurania* to port but she struck submerged rocks off Tobermory, Isle of Mull, and became a total loss.
Casualties: 8

One of three vessels built for either the Liverpool or London service to Boston or Montreal, the *Aurania*'s sisters were the *Andania* and *Alaunia*. *World Ship Society*

AUSONIA (1908) ex-*Tortona* (1911) Cunard Line, UK

8,153grt; 450ft (137.2m) lbp x 54ft (16.5m) beam
1,050 passengers in two classes
Swan Hunter & Wigham Richardson, Wallsend-on-Tyne (Yard No 837)
Triple-expansion steam reciprocating, single screw
The passenger ship *Ausonia*, bound from Liverpool to New York in ballast, was well out into the Atlantic, approximately 620 miles south-south-west of Fastnet, in the position 47.59N, 23.42W, when she was torpedoed and sunk by the German submarine U62 on 30 May 1918. The survivors of the attack spent eight days adrift in the lifeboats before they were picked up by the destroyer HMS *Zennia*.
Casualties: 44

The *Ausonia* was employed on the Cunard services from London and Southampton to Quebec and Montreal. *Real Photos*

AUSONIA (1928) Lloyd Triestino, Italy

12,995grt; 544ft (165.8m) loa x 66ft (20.2m) beam
390 passengers in three classes
Ansaldo, Sestri Ponente, Genoa (Yard No 283)
Steam turbines, twin screw

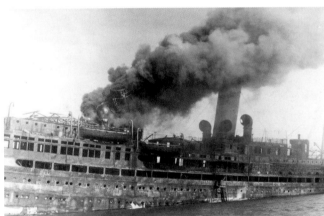

The sleek Italian passenger ship *Ausonia* operated on a route from Trieste to Alexandria, Egypt, via other Eastern Mediterranean ports. These unusual views, taken from a rescue craft or lifeboat, show her at the height of the blaze that destroyed her. *David Hutchings*

In the early hours of 18 October 1935, during the quarantine formalities following her arrival from Syria at the Egyptian port of Alexandria, the passenger ship *Ausonia*'s boiler exploded violently and started a blaze amidships that spread quickly. British naval ratings from the warships HMS *Queen Elizabeth*, *Valiant*, *Revenge* and *Shropshire* assisted in fighting the fire and evacuating the persons who were stranded aboard the stricken ship. All the passengers were rescued as were 234 members of the *Ausonia*'s crew.

The injured were treated aboard the nearby hospital ship *Maine*. Aboard the *Ausonia*, further explosions occurred in her oil tanks. At this point her anchor chain was cut and the listing ship was towed into shallow water at Ramleh Bay, where she settled alongside the breakwater with her after end under water. In January 1936 the wreck was raised and towed to Trieste where it was demolished.
Casualties: 6 (all crew)

AUSTRALIA (1892) P&O Line, UK

6,901grt; 465ft (141.9m) lbp x 52ft (15.9m) beam
450 passengers in two classes
Caird, Greenock (Yard No 267)
Triple-expansion steam reciprocating, single screw
The passenger steamship *Australia* stranded at the entrance to Port Philip Bay, Victoria, at Corsair Rock, Point Nepean, on 20 June 1904 when the local pilot made a navigational error, through confusion of channel-marking lights. Her entire complement of 294 persons was evacuated safely but the ship could not be refloated and was completely wrecked where it lay after it caught fire. The hulk was sold locally for clearance but remained on the shoal for some considerable time.
Casualties: 0

The P&O liner *Australia* of 1892, sister of the second *Himalaya* on the London to Australia mail service, via Colombo. *Tom Rayner collection*

AUSTRALIEN (1889) Messageries Maritimes, France

6,377grt; 482ft (146.9m) lbp x 49ft (15.0m) beam
586 passengers in four classes
Messageries Maritimes, La Ciotat (Yard No 66)
Triple-expansion steam reciprocating, single screw

In consort with her sister ships *Armand Behic*, *Polynesien* and *Ville de la Ciotat*, the *Australien* maintained Messageries Maritimes' services to Australia. *Alex Duncan*

The passenger steamship *Australien* was requisitioned in August 1914 for use as a wartime auxiliary and as such participated in the landings at the Dardanelles, evacuating casualties. Later she transported Serbian troops from Corfu to Salonica (Thessaloniki). She was torpedoed and sunk 26 miles north-east of Cape Bron by the German submarine U54 on 19 July 1918, while sailing in convoy from Marseilles to Malta and Port Said with 951 military passengers in addition to her normal crew. The explosion set fire to the *Australien*, which had to be abandoned. A prompt and efficient evacuation permitted the safe rescue of most of those who were aboard her, the survivors being transferred to a British sloop and four Japanese destroyers that together comprised the convoy escort. The *Australien* remained afloat while the fire aboard her raged, finally sinking the following day, thirteen hours after the attack.

Casualties: 64 (45 military personnel and 19 crew members)

AVA (1873) British India Line, UK

2,600grt; 350ft (106.7m) lbp x 36ft (11.0m) beam
Passenger numbers not known
William Denny, Dumbarton (Yard No 167)
Compound-expansion steam reciprocating, single screw
The *Ava* was at the start of a voyage from Calcutta to London via Madras, Colombo and the Suez Canal when she was struck by the sailing ship *Brenhilda* seventy miles off Sandheads, in the mouth of the Hooghly River. The disaster occurred in the early hours of 24 May 1879, and the *Ava* was virtually cut in two, sinking rapidly. Only three lifeboats could be safely launched, taking with them 53 survivors, the majority of those killed being deck passengers and crew.

Casualties: 70 (one report gives a figure of 90)

AVILA STAR (1927) ex-*Avila* (1929) Blue Star Line, UK

14,443grt; 569ft (173.4m) loa x 68ft (20.7m) beam
150 passengers in single class
John Brown, Clydebank (Yard No 514)
Steam turbines, twin screw
While the *Avila Star* was returning to Liverpool from Buenos Aires and Freetown on 5 July 1942, she was torpedoed by the submarine U201 north-east of the Azores and sank in the position 38.04N, 22.45W. Her evacuation and its aftermath were a graphic testimony to the kind of cruel ordeal that many merchant crews and their passengers experienced during the war at sea. Even as the 25 passengers and 171 crew members were abandoning ship, one lifeboat got caught up in the falls, spilling its occupants into the sea, while another, which had been successfully launched, was destroyed when a second torpedo fired into the *Avila Star* exploded close by it. For the occupants of the five lifeboats that remained, many of whom were sick or injured and required medical attention, there followed an epic struggle for survival on the open ocean. Every effort was made to keep the five boats together as they made for the Portuguese coast, the nearest landfall, but they gradually became separated as time passed.

Three of the boats were found on 8 and 9 July, three days after the sinking, by the Portuguese destroyer *Lima*, and the rescued survivors were landed at Ponta Delgada. Aboard the last two lifeboats, which had remained together for a time, it had been necessary to introduce a system of rationing to conserve the limited quantity of available food and water.

After 11 July, , they also lost contact with each other and one lifeboat was never seen again. The survivors on the last lifeboat, who must have been wondering if they would ever be rescued, were finally picked up on 25 July by the Portuguese sloop *Pedro Nunes* and conveyed to Lisbon. Many had died in the lifeboats, from injuries sustained in the torpedo attack and from exposure and illness. Some had lost their sanity in the harrowing circumstances, and one passenger had jumped overboard in a state of delirium and could not be rescued.

The outstanding courage and fortitude displayed by the Blue Star officers and crewmen, an uplifting example to their less confident compatriots and a fitting tribute to the traditions of their service, was recognised in the form of six awards: four OBEs, a Lloyd's War Medal for Bravery at Sea, and a British Empire Medal. A female passenger also received the British Empire Medal for her exceptional bravery in helping to save life at sea.

Casualties: 62

The third of Blue Star Line's five-ship class of passenger-cargo liners completed for the South American trade from London, the *Avila Star* was the fourth of the quintet to be sunk in the Second World War. *World Ship Society*

AWA MARU (1943) Nippon Yusen Kaisha, Japan

11,249grt; 535ft (163.1m) loa x 66ft (20.1m) beam
296 passengers in two classes (revised design)
Mitsubishi, Nagasaki (Yard No 770)
Motor-ship, twin screw
When war broke out in the Pacific in December 1941, the passenger-cargo ship *Awa Maru* was still under construction. She was completed as a troop transport, but because she did not survive the war she never saw commercial service. In February 1945 she was designated for a special 'mercy' voyage for which she was granted diplomatic status. Disarmed and repainted with a green hull on which were two prominent white crosses either side, she commenced a long voyage in this guise setting out from Moji bound for Kaohsiung, Hong Kong, Saigon, Singapore and Djakarta before making the return voyage to Tsuruga. On the outward leg of the voyage she transported a vast quantity of Red Cross parcels for prisoners of war, but it was intended that on the return leg she would use her safe, flag-of-immunity status as protection while conveying valuable, inaccessible and possibly illicit cargoes back to the Japanese homeland. She also attracted a large number of passengers, Japanese

nationals heading home who felt more secure aboard a ship flying the flag of the International Red Cross.

However, when sighted by the United States submarine *Queenfish* on 1 April 1945 as she passed through the Formosa Strait, she was mistaken for a warship in the overcast weather. Hit by four torpedoes fired by the *Queenfish* with deadly accuracy, the *Awa Maru* blew up and foundered within minutes, sinking in the position 25.26N, 120.08E. There was only one survivor. Among those who were killed was a newborn baby that had been delivered while the ship was at sea. The loss of the *Awa Maru* was the worst Japanese maritime disaster in both wartime and peacetime, and she has been called 'Japan's Titanic'. Various attempts to locate the wrecked ship were unsuccessful until, around the early 1980s, she was found about ten miles off the coast of Taiwan in the position 24.41N, 119.45E.

Casualties: 2,002

The loss of the *Awa Maru* still arouses controversy as she was sailing under 'safe conduct' clearance when she was torpedoed by an American submarine. Intended for Nippon Yusen Kaisha's Japan to Australia service, as it turned out she was never operated commercially. This photograph shows her before she adopted special diplomatic colouring.
Nippon Yusen Kaisha

AWATEA (1936) Union Steamship Co of New Zealand, UK

13,482grt; 545ft (166.1m) loa x 74ft (22.6m) beam
566 passengers in three classes
Vickers-Armstrongs, Barrow-in-Furness (Yard No 707)
Steam turbines, twin screw

The *Awatea* was one of the largest passenger liners to serve a New Zealand shipping company. She operated across the Tasman Sea between Sydney, Auckland and Wellington, a two-and-a-half-day run. From 1940 some voyages were extended as far as Vancouver for the Canadian-Australasian Line.
Ian Allan Library

The passenger steamship *Awatea* was commandeered for service as a troopship in September 1941. A year later she was deployed transporting commando units during the

Operation 'Torch' landings in North Africa in November 1942. After she had completed the disembarkation, on 11 November, the *Awatea* set sail from Bougie (Bejaia) bound for Gibraltar. When only a mile outside the Bougie breakwater, she came under attack from six German bombers, two of which were shot down by her own anti-aircraft guns. She was unable to completely repel the aircraft, however, and collectively they were able to inflict widespread damage with bombs and torpedoes, setting the *Awatea* on fire. After all of her crew had safely abandoned the blazing ship, she was left to drift, finally sinking near Cape Carbon.

Casualties: 0

B

BAEPENDY (1899) ex-*Tijuca* (1917) Lloyd Brasileiro, Brazil

4,801grt; 375ft (114.3m) lbp x 46ft (14.0m) beam
450 passengers in two classes
Blohm & Voss, Steinwerder, Hamburg (Yard No135)
Quadruple-expansion steam reciprocating, single screw
During a voyage from Rio de Janeiro and Bahia bound for Fernando Noronha and Manaos on 15 August 1942, the passenger-cargo ship *Baependy* was torpedoed and sunk by the German submarine U507 in the position 11.50S, 37.00W. She had been sailing in convoy with other Brazilian vessels, including the coastwise liner *Araraquara*, which was also sunk. The *Baependy* was carrying 246 passengers and troops, the latter destined for Fernando Noronha, and a 74-man crew. Of these, there were only 36 survivors. At the time of the attack, although diplomatic relations had been cut, Brazil was not at war with Germany and the sinking provoked a massive public outcry across the country such that war was declared within a matter of seven days.
Casualties: 284

Originally part of the Hamburg Sud-Amerika Line fleet, seized by Brazil in 1917, the *Baependy* sailed between Santos and Hamburg and other European ports for Lloyd Brasileiro. *National Maritime Museum*

BAGÉ (1912) ex-*Sierra Nevada* (1917) Lloyd Brasileiro, Brazil

8,235grt; 439ft (133.8m) lbp x 56ft (17.1m) beam
1,650 passengers in three classes
Vulkan Werke, Stettin (Yard No 328)
Triple-expansion steam reciprocating, twin screw
During a voyage from Pernambuco to Bahia on 1 August 1943, the passenger-cargo ship *Bagé* was torpedoed by the German submarine U185 in the position 11.29S, 36.58W, close to the Brazilian coast. After disabling the *Bagé* with its torpedo, the submarine surfaced and shelled the ship until it sank. Of her total complement of 135 persons, 28 were passengers, the remainder crew.
Casualties: 48

The former Hamburg Sud-Amerika liner *Sierra Nevada* passed to Lloyd Brasileiro in 1917 as the *Bagé* and was engaged in the service from Santos to Hamburg. *World Ship Society*

BAHIA PARAISO (1981) Argentine Government (Direccion Nacional del Antarctica)

5,270grt; 435ft (132.7m) loa x 64ft (19.5m) beam
Passenger numbers not known
Principe Menghi Penco, Avellaneda (Yard No 147)
Motor-ship, twin screw
The Argentine passenger vessel *Bahia Paraiso* was stranded in the Bismarck Strait, Antarctica, on 28 January 1989 during an Antarctic cruise. Four days later she slipped off the rocks and sank in deep water. During the Falklands Conflict she had served as a hospital ship and exchanged service casualties with Britain's *Uganda*.
Casualties: 70

BALLARAT (1911) P&O Line, UK

11,120grt; 515ft (157.0m) loa x 62ft (18.9m) beam
1,100 passengers in single class
Caird, Greenock (Yard No 318)
Quadruple-expansion steam reciprocating, twin screw
As she was approaching the entrance to the English Channel, near to the Scilly Isles, on 25 April 1917, the passenger steamship *Ballarat* was torpedoed by the German submarine UB32. At the time she was bound for London from Melbourne carrying troops, her total complement, including crew, amounting to 1,752 persons. All aboard her were safely transferred to escorting destroyers. The *Ballarat* sank 24 miles south-by-west of Wolf Rock lighthouse, in the position 49.33N, 05.36W.
Casualties: 0

The *Ballarat* operated on the branch line service to Australia via Cape Town. When she first entered service she displayed on her funnel the blue anchor symbol of the William Lund Company, which had been recently absorbed by P&O. *World Ship Society*

Looking somewhat altered for wartime service, the *Ballarat*, dead in the water, is seen sinking after she had been torpedoed. *Imperial War Museum (Q22837)*

BALOERAN (1930) Rotterdam Lloyd, The Netherlands

serving under the wartime name STRASSBURG
16,981grt; 574ft (174.9m) loa x 70ft (21.3m) beam
634 passengers in four classes
Maats Fijenoord, Rotterdam (Yard No 313)
Motor-ship, twin screw

The *Baloeran*, sister ship of the *Dempo*, was employed in the service from Rotterdam to the Dutch East Indies. This view shows her during wartime under German control as the hospital ship *Strassburg*. *WZ-Bilddienst*

The second view shows the wrecked *Strassburg* lying half-submerged off Ymuiden. *WZ-Bilddienst*

With the fall of The Netherlands in May 1940, the passenger liner *Baloeran*, which had been berthed at Rotterdam, was seized by the German Navy. She was converted into a hospital ship at the Wilton Fijenoord shipyard and returned to service in July 1941 renamed *Strassburg*, under the management of the Hamburg Amerika Line. While bound from Rotterdam to

Hamburg on 1 September 1943, the *Strassburg* struck a mine some ten to fifteen miles north of Ymuiden. The badly holed ship was taken in tow in an attempt to get her to port but, fearing that she would sink, she was beached in the position 52.30N, 04.36E. Efforts to salvage her were unsuccessful and the abandoned wreck was completely destroyed in British MTB attacks on 20 September 1943 and RAF bombing raids on 19 October 1943.
Casualties: not known

BATAVIER III (1939) Batavier Line (Wm H. Muller & Co), The Netherlands

2,687grt; 267ft (81.4m) lbp x 44ft (13.3m) beam
175 passengers
De Noord, Alblasserdam (Yard No 576)
Compound steam reciprocating, single screw
Captured by the Germans at the Hook of Holland on 27 May 1940, the North Sea passenger ferry *Batavier III* was pressed into service as a convoy rescue ship in the Baltic. Subsequently, from January 1941, she was employed as a troop transport, and while operating in this capacity she struck a mine in the Kattegat on 15 October 1942. The *Batavier III* sank, though she was not completely submerged, off the Danish coast, some twenty miles south of Aalborg, in the position 56.50N, 11.11E. A constructive total loss, she was later demolished.
Casualties: not known

BAUDOUINVILLE (1939) Cie Maritime Belge (Lloyd Royal), Belgium

serving under the wartime name LINDAU
13,761grt; 541ft (164.9m) loa x 67ft (20.4m) beam
395 passengers in two classes
John Cockerill, Hoboken (Yard No 675)
Motor-ship, twin screw
The Germans seized the almost new Belgian passenger ship *Baudouinville* at Bordeaux in June 1940, after she had eluded capture at Antwerp the previous month. She was commandeered by the German Navy on 28 October 1941 and converted into the hospital ship *Lindau*, managed by the Deutsche Ost-Afrika Line. Hospital ship duties were terminated in January 1943, after which she became an accommodation ship located at Nantes. During the retreat from Nantes, on 10 August 1944, the Germans deliberately set the vessel alight to scuttle her and she sank after an ammunition store ignited and exploded. The half-submerged wreck, lying in the position 47.13N, 01.34W, was refloated in 1946 and towed to Antwerp where breaking up commenced on 29 August 1946. Later, on 21 October 1947, the partly demolished ship was moved to Boom for the work to be completed.

A sister ship to the *Baudouinville*, the *Grisarville*, was apparently under construction when war broke out. How far it had progressed is not known, but it did not survive the conflict.
Casualties: not known

BAVARIAN (1899) Allan Line, UK

10,376grt; 520ft (158.5m) loa x 59ft (18.1m) beam
1,460 passengers in three classes

William Denny, Dumbarton (Yard No 606)
Triple-expansion steam reciprocating, twin screw
The passenger-cargo liner *Bavarian* was stranded on Wye Rock, Grosse Ile, near Montreal, on 3 November 1905 and broke her back just forward of the funnel. The wreck was refloated on 19 November 1906 and towed to Quebec, where it was broken up during 1907.
Casualties: 0

Built for the Canadian service from Liverpool, the Allan Line steamer *Bavarian* and her sister *Tunisian* were the company's first vessels to exceed 10,000 gross tons.
H. B. Christiansen Collection / Online Transport Archive

BELGRAVIA (1882) Anchor Line, UK

4,977grt; 400ft (121.9m) lbp x 45ft (13.7m) beam
436 passengers
D. & W. Henderson, Meadowside, Glasgow (Yard No 218)
Compound-expansion steam reciprocating, single screw
The passenger steamship *Belgravia* was wrecked on 22 May 1896 when she hit the rocks at Mispeck Point, near St John, New Brunswick. At the time she was returning to Liverpool with passengers and a cargo of timber.
Casualties: 0

BELLE ABETO (1952) ex-*Laënnec* (1966)
Cia de Nav Abetos SA, Panama

12,177grt; 538ft (163.9m) loa x 64ft (19.6m) beam
436 passengers in two classes (as built)
Chantiers de la Loire, St Nazaire (Yard No not known)
Motor-ship, twin screw
The pilgrim carrier *Belle Abeto*, engaged in the Indonesia to Jeddah service, caught fire while at an anchorage in Sasebo harbour, Japan, on 30 July 1976. Extensively damaged, she sank the following day.
Casualties: not known

The *Belle Abeto*, originally Messageries Maritimes *Laënnec*, was employed in the pilgrim trade to Jeddah from Indonesia. She is seen here at Singapore. *Ian Shiffman*

BELLE ISLE (1918) Chargeurs Réunis, France

9,589grt; 479ft (146.0m) lbp x 58ft (17.7m) beam
184 passengers
Forges et Chantiers de la Méditerranée, Le Havre
(Yard No 371)
Triple-expansion steam reciprocating, twin screw
On 24 November 1943 the passenger-cargo ship *Belle Isle* was in dry dock at Toulon when the port came under attack from Allied warplanes. She was hit by several bombs and set on fire. Her completely burned-out shell was scrapped after the end of the war.
Casualties: not known

BEN-MY-CHREE (1908) Isle of Man Steam Packet Co,
Isle of Man

2,651grt; 375ft (114.3m) lbp x 46ft (14.1m) beam
2,549 passengers
Vickers Maxim, Barrow-in-Furness (Yard No 363)
Steam turbines, triple screw
Early after the outbreak of the First World War, the Isle of Man passenger ferry *Ben-My-Chree* was taken over by the Admiralty for service as a seaplane carrier. Duly modified, with a flying-off ramp forward and a hangar aft, she sailed to the eastern Mediterranean for active service during the Gallipoli campaign. While on station at the Dardanelles, one of her aircraft successfully carried out an aerial torpedo attack, sinking a Turkish vessel. She continued with flying operations off the Turkish coast until 11 January 1917 when she was hit and sunk by Turkish coastal batteries while she in harbour at Castellanzo, on the Greek island of Kastelorizon (Kastelorgio). Raised in 1920, the former ferry was then only fit for scrap.
Casualties: 0

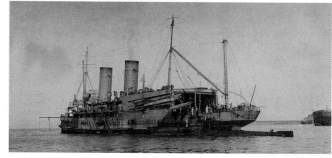

The Isle of Man ferry *Ben-My-Chree* seen as a floatplane aircraft carrier during the First World War. *Fleet Air Arm Museum*

BERENGARIA (1913) ex-*Imperator* (1921)
Cunard Line, UK

52,226grt; 909ft (277.1m) loa x 98ft (29.9m) beam
2,723 passengers in four classes
Vulcan, Hamburg (Yard No 314)
Steam turbines, quadruple screw
At times the damage caused by an onboard fire may be regarded as superficial if the ship appears from its exterior to be largely unscathed, but when the extent of the damage within the ship leaves it effectively beyond economic repair, necessitating disposal for breaking up, the outcome may be considered a disastrous loss, if primarily in financial terms. A case in point, one of a number described in these pages, was

that of the express Cunard liner *Berengaria*, which had a major fire in her passenger accommodation while berthed at New York on 3 March 1938. With the fire extinguished, she returned empty to Southampton and was then laid up. Offered for sale, there were no takers and she was moved to Jarrow in November 1938 for demolition. Her loss frustrated Cunard's intentions of keeping her in service until 1940, when she would have been replaced by the *Queen Elizabeth*. It also denied the United Kingdom a valuable troopship in the ensuing World War.

Casualties: not known

Built as Hamburg Amerika Line's *Imperator*, the *Berengaria* was awarded to Britain under the Treaty of Versailles together with near sister *Majestic* (ex-*Bismarck*) as compensation for the losses of the *Lusitania* and *Britannic*. *Author's collection*

BERMUDA (1927) Furness Withy, UK

19,086grt; 547ft (166.7m) loa x 74ft (22.6m) beam
691 passengers in two classes
Workman Clark, Belfast (Yard No 490)
Motor-ship, quadruple screw

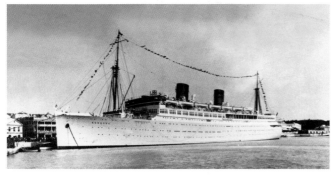

Furness Withy's luxury passenger service from New York to Bermuda, the 'Millionaire's Run' as it was called, was launched with the luckless *Bermuda*, seen here berthed at Hamilton. *Furness Withy Group*

During her fourth season, while berthed at Hamilton, the *Bermuda*'s superstructure was completely destroyed in an outbreak of fire that occurred on 16 June 1931. The fire started in a lift shaft and spread to the three adjoining decks. Her stern oil storage tanks were flooded to minimise the danger of explosion and the ship's aft end settled gently on the coral bottom. All the passengers were rescued, but there were crew casualties. Apart from her hull and machinery spaces, the *Bermuda* was extensively damaged. After pumping out, she proceeded to the UK under her own power for repairs to be carried out by her builders, but on 19

November of the same year, when the work was virtually complete, fire broke out again and the *Bermuda* was completely gutted and sank. The wreck was raised on 24 December 1931 and sold as a hulk for breaking up at Rosyth. However, while it was en route to the breakers yard on 30 May 1932, under tow of the tug *Seaman*, the *Bermuda* ran aground on the Badcall Islands, in Eddrachilles Bay, Scotland, and became a total loss.

Casualties: 2 (a fireman and a crew member)

BERNADIN DE SAINT PIERRE (1925) Messageries Maritimes, France,

serving under the wartime name TEIBI MARU
10,085grt; 476ft (145.1m) loa x 60ft (18.3m) beam
299 passengers in three classes
J. C. Tecklenborg, Geestemunde (Yard No 399)
Steam turbines, twin screw

After transporting Americans from Shanghai and Hankou to Manila in December 1941, following the attack on Pearl Harbor, the passenger-cargo ship *Bernardin de Saint Pierre* was blockaded at Haiphong, Vietnam, until she was able to return to Saigon in January 1942. There, on 10 April 1942, she was requisitioned by Japanese forces. She was pressed into Japanese government transport service as the *Teibi Maru*, only to be lost on 10 October 1943. She was torpedoed off the coast of Vietnam, north-east of Quin Hon (Annam) by the American submarine USS *Bonefish* and sank in the position 14.49N, 110.16E.

Casualties: not known

The *Bernardin de Saint Pierre* and her sister ship *Explorateur Grandidier* were employed in the service from Marseilles to Madagascar. *Ian Allan Library*

BERWICK CASTLE (1902) Union-Castle line, UK

5,891grt; 398ft (121.4m) lbp x 50ft (15.2m) beam
540 passengers in three classes
William Beardmore, Govan (Yard No 476)
Triple-expansion steam reciprocating, twin screw

The emigrant-cargo steamer *Berwick Castle* was gutted by fire at Mombasa, Kenya, on 20 October 1919. Beached and declared a constructive total loss, the wreck was refloated on 7 November of that year and sold to Italian ship-breakers for demolition. However, it was immediately resold and, following repairs, re-entered service in 1921 under the Italian flag, renamed *Andora Castle*. After four years of additional service, the *Andora Castle* was broken up at La Spezia in 1925.

Casualties: not known

The *Berwick Castle*, an 'extra' steamer on Union-Castle's emigrant trade to South Africa. *David Reed*

BIANCA C (1949) ex-Arosa Sky (1958) ex-*La Marseillaise* (1957) ex-*Marechal Petain* (launch name, 8 June 1944) Costa Line, Italy

18,427grt; 593ft (180.8m) loa x 76ft (23.0m) beam
1,232 passengers in two classes
Constructions Navales, La Ciotat (Yard No 161)
Motor-ship, triple screw

In the early hours of 22 October 1961, while anchored off St George, Grenada, following her arrival from Venezuela, the passenger liner *Bianca C* suffered a series of engine room explosions that precipitated an outbreak of fire. The fire spread with alarming rapidity and it became necessary to abandon ship. All but one of the 674 persons onboard, 362 of them passengers, were safely evacuated in the ship's lifeboats. Two days later the frigate HMS *Londonderry* managed to secure a line to the still blazing liner in an attempt to tow her to a suitable area for beaching, but the *Bianca C* sprang a leak and sank in deep water.

Casualties: 3 (two persons died later in hospital from burn injuries)

Seen here in an earlier phase of her career, the *Bianca C* is in the guise of the French hospital ship *La Marseillaise* at the time of the Suez Crisis. Later she became the *Arosa Sky* before entering Costa Line's Italy to Venezuela service. *ECPA*

BLACK PRINCE (1938) Fred Olsen Line (A/S Ganger Rolf), Norway

serving under the wartime name LOFJORD
5,039grt; 365ft (111.3m) lbp x 53ft (16.2m) beam
250 passengers in two classes
Akers MV, Oslo (Yard No 473)
Motor-ship, twin screw

The Norwegian ferry *Black Prince* was seized by the Kriegsmarine on 26 August 1941 following the invasion of Norway. She was taken to Danzig (Gdansk) for use as an

accommodation ship for U-boat crews, under the name *Lofjord*. There, on 14 December 1941, she was bombed and set on fire during an Allied air raid. Though salvaged in June 1942, the wreck of the former *Black Prince* was designated as a bombing target for the Luftwaffe. For this purpose, she was towed to shallow waters north of Gilleleje on Denmark's east coast where, on 1 July 1943, her sea cocks were opened, allowing her to settle on the bottom in 4 metres of water. Sand ballast was pumped aboard her to keep her upright. Found in this condition after the war, she was raised on 25 April 1946. Despite the extent of her damage, more than once consideration was given to rebuilding the *Black Prince*. Finally, however, she went to ship-breakers at Burght, Belgium, in November 1951.

Casualties: not known

Two elegant passenger ferries introduced by Fred Olsen on the Bergen to Newcastle route just prior to the Second World War were the *Black Prince*... *Bjørn Pedersen*

...and *Black Watch*. *Knut Klippenberg, Fred Olsen*

BLACK WATCH (1939) Fred Olsen Line (A/S Ganger Rolf), Norway

5,035grt; 365ft (111.3m) lbp x 53ft (16.2m) beam
246 passengers in two classes
Akers MV, Oslo (Yard No 474)
Motor-ship, twin screw

Unlike her sister ship, the *Black Watch* almost survived the Second World War unscathed, even though she too fell into enemy hands and was similarly employed as a submarine depot/accommodation ship. It was not to be, however, for on 4 May 1945, almost within hours of the end of hostilities, the *Black Watch* was attacked by British aircraft from the escort carriers HMS *Searcher*, *Queen* and *Trumpeter* while she lay in the apparent safety of a mooring in the Andfjord, in the north of Norway. She broke in two and sank at Kilbotn, near Harstad, in the position 68.48N, 16.38E.

Casualties: not known

BLENHEIM (1951) Fred Olsen Line (A/S Ganger Rolf), Norway

4,766grt; 374ft (114.0m) loa x 53ft (16.2m) beam
243 passengers
John I. Thornycroft, Southampton (Yard No 4123) and
Akers MV, Oslo (Yard No 490)
Motor-ship, single screw
The *Blenheim*, one of two replacements for losses sustained in the Second World War, was a modern, strikingly streamlined passenger ferry. Her seventeen years of successful service on the Oslo to Newcastle route came to an abrupt end when, east of Dundee on 21 May 1968, fire broke out aboard the *Blenheim*, which caused extensive damage. After the fire had been extinguished, she was towed to Kristiansand with a view to a full restoration as a passenger ferry by the Akers MV shipyard. However, examination of the wrecked vessel found her to be beyond this, so her hull was sold instead to J. M. Ugland Rederi and she was converted for them into the roll-on roll-off vehicle and freight carrier *Cilaos*. She continued in service in this form until she was scrapped at Karachi from September 1981.
Casualties: not known

A later Fred Olsen ferry, the post-war *Blenheim*, with sister *Braemar*, introduced a number of extremely modernistic features to vessels of this type. *Kenneth Wightman*

BLUE SEA (1952) ex-*Europa* (1976) Ahmed Mohamed Baaboud, Saudi Arabia

11,430grt; 518ft (158.0m) loa x 68ft (20.8m) beam
446 passengers in two classes
Ansaldo, La Spezia (Yard No 319)
Motor-ship, twin screw
The *Blue Sea* was a former passenger-cargo liner that was converted into a pilgrim ship. On 12 November 1976, after less than two months of her new duties, she caught fire while at Jeddah. All the passengers and crew were safely disembarked but the *Blue Sea* sank at her anchorage during the night of 14-15 November.
Casualties: 0

BOKHARA (1873) P&O Line, UK

2,944grt; 362ft (110.2m) lbp x 39ft (11.9m) beam
195 passengers in two classes
Caird, Greenock (Yard No 177)
Compound-expansion steam reciprocating, single screw

After leaving Shanghai for Hong Kong, Colombo and Bombay, on 8 October 1892, the passenger-cargo steamship *Bokhara* ran into a typhoon and was swamped in the mountainous seas, losing all power and left drifting at the mercy of the wind. After two days she was driven onto rocks on Sand Island in the Pescadores (Penghu) group, between Formosa (Taiwan) and the Chinese mainland, and was completely wrecked. At the time she was carrying 148 persons. Only two of the survivors were passengers, members of a touring cricket party. Besides them, five officers and sixteen Lascar seamen were also rescued, picked up by the steamer *Thales* and later transferred to the cruiser HMS *Porpoise*, which took them to Hong Kong. A valuable cargo of silk and gold also went down with the *Bokhara*.
Casualties: 125

BORUSSIA (1905) Hamburg Amerika Line, Germany

6,951grt; 421ft (128.4m) lbp x 54ft (16.5m) beam
1,878 passengers in three classes
Krupp Germania, Kiel (Yard No 106)
Quadruple-expansion steam reciprocating, twin screw
The passenger steamer *Borussia*, whose accommodation provided mainly for emigrants in Steerage class, foundered off Lisbon, Portugal, while coaling on 22 October 1907 during a voyage from Hamburg to South America.
Casualties: 3

BRAGA (1907) ex-*Europa* (1920) ex-*Laura* (1917) Fabre Line, France

6,122grt; 415ft (126.6m) lbp x 50ft (15.1m) beam
1,480 passengers in three classes
Russell, Port Glasgow (Yard No 580)
Triple-expansion steam reciprocating, twin screw
The passenger-cargo ship *Braga* was ceded to France as a First World War reparation. On 16 November 1926 she was on passage from Beirut and Constantza bound for other ports in the western Mediterranean before crossing to New York when she was wrecked at Aspronissi, near the island of Lipsi or Lipsos, to the east of Patmos in the Greek islands.
Casualties: not known

BRAZIL MARU (1939) Osaka Shosen Kaisha, Japan

12,752grt; 549ft (167.3m) loa x 68ft (20.7m) beam
901 passengers in three classes
Mitsubishi, Nagasaki (Yard No 735)
Motor-ship, twin screw

The *Brazil Maru* operated a service between Japan and South America with her near-sister the *Argentina Maru*. A planned wartime conversion into an escort carrier never transpired. *Mitsui-OSK Lines*

Like her sister ship the *Argentina Maru*, it had been the intention of the Imperial Japanese Navy to convert the *Brazil Maru* into an auxiliary aircraft carrier, but in the event these plans were abandoned and she remained deployed as she had been since December 1941, as a troopship. While she was midway between the islands of Guam and Truk on 5 August 1942, the *Brazil Maru* was torpedoed by the American submarine USS *Greenling* in the position 09.51N, 150.38E. Aboard her were 400 troops, 200 other passengers and her crew. Reports suggest that there was heavy loss of life.
Casualties: ~600

BRAZZA (1923) ex-*Camranh* (1927) Chargeurs Réunis, France

10,387grt; 492ft (150.0m) loa x 59ft (18.0m) beam
363 passengers in three classes
Chantiers de la Loire, Nantes (Yard No 544)
Motor-ship, twin screw
The *Brazza*, originally a cargo ship that was reconstructed for passenger service in 1927, continued with those duties after the outbreak of the Second World War. She was torpedoed by the German submarine U37 on 28 May 1940 while she was on passage from Bordeaux to Casablanca, West African ports and New Caledonia. Aboard the *Brazza* were 576 persons, 444 passengers and 132 crew. She sank within four minutes in the position 42.43N, 11.00W, about 100 miles west of Oporto. The survivors were picked up by the French gunboat *Enseigne Henry* and the British armed merchant cruiser HMS *Cheshire*.
Casualties: 379 (300 passengers, her Master and 78 crew)

BREMEN (1897) Norddeutscher Lloyd, Germany

10,552grt; 550ft (167.6m) loa x 60ft (18.4m) beam
2,330 passengers in three classes
Schichau, Danzig (Yard No 583)
Quadruple-expansion steam reciprocating, twin screw
The passenger-cargo steamer *Bremen*, together with many of her fleet-mates, was berthed at the Norddeutscher Lloyd pier at Hoboken, New Jersey, on 30 June 1900 when fire broke out. For the full account, see the entry for the *Saale*.

One of a number of Norddeutscher Lloyd passenger steamers caught up in the conflagration at the Hoboken, New Jersey, piers in January 1900 was the *Bremen*, seen here after she had been towed clear into the River Hudson. *Mariners Museum*

BREMEN (1929) Norddeutscher Lloyd, Germany

51,656grt; 938ft (285.9m) loa x 102ft (31.1m) beam
2,200 passengers in four classes
Deschimag AG Weser, Bremen (Yard No 872)
Steam turbines, quadruple screw

It had been the intention of the German Naval Command to utilise the transatlantic record-breaking liner *Bremen* and her sister *Europa* as troop transports for the planned invasion of Great Britain, Operation 'Sealion'. The conversion work appears to have been undertaken and the pair were painted in dazzle camouflage in readiness. However, when the operation was cancelled, the *Bremen* returned to lay up at Bremerhaven where she was to serve as an accommodation ship for the duration. She was destroyed there by fire on 16 March 1941 in an outbreak that was apparently started deliberately by a member of her crew, in a reprisal action precipitated by a reprimand over a relatively trivial matter. Neither the ship's skeleton crew nor shore personnel were sufficiently prepared for such an emergency and the *Bremen* was completely gutted, coming to rest, listing to starboard, against the quayside. Quite unrecoverable, she was broken up locally, her final remains cleared by explosives at the end of the war. It has been claimed that the fire was really an act of anti-Nazi sabotage, but there is no evidence to support this.
Casualties: 0

The *Bremen* was the famous Atlantic record-breaker that had wrested the Blue Riband from Cunard's *Mauretania* on her maiden voyage in May 1929. The largest German passenger vessel to be lost in the Second World War, her end could not have been more futile. *Ian Allan Library*

BRETAGNE (1922) ex-*Flandria* (1936) Compagnie Générale Transatlantique (French Line), France

10,171grt; 472ft (143.9m) loa x 59ft (18.0m) beam
440 passengers in single class
Barclay Curle, Whiteinch, Glasgow (Yard No 594)
Steam turbines, twin screw
On 14 October 1939, while on passage from Cristobal, Panama, and Kingston, Jamaica, to Le Havre, the *Bretagne* was torpedoed and sunk by the German submarine U45, 300 miles south-west of the Fastnet Rock in the position 50.20N, 12.45W. The submarine surfaced and shelled the sinking liner, hitting a lifeboat that was being lowered and killing some of its occupants. The survivors, many of them gravely wounded, were picked up by a British warship.
Casualties: 7

BRITANNIA (1926) Anchor Line, UK

6,525grt; 465ft (141.7m) lbp x 59ft (18.0m) beam
300 passengers
Alexander Stephen, Linthouse, Glasgow (Yard No508)
Quadruple-expansion steam reciprocating, single screw
The passenger-cargo ship *Britannia*, carrying 281 passengers and 203 crew members, was bound from Glasgow and Liverpool to Cape Town and Bombay on 25 March 1941, when she was intercepted and sunk by the German

commerce raider *Thor*, south-west of Freetown, Gambia. There was a brief exchange of fire between the two vessels but the hopelessly outgunned *Britannia* was forced to concede after an hour. Her boats were lowered so that the survivors could abandon ship, and once they were clear the *Thor* resumed its onslaught, pounding the *Britannia* with shells until she sank, going down in the position 07.24N, 24.03W. No assistance was rendered to the *Britannia*'s castaways by the *Thor*. One boat of 63 survivors was later picked up by the Spanish ship *Bachi*, while another, with 38 surviving occupants, managed to reach the coast of Brazil twenty-three days later, on 17 April 1941.

Casualties: 249 (127 passengers and 122 crew)

Anchor Line's *Britannia* operated between the United Kingdom and India, via Suez. *Ian Allan Library*

BRITANNIC (1915) White Star Line, UK

48,158grt; 903ft (275.2m) loa x 94ft (28.7m) beam
2,573 passengers in three classes (as designed)
Harland & Wolff, Belfast (Yard No 433)
Quadruple-expansion steam reciprocating with LP turbine, triple screw

The *Britannic* was the half-sister of the express mail liners *Olympic* and *Titanic*, having received structural improvements and other modifications in the wake of the disastrous sinking of the *Titanic*. Still in the early stages of construction at the time, these changes delayed her completion and she was still at her builder's yard in August 1914. A year later her completion as a hospital ship was ordered by the Admiralty and in this capacity she entered service on 12 December 1915, drafted to the eastern Mediterranean in support of the Allied armies in the Dardanelles. Using her great capacity, she transported back to Naples and Southampton large numbers of wounded men brought by smaller hospital vessels from the battle fronts in Gallipoli to the Greek Island of Lemnos, where she was based at Mudros. On 21 November 1916, on only her sixth round voyage, the outward-bound *Britannic*, with a complement of 1,125 persons, comprising 625 crew and 500 medical officers, nurses and RAMC personnel, struck a mine four miles west of Port St Nikolo in the Kea Channel. The mine was one of a large quantity that had been laid earlier by the German submarine U73. The explosion ripped open the *Britannic*'s starboard side, rupturing the bulkhead between two of the watertight compartments, which, in conjunction with a failure of the watertight door system in the forepart of the ship, caused the ship to flood rapidly, a situation worsened by her continuing forward movement. Efforts were made to beach her in shallow waters but she could not be saved, and only an hour after the explosion, with her bow under, she heeled over to starboard and disappeared beneath the

surface. The *Britannic* was the largest British merchant vessel sunk in the First World War.

Casualties: 21

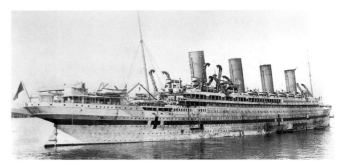

The third ship of the 'Olympic' class, the *Britannic* only saw service as a wartime hospital ship. She was the largest passenger ship lost in the First World War.
Imperial War Museum (HU90768)

BRITTANY (1952) ex-*Bretagne* (1962) Chandris Line, Greece

16,335grt; 581ft (177.0m) loa x 73ft (22.3m) beam
1,200 passengers in two classes
Penhoët, St Nazaire (Yard No X12)
Steam turbines, twin screw

On 28 March 1963 the passenger liner *Brittany* was taken in hand for engine repairs at the Hellenic Shipyards at Skaramanga, Greece, but while there she caught fire and was virtually gutted on 8 April. The burning wreck was beached in Vasilika Bay the following night. It was raised on 10 May, then laid up pending a decision on its future. As reconstruction was an uneconomic proposition, the Britanny was towed to La Spezia, Italy, arriving on 31 March 1964 for breaking up to commence.

Casualties: not known

Chandris Line's *Brittany* started her career as the French-flag *Bretagne*. After a year under charter to Chandris, she was purchased outright for the Europe to Australia service.
Tom Rayner collection

BROOKLYN (1869) ex-*City of Brooklyn* (1878) Dominion Line, UK

4,215grt; 400ft (121.9m) lbp x 42ft (12.8m) beam
480 passengers in two classes
Tod & McGregor, Meadowside, Glasgow (Yard No 145)
Compound-expansion steam reciprocating, single screw

The former Inman Line passenger-cargo steamship *Brooklyn* was wrecked on Anticosti Island, Quebec, on 8 November 1885, as she was arriving at the end of a westbound crossing.

Casualties: 0

BRUGES (1920) London & North Eastern Railway, UK

2,949grt; 322ft (98.0m) lbp x 43ft (13.1m) beam
1,500 passengers
John Brown, Clydebank (Yard No 494)
Steam turbines, twin screw

The third of a group of three vessels ordered by the Great Eastern Railway for the Harwich-Hook service, the *Bruges* and her sisters served the LNER from 1923. Taken over for transport duties after the outbreak of the Second World War, carrying units of the British Expeditionary Force to France, the *Bruges* was soon engaged in the operation to bring these same troops back to the UK from the continent in the summer of 1940. Assigned to Operation 'Cycle', conveying Allied troops from Cherbourg and Le Havre to Southampton, she came under attack from German aircraft on 11 June 1940 while at anchor off Le Havre. Sustaining a direct bomb hit, she was beached and abandoned as a total loss. She was not carrying troops at the time of the attack.
Casualties: 0

The LNER's *Bruges* was one of a class of steamers introduced by the company's forerunner, the Great Eastern Railway, in the early 1920s for the Harwich to Hook of Holland service.
Ambrose Greenway

BUENOS AIRES MARU (1930) Osaka Shosen Kaisha, Japan

9,626grt; 473ft (144.2m) loa x 62ft (18.9m) beam
1,136 passengers in two classes
Mitsubishi, Nagasaki (Yard No 456)
Motor-ship, twin screw

The *Buenos Aires Maru* at Cape Town. *Alex Duncan*

From 1942 the *Buenos Aires Maru* served with the Imperial Japanese Navy as a hospital ship. She was attacked and damaged in a torpedo attack in the South China Sea on 25 November 1943, which she survived. Two days later, while she was limping home for repairs, she was bombed by United States aircraft off the coast of the island of St Matthias, in the Bismarck Archipelago (Mussau islands, now part of Papua, New Guinea) and sank in the position 02.44S, 149.15E.
Casualties: not known

BURDIGALA (1898) ex-*Kaiser Friedrich* (1912) Compagnie Sud-Atlantique, France

12,481grt; 600ft (182.9m) loa x 64ft (19.4m) beam
1,350 passengers in three classes
Schichau, Danzig (Yard No 587)
Quadruple-expansion steam reciprocating, twin screw

The *Burdigala* had been laid up at Bordeaux from November 1913, but she was reactivated after the outbreak of the First World War, commandeered in March 1915 for service as an armed transport with the French Navy. She lasted only a year and a half, though, for she struck a mine on 14 November 1916, 2 miles from Kea, in the Kos channel, and was destroyed. She was the first of three passenger vessel victims of a minefield laid by the German submarine U73 between Mykonos and Tenos, in the Aegean Sea. Though eighteen years old when sunk, the *Burdigala*'s total commercial service had amounted to less than three years for she had also spent many of her early years laid up.
Casualties: not known

CABO SAN ANTONIO (1930) Ybarra y Cia, Spain

12,275grt; 500ft (152.5m) loa x 63ft (19.3m) beam
250 passengers in two classes
Soc Española de Construccion Naval, Bilbao (Yard No 33)
Motor-ship, twin screw

The passenger-cargo liner Cabo San Antonio caught fire on 29 December 1939 while bound from Buenos Aires to Genoa. When she was about 400 miles south-west of Dakar, Senegal, on the west coast of Africa, fire broke out in her galley and quickly spread throughout the vessel. In a very short time the fire was completely out of control and the passengers and crew were evacuated by the French destroyer *Cassard*, which had come to their assistance. As the *Cabo San Antonio* was considered to be a danger to navigation, the destroyer shelled and sank her on 31 December in the approximate position 10.10N, 21.00W.
Casualties: 5 (all passengers)

CABO SANTO TOMÉ (1931) Ybarra y Cia, Spain

12,589grt; 500ft (152.5m) loa x 63ft (19.3m) beam
512 passengers in two classes
Soc Española de Construccion Naval, Bilbao (Yard No 39)
Motor-ship, twin screw

After five years on the South America run, the *Cabo Santo Tomé* was commandeered by Republican forces during the Spanish Civil War and placed in service as a transport to convey ammunition, aircraft and military equipment from the Soviet Union. On 10 October 1937, while returning from Odessa, she was attacked off the Algerian coast at Cape Roca by two Nationalist gunboats, the *Dato* and *Canovas*. The crew of the *Cabo Santo Tomé* attempted to make for the Algerian seaport of Bône (Annaba), but the vessel was set on fire, which spread so quickly that they were forced to abandon ship. Soon afterwards an explosion within the *Cabo Santo Tomé* ripped her apart and she sank.
Casualties: not known

Ybarra Line's *Cabo Santo Tomé* sailed on the Genoa and Barcelona to La Plata service. *World Ship Society*

CALABRIA (1922) ex-*Werra* (1935) Lloyd Triestino, Italy

9,476grt; 480ft (146.3m) loa x 57ft (17.4m) beam
954 passengers in two classes
Deschimag AG Weser, Bremen (Yard No 324)
Triple-expansion steam reciprocating, twin screw

The Italian passenger-cargo ship *Calabria* was captured by the British at Calcutta, where she was in dry dock, on 11 June 1940. She was placed under the management of the British India Line by the Ministry of War Transport, the intention being to use her as a troopship, a function she had previously performed for the Italian Government. However, she was torpedoed and sunk on 8 December 1940 by the German submarine U103, in the position 52.43N, 18.07W, as she was nearing the end of a voyage to the River Clyde from Calcutta and Freetown. There were no survivors.
Casualties: 360 (230 Indian passengers and 130 crew)

The Norddeutscher Lloyd transatlantic steamship *Werra* was sold to Italy in 1935 and renamed *Calabria*. The photograph shows her as the *Werra*. *Arnold Kludas*

CALEDONIA (1905) Anchor Line, UK

9,223grt; 500ft (152.4m) lbp x 58ft (17.7m) beam
1,616 passengers in three classes
D. & W. Henderson, Meadowside, Glasgow (Yard No 438)
Triple-expansion steam reciprocating, twin screw

Requisitioned as a troopship during the First World War, the passenger liner *Caledonia* was equipped to carry 3,074 troops. On 4 December 1916, while she was returning from Salonica (Thessaloniki) bound for Marseilles, empty apart from bags of mail, she was torpedoed and sunk by the German submarine U65, which attacked her without warning. She sank in the position 35.40N, 17.05E, approximately 125 miles east-by-south of Malta.
Casualties: 1

The *Caledonia* of 1905 spent nine years on the run from Glasgow to New York with three similar vessels, the *California*, *Cameronia* and *Columbia*. *World Ship Society*

CALEDONIA (1922) ex-*Majestic* (1937) ex-*Bismarck* (1922) Admiralty, UK

56,551grt; 956ft (291.4m) loa x 100ft (30.5m) beam
2,000 naval cadets

Blohm & Voss, Steinwerder, Hamburg (Yard No 214)
Steam turbines, quadruple screw

After 14 years' service on the North Atlantic, the liner Majestic was sold for conversion into a boys' training ship stationed at Rosyth. Three years later, at the very time when consideration was being given to re-converting the *Caledonia*, as she had been renamed, into a troopship, she was completely burned out on 29 September 1939, sinking on an even keel in shallow water. Raised in March 1940 but found to be unfit for restoration, she was dismantled down to her lower hull where she lay. This remaining part of the wreck was towed to Inverkeithing in July 1943 where it too was scrapped, her contribution to the war effort reduced to scrap metal.
Casualties: not known

At the end of her transatlantic days, the White Star liner *Majestic* was sold to the Admiralty for conversion into the boys' training ship *Caledonia*, stationed at Rosyth. *Richard de Kerbrech collection*

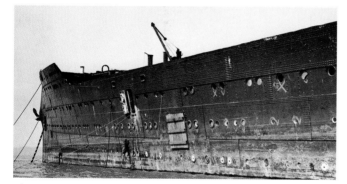

The remains of the *Caledonia* in the Firth of Forth, awaiting final disposal. She has already been stripped down to below main deck level. *Imperial War Museum (A9766)*

CALEDONIA (1925) Anchor Line, UK

serving under the wartime name HMS SCOTSTOUN
17,046grt; 578ft (176.2m) loa x 70ft (21.3m) beam
1,342 passengers in three classes
Alexander Stephen, Linthouse, Glasgow (Yard No 495)
Steam turbines, twin screw

The transatlantic passenger liner *Caledonia* was requisitioned for conversion into an armed merchant cruiser and commissioned under the name HMS *Scotstoun* in September 1939 with a complement of 350 officers and naval ratings. While patrolling the Northern Approaches on 13 June 1940, she was torpedoed and sunk by the German submarine U25 when she was 200 miles west of Inishtrahull, in the position 57.00N, 09.57W.
Casualties: 6

Anchor Line's replacement *Caledonia* was lost in June 1940 while serving as the armed merchant cruiser HMS *Scotstoun*. *Ian Allan Library*

CALEDONIEN (1882) Messageries Maritimes, France

4,248grt; 413ft (125.9m) lbp x 41ft (12.5m) beam
209 passengers in three classes
Messageries Maritimes, La Ciotat (Yard No 54)
Triple-expansion steam reciprocating, single screw

The *Caledonien*, which had been requisitioned by the French government to maintain essential postal services, was bound in convoy from Marseilles to Madagascar and Mauritius on 30 June 1917 when she struck two mines some 30 miles from Port Said, in the eastern Mediterranean. The mines had been laid by the German submarine UC34. The devastation to the *Caledonien* was enormous and her forward end sank within four minutes. Although her stern end remained afloat for around 25 minutes, there were no means of organising an orderly evacuation, besides which many had been killed by the explosions. The *General Gallieni*, another convoy ship, and the destroyers *Lansquenet* and *Thyelli* went to the assistance of the *Caledonien* but they were limited to picking up survivors from the sea.
Casualties: 51 (all crew)

The *Caledonien* was one of a large class of seven sister ships built for the route from Marseilles, via the Suez Canal, to Australia and New Caledonia. *World Ship Society*

CALGARIAN (1914) Canadian Pacific Line, UK

17,515grt, 600ft (182.9m) loa x 72ft (21.9m) beam
1,680 passengers in three classes
Fairfield, Govan (Yard No 487)
Steam turbines, quadruple screw

Taken over in September 1915 as an armed merchant cruiser and attached to the 9th Cruiser Squadron, the liner *Calgarian* was sunk while performing this role. As she had transferred ownership from the Allan Line during the First World War,

in July 1917, she never undertook any commercial sailings for Canadian Pacific, her new owners. She was torpedoed off Rathlin Head, Northern Ireland, on 1 March 1918 by the German submarine U19. She did not remain afloat for long and sank soon after the attack.
Casualties: 49 (2 officers and 47 naval ratings)

The *Calgarian*, seen here, and *Alsatian* were introduced to the Liverpool to Halifax and St John's, Nova Scotia, route in 1914. They passed to Canadian Pacific ownership in July 1917, when that company absorbed the Allan Line.
H. B. Christiansen Collection / Online Transport Archive

CALIFORNIA (1907) Anchor Line, UK

8,662grt; 485ft (147.8m) loa x 58ft (17.7m) beam
1,214 passengers
D. & W. Henderson, Meadowside, Glasgow (Yard No 459)
Triple-expansion steam reciprocating, twin screw
The passenger liner *California* was attacked by the German submarine U85 on 7 February 1917, nine days after she had set sail from Glasgow to New York with 205 persons on board. There were fatalities when the torpedo struck her aft end and there were more when, as she sank with alarming speed, lifeboats capsized in the hasty evacuation. She sank some 38 miles west-by-south of the Fastnet Rock, in the position 51.10N, 09.21W.
Casualties: 43

CALIFORNIA (1920) ex-*Albania* (1930) Lloyd Triestino, Italy

13,060grt; 539ft (164.3m) loa x 64ft (19.5m) beam
150 passengers in two classes
Scott's, Greenock (Yard No 479)
Steam turbines, twin screw

Construction of the Cunard Line's *Albania*, the fourth ship of the pre-First World War 'A' class, was interrupted by the hostilities. When completed in 1920, she emerged in a somewhat different configuration and did not fit into a balanced schedule. Laid up in 1925, she was acquired by Navigazione Libera Triestina, Italy, in January 1930 and placed in their service to Seattle under the name *California*. Five years later she passed to Lloyd Triestino. *Alex Duncan*

The passenger-cargo ship *California*, which had served for much of the time after her transfer to Italian registry in 1930 as a hospital ship and troopship, was sunk by British torpedo bombers at Syracuse, Sicily, on 11 August 1941. In January 1949 her wreck was still lying where it had been sunk, but it was raised and scrapped shortly thereafter.
Casualties: 1

CALIFORNIA (1923) Anchor Line, UK

16,792grt; 575ft (175.3m) loa x 70ft (21.3m) beam
1,785 passengers in three classes
Alexander Stephen, Linthouse, Glasgow (Yard No 494)
Steam turbines, twin screw
Following the outbreak of the Second World War, the passenger liner *California* spent almost three years as an armed merchant cruiser before she was converted into a troopship in 1942. Early on 12 July 1943 she was proceeding in a convoy, west of Portugal, bound for Freetown from the River Clyde, when she came under attack from German long-range bombers. The *California* was hit a number of times, caught fire and had to be abandoned by her 767 occupants, 449 troops and the crew of 318 men. As the convoy was obliged for safety reasons to maintain its forward progress, the *California* had to be sunk by shell fire from naval escorts in the position 41.15N, 15.24W to prevent her from falling into enemy hands if she remained afloat.
Casualties: 72 (26 passengers and 46 crew)

The *California* was the last ship of the 'Cameronia' class, four vessels introduced on the transatlantic services from Glasgow or London in the 1920s. *Alex Duncan*

CALINO (1940) Adriatica Line, Italy

5,186grt; 373ft (113.7m) lbp x 53ft (16.0m) beam
282 passengers in three classes
Cantieri Riuniti dell'Adriatico, Monfalcone
(Yard No 1241)
Motor-ship, twin screw
The passenger-cargo ship *Calino* was completed in May 1940, just prior to Italy's entry into the Second World War, and most probably saw no commercial service, instead taken up immediately for auxiliary employment. She was mined off Punta Campanella on 10 January 1943 and capsized, a total loss, three miles north-east of Capri.
Casualties: not known

CALITEA (1933) Adriatica SA di Navigazione, Italy

4,013grt; 334ft (100.0m) lbp x 50ft (15.2m) beam
150 passengers
Cantieri Riuniti dell'Adriatico, Monfalcone
(Yard No 1118)
Motor-ship, twin screw
The passenger ship *Calitea* was sunk on 11 December 1941, torpedoed by the British submarine HMS *Talisman* ninety miles south of Cape Matapan (Tainaron), in the position 36.23N, 20.33E.
Casualties: not known

CALPEAN STAR (1929) ex-*Highland Chieftain* (1959) Calpe Shipping Co, Gibraltar

14,232grt; 544ft (165.8m) loa x 69ft (21.1m) beam
439 passengers in two classes (in Royal Mail Lines service)
Harland & Wolff, Belfast (Yard No 806)
Motor-ship, twin screw
The Royal Mail Lines passenger liner *Highland Chieftain* was sold in October 1959 for service as a maintenance ship and crew transport supporting whaling fleets operating in the Antarctic. Less than six months after the *Calpean Star*, as she was renamed, commenced these duties, she suffered a damaged rudder and was obliged to make for Montevideo for repairs. On 1 June 1960, after leaving Montevideo on the conclusion of this work, there was a massive explosion in the ship's engine room that caused her to sink in shallow waters two nautical miles off the coast of Uruguay. Following salvage the *Calpean Star* was broken up.
Casualties: not known

The *Calpean Star*, formerly the *Highland Chieftain*.
H. B. Christiansen Collection /Online Transport Archive

CAMERONIA (1911) Anchor Line, UK

10,963grt; 532ft (162.1m) loa x 62ft (18.9m) beam
1,700 passengers in three classes
D. & W. Henderson, Meadowside, Glasgow (Yard No 472)
Triple expansion steam reciprocating, twin screw
Until 1917 the passenger liner *Cameronia* had continued to operate on commercial schedules, but she was then taken up for troopship service. In this role she was torpedoed and sunk on 15 April 1917 by the German submarine U33 while she was bound from Marseilles to Egypt with 2,630 troops. Without warning, the submarine launched its attack some 150 miles east of Malta. The *Cameronia* remained afloat for forty minutes, which permitted as full an evacuation as

possible. However, many lives were lost when the first lifeboat to be launched capsized upon reaching the water.
Casualties: 140 (129 troops, including one officer, and 11 crew members) Some reports give the death toll as 210.

The Anchor liner *Cameronia*, which entered the Glasgow to New York service in September 1911, was later employed on a joint service, in conjunction with Cunard, which included a call at Liverpool. *Wm. Robertson & Co.*

The *Cameronia*'s last moments as she sinks off Malta in April 1917. *Imperial War Museum (Q115414)*

CAO-BANG (1902) Messageries Maritimes, France

6,487grt; 445ft (135.9m) lbp x 47ft (14.4m) beam
1,990 officers and troops
Forges et Chantiers de la Méditerranée, La Seyne
(Yard No 960)
Triple-expansion steam reciprocating, twin screw
The passenger-cargo ship *Cao-Bang* was wrecked in fog on the island of Poulo Condore (Pulo Kampong), off French Indo-China (now Cambodia), on 4 January 1906, while bound from Hai Phong and Saigon for Marseilles.
Casualties: 0

CAP ARCONA (1927) Hamburg Sud-Amerika Line, Germany

27,561grt; 675ft (205.7m) loa x 84ft (25.6m) beam
1,315 passengers in three classes
Blohm & Voss, Steinwerder, Hamburg (Yard No 476)
Steam turbines, twin screw
From late November 1940 the passenger liner *Cap Arcona* was based at Gotenhafen (Gdynia), where she was utilised as a German Navy accommodation ship. She remained so engaged until January 1945 when she was reactivated to assist in Operation 'Hannibal', the evacuation of Germany's

eastern territories. Later, in April 1945, a new, 'special' task, apparently to provide accommodation for the concentration camp internees from Neuengamme, Mittelbau-Dora and Stutthof, was allocated to the *Cap Arcona* and *Deutschland* (qv), the latter to be converted into a hospital ship, together with the cargo ship *Thielbek* (see Appendix 2). Between 7,300 and 7,500 prisoners were embarked upon the *Cap Arcona* and *Thielbek*, among them numbers of Russian and Polish prisoners of war, all ferried to the two vessels anchored off Neustadt, in the Bay of Lubeck, aboard another cargo ship, the *Athen*. Conditions aboard the *Cap Arcona* were crowded, for with some 400 SS guards, a naval gunnery detail of 500 and a crew of 76, there were almost 6,000 persons on board.

In this situation the *Cap Arcona*, *Thielbek* and *Deutschland* came under attack from RAF Typhoon fighter-bombers in a series of raids on 3 May 1945, just five days before the war's end. The *Cap Arcona* was hit repeatedly by rockets and machine-gun fire and set ablaze. Virtually all means of escape were destroyed – only one lifeboat was launched – and panic broke out within the ship when the SS guards confined the prisoners below, threatening to shoot them if they tried to escape. Shortly afterwards the *Cap Arcona* capsized onto her side, claiming the lives of prisoners and guards alike. She drifted ashore in the position 54.04N, 10.50E, where she became a total wreck.

She remained thus until late 1949, when demolition commenced using divers. As a postscript, it was revealed after the war that the loading of concentration camp internees aboard the *Cap Arcona* and *Thielbek* had, in fact, had a more sinister purpose. As part of the Nazi efforts in the final days of the war to conceal the terrible crimes against humanity perpetrated within these camps, the ships were to have been towed to sea and deliberately sunk, killing all the prisoners. It is a bitter irony that almost the same outcome was inflicted by those who, only days later, could have liberated them.

Casualties: As with the *Wilhelm Gustloff*, precise numbers of casualties from the *Cap Arcona* disaster are not available. There were certainly in excess of 5,000. Figures of 5,136 and 5,594 have been quoted, but the basis of these computations is uncertain. It is reported that 350 prisoners and 490 guards, naval gunners or crew survived. Of the 2,800 prisoners placed on the *Thielbek*, only 50 survived.

The *Cap Arcona* was the largest German liner ever to be placed on the run to ports on the River Plate, South America, at a time when there was considerable competition on the route and other companies were introducing increasingly larger vessels. Her loss, late in the Second World War, was the second worst suffered by the German merchant marine and was all the more tragic because she was packed with concentration camp internees. *Ian Allan Library*

The wreck of the *Cap Arcona* during clearance operations after the war. *Imperial War Museum (HU58279)*

CAP FRIO (1899) Hamburg Sud-Amerika Line, Germany

5,732grt; 411ft (125.0m) lbp x 48ft (14.6m) beam
580 passengers in two classes
Reiherstiegwerft, Hamburg (Yard No 404)
Quadruple-expansion steam reciprocating, single screw
The passenger-cargo ship *Cap Frio* was wrecked on the Brazilian coast on 30 August 1908, near the Barra lighthouse, Bahia, during a tropical storm. At the time she had been bound from Bahia to Hamburg.
Casualties: not known

CAP LAY (1921) ex-*Halgan* (1926) Chargeurs Réunis, France

8,169grt; 417ft (127.3m) lbp x 55ft (16.8m) beam
850 passengers
Chantiers de la Loire, Nantes (Yard No 541)
Steam turbines, single screw
The cargo ship *Halgan*, together with four sister vessels, was converted into a passenger ship in 1925, in her case renamed *Cap Lay*. In this form she was lost in a typhoon off Catba Island, in the Bay of Along, Vietnam, in the Gulf of Tonkin, on 17 July 1928.
Casualties: not known

CAP PADARAN (1922) ex-*D'Iberville* (1925) Chargeurs Réunis, France

8,169grt; 417ft (127.1m) lbp x 55ft (16.8m) beam
850 passengers
Chantiers de la Loire, Nantes (Yard No 542)
Steam turbines, single screw
While bound from Taranto to Augusta, Sicily, on 9 December 1943, carrying a crew of 195, which included thirteen gunners, the passenger-cargo ship *Cap Padaran* was torpedoed and sunk by the German submarine U596. The attack took place east of Crotone, Calabria, in the position 39.15N, 17.30E. The stricken ship, her back broken, was taken in tow but the line parted and she sank soon after.
Casualties: 5

CAP TRAFALGAR (1914) Hamburg Sud-Amerika Line, Germany

18,710grt; 613ft (186.8m) loa x 72ft (21.9m) beam
1,586 passengers in three classes
Vulcan, Hamburg (Yard No 334)
Triple-expansion steam reciprocating, triple screw

The liner *Cap Trafalgar* was lost in a unique engagement between two converted passenger liners, a duel that very nearly cost both ships. She was fitted out as an auxiliary cruiser in August 1914, only five months after entering the Hamburg to South America service. The adaptation took place at sea: having received her orders at Buenos Aires and coaled at Montevideo, she was soon bound for Bahia Blanca, where she rendezvoused with the gunboat *Eber*, which transferred weapons and other equipment to her. To help conceal her identity, her third funnel was removed.

On 13 September the British armed merchant cruiser *Carmania* interrupted the *Cap Trafalgar* in the act of coaling, off the Brazilian island of Trinidad. After a brief chase, the two ships opened fire on one another and initially, at a distance of 4 miles, the British ship's gunnery was more effective, her shells causing considerable damage to the *Cap Trafalgar*'s hull. As the range closed, however, the battle became more even and the *Carmania* also began to sustain damage. The intense action lasted nearly 2 hours, after which the *Cap Trafalgar* was listing and ablaze from end to end, while the *Carmania*, hit no fewer than 79 times, was also on fire at her fore end. The British ship had also lost the use of her navigation and communication equipment, her water main had been ruptured, making it impossible to fight fires, and she had to be escorted to port by the cruiser HMS *Cornwall*. The *Cap Trafalgar* capsized onto her port side and sank bow-first in the position 20.10S, 29.50W. Her survivors were picked up by the *Eleonore Woermann*.
Casualties: 166 (159 Germans and 9 British)

The loss of the *Cap Trafalgar*, of the Hamburg Sud-Amerika Line, was unique, resulting from the only liner-versus-liner engagement of either World War. She and her adversary *Carmania* were both serving as auxiliary cruisers.
Hamburg Sud-Amerika Line

CAP VARELLA (1921) ex-*Kersaint* (1926) Chargeurs Réunis, France

serving under the wartime name TEIKA MARU
8,169grt; 417ft (127.1m) lbp x 55ft (16.8m) beam
727 passengers in two classes
Chantiers de la Loire, Nantes (Yard No 539)
Steam turbines, single screw
The passenger-cargo ship *Cap Varella* was seized by the Japanese at Yokohama on 10 April 1942 and placed in service as a transport under the name *Teika Maru*. She was sunk on 7 May 1945 when she struck a mine laid by the American submarine USS *Finback* in the position 34.06N, 130.47E, north-east of the island of Iki, between Karatsu and Shimonoseki.
Casualties: not known

CARAQUET (1894) ex-*Guelph* (1913) Royal Mail Line, UK

4,917grt; 400ft (122.1m) lbp x 47ft (14.4m) beam
353 passengers in three classes
Harland & Wolff, Belfast (Yard No 284)
Triple-expansion steam reciprocating, twin screw
On 25 June 1923, during a voyage from Halifax, Nova Scotia, bound for Bermuda and the Antilles, the passenger-cargo steamer *Caraquet* ran ashore on Northern Reef, twelve miles north of Hamilton, Bermuda, and became a total loss. An attempt was made to salvage the vessel, for which the salvors had insisted upon receiving a $5,000 guarantee payment due to the *Caraquet*'s age and her exposed position.
Casualties: 0

CARIBBEAN (1890) ex-*Dunottar Castle* (1913) Royal Mail Line, UK

5,825grt; 433ft (132.0m) loa x 49ft (14.9m) beam
350 passengers in three classes
Fairfield, Govan (Yard No 348)
Triple-expansion steam reciprocating, single screw
Just a year after her acquisition from Union-Castle Line, the passenger-cargo steamship *Caribbean* was requisitioned in August 1914 for service as a troop transport and armed merchant cruiser. While bound for Scapa Flow on 27 September 1915 she encountered extremely heavy weather off the aptly named Cape Wrath, Sutherland, and was disabled. The cruiser HMS *Birkenhead*, assisted by Navy tugs, attempted to tow the crippled former liner to port, but they were unsuccessful and the *Caribbean* foundered.
Casualties: 15

Royal Mail's *Caribbean*. Under her former name of *Dunottar Castle* she was distinguished as the vessel aboard which the reception marking the amalgamation of the Union and Castle Line fleets was held on 17 March 1900.
H. B. Christiansen Collection / Online Transport Archive

CARIBIA (1928) ex-*Vulcania* (1965) Sicula Oceanica (SIOSA), Italy

24,496grt; 632ft (192.5m) loa x 80ft (24.3m) beam
1,437 passengers in three classes
Cantieri Navale Triestino, Monfalcone (Yard No 161)
Motor-ship, twin screw
The former transatlantic liner *Caribia* ran onto submerged rocks off Cannes during the night of 23-24 September 1972, while she was on a Mediterranean cruise bound from Genoa and Nice to Barcelona. Her engine room was flooded and all

power was lost, throwing the entire vessel into darkness. Assistance arrived the following morning and the *Caribia* was towed to Genoa. Five days later she was laid up at La Spezia pending a decision on her future. A year of idleness followed, at the end of which she was sold for breaking up at Barcelona as repairs were considered uneconomical on a vessel of such advanced years. A further transaction did nothing to forestall this, for it only took the *Caribia* instead to a scrapyard in Taiwan. However, on her arrival in the Far East hull leaks that had worsened during the voyage caused her to sink outside the harbour at Kaohsiung.
Casualties: 0

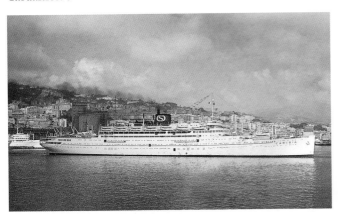

The former Italia transatlantic liner *Vulcania*, originally built for the Cosulich Line, was rebuilt and modernised as the SIOSA cruise ship *Caribia*. *Mick Lindsay*

CARINTHIA (1925) Cunard Line, UK

20,277grt; 624ft (190.2m) 73ft (22.3m) beam
1,650 passengers in three classes
Vickers, Barrow-in-Furness (Yard No 586)
Steam turbines, twin screw
In January 1940 the passenger liner *Carinthia* was commissioned for service as an armed merchant cruiser. On 7 June 1940, while she was patrolling west of the Irish Coast, she was torpedoed by the German submarine U46 and sank in the position 53.13N, 10.40W. Fortunately, she remained afloat for some time, permitting the full evacuation of all those aboard, apart from a number of casualties caused by the exploding torpedo.
Casualties: 4 (2 naval officers and 2 ratings)

The *Carinthia* was one of a class of five similar ships built for Cunard Line's intermediate transatlantic service from Liverpool, the other four being the *Scythia*, *Samaria*, *Laconia* and *Franconia*. During the Depression years, the *Carinthia* also went cruising, as seen here about to leave the Mersey.
Ian Allan Library

CARPATHIA (1903) Cunard Line, UK

13,603grt; 558ft (170.1m) loa x 64ft (19.5m) beam
1,704 passengers in two classes
C. S. Swan & Hunter, Wallsend-on-Tyne (Yard No 274)
Quadruple-expansion steam reciprocating, twin screw
While on passage from Liverpool to Boston with 57 passengers and a crew of 220, the liner *Carpathia* was torpedoed and sunk by the German submarine U55 on 17 July 1918. The attack took place 170 miles north-west of Bishop Rock, in the position 50.25N, 10.49W.
Casualties: 5 (all crew)

Whatever else is written about the *Carpathia*, she will always be best remembered as the ship whose mercy dash to the sinking *Titanic* resulted in the rescue of more than 700 survivors. She operated on the routes to New York from both Liverpool and Trieste. Berthed at New York, she is about to sail.
Richard de Kerbrech collection

CARTHAGE (1910) Compagnie Générale Transatlantique (French Line), France

5,601grt; 400ft (121.8m) lbp x 51ft (15.6m) beam
347 passengers in three classes
Swan Hunter & Wigham Richardson, Low Walker, Newcastle (Yard No 828)
Triple-expansion steam reciprocating, twin screw

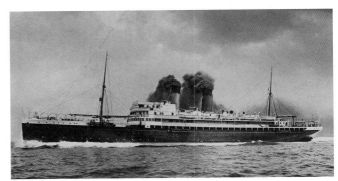

The Swan Hunter-built *Carthage* served Algeria, Tunisia and Morocco from Marseilles for the French Line. *Ian Rae*

The *Carthage* worked the North African routes to the French colonies from her home port of Marseilles until the outbreak of the First World War, when she was taken over for service as an auxiliary cruiser. Later she was utilised as a troop transport

and it was while engaged in these duties that she was torpedoed and sunk on 4 July 1915 while lying at anchor two nautical miles west of Cape Hellas in the Aegean Sea. Her assailant was the German submarine U212.
Casualties: 6 (all crew)

CARTHAGINIAN (1884) Allan Line, UK

4,444grt; 386ft (117.6m) lbp x 45ft (13.7m) beam
596 passengers in three classes
Govan Shipbuilding Co, Govan, Glasgow (Yard No 140)
Compound steam reciprocating, single screw
The passenger steamship *Carthaginian* was bound for Montreal from the River Clyde on 14 June 1917 when she struck a submarine-laid mine and sank as a result of the explosion. The location of the incident was 2½ miles north-west of Inishtrahull lighthouse.
Casualties: 0

CASTILIAN (1899) Allan Line, UK

7,441grt; 470ft (143.3m) lbp x 54ft (16.4m) beam
1,420 passengers in three classes
Workman Clark, Belfast (Yard No 150)
Triple-expansion steam reciprocating, single screw
The passenger-cargo ship *Castilian* was lost on 11 March 1899 on the homeward leg of her maiden voyage from Liverpool to Halifax and Portland, Maine, carrying 162 passengers. She stranded on Gannet Rock Ledge, in the entrance to the Bay of Fundy, about ten miles south-west of Yarmouth, Nova Scotia.
Casualties: 0

CATALUÑA (1883) Cia Trasatlantica Española, Spain

3,665grt; 384ft (117.1m) lbp x 42ft (12.9m) beam
1,230 passengers in three classes
William Denny, Dumbarton (Yard No 272)
Compound-expansion steam reciprocating, single screw
During a voyage to West Africa on 25 March 1923, the passenger-cargo ship *Cataluña* ran ashore and was wrecked at Rio del Oro, Spanish West Africa (Spanish Sahara). She had been built for North Atlantic service but was switched to the Marseilles and Cadiz to Buenos Aires route in 1892, for which her Steerage class accommodation was considerably enlarged. However, she appears to have completed only one round voyage before being redeployed again.
Casualties: 0

CATHAY (1925) P&O Line, UK

15,225grt; 545ft (166.1m) loa x 70ft (21.3m) beam
306 passengers in two classes
Barclay Curle, Whiteinch, Glasgow (Yard No 602)
Quadruple-expansion steam reciprocating, twin screw
After three years spent as an armed merchant cruiser, from October 1939, the passenger ship *Cathay* was converted into a troopship and in November 1942 was attached to the Allied amphibious task force engaged in the North African landings. After she had arrived off Bougie (Bejaia) from Glasgow on 11 November, she was attacked by German bomber aircraft while in the process of disembarking her troops. Ablaze from end to end, she sank the following day, settling on the bottom

in the position 36.44N, 05.07E. Initially listing to port, damage on her starboard side, caused by the explosions from near-misses during another air attack, first righted her, then caused her to list in the other direction. When a delayed-action bomb in her galley suddenly detonated and blew off her stern, any remaining hope of saving her was dashed.
Casualties: 1

The liner *Cathay*, with her sisters *Comorin* and *Chitral*, was built for the Australian service from London.
Tom Rayner collection

The *Cathay* on fire off Bougie, Algeria.
Imperial War Museum (A12834)

CAVOUR (1905) ex-*Florida* (1912) Transatlantica Italiana, Italy

5,156grt; 381ft (116.2m) lbp x 48ft (14.7m) beam
1,665 passengers in two classes
Esercizio Bacini, Riva Trigoso (Yard No 35)
Triple-expansion steam reciprocating, twin screw
After restoration following her collision with the White Star liner *Republic* (qv), the *Florida* passed to the Ligure Brasiliana Line in 1912 and was renamed *Cavour*. In 1914 she was transferred to Transatlantica Italiana, continuing to work on the run from Genoa to South America. Three years later, on 12 December 1917, she was involved in a second collision, with the Italian Navy's auxiliary cruiser *Caprera*, herself the fatally damaged vessel on this occasion. The accident occurred 2½ miles off La Almetlla de Mar, Spain, approximately 80 miles south-east of Barcelona.
Casualties: not known

CAWDOR CASTLE (1901) Union-Castle Line, UK

6,243grt; 415ft (126.4m) lbp x 51ft (15.6m) beam
540 passengers in three classes
Barclay Curle, Whiteinch, Glasgow (Yard No 429)
Triple-expansion steam reciprocating, twin screw
The *Cawdor Castle*, an 'Extra' steamer providing mainly very basic accommodation in the South African emigrant trade, ran

ashore at Conception Bay, South West Africa, on 30 July 1926 during a voyage from London to Mauritius. She could not be refloated and was broken up where she lay.
Casualties: not known

The *Cawdor Castle* was another Union-Castle 'Extra' steamer, sister of the *Alnwick*, *Berwick* and *Newark* 'Castles'. *David Reed*

C. DE EIZAGUIRRE (1904) ex-*Landana* (1910) ex-*Leopoldville* (1908) Cia Transatlantica Española, Spain

4,629grt; 400ft (121.9m) loa x 47ft (14.3m) beam
Passenger numbers not known
Raylton Dixon, Middlesbrough (Yard No 502)
Triple-expansion steam reciprocating, twin screw
While bound from Barcelona to Manila by way of the Cape of Good Hope on 27 May 1917, the *C. de Eizaguirre* struck a mine off Robben Island, some 15 miles from Cape Town. It was one of a quantity laid in that area by the German raider *Wolf*. The passenger ship's back was broken by the force of the explosion and she sank within minutes, her bow and stern pointing skyward. At the time she was carrying more than 150 passengers besides her crew, the majority of whom had been asleep in their cabins, the incident having occurred in the early hours before daybreak. It was a desperate race against time to launch the boats in a bid to save those aboard, who, rudely awakened, were generally dazed and in shock. It was possible to get only one lifeboat waterborne, holding just 24 persons, among them the Chief Engineer, and they turned out to be the only survivors of the disaster.
Casualties: 128

CELTIC (1901) White Star Line, UK

21,035grt; 700ft (213.4m) loa x 75ft (22.9m) beam
1,600 passengers in three classes
Harland & Wolff, Belfast (Yard No 335)
Quadruple-expansion steam reciprocating, twin screw
The *Celtic* was the first unit of the White Star Line's famed 'Big Four' and the first ship in the world to exceed 20,000 tons. While she was approaching Cobh Harbour in a gale on 10 December 1928, she was driven onto Roches Point, only yards from the lighthouse there. All attempts at salvage were unsuccessful and she was eventually abandoned as a total loss. The Danish company Petersen & Albeck was engaged to demolish the ship as she was a menace to navigation, and by 1933 the *Celtic* had been completely dismantled.
Casualties: 0

Lead ship of White Star Line's 'Big Four', the *Celtic* of 1901 is seen anchored in the River Mersey... *Ian Allan Library*

...and stranded at Roches Point in December 1928. She was demolished on the spot. *White Star Line*

CENTAUR (1924) Ocean SS Co (Alfred Holt & Co), UK

3,222grt; 316ft (96.3m) lbp x 48ft (14.6m) beam
161 passengers
Scott's, Greenock (Yard No 524)
Motor-ship, twin screw

During the Second World War the small *Centaur*, which had maintained Antipodean services for Blue Funnel, was sunk while serving as a hospital ship. *H. B. Christiansen Collection / Online Transport Archive*

During the Second World War the passenger-cargo ship *Centaur* was loaned to the Australian Government for service as a hospital ship. In this capacity she was attacked by the Japanese submarine I-177 on 14 May 1943, despite the fact that she was burning her lights and clearly marked in Red Cross colours. At the time of the attack, the *Centaur* was bound from Sydney to Cairns and New Guinea. She had aboard 257 service medical personnel, comprising nurses, doctors and orderlies: 65 from the Australian Army General Hospital and 192 from the Australian Army Field Ambulance. She also had a crew of 74. The un-forewarned attack occurred when she was 24 miles east-north-east of Point Lookout, Stradbroke Island, some 45 miles to the east of Brisbane. There was insufficient time to launch lifeboats because the *Centaur* foundered in less than 3 minutes but, while those who had been aboard the sinking ship struggled for their lives in the sea, the submarine surfaced, apparently to observe the *Centaur*'s last moments. Further loss of life could have been prevented had the crew of the submarine made the effort, but no such assistance was offered. The *Centaur*'s last position was 27.17S, 154.05E.

Casualties: 268 (223 medical staff and 45 crew) There was only one female survivor.

CERAMIC (1913) Shaw Savill & Albion, UK

18,713grt; 679ft (207.0m) loa x 69ft (21.0m) beam
340 passengers in single class
Harland & Wolff, Belfast (Yard No 432)
Triple-expansion steam reciprocating with LP turbine, triple screw

From February 1940 the passenger liner *Ceramic* served as a troopship. She was bound from Liverpool to St Helena, Durban and Sydney on 6 December 1942, carrying 378 military passengers and 278 crew, when she was torpedoed by the German submarine U515. The attack took place west of the Azores in the position 40.30N, 40.20W. The torpedoes struck the *Ceramic* with devastating impact, and before even a single distress call could be made she had foundered. The sole survivor (Sapper A. E. Munda) was picked up the next day by another U-boat after the lifeboat he was in capsized in a gale. He was taken prisoner, preventing the full facts of the disaster being made known for two and a half years.

Casualties: 655

The *Ceramic* was constructed for the White Star Line's Australia service, serving Sydney from Liverpool for almost 21 years. She was then sold to Shaw Savill & Albion in 1934, from which time Brisbane became her terminus port in Australia.
Ian Allan Library

CESARE BATTISTI (1920) Tirrenia Line, Italy

8,331grt; 434ft (135.6m) lbp x 53ft (16.2m) beam
c450 passengers
Ansaldo, Sestri Ponente, Genoa (Yard No 236)
Steam turbines, twin screw

On 23 December 1936 the passenger-cargo ship *Cesare Battisti* arrived at Massawa (Port Sudan) in Eritrea carrying Italian workmen bound for Addis Ababa. As they were being disembarked there was a huge explosion in the ship's boilers, which ripped a hole in her side. Apart from those killed, it left

more than 100 others injured and hospitalised in a serious condition. The *Cesare Battisti* developed an immediate list and sank, resting on her beam ends in shallow water. The ship was not salvaged but broken up on the spot.

Casualties: 26

CHAKDINA (1914) British India Line, UK

3,033grt; 331ft (100.8m) lbp x 46ft (14.1m) beam
36 cabin passengers in two classes plus 1,000 on deck
Ramage & Ferguson, Leith (Yard No 239)
Triple-expansion steam reciprocating, single screw

The small passenger vessel *Chakdina* was taken over by the Admiralty in January 1940 and commissioned as the Armed Boarding Vessel HMS *Chakdina*. She was sunk on 5 December 1941 by a torpedo launched from an Italian aircraft. The position was 32.11N, 24.30E, between Tobruk and Alexandria.

Casualties: not known

CHAKLA (1914) British India Line, UK

3,081grt; 331ft (100.7m) lbp x 46ft (14.1m) beam
36 cabin passengers in two classes plus 1,000 on deck
Alexander Stephen & Sons, Linthouse, Glasgow
(Yard No 462)
Triple-expansion steam reciprocating, single screw

Also taken over as the Armed Boarding Vessel HMS *Chakla*, in her case from September 1939, this sister ship of the *Chakdina* was bombed and sunk in Tobruk harbour on 29 April 1941. Her after-part was salvaged in 1950 and taken to Savona, where it was broken up.

Casualties: not known

CHAMPLAIN (1932) Compagnie Générale Transatlantique (French Line), France

28,124grt; 641ft (195.4m) loa x 83ft (25.3m) beam
1,053 passengers in three classes
Penhoët, St Nazaire (Yard No Y6)
Steam turbines, twin screw

The transatlantic passenger liner *Champlain* struck a mine off the entrance to La Pallice, three miles west of La Rochelle, on the French Atlantic coast, on 17 June 1940, while returning from New York with passengers, having already made a call at St Nazaire. There were 381 crew members and a small number of passengers still aboard her. She settled in shallow water, upright but with a slight list to starboard. In the absence of any attempt to salvage her, as far as is known she remained there throughout the war and well into the 1950s before demolition of the wreck commenced. By 1964 the final traces of the once-striking *Champlain* had been removed.

There are some anomalies in reports relating to the loss of the *Champlain*. Documents in Lloyd's War Loss Records state that she had been engaged on His Majesty's Service at the time of her sinking, but this is most unlikely for the date of the incident was five days prior to the signing of the Armistice that ended hostilities between France and Germany. Also, in some reports it is stated that around 300 persons lost their lives when the *Champlain* struck the mine, but this is incorrect.

Casualties: 11 (all crew)

The cabin-class liner *Champlain* sailed between Le Havre and New York, with occasional calls at Bordeaux. She was a striking vessel and, like many other French Line ships from the pre-war period, she pioneered new trends in décor and appearance. *Author's collection*

The *Champlain* during demolition off La Pallice where she struck a magnetic mine. Her remains were not cleared until the early 1960s. *Serra Frères, Toulon*

CHAMPOLLION (1924) Messageries Maritimes, France

12,546grt; 550ft (167.6m) loa x 63ft (19.1m) beam
949 passengers in four classes
Constructions Navales, La Ciotat (Yard No 149)
Triple-expansion steam reciprocating, twin screw
The passenger-cargo liner *Champollion* ran aground in the approaches to Beirut Harbour on 22 December 1952, and became a total wreck. As she approached the port in bad weather, a course bearing was wrongly set due to confusion over two navigation beacons, one at Khaede airport and the other the Ras Beirut lighthouse, which were using the same signal frequency. The *Champollion* became stranded, parallel with the shore, on Elchat Elmalhoun reef, two miles from the harbour entrance, where she assumed an acute list and broke in two at a point level with her funnel. The position was 33.51N, 35.28E. It was impossible to evacuate the 108 passengers and 250 crew because the seas were too rough to lower the boats. As the ship was close to the shore, some forty to fifty persons, desperate to reach safety, attempted to swim ashore, but fifteen of them were unsuccessful. Fearing that the *Champollion* would capsize and that the remainder of those aboard her would be drowned, a small fleet of rescue craft, including fishing vessels, tugs, cargo ships and the cruiser HMS *Kenya*, which had arrived from Port Said, surrounded the stricken liner. It was not until late the

following day, however, that any rescue effort could be undertaken, although it was then achieved without further loss of life. The wreck was scrapped on the spot by Lebanese breakers.
Casualties: 15

With her sister ship *Mariette Pacha*, the *Champollion* operated on the service from Marseilles to Alexandria and Levant ports. *Real Photos*

CHANTALA (1920) British India Line, UK

3,129grt; 330ft (100.6m) lbp x 46ft (14.0m) beam
48 cabin passengers in two classes plus 1,503 on deck
Barclay Curle, Whiteinch, Glasgow (Yard No 589)
Triple-expansion steam reciprocating, single screw
Another of British India's small passenger ships requisitioned for wartime service as an Armed Boarding Vessel was the *Chantala*. As HMS *Chantala*, she struck a mine near Tobruk on 7 December 1941, which sank her. Her remains were raised after the war and broken up at Savona from August 1951.
Casualties: not known

CHAOUIA (1896) ex-*Koningin Wilhelmina* (1911) Paquet & Cie, France

4,249grt; 382ft (116.4m) lbp x 45ft (13.8m) beam
Passenger numbers not known
Royal Schelde, Vlissingen (Yard No 84)
Quadruple-expansion steam reciprocating, single screw
While passing through the Straits of Messina on 15 January 1919, bound from Piraeus to Constantinople (Istanbul), the passenger-cargo ship *Chaouia* struck an uncleared mine, which exploded with devastating consequences. She was carrying some 690 passengers and crew but, as she sank in no more than 4 minutes, many lives were lost, besides which many of the 230 survivors were severely injured by the detonation and had to be hospitalised at Messina.
Casualties: 460

CHELLA (1935) Cie de Navigation Paquet, France

8,920grt; 453ft (132.0m) lbp x 62ft (18.9m) beam
468 passengers in three classes
Chantiers de la Méditerranée, La Seyne (Yard No 1217)
Steam turbines, twin screw
While lying at Marseilles on 2 June 1940, the passenger liner *Chella* was bombed and seriously damaged by German

aircraft. She was moved outside of the harbour and beached. The Orient Line's *Orford* was also bombed and burned out in the same air raids. Later, the *Chella* came under fire from enemy coastal artillery, sinking offshore in shallow waters. The wreckage of the destroyed ship was later cleared.
Casualties: not known

The *Chella* was employed on the route to Tangier, Agadir, Casablanca and Dakar from Marseilles. *World Ship Society*

CHENONCEAUX (1923) ex-*Aramis* (1925) Messageries Maritimes, France

14,825grt; 565ft (172.2m) loa x 65ft (19.8m) beam
317 passengers in three classes
Chantiers de la Gironde, Bordeaux (Yard No 178)
Triple-expansion steam reciprocating, twin screw
Following lay-up in May 1941, after service as a French troopship followed by a series of repatriation voyages from the UK and the Far East, the passenger-cargo liner *Chenonceaux* was used as an accommodation ship and school for Merchant Marine officer cadets. Under the Laval-Kaufman agreement, she was handed over to the Germans in 1944 and towed to Canal de Caronte. The same year, on 18 July, she was moved to Marseilles where, moored alongside the harbour's pier, she was scuttled on 21 August. Salvage work on the wreck commenced in October 1945 and by May 1948 she had been refloated. On 17 June 1948 she was sold for breaking up at La Seyne.
Casualties: not known

The *Chenonceaux* sailed on the Far East routes from Marseilles with her near sister ships *Athos II* and *D'Artagnan*. Following her launch on 30 March 1922 and her trials under the name *Aramis*, this passenger-cargo liner was laid up, Messageries Maritimes refusing to take delivery because of unsatisfactory performance. Following engine modifications, by which time she had been renamed *Chenonceaux*, she made her first commercial sailing in March 1927. *Author's collection*

CHEROKEE (1925) Clyde-Mallory Lines, USA

5,943grt; 402ft (122.5m) loa x (16.6m) beam
446 passengers in two classes
Newport News Shipbuilding & Drydock Co, Newport News, Virginia (Yard No 274)
Steam turbines, single screw
The American passenger ship *Cherokee* was torpedoed and sunk by the German submarine U87 off Cape Cod on 16 June 1942 while bound from Halifax, Nova Scotia, to New York. The survivors of the attack, less than half her complement, numbered 83. The Cherokee sank in the position 42.25N, 69.10W (some reports give the position as 42.47N, 66.18W).
Casualties: 86

CHICAGO (1866) Guion Line, UK

2,866grt; 335ft (102.1m) lbp x 42ft (12.8m) beam
872 passengers in two classes
Palmers, Jarrow (Yard No 198)
Inverted steam engines, single screw
As she was nearing the end of her eighth transatlantic round-trip voyage, the passenger steamship *Chicago* went ashore on Daunt's Rock in the Roches Point reef, outside Queenstown (Cobh), on 12 January 1868. She became a total loss.
Casualties: 0

CHICAGO MARU (1910) Osaka Shosen Kaisha, Japan

5,866grt; 410ft (127.9m) lbp x 49ft (15.1m) beam
181 passengers in two classes
Kawasaki, Kobe (Yard No 299)
Triple-expansion steam reciprocating, twin screw
The passenger-cargo ship *Chicago Maru* was torpedoed off the west coast of Formosa (Taiwan) on 15 October 1943 by the American submarine USS *Tullibee*. She sank in the position 24.35N, 120.31E.
Casualties: not known

CHIDAMBARAM (1966) ex-*Pasteur* (1973) Shipping Corporation of India

17,226grt; 571ft (174.0m) loa x 79ft (24.0m) beam
154 passengers berthed and 1,526 in dormitories
Chantiers de Dunquerque et Bordeaux, Dunkirk (Yard No 247)
Motor-ship, twin screw

Constructed originally as Messageries Maritimes' *Pasteur*, the *Chidambaram* was placed on service from India to Singapore with the majority of her passenger accommodation in dormitories. *Ian Shiffman*

After almost 12 years in the India to Singapore service, the passenger ship *Chidambaram* was extensively damaged by fire on 12 February 1985, in the position 11.35N, 82.20E, while she was bound from Singapore to Madras. Besides her crew she was carrying 702 passengers. The *Chidambaram* finally arrived at Madras on 14 February, where she was condemned as a constructive total loss. She was broken up at Bombay from 8 April 1985.
Casualties: 40 (all passengers)

CHIYO MARU (1908) Toyo Kisen Kaisha, Japan

13,426grt; 575ft (175.3m) loa x 62ft (18.8m) beam
1,150 passengers in three classes
Mitsubishi, Nagasaki (Yard No 191)
Steam turbines, triple screw
On 31 March 1916 the passenger-cargo liner *Chiyo Maru* was lost when she ran aground on Tam Kan Island (Lema), 20 miles south of Hong Kong. Two days later she broke in two and became a total loss. Casualties: 0

CHRISTIAAN HUYGENS (1928) Nederland Line, The Netherlands

16,287grt; 570ft (173.7m) loa x 68ft (20.7m) beam
572 passengers in three classes
Nederlandsche Dok & Scheeps, Amsterdam (Yard No 186)
Motor-ship, twin screw
The passenger-cargo liner *Christiaan Huygens* survived the Second World War only to become a mine casualty shortly after the cessation of hostilities. She was heading from Antwerp to Rotterdam on 26 August 1945 when she struck an uncleared mine near Westkapelle in the estuary of the River Scheldt. Severely damaged, she was beached on the Zuid Steenbank, in the position 51.37N, 03.16E, but on 5 September 1945 she broke in two, a total loss.
Casualties: 1 (crew member)

The *Christiaan Huygens* was constructed for the Amsterdam to Batavia (Djakarta) service. In effect, other than the former Italia Line ship *Raffaello* lost in Iraq in November 1982, she was the very last passenger ship to be sunk by war causes. The wreck of the *Christiaan Huygens* (below) seen near Westkapelle. *Both L. L. von Münching*

CHROBRY (1939) Gdynia Amerika Line, Poland

11,442grt; 505ft (153.9m) loa x 66ft (20.1m) beam
1,167 passengers in three classes
Nakskov Skibsvaerft, Nakskov (Yard No 89)
Motor-ship, twin screw
The passenger ship *Chrobry* was in Brazil when war broke out between Poland and Germany and, after her home country fell, she was sailed to Great Britain where she was fitted out as a troopship. During the Norwegian campaign, on 14 May 1940, the *Chrobry* was engaged to carry troops from Leith to Smaaland, Bodo and Harstad. Besides her 159-man crew, she embarked a large military contingent for the operation. On reaching Norway, she was bombed off Bodo by German aircraft and caught fire. Most of those aboard safely abandoned ship but many did not make it to the rescue vessels that went to her aid. The completely gutted *Chrobry* sank the following day in the position 67.40N, 13.50E.
Casualties: not known (11 of her crew were killed and an unspecified number of troops)

The new motor passenger ships *Chrobry* and her sister *Sobieski* saw only limited service on the Gdynia to South America route before the outbreak of war interrupted their commercial activities. *World Ship Society*

CIMBRIA (1867) Hamburg Amerika Line, Germany

3,057grt; 340ft (103.6m) loa x 40ft (12.2m) beam
678 passengers
Caird, Greenock (Yard No 136)
Compound-expansion steam reciprocating, single screw
The transatlantic steamship *Cimbria* left Hamburg on 18 January 1883 bound for New York with 402 passengers and 120 crew. Many of the passengers were East European emigrants. Early on 19 January, when off the island of Borkum near the entrance to the River Ems, she ran into thick fog. Soon after, with little warning, she was struck on her port side forward by the British coastal ship *Sultan* of the Hull & Hamburg Line. The *Cimbria* was holed below the waterline while the *Sultan*, which backed off and soon disappeared in the murk, had a hole in her bows and was fast taking water.

Aboard the *Cimbria* the situation was grave and the passengers, who had been startled awake, discovered as they emerged on deck that she was rapidly settling and heeling over to starboard. All seven lifeboats were launched, although one capsized. Besides these, every effort was made to provide means to sustain life. All deck objects that could float were cut free and jettisoned into the water. Despite these measures very few persons were saved. Two of the boats were picked up by the British barque *Theta*, another was picked up by the British cargo ship *Diamant*, while a fourth made it ashore to Borkum.
Casualties: 389, including the Master and almost all of the 72 women and 87 children on board. Lloyd's records state that

only 65 persons were rescued, which, if correct, would make the number of casualties 457, but this figure is not quoted elsewhere.

Like many of her Hamburg Amerika contemporaries on the Atlantic passage, the *Cimbria* carried a high percentage of emigrant passengers in Steerage class. *Hapag-Lloyd*

CINCINNATI (1908) Hamburg Amerika Line, Germany

serving under the wartime name COVINGTON
16,339grt; 600ft (182.9m) loa x 65ft (19.8m) beam
2,758 passengers in three classes
Schichau, Danzig (Yard No 804)
Quadruple-expansion steam reciprocating, twin screw
Seized at Boston by the American authorities on 6 April 1917, the Hamburg Amerika liner *Cincinnati*, which had been interned there since 1914, was commissioned as a US Navy transport under the name *Covington*, managed by the US War Shipping Board and deployed transporting American troops to the battlefields in Europe. While returning empty to the United States after she had completed a troop-carrying crossing, the *Covington* was torpedoed in the Western Approaches by the German submarine U86 on 1 July 1918. She sank in the position 47.24N, 07.44W.
Casualties: 6 (all crew)

Seen as the United States' troop transport *Covington*, the *Cincinnati* (on the left) had operated in the Hamburg to New York or Boston services prior to the First World War. *US National Archives*

CITTA DI CATANIA (1910) Tirrenia Line, Italy

3,397grt; 363ft (110.8m) lbp x 42ft (12.8m) beam
307 passengers in three classes
Ansaldo Armstrong, Sestri Ponente (Yard No 157)
Steam turbines, triple screw
The *Citta di Catania*, a former Italian State Railways ferry, survived the First World War only to become a casualty in the Second when she was torpedoed and sunk by the British submarine HMS *Unruffled* on 3 August 1943. The ship sank in the position 40.43N, 18.04E, some eight miles off Brindisi.
Casualties: not known

CITTA DI GENOVA (1930) Tirrenia Line, Italy

5,413grt; 412ft (125.5m) lbp x 51ft (15.5m) beam
565 passengers
Cantieri Navale Riuniti, Palermo (Yard No 101)
Motor-ship, twin screw
The passenger ship *Citta di Genova*, originally owned with her sisters by the Italian State Railways, was torpedoed and sunk by the submarine HMS *Tigris* on 21 January 1943. The attack took place as the *Citta di Genova* passed through the Strait of Otranto, about 25 miles west of Saseno Island, in the position 40.32N, 18.45E.
Casualties: 173

CITTA DI PALERMO (1910) Ferrovie dello Stato (Italian State Railways), Italy

3,415grt; 363ft (110.8m) lbp x 42ft (12.8m) beam
307 passengers in three classes
Riuniti, Palermo (Yard No not known)
Steam turbines, triple screw
Sister ship of the *Citta di Catania*, the ferry *Citta di Palermo* was sunk on 8 January 1916. While bound for Durazzo from Brindisi carrying troops, among them a 143-man British contingent, she entered a minefield and foundered almost immediately after striking one of the mines. The scene of the disaster made it dangerous for rescue craft to approach, but minesweepers that were in the vicinity were able to render some assistance. Of the 200 or more persons aboard the *Citta di Palermo*, about half were saved.
Casualties: c100 (including 59 British soldiers)

The Italian State Railways train ferry *Citta di Palermo* of 1910; her sister ship was the *Citta di Catania*.
M. Cicogna collection, Trieste

CITTA DI PALERMO (1930) Tirrenia Line, Italy

5,413grt; 412ft (125.5m) lbp x 51ft (15.6m) beam
565 passengers
Cantieri Navale Riuniti, Palermo (Yard No 102)
Motor-ship, twin screw

One of the most serious losses involving an Italian-flag merchant passenger ship in the Second World War was that of the *Citta di Palermo* while she was on passage from Brindisi for Patras escorting the Adriatica motor vessel *Calino* (qv). She was torpedoed by the British submarine HMS *Proteus* three miles west of Cephalonia, off Cape Dukato, on 5 January 1942, while serving as an auxiliary cruiser and troop transport. The *Citta di Palermo* sank rapidly in the position 38.33N, 20.36E and there were few survivors.

Casualties: More than 600

The *Citta di Palermo* of 1930 saw service with both the Tirrenia and Florio companies. Her wartime loss was among the worst involving Italian ships. *M. Cicogna collection, Trieste*

CITY OF BENARES (1936) Ellerman Lines, UK

11,081grt; 509ft (155.1m) loa x 62ft (18.9m) beam
219 passengers in single class
Barclay Curle, Whiteinch, Glasgow (Yard No 656)
Steam turbines, twin screw

The passenger-cargo ship *City of Benares* sailed from Liverpool on 13 September 1940, bound for Montreal and Quebec as part of convoy OB213, with 199 passengers, of whom 90 were children. She was also carrying a crew of 209. The youngsters were child evacuees, some escorted by their parents, who were being taken for the duration of the war to the apparent safety of Canada under the auspices of the Children's Overseas Reception Board (CORB), an operation sponsored by the British Government as part of its evacuation policy. Her loss in mid-Atlantic four days later helped to bring the CORB scheme to an early end to avoid similar disasters. When the convoy was about 600 miles out into the Atlantic and only a short time after its Royal Navy escort had been detached, the *City of Benares* was torpedoed and sunk by the German submarine U48 in the position 56.48N, 21.15W. The torpedo struck the ship on the port side adjacent to her No 5 hold and she did not remain afloat for long.

During the limited time available every effort was made to launch the boats but the seas were very rough and some lifeboats capsized, drowning their occupants and adding to the fatalities already caused when the torpedo had exploded. For those souls who survived the sinking, their ordeal was far from over for they now had to endure a harrowing experience on the open sea, exposed to wild and freezing conditions as they huddled together in open boats and rafts that were swamped with water. The children especially had little resistance against these inhospitable elements and little could be done to prevent them from succumbing to

hypothermia in the bitter cold. Fortunately, some were rescued the following day by the destroyer HMS *Hurricane*, but, for the occupants of one boat, the ordeal continued for another ten days before they were sighted by a Sunderland flying boat, which directed a warship to their aid.

Casualties: 248 (77 children – the worst loss of life in percentage terms – 58 adult passengers and 113 crew members) A figure of 258 casualties is also quoted, and 116 for the crew victims.

Before the Second World War the *City of Benares* had sailed between Liverpool and Bombay via the Mediterranean in conditions that were typically a far cry from those she experienced on the North Atlantic at the time of her destruction. *Real Photos*

CITY OF BIRMINGHAM (1911) Ellerman Lines, UK

7,498grt; 452ft (137.8m) lbp x 55ft (16.8m) beam
170 passengers in two classes
Palmers, Newcastle (Yard No 814)
Quadruple-expansion steam reciprocating, single screw

The *City of Birmingham* was sunk in a torpedo attack in the Mediterranean, 90 miles south-east of Malta, while bound from Liverpool to Karachi on 27 November 1916. She was carrying 315 persons, of whom 170 were passengers, many of them women and children. A heavy swell made it difficult to launch the boats but there was an orderly evacuation before the *City of Birmingham* sank in the approximate position 36.01N, 16.00E.

Casualties: 4 (all crew)

The Ellerman Lines' passenger-cargo ship *City of Birmingham*. *World Ship Society*

CITY OF BIRMINGHAM (1923) Ocean Steamship Co of Savannah, USA

5,861grt; 382ft (116.4m) lbp x 52ft (15.9m) beam
Passenger numbers not known
Newport News Shipbuilding & Drydock Co, Newport

News, Virginia (Yard No 267)
Triple-expansion steam reciprocating, single screw
The passenger-cargo steamship *City of Birmingham* was torpedoed by the German submarine U202 on 30 June 1942 while bound from Norfolk, Virginia, to Bermuda. She sank in the position 35.10N, 70.53W. The majority of those who were aboard her, 369 survivors in total, were subsequently rescued.
Casualties: 12 (7 passengers and 5 crew)

CITY OF BRUSSELS (1869) Inman Line, UK

3,747grt; 390ft (118.9m) lbp x 40ft (12.3m) beam
600 passengers
Tod & McGregor, Meadowside, Glasgow (Yard No 146)
Compound-expansion steam reciprocating, single screw
When nearing the end of a voyage from New York to Liverpool on 7 January 1883, the *City of Brussels* ran into extremely thick weather near the English coast. Off the Great Ormes Head her speed was substantially reduced until she came to a complete stop in the water when still about twenty miles from her destination. About an hour later the siren from another ship was heard but, before the *City of Brussels* could respond and make her presence known, it slammed into her starboard bow, breaching her hull to below the waterline and sealing her fate. The other ship turned out to be the *Kirby Hall* of the Hall Line, bound from Liverpool on her maiden voyage to India. The *Kirby Hall*'s boats were lowered and the surviving occupants of the stricken *City of Brussels* were transferred to her.
Casualties: 10 (2 passengers and 8 crew)

CITY OF CAIRO (1915) Ellerman & Bucknall Line, UK

8,034grt; 465ft (142.0m) loa x 55ft (16.8m) beam
176 passengers
Earle's, Hull (Yard No 608)
Quadruple-expansion steam reciprocating, single screw

The owners of the *City of Cairo* operated a wide range of services from Glasgow, Liverpool and London to Indian and African destinations. *Real Photos*

The passenger-cargo ship *City of Cairo* was torpedoed and sunk by the German submarine U68 on 6 November 1942, while on a voyage from Bombay and Cape Town to Pernambuco (Recife), Brazil, with a complement of 296 persons, including around 100 passengers, her ultimate destination being the United Kingdom. The attack took place in the position 23.30S, 05.30W. In another incredible episode of human endurance, while cast adrift on the ocean two of the survivors, the Third Officer and a woman passenger, survived for 51 days before they were picked up by a Brazilian minelayer on 27 December 1942. Three other survivors were taken aboard the German blockade runner *Rhakotis*, but two of them were killed later when British warships sank the *Rhakotis* on 1 January 1943, 200 miles north-west of Cape Finisterre.
Casualties: 104 (22 passengers and 82 crew)

CITY OF CHICAGO (1883) Inman Line, UK

5,202grt; 431ft (131.3m) lbp x 45ft (13.7m) beam
970 passengers
Charles Connell, Scotstoun (Yard No 132)
Compound-expansion steam reciprocating, single screw
The nine-year career of the passenger steamship *City of Chicago*, on the Liverpool to New York route, was ended on 1 July 1892 when she was stranded west of the Old Head of Kinsale, county Cork.
Casualties: 0

CITY OF HONOLULU (1896) ex-*Huron* (1922) ex-*Friedrich der Grosse* (1917) United States Shipping Board (chartered to Los Angeles Steamship Co), USA

10,696grt; 546ft (166.4m) loa x 60ft (18.3m) beam
2,423 passengers in three classes (as built)
Stettiner Vulcan, Stettin-Bredow (Yard No 231)
Quadruple-expansion steam reciprocating, twin screw
This former transatlantic passenger-cargo liner was reconstructed after the First World War for service between American west coast ports and Hawaii. During the return leg of her first voyage to Honolulu following reconditioning, on 12 October 1922, the *City of Honolulu* caught fire about 400 miles from San Pedro, California. The ship was completely burned out and after the passengers and crew had been removed she was sunk by gunfire from the American troopship *Thomas*. Subsequently, the survivors were taken aboard the *Thomas* to San Francisco.
Casualties: 0

CITY OF HONOLULU (1900) ex-*President Arthur* (1927) ex-*Princess Matoika* (1922) ex-*Prinzess Alice* (1917) ex-*Kiautschou* (1904) Los Angeles Steamship Co, USA

10,860grt; 540ft (164.6m) loa x 60ft (18.3m) beam
495 passengers in two classes
Stettiner Vulcan, Stettin-Bredow (Yard No 246)
Quadruple-expansion steam reciprocating, twin screw
The replacement *City of Honolulu* was a class-mate of her earlier namesake, but she too was destroyed by fire. On 25 May 1930, while she was tied up at her pier at Honolulu, fire broke out causing extensive damage. The virtually gutted ship returned to Los Angeles without passengers and was laid up until August 1933, when she was sold to be broken up by Japanese ship-breakers at Osaka.
Casualties: 0

CITY OF MONTREAL (1872) Inman Line, UK

4,489grt; 419ft (127.7m) lbp x 44ft (13.4m) beam
600 passengers
Tod & McGregor, Meadowside, Glasgow (Yard No 148)
Inverted compound-expansion steam reciprocating, single screw

The transatlantic passenger steamship *City of Montreal* was destroyed by fire while at sea on 10 August 1887, 400 miles from Newfoundland. The fire originated in her cargo of bales of raw cotton. Fortunately, all passengers and crew were rescued by the cargo ship *York City* of the Furness Line and taken to Queenstown (Cobh), Ireland.
Casualties: 0

CITY OF NAGPUR (1922) Ellerman Lines, UK

10,146grt; 490ft (149.3m) loa x 59ft (18.0m) beam
318 passengers in two classes
Workman Clark, Belfast (Yard No 464)
Quadruple-expansion steam reciprocating, single screw

The *City of Nagpur*, which had been taken over for military duties at the outset of the Second World War, was lost on 29 April 1941 while she was on passage from Glasgow to Freetown, Natal, Bombay and Karachi with 274 military personnel and a crew of 204. She was torpedoed and sunk by the German submarine U75 about 700 miles west of Fastnet, in the position 52.30N, 26.00W.
Casualties: 16

The *City of Nagpur* spent the first 12 years of her life on the route from Glasgow to Bombay. She was then diverted to the London to Africa service with a season of cruises each summer. *Alex Duncan*

CITY OF PARIS (1907) Ellerman Lines, UK

9,239grt; 493ft (150.3m) lbp x 57ft (17.4m) beam
290 passengers in two classes
Barclay Curle, Whiteinch, Glasgow (Yard No 466)
Quadruple-expansion steam reciprocating, single screw

The *City of Paris* was proceeding through the Mediterranean on 4 April 1917, bound from Karachi to Liverpool with a call to be made at Marseilles, when she was torpedoed and sunk by the German submarine U52. At the time of the attack, which occurred 46 miles south-by-east-south-east of Cap d'Antibes, she had been following a zig-zag course, having earlier received radioed warnings of enemy submarines in that vicinity. After the torpedo struck, there was little time to evacuate the ship, but it was reported that while those aboard were trying to organise their escape, the submarine surfaced and shelled the *City of Paris* before finishing her off with a second torpedo. She sank in the position 42.47N, 07.56E.

No survivors were found by French warships when they reached the scene later.
Casualties: 122

Ellerman Lines' steamship *City of Paris* was a First World War loss, her owner's most serious of that conflict. *Alex Duncan*

CITY OF RIO DE JANEIRO (1878) ex-*Rio de Janeiro* (launch name, 6 March 1878) Pacific Mail Steamship Co, USA

3,548grt; 345ft (105.2m) lbp x 38ft (11.6m) beam
600 passengers
Roach, Chester, Pennsylvania (Yard No 178)
Compound-expansion steam reciprocating, single screw

When she was nearing the end of a crossing from Yokohama to San Francisco on 22 January 1901, the passenger steamship *City of Rio de Janeiro* was stranded off Fort Point, near the Golden Gate, in thick fog. Against the advice of his pilot and despite the conditions, her Master had attempted manoeuvring through a dangerous channel. Having sustained extensive damage below the waterline when she struck the rocks, immediately flooding her forepart, she sank bow first in just 15 minutes. Aboard her were a total of 201 persons, only 97 of whom, less than half, were rescued.
Casualties: 104 (72 passengers and 32 crew) Some reports give a higher casualty figure of 131, which may be because among her passenger complement were Chinese and Japanese nationals who may not have been manifested.

CITY OF SIMLA (1921) Ellerman Lines, UK

10,138grt; 476ft (145.1m) lbp x 58ft (17.7m) beam
250 passengers
William Gray, West Hartlepool (Yard No 883)
Steam turbines, twin screw

The *City of Simla*, another Ellerman Lines 'City' ship, operated between Liverpool and London via Cape Town to Bombay. *H. B. Christiansen Collection / Online Transport Archive*

While she was on passage from London to Bombay via Cape Town, on 21 September 1940, carrying 167 passengers and a crew of 183, the passenger-cargo steamship *City of Simla* was torpedoed by the German submarine U138. She was about fifty miles north-west of Malin Head, Northern Ireland, at the time and sank in the position 55.59N, 08.16W.
Casualties: 3

CITY OF TOKIO (1874) Pacific Mail Steamship Co, USA

5,079grt; 408ft (122.8m) lbp x 47ft (14.3m) beam
1,650 passengers
Roach, Chester, Pennsylvania (Yard No 131)
Compound-expansion steam reciprocating, single screw
The trans-Pacific passenger steamship *City of Tokio*, her owners' largest vessel up to that time, with a sister ship *City of Peking*, was wrecked on the coast of Honshu Island, near Yokohama, on 24 June 1885.
Casualties: not known

CITY OF VENICE (1924) Ellerman Lines, UK

8,308grt; 473ft (144.2m) loa x 58ft (17.7m) beam
165 passengers
Workman Clark, Belfast (Yard No 468)
Quadruple-expansion steam reciprocating, single screw
The German submarine U375 torpedoed and sank the passenger-cargo ship *City of Venice* in the Mediterranean, off North Africa, on 4 July 1943. At the time she was bound from the River Clyde to Sicily carrying troops and munitions in support of Operation 'Husky', the Allied landings there. Also aboard was her crew of 180 men. The *City of Venice* sank in the position 36.44N, 01.31E.
Casualties: 11 (all crew) It has been reported that there were also fatalities among the troops, but no figures are available.

The *City of Venice*, lost while serving as a troopship during the Sicily landings, is seen here in October 1935.
H. B. Christiansen Collection / Online Transport Archive

CITY OF WASHINGTON (1855) Inman Line, UK

2,870grt; 358ft (109.1m) lbp x 40ft (12.2m) beam
600 passengers
Tod & McGregor, Meadowside, Glasgow (Yard No 77)
Steam reciprocating, single screw
The passenger steamship *City of Washington* inaugurated the Inman Line's transatlantic service from Liverpool to New York, having previously served Philadelphia. She was lost on 7 July 1873 when she was stranded near Cape Sable, Nova

Scotia, and was completely wrecked. The accident was attributed to a defective compass that had led to a navigational error.
Casualties: 0

CIUDAD DE CADIZ (1878) Cia Trasatlantica Española, Spain

3,202grt; 364ft (110.8m) lbp x 38ft (11.6m) beam
417 passengers in three classes
Lobnitz Coulborn, Renfrew (Yard No 143)
Triple-expansion steam reciprocating, single screw
The transatlantic passenger steamship *Ciudad de Cadiz* foundered off San Carlos, near Fernando Po (Biako), Equatorial Guinea, on 10 October 1924 in extremely heavy weather. At the time she was bound for Fernando Po from Barcelona.
Casualties: not known

CLIMAX OPAL (1952) ex-*Monte Ulia* (1976) ex-*Monasterio de el Escorial* (launch name, 9 January 1951) Climax Shipping Corp, Liberia

10,123grt; 487ft (148.5m) loa x 62ft (19.0m) beam
210 passengers in two classes
Soc Española de Construccion Naval, Bilbao (Yard No 66)
Motor-ship, single screw
Shortly after she had been purchased from Naviera Aznar, Spain, in July 1976, the passenger-cargo ship *Climax Opal* was destroyed by fire at Belfast on 3 April 1977, while undergoing a refit. Unfit for restoration, she was sold for breaking up and arrived at Santander on 7 June 1977.
Casualties: not known

COAMO (1925) New York & Porto Rico Line, USA

7,057grt; 429ft (130.8m) lbp x 59ft (18.1m) beam
361 passengers
Newport News Shipbuilding & Drydock Co, Newport News, Virginia (Yard No 280)
Steam turbines, single screw
The loss of the American coastwise passenger ship *Coamo*, serving as a troopship during the Second World War, was at first recorded as a disappearance at sea, but it was later revealed that she had been the victim of a torpedo attack. She formed part of the large Allied invasion convoy assembled for the invasion of North Africa in November 1942, joined by other American-flag vessels that had also operated pre-war on the coastal run from New York to the West Indies. After they had unloaded their troops, the *Coamo* and the *Shawnee*, sister of the *Cherokee* and *Mohawk* (qv), returned to Gibraltar, where they formed part of an England-bound convoy that sailed on 26 November 1942.

However, one day out the *Coamo* was ordered to sail independently to Norfolk, Virginia. Her last known position, when seen from another ship on 1 December 1942, was 53.00N, 13.19W. She had no passengers, with only her crew aboard, and when she failed to arrive at Norfolk as expected she was treated as missing, lost with all hands, though never formally 'posted' as such. The log of the German submarine U604 later indicated what her true fate had been. In fact, the *Coamo* had been torpedoed late on 2 December 1942 when east of Bermuda. The position has been reported in American sources as 49.00N, 24.00W, but according to the German naval authorities the U604 reported the sinking in grid square BE1739, which equates to the more precise position of 48.59N, 23.35W.

Casualties: not known (all her crew – no survivors)

Documented as a 'missing' ship, presumed disappeared without explanation, the New York & Porto Rico Line's *Coamo* turned out to have been a torpedo victim.
Frank Braynard collection

COBEQUID (1893) ex-*Goth* (1913) Royal Mail Line, UK

4,738grt; 400ft (122.1m) lbp x 47ft (14.4m) beam
353 passengers
Harland & Wolff, Belfast (Yard No 263)
Triple-expansion steam reciprocating, twin screw
The passenger-cargo ship *Cobequid* was lost on her first voyage on the Canada to West Indies route. While returning to St John, New Brunswick, from Demerara on 13 January 1914, with passengers and a cargo of sugar, she struck the Trinity Ledge Rocks, in the Bay of Fundy, and was wrecked.
Casualties: 0

COLIMA (1873) Pacific Mail Steamship Co, USA

2,905grt; 299ft (91.1m) lbp x 39ft (11.9m) beam
Passenger numbers not known
Roach, Chester, Pennsylvania (Yard No 128)
Steam engines, single screw
The passenger steamship *Colima* made her last departure from San Francisco, bound for Mexico and Panama, on 18 May 1895. There were 134 persons aboard making the southbound voyage, but they were added to at ports-of-call en route, increasing her total complement to 192. In the late evening of 27 May, when the *Colima* was about fifty miles south of Manzanillo, Mexico, her boilers exploded and she began to take water. The blast felled one of her two masts, killing her Master, the Chief Engineer and the Pilot. Although she was immediately steered for the coast in a bid to find a safe haven, panic broke out among the passengers as the ship's dire situation became evident, and as a result of an appalling scramble to get in the lifeboats many of those aboard were unable to abandon ship. The *Colima* foundered before safety was reached, taking most of her occupants with her. Casualties: 173

COLOMBIA (1915) Panama Mail Steamship Co, USA

5,644grt; 379ft (115.8m) lbp x 49ft (14.8m) beam
189 passengers in two classes (as built)

Nederlandsche SB, Amsterdam (Yard No 133)
Triple-expansion steam reciprocating, single screw
The former Dutch passenger-cargo ship *Colombia*, engaged in the American inter-coastal trade via the Panama Canal, was wrecked at Point Tosco, Margarita Island, Baja California, on 13 September 1931. Casualties: not known

COLOMBIA (1930) Royal Netherlands Steamship Co, The Netherlands

10,782grt; 457ft (139.3m) loa x 61ft (18.6m) beam
309 passengers in three classes
P. Smit Jr, Rotterdam (Yard No 454)
Motor-ship, twin screw
In 1940, after the Netherlands had fallen to German forces, the passenger ship *Colombia* was commissioned as a submarine depot ship with the exiled Royal Dutch Navy. The German submarine U516 torpedoed and sank her in the position 33.36S, 27.29E on 27 February 1943, during a voyage from East London to Simonstown, South Africa.
Casualties: 8 (all crew)

COLOMBO (1917) ex-*San Gennaro* (1921) Lloyd Triestino, Italy

12,003grt; 536ft (163.4m) loa x 64ft (19.5m) beam
2,800 in three classes
Palmers, Hebburn-on-Tyne (Yard No 843)
Quadruple-expansion steam reciprocating, twin screw
The passenger ship *Colombo* was docked in the port of Massowah (Massawa), Eritrea, when it fell to British forces on 8 April 1941. Her crew deliberately sank her by detonating explosive charges in order to prevent the ship from being captured. The wreck, which was raised by the British after the war, was broken up for scrap from 1949.
Casualties: not known

Originally a cargo ship operated by the Transoceanica Company, a subsidiary of Navigazione Generale Italiana, the *San Gennaro* was reconstructed as the passenger ship *Colombo* in August 1921. Thereafter she sailed on the Naples to New York or Genoa to Valparaiso services until transferred to Italia Line in 1932. A further move in 1937 took her to Lloyd Triestino for the Genoa to Massowah and Djibouti service.
World Ship Society

COLORADO (1868) Guion Line, UK

2,927grt; 330ft (100.6m) lbp x 43ft (13.1m) beam
c870 passengers in two classes
Palmers, Jarrow (Yard No 219)
Inverted steam engines, single screw

The transatlantic steamship *Colorado*, one of a group of four working the Liverpool to New York route, was sunk on 7 February 1872 after colliding with the Bibby Line steamship *Arabian* in the River Mersey. Casualties: 6

COLUMBUS (1922) Norddeutscher Lloyd, Germany

32,565grt; 775ft (236.2m) loa x 83ft (25.3m) beam
1,792 passengers in three classes
Schichau, Danzig (Yard No 929)
Steam turbines, twin screw

One of the highest-profile cases of the many German passenger ships that tried to make runs for safe havens in the early part of the Second World War was that of the *Columbus*. When war broke out in September 1939 she was on a Caribbean cruise, which was prematurely terminated and her passengers disembarked at Havana, Cuba. She then made for Vera Cruz to seek temporary sanctuary in neutral Mexican waters; while there, attempts were made to disguise her by painting the tops of her buff funnels black. By that December, however, her continued presence off Mexico was causing tensions, besides which her supplies were also dwindling. The decision was therefore taken to attempt to make a run for home, breaking through the British naval blockade, then taking a course that hugged the coastline of the still-neutral United States before heading north-east past Iceland towards either Murmansk or occupied Oslo.

The *Columbus* set sail on 14 December but the voyage did not unfold as planned. Shadowed by American warships, initially a sequence of different destroyers and later by the cruiser USS *Tuscaloosa*, she was intercepted by the British destroyer HMS *Hyperion* on 19 December, some 320 miles east of Cape Hatteras, Delaware. To prevent capture by the British as well as to avoid unnecessary loss of crewmen's lives, orders were given to scuttle the *Columbus*, a drill that had been well rehearsed during the months of idleness off Mexico. She was soon blazing from end to end and, with her sea cocks open, she sank just before midnight in the position 38.01N, 65.41W. All but two of the 579 persons who had been aboard the *Columbus* were picked up by the *Tuscaloosa* and landed at New York. As a mark of respect – behaviour that would be all too rarely seen over the next six years – both the *Hyperion* and *Tuscaloosa* dipped their ensigns in salute as they steamed past the dying liner. Casualties: 2

Unlike her British twin, the *Columbus* was given a more modern external appearance during a 1929 refit. She is seen ablaze off the coast of Delaware when she was deliberately scuttled to prevent capture by the Royal Navy.
Imperial War Museum (OG245)

COLUMBUS C (1953) ex-*Europa* (1981) ex-*Kungsholm* (1965) Independent Continental Lines, Panama (subsidiary of Costa Armatori SpA), Italy

21,514grt; 600ft (182.9m) loa x 77ft (23.5m) beam
785 passengers in single class
'De Schelde', Vlissingen (Yard No 273)
Motor-ship, twin screw

The cruise ship *Columbus C*, formerly a transatlantic liner under the Swedish and German flags, became a constructive total loss on 29 July 1984 when she struck a breakwater as she entered the port of Cadiz, Spain, in bad weather. Holed below the waterline, she subsequently flooded and sank at her berth. All her passengers and crew were safely disembarked. An inspection on 14 September of that year indicated that she was beyond economic recovery and, after she had been raised by Smit Tak International in November, she was sold to Spanish ship-breakers, demolition commencing in March 1985.

Casualties: 0

The *Columbus C*, originally the Swedish America Line passenger liner *Kungsholm*, seen at Rio de Janeiro. *Ian Shiffman*

In the years immediately prior to the First World War, Norddeutscher Lloyd laid down the hulls of two new giant liners for its transatlantic express service. The first ship, named *Columbus*, passed into British ownership under the Treaty of Versailles and was completed for the White Star Line as the *Homeric*. The second, unlaunched hull, for which the name *Hindenburg* had been intended, adopted the name of her former sister. The *Columbus* finally entered service on the Bremerhaven to New York route in April 1924.
B. & A. Feilden

COMMISSAIRE RAMEL (1920) Messageries Maritimes, France

14,825grt; 500ft (152.4m) loa x 59ft (18.0m) beam
552 passengers in three classes
Soc Provencale de Construction Navale, La Ciotat
(Yard No not known)
Triple-expansion steam reciprocating with LP turbines, single screw

The *Commissaire Ramel*, a former cargo ship rebuilt to carry passengers by the addition of promenade and boat decks, was seized at Suva on 18 July 1940 on the instructions of the British Governor of Fiji. Having set out originally from Marseilles, she arrived at Suva via Papeete, and subsequently, after refuelling, proceeded to Port Vila, then Sydney, Australia. There, with 26 members of her crew and her Master deciding to side with the British, she was allocated to the Ministry of War Transport and placed under the management of Shaw, Savill & Albion with a view to conversion into a troopship.

While she was bound from Sydney to the UK via South Africa on 19 September 1940, the *Commissaire Ramel* was intercepted by the German auxiliary cruiser *Atlantis* in the Indian Ocean. When an attempt was made to radio for help, the *Atlantis* opened fire on her with its guns and set her alight. She sank in the position 28.25S, 74.27E, some 1,000 miles south-east of Mauritius. The 63 members of the *Commissaire Ramel*'s crew who had survived the sinking were taken aboard the German vessel as prisoners, later transferring with others to the Yugoslavian-flag prize *Durmitor*, which became stranded at Uarsciek, thirty miles north of Mogadishu (Mogadiscio), Italian Somaliland, on 22 November 1940. A total of 263 prisoners disembarked and were interned at a camp at Merca where they remained in captivity until 25 February 1941, when they were freed by British troops.
Casualties: 3

The *Commissaire Ramel*. *Alex Duncan*

COMORIN (1925) P&O Line, UK

15,132grt; 545ft (166.1m) loa x 70ft (21.3m) beam
306 passengers in two classes
Barclay Curle, Whiteinch, Glasgow (Yard No 603)
Quadruple-expansion steam reciprocating, twin screw
While she was in mid-Atlantic on 6 April 1941, in the position 53.34N, 21.20W, the passenger-cargo liner *Comorin*, which had been serving as an auxiliary cruiser since December 1939, caught fire, an unfortunate occurrence given the other hazards she was facing, and she was soon a raging inferno. The British destroyers HMS *Brooke* and *Lincoln* stood by to assist the *Comorin*'s naval crew to abandon ship, although they were unable to safely approach close up. In these circumstances, to aid the evacuation the *Lincoln* drifted floats, rafts and other buoyancy aids towards the blazing ship, helping the majority to escape by these means to be picked up from the sea. The *Comorin* was not so lucky. Engulfed in flames, her derelict hulk was torpedoed and sunk by the *Brooke* the following day.
Casualties: 20

In the mid-1920s P&O built three new intermediate liners with reciprocating engines for the London to Sydney service, the *Cathay*, *Chitral* and *Comorin*. This is the last-named. *Tom Rayner collection*

CONNAUGHT (1860) Galway Line, UK

2,860grt; 378ft (115.2m) lbp x 40ft (12.2m) beam
857 passengers in two classes
Palmers, Jarrow (Yard No 81)
Inverted compound-expansion steam reciprocating, paddles
After leaving St John's, Newfoundland, on 5 October 1860, en route for Boston on her second voyage, the *Connaught* sprang a leak and developed a serious list. After two days of fruitless efforts to try and right the ship, a further menace was encountered when she caught fire due to the funnel overheating and igniting the lagging over the boiler. Simultaneously, water entered the engine room and all power was lost. With the fire spreading rapidly throughout the helpless vessel, the 591 persons on board were in grave danger and, but for the opportune arrival of the American brigantine *Minnie Schiffer*, the most appalling loss of life would have resulted. The brigantine managed to rescue all of the *Connaught*'s occupants and they were disembarked at Scituate, Massachusetts. The *Connaught* was last seen ablaze from stem to stern.
Casualties: 0

An early transatlantic passenger steamship, both the *Connaught* and her owner, the Galway Line, were short-lived as the fortunes of would-be operators on the routes from Europe to America fluctuated. *National Maritime Museum*

CONNAUGHT (1897) City of Dublin Steam Packet Co, UK

2,646grt; 360ft (109.7m) lbp x 42ft (12.7m) beam
1,400 passengers
Laird, Birkenhead (Yard No 614)
Triple-expansion steam reciprocating, twin screw
Sister ship of the *Leinster* (qv), the Irish Sea ferry *Connaught* was bound from Le Havre to Southampton on 3 March 1917

when she was torpedoed and sunk by the German submarine U48. The attack took place 29 miles west-south-west of the Owers light vessel in the position 50.08N, 00.45W.
Casualties: 3

CONTE DI SAVOIA (1932) Italia Line, Italy

48,502grt; 860ft (262.1m) loa x 96ft (29.3m) beam
2,200 passengers in four classes
Cantieri Riuniti dell'Adriatico, San Marco, Trieste
(Yard No783)
Steam turbines, quadruple screw
Considered to be too large and vulnerable for military service in the Mediterranean, the transatlantic express liner *Conte di Savoia* was laid up at Malamocco, near Venice, following Italy's entry into the Second World War. While lying there she was attacked by United States fighter-bombers on 11 September 1943 and set on fire. The blazing liner gradually heeled over and sank in the shallow waters of the lagoon. The wreck was raised on 16 October 1945, with a serious prospect of reconstruction for continued service, even in a utilitarian capacity. However, it had been necessary to strip off a large amount of her upper structure in order to right her, and the cost of replacing this, together with the repairs to the immense amount of internal damage, would have proved too expensive. So it was, after lengthy deliberations on her future, that the *Conte di Savoia* was towed to Monfalcone, Trieste, on 24 April 1950 to be broken up.
Casualties: not known

Ordered by Lloyd Sabaudo, the *Conte di Savoia* served on the New York route from the Mediterranean alongside the *Rex*, Italy's only Blue Riband holder, under the Italia banner. Though marginally slower, the *Conte di Savoia* was considered to be the better proportioned of the pair. *L. L. von Münching*

The bomb-wrecked and fire-burned hulk of the *Conte di Savoia*, photographed after the war's end. For a time there were hopes that she could be restored in some way, but ultimately there was no cost justification for the huge amount of work that would have been involved. *Real Photos*

CONTE ROSSO (1922) Lloyd Triestino, Italy

17,856grt; 591ft (180.1m) loa x 74ft (22.6m) beam
640 passengers in three classes
William Beardmore, Dalmuir (Yard No 611)
Steam turbines, twin screw
One of three ships sunk by the British submarine HMS *Upholder* (see also the *Neptunia* and *Oceania*), the passenger liner *Conte Rosso*, serving as a troopship, was torpedoed and sunk on 24 May 1941 about fifteen miles east of Syracuse, in the position 36.41N, 15.42E. She had been bound in convoy for Tripoli with 2,500 troops and there was heavy loss of life, making it one of the worst Italian merchant shipping disasters of the Second World War.
Casualties: 1,291

In her 17 years as a commercial passenger liner, the *Conte Rosso* served three companies on three different routes. Between the years 1922 and 1932 she operated between Genoa and New York or Buenos Aires for Lloyd Sabaudo. She then briefly joined the new Italia Line fleet, switching to the Trieste to Shanghai service. From 1932, after transfer to Lloyd Triestino, she was engaged mainly under charter to the Italian government transporting soldiers between Italy and North Africa. *World Ship Society*

CONTE VERDE (1923) Lloyd Triestino, Italy

serving under the wartime name KOTOBUKI MARU
18,765grt; 593ft (180.7m) loa x 74ft (22.6m) beam
640 passengers in three classes
William Beardmore, Dalmuir (Yard No 612)
Steam turbines, twin screw
Interned at Shanghai in June 1940, the passenger liner *Conte Verde* was controversially escorted to Japan by Japanese warships in April 1941 in breach of the Hague Convention, since at that time Japan was not a combatant. On her arrival she was laid up until 1942, when she was chartered to the Japanese government for prisoner exchange voyages with the Chinese. Laid up again in the Huangpo River, Shanghai, on their conclusion, the *Conte Verde* was scuttled there by her crew on 11 September 1943 to deny possession of her to the Japanese. The ship was salvaged, however, and on the completion of temporary repairs at Shanghai was taken to Maizuru, Honshu, Japan, to be rebuilt as the troop transport *Kotobuki Maru*. During an American air raid on Maizuru in December 1944, she sustained a certain amount of damage and, during a subsequent raid on 8 May 1945, she was sunk in Nakata Bay, in the position 34.30N, 126.30E. It has been reported that an aircraft-laid mine was responsible for sinking the *Kotobuki Maru*. Refloated in June 1949 and taken to the

Maizuru shipyard, she was formally returned to the Italian Government in 1950 but remained laid up in Japan. Considered to be beyond economic reconstruction, she was finally sold to Mitsui in 1951 and breaking up commenced that August.

Casualties: not known

The *Conte Verde*, sister of the *Conte Rosso*, had a similar career. She is seen in the all-white livery of Lloyd Triestino in which she was painted for Far East service. *Bettina Rohbrecht*

The wreck of the *Kotobuki Maru*, the former *Conte Verde*, at Maizuru in 1949 prior to being broken up. *Real Photos*

CONWAY CASTLE (1877) Castle Line, UK

2,966grt; 349ft (106.4m) lbp x 39ft (12.0m) beam
250 passengers in three classes
Robert Napier, Govan (Yard No 364)
Compound-expansion steam reciprocating, single screw
During a voyage from London to Mauritius on 11 May 1893, the passenger and emigrant ship *Conway Castle* ran aground at Vaudreuil Reef, near Vatoumandry, fifty miles south of Tamatave, Madagascar. She was abandoned as a total loss.

Casualties: 0

COPENHAGEN (1907) Great Eastern Railway, UK

2,570grt; 325ft (100.9m) lbp x 47ft (13.2m) beam
450 berthed passengers in two classes plus 300 on deck
John Brown, Clydebank (Yard No 380)
Steam turbines, triple screw
The North Sea ferry *Copenhagen* was torpedoed without warning and sunk on 5 March 1917. The attack occurred some eight nautical miles east-half-north of the Noord Hinder light vessel, south-west of Vlissingen (Flushing) near the Dutch/Belgian border.

Casualties: 6

The North Sea ferry *Copenhagen* operated between Harwich and the Hook of Holland for the Great Eastern Railway. *H. B. Christiansen Collection / Online Transport Archive*

CORDILLERA (1869) Pacific Steam Navigation Co, UK

2,860grt; 353ft (17.6m) lbp x 41ft (12.5m) beam
520 passengers in three classes
Randolph Elder, Govan (Yard No 96)
Compound-expansion steam reciprocating, single screw
On 20 September 1884, 15 years after first entering service, the *Cordillera* was wrecked in the Straits of Magellan while bound from Liverpool to Valparaiso, Chile.

Casualties: not known

CORINTHIAN (1900) Canadian Pacific Line, UK

7,333grt; 430ft (131.1m) lbp x 54ft (16.5m) beam
940 passengers in three classes
Workman Clark, Belfast (Yard No 160)
Triple-expansion steam reciprocating, single screw
On 14 December 1918 the passenger-cargo ship *Corinthian* was wrecked on the North West Ledges, near Brier Island, Bay of Fundy, while returning to Liverpool on her first round-trip following the Armistice.

Casualties: not known

COSTA RICA (1910) ex-*Prinses Juliana* (1930) Royal Netherlands SS Co, The Netherlands

8,672grt; 455ft (138.7m) lbp x 55ft (16.8m) beam
254 passengers
Nederlandsche Schps Maats, Amsterdam (Yard No 105)
Quadruple-expansion steam reciprocating, twin screw
On 27 April 1941 the passenger-cargo ship *Costa Rica*, bound for the southern shores of the Mediterranean from Kalamata, Greece, transporting troops, was sunk in an air attack in the position 35.54N, 23.49E. All the troops were saved as was her entire 178-man crew.

Casualties: 0

COTE D'ARGENT (1932) Société Anonyme de Gerance et d'Armament (SAGA), France

serving under the wartime name OSTMARK
3,047grt; 326ft (99.3m) lbp x 45ft (13.7m) beam
1,000 passengers
Forges et Chantiers de la Méditerranée, Le Havre
(Yard No not known)
Steam turbines, twin screw

With the fall of France in the summer of 1940, in July the French-flag cross-Channel ferry *Cote d'Argent* was captured by the invading Germans in the port of Cherbourg. She was placed in German naval service as an accommodation ship for minesweeper flotillas based on the French Atlantic coast. Later, after she had been damaged by fire, she was repaired and converted into a minelayer between March and October 1941, emerging as the *Ostmark*. By 1942 she had been converted again, at Kiel, into a torpedo target training vessel for the Luftwaffe, based in the Baltic. She did not survive the war for, on 21 April 1945, after sailing from Kristiansand, Norway, she was bombed in the Kattegat by warplanes of RAF Coastal Command and sank west of Anholt Island, in the approximate position 56.00N, 11.00E.

Casualties: 109 (crew and service personnel)

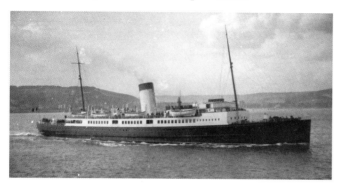

The *Cote D'Argent* and her sister *Cote D'Azur* maintained SAGA's cross-Channel services between Calais and Dover. They were both unfortunate to be trapped in French ports at the time of the German blitzkrieg through the Low Countries into northern France. *World Ship Society*

COTE D'AZUR (1931) Société Anonyme de Gerance et d'Armament (SAGA), France

serving under the wartime name ELSASS
3,047grt; 326ft (99.3m) lbp x 45ft (13.7m) beam
1,000 passengers
Forges et Chantiers de la Méditerranée, Le Havre (Yard No not known)
Steam turbines, twin screw
Like her sister, *Cote d'Argent*, the short-sea ferry *Cote d'Azur* fell into German hands after she had been bombed and sunk at Dunkirk on 27 May 1940 during the Operation 'Dynamo' evacuation of British and French troops. Salvaged by the German Navy in January 1941 and repaired for service as an accommodation ship, she was later converted at Flushing (Vlissingen) into a minelayer, being commissioned on 18 October 1942 as the *Elsass*. Later, for periods in both 1943 and 1944, she was employed as a form of helicopter carrier, performing observation duties for U-boats operating in the Baltic Sea. On 5 January 1945 she struck a mine and sank east of the island of Samso, in the position 55.43N, 10.40E.

Casualties: 87 (naval crew) One report gives the number of casualties as 18.

COTOPAXI (1873) Pacific Steam Navigation Co, UK

4,045grt; 402ft (122.5m) lbp x 42ft (12.8m) beam
184 passengers plus emigrants
John Elder, Govan (Yard No 146)
Compound-expansion steam reciprocating, single screw

On 8 April 1889, following a collision with the German ship *Olympia* in the Strait of Magellan, the passenger steamship *Cotopaxi* was beached. She was careened and re-plated on the spot but, after she had been refloated, on 15 April, she struck a rock in the Smyth Channel in the same area, and sank. All 202 persons aboard her were rescued by the Kosmos Line ship *Setos*. The *Cotopaxi* had been bound for Valparaiso at the time of the incident.

Casualties: 0

CRIJNSSEN (1919) Royal Netherlands SS Co, The Netherlands

4,298grt; 342ft (104.2m) lbp x 47ft (14.3m) beam
203 passengers in two classes
Maats Fijenoord, Rotterdam (Yard No 283)
Triple-expansion steam reciprocating, single screw
The passenger-cargo ship *Crijnssen* was on passage from Demerara and Curacao to New Orleans with 27 passengers and 66 crew on 10 June 1942, when she was torpedoed and sunk in the position 18.14N, 84.11W. Her attacker was the German submarine U504. Of the survivors, 49 were picked up by the American ore carrier *Lebore*, only to become victims of a second attack when that ship was sunk by the submarine U172 on 14 June 1942, as it headed for Cruz Grande from Baltimore.

Casualties: 2

CRISTOBAL COLON (1923) Cia Trasatlantica Española, Spain

10,883grt; 520ft (158.5m) loa x 61ft (18.6m) beam
1,100 passengers in three classes
Soc Española de Construccion Naval, Ferrol (Yard No 5)
Steam turbines, twin screw
The passenger-cargo liner *Cristobal Colon* was lost in unusual circumstances on 24 October 1936. Three months earlier, on 25 July, after she had left New York bound for Bilbao, she had been informed by radio of the outbreak of the Spanish Civil War and was re-directed to Southampton. From Southampton she proceeded to Le Havre, then to St Nazaire, where her 500 or so passengers were landed. When elements of her crew, who were supporters of General Franco, refused to take the ship to Spain, the *Cristobal Colon* sailed instead to Cardiff to bunker, for she was a coal-burning ship. On the completion of this it was decided that she should return to Vera Cruz, Mexico, to await developments or further instructions. En route, the liner was stranded on North Rock in the North East Reefs, ten miles off the coast of Bermuda. She was holed in No 3 hold and soon flooded and, due to the deep swell and her exposed position, in immediate danger. The crew dumped more than 1,500 tons of material overboard in a bid to lighten her but to no avail. The British cruiser HMS *Dragon* and two tugs arrived on the scene to offer assistance with the salvage effort but, after two days, in which her other holds were also breached, all attempts to save her were abandoned and the crew of 160 were landed. Due to heavy weather, on 26 October 1936, the *Cristobal Colon* hogged and broke her back. She was written off as a total loss.

Casualties: 0

The *Cristobal Colon* of the Bilbao to Havana and Vera Cruz service was, like sister ship the *Habana*, a victim of the Spanish Civil War. *Ian Allan Library*

CUBA (1897) ex-*Sachem* (1920) ex-*Coblenz* (1917) Pacific Mail Steamship Co, USA

3,168grt; 308ft (93.8m) lbp x 42ft (12.9m) beam
724 passengers in two classes
Blohm & Voss, Steinwerder, Hamburg (Yard No 121)
Triple-expansion steam reciprocating, twin screw
On 8 September 1923, while heading north from Panama to San Francisco, the passenger steamship *Cuba*, engaged in coastwise service, was wrecked on San Miguel Island, south of Santa Barbara, California.
Casualties: not known

CUBA (1923) Compagnie Générale Transatlantique (French Line), France

11,420grt; 495ft (150.9m) loa x 62ft (18.9m) beam
1,086 passengers in four classes
Swan Hunter & Wigham Richardson, Low Walker, Tyneside (Yard No 1108)
Steam turbines, twin screw

The *Cuba* operated on the French Line service from St Nazaire to the West Indies and Vera Cruz, Mexico, for many years in consort with the *Mexique*. *Ian Rae*

As a Vichy-controlled vessel following the fall of France, the passenger-cargo liner *Cuba* was arrested and seized by the British warship HMS *Moreton Bay* west of the Canaries on 31 October 1940 while she was bound from Martinique to Casablanca. Taken to Freetown, she was placed under Cunard Line management for the Ministry of War Transport and employed as a troopship. On 6 April 1945, when she was about fifty miles south of St Catherine's Point, Isle of Wight, during a convoy crossing from Southampton to Le Havre, the *Cuba* was torpedoed by the German submarine U1195, becoming one of the last Allied passenger ship losses of the war. On board were 265 persons, her crew of 252 men and a small number of military passengers, the majority of whom

were taken off by the destroyer HMS *Watchman*. The *Cuba* sank in the position 50.36N, 00.57W, but because the wreck was a potential hazard, it was later dispersed to a greater depth.
Casualties: 1 (crew member)

CUNARD AMBASSADOR (1972) Cunard Line, UK

14,160grt; 484ft (147.5m) loa x 71ft (21.5m) beam
831 passengers in single class
P. Smit Jr, Rotterdam (Yard No 666)
Motor-ship, twin screw
When barely two years old, the Cunard Line cruise ship *Cunard Ambassador* caught fire as she was bound from Port Everglades to New Orleans, on 12 September 1974. As it was a positioning voyage, she was not carrying passengers. The fire started in her engine room but rapidly spread to the accommodation decks. After three days, in which the fire wreaked havoc inside her, the blaze was brought under control and the *Cunard Ambassador* was taken in tow to Key West where, following an inspection, she was declared to be a total loss. Seemingly destined for the scrapyard after an extremely short career, her interiors and hull extensively damaged, she was sold instead to C. Clausen D/S A/S of Copenhagen for reconstruction. In March 1975 she was towed by the *Willem Barendz* to Landskrona where she was transformed into the livestock carrier *Linda Clausen*, the work completed at Hamburg from January 1976. She returned to operational service on 15 June 1976, surviving for another eight years.
Casualties: 0

CYMRIC (1898) White Star Line, UK

13,096grt; 599ft (182.6m) loa x 64ft (19.5m) beam
1,418 passengers in two classes
Harland & Wolff, Belfast (Yard No 316)
Quadruple-expansion steam reciprocating, twin screw

Employed on scheduled service voyages between Liverpool and New York or Boston, the *Cymric* also served as a troopship in the Boer War and the First World War. *H. B. Christiansen Collection / Online Transport Archive*

After the outbreak of hostilities between Britain and Germany in August 1914, the *Cymric* continued about her commercial schedules regardless of the submarine menace. While bound from New York for Liverpool on 8 May 1916, without passengers but carrying a general cargo and manned by a crew of 110, she was torpedoed by the German submarine U20 when she was 140 miles west-north-west of Fastnet. The U20 was the submarine that had been responsible for the sinking of the *Lusitania* a year earlier. The *Cymric* sank the day after the attack.

Casualties: 5

CYRIL (1883) ex-*Hawarden Castle* (1902) Booth Line, UK

4,380grt; 381ft (116.0m) lbp x 43ft (13.0m) beam
More than 250 passengers in three classes
John Elder, Govan (Yard No 269)
Triple-expansion steam reciprocating, single screw

A former Union-Castle vessel, the passenger-cargo ship *Cyril* was lost on 5 September 1905 while bound from Liverpool to Para (Belém) and Manaos. She was sunk in the River Amazon, 4 miles below Curralinho, on 16 September 1905 after colliding with her fleet-mate *Anselm*.

Casualties: 0

DAIREN MARU (1925) Dairen Kisen Kaisha, Japan

3,748grt; 360ft (109.7m) lbp x 46ft (14.0m) beam
Passenger numbers not known
Mitsubishi, Kobe (Yard No 157)
Steam turbines, twin screw

The passenger-cargo ferry *Dairen Maru* was torpedoed and sunk on 30 November 1944 by the American submarine USS *Sunfish*. The attack took place about 100 miles south-west of Chinampo, Korea, in the position 38.06N, 124.39E.

Casualties: not known

DAKOTA (1875) Guion Line, UK

4,332grt; 401ft (122.2m) lbp x 43ft (13.1m) beam
1,050 passengers in three classes
Palmers, Jarrow (Yard No 283)
Compound-expansion steam reciprocating, single screw

On 9 May 1877, while passing Port Lynas Light, in fog, outward bound from Liverpool to New York with 218 passengers and 109 crew, the passenger steamship *Dakota* was inadvertently steered onto the rocks, when a helm instruction from her Master was misunderstood by the quartermaster. She was stranded at Amlwch, on Anglesey, where the following day she broke her back and became a total wreck.

Casualties: 0

DAKOTA (1905) Great Northern Steamship Co, USA

20,714grt; 630ft (192.0m) loa x 74ft (22.4m) beam
2,700 passengers in two classes
Eastern Shipbuilding Co, New London (Yard No 2)
Triple-expansion steam reciprocating, twin screw

The passenger-cargo steamship *Dakota* carried mainly emigrant passengers besides having a vast cargo capacity. She was stranded on a reef at Noshima, forty miles from Yokohama, on 7 March 1907. Abandoned by her passengers and crew without mishap, she could not be saved herself. Sixteen days later she broke up in a storm and was subsequently dismantled where she lay.

Casualties: 0

One of the largest ships of her day, the *Dakota* operated a trans-Pacific service from San Francisco to the Far East with her sister *Minnesota*. Their accommodation was predominantly in Steerage. *University of Washington*

DANAE (1955) ex-*Therisos Express* (1974) ex-*Port Melbourne* (1972) Prestige Cruises NV, Liberia

9,603grt; 533ft (162.3m) loa x 70ft (21.3m) beam
497 passengers in single class
Harland & Wolff, Belfast (Yard No 1483)
Motor-ship, twin screw

A former Port Line cargo liner, the *Danae* was rebuilt as a cruise ship, together with her sister ship *Port Sydney*, which became the *Daphne*. While in dry dock at Genoa on 10 December 1991 undergoing overhaul prior to embarking upon a three-month cruise, she was engulfed by a major fire and declared a constructive total loss. Subsequently sold for breaking up, while bound for Piraeus under tow on 9 July 1992 under the name *Anar* she was given a reprieve when she was acquired for reconstruction. Renamed *Starlight Princess*, she was diverted to Gythion where she arrived on 1 September 1992, subsequently sailing to Venice under her own power and once again renamed *Danae*. She re-emerged after repairs and renovation in 1994 as the *Baltica*, being further renamed in 1996 when she became the *Princess Danae*.
Casualties: 0

DANMARK (1880) ex-*Jan Breydel* (1888) Thingvalla Line, Denmark

3,414grt; 340ft (103.6m) lbp x 40ft (12.2m) beam
1,100 passengers
Mitchell, Low Walker, Tyneside (Yard No 385)
Compound-expansion steam reciprocating, single screw

On a westbound crossing on 6 April 1889, bound from Copenhagen to New York carrying 669 passengers and 66 crew, the emigrant passenger steamer *Danmark* suffered a broken propeller shaft, which led to her flooding and foundering in mid-Atlantic. She was last seen on 8 April in the position 45.45N, 37.16W, some 800 miles east of Newfoundland. Thanks to the timely arrival of the Atlantic Transport liner *Missouri*, the *Danmark*'s entire complement was picked up safely and landed in the Azores some days later.
Casualties: 0

DARA (1948) British India Line, UK

5,030grt; 399ft (121.6m) lbp x 55ft (16.7m) beam
74 berthed passengers in two classes plus 1,377 deck passengers
Barclay Curle, Whiteinch, Glasgow (Yard No 711)
Motor-ship, twin screw

After the passenger-cargo ship *Dara*, whose accommodation catered for a large number of native deck passengers, arrived at Dubai on 7 April 1961, on a return voyage to Bombay, she anchored in the roadstead in readiness to receive lighters and launches by means of which her cargo and passengers could be transferred to and from shore. When a sudden storm struck the port it was decided that the ship should leave the harbour and ride it out in deeper water. Early on the following day, when the weather had moderated, the *Dara* headed back to Dubai, but as she was re-entering harbour she was shaken by a huge explosion. The most likely cause was a mine placed by saboteurs in an alleyway at the forward end of her bridge deck (although sabotage was suspected it was never actually proven for lack of forensic evidence).

The detonation started fires and threw the ship into darkness, which led to panic among elements of the passengers. The fire spread rapidly into the cabin accommodation, as the holes blown through the bridge and promenade decks permitted a draught to fan the flames. There was no opportunity to send distress calls because the radio office had been destroyed early on and the officers on the *Dara* concentrated their efforts on evacuating the ship. Great difficulty was experienced in lowering the boats for a variety of reasons. It was impossible to lower some of the double-banked boats, while those on the starboard side amidships could not be launched because the strong wind was blowing the flames in that direction. The flames also denied access to the boats from the normal stations and loading had to be undertaken at the poop. Overcrowding was a problem and two boats that were safely floated later capsized for this reason.

Fortunately there were many ships nearby that had witnessed the explosion and help was soon on its way. Among those that rendered assistance were the tankers *British Energy* and *Yoyo Maru*, the Norwegian-registered *Thorsholm*, and another British India vessel, the *Berpeta*. Between them they managed to save 528 of the 745 passengers and crew. A further 53 persons were saved from the 74 shore personnel that had boarded the *Dara* when she had first arrived at the port. All were landed at Bahrain. Fire parties from three Royal Navy frigates and an American destroyer who had boarded the *Dara* managed to extinguish the fire, following which the salvage vessel *Ocean Salvor* took her in tow to deeper water where she sank, three miles off shore, in the position 25.34N, 55.27E, on 10 April 1961.
Casualties: 238, including 165 of the 537 un-berthed deck passengers

The British India passenger ship *Dara*, which operated between India, Africa, the Red Sea and the Persian Gulf, was probably the victim of an act of terrorism. Fortunately, very few passenger ships have been the targets of such action.
World Ship Society

D'ARTAGNAN (1925) Messageries Maritimes, France

serving under the wartime name TEIKO MARU
15,105grt; 565ft (172.2m) loa x 65ft (19.8m) beam
420 passengers in three classes
Chantiers de la Gironde, Bordeaux (Yard No 181)
Triple-expansion steam reciprocating, twin screw

The passenger-cargo liner *D'Artagnan* continued to sail between Saigon, Manila and Shanghai after June 1940, maintaining the service until 20 October 1941, when she suffered an outbreak of fire while docked in the Huangpo River at Shanghai. Early in the following year, after the Japanese had taken complete control of Shanghai, the burned-out *D'Artagnan*, thought to be only fit for demolition, was seized and repaired, and handed to the Japanese Navy for service as a troop transport under the name *Teiko Maru*. She remained so employed until 22 February 1944 when she was torpedoed and sunk off the Natuna Islands in the position 03.13N, 109.18E by the American submarine USS *Puffer*. Although the taking of the *D'Artagnan* is described as a 'seizure', the acquisition of the ship might more correctly be described as a 'transfer' in that it was apparently carried out in accordance with a charter arrangement concluded with the Vichy Government in France.

Casualties: not known

DASHUN (1983) ex-*Volans* (1999) Yanda Ferry Co, People's Republic of China

9,843grt; 414ft (126.2m) loa x 66ft (20.0m) beam
520 passengers
Naikai Shipbuilding, Setoda, Japan (Yard No 483)
Motor-ship, twin screw

After leaving port at 13.40 local time on 24 November 1999, bound from Yantai, in China's Shandong province, across the Bohai Strait to the port of Dalian, the ro-ro passenger/vehicle ferry *Dashun* encountered a severe typhoon in extremely cold conditions. Aboard her were 264 passengers and 40 crew. The weather forecast prior to departure had advised of bad weather but it turned out to be far worse than had been expected with wind gusts over force 10 and temperatures near freezing. The wind direction, from north to north-east, had aggravated the sea state and it was not long before the *Dashun* was heading into mountainous waves that shook the vessel violently. It was soon reported from the car decks, where 61 vehicles of different sizes were stowed, that some had broken free and were colliding against each other. The *Dashun*'s Master decided that the weather, which was worsening, was too severe to continue and, at around 15.20, when about twenty miles out from port, resolved to take the ship back to the shelter of Yantai and wait for the storm to pass.

In order to turn her, the *Dashun* was helmed to starboard (in an easterly direction) which brought her broadside on to the wind and waves. Consequently, the violent pitching was replaced by an extreme rolling motion, which made it difficult to steer the ship and increased the movement of vehicles on the car deck. Less than an hour later, while making laboured progress and still struggling to fully turn the ship, the smoke alarm on the bridge sounded, indicating that fire had broken out on the lower vehicle deck. It was speculated that the cause had been the ignition of leaking fuel oil from tanks that had been ruptured through the constant pounding. The affected area was sealed and the sprinkler system activated, but it failed to operate. In these grave circumstances, the Master ordered the transmission of 'May Day' signals, advising that his ship was in immediate danger and required assistance. All passengers were instructed to don their lifejackets and members of the crew were ordered to rig hoses to keep the bulkheads on C deck, where the fire had originated, cool, and to endeavour to tackle the blaze at the first opportunity.

The *Dashun*'s position at this time was 37.41N, 121.37E.

Three ships, the *Qilu*, *Xing Lu* and *Dai Jiang* responded to the calls for help, but because of the wild sea-state found it difficult to make headway towards the stricken ferry. A short time after sending the distress calls, the *Dashun*'s steering gear failed and her emergency rudder could not be reached because access to it was through the compartment containing the fire. The ship was now at the mercy of the elements and her only hope depended on the vessels trying to reach her. At 17.25, by now in failing light that added to the already poor visibility, one of her anchors was dropped in a bid to reduce the rolling and arrest her drift, but by then she had an extreme list to port and the anchor was dragged by the power of the waves. The ships that had gone to her aid managed to manoeuvre as close to the *Dashun* as they could without endangering themselves, and for two hours they repeatedly fired lines to her using rope guns in a bid to secure a cable and get her in tow. But the lines either never reached her or, when they did, the cables failed as the ships were buffeted in the wild seas, by now driven by violent storm force 11 winds.

Aboard the *Dashun*, the passengers, who had been readied for evacuation, were feeling the effects of exposure to the perishing cold, no doubt worsened by their anxiety, and they were instructed to return to their cabins despite the fact that the ship was increasingly taking water and the fire was still being fought below. By 23.00 the crew had managed to extinguish the fire but all power was lost soon after and the ship's pumps failed. With a 90-degree list to port, the *Dashun* suddenly rolled over onto her beam ends and sank, taking many of those aboard with her. Others attempted to save themselves by leaping into the raging and freezing sea to reach the lifebuoys and rafts that had been cut free in a last desperate attempt to save lives, but few were successful. By the time she sank, the *Dashun* was only some two miles off the coast, just north of Zhuangyun village, her last recorded position 37.28N, 121.47E.

While it may be pondered whether the *Dashun* should ever have put to sea in the first place in such weather, this more detailed account has been included as her loss serves to demonstrate how, in maritime emergencies, the situation can swiftly deteriorate through a sequence of contributory factors, often as the result of consecutive system failures.

Casualties: 282 (247 passengers and 35 crew)

The Chinese ro-ro ferry *Dashun* was originally the Japanese-flag *Volans*, as shown here. Her loss in the Bohai Strait was one of China's worst maritime disasters for many years. As the *Dashun*, the large apertures in groups of four, at main deck level, including those just below and aft of the funnels, were sealed. *Klas Brogren, ShipPax*

DE LA SALLE (1924) Compagnie Générale Transatlantique (French Line), France

8,400grt; 440ft (134.1m) lbp x 56ft (17.1m) beam
More than 891 passengers in three classes
Barclay Curle, Whiteinch, Glasgow (Yard No 582)
Triple-expansion steam reciprocating, twin screw

After the fall of France the Germans requisitioned the passenger-cargo ship *De La Salle* with the intention of using her for the planned invasion of England, but in November 1940, while she was at Casablanca, she passed into the control of the British War Ministry for service as a troopship. During a convoy voyage from Liverpool to Freetown, Walvis Bay and East London on 9 July 1943, she was torpedoed and sunk by the German submarine U508 in the Gulf of Benin, in the position 05.50N, 02.22E. At the time the *De La Salle* was carrying 150 crew and 99 passengers.
Casualties: 10 (2 passengers and 8 crew)

The *De La Salle* was one of a pair of ships, although her sister, the *Sinaia*, was, unusually, owned by the Fabre Line. The French Line employed the *De La Salle* on the West Indies and Central America services. *World Ship Society*

DELHI (1905) P&O Line, UK

8,090grt; 470ft (143.3m) lbp x 56ft (17.1m) beam
240 passengers in two classes
Caird, Greenock (Yard No 307)
Quadruple-expansion steam reciprocating, twin screw

Built for the Far Eastern service, the *Delhi* was lost while carrying members of the Royal Family. *Tom Rayner collection*

The passenger-cargo steamship *Delhi* was lost on 13 December 1911 while carrying the Princess Royal and her family in addition to 81 other passengers, bound from London to Bombay via Marseilles. She ran ashore and was wrecked two miles south of Cape Spartel, Tangiers, in a gale. Calls for help were transmitted by wireless and responded to by the French cruiser *Friant*, the British cruiser HMS *Duke of Edinburgh* and the battleship HMS *London*. The *Friant* attempted to take off those stranded aboard the *Delhi* in her

own boats, but in the course of these efforts one launch capsized and three naval ratings were drowned. Meanwhile, the *Duke of Edinburgh*'s boats joined the rescue operation, one of them collecting the Royal party. This lifeboat turned over in the surf as it neared the shore and its occupants had a narrow escape from drowning. Everyone else aboard the *Delhi* was eventually taken off in safety, brought ashore and taken to Tangiers.
Casualties: 3 (from the *Friant*)

DEMPO (1931) Rotterdam Lloyd, The Netherlands

17,024grt; 574ft (174.9m) loa x 70ft (21.3m) beam
634 passengers in four classes
Royal Schelde, Vlissingen (Yard No 189)
Motor-ship, twin screw

After the fall of the Netherlands, the Dutch motor passenger ship *Dempo* was taken over as an Allied troopship. She was in convoy SNF17, bound from Naples to Oran, North Africa, on 17 March 1944, when she was torpedoed and sunk by the German submarine U371. The attack occurred between Algiers and Phillipeville (Skikda) in the position 37.08N, 05.27E.
Casualties: 0

The sister ships *Baloeran* and *Dempo*, the latter shown here, joined the service from Rotterdam to the Dutch East Indies in 1930 and 1931 respectively. *Bettina Rohbrecht*

DEUTSCHLAND (1866) Norddeutscher Lloyd, Germany

2,898grt; 337ft (102.7m) loa x 40ft (12.2m) beam
c650 passengers
Caird, Greenock (Yard No 132)
Compound-expansion steam reciprocating, single screw

The passenger steamship *Deutschland* was crossing the North Sea, bound from Bremen to Southampton and New York on 6 December 1875, when she lost her bearings in snow squalls. In the poor visibility, which concealed the Sunk, Cork and Kentish Knock lightships marking the approaches to the Thames Estuary, the *Deutschland* ran onto the Kentish Knock Sands, in the North Goodwins. At the time she was carrying both the Weser and Channel pilots. In a bid to free herself, her propeller was broken and the ship was left in a helpless situation. She was too far from shore for her distress rockets to be seen, but by a process of relaying rocket signals from lightship to lightship along the coast, people ashore at Harwich were alerted to her plight. The paddle tug *Liverpool* proceeded to locate the wrecked liner, also by following the course of the line of lightships, but by the time she arrived to give help, on 7 December, many of the *Deutschland*'s occupants had already frozen to death in the rigging. Using

lifeboats, and by coming alongside, the *Liverpool* managed to take off the remaining 173 persons aboard the stricken ship, including her Master. The transfer operation was fraught with danger for the wind had freshened and the sea had roughened in the hours following the stranding, but was finally accomplished without further loss of life. The *Deutschland* was abandoned, a total wreck.
Casualties: 157

DEUTSCHLAND (1923) Hamburg Amerika Line, Germany

21,046grt; 677ft (206.3m) loa x 72ft (21.9m) beam
1,515 passengers in three classes
Blohm & Voss, Steinwerder, Hamburg (Yard No 405)
Steam turbines, twin screw
The passenger liner *Deutschland* had completed five years as a naval accommodation ship stationed at Gotenhafen (Gdynia), followed by seven voyages ferrying refugees from the German eastern territories during Operation 'Hannibal', when she was ordered to the Bay of Lubeck to join the *Cap Arcona* (qv) and *Thielbek*. These ships were being used as prison ships, holding a large number of concentration camp inmates and political prisoners, while the *Deutschland*, so it is reported, was to have been deployed as a hospital ship for the injured and sick among their number. In reality, the three ships were to have been sacrificed as part of a despicable plot to conceal war crimes by deliberately scuttling them and killing the prisoners from three concentration camps. In the event, this was thwarted but at a terrible cost in human lives, when the three ships were attacked by British aircraft with rockets and bombs in air raids at Neustadt on 3 May 1945. The *Deutschland* caught fire and capsized, sinking in a munitions dumping area, in the position 54.03N, 10.48E. It is understood that the *Deutschland*, of the three vessels, did not have prisoners aboard her at the time of the attacks. Her wreck was raised and broken up in 1948.
Casualties: not known

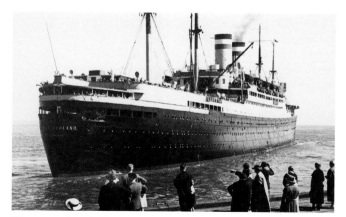
The transatlantic liner *Deutschland* was, like the *Cap Arcona*, lost in unsavoury circumstances after her involvement in the Operation 'Hannibal' refugee evacuation. *Hapag-Lloyd*

DEVON (1897) Federal Steam Navigation Co, UK

6,059grt; 420ft (128.0m) lbp x 54ft (16.5m) beam
168 passengers in two classes
Hawthorn Leslie, Hebburn-on-Tyne (Yard No 340)
Triple-expansion steam reciprocating, single screw

The passenger-cargo steamship *Devon* was lost on 25 August 1913 while bound from Montreal to Wellington, New Zealand. She stranded on Pencarrow Point, Wellington Heads, and became a total loss.
Casualties: not known

DIAMOND PRINCESS (2003) P&O Princess Cruises (Fairline Shipping International), Bermuda

115,875grt; 952ft (290.0m) loa x 124ft (37.8m) beam
3,078 passengers
Mitsubishi, Nagasaki (Yard No 2180)
Diesel-electric, twin Azipods
Due to enter service in May 2003, the giant cruise ship *Diamond Princess* was swept by fire on 1 October 2002 and sustained widespread and severe damage while still under construction at her builder's shipyard. After the blaze had been brought under control the following day, it was estimated that more than 70 per cent of the ship's interiors were gutted and, while her engine room and power-plant were undamaged, it was considered initially that the ship was beyond recovery and that all work should cease pending her disposal. However, it was announced subsequently that construction would continue and on 21 October the *Diamond Princess* was towed to the Mitsubishi shipyard at Koyagi for the damage to be repaired and the ship finished as intended. She finally entered service on 27 May 2004, by then renamed *Sapphire Princess*. In the meantime her original name had been allocated to Yard No 2181, which had been launched (floated) as the *Sapphire Princess*. No doubt the exercise was to confuse the two ships and help conceal the identity of the one that had been affected by the blaze. In tonnage terms, the *Diamond Princess* is the largest ship described in these pages. It is perhaps as well that, given her large passenger capacity, she caught fire in dock while under construction rather than in service, fully loaded.
Casualties: 0

The *Sapphire Princess*, seen off the coast of Alaska, started life as the *Diamond Princess*. She is the largest passenger ship to be described in these pages. It has to be said that Princess Cruises has an outstanding safety record but it is fortunate that the fire aboard the *Diamond Princess* occurred in the shipyard rather than at sea. *Princess Cruises*

DISCOVERY I (1970) ex-*Venus Venturer* (1986) ex-*Scandinavian Sea* (1984) ex-*Blenheim* (1981) Discovery Cruise Line Partnership, Panama

12,244grt; 506ft (154.2m) loa x 66ft (20.0m) beam
1,350 unberthed passengers
Upper Clyde Shipbuilders, Clydebank (Yard No 744)
Motor-ship, twin screw

The cruise ship *Discovery I*, which earlier in her career had been rescued from demolition after a major fire reduced her to a constructive total loss under the name *Scandinavian Sea* (qv), was lost on 9 May 1996. During one of her gambling cruises from Fort Lauderdale with 821 passengers plus crew, she was disabled by an engine room fire on 8 May and was towed to Freeport in the Bahamas, her intended destination, where an inspection concluded that she was beyond economic recovery. She was subsequently sold for breaking up at Alang where she arrived on 1 September 1997.
Casualties: not known

DJEMNAH (1875) Messageries Maritimes, France

3,785grt; 394ft (120.1m) lbp x 39ft (11.9m) beam
163 passengers in three classes
Messageries Maritimes, La Ciotat (Yard No 45)
Compound steam reciprocating, single screw
On the night of 14 July 1918 the small French passenger ship *Djemnah* was returning from Madagascar with around 1,000 troops as part of a convoy bound for Marseilles escorted by HMS *Mallow* together with three French armed trawlers. Having passed through the Red Sea and the Suez Canal, the convoy was some 69 miles north-east of Derna, passing to the south of Crete, when the German submarine UB105 attacked. The submarine's torpedo struck the *Djemnah* on her starboard side, the explosion cutting her in two, and she disappeared beneath the surface after barely 2 minutes. There was no opportunity in so little time for all those aboard to make their escape and, as a consequence, there was heavy loss of life. Indeed, the sinking of the *Djemnah* ranks with the losses of the *Gallia*, *La Provence* and *Amiral Magon* as being among France's most serious maritime disasters of the First World War.
Casualties: 548 (489 soldiers and 59 crew members)

The third of a class of five ships, Messageries Maritimes' *Djemnah* was destined for service from Marseilles to the Orient. *World Ship Society*

DNYEPR (1931) ex-*Cabo San Agustin* (1939) Black Sea Shipping Co (Sovtorgflot), USSR

12,589grt; 500ft (152.4m) loa x 63ft (19.2m) beam
512 passengers in two classes (as a Spanish ship)
Soc Española de Construccion Naval, Bilbao (Yard No 38)
Motor-ship, twin screw
On 3 October 1941 the Russian passenger ship *Dnyepr* (also rendered as *Dnepr*), a former Spanish vessel that had been seized at Feodosiya, Crimea, was bound from Novorossiysk to Odessa to evacuate Russian troops trapped by the German Army's push on Stalingrad (Volgograd). En route, while off Anapa, south of the Straits of Kerch, she was sunk by a torpedo launched from a German aircraft.
Casualties: not known

Having survived the Spanish Civil War, in which she performed troop-carrying duties for the Republican forces, the *Cabo San Agustin* was laid up at Feodosiya, in the Crimea, where she was seized by the Russians. Renamed *Dnyepr*, she was placed in Soviet passenger service based on Odessa.
Edward Wilson

DOMINION (1874) E. Thirkell & Co, UK

2,999grt; 335ft (102.1m) lbp x 38ft (11.6m) beam
680 passengers in two classes
A. McMillan, Dumbarton (Yard No 176)
Triple-expansion steam reciprocating, single screw
After serving for more than 20 years on the transatlantic service from Liverpool to Canada, the passenger-cargo steamship *Dominion* was wrecked at Castletown Berehaven, County Cork, on 4 January 1896, a year after she had been sold to new owners. It is assumed that she was still in the passenger-carrying business at the time of her loss.
Casualties: not known

DOM PEDRO (1878) Chargeurs Réunis, France

2,999grt; 329ft (100.4m) lbp x 39ft (11.9m) beam
Passenger numbers not known
Forges et Chantiers de la Méditerranée, Le Havre
(Yard No not known)
Compound-expansion steam reciprocating, single screw
On 27 May 1895 the passenger-cargo ship *Dom Pedro* was bound for La Plata ports with 126 persons on board. She had already called at Pasajes and was heading for Carril (Villagarcia), where she was scheduled to pick up an additional 200 emigrant passengers. As she was nearing the port, she struck the rocks at Fraquina Reef, Currubedo, Cape Finisterre, due to a navigational error. The sudden impact caused the ship's boilers to explode, which in turn set off panic among those passengers already aboard the *Dom Pedro*. The Master and his officers endeavoured to calm the terrified mob but their appeals went unheeded with the result that there was considerable loss of life in the unruly evacuation. The death toll would have been higher but for the help of boats that had come from the shore, some ten miles distant.
Casualties: 87

DONA MARILYN (1966) ex-*Dona Ana* (1980) ex-*Otohime Maru* (1976) Sulpicio Lines, Philippines

2,991grt; 320ft (97.6m) loa x 45ft (13.7m) beam
807 passengers

Onomichi Zosen, Onomichi (Yard No 175)
Motor-ship, single screw

The passenger-cargo ferry *Dona Marilyn* took over on the Manila to Tacloban route to fill the space vacated by the loss of the *Dona Paz* (qv), which had occurred in December 1987. Ten months later, on 24 October 1988, the *Dona Marilyn* was caught in typhoon 'Ruby' while she was outbound from Manila with 451 passengers and 67 crew members. Caught in the storm, the ship reported that she was experiencing engine trouble but shortly afterwards she was completely overwhelmed and sank off Leyte. Initial announcements stated that there had only been fifteen survivors, but gradually more persons were recovered from remote islands surrounding the area where the ship had foundered.
Casualties: 254 (official number)

DONA PAZ (1963) ex-*Don Sulpicio* (1981) ex-*Himeyuri Maru* (1975) Sulpicio Lines, Philippines

2,602grt; 305ft (93.1m) loa x 45ft (13.6m) beam
1,518 passengers
Onomichi Zosen, Onomichi (Yard No 118)
Motor-ship, single screw

The *Dona Paz* holds the dubious distinction of being the worst ever peacetime passenger ship loss. A quite indistinct vessel, it is hard to imagine that a ship of this size could carry so many passengers. *Sulpicio Lines*

The loss of this relatively insignificant inter-island ferry ranks as the worst peacetime shipping tragedy of all time, the unofficial death toll amounting to 4,386 persons. For such a small ship to be carrying so many passengers (three times her licensed number) defies the imagination but, under the insufficiently regulated Philippine ferry industry, vessels are typically overloaded to excess and proper passenger manifests are rarely kept or are unreliable. For this reason, the Philippine authorities were able to publish an official count of 1,565 casualties, still greater than the loss from the *Titanic*, but a figure known to be massively wide of the mark, as demonstrated by the vast volume of claims from bereaved relatives. Such denial does not help the cause of implementing higher safety standards and preventative measures.

The incident arose when the *Dona Paz*, on passage from Tacloban to Manila with families heading home for Christmas, was in collision with the small oil tanker *Vector* on 20 December 1987 off Dumali Point, East Mindoro, while she was between Mindoro and the Marinduque islands. Both ships were engulfed in flames and sank within minutes. Only 21 survivors were helped from the shark-infested waters, and only 270 bodies were ever recovered, a testimony to the speed with which the *Dona Paz* sank.

Casualties: 4,386 (the published figure now recognised as being most accurate)

DONAU (1869) H. Bischoff & Co, Germany

3,073grt; 347ft (105.8m) lbp x 40ft (12.2m) beam
760 passengers in three classes
Caird, Greenock (Yard No 147)
Compound steam reciprocating, single screw

The former Norddeutscher Lloyd transatlantic steamship *Donau* was destroyed by a fire that broke out during a westbound crossing on 15 March 1895, in the position 49.26N, 24.13W. The fire, of unknown cause, was discovered in the cargo early in the morning and immediately all passengers were ordered on deck. To avoid ventilating the fire, the hold covers were sealed and the *Donau* was steered before the wind on half-engines. Hoses were rigged through holes cut in the deck but they were largely ineffective as dense smoke made it impossible to see the seat of the blaze. All inflammable materials and some explosives were also dumped over the side.

As the fire intensified, the tactics were revised, concentrating on getting to land, and the *Donau* was turned into the wind to keep the smoke astern while an attempt was made to reach the coast of Ireland. A final effort was made to extinguish the fire using the steam supply that operated the winch, but this too was of no avail, and by early on 16 March it was realised that there was little prospect of successfully extinguishing the fire. Conditions in the engine and boiler rooms had become untenable and one dead engineer had already been brought up from below. The ship's sides were blistering outwards and smoke belched out of the hull in many places. There were numerous explosions between decks and the intense heat made much of the accommodation areas impenetrable.

At this stage it was decided that the ship's company should abandon her. Fortunately, the eastbound British oil tanker *Delaware* was sighted and she took on all survivors without mishap, landing them in the Mersey on 19 March. The *Donau* was last seen shrouded in smoke in the approximate position 51.00N, 20.00W near where she eventually sank.
Casualties: 1

DORCHESTER (1926) Merchant & Miners Transportation Co, USA

5,649grt; 350ft (106.7m) lbp x 52ft (15.9m) beam
314 passengers
Newport News Shipbuilding & Drydock Co, Newport News, Virginia (Yard No 289)
Triple-expansion steam reciprocating, single screw

The coastal passenger ship *Dorchester* was deployed as a troopship after the entry of the USA into the Second World War. While operating in this capacity, she was torpedoed and sunk by the German submarine U223 on 3 February 1943 in the position 59.22N, 48.42W, between Newfoundland and Greenland. She was bound from New York and St John's to Bluie West carrying a total of 904 persons. The loss of the *Dorchester* was one of the worst disasters to befall an American-flag passenger ship. The majority of those who were killed drowned in the freezing seas.
Casualties: 675 (crew and service personnel). A figure of 605 is given in some reports.

The American coastwise passenger ship *Dorchester*.
Northrop Grumman Shipbuilding

DORIC (1923) White Star Line, UK

16,484grt; 601ft (183.1m) loa x 68ft (20.6m) beam
2,300 passengers in two classes
Harland & Wolff, Belfast (Yard No 573)
Steam turbines, twin screw

While returning from a Mediterranean cruise on 5 September 1935, the passenger-cargo liner *Doric* was in collision in thick fog with the Chargeurs Réunis steamer *Formigny* off Cape Finisterre, Portugal, in the position 41.19N, 09.34W. The *Doric* was badly damaged and began to list. Calls for assistance brought three other British liners to the scene, the P&O ships *Mooltan* and *Viceroy of India* and Orient Line's *Orion*. While the *Mooltan* stood by, the *Viceroy of India* and *Orion* between them evacuated the *Doric*'s passengers, around 250 on the former and 475 on the latter, and returned them to Gravesend. The *Doric*'s crew remained on board and, under her own steam, with the aid of the salvage vessel *Valkyrien*, she proceeded to Vigo where a cofferdam was fitted prior to her making the return voyage to Tilbury. On arrival at Tilbury the *Doric* was examined with a view to sending her to Belfast for repairs. In the event, due to the scale of the damage and the projected cost of the extensive reconstruction work involved, she was sold instead for breaking up and left Tilbury on 7 October 1935 bound for a scrapyard at Newport, Monmouthshire.

Casualties: 0

The *Doric*, like the similar but larger *Laurentic* of 1927, had distinctive double-tiered gravity lifeboat davits. *Ian Allan Library*

DOURO (1865) Royal Mail Line, UK

2,846grt; 326ft (99.5m) lbp x 40ft (12.3m) beam
313 passengers in three classes
Caird, Greenock (Yard No 110)
Compound-expansion inverted steam engines, single screw

Shortly after leaving Lisbon on the last leg of her voyage from Brazil to the UK, the passenger ship *Douro* collided with the Spanish cargo steamer *Yrurac Bat*, bound from La Coruna to Havana, on 1 April 1882. The accident occurred in the late evening, about 45 miles off Cape Finisterre, Portugal. The lights of the then unidentified *Yrurac Bat* were seen approaching close off the starboard bow and evasive action was taken, but too late to prevent a collision. The *Douro* was struck amidships on her starboard side with considerable impact and began to settle immediately. Before she foundered, stern-first, seven of her boats were launched and got away safely with 112 persons. The *Yrurac Bat* also sank within thirty minutes and her occupants were cast into the sea. The steamship *Hidalgo* arrived on the scene and picked up a total of 144 survivors from the two ships; but for her timely appearance, given the high seas that were running, the death toll would have been higher.

Casualties: 59 (23 from the *Douro*, including her Master, six officers and seven crew, and 36 from the *Yrurac Bat*)

DOVER CASTLE (1904) Union-Castle Line, UK

8,271grt; 490ft (149.3m) loa x 56ft (17.1m) beam
220 passengers in single class
Barclay Curle, Whiteinch, Glasgow (Yard No 443)
Quadruple-expansion steam reciprocating, twin screw

During the First World War the *Dover Castle* served as a hospital ship. On 26 May 1917, during a voyage from Malta to Gibraltar in company with the hospital ship *Karapara* and the destroyers HMS *Camelon* and *Nemesis*, she was torpedoed by the German submarine UC67 as the convoy was passing fifty miles north of Bona (Annaba), Algeria. The *Dover Castle* was carrying many wounded soldiers and they, together with the hospital staff and the majority of the crew, were transferred to the *Camelon*. Meanwhile, a skeleton crew remained aboard the hospital ship in a bid to save her, but these efforts proved to be in vain for a second torpedo was fired into the *Dover Castle* and she sank soon afterwards. The position was 37.54N, 07.36E.

Casualties: 7 (all engine room crew)

The *Dover Castle*, one of three sisters, was employed on both the London to Cape Town and Mombasa services. She is seen here during the First World War, as a hospital ship.
Ian Allan Library

DRESDEN (1920) ex-*Ormuz* (1927) ex-*Zeppelin* (1917) Norddeutscher Lloyd, Germany

14,690grt; 570ft (173.7m) loa x 67ft (20.5m) beam
971 passengers in single class
Bremer Vulkan, Vegesack (Yard No 579)
Quadruple-expansion steam reciprocating, twin screw
Following a stranding accident on 20 June 1934, during an excursion trip to the Norwegian fjords, the cruise ship *Dresden* was beached at the southern end of Karmesund, Utsire, 5 miles north of Hvidingsö, on Norway's west coast. She had been returning from Ryfylke to Hardanger when she ran aground at Klep on Boken Island in the Karmesund, but was refloated without assistance. Visibility was clear but strong north-westerly winds and a powerful current had driven the ship off course onto uncharted rocks. She was subsequently beached only forty metres away from the shore at Blikshavn, leaving her firmly wedged, holed underwater and listing. Numerous ships went to her assistance, among them the Norwegian steamers *Kong Harald* and *Kronprinsesse Martha*, which took off 700 passengers, the French warship *Ardent*, the salvage vessels *Achilles* and *Herkules*, and the tug *Hermes*. The survivors from her 1,000 or so passengers were taken to Stavanger where they were collected by the liner *Stuttgart* for return to Bremen. The day after she stranded, the *Dresden* capsized onto her port side, lying half exposed in shallow water with her stern almost completely submerged. Declared a total loss, she was scrapped by local breakers. It later transpired that her pilot had not been in possession of a certificate for those waters.
Casualties: 4 (all women passengers)

A ship that had a multi-faceted career was the *Dresden*. Ordered as the *Zeppelin* for Hamburg Amerika Line, she was seized as a First World War reparation to become Orient Line's *Ormuz* before returning to German ownership in 1927.
Ian Allan Library

The *Dresden* became one of the earliest German ships to be taken up for the Deutsche Arbeitsfront scheme for Nazi party members' and workers' cruises under the 'Kraft durch Freude' banner. She is seen capsized after being stranded on Boken Island, Norway, during one such cruise. *Author's collection*

DRINA (1913) Royal Mail Line, UK

11,483grt; 517ft (157.6m) loa x 62ft (18.9m) beam
995 passengers in three classes
Harland & Wolff, Belfast (Yard No 428)
Quadruple-expansion steam reciprocating, twin screw
After a year's service as a hospital ship at the outset of the First World War, the passenger liner *Drina* reverted to her owners' commercial services on the run to South America. While returning from Buenos Aires to her home port of Liverpool on 1 March 1917, she was torpedoed and sunk two miles west-south-west of the island of Skokholm, near the Pembrokeshire coast, in the position 51.41N, 05.20W, by the German submarine UC65.
Casualties: 15

The *Drina* was the last of a class of five Royal Mail ships built for the service from Liverpool to the River Plate ports.
Furness Withy Group

DRUMMOND CASTLE (1881) Castle Line, UK

3,663grt; 365ft (111.3m) lbp x 44ft (13.3m) beam
380 passengers in three classes
John Elder, Govan (Yard No 246)
Triple-expansion steam reciprocating, single screw

The *Drummond Castle*, engaged in the Castle Line's mail service to South Africa, is seen moored in Dartmouth harbour, embarking passengers prior to departure. Her loss was one of the worst involving a British ship up to that time.
British & Commonwealth Shipping

While she was returning from Cape Town with 143 passengers and 103 crew, the passenger steamship *Drummond Castle* ran onto the Pierre Vertes Reef, Ushant, at the southern entrance to Fronveur Sound, shortly before midnight on 16 June 1896. The visibility was poor at the time. Believing the vessel to be securely grounded, as she had struck the shoal at 12 knots, and little realising that she was to remain on the surface for less than four minutes, little immediate attention was given to organising an abandonment; although the boats were readied, they were not lowered. While steam was being released from the boilers, to prevent an explosion, the *Drummond Castle* suddenly foundered, taking almost all her occupants with her. Breton fishermen picked up the survivors, a male passenger, a quartermaster and a seaman. Some 33 years later, during the search for the wreck of the P&O liner *Egypt*, the salvors located the *Drummond Castle* and discovered that she had a huge tear in her side, extending from the waterline to the keel, providing an explanation for why she had sunk with such speed.

Casualties: 243

DUCA DI GENOVA (1907) La Veloce Line, Italy

8,337grt; 476ft (145.1m) lbp x 53ft (16.2m) beam
1,928 passengers in three classes
Cantieri Navali Riuniti, Muggiano, La Spezia
(Yard No 33)
Quadruple-expansion steam reciprocating, twin screw
The passenger steamer *Duca di Genova* was torpedoed by the German submarine U64 on 6 February 1918 as she was bound for Genoa at the end of a voyage to New York. The attack occurred near Cape Canet, north of Valencia, about a mile off shore in the position 39.36N, 00.11W. The *Duca di Genova* was beached but became a total loss.

Casualties: not known

DUCHESS OF ATHOLL (1928) Canadian Pacific Line, UK

20,119grt; 601ft (183.2m) loa x 75ft (22.9m) beam
1,570 passengers in three classes
William Beardmore, Dalmuir (Yard No 648)
Steam turbines, twin screw
The passenger liner *Duchess of Atholl* was converted into a troopship in December 1939. While serving in this capacity, sailing in convoy from Cape Town to the United Kingdom via Freetown on 10 October 1942, she was torpedoed and sunk 200 miles east of Ascension Island, in the position 07.03S, 11.12W, by the German submarine U178. The *Duchess of Atholl*'s complement comprised 534 passengers and 296 crew, the majority of whom survived the attack and were rescued by other ships in the convoy.

Casualties: 4

Canadian Pacific introduced the 'Duchess' ships to the Liverpool to Montreal service between 1928 and 1929. The *Duchess of Atholl* was the lead ship of the class. *Ian Allan Library*

DUCHESS OF YORK (1929) Canadian Pacific Line, UK

20,021grt; 601ft (183.2m) loa x 75ft (22.9m) beam
1,570 passengers in three classes
John Brown, Clydebank (Yard No 524)
Steam turbines, twin screw
The passenger liner *Duchess of York* was sunk while serving as a troopship on 11 July 1943. Bound from Glasgow to Freetown with 607 troops and her crew of 281, she was attacked by German long-range bombers west of Oporto, Portugal, as she was passing the Portuguese coast. The bomb hits set her on fire and, when this could not be controlled, she was abandoned. The destroyers HMS *Douglas* and HMCS *Iroquois*, together with the frigate HMS *Moyola*, went to her assistance and were able to rescue the majority of her occupants. The blazing *Duchess of York* was torpedoed by one of the convoy escorts the following day and sank in the position 41.18N, 15.24W.

Casualties: 34 (23 troops and 11 crew)

The *Duchess of York* was the last vessel to be completed of her class of four ships built for the Canada run from Liverpool. *B. & A. Feilden*

DUILIO (1923) Lloyd Triestino, Italy

24,281grt; 635ft (193.5m) loa x 76ft (23.2m) beam
757 passengers in three classes
Ansaldo, Sestri Ponente, Genoa (Yard No 175)
Steam turbines, quadruple screw

The liners *Duilio* and *Giulio Cesare* were the first large modern passenger vessels to fly the Italian flag. They first entered the New York service from Genoa and Naples for their original owners, Navigazione Generale Italiana. From 1928 to 1932 they sailed on the South American service, then, following absorption into the Italia Line Fleet, they switched to the African service from Genoa to Cape Town. A further move in their chequered careers took them to Lloyd Triestino ownership in 1937. This saw the only break in their partnership for, while the *Duilio* continued in the African passenger service, the *Giulio Cesare* was switched to the Italy to Far East route. This is the *Duilio* on 6 March 1932. *Ian Allan Library*

Bombed and capsized at Vallone di Zaule in late 1944 is the former Italia liner *Duilio*. The area became something of a passenger ship graveyard, for lying near the *Duilio* were the wrecks of her near sister *Giulio Cesare* and the *Sabaudia* (ex-*Stockholm*). *Aldo Fraccaroli*

In 1940 the passenger liner *Duilio* was laid up at Genoa only to be reactivated in March 1942 when, painted in the colours of the International Red Cross, she was chartered for a number of repatriation voyages between East Africa and Italy with her near sister ship *Giulio Cesare*. From June 1943 the *Duilio* returned to lay-up at Trieste. By July 1944 she was at an anchorage near San Sabbia, at Vallone di Zaule, Muggia, along with the *Giulio Cesare* and *Sabaudia* (both qv). When Allied aircraft attacked the anchorage on 10 July 1944, the *Duilio*, still painted in her distinctive 'mercy ship' markings, was bombed and sunk. She sustained further damage during a second raid on 11 September 1944, which left her listing to starboard and partially submerged. The *Duilio* was refloated in 1948 and taken to the San Rocco shipyard where demolition commenced on 11 February of that year.
Casualties: not known

DUNBAR CASTLE (1930) Union-Castle Line, UK

10,002grt; 484ft (147.5m) loa x 61ft (18.6m) beam
460 passengers in two classes
Harland & Wolff, Govan (Yard No 851)
Motor-ship, twin screw
While she was sailing in a convoy, outward bound from London to Beira, the *Dunbar Castle* was torn apart by an explosion when she struck a mine soon after leaving the Thames Estuary on 9 January 1940. She was two miles northeast of the North Goodwins, in the position 51.23N, 01.34E, heading for the Strait of Dover. The critically damaged ship settled rapidly and within half an hour foundered in shallow water. Coastal patrol vessels picked up the 189 survivors. The wreck, which for years could be seen above the water in the position 51.22N, 01.36E, was broken up after the war.
Casualties: 9

Between the World Wars Union-Castle was in the forefront of promoting diesel propulsion with its distinctive twin-funnelled motor-ships. Two of the smaller vessels built for the round-Africa service from London were the *Dunbar Castle*, shown here, and *Llangibby Castle*. *David Reed*

DUNVEGAN CASTLE (1936) Union-Castle Line, UK

15,050grt; 560ft (170.7m) loa x 71ft (21.6m) beam
508 passengers in two classes
Harland & Wolff, Belfast (Yard No 960)
Motor-ship, twin screw
The *Dunvegan Castle*, which had been commandeered by the Admiralty in December 1939 for service as an armed merchant cruiser, was torpedoed by the German submarine U46 west of Ireland on 27 August 1940. She had a complement of 277 officers and men. She sank the day after the attack in the position 54.50N, 11.00W.
Casualties: 27 (4 officers and 23 ratings)

The sister ships *Dunvegan Castle*, seen here, and *Dunnottar Castle* were built for the round-Africa service from London. *Ian Allan Library*

DWINSK (1897) ex-*C. F. Tietgen* (1913) ex-*Rotterdam* (1906) Russian East Asiatic Steamship Co, Russia (under the wartime management of Cunard Line for the Shipping Controller, UK)

8,173grt; 486ft (148.1m) loa x 53ft (16.2m) beam
281 passengers in two classes plus 610 on deck
Harland & Wolff, Belfast (Yard No 312)
Triple-expansion steam reciprocating, twin screw
The Russian-flag passenger steamship *Dwinsk* was requisitioned by the British Government in 1917 for service as a troopship. As such, she was torpedoed and sunk without warning by the German submarine U151 on 18 June 1918 while bound from Brest to New York and Newport News, Virginia, carrying only her crew. The attack took place some 400 miles north-east of Bermuda, in the position 39.10N, 63.01W.
Casualties: 24

The *Dwinsk* was acquired from the Scandinavian American Line (forerunner of DFDS), continuing on the New York run but with her base port switched from Copenhagen to Libau. *Edward Wilson*

EDAM (1881) Holland Amerika Line, The Netherlands

2,950grt; 320ft (87.5m) lbp x 39ft (11.9m) beam
694 passengers in two classes
Archibald McMillan, Dumbarton (Yard No 232)
Compound-expansion steam reciprocating, single screw
The transatlantic passenger ship *Edam*, which had entered the Rotterdam to New York service on 29 October 1882, was sunk less than 11 months later, on 21 September 1882, after she was in collision with the Wilson Line steamship *Lepanto*. The accident occurred in dense fog, off Cape Cod, as she was heading for Sandy Hook, in the approaches to New York harbour. The *Edam* foundered in the approximate position 44.00N, 66.00W.
Casualties: 2

EDAM (1883) Holland Amerika Line, The Netherlands

3,130grt; 328ft (100.0m) lbp x 41ft (12.5m) beam
474 passengers in two classes
Nederlandsche SM, Rotterdam (Yard No 123)
Compound-expansion steam reciprocating, single screw
The replacement *Edam* fared little better than her predecessor. After 12 years of service, she too was lost as a result of a collision, in her case in the English Channel, fifty miles south-east of Start Point, where she struck the Strick Line's *Turkistan* on 19 September 1895. She sank south of Portland Bill.
Casualties: 0

EGEMEN (1939) Denizbank Denizyollari Isletmesi Müdürlügü, Turkey

serving under the wartime name SWAKOPMUND
6,133grt; 400ft (125.0m) loa x 53ft (16.1m) beam
629 passengers in four classes
Blohm & Voss, Steinwerder, Hamburg (Yard No 521)
Triple-expansion steam reciprocating, twin screw

Here seen in a poor wartime view as the *Swakopmund* is the Turkish passenger ship that never was, the *Egemen*. She was one of a class of three, none of which saw service for the company that ordered them. *Arnold Kludas*

The passenger steamer *Egemen*, one of three new German-built ships intended for operation in the Mediterranean, was lost while under German Government control, having been seized complete but undelivered on the outbreak of the Second World War. Taken over by the Kriegsmarine under the name *Swakopmund*, she was used as a U-boat depot ship at Pillau (Baltiysk) and as a target ship based at Kiel. While engaged in the evacuation of Germany's eastern territories, Operation 'Hannibal', during the closing months of the war in Europe, the *Swakopmund* was bombed and sunk south of Staberhuk, north-east of Fehmarn, on 3 May 1945. She had been carrying civilian refugees but, having discharged, was returning to the embarkation port empty. The wreck was broken up in 1950.
Casualties: 0

EGYPT (1871) National Line, UK

4,670grt; 440ft (134.1m) lbp x 44ft (13.4m) beam
More than 550 passengers in two classes
Liverpool Shipbuilding, Liverpool (Yard No not known)
Compound-expansion steam reciprocating, single screw
This transatlantic steamship *Egypt*, which enjoyed a reputation for being a fast ship in her time, was destroyed by fire and abandoned on 19 July 1890 while she was on an eastbound crossing from New York to Liverpool.
Casualties: 0

EGYPT (1897) P&O Line, UK

7,941grt; 500ft (152.3m) lbp x 54ft (16.6m) beam
526 passengers in two classes plus 2,500 troops
Caird, Greenock (Yard No 285)
Triple-expansion steam reciprocating, single screw
Disaster met the passenger and troopship *Egypt* off the French Coast on 20 May 1922, the day after she had departed from Tilbury bound for Bombay. On board were 44 passengers, a rather low figure given her normal complement of more than 500, but the majority were expected to join her at Marseilles, the practice in those days being to travel overland to avoid the unpleasant conditions of the Bay of Biscay. In addition, her crew numbered 294, the majority of whom were Lascars or Goanese, in keeping with the P&O tradition.

Off Ushant, about twenty miles from the Armen lighthouse, in the position 48.10N, 05.30W, the *Egypt* ran into thick fog and her engines were stopped while she hove to until it was safe for her to proceed. Another ship was heard approaching and the *Egypt*'s fog horn was sounded, but to no avail. The advancing vessel turned out to be the French steamer *Seine*, bound from La Pallice to Le Havre. She was proceeding at excessive speed given the conditions and, barely seconds after she was spotted, she struck the *Egypt* amidships on the port side, her ice-strengthened bow penetrating deep into the boiler rooms, instantly flooding them, and setting off panic among the Asiatic contingent of the engine room crew.

Help was summoned, her calls responded to by the Royal Mail passenger liner *Andes* and the cargo steamer *Cahirecon*. The situation aboard the *Egypt* was grave, the heavy list and ill-disciplined behaviour of some elements of the crew severely hampering efforts to lower the boats. When the stricken ship foundered, inside twenty minutes, all remaining boats, rafts and buoyant deck fittings were cut free in a final bid to provide aid for those struggling in the water. The survivors were eventually picked up by the *Seine* and taken to Brest, the help of the other ships not being required. At the time of the collision, the *Egypt* was carrying a valuable cargo of gold and silver bullion. Much of this treasure was retrieved between 1929 and 1933 in a daring and celebrated salvage operation.

Casualties: 86 (15 passengers and 71 officers and crew)

The loss of P&O's *Egypt* in May 1922 was followed eight years later by an epic salvage operation to recover the gold bullion she was carrying. *Ian Allan Library*

EIDER (1884) Norddeutscher Lloyd, Germany

4,719grt; 430ft (131.0m) lbp x 47ft (14.3m) beam
1,204 passengers in three classes
John Elder, Govan (Yard No 283)
Compound-expansion steam reciprocating, single screw
The passenger steamship *Eider* became stranded on the Atherfield Ledge, Isle of Wight, on 31 January 1892, while she was bound from Bremen and Southampton to New York. Thanks to the efforts of local lifeboatmen, all her occupants were safely evacuated. Though refloated, the *Eider* was a total loss and was broken up in the UK commencing in January 1893.

Casualties: 0

The transatlantic steamer *Eider* came to grief on Atherfield Ledge, Isle of Wight. Local lifeboatmen were rewarded by the German Kaiser Wilhelm II for their endeavours in saving the lives of passengers and crew. Many were also decorated for their bravery. *Hapag-Lloyd*

ELANDSFONTEIN (launched 30 March 1940) Holland Afrika Line, The Netherlands

10,500 grt; 528ft (160.9m) loa x 63ft (19.1m) beam
160 passengers in two classes
Schichau, Danzig (Yard No not known)
Motor-ship, twin screw
Conceived originally as the *Rietfontein*, her name changed by the date of her launch, the *Elandsfontein* was seized by the German Navy though she remained incomplete, laid up in the Baltic port. On 14 March 1945, she was severely damaged in the crossfire of Soviet and German artillery as fighting in the area intensified. The *Elandsfontein* sank in the mouth of the Vistula river where she remained until refloated on 20 March 1947. Given temporary repairs to ensure her seaworthiness,

she was towed to Flushing (Vlissingen) to be completed by the De Schelde shipyard. She entered service on the Europe to East Africa service via the Cape under the name *Jagersfontein* on 11 March 1950.

Casualties: not known

The *Jagersfontein*, ordered as the *Rietfontein* and sunk as the *Elandsfontein*, finally emerged, fully restored from her extensive wartime damage, to enter the Europe to Africa service in March 1950. *Real Photos*

ELBE (1881) Norddeutscher Lloyd, Germany

4,897grt; 440ft (134.0m) loa x 45ft (13.7m) beam
1,117 passengers in three classes
John Elder, Govan (Yard No 248)
Compound-expansion steam reciprocating, single screw
On 30 January 1895, as the transatlantic passenger steamer *Elbe* was crossing the North Sea, bound from Bremerhaven to Southampton and New York, she was run into by the small steamship *Crathie*, about 5 miles south-west of the Haaks light vessel. The *Elbe* was carrying a total of 354 persons, comprising 199 passengers, of whom 149 were from Steerage, and 155 crew. The collision occurred early in the morning when it was still quite dark, although the weather was clear. The *Crathie* was heading for Aberdeen, having left Rotterdam the previous evening. Her route thus took her across that of the *Elbe*. She was sighted from the *Elbe* some time before the two vessels struck but, as the *Elbe* had the right of way, she proceeded regardless. Unfortunately, the *Crathie* was not being navigated with a similar degree of alertness and those aboard her were apparently totally unaware of the presence of the *Elbe*. When an attempt was finally made to take avoiding action it was too late and the *Crathie* struck the *Elbe* bow first on her port side, at a point about 100 feet from the stern.

The *Crathie* was badly damaged but was in no immediate danger of sinking. Seemingly ignorant of the severity of the impact to the other ship and making no attempt to see if assistance was required, even though maroons were fired, the *Crathie* limped back to Rotterdam, calling first at Maasluis. The *Elbe* had indeed been struck a fatal blow and soon developed a severe list to port. The terror of the startled and anxious passengers was increased by the failure of her electric lighting system, throwing the entire ship into darkness. The night was bitterly cold, which complicated attempts to evacuate the ship, for many of the falls from the boats were frozen solid and had to be chopped through to release them. In the circumstances it was only possible to launch two boats, one of which capsized, for the *Elbe* foundered barely twenty minutes after the collision, sinking stern-first.

The twenty survivors who were picked up by the fishing smack *Wild Flower* from Lowestoft were near to death by exposure when they were rescued. The regulations for the prevention of collisions require that the stand-on ship, in this case the *Elbe*, should maintain her course and speed. The fact that she did and took no evasive action herself in spite of evident danger and its dire consequences was most unfortunate, although mariners know that there are also considerable risks in taking pre-emptive action.
Casualties: 334

Germany's worst passenger shipping disaster of the 19th century was the loss of the *Elbe* in January 1895. *Hapag-Lloyd*

This graphic impression of the *Elbe* in her death throes was painted by Fred T. Jane. *Author's collection*

ELEONORE WOERMANN (1902) Woermann Line, Germany

4,624grt; 364ft (111.2m) lbp x 47ft (14.4m) beam
214 passengers in three classes
Blohm & Voss, Steinwerder, Hamburg (Yard No 156)
Triple-expansion steam reciprocating, single screw
To avoid capture by the British, the passenger-cargo ship *Eleonore Woermann* was scuttled on 6 January 1915 in the position 42.50S, 52.50W, some 250 miles to the east of the Golfo San Matias, Argentina, after attempting to make a break

for home, it is thought, from Buenos Aires. Her progress was halted when she was spotted by a British warship.
Casualties: not known

EL HIND (1938) Scindia Steam Navigation Co, India

5,319grt; 415ft (126.4m) loa x 52ft (15.9m) beam
Passenger numbers not known (pilgrims carried)
Lithgows, Port Glasgow (Yard No 912)
Triple-expansion steam reciprocating, single screw
The pilgrim ship *El Hind* was requisitioned by the Royal Indian Navy and engaged in war work as an Infantry Landing Ship (Large). She was unfortunate to be berthed in Bombay docks on 14 April 1944. This was the day when the ammunition ship *Fort Stikine* caught fire and blew up with incredible force, wrecking numerous adjacently berthed ships, warehouses, quay installations and large quantities of cargo and produce that were held in store. In total 336 persons were reported to have been killed and more than 1,000 injured. The *El Hind*, which caught fire, burned out and sank, was one of eighteen merchantmen and three warships caught in the blast, of which at least nine others were either sunk or damaged beyond repair.
Casualties: not known (for the *El Hind*)

ELINGAMITE (1887) Huddart Parker & Co, Australia

2,585grt; 311ft (94.6m) lbp x 46ft (12.4m) beam
301 passengers (118 on sofa-beds in the Saloon, 102 in the poop and 81 in the fo'c'sle)
C. S. Swan & Hunter, Wallsend-on-Tyne (Yard No 106)
Triple-expansion steam reciprocating, single screw
Four days after leaving Sydney bound for Auckland, New Zealand, on 5 November 1902, the steamship *Elingamite* ran onto rocks off the Three Kings islands, to the north of Auckland, in thick fog. Unable to extract herself because her engines could not be reversed, she sank within twenty minutes. In this short space of time it was possible to launch a number of lifeboats and rafts permitting the majority of her complement to abandon the ship. The *Elingamite* had been carrying 136 passengers and a crew numbering 59. Some survivors made it to the mainland at Hohura, another party managed to get ashore on the Great King Island, while others were picked up by the naval ship HMS *Penguin*. It was subsequently established that the position of the Three Kings islands had been incorrectly marked on navigational charts, leading to the reinstatement of the Master's ticket, which had been suspended.
Casualties: 45

ELISABETHVILLE (1949) Cie Maritime Belge, Belgium

10,901grt; 504ft (153.7m) loa x 64ft (19.6m) beam
179 passengers in single class
Cockerill, Hoboken (Yard No 719)
Motor-ship, twin screw
Soon after arrival at berth 214, Antwerp docks, on 20 March 1968, the passenger-cargo liner *Elisabethville* was badly damaged by fire while unloading a cargo of copper and palm oil from Matadi, Zaire. The fire started in No 3 hold, from which twenty dock workers were rescued by the swift action of a crane operator. The structural damage to the ship was extensive with the midships section and navigation bridge

completely gutted, and she was adjudged to be beyond economic repair. The wreck of the *Elisabethville* was dismantled, partly at Antwerp and finally, from December 1968, at Ghent.

Casualties: 0

EL MADINA (1937) Scindia Steam Navigation Co, India

3,962grt; 374ft (114.1m) loa x 50ft (15.3m) beam
12 First-class passengers and 1,000 pilgrims
Barclay Curle, Whiteinch, Glasgow (Yard No 666)
Triple-expansion steam reciprocating plus LP turbines, twin screw

The Indian-flag pilgrim carrier *El Madina*, serving as a wartime troopship, was sunk in the Bay of Bengal on 16 March 1944 during a troop-carrying voyage from Calcutta to Chittagong, torpedoed by the Japanese submarine Ro111. She was heavily loaded, carrying 1,161 troops, 125 crew and 7 gunners, and casualties were high. The *El Madina*'s last position was 20.54N, 89.36E, 100 miles south of the Ganges delta.

Casualties: 417 (364 soldiers, 6 gunners and 47 crew).

EMPIRE WAVENEY (1929) ex-*Milwaukee* (1945) Ministry of Transport, UK (managed by Cunard White Star Line)

16,754grt; 575ft (175.1m) loa x 73ft (22.1m) beam
957 passengers in three classes (as built)
Blohm & Voss, Steinwerder, Hamburg (Yard No 483)
Motor-ship, twin screw

Following service as a naval accommodation ship and a refugee ship, the former German passenger liner *Milwaukee* was taken over as a war prize in May 1945. This was after the RAF had bombed her to prevent her use by top-ranking Nazis as a means of escape. She was adapted into a troopship under US Navy control only to be transferred to Great Britain while at New York in October 1945, when she was renamed *Empire Waveney*. Sent to Liverpool for a refit, she was completely gutted by fire and sank on 1 March 1946 while it was in progress. During May of that year her wreck was raised and on 27 January 1947 it was towed to Dalmuir on the Clyde for scrapping. The work was completed at Troon from late September 1947.

Casualties: 0

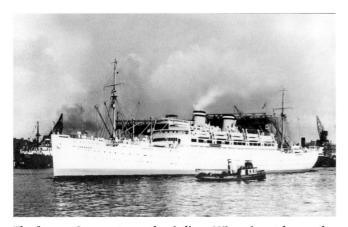

The former German transatlantic liner *Milwaukee*, taken as the war-prize *Empire Waveney*, was lost by fire while in the process of being converted into a permanent troopship.
Real Photos

EMPIRE WINDRUSH (1931) ex-*Monte Rosa* (1946) Ministry of Transport, UK (managed by New Zealand Shipping Co)

14,651grt; 524ft (152.5m) loa x 66ft (20.1m) beam
2,408 passengers in two classes (as built)
Blohm & Voss, Steinwerder, Hamburg (Yard No 492)
Motor-ship, twin screw

The troopship *Empire Windrush*, the former Hamburg Sud-Amerika liner *Monte Rosa*, also brought some of the earliest West Indian immigrants to the UK. *Southern Newspapers*

Fire ends the career of the *Empire Windrush*, seen from the air ablaze in the Mediterranean on 28 March 1954.
Imperial War Museum (A32891)

The former German liner *Monte Rosa* was taken as a war prize at Kiel on 18 November 1945. After conversion into the dedicated troopship *Empire Windrush*, she undertook trooping voyages but also conveyed some of the first West Indian migrants to the UK. Fire broke out aboard her on 28 March 1954, following an engine room explosion, when she was thirty miles north-west of Cape Caxine, midway between Oran, Algeria, and Cartegena, Spain, in the position 37.05N, 02.25E. The incident occurred during a voyage from Yokohama, Japan, to England with 1,265 passengers aboard – troops, service wives and children – besides her 234-strong crew. As a consequence of the explosion, power was lost to a number of vital services including the electric alarm system, the telephone system, the watertight doors and the public address system, the combined effect of which was to permit the situation to deteriorate unchecked and to make it difficult to alert and muster the passengers in preparation for a possible evacuation. Later, the water supply to the hoses was also lost, at which time the *Empire Windrush* also ceased to respond to the helm. In this hopeless situation, the order was given to abandon ship. Of the ship's total complement, 1,494 persons were picked up by other ships that had come to the aid of the stricken troopship, among them the cargo vessels *Mentor*, *Socotra* and *Hemesfjell*, and the oil tanker *Taigete*, and they were landed in Algiers. Meanwhile the *Empire Windrush* was taken in tow for Gibraltar by the destroyer HMS *Saintes*, but she foundered two days after the disaster in the position 37.00N, 02.11E.

Casualties: 5 (all engine room crew)

EMPRESS EKATERINA II (1913) Russian Steam Navigation & Trading Co, Russia

5,545grt; 381ft (116.1m) lbp x 31ft (9.3m) beam
Passenger numbers not known
William Denny, Dumbarton (Yard No 975)
Triple-expansion steam reciprocating, twin screw

The passenger-cargo ship *Empress Ekaterina II* was requisitioned by the French Government from the beginning of 1918, following the Russian Revolution and Russia's disengagement from the conflict with Germany. She had been under French control for less than a month when, on 30 January 1918, while bound from Bizerta, Algeria, to Greece, she was torpedoed and sunk north of Bougie, Algeria, by the German submarine UB52. At the time she was not carrying passengers.

Casualties: 0

EMPRESS OF ASIA (1913) Canadian Pacific Line, UK

16,909grt; 592ft (180.4m) loa x 68ft (20.7m) beam
1,238 passengers in four classes
Fairfield, Govan (Yard No 485)
Steam turbines, quadruple screw

The liner *Empress of Asia*, which had been converted into a troopship in 1941, was directed to sail from Bombay to Singapore in early 1942 with 2,235 troops, reinforcements for the British garrison there, together with a total crew complement of 563 men. As she was arriving off Singapore on 5 February 1942, about 6 miles from her destination, she came under attack from a large number of Japanese dive-bombers and sustained five direct hits. Four of the bombs exploded in the vicinity of her bridge, while the fifth penetrated within the vessel, setting her on fire. The Australian sloop HMAS *Yarra* came alongside and, despite the continuing aerial bombardment and the raging fires, managed to assist in an almost full evacuation. The minesweeper HMAS *Burnie* also stood by to help. A large number of the survivors were, however, taken prisoner by the Japanese when Singapore was captured ten days later. The *Empress of Asia* was abandoned ablaze and she drifted to the west of Keppel Harbour, where she went ashore just under a mile from the Sultan Shoal lighthouse. Over the next two days she was completely burned out, her wreck abandoned until after the war. It was scrapped from 1952, the work continuing until as late as March 1960.

Casualties: 16 (15 troops and 1 crew member who died later in hospital)

The sister ships *Empress of Asia*, seen here, and *Empress of Russia* were the first large passenger liners to have cruiser sterns. They sailed on the Vancouver to Yokohama service. *H. B. Christiansen Collection / Online Transport Archive*

These rare photographs, taken from an Australian minesweeper, show the *Empress of Asia* burning in Singapore Roads at the time of the Japanese attack on Singapore in early February 1942. *Jim Payne - Through Their Eyes*

EMPRESS OF BRITAIN (1931) Canadian Pacific Line, UK

42,348grt; 758ft (231.0m) loa x 97ft (29.6m) beam
1,182 passengers in three classes
John Brown & Co, Clydebank (Yard No 530)
Steam turbines, quadruple screw

The transatlantic liner *Empress of Britain* was requisitioned on 25 November 1939 for service as a troopship. Just under a year later, on 26 October 1940, she was crossing the Atlantic, returning to the United Kingdom from Canada, at the end of a long voyage that had begun from Cape Town. When she was about 100 miles north-west of the Irish coast, in the position

54.53N, 10.49W, she was attacked by a long-range German bomber, which hit her with high-explosive and incendiary bombs. The attack left her in a damaged and burning condition and it was necessary for the majority of her complement of 643 persons to abandon ship. For this purpose she was manoeuvred into the wind as the personnel for evacuation were mustered on the foredeck. Her boats were then lowered and the survivors picked up by naval escorts. Meanwhile, a small party of crew members remained aboard to fight the fires, while the Polish destroyer *Burza* took her in tow in the hope of getting her to port where more effective fire-fighting would be possible. This effort was proceeding reasonably well until, two days later, she was hit by two torpedoes fired by the German submarine U32, blew up and sank in the position 55.16N, 09.50W. The *Empress of Britain* was the largest active British merchant ship to be lost in the Second World War.

Casualties: 49 (Some reports give the number killed as 45)

Canadian Pacific's second *Empress of Britain* was the largest liner to be placed permanently on regular service between Southampton and Quebec. A feature of her annual programme was her luxury cruises during the winter months. She was the largest active British passenger ship to be lost in the Second World War. *National Archives of Scotland*

The *Empress of Britain* lists to starboard and is on fire following the initial attack on her by German long-range bombers. Two days later she was gone. *Imperial War Museum (HU17754)*

EMPRESS OF CANADA (1922) Canadian Pacific Line, UK

21,517grt; 653ft (199.0m) loa x 77ft (23.5m) beam
1,758 passengers in four classes
Fairfield, Govan (Yard No 528)
Steam turbines, twin screw

The passenger liner *Empress of Canada* was converted into a troopship following the outbreak of the Second World War. On 14 March 1943 she was bound from Durban to Takoradi, Ghana, carrying about 1,400 Greek and Polish refugees in addition to a contingent of Italian prisoners of war, military guards and her crew of 318 men. When she was about 400

miles south of Cape Palmas, in the position 01.13S, 09.57W, she was torpedoed by the Italian submarine *Leonardo da Vinci*. About an hour after the initial attack, the submarine fired a second torpedo and, after it exploded, the *Empress of Canada* remained afloat for barely twenty minutes. Even so, a substantial number of her complement were safely evacuated during this extremely brief interlude.

Casualties: 392 (340 of the various passengers, including many of the Italian prisoners, 44 crew and 8 gunners)

The *Empress of Canada* was the first major unit to join the Canadian Pacific fleet after the First World War. She spent most of her life in the trans-Pacific service between Vancouver and Yokohama. Her accommodation included a large number of spaces for Asiatic steerage passengers. *Ian Allan Library*

EMPRESS OF CANADA (1928) ex-*Duchess of Richmond* (1947) Canadian Pacific Line, UK

20,325grt; 600ft (183.1m) loa x 75ft (22.9m) beam
700 passengers in two classes
John Brown, Clydebank (Yard No 523)
Steam turbines, twin screw

The *Empress of Canada* (formerly the *Duchess of Richmond*) was placed post-war on Canadian Pacific's premier service from Liverpool to Montreal and Quebec with sister ship *Empress of France* (ex-*Duchess of Bedford*). They were the only two of their class to survive the Second World War. *Ian Allan Library*

The wreck of the burned-out *Empress of Canada* in Gladstone Dock, Liverpool. It took a year for the Mersey Docks & Harbour Board salvage team to right and refloat her. *Maritime Photo Library*

The transatlantic liner Empress of Canada was lying at a berth in the No 1 North Branch of the Gladstone Dock, Bootle, nearing the end of a refit and overhaul, when fire broke out aboard her on 25 January 1953. The outbreak seems to have originated in the ship's dispensary on B deck. The conditions on board for fire-fighting were both difficult and hazardous due to exploding acetylene and oxygen cylinders left behind by welders still working aboard the ship. All efforts to control the fire failed, and because of the immense volume of water pumped aboard the *Empress of Canada*, destabilising her, she capsized early on the following day. She had been in a 'tender' condition at the time when the fire started, being unladen, and consideration was given to scuttling the ship on an even keel, but because the depth below the ship was only 50 feet, there was doubt as to whether this would have been sufficient to keep her upright. During March 1954 the damaged ship was righted by the Mersey Docks & Harbour Board and was refloated by the end of that June. Judged to be a constructive total loss, though, she was sold for breaking up in Italy and arrived in tow at ship-breakers at La Spezia on 10 October 1953.

Casualties: 0

EMPRESS OF CHINA (1890) Canadian Pacific Line, UK

5,947grt; 455ft (138.8m) lbp x 51ft (15.6m) beam
600 passengers in three classes
Naval Construction & Armaments, Barrow-in-Furness (Yard No 181)
Triple-expansion steam reciprocating, twin screw
The yacht-like passenger steamship *Empress of China* was wrecked on Mera Reef, Cape Nojima, Tokyo Bay, some 35 miles south-east of Yokohama, on 27 July 1911, while she was sailing near the Japanese coast in fog. All her passengers and crew were rescued and the mails were also taken off without loss. She was refloated in October 1912 and taken to Yokohama for breaking up.

Casualties: 0

With their clipper bows, the three sisters *Empress of China*, *Japan* and *India* were considered to be among the most graceful ships placed on the trans-Pacific passenger service from Vancouver to Yokohama. This is the ill-fated *Empress of China*. *World Ship Society*

EMPRESS OF IRELAND (1906) Canadian Pacific Line, UK

14,191grt; 570ft (173.7m) loa x 68ft (20.0m) beam
1,580 passengers in four classes
Fairfield, Govan (Yard No 443)
Quadruple-expansion steam reciprocating, twin screw
Eight years after entering service, the passenger liner

Empress of Ireland was rammed and sunk in thick but patchy fog in the St Lawrence River when outward bound for Liverpool on 29 May 1914. She was carrying 1,477 persons, of whom 1,050 were passengers. They included a group of Salvation Army officers who were returning from a convention in Canada. In one of the intermittent clear areas, about twenty miles downstream from Rimouski, near Father Point, the lights of another ship heading upriver were seen from the *Empress of Ireland*, but immediately afterwards the fog enveloped both ships. Aboard the *Empress of Ireland* the engines were ordered full astern to bring her to a stop and this action was signalled to the approaching vessel, the collier *Storstad* of A/S Maritim, Norway, by three long blasts on the ship's siren. Suddenly the *Storstad* emerged from the gloom heading directly at the *Empress of Ireland* and crashed into her starboard side at a point between the funnels, leaving a gaping hole that extended far below the waterline.

The liner's engine rooms and boiler rooms were instantly flooded and, as the impact had breached the watertight bulkheads in that part of the ship, there was nothing to restrain the sudden inflow of water. Realising that the *Empress of Ireland* was in a critical condition, a request was made for the *Storstad* to be kept with her engines going forward in order to plug the hole in the liner's side and provide vital breathing space in which the passengers could be evacuated. Apparently this was impossible because of the extent of the damage to the *Storstad*'s bows and, unable to inhibit the flooding, the doomed *Empress of Ireland* foundered fifteen minutes after the collision. It was only possible to launch four lifeboats in this time and only one distress call could be made from the *Empress of Ireland* before her wireless equipment failed. This brought the steamships *Eureka* and *Lady Evelyn* to the scene from Father Point and between them they picked up the survivors, aided by lifeboats from the *Storstad*.

Casualties: 1,014 (840 passengers and 174 crew)

The second-worst passenger ship disaster at the time of her loss, the sinking of the *Empress of Ireland* was overshadowed by the outbreak of the Great War just three months later. This is probably an altered photograph of her sister, the *Empress of Britain*. *Library of Archives of Canada*

EMPRESS OF RUSSIA (1913) Canadian Pacific Line, UK

16,810grt; 592ft (180.4m) loa x 68ft (20.8m) beam
1,238 passengers in four classes
Fairfield, Govan (Yard No 484)
Steam turbines, quadruple screw

After auxiliary duties as a troopship throughout the Second World War came to an end, the trans-Pacific liner *Empress of Russia* was sent to the Vickers-Armstrongs yard at Barrow-in-Furness for refit and repairs prior to resuming commercial service. During the course of the refurbishment, on 8 September 1945, she caught fire and was completely burned out. The hulk was broken up at Barrow during 1946.
Casualties: 0

Sister ship of the *Empress of Asia*, the *Empress of Russia* is seen in an evocative view in a Far Eastern port in the 1930s. *Ian Allan Library*

Requisitioned as a Second World War troopship, the *Empress of Russia* survived the conflict only to be gutted by fire during post-war renovation at Barrow-in-Furness. *Real Photos*

ENGLAND (1932) Det Forenede Dampskibs-Selskab (DFDS), Denmark

serving under the wartime name GRENADIER
2,767grt; 324ft (98.8m) loa x 44ft (13.5m) beam
190 passengers in two classes
Helsingor Vaerft, Elsinore (Yard No 204)
Motor-ship, twin screw
After spending almost four years laid up at Copenhagen , the Danish-flag North Sea ferry *England* was seized by German forces in January 1944 and towed to Stettin (Szczecin) where she was employed as the accommodation ship for the 4th U-boat flotilla under the name *Grenadier*, managed by J. T. Essberger. This activity was short-lived, for in May 1944 the Kriegsmarine had her taken to the Howaldtswerke shipyard at Kiel for conversion for active naval duties. While there she sustained heavy bomb damage during an air raid on 27 August 1944. Towed out of the harbour while still ablaze and beached, she was left for the fire to burn itself out. When the gutted hulk was inspected on 22 September it was decided that she was beyond economic recovery and the former

England was abandoned until after the war had ended. Refloated in June 1949, her wreck was towed to Flensburg in June 1950, where the engines were removed, then on to Odense where it was broken up from that July.
Casualties: not known

The DFDS North Sea ferry *England* of 1932, a war loss under the German flag. *Bjørn Pedersen*

ERIDANIA (1916) ex-*Palestina* (1940) ex-*Amazzonia* (1935) ex-*Aquileia* (1933) ex-*Innsbruck* (1921) Adriatica SA di Navigazione, Italy

7,039grt; 411ft (125.3m) lbp x 53ft (16.2) beam
About 800 passengers
Cantieri San Rocco, San Rocco, Trieste (Yard No 28)
Triple-expansion steam reciprocating, twin screw
Following the surrender of Italy, the passenger steamship *Eridania*, which had been in service with the Italian Navy as a transport since July 1940, attempted to make for a friendly port on 11 September 1943 when a bid was made to sail her to Zara. However, she was intercepted and ordered to Venice. A month later, on 7 October 1943, when she was between Veruda and Pola, she was torpedoed and sunk off Cape Promontore by the Polish submarine *Sokol*.
Casualties: not known

ERIN (1864) National Line, UK

4,577 grt; 391ft (119.2m) lbp x 41ft (12.5m) beam
1,200 passengers in single class
Palmers, Jarrow (Yard No 143)
Compound-expansion steam reciprocating, single screw
The Steerage-class passenger ship *Erin*, sister-ship of the *Ontario* (qv), disappeared at sea in 1889 during a voyage from New York to London. She was last seen on 31 December 1889 and the cause of her loss is unknown.
Casualties: 72

ERINPURA (1911) British India Line, UK

5,143grt; 411ft (125.3m) lbp x 53ft (16.0m) beam
1,590 passengers in three classes, the majority on deck
William Denny, Dumbarton (Yard No 945)
Triple-expansion steam reciprocating, twin screw
The *Erinpura* was lost on 1 May 1943 while sailing in convoy

with a naval escort bound for Malta carrying 1,025 officers and troops from the Basuto Pioneer Corps, plus her crew. She was bombed by German warplanes when thirty miles north of Benghazi and sank rapidly in the position 32.40N, 19.53E. Like the *Suevic* (qv), the *Erinpura* had received a new bow section in 1920, after grounding in the Red Sea.
Casualties: About 664, including 57 crew and 7 gun-crew. The casualties figure is also reported as 657, with the loss of 54 crew and 3 gun-crew lives.

The British India passenger ship *Erinpura*. *World Ship Society*

ERNESTO ANASTASIO (1955)
Compania Trasmediterranea, Spain

7,295grt; 413ft (126.0m) loa x 55ft (16.8m) beam
233 passengers in two classes
Union Levante, Valencia (Yard No 55)
Motor-ship, twin screw
The motor passenger ship *Ernesto Anastasio* was lost on 24 April 1980 while on a voyage from Pasajes to Villagarcia. She was stranded on the Bancha del Oeste Shoal, near Pasajes. After she had been refloated and returned to port, where her cargo was discharged, an inspection revealed her to be a constructive total loss. She was broken up at Bilbao.
Casualties: 0

The Spanish passenger ship *Ernesto Anastasio* photographed at Barcelona in July 1975. *Frank Heine FERRIES*

ERNEST SIMONS (1894) Messageries Maritimes, France

5,543grt; 443ft (135.0m) lbp x 47ft (14.4m) beam
About 585 passengers in four classes
Messageries Maritimes, La Ciotat (Yard No 71)
Triple-expansion steam reciprocating, single screw
While bound from Marseilles to Madagascar on 3 April 1917, the passenger-cargo steamer *Ernest Simons* was torpedoed

in the Mediterranean by a German submarine, but while they agree on the date, there is some conflict between the German and French accounts of the sinking. The German records state that she was sunk 17 miles north-east of Cape Sera, Algeria, by the UC37, sinking in the position 37.08N, 08.28E. The French version, on the other hand, states that the submarine concerned was the UC27 and that the attack took place in the vicinity of Crete, considerably further to the east. It also notes that the survivors were picked up by the armed trawler *Auguste Leblond* and the Greek ship *Marionga Goulandris*.
Casualties: 0 (German account); 12 (French account)

ESBJERG (1929) Det Forenede Dampskibs-Selskab (DFDS), Denmark

serving under the wartime name KURASSIER
2,762grt; 324ft (98.8m) loa x 44ft (13.5m) beam
220 passengers in two classes
Helsingor Vaerft, Elsinore (Yard No 186)
Motor-ship, twin screw
The North Sea ferry *Esbjerg*, which had been commandeered by German forces in March 1944 and renamed *Kurassier*, was sunk on 25 July 1945, two days after leaving Lübeck bound for Copenhagen. Recovered following the end of the war in Europe, she was on passage for return to her owners, manned by a Danish crew, when she struck a mine off Stevns and sank in the position 55.14N, 12.36E. Despite the extent of the damage she was raised in August 1946 and towed to Copenhagen, having by then reverted to her original name. However, it was decided that she was not worth the cost of repairing her for return to her former service and her wreck was sold in July 1947 to the Spanish concern Compania Trasmediterranea SA. This company had her completely rebuilt as the *Ciudad de Ibiza* for the Valencia to Ibiza service and, as such, she survived until November 1978, when she was sold for breaking up at Villanueva y Geltrú.
Casualties: not known

ESPERANZA (1901) Ward Line, USA

4,702grt; 341ft (103.9m) lbp x 48ft (14.5m) beam
194 passengers in three classes
William Cramp, Philadelphia (Yard No 309)
Triple-expansion steam reciprocating, twin screw
The coastwise passenger-cargo ship *Esperanza* was lost on 24 November 1925 when she was stranded at Tampico, Mexico, on the Gulf coast.
Casualties: not known

ESPERIA (1921) Adriatica Line, Italy

11,398grt; 528ft (160.9m) loa x 62ft (18.9m) beam
479 passengers in four classes
Ersercicio Bacini, Riva Trigoso (Yard No 66)
Steam turbines, twin screw
The passenger ship *Esperia* was taken over by the Italian Government to serve as a troopship to carry reinforcements to the Italian armies fighting in North Africa. On 20 August 1941, while she was sailing in a convoy to Libya with a large contingent of troops, she was torpedoed and sunk by the British submarine HMS *Unique* 11 miles north-west of Tripoli lighthouse.
Casualties: 31

ESTONIA (1980) ex-*Wasa King* (1991) ex-*Silja Star* (1990) ex-*Viking Sally* (1990) Estline, Estonia

21,794grt; 510ft (155.4m) loa x 79ft (24.2m) beam
2,000 passengers of whom 1,190 in berths
J. L. Meyer, Papenburg (Yard No 590)
Motor-ship, twin screw

The loss of the ro-ro ferry *Estonia* in stormy Baltic seas while crossing from Tallinn to Stockholm in September 1994 was the worst passenger ship disaster for twenty years. She is seen here at Oxdjupet on 13 May 1994. *Frank Heine FERRIES*

The Baltic ro-ro ferry *Estonia* was lost on 29 September 1994 during an overnight crossing from Tallinn, Estonia, to Stockholm in tempestuous weather. Aboard her were 989 persons, comprising 802 passengers and a crew of 187. Prior to her departure, the evening before, inspectors had found problems with the seals that lined the bow visor, which incorporated her forward loading ramp. When, around midnight, engineers discovered that water was leaking into the vehicle deck through this structure, the ship's pumps were immediately activated. As an indication of how rapidly the situation worsened, though, they were completely overwhelmed within fifteen minutes. An hour later, distress calls were transmitted but soon after the huge seas caused the total failure of the bow visor and ramp, flooding the vehicle deck. Critically destabilised, the *Estonia* foundered 20 miles from Utoe Island, south-west Finland, in the position 59.23N, 21.42E. The *Estonia* carried Emergency Position-Indicating Radio Beacons (EPIRBs) to help pinpoint her position but they required manual activation, something which at the height of the emergency was overlooked and, as a consequence, it was an hour after she had sunk before the first rescue vessel arrived at the scene. It was unable to do more than pick up some of the survivors and those bodies of casualties floating in the water. The bodies of the majority of the victims, there being 757 persons listed as missing, remain trapped in the hull on the sea bed. Ranking as the world's worst maritime disaster since that date, the loss of the *Estonia* gave rise to the incorporation of the 'Stockholm Agreement' into the European Union's ferry stability regulations. It has also influenced the reasoning behind IMO's 'Citadel Concept'.

Casualties: 852, the majority being of Swedish and Estonian nationality, 501 and 285 respectively.

ETTRICK (1938) Ministry of Transport (managed by P&O Line), UK

11,279grt; 517ft (157.6m) loa x 63ft (19.2m) beam
194 passengers in two classes plus 1,150 troops
Barclay Curle, Whiteinch, Glasgow (Yard No 669)
Motor-ship, twin screw

The *Ettrick* had been purpose-built for the Ministry of Transport as a troop-carrying passenger ship for the peacetime transportation of troops overseas to maintain Britain's various military outposts. During the Second World War she and her three near sisters became full-time troopships. The *Ettrick* was deployed for support and transport duties during the Allied operations in French North Africa in November 1942. On 15 November, when she was 150 miles west of Gibraltar, she was torpedoed by the German submarine U155, sinking vertically, stern first, in the position 36.13N, 07.54W. She had been returning to the River Clyde, following the completion of the landings, where she was to disembark the 40 military personnel that she was carrying in addition to her crew of 209.

Casualties: 24 (17 naval ratings and 7 Indian crew members)

In the late 1930s a class of four troop-carrying passenger motor-ships was built to the order of the Ministry of Transport. They were the *Dilwara* and *Dunera* managed by the British India Line, the *Devonshire* of the Bibby Line and the *Ettrick*, managed by P&O, seen here in a wartime view. When they were not engaged in trooping activities they offered relatively inexpensive cruise voyages in basic accommodation. *Imperial War Museum (E56)*

EUBEE (1922) Chargeurs Réunis, France

9,582grt; 483ft (147.2m) lbp x 59ft (18.0m) beam
225 passengers in three classes
Chantiers de France, Dunkirk (Yard No not known)
Triple-expansion steam reciprocating, twin screw

On 14 August 1936 the passenger-cargo ship *Eubee* was in collision in fog with the British cargo vessel *Corinaldo* in the position 32.40S, 54.24W, about 95 miles north of the Rio Grande. The *Eubee* was bound from Bordeaux to Buenos Aires with 178 passengers and a crew of 145, while the *Corinaldo* was bound from La Plata ports to Liverpool. The sudden inrush of water caused by the collision put the *Eubee*'s engines out of action and drowned those crew members who were in the stoke-hold. All her passengers and 42 members of the crew were transferred to the *Corinaldo* and taken to

Montevideo. The remaining 98 crew members stayed aboard the *Eubee*, which was taken in tow in an attempt to get her to Rio de Janeiro; however, two days after the collision she foundered and the crew were picked up by the tug *Antonio Azambuja*, which landed them at Rio Grande.

Casualties: 5 (all crew)

EUROPA (1930) Norddeutscher Lloyd, Germany

49,746grt; 941ft (286.7m) loa x 102ft (31.1m) beam
2,024 passengers in four classes
Blohm & Voss, Steinwerder, Hamburg (Yard No 479)
Steam turbines, quadruple screw

The new transatlantic passenger liner *Europa* was nearing completion at the Blohm & Voss shipyard when a serious outbreak of fire aboard her on 26 March 1929 caused very severe damage. She sank on an even keel alongside the fitting-out quay, with much of the metal in her upper deck areas badly buckled and twisted, and many of her interior fittings destroyed. Initial inspections suggested that she was fit only for salvage and scrapping. She was, however, reprieved after subsequent surveys revealed that her hull and engines were largely intact and that sufficient of the lower deck areas had escaped the ravages of the fire to make restoration economically practicable. She was raised on 10 April 1929 and eventually entered service, fully repaired, after a delay of almost a year, making her maiden voyage on 19 March 1930. Later in her life, as the French liner *Liberté*, she experienced a second flooding after striking the wreck of the *Paris* and ripping open her hull during a storm at Le Havre on 8 December 1946. Raised on 15 April 1947, she underwent repairs and reconstruction that lasted until 17 August 1950 before she resumed operation in the post-war period.

Casualties: not known

These photographs show the extent of the damage caused by the fire aboard the incomplete *Europa*. But for the fact that her engines and associated machinery survived intact, she could well have been abandoned for scrap as a constructive total loss. *Both Blohm & Voss*

The *Europa* as finally completed, with short funnels, at the Columbus Quay, Bremerhaven. *Hapag-Lloyd*

EUROPE (1864) Compagnie Générale Transatlantique (French Line), France

5,333grt; 394ft (120.1m) lbp x 44ft (13.4m) beam
211 passengers in three classes
Scott's, Greenock (Yard No 92)
Compound-expansion steam reciprocating, single screw

Having started life as a paddle steamer, the transatlantic passenger-cargo ship *Europe* was converted to screw propulsion in 1873, when she was also lengthened. During a voyage from Le Havre to New York on 10 April 1874, the *Europe* was abandoned at sea after she sprang a leak and began to sink in severe weather. Apparently the ship's keel had touched the bottom as she left Le Havre, which may have weakened her plates. The passengers and crew were taken off by the National Line steamer *Greece*. Fully evacuated, the derelict ship drifted for several days before it foundered.

Casualties: 0

A ship blessed with a series of misfortunes was the Norddeutscher Lloyd express passenger liner and transatlantic Blue Riband-holder *Europa*, which caught fire while fitting out. *Both: Blohm & Voss*

EXCALIBUR (1930) American Export Line, USA

serving under the wartime name JOSEPH HEWES [AP-50]
9,359grt; 474ft (144.5m) loa x 61ft (18.6m) beam
147 passengers in single class
New York SB Corp, Camden, New Jersey (Yard No 394)
Steam turbines, single screw
The passenger-cargo ship *Excalibur* was taken over for war service in 1942 as the troop transport *Joseph Hewes*. She took part in the Allied landings in North Africa in November 1942, in consort with a number of other converted American liners. While she was lying in Fedalah Roads, near Rabat, on 11 November, the *Joseph Hewes* was torpedoed by the German submarine U173, which had penetrated a defensive screen in order to launch its attack. She sank in the position 35.10N, 04.00W.
Casualties: More than 100. (This figure could be the total from all the American troop transport losses during Operation 'Torch')

The *Excalibur* was one of a group of four pre-Second World War passenger ships known as the 'Four Aces', employed on the transatlantic service from New York to the Mediterranean. *World Ship Society*

EXCAMBION (1931) American Export Line, USA

serving under the wartime name JOHN PENN [AP-51]
9,360grt; 450ft (137.2m) lbp x 61ft (18.6m) beam
147 passengers
New York SB Corp, Camden, New Jersey (Yard No 397)
Steam turbines, single screw
The United States Navy took over the passenger-cargo ship *Excambion* in 1941 for service as an armed transport under the name *John Penn*. While serving in this capacity, she was bombed and sunk by Japanese dive- and torpedo-bombers off Lunga Point, Guadalcanal, Solomon Islands, on 13 August 1943.
Casualties: not known

EXCELSIOR NEPTUNE (1959) ex-*Feliks Dzerzhinskiy* (1988) Excelsior Shipping Co, Honduras

4,195grt; 401ft (122.2m) loa x 53ft (16.0m) beam
333 passengers in single class (as built)
Mathias Thesen Werft, Wismar (Yard No 102)
Motor-ship, twin screw
The ferry *Excelsior Neptune*, acquired from the USSR in 1988, was lost in January 1993 during a delivery voyage to new owners in the People's Republic of China to whom she had been sold. While under tow from Taiwan to Canton, she was seen as she passed Hong Kong during that January but was subsequently lost in circumstances that are not fully known.
Casualties: not known

EXETER (1931) American Export Line, USA

serving under the wartime name EDWARD RUTLEDGE [AP-52]
9,360grt; 450ft (137.2m) lbp x 61ft (18.6m) beam
147 passengers
New York SB Corp, Camden, New Jersey (Yard No 396)
Steam turbines, single screw
The passenger-cargo steamship *Exeter* was taken over as an American naval transport in 1942 and renamed *Edward Rutledge*. She was engaged in the Allied landings at Casablanca, Morocco, in November 1942 together with her sister ship, the former *Excalibur* (qv), and other requisitioned American and Allied passenger ships. While she was approaching the beachhead off Fedalah, on 12 November 1942, the *Edward Rutledge* was torpedoed by the German submarine U130 and sank in the position 33.40N, 07.35W.
Casualties: not known

EXPLORATEUR GRANDIDIER (1924) Messageries Maritimes, France

10,267grt; 476ft (145.1m) loa x 60ft (18.3m) beam
299 passengers in three classes
Penhoët, St Nazaire (Yard No C5)
Triple-expansion steam reciprocating, twin screw
Used initially as a wartime troopship, the passenger steamship *Explorateur Grandidier* returned to Brest on 19 May 1940 and was subsequently engaged in repatriation voyages from Beirut before being laid up. She was disarmed and ceded to Germany on 10 May 1943, but returned to French control that December. However, on 16 July 1944 the Germans seized the ship and sailed her to Marseilles where, on 21 August, she was scuttled in the North Pass, Mirabeau Basin. The wreck was cleared and broken up in 1948.
Casualties: not known

EXPRESS SAMINA (1966) ex-*Golden Vergina* (2000) ex-*Corse* (1982) Minoan Flying Dolphins Maritime SA, Greece

4,555grt; 377ft (115.0m) loa x 59ft (18.1m) beam
1,408 passengers
Chantiers de L'Atlantique, St Nazaire (Yard No F23)
Motor-ship, twin screw
The ro-ro passenger ferry *Express Samina* was lost on 26 September 2000 when she stranded on a reef off Paros Island in the position 37.05N, 25.19E. She was carrying 473 passengers.
Casualties: 143 (82 passengers and 61 crew)

F

FAGR (1970) ex-*Mecca I* (1998) ex-*Al-Qamar Al-Saudi II* (1994) ex-*Al-Qamar Al-Saudi Al-Misri I* (1993) ex-*Al Hussein II* (1991) ex-*Mecca I* (1986) ex-*Khalid I* (1985) ex-*Viking I* (1984) ex-*Wasa Express* (1984) ex-*Viking I* (1983) Brave Commander SA, Honduras

5,993grt; 357ft (108.7m) loa x 57ft (17.3m) beam
404 berthed and 796 deck passengers (as built)
J. L. Meyer, Papenburg (Yard No 562)
Motor-ship, twin screw
The ro-ro passenger ferry *Fagr*, which had been engaged in conveying Muslim pilgrims across the Red Sea for some years, was lost on 19 April 2000. By that date she had been idle since January 1999, riding at anchor off Port Tewfik. Caught in strong winds, she capsized and sank, and was subsequently declared a constructive total loss.
Casualties: 0

Originally the *Viking I*, one of the 'Papenburg' sisters, the much-renamed ro-ro ferry *Fagr* is shown here under another earlier guise as the *Mecca I* at Suez on 20 May 1998. *Frank Heine FERRIES*

FAIRSEA (1942) ex-*Charger* (1949) Sitmar Line (Passenger Liner Services Inc), Panama

13,317grt; 492ft (150.0m) loa x 69ft (21.1m) beam
1,212 passengers in single class
Sun Shipbuilding & Drydock Co, Chester, Pennsylvania (Yard No 188)
Motor-ship, single screw
Ordered as a wartime emergency C3 cargo ship but completed as an auxiliary escort carrier, the passenger ship *Fairsea* was acquired for the emigrant services from Bremerhaven and Southampton to Quebec or Sydney. Fully refurbished in 1958, she survived another 11 years until 29 January 1969 when, during a voyage from Sydney to Southampton, she was severely disabled by a fire that broke out in her engine room when she was 900 miles west of Panama. Towed to Balboa, she was laid up but, declared a constructive total loss, she was sold for breaking up and towed to La Spezia where she arrived on 6 August of that year.
Casualties: 0

Reconstructed from a C-3 emergency cargo ship hull and wartime escort carrier, the *Fairsea* was one of a number of such vessels engaged in the Australian emigrant services of the 1950s and early 1960s. *Mike Lennon*

FALABA (1906) Elder Dempster Line, GB

4,806grt; 381ft (116.1m) lbp x 47ft (14.3m) beam
210 passengers
Alexander Stephen, Glasgow (Yard No 414)
Triple-expansion steam reciprocating, single screw
The passenger steamship *Falaba* was the victim of a torpedo attack on 28 March 1915 while bound from Liverpool for Sierra Leone with 151 passengers and 96 crew. When some 38 miles west of the Smalls lighthouse, she sighted a submarine but there was no immediate concern as it was flying the White Ensign. However, as it approached the *Falaba* its true identity was revealed as being the U28, the flag exchanged for the German naval ensign. The *Falaba* was hove to and the lowering of her boats was commenced in anticipation of an attack. After only five boats had been swung out, the U28 fired a torpedo that struck the *Falaba* amidships and she sank rapidly, disappearing beneath the surface within 10 minutes. The survivors were picked up by the drifters *Eileen Emma* and *Wenlock*.
Casualties: 104

The Elder Dempster ship *Falaba* was engaged on the West African services from Liverpool. *H. B. Christiansen Collection / Online Transport Archive*

FATSHAN (1933) ex-*Koto Maru* (1945) ex-*Fatshan* (1942) Tai Tak Hing Shipping Co, UK

2,639grt; 250ft (73.5m) lbp x 47ft (13.9m) beam
122 berthed passengers in three classes plus 1,261 deck passengers
Taikoo Dock & Engineering Co, Hong Kong

(Yard No 262)
Triple-expansion steam reciprocating, twin screw
The Hong Kong-registered coastal passenger steamship *Fatshan* was lost on 17 August 1971 when caught in typhoon 'Rose' with some 84 persons aboard during a crossing from Hong Kong to Macao. She was overwhelmed by the weather and capsized and sank near Lantau Island. One of the four survivors later claimed that a drifting ship had in fact struck the vessel while it was riding out the storm. The *Fatshan* was a total loss and her wreck was sold for scrap.
Casualties: About 80

FELTRIA (1891) ex-*Uranium* (1916) ex-*Atlanta* (1908) ex-*Avoca* (1907) ex-*San Fernando* (1896) ex-*Avoca* (1896) Cunard Line, UK

5,254grt; 420ft (128.0m) lbp x 48ft (14.7m) beam
400 passengers in single class
William Denny, Dumbarton (Yard No 448)
Quadruple-expansion steam reciprocating, single screw
The emigrant passenger ship *Feltria* was lost on 5 May 1917. She was torpedoed by the German submarine UC48 when eight miles off Mine Head, Waterford, on the south-east coast of Ireland, in the position 51.56N, 07.24W. She was bound from New York for Avonmouth with a general cargo but no passengers.
Casualties: 45

FLANDRE (1914) Compagnie Générale Transatlantique (French Line), France

8,503grt; 480ft (146.3m) loa x 57ft (17.4m) beam
550 passengers
Penhoët, St Nazaire (Yard No E3)
Compound-expansion steam reciprocating with LP turbine, quadruple screw

French Line's first *Flandre* served on the run to the West Indies and Central America. Prior to the Second World War, like the *St Louis*, she had undertaken some mercy voyages carrying Jewish refugees. *World Ship Society*

On the outbreak of the Second World War, the passenger ship *Flandre* was taken up by the French naval authorities as a troopship and in this role took part in the Norwegian campaign of April 1940. After the fall of France and in the hands of the occupying Germans, she was requisitioned with a view to her participation in the planned invasion of England,

Operation 'Sea Lion'. However, the *Flandre* was sunk after striking a magnetic mine at the mouth of the River Gironde on 14 September 1940. The badly damaged ship was beached near La Coubre but she broke up and became a total loss.
Casualties: 0

FLAVIA (1906) ex-*Campanello* (1916) ex-*Campania* (1910) ex-*British Empire* (1906) Cunard Line, UK

7,347grt; 470ft (143.3m) lbp x 57ft (17.3m) beam
2,270 passengers in two classes
Palmers, Jarrow (Yard No 755)
Triple-expansion steam reciprocating, twin screw
The passenger-cargo ship *Flavia* was acquired by Cunard Line during the First World War, possibly with a view to a return to the European emigrant trade after the war, for she had the bulk of her large passenger capacity in the Steerage grade. However, she was torpedoed and sunk by the German submarine U107 on 24 August 1918 while she was on passage from Montreal to Avonmouth with cargo and livestock but no passengers. She was attacked thirty miles north-west-by-west of Tory Island, off the north coast of Ireland, in the position 55.23N, 09.40W.
Casualties: 1

FLORIDE (1907) Compagnie Générale Transatlantique (French Line), France

7,029grt; 437ft (133.2m) loa x 52ft (15.9m) beam
910 passengers in two classes
Chantiers de Provence, Port de Bouc (Yard No 23)
Triple-expansion steam reciprocating, single screw
The passenger-cargo ship *Floride* was sunk on 19 February 1915 by the German auxiliary commerce raider *Prinz Eitel Friedrich*, another former liner, while she was bound from Le Havre to the River Plate. Intercepted north-east of Fernando de Noronha, near Dakar, Senegal, her 86 passengers and 78 crew were removed, after which the *Floride* was shelled and sunk in the position 02.28S, 31.10W. Her occupants were held prisoner aboard the *Prinz Eitel Friedrich* until, her fuel and supplies exhausted, she was interned at Newport News, Virginia, on 11 March 1915.
Casualties: 0

FONTAINEBLEAU (1923) ex-*Islande* (launch name, 9 November 1923) Messageries Maritimes, France

10,015grt; 501ft (152.6m) loa x 59ft (18.1m) beam
576 passengers in four classes
Chantiers de la Loire, Saint-Nazaire (Yard No 244)
Steam turbines, twin screw
The passenger-cargo ship *Fontainebleau* was bound for Ceylon, the Straits, China and Japan on 12 July 1926 when she caught fire off the coast of Djibouti where she was headed after leaving Port Said. The source of the outbreak was bales of cotton in her hold. After arriving at the east African port, the fire was fought with the assistance of help from ashore, but during the evening it was fanned by a strong offshore wind, spreading to the passenger and crew accommodation. Destabilised by the volume of water pumped aboard her, the *Fontainebleau* sank in the roadstead in forty feet of water with a 70-degree list to starboard. All aboard were saved unhurt, apart from some injuries to three passengers and

some crew members. The passengers, together with their luggage, continued their voyage aboard the *Amiral Nelly* while the crew was repatriated to Marseilles aboard the *Athos*. Salvage was considered to be possible but, after several unsuccessful attempts to refloat the *Fontainebleau*, her owners abandoned her to the underwriters as a total loss. The wreck was later utilised as the foundation of a breakwater.
Casualties: 0

FORT VICTORIA (1913) ex-*Willochra* (1920) Furness Withy (Bermuda & West Indies Steamship Co), UK

7,784grt 412ft (125.5m) lbp x 57ft (17.3m) beam
429 passengers
William Beardmore, Dalmuir (Yard No 507)
Quadruple-expansion steam reciprocating, twin screw
The passenger-cargo ship *Fort Victoria* was outward bound from New York to Bermuda on 18 December 1929, when she was rammed in thick fog by the American coastwise liner *Algonquin*, owned by Cherokee Seminole Steamship Corp, part of the Clyde-Mallory group. The *Fort Victoria* was carrying some 200 passengers and the *Algonquin* had a further 289 aboard her. The accident occurred in the Ambrose Channel, off Sandy Hook, about two miles from the Ambrose light vessel. The *Fort Victoria*, which had stopped, was transferring her pilot to a cutter when the *Algonquin* suddenly appeared out of the fog bearing down on her and striking her with a severity that proved fatal. Before she foundered, the *Fort Victoria*'s passengers were transferred to the pilot boat, 144 of them being landed at Staten Island and the remainder at the Hudson River Pier from which she had earlier sailed. Her wreck was regarded as a menace to shipping and demolition with explosives was proposed, but subsequent storms completed the job of breaking her up without aid.
Casualties: 0

FOUCAULD (1922) ex-*Hoedic* (1929) Chargeurs Réunis, France

11,028grt; 501ft (152.7m) loa x 58ft (17.7m) beam
450 passengers in three classes
Forges et Chantiers de la Méditerranée, La Seyne (Yard No 1136)
Triple-expansion steam reciprocating, twin screw
The passenger ship *Foucauld* was bombed and burned out during a German air raid on La Pallice on 20 June 1940. She was beached on the Ile de Ré, where she settled in shallow water with her back broken. Earlier in her career, under her previous name, she had capsized while under tow at Le Havre on 5 June 1928. After a complicated salvage operation and a lengthy refit at Rotterdam by Wilton Fijenoord, she had emerged as the *Foucauld*, making her first sailing in January 1930.
Casualties: not known

FRANCESCO CRISPI (1925) Lloyd Triestino, Italy

7,464grt; 447ft (136.2m) loa x 52ft (15.9m) beam
450 passengers
Ansaldo San Giorgio, Muggiano (Yard No 194)
Steam turbines, twin screw
The passenger-cargo ship *Francesco Crispi*, serving as a

wartime troopship, was torpedoed and sunk by the British submarine HMS *Saracen* on 19 April 1943. She was attacked off Punta Nere, about eighteen miles from Cape Le Serre, Elba, in the position 42.46N, 09.46E. At the time, she was bound in convoy from Livorno to Bastia, Corsica, carrying troops.
Casualties: More than 800

The *Francesco Crispi*, with her sister ship *Giuseppe Mazzini*, was originally built for the Transatlantic Italiana Company, passing to Lloyd Triestino in the early 1930s. They operated between Italy and Latin America. *Tom Rayner collection*

FRANCONIA (1911) Cunard Line, UK

18,150grt; 625ft (190.5m) loa x 71ft (21.6m) beam
2,850 passengers in three classes
Swan Hunter & Wigham Richardson, Wallsend-on-Tyne (Yard No 857)
Quadruple-expansion steam reciprocating, twin screw
The passenger liner *Franconia* was requisitioned in February 1915 for war service as a troopship for operations in the Mediterranean. As such, she was torpedoed and sunk by the German submarine UB47 on 4 October 1916, when she was some 195 miles south-east of Malta, in the position 35.56N, 18.30E. She had been bound from Alexandria to Marseilles, fortunately without troops, only her 314-man crew having been aboard her at the time of the attack.
Casualties: 12

Cunard introduced the sister ships *Franconia* (seen here) and *Laconia* to the Liverpool to New York or Boston services in 1911. *Real Photographs*

FRESHFIELD (1896) ex-*Clement* (1915) ex-*La Plata* (1900) Lawrence Smith & Co, Canada

3,445grt; 346ft (105.4m) lbp x 44ft (13.4m) beam
735 passengers in two classes
Robert Napier, Govan (Yard No 449)
Triple-expansion steam reciprocating, single screw
The small passenger cargo ship *Freshfield*, built originally for

the Royal Mail Line, was lost on 5 August 1918 when she was torpedoed without warning four miles north-east-by-north of Cape Colonne, south of Crotone, in southern Italy, while bound from Messina to Taranto in ballast. Her attacker was the German submarine UC25 under the command of Karl Dönitz, later the Grand Admiral of the Kriegsmarine.
Casualties: 3

FUJI [HUZI] MARU (1937) Nippon Yusen Kaisha, Japan

9,138grt; 453ft (138.1m) lbp x 60ft (18.3m) beam
984 passengers
Mitsubishi, Nagasaki (Yard No 650)
Steam turbines, twin screw
The passenger-cargo ship *Fuji Maru* was torpedoed and sunk on 27 October 1943 when she was north-west of the Ryukyu Islands, in the position 28.20N, 128.05E. Her attackers were the American submarines USS *Shad* and *Grayback*.
Casualties: not known

The passenger steamship *Fuji [Huzi] Maru* was employed on the service to Europe via the Suez Canal. *World Ship Society*

FULDA (1882) Norddeutscher Lloyd, Germany

4,816grt; 455ft (138.7m) loa x 46ft (14.0m) beam
1,255 passengers in three classes
John Elder, Govan (Yard No 267)
Compound-expansion steam reciprocating, single screw
On 2 February 1899 the transatlantic passenger steamship *Fulda* sustained serious damage in a dry-dock accident at Birkenhead, shortly after a provisional sale to the Canadian Steamship Company had been arranged, a sale that in part depended upon the inspection she was to have undergone. She had fallen against the dock side, presenting a considerable challenge to extricate her. When examined subsequently, she was considered to be beyond repair and the sale was therefore abandoned. She was sold instead for scrap, arriving at Bremerhaven on 20 May 1899, breaking up not commencing until four months later.
Casualties: 0

FULVIA (1949) ex-*Oslofjord* (1969) Norwegian America Line, Norway (under charter to Costa Line)

16,923grt; 577ft (175.9m) loa x 72ft (22.0m) beam
625 passengers in two classes
Nederlandsche Stoom Maats, Amsterdam (Yard No 410)
Motor-ship, twin screw
The former transatlantic liner *Oslofjord* was chartered for

cruising under the name *Fulvia*. During a cruise with a full complement of 721 passengers on 20 July 1970, she caught fire following an explosion in her engine room. The ship's position was 30.17N, 16.23W, about 100 miles due north of the Canary Islands. All passengers and crew were rescued by the French passenger liner *Ancerville*, which had answered the calls for assistance transmitted from the stricken cruise ship. An attempt was made to tow the *Fulvia* to Tenerife, but she foundered later the same day in position 29.57N, 16.30W.
Casualties: 0

At the end of her transatlantic career, Norwegian America Line chartered the *Oslofjord* to Costa Armatori for service as the cruise ship *Fulvia*, but fire brought this phase of her life to an abrupt end after less than a year. The photograph shows the *Oslofjord* at one of the New York piers while still working as a scheduled service liner. *Ian Shiffman*

FUSHIMI [HUSIMI] MARU (1914) Nippon Yusen Kaisha, Japan

10,936grt; 525ft (160.0m) loa x 63ft (19.2m) beam
512 passengers in three classes
Mitsubishi, Nagasaki (Yard No 237)
Triple-expansion steam reciprocating, twin screw
The passenger-cargo ship *Fushimi Maru* was torpedoed and sunk by the American submarine USS *Tarpon* on 1 February 1943. She was attacked off the coast of Honshu, in the position 34.08N, 138.11E.
Casualties: not known

FUSO [HUSO] MARU (1908) ex-*Latvia* (1923) ex-*Russ* (1921) ex-*Russia [Rossiya]* (1914) Osaka Shosen Kaisha, Japan

8,596grt; 475ft (144.8m) lbp x 57ft (17.4m) beam
1,291 passengers in two classes (as a Polish ship)
Barclay Curle, Whiteinch, Glasgow (Yard No 470)
Triple-expansion steam reciprocating, twin screw
The passenger-cargo ship *Fuso Maru*, converted into a naval troop transport, was lost while sailing in convoy on 31 July 1944. She was torpedoed and sunk by the American submarine USS *Steelhead* off the north coast of Luzon, in the Philippines Group, in the position 18.57N, 120.50E.
Casualties: not known

G

concerted salvage attempts she became a total wreck.
Casualties: 0 (This figure is from the Lloyd's records, but other reports say there were 19 deaths)

GALAPAGOS DISCOVERY (1962) ex-*Bali Sea Dancer* (1998) ex-*Illiria* (1994) Galatours SA, Ecuador

3,763grt; 333ft (101.4m) loa x 48ft (14.7m) beam
181 passengers (as built)
Cantieri Nav Pellegrino, Naples (Yard No 116)
Motor-ship, twin screw
The small cruise ship *Galapagos Discovery* was lost on 19 October 1999 while undergoing repairs at Rooman Pier No 3, Balboa, in the Panama Canal. She caught fire and, while still ablaze, was moved to a position on the west bank of the Canal, near the Miraflores Locks, for the fire to burn itself out. She sank the following day and was abandoned as a half-submerged and gutted hulk.
Casualties: not known

The stylish *Illiria*, which became the *Galapagos Discovery* in 1998, is seen at St Malo in August 1993. *Frank Heine FERRIES*

The wreck of the *Galapagos Discovery* near Balboa in the Panama Canal, photographed on 20 January 2001.
Mick Lindsay (Harley Crossley)

GALEKA (1899) Union-Castle Line, UK

6,722grt; 440ft (134.1m) loa x 53ft (16.2m) beam
210 passengers in two classes
Harland & Wolff, Belfast (Yard No 347)
Triple-expansion steam reciprocating, twin screw
Initially taken up as a First World War troopship, the *Galeka* was redeployed as a hospital ship in 1915 for service in the Mediterranean during the Gallipoli campaign. On 28 October 1916 she struck a mine five miles north-west of Cap de le Hogue, in the position 49.34N, 00.05E. The *Galeka* was beached near Le Havre in a bid to save her, but in spite of

The last vessel to enter service with the Union Line prior to its amalgamation with the Castle Line was the *Galeka*, which operated on the intermediate service to South Africa.
Real Photos

GALILEA (1918) ex-*Pilsna* (1935) Adriatica SA di Navigazione, Italy

8,040grt; 433ft (131.9m) lbp x 51ft (15.6m) beam
440 passengers
San Rocco Cantieri, San Rocco (Yard No 30)
Triple-expansion steam reciprocating, twin screw
The liner *Galilea* was lost on 28 March 1942 while serving as a wartime troopship, on a voyage from North Africa to Italy transporting Italian troops. She was torpedoed by a British submarine near Antipaxo, near Corfu, and sank in the position 39.04N, 20.05E.
Casualties: 768 (troops and crew)

Lloyd Triestino's *Galilea*. In terms of gravity, her loss in the Second World War ranked only behind those of the *Conte Rosso* and *Francesco Crispi* where Italian ships were concerned. *World Ship Society*

GALLIA (1878) ex-*Don Alvaro de Bazan* (1896) ex-*Gallia* (1896) Allan Line, UK

4,809grt; 430ft (131.1m) lbp x 45ft (13.6m) beam
1,500 passengers in two classes
J. & G. Thomson, Clydebank (Yard No 163)
Compound-expansion steam reciprocating, single screw
The liner *Gallia*, originally a Cunard Line ship, was wrecked on 18 May 1899 on the outbound leg of her first voyage, from Liverpool, for her new owners. She was stranded at Sorel Point, near Quebec. Though salvaged, she was not considered to be fit for repair. She was returned across the Atlantic – it is not certain whether this was achieved under her own steam or under tow – for breaking up at Cherbourg, France, which commenced in May 1900.
Casualties: 0

GALLIA (1913) Cie Sud-Atlantique, France

14,996grt; 600ft (182.9m) loa x 62ft (18.9m) beam
1,086 passengers in four classes
Forges et Chantiers de la Méditerranée, La Seyne (Yard No 1056)
Triple-expansion steam reciprocating with LP turbine, quadruple screw

The passenger liner *Gallia*, taken up as a troopship, was bound from Marseilles for Salonica (Thessaloniki) carrying in excess of 2,700 persons, the majority of them French and Serbian troops destined to join the fighting at Gallipoli. A day out, on 4 October 1916, she was torpedoed and sunk 35 miles south-west of San Pietro Island, off the coast of Sardinia. Her adversary was the German submarine U35. The *Gallia* was unescorted at the time but had been pursuing a zig-zag course at 18 knots. Two torpedoes struck her, the explosions so violent that her radio equipment was destroyed, preventing her from putting out calls for help. The ship began to settle rapidly and there was much confusion and a fair amount of indiscipline as many of the panicking soldiers jumped into the sea without lifejackets or other buoyancy aids. The *Gallia*'s crew struggled to launch lifeboats in these difficult circumstances and a number were still in their davits as she slipped beneath the surface, denying many a means of refuge until rescue arrived. When the French cruiser *Chateaurenault* reached the scene the next day, she was able to pick up only 1,362 survivors. The loss of the *Gallia* was thus France's worst maritime disaster of the First World War.
Casualties: 1,428

The *Gallia* was built for the express service between Bordeaux and the River Plate. Her sinking in October 1916 was France's worst ever shipping disaster. *World Ship Society*

GALWAY CASTLE (1911) Union-Castle Line, UK

7,988grt; 452ft (137.8m) lbp x 56ft (17.1m) beam
About 300 passengers
Harland & Wolff, Belfast (Yard No 419)
Quadruple-expansion steam reciprocating, twin screw

Initially, on the outbreak of the First World War, the intermediate liner *Galway Castle* was engaged as a troopship to take infantry units to German South West Africa to join the campaign in that region. Subsequently she reverted to her owners and resumed commercial sailings. While she was outward bound from Plymouth to Port Natal on 12 September 1918, the *Galway Castle* was torpedoed by the German submarine U82. The attack was made 160 miles south-south-west of Fastnet and she sank in the position 48.50N, 10.40W. The explosion of the torpedo broke her back

and she was not expected to remain afloat for long. There was also considerable anxiety about the possibility of the U-boat continuing the attack as long as the crippled liner remained on the surface. In these circumstances, a hasty evacuation was commenced in which the lifeboats were hurriedly launched, many of them spilling their occupants as they reached the water. The devastation caused by the torpedo had also severed communications between the ends of the ship on either side of the point of impact such that there was difficulty in accounting for everyone on board.

Distress calls were transmitted and were answered by destroyers sent to the scene from Devonport, and they rescued many of those who would otherwise have drowned had the *Galway Castle* suddenly sunk, as thought, or if the U-boat had resumed its attack. In the event, she remained afloat for three days and the unduly rushed evacuation, which, ironically, was responsible for many of the deaths, could have been conducted in a more orderly fashion. However, it has to be said that hindsight is a wonderful thing and, at the time, the most important priority for the officers aboard the *Galway Castle* was to get survivors away as quickly as possible while they were still confronted by a hostile adversary.
Casualties: 143

The *Galway Castle* and her sister ships *Gloucester Castle* and *Guildford Castle* were employed on the intermediate service to South Africa. *David Reed*

GANDIA (1907) ex-*Konigstein* (1940) ex-*Arawa* (1928) Cie Maritime Belge, Belgium

9,626grt; 459ft (139.9m) lbp x 59ft (18.0m) beam
220 passengers in three classes
Swan Hunter & Wigham Richardson, Wallsend-on-Tyne (Yard No 783)
Triple-expansion steam reciprocating, twin screw

The Bernstein Line bought the *Arawa* from Shaw Savill & Albion in 1928 for service across the Atlantic and had her passenger accommodation extended in 1931. Renamed *Konigstein*, she was transferred a second time, to Cie Maritime Belge, in 1940. As the *Gandia* she was intended for the West African service from Antwerp, but the outbreak of the Second World War interfered with these plans. *Alex Duncan*

The passenger-cargo ship *Gandia* was lost while bound in convoy from Liverpool to St John, New Brunswick, on 22 January 1942, carrying a crew of 88 men. Maintaining her position in the convoy had proved to be difficult and shortly after she became separated she was torpedoed by the German submarine U135. She sank in the position 42.45N, 53.00W, some 420 miles south of Cape Race. Apart from those lost when she sank, another 24 died in the lifeboats on the open seas. Casualties: 66

GANGES (1882) P&O Line, UK

4,168grt; 390ft (118.9m) lbp x 42ft (12.8m) beam
168 passengers in two classes plus 500 troops
Barrow Shipbuilding Co, Barrow-in-Furness (Yard No 86)
Inverted compound-expansion steam reciprocating, single screw

On 1 July 1898 the passenger and troopship *Ganges* caught fire in Bombay Harbour and was completely burned out. The crew from her fleet-mate *Brindisi*, which was also in port at the time, assisted in the fire-fighting but their efforts were in vain. There were no passengers aboard the *Ganges* and the only fatality was a stewardess in whose cabin the fire had reputedly began. The unsubstantiated account suggested that she had fallen asleep while smoking under her mosquito net. As the vessel was almost seventeen years old, it was decided that there was no economic justification for repairing her. Thus, after she was refloated, she was sold to local ship-breakers for demolition.
Casualties: 1

P&O's *Ganges* was one of a class of five vessels employed on the Indian and Australian services. *Tom Rayner collection*

GARIBALDI (1906) ex-*Virginia* (1911) Tirrenia SA di Navigazione, Italy

5,278grt; 381ft (116.2m) lbp x 48ft (14.7m) beam
1,665 passengers in two classes
Esercizio Bacini, Riva Trigoso (Yard No 39)
Triple-expansion steam reciprocating, twin screw

Formerly owned by the Genoese company Lloyd Italiano and later by the Cia Italiana Transatlantica, the *Garibaldi*, sister ship of the *Cavour* (qv), was lost on 2 August 1944 when she was bombed and sunk at Genoa.
Casualties: not known

GEELONG (1904) ex-*Australia* (launch name, 19 March 1904) P&O Line, UK

7,954grt; 450ft (137.2m) lbp x 55ft (16.6m) beam
700 passengers in single class
Barclay Curle, Whiteinch, Glasgow (Yard No 444)
Triple-expansion steam reciprocating, twin screw

Built for the so-called 'Branch Line' service to Australia, essentially an emigrant-carrying service, the passenger steamship *Geelong* was taken up as a troopship in 1915, conveying units of the Australian Expeditionary Forces to the war theatre in Europe. While performing these duties on 1 January 1916, she was sunk following a collision with the Cardiff-registered cargo ship *Bonvilston* as she was steaming in convoy about 100 miles north-west of Alexandria in the position 32.46N, 30.05E. The accident occurred in darkness, neither ship displaying lights because of the risk of submarine attack. All those aboard both vessels were rescued.
Casualties: 0

GEISER (1881) Thingvalla Line, Denmark

2,831grt; 324ft (98.8m) lbp x 39ft (11.9m) beam
About 1,000 passengers in three classes
Burmeister & Wain, Copenhagen (Yard No 118)
Compound-expansion steam reciprocating, single screw

When outward bound from New York to Christiansand (Kristiansund) and Copenhagen on 14 August 1888, the passenger steamship *Geiser* was struck by her inward-bound fleet-mate, the *Thingvalla*. The accident occurred about thirty miles south of Sable Island in hazy conditions. Neither vessel was sighted by the other until just before the moment of impact, when the *Geiser*'s helm was put hard to starboard, but, as the *Thingvalla* was simultaneously steered hard to port, a collision was unavoidable. The *Geiser* was almost cut in two, at a point midway along her starboard side, and she capsized and sank within ten minutes, allowing sufficient time to launch only three of her boats. Many of her complement of 107 passengers and 53 crew fell through the gaping hole in her side into the sea, where they drowned. The *Thingvalla*'s bows were badly damaged but the forward bulkhead held and she remained afloat and was able to rescue the *Geiser*'s survivors, adding them to the 455 passengers she was already carrying. Later, the *Thingvalla* transferred all her passengers to the Hamburg Amerika Line's *Wieland*, which took them to New York, while she proceeded to Halifax, Nova Scotia, for repairs.
Casualties: 129

GENERAL ARTIGAS (1923) ex-*Westphalia* (1930) Hamburg Sud-Amerika Line, Germany

11,254grt; 495ft (150.9m) loa x 60ft (18.3m) beam
561 passengers in two classes
Howaldtswerke, Kiel (Yard No 611)
Steam turbines, single screw

From late January 1940, the passenger-cargo ship *General Artigas* was used as a naval accommodation ship based at Hamburg, in the Kuhwerder Harbour. During a British air raid on the city on 25 July 1943 she was hit by bombs, caught fire and sank. A total loss, the wreck was raised in 1946 and scrapped locally.
Casualties: not known

GENERAL M. C. MEIGS (1944) US Maritime Administration, USA

17,707grt; 622ft (189.7m) loa x 76ft (23.0m) beam
5,200 troops
Federal Shipbuilding & Drydock Co, Kearny, New Jersey

(Yard No 274)
Geared steam turbines, twin screw
One of a large group of wartime-built standard troopships of the P-2 type, the *General M. C. Meigs* was lost on 9 January 1972 while under tow from Olympia, in Puget Sound, where she had been laid up, to San Francisco, where her lay-up as a reserve vessel was to continue. She was stranded at Cape Flattery, broke in two and became a total loss.
Casualties: not known

GENERAL METZINGER (1906) ex-*Sobral* (1923) ex-*Cap Vilano* (1917) Messageries Maritimes, France

9,467grt; 475ft (144.8m) lbp x 55ft (16.8m) beam
297 passengers in three classes
Blohm & Voss, Steinwerder, Hamburg (Yard No 183)
Quadruple-expansion steam reciprocating, twin screw
The French passenger-cargo ship *General Metzinger* was sunk at Le Havre when she was bombed there by German aircraft on 11 June 1940 during the operation to evacuate Allied troops trapped by the German advance. She caught fire and sank in shallow water. Her wreck was broken up for scrap in 1950. Casualties: 6 (all crew)

GENERAL OSORIO (1929) Hamburg Sud-Amerika Line, Germany

11,590grt; 528ft (160.9m) loa x 65ft (19.8m) beam
980 passengers in two classes
Bremer Vulkan, Vegesack (Yard No 669)
Motor-ship, twin screw
In April 1940 the passenger-cargo liner *General Osorio* became a naval accommodation ship, stationed at Kiel. From late December 1943 she was transferred to Flensburg but was back at Kiel, in the Howaldtswerke shipyard, when the port suffered an RAF bombing raid on 24 July 1944. Hit by bombs, the *General Osorio* was set on fire and partially gutted. Beached with her stern end high and dry, she was raised that October, but while she was undergoing repairs she was hit a second time during another raid on Kiel by British warplanes on 9 April 1945. Sustaining more extensive damage, she completely burned out and sank. Her wreck was refloated in 1947 and in August of that year was towed to the UK for demolition at Inverkeithing.
Casualties: not known

The twin-funnelled motor-ship *General Osorio* was built for Hamburg Amerika Line's service to South America. Five years after entering service she was chartered to Hamburg Sud-Amerika Line and, later still, was sold to them outright. *Hapag-Lloyd*

GEORGES PHILIPPAR (1932) Messageries Maritimes, France

17,359grt; 567ft (172.7m) loa x 68ft (20.8m) beam
1,045 passengers in four classes
Chantiers de la Loire, St Nazaire (Yard No 148)
Motor-ship, twin screw
The passenger liner *Georges Philippar* succumbed to fire on 16 May 1932 during the return leg of her maiden voyage from Marseilles to Yokohama and Shanghai, via Djibouti, Colombo and Saigon. When the ship was about five miles off Cape Guardafui, Italian Somaliland (now the Somali Republic), in the Gulf of Aden, a First class passenger discovered a fire in an electric commutator on D deck aft. In spite of prompt action to isolate the fire, the flames spread along the electrical wiring and soon gained hold more widely on the deck of the outbreak. A prompt evacuation was ordered while, simultaneously, the radio operator sent out repeated distress calls until the destruction of the wireless apparatus and generators prevented him from continuing any longer. A less auspicious move, however, was the order to close the watertight doors in the vicinity of the blaze. An essential action in the circumstances, it also unfortunately trapped many of the passengers in their cabins or in the alleyways in that section of the ship and, apart from a small number who managed to escape through portholes into the shark-infested waters, the majority were killed by asphyxiation.

The British ships *Mahsud* and *Contractor*, together with the Russian tanker *Sovietskaya Neft*, hurried to the scene and picked up 698 persons between them. The *Mahsud* and *Contractor* took their survivors, 129 and 149 respectively, to Aden, while the 420 who were aboard the *Sovietskaya Neft* were transhipped in mid-ocean to the *André Lebon* and were later landed at Djibouti. The *Georges Philippar* eventually foundered in the afternoon of 19 May, 145 miles north-east of Cape Guardafui, in the position 14.20N, 50.25E.
Casualties: 54 (all passengers)

The *Georges Philippar* of Messageries Maritimes was one of a small number of passenger ships with the distinction of having been lost on their maiden voyages. In her case it was on the homeward-bound leg. *Musée de la Marine*

GEORGE WASHINGTON (1908) ex-*Catlin* (1941) ex-*George Washington* (1941) US Maritime Administration, USA

23,788grt; 723ft (220.2m) loa x 73ft (23.8m) beam
2,679 passengers in four classes (as built)
Stettiner Vulcan, Stettin-Bredow (Yard No 286)
Quadruple-expansion steam reciprocating, twin screw

Prior to the Second World War the transatlantic liner *George Washington* was laid up in the US Reserve Fleet in the Patuxent River, Maryland, only to be given a new lease of life when she was recommissioned for trooping operations in 1941. After the war she was again laid up, first at New York where, in March 1947, she sustained considerable damage in an outbreak of fire. After repairs, she was moved to a new lay-up berth at the US Government Pier at Hawkins Point, Baltimore, Maryland. There, on 16 January 1951, a fire of unknown origin broke out on the pier structure and, as a result of bureaucratic indecision, together with the fact that there was only a skeleton crew aboard the ship at the time, the flames had enveloped the *George Washington* before she could be moved. All fire-fighting effort was concentrated on the burning troopship in an attempt to save her, but when she developed a serious list it was decided that she should be left to burn herself out rather than risk having her capsize. The wreck was later broken up for scrap.

Casualties: 0

Formerly a Norddeutscher Lloyd ship, the *George Washington*, or 'Big George' as she was popularly known, continued intermittently on the North Atlantic run under United States Lines ownership. She is seen, unusually, docking at Cardiff on 23 May 1930. The bunting suggests a special occasion.
Ian Allan Library

Fire-fighters on the quayside tackle the second, fatal blaze aboard the laid-up *George Washington* at the US Government Pier at Hawkins Point, Baltimore, in January 1951.
Frank Braynard

This view shows how the fire on the redundant troopship spread despite fire-fighting efforts and became uncontrollable.
Author's collection

GEORGIC (1932) Cunard White Star Line, UK

27,759grt; 711ft (216.7m) loa x 82ft (25.1m) beam
1,542 passengers in three classes
Harland & Wolff, Belfast (Yard No 896)
Motor-ship, twin screw

The last passenger ship to enter service with the White Star Line, the liner *Georgic* was extremely severely damaged on 14 July 1941 at Port Tewfik at the southern end of the Suez Canal while serving as a Second World War troopship. After she had discharged troops and during embarkation for the return voyage to the Clyde, she came under attack from German aircraft and was bombed and caught fire. To avoid blocking the shipping channel, the *Georgic*, already listing to port and down at the stern, was moved outside the harbour and beached on a sandbank at Kabireh while, as far as possible, fire-fighting efforts continued. She struck another ship in the manoeuvre, twisting her stem. Incredibly, all aboard her managed to escape unharmed. Left to burn herself out over the next two days, the half-submerged and gutted ship was left a constructive total loss.

The last passenger liner to be completed for the White Star Line was the motor-ship *Georgic*. *Real Photos*

However, because of the shortage of troop-carrying tonnage, it was decided to recover and rebuild her. Refloated on 27 October 1941 and patched up, she was towed back to the UK, via Port Sudan, Karachi, Bombay and the Cape of Good Hope, receiving temporary repairs en route, finally arriving at Belfast in early 1943 for reconstruction to commence. The *Georgic* returned to service less her forward funnel in December 1944, dubbed the 'Super Trooper'. After the war she continued to operate as an austere emigrant

carrier with only a utility standard of accommodation, alternately making passages to Australia and to Canada and the USA until November 1955 when she was sold for breaking up at Faslane.
Casualties: 0

The scene at Port Tewfik in July 1941 as the *Georgic* burns following the German bombing attack. The second of these rare views shows her anchored after she had been refloated that October. *Both: Jim Payne – Through Their Eyes*

GERMANIA (1871) Hamburg Amerika Line, Germany (under charter to Hamburg Sud-Amerika Line)

3,810grt; 350ft (106.7m) loa x 39ft (11.9m) beam
370 passengers in three classes
Caird, Greenock (Yard No 161)
Compound-expansion steam reciprocating, single screw
The passenger steamship *Germania*, second of the name, was wrecked off the coast at Bahia, Brazil, on 10 August 1876, within months of being switched from the North Atlantic route to service on the South America run from Hamburg to River Plate ports.
Casualties: not known

GERMANY (1866) Allan Line, UK

3,244grt; 343ft (104.6m) lbp x 42ft (12.8m) beam
450 passengers in two classes
Pearse & Co, Stockton-on-Tees (Yard No 56)
Inverted steam engines, single screw
On 22 December 1872, during a voyage to the Gulf of Mexico, bound from Liverpool for Havana and New Orleans, the passenger steamship *Germany* was wrecked at Ponte de Coubre in the River Gironde, near Bordeaux. The survivors were rescued by the Messageries Maritimes steamer *Mendoza*.
Casualties: 30

GERTRUD WOERMANN (1893) ex-*Pfalz* (1904) Woermann Line, Germany

4,604grt; 417ft (127.2m) loa x 43ft (13.3m) beam
860 passengers in two classes
Wigham Richardson, Low Walker, Tyneside (Yard No 291)
Triple-expansion steam reciprocating, single screw
The passenger steamship *Gertrud Woermann* was lost on 19 November 1904, when she stranded off Swakopmund, Namibia, to the north of Walvis Bay, where she was reduced to a complete wreck.
Casualties: not known

GINYO MARU (1921) Nippon Yusen Kaisha, Japan

8,613grt; 445ft (135.6m) lbp x 58ft (17.7m) beam
531 passengers in three classes
Asano Shipbuilding Co, Tsurumi, Asano (Yard No 38)
Steam turbines, twin screw
The passenger-cargo ship *Ginyo Maru* was torpedoed and sunk by the American submarine USS *Flying Fish* on 16 December 1943. She was off Kaohsiung, Formosa (Taiwan), at the time, and foundered in the position 22.14N, 120.06E.
Casualties: not known

GIULIO CESARE (1920) Lloyd Triestino, Italy

21,657grt; 634ft (193.2m) loa x 76ft (23.2m) beam
640 passengers in three classes
Swan Hunter & Wigham Richardson, Wallsend-on-Tyne (Yard No 967)
Steam turbines, quadruple screw

After a mixed career for several owners, working in conjunction with her near sister ship the *Duilio*, the passenger liner *Giulio Cesare* entered the Italy to Far East service for Lloyd Triestino in 1937. *Ian Rae*

One of the duties performed during the Second World War by the *Giulio Cesare*, seen here, and the *Duilio*, was prisoner exchange voyages to East Africa under diplomatic clearance. This required them to be painted in a special livery as shown. *Imperial War Museum (GM625)*

Laid up at Genoa after the outbreak of war, the passenger liner *Giulio Cesare*, like her near sister *Duilio*, undertook prisoner repatriation voyages for the International Red Cross in March 1942, after which she was laid up again, at Trieste. She was destroyed in bombing raids at Vallone di Zaule, Muggia, in the late summer of 1944. Though extensive damage was caused in the raid of 25 August 1944, she remained afloat, but the raid on 11 September finished her off. It left her burnt and sunk on her side in shallow water, listing to starboard, close to the *Duilio* and *Sabaudia* (both qv). The wreck was removed and demolished in 1949.

Casualties: not known

GLENART CASTLE (1900) ex-*Galician* (1914)
Union-Castle Line, UK

6,757grt; 440ft (134.1m) lbp x 53ft (16.2m) beam
195 passengers in three classes
Harland & Wolff, Belfast (Yard No 348)
Triple-expansion steam reciprocating, twin screw
The passenger steamship *Glenart Castle* served as a hospital ship from late 1914. While engaged in this role, and despite being clearly marked as a hospital ship with all lights showing, she was torpedoed by the German submarine UC56 on 26 February 1918 and sank twenty miles west of Lundy Island. At the time she had been bound from Newport, Monmouthshire, to Brest where she was to take on wounded for return to England. The *Glenart Castle* had 186 persons on board, made up of medical staff and her civilian crew. Had she been on the return run to the UK, this number would have been significantly higher, swollen by Army casualties. As it was, there was still considerable loss of life for she sank soon after the attack and before all her boats could be lowered.

Casualties: 148 (53 medical staff, her Master and 94 crew) These are the official figures from Lloyds and the company's own records.

The *Glenart Castle* was formerly the *Galician*, the sixth unit of a class of ships ordered by the Union Line prior to its merger with the Castle Line. She was intercepted near Tenerife by the German auxiliary cruiser *Kaiser Wilhelm der Grosse* during a homeward-bound voyage from Cape Town on 15 August 1914. After two military passengers had been seized, the *Galician* was permitted to proceed on her way. Here she is seen in hospital ship colours. *David Reed*

GLOUCESTER CASTLE (1911) Union-Castle Line, UK

7,999grt; 452ft (137.7m) lbp x 56ft (17.1m) beam
300 passengers in three classes
Fairfield, Govan (Yard No 478)
Quadruple-expansion steam reciprocating, twin screw
On the outbreak of the Second World War the passenger ship *Gloucester Castle*, which had been laid up off Netley, in Southampton Water, since earlier that year, was reactivated for

war service. During a voyage from Birkenhead to Cape Town, East London and Simonstown on 15 July 1942, carrying twelve passengers and a crew of 142, she was attacked at night near Ascension Island by the German raider *Michel*. She did not survive for longer than ten minutes and during that time the raider's shells destroyed her wireless transmitter and all the lifeboats on the starboard side. She sank in the approximate position 10.00S, 05.00E. The small number of her complement who managed to get away, just 61 in total, made their escape in two portside lifeboats, but they were plucked from the water and imprisoned aboard the *Michel*. Later they were transferred to the supply tanker *Charlotte Schliemann* and taken to Yokohama, Japan, where they were interned for the remainder of the war, the release of all but two of them, who died in captivity, not coming until after the defeat of Japan.

Casualties: 93 (The 12 passengers were all women and children. It is not known how many of them survived.)

The *Gloucester Castle*, with her sister ships *Galway Castle* and *Guildford Castle*, was employed in the intermediate service to Africa. She is seen departing Southampton's River Itchen. *British & Commonwealth Shipping*

GNEISENAU (1935) Norddeutscher Lloyd, Germany

18,160grt; 652ft (198.7m) loa x 74ft (22.6m) beam
293 passengers in two classes
Deschimag AG Weser, Bremen (Yard No 893)
Steam turbines, twin screw

Norddeutscher Lloyd introduced the sister ships *Gneisenau* and *Scharnhorst* to the run from Hamburg to the Far East in the mid-1930s, the former steam-turbine-driven, the latter powered by turbo-electric engines. They were distinctive for having Maier-formed bows. *Hapag-Lloyd*

In 1940 the passenger liner *Gneisenau* was adapted for service as a naval accommodation ship in the Baltic. Later, in 1942, conversion into an aircraft carrier at Wilhelmshaven was planned, as happened to her sister *Scharnhorst* (qv) for the Imperial Japanese Navy, but this never transpired. She was lost on 2 May 1943 during a voyage from Hamburg to Norway via the Kiel Canal, carrying troops. As she was passing west of Gedser on the island of Lolland in the Baltic, in the position 54.38N, 12.26E, she struck a mine laid by a British aircraft. Though beached, she became a total loss. In 1946 the wreck was purchased by the Danish Government for breaking up and by December 1956 the last traces of the *Gneisenau* had been removed.

Casualties: not known

GOETHE (1873) Hamburg Amerika Line, Germany

3,408grt; 376ft (114.6m) lbp x 40ft (12.2m) beam
990 passengers in three classes
Robert Napier, Govan (Yard No 322)
Compound-expansion steam reciprocating, single screw
The former Adler Line passenger steamship *Goethe*, sister of the *Schiller* (qv), bound from Hamburg to Buenos Aires, became stranded off Lobos Island in the mouth of the River Plate on 23 December 1876. She became a total wreck.

Casualties: not known

GOKOKU MARU (1942) Osaka Shosen Kaisha, Japan

10,438grt; 537ft (163.7m) loa x 66ft (20.1m) beam
400 passengers in three classes (as designed)
Tama SB Co, Tama/Mitsui, Tamano (Yard No not known)
Motor-ship, twin screw
Still under construction at the date when the Pacific war broke out, the passenger-cargo ship *Gokoku Maru* never saw commercial service. Completed as an auxiliary cruiser for the Imperial Japanese Navy in September 1942, later reverting to the role of troop transport, she was an unlucky ship. She was badly damaged by US aircraft at Madang on 18 December 1942 and struck a mine off Omae Zaki on 27 December 1943. Her end came on 10 November 1944 when, in the position 33.23N, 129.03E, about 50 miles west of Sasebo, she was torpedoed and sunk by the American submarine USS *Barb*.

Casualties: not known

The third ship of the group that comprised the *Aikoku Maru* and *Hokoku Maru* was the *Gokoku Maru*. No photographs exist showing her completed. The builder's model shows her to be broadly the same as her two class-mates. *Mitsui-OSK Lines*

GOLDEN GATE (1851) Aspinwall Line, USA

2,850grt; 285ft (86.9m) lbp x 43ft (13.1m) beam
Passenger numbers not known
W. H. Brown & Co (Yard No not known)
Steam beam engine, paddles
While bound from San Francisco to New York via Cape Horn, the paddle steamship *Golden Gate*, which had embarked 242 passengers together with her 95-strong crew, caught fire off Manzanilla, Mexico, on 27 July 1862. The fire spread with alarming rapidity and she was steered towards the shore, about 3½ miles distant, in an attempt to beach her. However, while making this manoeuvre her superstructure collapsed, trapping a large number of passengers in the ship's saloon. On reaching the vicinity of the shore, those who were able to swim appear to have made good their own escape from the blazing ship, regardless of the fate of those less able souls left behind. A small number of other passengers and crew escaped by lifeboat. The survivors had to endure considerable hardship in the desolate area in which they had landed before they were eventually rescued. The *Golden Gate* was a total loss, but some of the US$1,400,000-worth of gold bullion she was carrying was salvaged at a later date.

Casualties: 257

GRADISCA (1913) ex-*Gelria* (1935) Italian Government (managed by Lloyd Triestino)

13,868grt; 560ft (170.7m) loa x 66ft (20.0m) beam
1,287 passengers in three classes
Alexander Stephen, Linthouse, Glasgow (Yard No 454)
Quadruple-expansion steam reciprocating, twin screw
Purchased in 1935 by the Italian Government for service as a troopship and hospital ship during the Abyssinian conflict, the passenger-cargo liner *Gradisca* took on the latter duties full-time during the Second World War, under both the Italian and German flags. She became the subject of diplomatic exchanges in late 1944 when she was detained by a British submarine in spite of her legitimate hospital ship status. Though returned to Germany she became a war prize in May 1945. Once more in British hands she was reactivated to carry troops, and it was while performing this task, on 23 January 1946, that the *Gradisca* was stranded off the island of Gavdhos, Crete, during a voyage from Port Said to Malta. She was not refloated until June of the following year, after which she was laid up at Venice requiring major repairs and overhaul but not economically worth this effort because of her age and value. Consequently she was sold for breaking up locally in 1949.

Casualties: 0

GRAMPIAN (1907) Canadian Pacific Line, UK

10,947grt; 502ft (153.0m) loa x 60ft (18.3m) beam
1,460 passengers in three classes
Alexander Stephen, Linthouse, Glasgow (Yard No 422)
Triple-expansion steam reciprocating, twin screw
The passenger-cargo liner *Grampian* was badly damaged by fire on 14 March 1921, the outbreak having occurred while she was in dock in Antwerp undergoing a refit. The fire started in her saloon and spread to the rest of the cabin accommodation. She sank alongside the quay with her keel resting on the bottom. The *Grampian* was ultimately

condemned following the underwriter's survey and her wreck was broken up at Hendrik Ido Ambacht, Rotterdam.
Casualties: 1

GREAT REPUBLIC (1866) New York-Pacific Mail Steamship Co, USA

4,750grt; 376ft (114.6m) loa x 48ft (14.6m) beam
1,450 passengers
Henry Steers, Greenpoint, Long Island (Yard No not known)
Vertical beam steam engine, paddles
On 19 April 1879, after arriving at the entrance to the Columbia River at the end of a trans-Pacific voyage from Japan and China carrying almost 600 passengers, the large paddle steamer *Great Republic* ran hard aground on Sand Island. It was decided that she should be abandoned although there seemed to be no immediate danger and consequently her lifeboats were launched. During the evacuation operation, one boat capsized, drowning its occupants, but all the other persons aboard the *Great Republic* were landed safely. The accident occurred in calm weather and had it remained so the *Great Republic* might have been saved, but within days, as the wind freshened and the sea became rougher, she began to break up. The *Great Republic* was the first ship to inaugurate a regular trans-Pacific service between the US west coast and Asia.
Casualties: 14 (all crew)

GRECIA EXPRESS (1966) ex-*Norwind* (1987) Strive Shipping Corporation, Greece

4,111grt; 357ft (108.8m) loa x 62ft (19.0m) beam
187 berthed and 48 deck passengers
Weser Seebeck, Bremerhaven (Yard No 899)
Motor-ship, twin screw

The *Grecia Express* was originally the British ro-ro ferry *Norwind*. Her sister was the *Italia Express* (the former *Norwave*), which was deliberately mined in March 1988.
Frank Heine FERRIES

The ro-ro passenger ferry *Grecia Express* had been moored for the winter at the Greek port of Aegion (Aegio or Aiyio), on the southern shore of the Gulf of Corinth, since 20 January 1994. She was lost overnight on 4-5 March 1994 when she heeled over and sank on her starboard side in shallow water in the position 38.15N, 22.06E, the cause unknown. The insurers rejected the claim on the lost vessel, alleging that the owners had been complicit in the sinking, by assisting those

who were responsible. In the court case that followed it was stated that a person unknown had cut the vessel's mooring ropes and opened one of the four seawater drencher valves located in the vessel's auxiliary engine room. As a result the vessel had flooded, causing her to capsize. The sole watchman had not been on board during the night, in dereliction of his duty, but had spent the time ashore with a female friend. The insurers asserted that they were not liable for a loss attributable to the wilful misconduct of the insured, but the court, having no hesitation in clearing the vessel's owners of any involvement in the loss, found against them. After she was refloated, inspection revealed that she could not be economically restored and the *Grecia Express*, accepted as a constructive total loss, was consequently sold for breaking up at Aliaga, where she arrived on 6 June 1995.
Casualties: 0

GRECIAN (1880) Allan Line, UK

3,613grt; 366ft (111.6m) lbp x 40ft (12.2m) beam
820 passengers in two classes
William Doxford, Pallion, Sunderland (Yard No 116)
Compound-expansion steam reciprocating, single screw
While bound from Halifax, Nova Scotia, to Liverpool on 9 February 1902, the passenger steamship *Grecian* was wrecked at Sandwich Point, seven miles south-east of Halifax, Nova Scotia.
Casualties: 0

GREGOR (1895) ex-*Bonn* (1913) Jebsen Diederichsen, Germany

3,969grt; 355ft (108.2m) lbp x 44ft (13.3m) beam
1,063 passengers in two classes
Krupp Germania, Kiel (Yard No 65)
Triple-expansion steam reciprocating, single screw
The former Norddeutscher Lloyd passenger and emigrant steamer *Gregor* was seized by the Russians at Odessa in 1914. Six years later, on 11 February 1920, her ownership apparently changed, she was being towed from Odessa to an unknown destination, probably Istanbul, when she broke free in rough weather. She became stranded in the Black Sea, nine miles west of the entrance to the Bosporus. A large party of British refugees from the civil war in Russia, about 200 in number, was aboard the *Gregor* at the time, but the majority were taken off without mishap.
Casualties: not known

GRUZIA [GRUZIJA] (1928) Black Sea Shipping Co (Sovtorgflot), USSR

5,008grt; 380ft (115.9m) lbp x 51ft (15.6m) beam
450 passengers in single class
Friedrich Krupp AG, Kiel (Yard No 493)
Motor-ship, twin screw
The Russian passenger ship *Gruzia*, the second of a class of six ships built in Germany and at Leningrad, was lost near Sevastopol on 13 June 1942. Some reports say she was torpedoed and sunk by an Italian motor torpedo boat, but Russian accounts state that she was, in fact, hit by bombs from German aircraft in two attacks. She was carrying around 4,000 Soviet troops and a considerable quantity of ammunition. After the first attack, though heavily damaged,

she attempted to return to Sevastopol escorted by a destroyer. Near the harbour entrance she was sunk after further bomb hits detonated the ammunition in the forward hold. It is claimed that the majority of the soldiers and most of her crew were killed, so violent were the explosions. When she was raised in 1949, the salvors found a large quantity of unexploded gas shells and bombs in the stern hold and, because they were judged to be extremely dangerous and unstable, the vessel was allowed to settle once more on the seabed. In 1956 Soviet salvors, under instructions to gather the suspect ordinance for its contents to be used in chemical weapons, attempted again to raise the *Gruzia*. However, she broke in two and once more sank to the floor of the Black Sea, her deadly cargo still within her.

Casualties: not known

The Soviet passenger ferry *Gruzia* [*Gruzija*] was engaged on the Black Sea service from Odessa. The loss of her sister ship *Armenia*, of which there are few, if any, photographs, was the worst disaster to befall a Russian passenger ship and it ranks with that of the *Wilhelm Gustloff* for the number of persons killed. *Infoflot*

GUADELOUPE (1907) ex-*Pointe a Pitre* (launch name, 15 December 1906) Compagnie Générale Transatlantique (French Line), France

6,600grt; 433ft (132.0m) lbp x 52ft (15.9m) beam
243 passengers in three classes
Chantiers de L'Atlantique, St Nazaire (Yard No G47)
Triple-expansion steam reciprocating, twin screw
While homeward bound to Bordeaux from Buenos Aires and Rio de Janeiro on 22 February 1915, the liner *Guadeloupe* was intercepted and captured by the German auxiliary cruiser *Kronprinz Wilhelm* some 300 miles south-east of Fernando de Noronha, Brazil, in the position 05.58S, 27.27W. The raider retained the *Guadeloupe* for two weeks, consuming her stores. Then, on 9 March 1915, her occupants, of whom 143 were passengers and 151 members of her crew, not including the officers, were transferred to the British collier *Chasehill*, another captured vessel, and the *Guadeloupe* was sunk in the approximate position 07.00S, 26.00W. The *Chasehill* made for Pernambuco, Brazil, where she arrived on 12 March.

Casualties: 0

GUILDFORD CASTLE (1911) Union-Castle Line, UK

7,995grt; 452ft (137.8m) lbp x 56ft (17.1m) beam
300 passengers in three classes
Barclay Curle, Whiteinch, Glasgow (Yard No 488)
Quadruple-expansion steam reciprocating, twin screw
On 30 May 1933 the passenger-cargo ship *Guildford Castle* was in collision in foggy conditions with the Blue Funnel Line motor-vessel *Stentor* near Oste Riff, in the River Elbe. The *Guildford Castle* was bound from Hamburg to London with 31 passengers and 60 crew while the *Stentor* was heading upriver to Cuxhaven. The latter received only bow damage and remained afloat, assisted under tow by two tugs, but the less fortunate *Guildford Castle* was beached with extensive damage. Her passengers were all safely transferred to the *Stentor* and subsequently landed at Cuxhaven, from where they were taken to Southampton aboard the Hamburg Amerika liner *New York*. The salvage tug *Seefalke* was sent to the assistance of the crippled *Guildford Castle* but she sank in the fairway the following day and broke up where she lay.

Casualties: 3 (all crew, including 2 deck boys)

The Union-Castle intermediate passenger ship *Guildford Castle* at Cape Town. *David Reed*

HABANA (1923) ex-*Alfonso XIII* (1931) Cia Transatlantica, Spain

10,551grt; 500ft (152.4m) loa x 61ft (18.6m) beam
1,100 passengers in three classes
Soc Española de Construccion Naval, Bilbao (Yard No 1)
Steam turbines, twin screw
The passenger-cargo liner *Habana* was laid up at Bordeaux in July 1936 due to the Spanish Civil War and, almost three years later, she was laid up again at Bilbao because of the Second World War. While laid up on this second occasion, she was gutted by a fire that left her really fit only for scrap. Even so, she was repaired and refitted as a cargo ship, returning to service in May 1943. After the Second World War some of her passenger cabins were restored, for around 100 passengers, and she continued in that configuration until 1962 when she was sold for conversion into a refrigerated fish factory ship. Earlier in her life, under her original name, she had caught fire while fitting out, on 26 October 1920, delaying her entry into service by nearly three years.
Casualties: not known

HAKONE MARU (1921) Nippon Yusen Kaisha, Japan

10,420grt; 520ft (158.5m) loa x 62ft (18.9m) beam
305 passengers in three classes
Mitsubishi, Nagasaki (Yard No 346)
Steam turbines, twin screw
The passenger-cargo ship *Hakone Maru* was bombed by aircraft of the United States Army Air Force on 27 November 1943 as she was passing through the Formosa Strait. She sank in the position 25.04N, 119.40E.
Casualties: not known

The *Hakone Maru* was the first unit of Nippon Yusen Kaisha's 'H' class, which sailed on the Yokohama to Hamburg service via the Suez Canal. The others were the *Haruna Maru*, *Hakozaki Maru* and *Hakusan Maru*. *Maritime Photo Library*

HAKOZAKI MARU (1922) Nippon Yusen Kaisha, Japan

10,413grt; 520ft (158.5m) loa x 62ft (18.9m) beam
305 passengers in three classes
Mitsubishi, Nagasaki (Yard No 348)
Steam turbines, twin screw
Converted into a naval troop transport in 1940, the passenger-cargo ship *Hakozaki Maru* was sunk in the East China Sea, in

the position 33.09N, 122.08E, on 19 March 1945. She was torpedoed by the American submarine USS *Balao*.
Casualties: not known

HAKUSAN MARU (1923) Nippon Yusen Kaisha, Japan

10,380grt; 520ft (158.5m) loa x 62ft (18.9m) beam
305 passengers in three classes
Mitsubishi, Nagasaki (Yard No 383)
Steam turbines, twin screw
Taken over as a troop transport with the Imperial Japanese Navy, the *Hakusan Maru* became a torpedo victim on 4 June 1944, when she was sunk by the American submarine USS *Flier*. She was attacked 400 miles south-west of Iwojima, in the position 22.55N, 136.44E.
Casualties: not known

HAMBURG (1926) Hamburg Amerika Line, Germany

22,117grt; 677ft (206.5m) loa x 73ft (22.1m) beam
950 passengers in three classes
Blohm & Voss, Steinwerder, Hamburg (Yard No 473)
Steam turbines, twin screw
The transatlantic liner *Hamburg* had been engaged as a refugee ship assisting in the evacuation of Germany's eastern territories when she was sunk on 7 March 1945. Having disembarked her passengers at Sassnitz, part of a total of 23,000 that she had conveyed westwards over several voyages, she struck two mines while being towed to an anchorage. Severely damaged, she sank and remained so until 1950 when she was raised by Soviet salvors. She was taken in hand for reconstruction as a passenger liner along the lines of her former sister *Hansa*, which became the *Sovietski Sojuz*. Renamed *Yuri Dolgorukiy*, this work was nearing completion when the plans were altered and she was converted instead into a whaling mother ship based at Kaliningrad. Casualties: not known

The '*Albert Ballin*' class transatlantic passenger liner *Hamburg* was mined and abandoned off Sassnitz in March 1945. Raised by Soviet salvors in 1950, she was taken in hand for reconstruction for passenger service, but when the plans were revised she emerged as the whale factory ship *Yuri Dolgorukiy*. *Edward Wilson*

HAMMONIA (1909) ex-*Hollandia* (1922) Hamburg Amerika Line, Germany

7,291grt; 419ft (127.9m) lbp x 54ft (16.5m) beam
1,207 passengers in three classes
Alexander Stephen, Linthouse, Glasgow (Yard No 430)
Triple-expansion steam reciprocating, twin screw

While bound for Puerto Mexico (Coatzacoalcos), Gulf of Campech, from Hamburg and Vigo, with passengers and a general cargo, the passenger-cargo ship *Hammonia* struck submerged rocks 75 miles west of Vigo, off the Portuguese coast, in the position 41.55N, 10.50W, on 9 September 1922. She foundered the next day but not before her passengers and crew had been picked up by the British cargo ship *Soldier Prince* and the Union-Castle liner *Kinfauns Castle*.
Casualties: 0

HAMONIC (1909) Canada Steamship Lines, Canada

6,905grt; 362ft (106.6m) lbp x 50ft (15.2m) beam
475 passengers
Collingwood Shipbuilders, Collingwood, Ontario (Yard No 22)
Quadruple-expansion steam reciprocating, single screw
The Great Lakes scheduled service and excursion steamer *Hamonic* was engulfed by fire on 17 July 1945 while tied up alongside a quay at Point Edward, near Sarnia, Ontario. The fire spread to her from the pier where it had started, and the *Hamonic* was completely burned out. Her passengers and crew were rescued a few at a time using a dockside crane. The wreck was sold for scrapping at Windsor, Ontario.
Casualties: 1

One of three similar vessels employed on Lake Ontario by Canada Steamship Lines, the *Hamonic* ran scheduled services and an annual itinerary of excursions.
Bowling Green State University

HANKOW (1874) China Navigation Co (John Swire & Co), UK

3,073grt; 308ft (93.9m) lbp x 42ft (12.8m) beam
Passenger numbers not known
A. & J. Inglis, Pinthouse, Glasgow (Yard No 107)
Compound-expansion steam reciprocating, paddles
The passenger-cargo steamer *Hankow*, which traded on the Chinese coast and along the large tidal rivers, was berthed at the Canton Steamer Wharf at Hong Kong on 14 October 1906 when she was gutted by fire. The wreck was not cleared but was reduced to a hulk where it lay and was used in this fashion for storage until the late 1930s.
Casualties: 130

HANOVERIAN (1882) Allan Line, UK

3,603grt; 366ft (111.6m) lbp x 41ft (12.5m) beam
820 passengers in two classes
William Doxford, Pallion, Sunderland (Yard No not known)

Compound-expansion steam reciprocating, single screw
The passenger steamship *Hanoverian*, sister ship of the *Grecian* (qv), was lost on 2 September 1885. During a voyage from Baltimore to Liverpool she was wrecked in Trepassey Bay, Newfoundland.
Casualties: 0

HANSA (1923) ex-*Albert Ballin* (1935) Hamburg Amerika Line, Germany

21,131 grt; 677ft (206.3m) loa x 73ft (22.2m) beam
965 passengers in three classes
Blohm & Voss, Steinwerder, Hamburg (Yard No 403)
Steam turbines, twin screw
Having survived more than five years of war as a static German Navy training and accommodation ship, the *Hansa* was reactivated in 1945 to run evacuation voyages from Gotenhafen (Gdynia) to ports in the western Baltic. On 6 March of that year, while underway on such a voyage, the *Hansa* struck a mine off Warnemunde. Her refugees took to the boats and an attempt was made to tow the ship to port but she sank in shallow water. There she remained for the next four years, already badly damaged but slowly deteriorating until, in 1949, Soviet salvors raised her. After she was patched up locally, she was sent to Antwerp for reconstruction into the Russian-flag passenger ship *Sovietski Sojuz* for service on the Vladivostok to Kamchatka route. Delayed by an explosion and fire while in the shipyard, she finally re-entered service in September 1955.
Casualties: not known

Sunk by mine at Warnemunde in 1945 and virtually written off, the Hamburg Amerika Line ship *Hansa* was salvaged by the Soviets and re-entered passenger service as the *Sovietski Sojuz* operating on Russia's Pacific coast, based at Vladivostok.
World Ship Society

HANSEATIC (1930) ex-*Scotland* (1958) ex-*Empress of Scotland* (1958) ex-*Empress of Japan* (1942) Hamburg Atlantik Line, Germany

30,030grt; 673ft (205.2m) loa x 84ft (25.5m) beam
1,252 passengers in two classes
Fairfield, Govan (Yard No 634)
Steam turbines, twin screw
While she was berthed at pier 84, New York, on 7 September 1966, the passenger liner *Hanseatic* was badly damaged by a fire that originated in her engine room, precipitated when leaking fuel ignited on contact with the engines. The fire engulfed both engine rooms and spread upward through five of the accommodation decks. Only three of her 425 booked passengers were on board and they were evacuated together

with the crew. After the fire was extinguished and the damage assessed at a Brooklyn shipyard, the *Hanseatic* was towed empty back to Hamburg by the Bugsier tugs *Atlantic* and *Pacific*. It was considered that repairs could have been effected, although smoke had permeated throughout the entire ship. In the final analysis, it was determined that the huge expense involved, relative to the ship's value, could not be justified and instead, as a constructive total loss, she was sold for breaking up locally in December 1966.
Casualties: 0

The *Hanseatic* was a striking ship, both as rebuilt and re-sculptured for the Hamburg Atlantik Line and in her original form as Canadian Pacific's *Empress of Japan*. *Mick Lindsay*

HARUNA MARU (1922) Nippon Yusen Kaisha, Japan

10,421grt; 520ft (158.5m) loa x 62ft (18.9m) beam
309 passengers in three class
Mitsubishi, Nagasaki (Yard No 347)
Steam turbines, twin screw
The passenger-cargo ship *Haruna Maru*, which had been engaged by the Japanese Government for military duties for the duration of the Second World War, was stranded on the coast of Suruga Wan, fifty or so miles south-west of Yokohama, on 7 July 1942, where she became a total loss. The stated position of the wreck, at 34.36N, 138.06E, has to be treated with caution because it in fact places her south of Suruga Wan, in open seas, suggesting that the *Haruna Maru* foundered rather than was stranded.
Casualties: not known

Another of Nippon Yusen Kaisha's 'H' class of European-service steamships was the *Haruna Maru*. *Nippon Yusen Kaisha*

HAWAII MARU (1915) Osaka Shosen Kaisha, Japan

9,482grt; 475ft (144.8m) lbp x 61ft (18.6m) beam
167 passengers in two classes
Kawasaki, Kobe (Yard No 374)
Triple-expansion steam reciprocating, twin screw

Requisitioned for war duties in December 1941, the passenger-cargo ship *Hawaii Maru* was torpedoed and sunk by the American submarine USS *Sea Devil* on 2 December 1944. At the time she was about 150 miles south-west of Kagoshima, Japan, in the position 30.51N, 128.45E.
Casualties: not known

HECTOR (1924) Blue Funnel Line, UK

11,198grt; 530ft (161.5m) loa x 62ft (18.9m) beam
175 passengers in single class (as built)
Scott's, Greenock (Yard No 521)
Steam turbines, twin screw
Requisitioned early in the Second World War for service as an armed merchant cruiser, the *Hector* operated initially in home waters but was transferred to the Indian Ocean after Japan entered the conflict in December 1941. She was in the harbour at Colombo, Ceylon (Sri Lanka), on 5 April 1942 when it was attacked by Japanese aircraft from a carrier task force. She was hit by several bombs, caught fire and sank. In 1946 her wreck was raised and beached at Uswetakeiyawa, five miles to the north of Colombo, prior to being broken up on the spot. Casualties: not known

HEIAN MARU (1930) Nippon Yusen Kaisha, Japan

11,616grt; 536ft (163.4m) loa x 66ft (20.1m) beam
330 passengers in three classes
Osaka Iron Works, Sakurajima, Osaka (Yard No 1128)
Motor-ship, twin screw
On 15 December 1941 the Imperial Japanese Navy requisitioned the passenger-cargo liner *Heian Maru* for conversion into a submarine tender. She was sunk on 17 February 1944 near the island of Truk in the Caroline Islands, in the position 07.35N, 151.51E, attacked and bombed by warplanes from American aircraft carriers.
Casualties: not known

The motor-vessel *Heian Maru* entered the Hong Kong and Kobe to Seattle service in 1930, joining two sister ships. She also called at ports on the Pacific coast of South America. *Nippon Yusen Kaisha*

HEIYO MARU (1930) Nippon Yusen Kaisha, Japan;

9,816grt; 460ft (140.2m) lbp x 60ft (18.3m) beam
175 passengers in three classes
Osaka Iron Works, Sakurajima, Osaka (Yard No 1127)
Motor-ship, single screw

Taken over for military purposes when war broke out between Japan and America, the passenger-cargo ship *Heiyo Maru* was torpedoed near the Marshall Islands on 17 January 1943 by the American submarine USS *Whale*. She sank in the position 10.10N, 151.25E.
Casualties: not known

HELEANNA (1954) ex-*Munkedal* (1966)
C. S. Efthymiadis, Greece

11,674grt; 549ft (167.4m) loa x 66ft (20.2m) beam
620 passengers in a single class
Gotaverken, Gothenburg (Yard No 679)
Motor-ship, single screw

The passenger-vehicle ferry *Heleanna* had started life as an oil tanker, converted for her new role in 1966. On 28 August 1971, when she was off the Italian port of Brindisi, fire broke out in the galley caused by an electrical fault. The ship was overcrowded, there being 1,128 persons on board, well in excess of her certificated number. Panic broke out and evacuation of the burning ship was badly organised. The survivors were picked up by fishing boats and other small ships in the vicinity. The wrecked *Heleanna* was sold for breaking up at La Spezia, where she arrived on 16 February 1974, but instead she was re-sold for conversion into a dumb lighter for use in the port of Toulon.
Casualties: 26

The doomed passenger ferry **Heleanna** was originally the oil tanker **Munkedal**, as revealed by her overall appearance.
Bettina Rohbrecht

HELGOLAND (1939) Hamburg Amerika Line, Germany

2,947grt; 370ft (112.8m) loa x 43ft (13.2m) beam
1,200 passengers
P. Lindenau, Memel, Stettin (Szczecin) (Yard No 72)
Turbo-electric, twin Voith Schneider vertical blade propulsion units

The passenger ship *Helgoland*, built for the pre-war Hamburg to Heligoland service, survived the Second World War and was ceded to Great Britain as a war reparation. However, she remained at Hamburg, being later moved to Cuxhaven. At the latter port, on 18 March 1946, she caught fire and was completely burned out. A survey in 1947 deemed that she was beyond economic repair, so it was decided to scuttle her wreck in the Skagerrak after quantities of seized gas and chemical ammunition had been stowed aboard her. As part of a major weapons disposal programme, this took place in 1948, the exact date unknown, together with a large number of other enemy and redundant Allied ships. The precise location of the *Helgoland*'s wreck is not known, but the ships

were scuttled off the Norwegian coast in an allocated dumping ground fourteen by four kilometres in area, 25 miles south-east of Arendal, in the position 58.18N, 09.38E. Recent surveys have shown that the canisters and shell casings are now in an advanced state of corrosion and that there is the looming threat of an environmental disaster.
Casualties: not known (for fire), 0 (when scuttled)

HELOUAN (1912) Lloyd Triestino, Italy

7,367grt 442ft (135.0m) lbp x 53ft (16.2m) beam
300 passengers
Lloyd Austriaco, Trieste (Yard No 126)
Quadruple-expansion steam reciprocating, twin screw

The passenger-cargo ship *Helouan* was destroyed by fire at Naples on 12 August 1937 while engaged as a hospital ship for the Italian Navy. The fire broke out in her medicine store, adjacent to the operating theatre, possibly through an electrical short-circuit. The *Helouan* was lying at anchor within the harbour and, because of the danger she posed, all access to the port was denied to other shipping. Her entire crew jumped overboard and all safely reached the shore. Attempts to extinguish the fire were in vain and as soon as she could be approached the *Helouan* was towed to the outer harbour where she was scuttled. Any hope of saving her was abandoned.
Casualties: 0

HERAKLION (1949) ex-*Leicestershire* (1965)
Typaldos Lines, Greece

8,922grt; 498ft (151.8m) loa x 60ft (18.4m) beam
300 passengers in single class
Fairfield, Govan (Yard No 745)
Steam turbine, single screw

The former Bibby Line **Leicestershire** was converted into the Greek inter-island ferry **Heraklion** (sometimes rendered as **Iraklion**) in 1965. *World Ship Society*

Converted into a vehicle-passenger ferry, the *Heraklion* (sometimes rendered *Iraklion*, but not so spelled on the ship itself) was lost on 8 December 1966 when she foundered in a storm during a voyage from Crete to Piraeus. Aboard her at the time were 194 passengers, around 100 Greek Navy recruits and a crew of 70. After water entered her open vehicle deck through the failed forward starboard-side loading door, smashed open by a poorly secured truck that had broken free in the heavy seas, she capsized and sank with great rapidity, preventing many of those aboard her from escaping. She went down in the position 36.52N, 24.08E, near

Falconcra, in the Cyclades Islands. Despite an urgent response to her calls for assistance, nothing remained of the *Heraklion* when rescue ships arrived on the scene.
Casualties: 217

HERALD OF FREE ENTERPRISE (1980) P&O European Ferries, UK

7,951grt; 433ft (131.9m) loa x 76ft (23.2m) beam
1,350 passengers
Schichau Unterweser, Bremerhaven (Yard No 2280)
Motor-ship, twin screw

The loss of the North Sea ferry *Herald of Free Enterprise*, one of a class of three ships, was the worst British shipping disaster since the *Princess Victoria* foundered in January 1953.
Both: Leo van Ginderen

Salvage work under way on the capsized *Herald of Free Enterprise* near the entrance to Zeebrugge harbour.
Leo van Ginderen

The ro-ro passenger ferry *Herald of Free Enterprise* was lost on 6 March 1987. She capsized while departing Zeebrugge, bound for Dover, when her car deck was flooded by ingress of water through her open bow doors, rapidly destabilising her. The doors had not been closed and secured prior to sailing. She had aboard her 459 passengers and 80 crew, of whom around 346 were rescued. The Department of the Environment subsequently revealed that trucks aboard the ship had been carrying cyanide and other poisonous chemicals. The *Herald of Free Enterprise* sank in the outer harbour in the position 51.23N, 03.11E. Raised that year, she was renamed *Flushing Grange* but only for the delivery voyage to ship-breakers at Kaohsiung, where she arrived on 22 March 1988. It was a matter of great concern that a British shipping operator had maintained such unreliable manifest data that it took a long time to determine the actual number of casualties in the sinking; the establishment of a final figure came to depend on the recovery of bodies from the wreck during the salvage operation.
Casualties: 193 (the figure issued by the Marine Accident Investigation Branch of the Department of Transport in 'Report of Court No 8074', although it was qualified by the statement 'not less than 150 passengers and 38 members of the crew lost their lives'.)

HERDER (1873) Hamburg Amerika Line, Germany

3,494grt; 375ft (114.3m) lbp x 40ft (12.2m) beam
990 passengers
Alexander Stephen, Linthouse, Glasgow (Yard No 169)
Compound-expansion steam reciprocating, single screw
The passenger steamship *Herder* was wrecked off Cape Race, Newfoundland, on 10 October 1882. She had been on passage from New York to Hamburg.
Casualties: 0

HERMES (1915) ex-*Jupiter* (1955) Epirotiki Lines, Greece (G. Potamianos)

2,557grt; 321ft (97.8m) loa x 42ft (12.7m) beam
225 passengers
Lindholmens MV, Gothenburg (Yard No 423)
Triple-expansion steam reciprocating, single screw
Converted into a cruise ship from a former Bergen Line Newcastle-service ferry by enclosing her fore and aft 'tween deck spaces to provide increased accommodation, the *Hermes* survived until 4 March 1960 when she was lost by fire during repairs at Piraeus. She was beached on Salamis Island, refloated four days later when the fire had subsided, and was then towed to Perama where a survey revealed her to be a constructive total loss. She was sold for breaking up at Split, in Yugoslavia.
Casualties: not known

HESPERIAN (1908) Allan Line, UK

10,920grt; 502ft (153.0m) loa x 60ft (18.3m) beam
1,460 passengers in three classes
Alexander Stephen, Glasgow (Yard No 425)
Triple-expansion steam reciprocating, twin screw
The *Hesperian* was bound for Montreal with 653 passengers and crew when she was torpedoed on 4 September 1915 by the German submarine U20, some 85 miles south-west-by-

south of Fastnet, in the position 50.03N, 10.10W. The *Hesperian* did not sink immediately and was taken in tow for Queenstown (Cobh) by warships that had gone to her aid. After a distance of approximately forty miles, she began to settle and the volunteer skeleton crew that had remained on board was forced to abandon her. Meanwhile, the other survivors of the stricken vessel, who had taken to the boats, were safely picked up. The *Hesperian* finally sank about 130 miles west of Malin Head, Donegal.
Casualties: 32

HIGHLAND BRAE (1910) Nelson Line, GB

7,634grt; 413ft (125.9m) lbp x 56ft (17.1m) beam
516 passengers in three classes
Cammell Laird, Birkenhead (Yard No 765)
Triple-expansion steam reciprocating, single screw
The passenger steamship *Highland Brae* was captured on 14 January 1915 by the German auxiliary cruiser (and former liner) *Kronprinz Wilhelm* while bound from London to Buenos Aires with passengers. She was retained for two weeks as a source of stores and as accommodation both for her own complement and for other prisoners captured on earlier victim ships. Finally, on 31 January, the *Highland Brae* was scuttled and sunk 630 miles north of Recife in the position 02.46N, 24.11W.
Casualties: 0

The Nelson Line steamship *Highland Brae* was a victim of one of Germany's commerce raiders that were deployed so effectively in the early part of the First World War.
Furness Withy Group

HIGHLAND CORRIE (1910) Nelson Line, UK

7,583grt; 414ft (126.2m) lbp x 56ft (17.1m) beam
520 passengers in two classes
Russell, Port Glasgow (Yard No 614)
Triple-expansion steam reciprocating, single screw
The passenger-cargo ship *Highland Corrie* was heading for London on 16 May 1917, at the end of a voyage from South America with a small passenger complement but a valuable cargo of frozen meat, when she was torpedoed by the German submarine UB40 in the English Channel. The attack took place four miles south of the Owers light vessel, off Selsey Bill, and she sank in the position 50.28N, 00.38W.
Casualties: 5 (all crew)

HIGHLAND HOPE (1930) Nelson Line, UK

14,129grt; 544ft (165.8m) loa x 69ft (21.2m) beam
701 passengers in three classes
Harland & Wolff, Govan (Yard No 813g)
Motor-ship, twin screw
When less than a year old, the passenger-cargo liner *Highland Hope*, the third ship of her class, ran onto one of the North East Farilhoes rocks, near Peniche on the Portuguese coast, in dense fog on 19 November 1930. She was outward bound at the time of the incident, carrying some 370 passengers in addition to her crew of 139, heading for Lisbon, having already made calls at Boulogne and Vigo. Many of the passengers were Spanish emigrants. Although the *Highland Hope* was irretrievably impaled on the rocks, the greater part of her hull having run over them, she was still partially afloat and moving in the swell. The passengers and crew took to the boats in good order and abandoned the ship. It was during the evacuation that the only casualty of the episode was sustained. In attempting to jump from the boat deck into a lifeboat, one emigrant passenger was critically injured and died in hospital the following day. The deserted *Highland Hope* was later reboarded by Portuguese fishermen who proceeded to loot the ship, but they were driven off by the salvage ship *Patrao Lopez*. With no hope of salvaging the *Highland Hope* intact, she was broken up.
Casualties: 1

HIGHLAND PATRIOT (1932) Royal Mail Line, UK

14,172grt; 544ft (165.8m) loa x 69ft (21.0m) beam
701 passengers in three classes
Harland & Wolff, Belfast (Yard No 916)
Motor-ship, twin screw
The *Highland Patriot* was returning to Glasgow from South America on 1 October 1940 when she was torpedoed by the German submarine U38 about 500 miles west of the Bishop Rock. She sank in the position 52.20N, 19.04W. At the time of the attack, the *Highland Patriot* was not carrying passengers, only her crew of 143 men. Casualties: 3

The *Highland Patriot* was the last of six motor passenger ships originally ordered by the Nelson Line for the service from London to Buenos Aires. *Real Photos*

HIGHLAND PRIDE (1910) Nelson Line, UK

7,469grt; 405ft (123.4m) lbp x 56ft (17.1m) beam
520 passengers in three classes
Russell, Port Glasgow (Yard No 602)
Triple-expansion steam reciprocating, single screw

The passenger-cargo ship *Highland Pride* left London bound for Buenos Aires in September 1929, carrying 63 passengers and 89 crew. After leaving Vigo, north Spain, she struck Roca Negra in the Carallones, a rocky outcrop off the Cies Islands in the approaches to Vigo, in the early hours of 9 September. At the time the visibility was poor with widespread mist and heavy rain. When it was appreciated that the ship was beyond recovery she was abandoned, the evacuation operation passing without accident thanks to the disciplined behaviour of all aboard. The survivors were taken to the fishing village of Bayone. Though she was on an even keel, the *Highland Pride* was flooded and submerged at the fore end with her stern out of the water. On 10 September she broke in two and the after section sank.
Casualties: 0

HIGHLAND SCOT (1910) Nelson Line, UK

7,604grt; 414ft (126.2m) lbp x 56ft (17.1m) beam
520 passengers in three classes
Russell, Port Glasgow (Yard No 615)
Triple-expansion steam reciprocating, single screw
The passenger-cargo ship *Highland Scot* was lost on 6 May 1918 while bound from Buenos Aires to Rio de Janeiro, on a return voyage to the United Kingdom. She was stranded on Maricas Island, Brazil, and became a total loss.
Casualties: not known

HIGHLAND WARRIOR (1911) Nelson Line, UK

7,485grt; 414ft (126.2m) lbp x 56ft (17.2m) beam
520 passengers in three classes
Russell, Port Glasgow (Yard No 622)
Triple-expansion steam reciprocating, single screw
While on a voyage from London to Buenos Aires via Corunna, on 3 October 1915, the passenger-cargo ship *Highland Warrior* ran ashore at Cape Prior, northern Spain, and became a total loss.
Casualties: 0

HILARY (1908) Booth Line, UK

6,329grt; 433ft (132.0m) loa x 52ft (15.9m) beam
582 passengers in two classes
Caledon, Dundee (Yard No 200)
Triple-expansion steam reciprocating, twin screw
The passenger ship *Hilary* was sunk within months of her two sisters, *Antony* and *Lanfranc*. The *Hilary* was taken up as an armed merchant cruiser attached to the 10th Cruiser Squadron and in this capacity she was sunk on 25 May 1917, torpedoed by the German submarine U88 while she was patrolling west of the Shetland Islands. She sank in the position 60.33N, 03.00W.
Casualties: 4

HILDEBRAND (1951) Booth Line, UK

7,735grt; 439ft (133.8m) loa x 60ft (18.4m) beam
170 passengers
Cammell Laird, Birkenhead (Yard No 1213)
Steam turbines, single screw
The passenger-cargo steamship *Hildebrand* became a stranding loss in only her sixth season when, in dense fog,

while bound from Liverpool to the River Amazon, she ran onto rocks off the Portuguese coast, at Cascaes Point, outside Lisbon, on 25 September 1957. Salvage operations were instigated in a bid to recover the ship, but by December of the following year they were abandoned when no progress was made, by which time the *Hildebrand* had broken her back and become a complete wreck.
Casualties: 0

HINDOSTAN (1869) P&O Line, UK

3,113 grt; 354ft (107.8m) lbp x 43ft (13.1m) beam
227 passengers in two classes
Day Summers, Northam, Southampton (Yard No 29)
Compound-expansion steam reciprocating, single screw
While serving on the Venice to India route via the Suez Canal, the passenger-cargo ship *Hindostan* ran onto a reef, forty miles south of Madras, on 21 October 1879. She was totally wrecked.
Casualties: not known

HIRAN MARU (1924) Department of Communications & Railways, Government of Japan

3,459 grt; 350ft (106.7m) lbp x 52ft (15.9m) beam
passenger numbers not known
Uraga Dock, Uraga (Yard No 201)
Steam turbines, twin screw
The passenger ferry *Hiran Maru* was one of three sister passenger ferries sunk on the same day while they were serving as wartime transports. They were bombed on 14 July 1945 by US carrier-based aircraft while they were steaming together in Rikuoka Bay on the western coast of Honshu and to the south of the Tsugaru Strait. The other two were the *Shoho Maru* and *Tsugaru Maru*. The *Hiran Maru* sank in the position 40.51N, 140.45E and the *Shoho Maru* in the position 40.51N, 140.47E, both near Noshiro. The *Tsugaru Maru* sank in the position 41.17N, 140.32E.
Casualties: not known for any of the three ships

HIRANO MARU (1908) Nippon Yusen Kaisha, Japan

8,520grt; 474ft (144.5m) lbp x 54ft (16.5m) beam
265 passengers in three classes
Mitsubishi, Nagasaki (Yard No 196)
Triple-expansion steam reciprocating, twin screw
After the outbreak of the First World War, the passenger-cargo ship *Hirano Maru* continued to make commercial sailings on the route from Japan to the UK and Europe. On 4 October 1918, while on the return voyage from Liverpool to Yokohama carrying a total complement of some 320 persons, she was torpedoed and sunk 200 miles south of the Irish coast by the German submarine UB91. At the time of the attack the weather conditions were severe, with strong winds and a rough sea, which hampered the efforts to lower the boats. Furthermore, the *Hirano Maru* was taking water fast, having been hit by two torpedoes, the second in her boiler room. With such severe damage she did not remain afloat for long and after just seven minutes she had disappeared, sinking bow-first and plunging almost vertically. It was impossible, in these circumstances, for many of her occupants to make good their escape and there was heavy loss of life. An American destroyer picked up the few survivors, only eleven of whom

were passengers. The loss of the *Hirano Maru* was the most serious disaster involving a Japanese merchant ship in the First World War.
Casualties: 292

The *Hirano Maru* was built for the route from Japan to Europe via the Suez Canal, maintaining this service with five sister ships. *Nippon Yusen Kaisha*

HITACHI MARU (1906) Nippon Yusen Kaisha, Japan

6,557grt; 450ft (137.2m) lbp x 50ft (15.2m) beam
160 passengers
Mitsubishi, Nagasaki (Yard No 188)
Triple-expansion steam reciprocating, twin screw
While bound from Yokohama to London, as she was passing the southernmost point of the Maldive Islands on 26 September 1917 the passenger-cargo ship *Hitachi Maru* was observed by the German auxiliary cruiser *Wolf*, which immediately went in pursuit of her. Despite efforts to drive off the raider with her single gun, the Japanese ship was soon overwhelmed by the better-armed *Wolf*. Having already sustained casualties, the *Hitachi Maru* was surrendered by her Master in order to prevent further loss of life. The captured ship and her occupants were taken to a lonely atoll where they remained for a month. During this time her cargo and much of the coal in her stokehold were discharged. After her passengers and crew had been transferred to the *Wolf*, the two ships put to sea again, bound for the Cargados Carajos Islands. The *Hitachi Maru* was eventually scuttled using time bombs on 7 November 1917. Prior to her capture, the ship had managed to transmit calls for help, which were intercepted by the Japanese and French cruisers *Tsushima* and *D'Estrees*. They searched the Indian Ocean at length to find the missing vessel but to no avail; that she had been a victim of the *Wolf* was only revealed later.
Casualties: 15 (including her Master, who jumped to his death over the ship's side)

The large group of liners that included the *Hitachi Maru* was employed initially on the Japan to Europe route, but later they were transferred to the Japan to Seattle service. *Nippon Yusen Kaisha*

An artist's impression showing the *Hitachi Maru* under attack by the raider *Wolf*. *WZ-Bilddienst*

HIYE [HIE] MARU (1930) Nippon Yusen Kaisha, Japan

11,622grt; 536ft (163.4m) loa x 66ft (20.1m) beam
330 passengers in three classes
Yokohama Dock Co, Yokohama (Yard No 178)
Motor-ship, twin screw
In late 1941 the passenger-cargo liner *Hiye Maru* was taken over by the Imperial Japanese Navy and converted into a submarine tender. Later she was modified into a supply ship and deployed carrying vital stores and materials to the outposts of the Japanese Empire. She was torpedoed and sunk on 17 November 1943 by the American submarine USS *Drum*, about 300 miles north-west of New Ireland in the position 01.45N, 148.45E.
Casualties: not known

HOHENZOLLERN (1889) ex-*Kaiser Wilhelm II* (1901) Norddeutscher Lloyd, Germany

6,668grt; 449ft (137.4m) lbp x 52ft (15.7m) beam
1,200 passengers
Stettiner Vulcan, Stettin-Bredow (Yard No 184)
Triple-expansion steam reciprocating, single screw
Having survived a flooding incident at Genoa on 5 June 1893 under her previous name, the passenger steamship *Hohenzollern* was stranded on the coast of Sardinia, at Alghero, on 10 May 1908. She was raised a month later but, fit only for disposal, was taken to Genoa for breaking up.
Casualties: 0

HOKOKU MARU (1940) Osaka Shosen Kaisha, Japan

10,438grt; 537ft (163.7m) loa x 66ft (20.1m) beam
400 passengers in three classes
Tama Zosensho, Tama (Yard No 251)
Motor-ship, twin screw
The passenger-cargo ship *Hokoku Maru* was commissioned as an Imperial Japanese Navy auxiliary cruiser on 10 March 1942. Thereafter she was deployed patrolling the Indian Ocean in partnership with her similarly converted sister ship *Aikoku Maru* (qv). On 11 November, in the position 19.45S, 92.40E, they intercepted the Dutch tanker *Ondina* under escort by the Indian minesweeper *Bengal*. As they closed in on this seemingly vulnerable prey, the Japanese vessels opened fire at a range of 3,500 yards with their 6-inch guns.

Although they were more heavily armed and realistically totally outmatched the *Bengal*, the minesweeper returned fire most effectively, hitting the *Hokoku Maru* repeatedly and causing an explosion that set her on fire. The *Ondina*, which was also armed, also managed to score hits on both Japanese cruisers but she was hit in reply, by both shells and torpedoes, and, after her ammunition had been exhausted, she was abandoned by the surviving members of her crew, some of whom subsequently lost their lives in the boats. In the confusion and smoke of the gunfire, the four ships became separated and, following a second explosion, the *Hokoku Maru* sank in the approximate position 20.00S, 93.00E. Believing that both the *Bengal* and *Ondina* had also been sunk, the *Aikoku Maru* withdrew and sailed away. In fact, both vessels had survived the engagement. The badly damaged *Bengal* limped back to Colombo, while the survivors of the *Ondina*'s crew reboarded her and succeeded in getting the crippled tanker to Fremantle.

Casualties: not known

The sister ships *Hokoku Maru*, shown here, *Aikoku Maru* and *Gokoku Maru* were intended for the Japan to Europe service. *Nippon Yusen Kaisha*

HOMERIC (1931) ex-*Mariposa* (1954) Home Lines, Panama

18,563grt; 641ft (195.5m) loa x 79ft (24.2m) beam
1,243 passengers in two classes
Bethlehem Shipbuilding Corp, Quincy, Massachusetts (Yard No 1440)
Steam turbines, twin screw

The passenger liner *Homeric*, built as the *Mariposa*, operated from Cuxhaven, Southampton and Le Havre to New York or Montreal. She is seen here during an off-peak cruise, an activity she concentrated on from October 1963. *Mick Lindsay*

During a cruise on 1 July 1973, while off Cape May at the entrance to Delaware Bay, fire broke out in the kitchens of the passenger liner *Homeric*. The kitchens and the adjoining dining rooms and passageways in the area of the fire were totally destroyed and much of the vessel was affected by smoke. After returning to New York and disembarking her

passengers – the fire had been contained without the necessity for an evacuation – the *Homeric* sailed for Genoa for a repair assessment. Examination of the damage and the peripheral renovation work that was required indicated that the vessel, more than forty years old, though capable of being restored, was beyond economic repair. Sold to ship-breakers in Taiwan, she arrived at Kaohsiung for breaking up in January 1974.

Casualties: 0

HONG KHENG (1903) ex-*Ling Nam* (1928) ex-*Field Marshall* (1922) ex-*Feldmarschall* (1916) Ho Hong Steamship Co, UK

6,167grt; 416ft (126.7m) lbp x 50ft (15.4m) beam
1,800 deck passengers
Reiherstiegwerft, Hamburg (Yard No 410)
Triple-expansion steam reciprocating, twin screw

The former Deutsche Ost-Afrika Linie steamship *Feldmarschall*, seized by Great Britain during the First World War, made passenger-carrying voyages in Far Eastern waters as the *Hong Kheng* from 1928 until 19 July 1947, when she was lost. She became stranded at Chilang point while bound from Rangoon to Swatow.

Casualties: not known

Earlier in her career, the *Hong Kheng* operated under the name *Field Marshall*, shown here in her First World War dazzle camouflage. *Tom Rayner collection*

HONG MOH (1881) ex-*City of Calcutta* (1902) Ho Hong Steamship Co, UK

3,954grt; 400ft (121.9m) lbp x 42ft (12.8m) beam
Passenger numbers not known
C. Connell, Scotstoun (Yard No 125)
Triple-expansion steam reciprocating, single screw

The passenger ship *Hong Moh* was lost on 3 March 1921 when she was stranded in a storm on the White Rocks, Lamock Island, off Swatow (Shantou, China), during a voyage from Singapore to Amoy (Xiamen) with 1,120 occupants, mainly Chinese. The British warships HMS *Carlisle* and *Foxglove* went to her assistance and were able to rescue many of the *Hong Moh*'s complement, but worsening weather forced them reluctantly to abandon their efforts before the operation was complete. The *Hong Moh* broke in two and sank before it could be resumed. Members of the *Carlisle*'s ship's company exhibited exemplary bravery in their efforts to rescue those trapped aboard the *Hong Moh*. Most notable were the actions of her commander, Captain Edward Evans, who dived into the sea and swam to the wreck to help attach lines and assist survivors to get into a motor-launch and a cutter used to ferry them to safety. In total 221 persons were taken to the *Carlisle*, while 28 were put aboard the *Foxglove*. A merchant ship, the *Shansi*, which also came to the aid of the *Hong Moh*, took off a further 45 survivors. The Board of Trade Silver Medal for Gallantry in Saving Life at Sea was awarded to Captain Evans, and the Bronze Medal was awarded to two of his ship's complement, a Lieutenant-Commander and a Naval Gunner.

Casualties: 862

HORAI MARU (1912) ex-*Pays de Waes* (1923) ex-*Indarro* (1920) Osaka Shosen Kaisha, Japan

9,204grt; 451ft (137.5m) lbp x 60ft (18.3m) beam
843 passengers in three classes
William Denny, Dumbarton (Yard No 966)
Quadruple-expansion steam reciprocating, twin screw
The passenger-cargo ship *Horai Maru* was sunk on 1 March 1942 through a combination of aircraft bombs and gunfire from Allied warships as she was making her way through the Sunda Strait, between Sumatra and Java, going down in the position 05.56S, 106.12E. Raised on 10 December 1946, her wreck was beached at Siglap before it was removed completely for breaking up in 1948.

Casualties: not known

HOTEN MARU (1928) Dairen Kisen Kaisha, Japan

3,975grt; 360ft (109.7m) lbp x 46ft (14.0m) beam
Passenger numbers not known
Mitsubishi, Kobe (Yard No 185)
Steam turbines, twin screw
On 18 October 1944 the passenger-cargo ferry *Hoten Maru* was with her sister ship *Tsingtao Maru* (qv), approximately forty miles north of Luzon Island, Philippines, when they were attacked and bombed by US carrier-based aircraft. They sank in the position 18.54N, 121.51E.

Casualties: not known

I

IDAHO (1869) Guion Line, UK

3,132grt; 360ft (109.7m) loa x 43ft (13.1m) beam
About 800 passengers in two classes
Palmers, Jarrow (Yard No 235)
Inverted steam engine, single screw
The passenger steamship *Idaho* was lost on 1 June 1878 when she was wrecked on the coast of county Wexford. At the time she had been bound from New York to Liverpool.

Casualties: 0

IL'ICH (1895) ex-*Veche* (1924) ex-*Imperator Nikolai II* (1917), Sovtorgflot, USSR

4,166grt; 390ft (113.1m) lbp x 45ft (13.7m) beam
Passenger numbers not known
William Denny & Bros, Dumbarton (Yard No 510)
Triple-expansion steam reciprocating, single screw
The Soviet-flag passenger ship *Il'ich* was lost on 24 June 1944 when she capsized in a shipyard at Portland, Oregon, during a refit. As it was not economical to repair her because of her age, she was raised and broken up.

Casualties: not known

ILLIMANI (1873) Pacific Steam Navigation Co, UK

4,022grt; 402ft (122.5m) lbp x 42ft (12.8m) beam
990 passengers in three classes
John Elder, Govan (Yard No 145)
Compound-expansion steam reciprocating, single screw
The passenger-cargo ship *Illimani* was stranded on the Mocha Island, Chile, on 18 July 1879 and was abandoned as a total loss.

Casualties: not known

INCOMATI (1934) Bank Line (Andrew Weir & Co), UK

7,369 grt; 435ft (132.6m) loa x 57ft (17.4m) beam
85 passengers in two classes plus 600 native deck passengers (some sources give figures of 70 + 500)
Workman Clark, Belfast (Yard No 532)
Motor-ship, twin screw
One of three sister-ships built for the India-Natal Line service, the passenger-cargo ship *Incomati* was torpedoed and sunk by the German submarine U508 on 18 July 1943. Bound for Walvis Bay and Durban, while en route from Takoradi, where she had left two days earlier, to the Middle East, she was carrying 112 passengers, eight gunners and a crew of 101 and a general cargo. The torpedo attack left her damaged, whereupon the submarine surfaced and turned its deck gun on the helpless *Incomati*, setting her afire and leaving her in a sinking condition in the position 03.09N, 04.15E. The survivors were rescued by the destroyer HMS *Boadicea* and the naval sloop HMS *Bridgewater* and returned to Takoradi.

Casualties: 1 (a crew member)

INDIA (1896) P&O Line, UK

7,940grt; 500ft (152.4m) lbp x 54ft (16.5m) beam
526 passengers in two classes and/or 2,500 troops
Caird, Greenock (Yard No 281)
Triple-expansion steam reciprocating, single screw
The passenger-cargo steamship *India* was taken over by the Admiralty in August 1914 for service as an auxiliary cruiser attached to the 10th Cruiser Squadron. In this capacity she was torpedoed and sunk by the German submarine U22 off the island of Hellevoer, near Bodo, Norway, in the position 67.30N, 13.20E, on 8 August 1915. At the time she had been stopped, examining a suspected blockade runner. The 141 survivors were taken to Narvik aboard the steamer *Gotaland*.
Casualties: 160

The *India* was the lead ship of a new class for the Indian and Australian services, P&O's largest passenger ships up to that time. *Tom Rayner collection*

INDIANA (1873) Pacific Mail Steamship Co, USA

3,335grt; 357ft (108.8m) lbp x 43ft (13.1m) beam
854 passengers in single class
William Cramp, Chester, Philadelphia (Yard No 182)
Compound steam reciprocating, single screw
The former transatlantic passenger ship *Indiana* survived a stranding at Cape Tosco on Santa Margarita Island, Mexico, on 3 April 1909, only to become a fire loss in Iquique Bay, Chile, in 1918.
Casualties: not known

INDUS (1871) P&O Line, UK

3,462grt; 360ft (109.8m) lbp x 40ft (12.2m) beam
179 passengers in two classes
William Denny, Dumbarton (Yard No 149)
Compound-expansion inverted steam reciprocating, single screw

The *Indus* was a one-off ship, acquired by P&O while still on the stocks and placed on the Bombay service via Suez.
Tom Rayner collection

The passenger-cargo steamship *Indus* entered the Bombay service via Suez in June 1871. Fourteen years later, on 8 November 1885, she was stranded on Muliavattu shoal, sixty miles north of Trincomalee, Sri Lanka, while en route from Calcutta to London, and was totally lost.
Casualties: 0

INNISFALLEN (1930) City of Cork Steam Packet Co, UK

3,071grt; 321ft (97.8m) lbp x 46ft (14.0m) beam
500 passengers
Harland & Wolff, Belfast (Yard No 870)
Motor-ship, twin screw
The Irish Sea ferry *Innisfallen* was lost on 21 December 1940 when she struck an aerially laid magnetic mine off the shore of the Wirral, near New Brighton, as she was leaving Liverpool bound for Cork. Although she was a vessel flying the British flag and her owners were part of the Coast Lines group, which comprised companies whose fleets were engaged in supporting the British war effort, the *Innisfallen* was registered at Cork, a port in a neutral country, and she had not been taken up for war duties. Fortunately no passengers were killed; all 157 were rescued, together with the remainder of her crew.
Casualties: 4 (all crew)

The Irish Sea ferry *Innisfallen*, engaged on the Cork to Liverpool service, was a neutral victim of the Second World War. *H. B. Christiansen Collection / Online Transport Archive*

IOANNINA (1897) ex-*Hittfeld* (1913) ex-*Arkoniya* (1911) ex-*Juliette* (1905) ex-*Dunolly Castle* (1905) National Greek Line, Greece

4,167grt; 368ft (112.2m) lbp x 47ft (14.3m) beam
205 passengers in three classes (as built)
Barclay Curle, Whiteinch, Glasgow (Yard No 407)
Triple-expansion steam reciprocating, single screw
The Greek passenger ship *Ioannina* was intercepted and torpedoed by the German submarine U156 about 150 miles north-west of Madeira, in the Azores, on 15 December 1917 while she was bound for New York from Piraeus. She sank in the position 34.40N, 19.45W.
Casualties: not known

IONIAN (1901) Canadian Pacific Line, UK

8,268 grt; 470ft (143.3m) lbp x 58ft (17.5m) beam
1,092 passengers in three classes
Workman Clark, Belfast (Yard No 177)
Triple-expansion steam reciprocating, twin screw

The passenger-cargo ship *Ionian*, which passed into Canadian Pacific ownership when the Allan Line was absorbed, was lost on 20 October 1917 when she struck a mine laid by the German submarine UC51 in the area to the south of Milford Haven. She had been bound from Liverpool to Plymouth at the time of the incident and her last position was 51.35N, 04.59W, two miles west of St. Govan's Head.
Casualties: 7

IONIAN EXPRESS (1975) ex-*Pegasus* (1994) ex-*Sundancer* (1984) ex-*Svea Corona* (1984) Strintzis Lines Maritime SA, Greece

12,576grt; 502ft (153.1m) loa x 72ft (22.0m) beam
810 passengers
Dubigeon-Normandie SA, Nantes (Yard No 141)
Motor-ship, twin screw
This luckless passenger ship was finally lost as the culmination of a sequence of unfortunate incidents during her career. Having been recovered first after stranding as the *Sundancer*, then after a fire as the *Pegasus* (qv), both of which incidents had resulted in her being declared a constructive total loss, she spent a period of lay-up at Eleusis until she was taken in hand for a refit, destined to emerge in her third cruise ship incarnation as the *Ionian Express*. However, following a second fire that originated in her engine room while in the shipyard at Perama on 20 November 1994, she was finally judged to be beyond economic recovery. She was sold for breaking up at Aliaga where she arrived on 29 March 1995. Casualties: not known

The *Ionian Express* was the renamed *Pegasus*, seen here at Elefsina in July 1992. The damage on her side is from the fire aboard her on 2 June 1991, which left her a constructive total loss. *Frank Heine FERRIES*

IONION (1972) Manis Stathakis & Vassilios Manousas, Greece

3,277grt; 283ft (86.2m) loa x 48ft (14.5m) beam
270 berthed and 600 deck passengers
Hellenic General, Perama (Yard No 1125)
Motor-ship, twin screw
The ro-ro passenger ferry *Ionion* was lost on 6 October 1992. Earlier that year, on 21 April, she had caught fire when five miles off Aegina Island, during a crossing from Kithira to Piraeus. The seventy passengers she was carrying at that time were safely evacuated and the burning ship was towed to Perama. It is not known whether the *Ionion* was then repaired for return to service, but barely five months later she was wrecked near Kastellion, Crete, and abandoned in a semi-submerged condition. The wreck finally sank completely in bad weather on 3 December 1992.
Casualties: not known

ISLA DE PANAY (1882) Cia Trasatlantica Española, Spain

3,545grt; 362ft (110.5m) lbp x 43ft (13.2m) beam
162 passengers in three classes
Scott's, Greenock (Yard No 216)
Triple-expansion steam reciprocating, single screw
On 7 December, while the passenger-cargo steamship *Isla de Panay* was bound from Barcelona to Fernando Po, Equatorial Guinea, she ran onto the Los Primos shoals two miles from the coast, between the islands of San Carlos and Santa Isabel. She became a total wreck.
Casualties: 0

ISTANBUL (1973) Turkiye Denizcilik Isletmeleri, Turkey

3,445grt; 301ft (91.7m) loa x 54ft (16.5m) beam
413 passengers
Denizcilik Bankasi, Camialti (Yard No 181)
Motor-ship, twin screw
The passenger ferry *Istanbul* was lost on 29 May 1992. She caught fire in the Sea of Marmara while bound from Istanbul to Izmir. The outbreak started in her engine room and caused considerable damage. Her passengers were evacuated and she was taken in tow to Tekindag, where a survey concluded that she was a constructive total loss. She was sold to Aliaga breakers where demolition commenced on 30 March 1993.
Casualties: not known

The Turkish ferry *Istanbul* operated via the Sea of Marmara and the Dardanelles to Izmir from Istanbul. *Michael Cassar*

ITALIA (1905) Lloyd Triestino, Italy

5,203grt; 393ft (119.8m) lbp x 47ft (14.3m) beam
550 passengers
N. Odero, Sestri Ponente, Genoa (Yard No 203)
Triple-expansion steam reciprocating, twin screw
The passenger steamship *Italia*, which had been seized by the Germans late in 1943, was sheltering in an inlet west of Brovigne, near Trieste, when she was attacked by British aircraft on 6 July 1944. Hit by rockets, she was shaken by an internal explosion. She caught fire, heeled over and sank. Attempts to salvage her on 18 September 1944 were unsuccessful and the *Italia* was not raised until 1950, only to be broken up.
Casualties: not known

The passenger liner *Italia* served four different Italian shipping lines in her 39-year career: La Veloce, Navigazione Generale Italiana, Soc Italiana di Servizi Marittimi, and Lloyd Triestino. She worked the North and South Atlantic routes.
H. B. Christiansen Collection / Online Transport Archive

ITALIA EXPRESS (1965) ex-*Norwave* (1987) Gitanic Shipping Co (Honduras), Greece

3,540grt; 357ft (108.8m) loa x 63ft (19.3m) beam
187 berthed and 48 deck passengers
Weser Seebeck, Bremerhaven (Yard No 898)
Motor-ship, twin screw
The passenger ro-ro ferry *Italia Express*, owned by members of the Ventouris family – five brothers involved in ferry shipping – was apparently the victim of a terror attack. She was reported to have been blown up by a limpet-mine attached to her hull while she was docked at Drapetzona, near Piraeus, on 24 March 1988. Clearly a deliberate act of terrorism, it was not clear who would have perpetrated such an act in a Greek port and, suspecting fraud, the underwriters challenged the owners' claim on the hull. When the case subsequently went to trial, the court totally vindicated the owners and the *Italia Express* was declared a war constructive total loss. As a matter of interest, a similar dispute arose six years later when the sister of the *Italia Express*, the *Grecia Express* (qv), was lost.
Casualties: not known

IVERNIA (1900) Cunard Line, UK

14,278grt; 600ft (182.9m) loa x 64ft (19.5m) beam
1,964 passengers in three classes
C. S. Swan & Hunter, Wallsend-on-Tyne (Yard No 247)
Quadruple-expansion steam reciprocating, twin screw

Cunard introduced the *Ivernia* and her sister ship *Saxonia* on the Liverpool to Boston service, but they were later switched to the service from Trieste to New York. *World Ship Society*

Commissioned as an auxiliary transport in the First World War, the *Ivernia* was taking 2,400 troops to Alexandria on 1 January 1917 when the German submarine UB47 torpedoed and sank her 58 miles south-by-east of Cape Matapan (Akra Tainaron).
Casualties: 121 (85 military personnel and 36 crew)

IXION (1912) Blue Funnel Line, UK

10,221grt; 518ft (157.9m) loa x 60ft (18.3m) beam
600 passengers in single class
Scott's, Greenock (Yard No 442)
Triple-expansion steam reciprocating, twin screw
While bound from Glasgow to New York on 7 May 1941, the pre-war emigrant steamer *Ixion*, steaming a northerly route, was torpedoed by the German submarine U94 when she was 200 miles south of Reykjavik, and sank the next day in the position 61.29N, 22.40W. She was not carrying passengers at the time and all 105 members of her crew survived the attack.
Casualties: 0

IZUMO MARU (1942) Nippon Yusen Kaisha, Japan

serving under the wartime name IJNS HIYO
27,700grt; 722ft (220.1m) loa x 88ft (26.8m) beam
890 passengers in three classes (as designed)
Kawasaki, Kobe (Yard No not known)
Steam turbines, twin screw
The *Izumo Maru* and her sister liner, the *Kashiwara Maru*, were designed with future conversion into aircraft carriers in mind and, to that end, their construction costs were partly defrayed by the Japanese Government. Hardly had their construction begun when the option to convert them for service with the Imperial Japanese Navy was taken. First to enter service, in May 1942, was the *Izumo Maru*, which had been launched on 24 June 1941 as the *Hiyo*. The *Hiyo* was present at many of the sea battles in the Pacific: the Battle of the Eastern Solomons in August 1942, the Battle of Santa Cruz in October 1942, during the lengthy Guadalcanal Campaign, and at the Battle of Tassafaronga. On 11 June 1943, when she was south of Tokyo Bay, she was damaged by a torpedo fired by the American submarine USS *Trigger*, but with the aid of a cruiser managed to reach Yokosuka where she was repaired. Her end came during the Battle of the Philippine Sea. On the afternoon of 20 June 1944 the *Hiyo* was hit repeatedly by dive- and torpedo-bombers from the American carrier USS *Belleau Wood*. Despite its intensity, she survived the onslaught but she had been mortally wounded. Petroleum vapour leaking from fractured fuel tanks, trapped low down inside her, suddenly ignited, shaking her with a series of massive explosions. Blazing from end to end, she rolled over and sank 450 miles north-east of Yap in the position 15.30N, 133.50E. Few survived the *Hiyo*'s dramatic end.
Casualties: the majority of her 1,224-strong complement

The *Izumo Maru*, originally conceived as an express trans-Pacific passenger liner for Nippon Yusen Kaisha, with a sister ship, the *Kashiwara Maru*, was completed as the short-lived light fleet aircraft carrier *Hiyo*. *Fujiphotos*

JAN PIETERSZOON COEN (1915) Nederland Royal Mail Line, The Netherlands

11,140grt; 522ft (168.2m) loa x 60ft (18.3m) beam
412 passengers in three classes
Nederlandsche Schps Maats, Amsterdam (Yard No 130)
Triple-expansion steam reciprocating, twin screw
The passenger ship *Jan Pieterszoon Coen* was deliberately sunk as a blockship between the pierheads at Ymuiden (Ijmuiden) on 14 May 1940, just days after she had arrived at Amsterdam from Genoa. She was sacrificed in an attempt to deny, or at least to hinder, the use of the port to the Germans. The wreck had been almost completely cleared by 1945 and was no longer an obstruction.
Casualties: 0

The Dutch passenger ship *Jan Pieterszoon Coen* operated on the service from Amsterdam to the Dutch East Indies.
World Ship Society

JAPAN (1868) Pacific Mail SS Co, USA

4,351grt; 362ft (110.3m) lbp x 49ft (14.9m) beam
Passenger numbers not known
Builders and Yard No not known
Propulsion machinery not known, paddles
The trans-Pacific wooden paddle steamer Japan caught fire while at sea between Yokohama and Hong Kong on 17 December 1874. She was completely burned out and sank.
Casualties: many

JEAN LABORDE (1930) Messageries Maritimes, France

11,591grt; 491ft (149.7m) loa x 61ft (18.6m) beam
900 passengers in four classes
Soc Provencale de Constructions Navales, La Ciotat (Yard No 107)
Motor-ship, twin screw
On 28 August 1940, after the fall of France, the passenger-cargo ship *Jean Laborde* was at Pointe Noire, French Equatorial Africa (Republic of Congo), when the Free French Forces were rallying in Gabon. However, because factions of her officers and crew favoured Vichy, she was sailed furtively

for Dakar, and by that September had returned to France. It was expected that she would be ceded to one of the Axis countries, either Germany or Italy, but in the event this never happened. In 1943 she was moored at Etang de Berre, Marseilles, but when her anchor chain broke on 5 March 1944 she was berthed in the Canal de Caronte. There, on 19 August 1944, the Germans deliberately set her on fire and the gutted ship sank in the waterway. Raised in early 1946, the wreck was towed to La Seyne in April of the same year for inspection. The damage to the ship was too extensive to justify recovery and the *Jean Laborde* was finally sold for breaking up at Savona on 19 April 1948.
Casualties: not known

The *Jean Laborde* and her sister ship *Marechal Joffre* were motor-ships employed on the service from France to Madagascar and the Far East via the Suez Canal.
Ian Allan Library

JERVIS BAY (1922) Aberdeen & Commonwealth Line, UK

14,129grt; 548ft (167.0) loa x 68ft (20.7m) beam
542 passengers in single class
Vickers, Barrow-in-Furness (Yard No 575)
Steam turbines, twin screw
The *Jervis Bay* was commissioned as an armed merchant cruiser in October 1939 and assigned to convoy escort duties. In this capacity she was escorting convoy HX84 bound from Halifax, Nova Scotia, to the UK when, on 5 November 1940, she encountered the German pocket battleship *Admiral Scheer*, which immediately attacked. The convoy was by then some 1,000 miles east of Newfoundland and, apart from the *Jervis Bay*, had no other naval escort. In order to provide some opportunity for the undefended merchantmen to disperse, the only way to save them, the *Jervis Bay* turned and steamed directly towards the enemy ready to engage. Essentially it was no more than a sacrificial diversion to gain time, for in the brief and one-sided exchange that ensued she was hopelessly out-matched in terms of the number and size of guns as well as in range-finding capabilities. Pounded by shells from the *Scheer*'s 11-inch guns, she was very soon a blazing wreck and sank in the position 52.26N, 32.34W. The objective of her brave gesture was achieved, however, for by the time the *Jervis Bay* had sunk, night had fallen and the majority of the 38 ships of the convoy had made good their escape in the gathering murk or concealed behind smoke screens. In the event, six other vessels were lost, the *Beaverford*, which had aided the *Jervis Bay* in the defence of the convoy, the *Maidan, Mopan, Fresno City, Kenbane Head* and *Trewellard*, costing the lives of 168 officers and seamen,

but it could have been far worse. The 65 survivors from the *Jervis Bay* were rescued by a neutral Swedish vessel that had been crossing with the convoy.

Casualties: 190 (34 officers and 156 naval ratings)

One of five 'Bay' class ships, the heroic *Jervis Bay* was engaged in the London to Australia service via Suez. *Imperial War Museum (Q105811)*

This well-known painting shows the *Jervis Bay* during the brief action with the German pocket battleship *Admiral Scheer*. *P&O*

JOHN ELDER (1870) ex-*Sacramento* (launch name, 29 August 1870) Pacific Steam Navigation Co, UK

4,151grt; 406ft (123.9m) lbp x 42ft (12.6m) beam
About 430 passengers in three classes
John Elder, Govan (Yard No 110)
Compound-expansion steam reciprocating, single screw
On 16 January 1892 the passenger steamer *John Elder* was bound from Valparaiso to Talcuhuanco with 139 passengers when she was wrecked on rocks at Cape Carranza, on the coast of Chile.

Casualties: not known

The Pacific Steam Navigation Company's *John Elder*. *H. B. Christiansen Collection / Online Transport Archive*

JOSIF STALIN (1939) Baltic Steamship Co (Sovtorgflot), USSR

7,645grt; 492ft (130.8m) lbp x 60ft (15.3m) beam
450 passengers in single class
Nederlandsche Schps Maats, Amsterdam (Yard No 275)
Turbo-electric, twin screw

The Soviet passenger ship *Josif Stalin* (also rendered *Iosif Stalin*), destined for the Leningrad to London service with her sister ship *Vyacheslav Molotov*, was instead lost on 3 December 1941 after the Soviet Union entered the war with Germany. Converted into a troopship, she departed Hanko (Hango), Finland, transporting 5,589 service personnel plus her crew, when she ran onto three naval mines. Severely damaged at the stern, she came under fire from Finnish coastal artillery, which scored a hit on the *Josif Stalin*'s ammunition storage area, causing a huge explosion. She immediately sank, settling on the bottom, but remaining visible above her main deck. There were many casualties because, located in the middle of a dense minefield, rescue vessels were unable to approach the stricken ship. It is not certain why there were such high casualties as many could still be seen on deck after she had sunk, suggesting something catastrophic occurred after this point. Those survivors who did make it ashore were taken prisoner by the Germans. Some reports state that the *Josif Stalin* was raised in July 1945 and taken to Tallinn, Estonia, for scrapping. However, as recently as 2008, photographs on the Internet show part of her wreckage to be still lying off the coast of Estonia, some 200 metres from the beach at Lohusalu.

Casualties: about 3,000

The *Josif Stalin* operated briefly on the Leningrad to London service with her sister ship *Vyacheslav Molotov*, later renamed *Baltika*. *Maritiem Museum Rotterdam*

The *Josif Stalin*, still fully loaded with servicemen, settled on the bottom with her stern blown away after her ammunition store exploded. Depicting a situation that appears to be under control, the events that followed must have been catastrophic for such a high number of casualties to have resulted. There appears to be inadequate lifeboats and she was inaccessible, surrounded by unexploded mines. *Maritiem Museum Rotterdam*

JUPITER (1961) ex-*Alexandros* (1970) ex-*Moledet* (1970) Epirotiki Lines, Greece

6,306grt; 415ft (126.6m) loa x 65ft (19.9m) beam
473 passengers
Chantiers de Bretagne, Prairie-au-Duc (Yard No 12400)
Motor-ship, twin screw

The Greek cruise ship *Jupiter*, formerly an Israeli passenger ferry working regular schedules on Mediterranean routes, was lost in a collision on 31 October 1988. Shortly after leaving Piraeus bound for Rhodes, she was struck by the vehicle carrier *Adige* and sank outside the Greek port. Casualties: 4 (2 passengers and 2 crew)

Epirotiki Line's cruise ship *Jupiter*, the former *Moledet* of Zim Israel Lines, was lost in a collision. *Frank Heine FERRIES*

JYLLAND (1926) Det Forenede Dampskibs-Selskab (DFDS), Denmark

serving under the wartime name MUSKATIER
2,762grt; 324ft (98.8m) loa x 44ft (13.4m) beam
220 passengers in two classes
Helsingor Vaerft, Elsinore (Yard No 176)
Motor-ship, twin screw

The Danish passenger-cargo ship *Jylland* was lost while in the hands of German occupying forces under the name *Muskatier*, which she had been given in April 1944. Captured at Copenhagen, where she had been laid up, the *Jylland* was towed to Danzig (Gdansk) where she was used as a target ship and later as an accommodation ship at Gotenhafen. While under tow from Wismar to Kiel, carrying about 800 refugees from East Prussia, she was bombed off Travemünde by Allied aircraft on 3 May 1945 and sank in the position 54.31N, 10.21E. Casualties: not known

KAISER WILHELM DER GROSSE (1897) Norddeutscher Lloyd, Germany

14,349grt; 648ft (197.5m) loa x 66ft (20.1m) beam
1,749 passengers in three classes
Stettiner Vulcan, Stettin-Bredow (Yard No 234)
Triple-expansion steam reciprocating, twin screw

After seventeen years on the North Atlantic, the *Kaiser Wilhelm der Grosse* was converted into an auxiliary cruiser for the German Navy, entering service on 4 August 1914. She sank three vessels over the next few weeks but allowed the *Galician* and *Arlanza* to proceed unharmed, having first destroyed their radio equipment, because they were both carrying passengers. However, the *Arlanza* encountered the cruiser HMS *Cornwall* off Las Palmas on 17 August and advised her of the raider's whereabouts. This was communicated to another cruiser, HMS *Highflyer*, which finally located the *Kaiser Wilhelm der Grosse* on 26 August while she was bunkering off Rio del Oro, Spanish West Africa. The German raider and the colliers were ordered to surrender, the *Highflyer* refraining from opening fire in respect of the sovereignty of Spanish territorial waters inside which they were located. This was refused, and two hours later the *Highflyer* opened fire anyway, which was swiftly returned. After exchanges lasting about 90 minutes, the *Kaiser Wilhelm der Grosse* rolled over and sank in shallow water, but the cause was disputed. The British claimed that her loss had been the result of the heavy damage inflicted upon her, accompanied by considerable loss of life, while the Germans insisted that her own crew had scuttled her when she ran out of ammunition, and that the *Kaiser Wilhelm der Grosse* had suffered only negligible damage from the cruiser's gunfire. Whichever version of events is nearer the truth, the survivors from the German crew rowed ashore in the boats and later made good their escape aboard the stores ship *Bethania*.

Casualties: not known

The Danish ferry *Jylland*, lost in German hands, operated between Esbjerg and Harwich with three sister ships. *Ian Allan Library*

The first German ship to capture the Atlantic Blue Riband, the *Kaiser Wilhelm der Grosse* was also the first of five liners to have four funnels arranged in pairs. *Alex Duncan*

**KAMAKARU MARU (1930) ex-*Chichibu [Titibu] Maru*
(1939) Nippon Yusen Kaisha, Japan**

17,526grt; 584ft (178.0m) loa x 74ft (22.6m) beam
817 passengers in three classes
Yokohama Dock Co, Yokohama (Yard No 170)
Motor-ship, twin screw
On the outbreak of war in the Pacific the *Kamakura Maru*, initially earmarked for conversion into an escort carrier, became a Japanese Navy transport, also making occasional repatriation voyages to Lourenço Marques under the auspices of the International Red Cross. On 28 April 1943, while bound from Manila to Singapore, she was torpedoed and sunk by the United States submarine USS *Gudgeon* when she was east of Palawan, in the Sulu Sea, in the position 10.25N, 121.50E. Casualties: not known

The *Chichibu Maru*, named after Crown Prince Chichibu, entered the Yokohama to San Francisco service in April 1930. When the new system of Romaji transliteration, introduced in 1937, led to the ship's name being respelled *Titibu*, it prompted a certain amount of smuttiness among American travellers to the embarrassment of NYK officials. As a consequence, the company prudently renamed the vessel *Kamakura Maru*. *Nippon Yusen Kaisha*

KAMO MARU (1908) Nippon Yusen Kaisha, Japan

8,524grt; 465ft (141.7m) lbp x 54ft (16.5m) beam
206 passengers in three classes
Mitsubishi, Nagasaki (Yard No 195)
Triple-expansion steam reciprocating, twin screw
The passenger-cargo ship *Kamo Maru* was torpedoed by the American submarine USS *Tinosa* while she was proceeding in convoy some 100 miles west of Kagoshima, Japan, on 3 July 1944. She sank in the position 32.24N, 128.46E. Casualties: not known

**KANOWNA (1903) Australasian United Steam
Navigation Co, Australia**

6,942 grt; 416ft (126.7m) lbp x 52ft (15.9m) beam
passenger numbers not known
William Denny, Dumbarton (Yard No 671)
Quadruple-expansion steam reciprocating, twin screw
The coastwise passenger-cargo ship *Kanowna* struck a rock at Wilson's Promontory on 18 February 1929 while on passage from Sydney to Melbourne. The stranded vessel sank the following day. Casualties: not known

KARANJA (1931) British India Line, UK

9,891grt; 486ft (148.1m) loa x 64ft (19.5m) beam
250 berthed passengers in two classes plus 2,329 deck passengers

Alexander Stephen, Linthouse, Glasgow (Yard No 530)
Steam turbines, twin screw
The passenger ship *Karanja* was requisitioned for auxiliary service as a troopship in 1940, later becoming the infantry landing ship HMS *Karanja* in July 1941. In this role she participated in the North African landings, Operation 'Torch', but she was one of several large passenger vessels lost during the operation. On 12 November 1942 she was off Bougie (Bejaia), having just picked up the survivors from the *Cathay* (qv), when she came under sustained attack by German aircraft. After a sequence of bomb hits she caught fire and all aboard her were forced to abandon ship. Blazing furiously, she sank in the bay but hundreds of survivors from both the *Cathay* and the *Karanja* managed to make it ashore. Casualties: 50

The liners *Karanja*, pictured here, and *Kenya* were partners in British India Line's East African service. *World Ship Society*

The *Karanja* on fire off Bougie, Algeria, on 12 November 1942. *H. B. Christiansen Collection / Online Transport Archive*

**KARNAK (1899) ex-*Tourane* (1912) ex-*Annam* (1904)
Messageries Maritimes, France**

6,054grt; 446ft (135.9m) loa x 50ft (15.2m) beam
394 passengers in three classes
Messageries Maritimes, La Ciotat (Yard No 77)
Triple-expansion steam reciprocating, twin screw
The passenger steamship *Karnak*, bound from Marseilles to Piraeus and Salonika, was torpedoed and sunk 60 miles south-east of Malta, after leaving Valletta on 27 November 1916, by the German submarine U32. The survivors were picked up by the British hospital ship *Letitia*. Casualties: 17

**KASHIMA [KASIMA] MARU (1913) Nippon Yusen
Kaisha, Japan**

9,908grt; 522ft (159.1m) loa x 59ft (18.0m) beam
380 passengers in three classes
Kawasaki, Kobe (Yard No 362)
Triple-expansion steam reciprocating, twin screw

The American submarine USS *Bonefish* torpedoed the passenger-cargo ship *Kashima Maru* on 27 September 1943 when she was some 200 miles east of Saigon. She sank in the position 10.10N, 109.40E.
Casualties: not known

KASHIWARA MARU (1942) Nippon Yusen Kaisha, Japan

serving under the wartime name IJNS JUNYO
27,700grt; 722ft (220.1m) loa x 88ft (26.8m) beam
890 passengers in three classes (as designed)
Mitsubishi, Nagasaki (Yard Nos 900 and 901)
Steam turbines, twin screw

While still under construction, the passenger liner *Kashiwara Maru* was taken over for conversion into the aircraft carrier *Junyo*, and was commissioned with the Imperial Japanese Navy on 5 May 1942. After being involved in many of the naval actions in the Pacific with her sister ship *Hiyo*, the former *Izumo Maru* (qv), the *Junyo* was torpedoed by the American submarines USS *Redfish* and *Sea Devil* on 9 December 1944 off Cape Nomozaki, south of Nagasaki, sustaining damage that was so extreme that she could take no further part in the war. She was able to reach Sasebo but, because of the limited facilities available and shortages of materials, she could not be restored for active service and work was abandoned in March 1945. She may well have been damaged further during later American air-raids on Sasebo. In her immobile state she was surrendered in August 1945. There was no contemplation of reconversion into a liner, but it has been suggested that she was reactivated as a repatriation transport under Allied authority prior to being broken up in 1947. It is not possible to confirm whether or not she was used in this fashion. Other Japanese aircraft carriers were utilised for this work, but all post-war photographs of the *Junyo* show her either as found at Sasebo or in the process of demolition, suggesting otherwise.
Casualties: 19 (in torpedo attack)

The *Kashiwara Maru* under construction as a passenger liner prior to the order being issued for her to be completed as an aircraft carrier. *Mitsubishi Heavy Industries*

The aircraft carrier *Junyo* at Sasebo at the end of the Pacific War. Although relatively intact, the cost to reconstruct her as a passenger ship could not be justified, especially at a time when few passengers would have been prepared to travel on a Japanese ship. *US National Archives*

KASUGA MARU (1941) Nippon Yusen Kaisha, Japan

serving under the wartime name IJNS TAIYO
17,127grt; 590ft (179.8m) loa x 74ft (22.6m) beam
285 passengers in three classes (as designed)
Mitsubishi, Nagasaki (Yard Nos 752 and 888) and Sasebo Navy Yard
Steam turbines, twin screw

The third ship of a trio of new passenger liners ordered for the European trade, the *Kasuga Maru* was still under construction when the Imperial Japanese Navy took her over for completion as an aircraft carrier in November 1940. Renamed *Taiyo*, she was commissioned on 15 September 1941, the first of the three ships to enter service in the carrier role and the only one that was never engaged in commercial service as originally intended. The escort carrier *Taiyo* was torpedoed by the American submarine USS *Rasher* on 18 August 1944, about 22 miles south-west of Cape Bojeador, Luzon, and sank in the position 18.16N, 120.20'E.
Casualties: there were only a small number of survivors from her 747-strong complement

In 1938 Nippon Yusen Kaisha ordered two large express passenger liners for the trans-Pacific service from Yokohama to San Francisco with completion scheduled for 1940, the year that the Olympic Games were to be held in Tokyo. The two vessels were partly financed by the Japanese Government on the understanding that they would be available for conversion into aircraft carriers at a time of national emergency, and the vessels' design reflected these contingency plans. This is an impression of the *Kashiwara Maru*. *Nippon Yusen Kaisha*

The passenger liner *Kasuga Maru* never saw commercial service, being taken over by the Imperial Japanese Navy while still incomplete as the escort carrier *Taiyo*, seen here.
US National Archives

KATORI MARU (1913) Nippon Yusen Kaisha, Japan

9,834grt; 520ft (158.5m) loa x 59ft (18.0m) beam
380 passengers in three classes
Mitsubishi, Nagasaki (Yard No 230)
Triple-expansion steam reciprocating with LP turbine, triple screw

On 23 December 1941, only two days after war had been declared between Japan and the United States of America, the passenger-cargo ship *Katori Maru* was torpedoed and sunk by a Dutch submarine, becoming Japan's first passenger ship loss in the Second World War under conditions of belligerency. Before the war's end there would be a great many more, decimating Japan's large pre-war passenger fleet. The *Katori Maru* went down off Kuching, Sarawak, in the position 02.30N, 110.00E.
Casualties: not known

The *Katori Maru* met a like fate to the four other ships of her class, the *Kashima*, *Suwa*, *Fushimi* and *Yasaka Marus*. They all had a broadly similar appearance. *Nippon Yusen Kaisha*

KEMMENDINE (1924) Henderson Line, UK

7,837grt; 453ft (138.1m) lbp x 59ft (18.0m) beam
150 passengers in single class
William Denny, Dumbarton (Yard No 1153)
Triple-expansion steam reciprocating, single screw

While bound from Liverpool to Burma via Cape Town, on 13 July 1940, the *Kemmendine* was sunk by the German raider *Atlantis*, which first opened fire with her guns, then launched a torpedo into the damaged passenger ship. The *Kemmendine* had a total of 147 persons aboard her, among them a number of passengers and prisoners of war. The attack took place in the position 04.12S, 81.47E.
Casualties: 82 (22 passengers, 3 prisoners of war and 57 crew)

The *Kemmendine*, sister of the *Pegu* and *Yoma*.
B. & A. Feilden

KHAI DINH (1914) ex-*Lamartine* (1939) ex-*Emperor Alexander III* (1921) ex-*Respublikanets* (1918) ex-*Imperator Aleksandr III* (1917) Messageries Maritimes, France

5,153 grt; 381ft (116.2m) lbp x 52ft (15.8m) Beam
200 passengers
William Denny, Dumbarton (Yard No 976)
Triple-expansion steam reciprocating, twin screw

Built originally for the Russian Steam Navigation & Trading Company of Odessa, over a four-year period from 1917 the passenger ship *Imperator Aleksandr III* served the Russian Navy as a seaplane tender and worked for both the German and French governments. Acquired by Messageries Maritimes in 1921, she had been relegated to 'station ship' in Indo-China by 1939 under the name *Khai Dinh*, operating from Saigon on a route that took her north along the Vietnamese coast. Seized by the Japanese, she was bombed south of Haiphong, in the Baie d'Alang, by Chinese and American aircraft on 22 November 1942 and sank in the position 20.58N, 106.40E.
Casualties: 7

KHEDIVE (1871) Duda Abdullah & Co, India

3,742 grt; 378ft (115.1m) lbp x 42ft (12.9m) beam
218 passengers in two classes (as built)
Caird, Greenock (Yard No 159)
Compound-expansion steam reciprocating, single screw

The former P&O Line passenger-cargo ship *Khedive* had been with new owners for just ten days when she stranded on the coast off Porbandar, approximately 200 miles northwest of Bombay, on 11 January 1897. Bound at the time from Bombay for Karachi on her first voyage for Duda Abdullah, she became a total loss.
Casualties: not known

KHEDIVE ISMAIL (1922) ex-*Aconcagua* (1935) Khedivial Mail Steamship Co, Egypt (managed by British India Line for the Ministry of War Transport)

7,513grt; 423ft (122.9m) lbp x 56ft (17.1m) beam
243 berthed in two classes plus deck passengers
Scott's, Greenock (Yard No 516)
Steam turbines, twin screw

While temporarily operating under the Red Ensign as a troopship, the *Khedive Ismail* was lost on 12 February 1944 when she was torpedoed by the Japanese submarine I-27 in the Indian Ocean, near the Maldive Islands. At the time of the attack she had aboard a total of 1,507 persons, of whom 1,324 were troops and the remainder a crew of 183, which included a number of gunners. She sank with heavy loss of life in the position 00.57N, 72.16E. Among the dead were 77 women, making it the single worst loss of female military personnel on a British ship.

Casualties: 1,271 (1,134 troops plus 137 crew)

Originally owned by a Chilean company, the *Khedive Ismail*, seen here at Valletta, was acquired by Egyptian owners together with a sister ship that became the *Mohamed Ali el Kabir*. Both were sunk by torpedoes. *Michael Cassar*

KIANG HSIN (1905) China Merchants Steam Navigation Co, UK

3,373grt; 325ft (99.1m) lbp x 44ft (13.4m) beam
Passenger numbers not known
S. C. Farnham, Shanghai (Yard No 984)
Triple-expansion steam reciprocating, twin screw

There appears to be some dispute as to whether the Chinese coastal passenger ship *Kiang Hsin*, first sunk on 23 June 1938, was raised and repaired after the incident only to be totally lost nine years later, or was salvaged a second time, returning to service until as late as 1967, when she was last heard of. What can be stated for certain is that the *Kiang Hsin* was bombed and sunk by Japanese aircraft near Yochow on the River Yangtse during the Sino-Japanese War. Recovered subsequently, she is reported to have been destroyed totally during bombing at Shanghai on 5 September 1949 at the height of the Chinese Civil War. This latter sinking was accompanied by a huge loss of life (see below). The alternative version of events states that, following the second aerial attack on the *Kiang Hsin*, she was salvaged and restored to service under her original name, but was later sold to become first the *Chiang Hsin* in 1955, then the *Dong Fang Hong 3* in 1967, in both cases registered in the People's Republic of China. After the latter date there is no trace of her.

Casualties: About 1,000 refugees

KIANG YA (1939) ex-*Hsing Ya Maru* (1947) ex-*Koa Maru* (?) China Merchants Steam Navigation Co, UK name also rendered as CHIANG YA or JIANGYA LUN

3,731grt; 322ft (98.1m) lbp x 50ft (15.2m) beam
3,920 passengers, the majority on deck
Harima Shipbuilding & Engineering Co, Aioi (Yard No 274)
Triple-expansion steam reciprocating, twin screw

The Chinese passenger ship *Kiang Ya* was sunk on 3 December 1948 while bound from Shanghai to Ningbo, Chekiang (Zhejiang) Province, some 100 miles (150 kilometres) to the south, crammed with refugees during the Chinese Civil War. She was shaken by a huge explosion, possibly after striking a mine, when 15 miles off the Woosung (Wusong) breakwater, north of Shanghai on the southern shore of the River Yangtse. It was stated in contemporary reports that the explosion was definitely not her boiler. Raised by the Communist authorities in October 1956, the *Kiang Ya* was comprehensively repaired and returned to passenger service in 1959. She was apparently renamed *Dong Fang Hong 8* in 1967 but there is no further trace of her after 1992. Aspects of her origins remain obscure.

Casualties: 3,520 (this figure is recorded as the number of persons missing)

KITSURIN [KITURIN] MARU (1935) Osaka Shosen Kaisha, Japan

6,783grt; 427ft (130.1m) lbp x 56ft (17.1m) beam
850 passengers
Mitsubishi, Nagasaki (Yard No 593)
Steam turbines, twin screw

On 11 May 1945 the passenger ship *Kitsurin Maru* struck a mine placed off Kobe by US forces. She sank in the position 34.39N, 135.11E.

Casualties: not known

KLIPFONTEIN (1939) Holland Afrika Line, The Netherlands

10,544grt; 520ft (158.5m) loa x 63ft (19.2m) beam
148 passengers in two classes
P. Smit Jr, Rotterdam (Yard No 517)
Motor-ship, twin screw

The passenger-cargo ship *Klipfontein* was lost on 8 January 1953 while bound from Lourenço Marques to Beira, both Mozambique. As she was clearing Cape Barra, she struck a submerged reef near Inhambane. The impact set off an explosion in the forward oil bunker and, as a result of this and the damage caused to her hull, the *Klipfontein* foundered within an hour, sinking bow-first almost vertically. There was no loss of life, for the Union-Castle Line's *Bloemfontein Castle* arrived on the scene in time to take off the 114 passengers and 119 crew.

Casualties: 0

A sister ship of the *Jagersfontein*, the *Klipfontein* was engaged on the service to South and East Africa from Hamburg and Rotterdam. *World Ship Society*

KNOSSOS (1952) ex-*La Bourdonnais* (1968) C. S. Efthymiadis, Greece

10,886grt; 492ft (150.1m) loa x 64ft (19.6m) beam
499 in three classes (as built)
Arsenal de Lorient, Lorient (Yard No MD2)
Motor-ship, twin screw
The *Knossos* was lost five years after she had been acquired from Messageries Maritimes for service on eastern Mediterranean routes. On 3 May 1973, while bound from Piraeus to Limassol with 186 passengers and a crew of 26, fire broke out in her engine room causing extensive damage well beyond its source and necessitating complete evacuation of the ship. The crippled *Knossos* was towed back to Piraeus where she was laid up and left unrepaired for the next four years. She was finally sold for breaking up at Perama, commencing July 1977.
Casualties: 0

KOKURYU MARU (1937) Osaka Shosen Kaisha, Japan

7,369grt; 426ft (129.8m) lbp x 57ft (17.4m) beam
805 passengers in three classes
Mitsubishi, Nagasaki (Yard No 680)
Steam turbines, twin screw
The passenger ship *Kokuryu Maru*, sister ship of the *Oryoku Maru* (qv), was sunk on 24 October 1944. She was torpedoed by the American submarine USS *Seadragon* about 150 miles north-west of Luzon Island, in the Philippines, in the position 20.33N, 118.34E.
Casualties: not known

KONGO MARU (1936) Department of Communications & Railways, Government of Japan

7,105grt; 415ft (126.5m) lbp x 57ft (17.4m) beam
1,750 passengers
Mitsubishi, Nagasaki (Yard No 630)
Steam turbines, twin screw
On 27 May 1945 the ferry *Kongo Maru* struck a mine laid by American aircraft off Fukuoka, near Sasebo, Kyushu. She was raised after the war and returned to service only to be wrecked on 14 October 1951 when she was stranded near Koshikishima, Goto Island.
Casualties: not known (for either incident)

KONIG WILHELM I (1871) Norddeutscher Lloyd, Germany

2,550grt; 312ft (95.1m) lbp x 39ft (11.9m) beam
555 passengers in three classes
Caird, Greenock (Yard No 155)
Inverted steam engines, single screw
The brief career of the passenger steamer *Konig Wilhelm I* ended on 26 November 1973 when she was wrecked on the Dutch coast at Nieuwediep while returning to Bremen from New York. She was refloated in March 1874, only to sink again. The wreck was finally removed by the Dutch Navy in 1951.
Casualties: 0

KONINGIN EMMA (1913) Nederland Royal Mail Line, The Netherlands

9,181grt; 470ft (143.3m) lbp x 57ft (17.4m) beam
310 passengers
Fijenoord, Rotterdam (Yard No 254)
Quadruple-expansion steam reciprocating, twin screw
While returning to Amsterdam from Batavier on 22 September 1915, the *Koningen Emma* struck a mine in the Thames estuary, between one and two miles west of the Sunk light vessel, in the position 51.54N, 01.32E. The mine had been laid by the German submarine UC7. Her partially submerged wreck was broken up and removed later. All her 155 passengers and crew survived.
Casualties: 0

Engaged on the Netherlands to Dutch East Indies service, prior to the First World War, this is the *Koningin Emma* of the Nederland Royal Mail Line. *L. L. von Münching*

The *Koningin Emma* is seen sinking in the Thames estuary after striking a mine. *L. L. von Münching*

KONRON MARU (1943) Department of Communications & Railways, Government of Japan

7,908grt; 443ft (135.1m) lbp x 60ft (18.2m) beam
2,048 passengers
Mitsubishi, Nagasaki (Yard No 891)
Steam turbines, single screw
The short-lived passenger ferry *Konron Maru* was lost on 5 October 1943, less than six months after she had first entered service on 30 March of that year. She was torpedoed and sunk east of Tsushima in the Korea Strait, in the position 34.20N, 130.18E, by the American submarine USS *Wahoo*. It was reported that, although she had been ordered for the Shimonoseki to Fusan ferry route, she was serving as a transport at the time of the attack.
Casualties: 544

KOOMBANA (1908) Adelaide Steamship Co, Australia

3,668grt; 340ft (103.7m) lbp x 48ft (14.7m) beam
188 passengers in two classes
Alexander Stephen, Linthouse, Glasgow (Yard No 429)
Triple-expansion steam reciprocating, single screw

The Australian coastal steamer *Koombana* foundered off Western Australia in a violent typhoon while bound from Port Headland to Broome with 48 passengers and 77 crew. She left Port Headland on 20 March 1912 and was seen the next day by another local passenger vessel, the Burns & Philip's *Montoro*. Thereafter nothing was heard of her for nearly a fortnight, long after she should have arrived at her destination, but her fate became apparent when a small number of items identified as coming from the *Koombana* were washed ashore on 3 April 1912, although no trace of the vessel itself has ever been found.
Casualties: 138 (118 passengers and 20 crew)

KOREYA (1899) ex-*Korea* (1899) Russian American Line (Russian East Asiatic Co), Russia

6,123grt; 409ft (124.7m) lbp x 50ft (15.1m) beam
1,400 passengers
Flensburger, Flensburg (Yard No 191)
Triple-expansion steam reciprocating, single screw

The passenger-cargo ship *Koreya*, originally ordered for the East Asiatic Company, was transferred virtually on her completion to the Russian American Line, which had been founded by the Danish concern. She was lost on 1 March 1910 when she foundered in mid-Atlantic in the position 52.15N, 28.19W while on passage from Narvik to Philadelphia.
Casualties: 0

KOVNO (1893) ex *Allemannia* (1906) ex *Orellana* (1905) Russian East Asiatic Co, Russia

serving under the wartime name OWASCO
4,821 grt; 398ft (122.2m) lbp x 48ft (14.5m) beam
745 passengers in two classes (as built)
Harland & Wolff, Belfast (Yard No 259)
Triple-expansion steam reciprocating, single screw

The former Pacific Steam Navigation Company's passenger-cargo ship *Orellana*, which by 1906 was operating under the Russian flag as the *Kovno*, was taken over by the United States government in 1917 and operated by the US Shipping Board under the name *Owasco*. While bound from Norfolk, Virginia, to Genoa, she was torpedoed and sunk on 10 December 1917 off Alicante, Spain, in the position 38.28N, 00.13W. Her attacker was the German submarine U64. Casualties: 2

KRISTIANAFJORD (1913) Norwegian Amerika Line, Norway

10,669grt; 530ft (161.5m) loa x 61ft (18.5m) beam
1,021 passengers in three classes
Cammell Laird, Birkenhead (Yard No 784)
Quadruple-expansion steam reciprocating, twin screw

The passenger-cargo liner *Kristianafjord* ran aground near Mistaken Point, seven miles west of Cape Race, on 15 July 1917 and sustained such severe damage that she was abandoned as a total loss. At the time she had been bound for Bergen from New York. Casualties: 0

The Norwegian passenger ship *Kristianafjord* operated the service from Oslo and Bergen to New York. *Bjørn Pedersen*

KRONPRINS FREDERIK (1941) Det Forenede Dampskibs-Selskab (DFDS), Denmark

3,895grt; 376ft (114.4m) loa x 50ft (15.2m) beam
302 passengers in two classes plus 56 deck passengers
Helsingørs Vaerft, Elsinore (Yard No 262)
Motor-ship, twin screw

The North Sea ferry *Kronprins Frederik* was severely damaged by a fire that broke out aboard her at Harwich on 19 April 1953. Completely gutted and top-heavy through the volume of water pumped aboard her, she capsized and sank the following day. It was estimated that 33 per cent of her accommodation had been destroyed. In August 1953 she was refloated and towed to Elsinore to be rebuilt, a task that took until late April 1954. The *Kronprins Frederik* resumed the DFDS Esbjerg to Harwich service on 7 May 1954, later working other routes until she was sold in March 1976 to become the *Patra* (qv).
Casualties: not known

The DFDS North Sea passenger ferry *Kronprins Frederik* in the River Tyne at South Shields in June 1962. *John Edgington*

KUNG WO (1921) Indo-China Steam Navigation Co, UK

4,636grt; 350ft (106.7m) lbp x 49ft (14.8m) beam
Passenger numbers not known
Hong Kong & Whampoa Dock Co, Kowloon
(Yard No 579)
Triple-expansion steam reciprocating, twin screw

While serving as an auxiliary minelayer in the Second World War, the passenger-cargo steamer *Kung Wo* was lost on 14 February 1942 at the time of the fall of Singapore. She was bombed and sunk by Japanese aircraft six miles north-west of Banka Island (Pompong Islands), near the Lingga Archipelago, while bound from Singapore to Australia carrying evacuees. It is also reported that she was berthed alongside the Dockyard Accommodation Building at Singapore when she was hit by a stick of bombs.

Casualties: not known (4 crew, a naval surgeon and an unspecified number of Asiatic personnel)

A poor-quality impression of the Chinese passenger ship *Kung Wo*, sunk at Singapore in February 1942. *Author's collection*

KURFURST (1901) Deutsche Ost-Afrika Line, Germany

5,655grt; 410ft (125.2m) lbp x 48ft (14.7m) beam
About 235 passengers in three classes
Reiherstiegwerft, Hamburg (Yard No 407)
Triple-expansion steam reciprocating, twin screw
After only three years in service, the passenger-cargo steamship *Kurfurst* was wrecked in fog north of Sagres, Portugal, on 5 May 1904.
Casualties: 0

KYARRA (1903) Australasian United Steam Navigation Co, UK

6,953grt; 416ft (126.6m) lbp x 52ft (16.0m) beam
511 passengers in three classes
William Denny & Bros, Dumbarton (Yard No 672)
Triple-expansion steam reciprocating, twin screw
The passenger-cargo ship *Kyarra* was lost in the First World War while serving as a hospital ship. While bound from London to Sydney, she was torpedoed without warning by the German submarine UB57 on 26 May 1918 and sank two miles south-south-east from Anvil Point, in the English Channel.
Casualties: 6 (all crew)

LA BOURGOGNE (1885) Compagnie Générale Transatlantique (French Line), France

7,395grt; 495ft (150.0m) lbp x 52ft (16.0m) beam
1,060 passengers in three classes
Forges et Chantiers de la Méditerranée, La Seyne
(Yard No not known)
Quadruple-expansion steam reciprocating, single screw
The French passenger steamship *La Bourgogne* was a victim of a collision on 4 July 1898 while she was bound from New York for Le Havre with a total of 711 persons on board, of whom around 500 were passengers. Off the Newfoundland Banks she ran into dense fog, but in spite of the conditions she was navigated somewhat imprudently. An excessive speed was maintained, which, coupled with either faulty steering or course plotting, took her some 150 miles north of her intended route and into the path of the sailing ship *Cromartyshire*, which was bound from Dunkirk to Philadelphia. When the *Cromartyshire* came upon the *La Bourgogne* that morning there was little opportunity for her to avoid the approaching liner and she smashed into its starboard side, flooding the engine room and carrying away the lifeboats on that side of the ship. The *La Bourgogne* started to sink immediately and panic broke out among the passengers. A delay in launching the port-side boats, while an attempt to make for Sable Island some sixty miles to the north was considered, only added to the already desperate situation. When finally lowered, few of the port-side boats were successfully launched and, as no lifejackets had been issued, many people were drowned as soon as they entered the water. Of those saved, 61 were passengers and 104 were crew. These survivors were picked up by the *Cromartyshire* but later transferred to the Allan Line's *Grecian*, which also took the crippled sailing ship in tow for Halifax, Nova Scotia.
Casualties: 546

One of a class of four ships built for the Le Havre to New York service, the *La Bourgogne*, unlike the other four, was not modified by the removal of two of her four masts. Her loss in July 1898 was the worst peacetime disaster involving a French ship. *Cie Générale Transatlantique*

LABRADOR (1891) Dominion Line, UK

4,737grt; 401ft (122.2m) lbp x 47ft (14.4m) beam
1,150 passengers in three classes
Harland & Wolff, Belfast (Yard No 238)
Triple-expansion steam reciprocating, single screw

While returning to Liverpool from St John, New Brunswick, on 1 March 1899, the passenger steamship *Labrador* was wrecked on Mackenzie Rock, Skerryvore, 25 miles west of Iona.
Casualties: 0

LA CHAMPAGNE (1886) Compagnie Générale Transatlantique (French Line), France

7,087grt; 508ft (154.8m) loa x 52ft (15.8m) beam
1,955 passengers in three classes
Chantiers de Cie Générale Transatlantique, St Nazaire
(Yard No 8)
Quadruple-expansion steam reciprocating, single screw
The transatlantic passenger steamer *La Champagne* was chartered to the Cie Sud-Atlantique in 1912 for service on the routes to South America from Bordeaux as cover for the *Burdigala* (qv), but on 28 May 1915 she ran aground near the entrance to the harbour at St Nazaire and broke her back. The wreck was sold for demolition. Earlier in her career, in August 1887, she had been involved in a collision near Le Havre, and 11 years later she had drifted totally out of control in mid-Atlantic when her propeller shaft fractured.
Casualties: 0

The French Line's *La Champagne*. *World Ship Society*

LACONIA (1911) Cunard Line, UK

18,099grt; 625ft (190.5m) loa x 71ft (21.6m) beam
2,850 passengers in three classes
Swan Hunter & Wigham Richardson, Wallsend-on-Tyne
(Yard No 877)
Quadruple-expansion steam reciprocating, twin screw

Besides scheduled-service line voyages, the sister ships *Laconia*, seen here, and *Franconia* also made occasional cruise voyages in the low season. *H. B. Christiansen Collection / Online Transport Archive*

The liner *Laconia* was taken over by the Admiralty in October 1914 for conversion into an armed merchant cruiser, but in September 1916 she resumed Cunard's North Atlantic passenger schedules. On 25 February 1917, while returning to Liverpool from New York with 75 passengers and a crew of 217, the *Laconia* was torpedoed by the German submarine U50 and sank 160 miles north-west-by-west of Fastnet, in the approximate position 52.00N, 13.40W. Hit twice on her starboard side, she remained afloat for barely an hour after the second explosion, but there was sufficient time to manage an almost full evacuation.
Casualties: 12 (6 passengers and 6 crew)

LACONIA (1922) Cunard Line, UK

19,680grt; 623ft (189.9m) loa x 73ft (22.3m) beam
2,200 passengers in three classes
Swan Hunter & Wigham Richardson, Wallsend-on-Tyne
(Yard No 1125)
Steam turbines, twin screw

Third vessel of Cunard's 'Scythia' class, the *Laconia* made her maiden voyage to New York from Liverpool in May 1922. She also made crossings from Hamburg and Southampton and cruises during the Depression years. *B. & A. Feilden*

The liner *Laconia* was commandeered by the Admiralty in late 1939 for service as an armed merchant cruiser, but she was transferred to the Ministry of War Shipping for use as a troopship from 1941. In that role she was engaged in September 1942 to carry 1,793 Italian prisoners of war from Suez to the UK, via South Africa. Besides the prisoners, she also had 769 other passengers aboard, among them women and children, and Polish guards, plus her 692-strong crew. On 12 September 1942, when she was about 800 miles south-west of Freetown, in the position 05.05S, 11.38W, the *Laconia* was torpedoed by the German submarine U156.

Following the attack, the U156 surfaced and approached the sinking merchantman, presumably with the intention of taking prisoners, but, when it was discovered that she was carrying Italian prisoners, other nearby U-boats were summoned to assist in a humanitarian rescue, despite the fact that they would all be exposed to attack themselves. Three submarines answered the call for help, the U506 and U507, and the Italian boat *Capellini*. Three Vichy-French surface warships, the cruiser *Gloire*, the sloop *Dumont D'Urville* and the minesweeper *Annamite* also put out from Casablanca in response. Meanwhile the four submarines took aboard as many survivors as they could while they also took the ship's lifeboats in tow, displaying prominent Red Cross flags on their topsides to indicate their status. Despite this, they came under attack from American aircraft and the U156 sustained damage. Nevertheless, the rescue operation proceeded until the French naval vessels arrived on the scene on 17 September. During the preceding five days, the German naval crews had distributed provisions among the survivors and had provided medical care for the injured.

The *Laconia*'s survivors were transhipped to the warships and taken to Casablanca, relieving the submarines, which resumed their operational duties. Whether or not the German U-boat commanders were motivated only by a desire to help their comrades in arms and would, perhaps, have behaved differently if all the survivors had been Allied personnel, will never be known. What is not open to debate is that, but for the brave rescue operation they mounted, a great many more persons, both Allied and Axis, would have perished in the sea. The number of survivors, according to Lloyd's records, was 975, of whom around 400 were Italian prisoners. Other reports say there were 1,111 survivors, but this figure cannot be substantiated.
Casualties: 2,279

LA CORUNA (1921) Hamburg Sud-Amerika Line, Germany

7,359grt; 414ft (126.2m) lbp x 55ft (16.8m) beam
584 passengers in two classes
Reiherstiegwerft, Hamburg (Yard No 508)
Triple-expansion steam reciprocating, single screw
On 13 April 1940 the passenger-cargo ship *La Coruna* was returning to Germany from Rio de Janeiro when the British armed merchant cruiser *Maloja* intercepted her east of Iceland. To prevent the *Maloja*, a converted P&O liner, from taking her as a war prize, the *La Coruna* was scuttled, sinking in the approximate position 63.00N, 10.20W. Her occupants, rescued by the *Maloja*, were taken prisoner and interned.
Casualties: 0

LADY DRAKE (1929) Canadian National Line, Canada

7,985grt; 419ft (127.7m) lbp x 59ft (18.0m) beam
237 passengers
Cammell Laird, Birkenhead (Yard No 940)
Steam turbines, twin screw

Ships of the Canadian National Line's 'Lady Nelson' class sailed between St Lawrence ports, Newfoundland and Nova Scotia and South America. This is the *Lady Drake* berthed at Hamilton, Bermuda, on 25 July 1931. *Ian Allan Library*

On 5 May 1942 the passenger-cargo ship *Lady Drake* was on passage from Demerara and Bermuda, returning to St John, New Brunswick, with a total complement of 272 persons, when she was torpedoed by the German submarine U106 north of Bermuda. She sank in the position 35.43N, 64.43W.
Casualties: 12 (6 passengers and 6 crew)

LADY HAWKINS (1929) Canadian National Line, Canada

7,989grt; 419ft (127.7m) lbp x 59ft (18.0m) beam
237 passengers
Cammell Laird, Birkenhead (Yard No 939)
Steam turbines, twin screw
The *Lady Hawkins* was bound from Halifax and Boston to Bermuda on 19 January 1942 when she was torpedoed by the German submarine U66 150 miles from Cape Hatteras, in the position 35.00N, 72.30W. She was carrying 210 passengers and 112 crew members. Two torpedoes struck the ship in her forward holds and the engine room. Three lifeboats were launched but only one was ever recovered. The New York & Porto Rico Line passenger ship *Coamo* picked up the seventy survivors and took them to San Juan.
Casualties: 252

The five vessels of the 'Lady Nelson' class were the *Lady Drake*, *Lady Hawkins* (seen here), *Lady Rodney*, *Lady Somers* and the nameship. *Maritime Photo Library*

LAFAYETTE (1930) Compagnie Générale Transatlantique (French Line), France

25,178grt; 613ft (186.8m) loa x 77ft (23.6m) beam
1,079 passengers in three classes
Penhoët, St Nazaire (Yard No J6)
Motor-ship, twin screw
While being overhauled in dry dock at Le Havre, on 4 May 1938, fire broke out in the stokehold of the passenger liner *Lafayette* when an accident while lighting oil burners caused the combustion of some spilled fuel oil. This in turn ignited the main fuel tanks and very soon a fire of great intensity had a grip on the entire vessel. Simultaneous with the outbreak, an electrical short-circuit put all the ship's pumps out of action. As none of the *Lafayette*'s hoses had been connected with shore mains during the overhaul, it was only possible to fight the fire from outside the ship and it had spread considerably from its source before this could be effective. During the early morning of 5 May the blazing ship was rocked by more than twenty internal explosions. The extent of the damage could be clearly observed from the dockside: the Boat and Promenade decks had collapsed, her superstructure was distorted, the bridge was wrecked and all wooden fittings such as masts, lifeboats, deck planking and handrails were destroyed.

Once the fire had abated sufficiently to permit an on-board inspection, a detailed survey of the *Lafayette* was carried out. This confirmed that the ship was fit only for scrap. With her metalwork weakened, she presented a formidable obstacle to extricate from the dock, but this was eventually achieved on 25 May. The *Lafayette* was then towed to Bolnes, Holland, where she was broken up. During the demolition, fire broke out aboard her again on 18 August 1938.
Casualties: 0

French Line's first purpose-built Cabin-class ship was the *Lafayette*. She served on the Le Havre to New York route via Plymouth. *Author's collection*

The wreck of the gutted *Lafayette* under tow to Dutch breakers at Rotterdam. *Smit International*

LA JANELLE (1931) ex-*Bahamas Star* (1969) ex-*Arosa Star* (1959) ex-*Puerto Rico* (1954) ex-*Borinquen* (1949) Western Steamship Co (Sorensen & Bayles), Panama

7,114grt; 466ft (126.1m) lbp x 60ft (18.2m) beam
806 passengers in two classes (as Arosa Star)
Bethlehem Shipbuilding Corp, Quincy, Massachusetts (Yard No 1432)
Steam turbines, single screw
The *La Janelle* was lost on 13 April 1970 while laid up idle at Port Hueneme, California. She broke her moorings in a severe storm and was driven ashore. A helicopter was used to evacuate the only two people aboard her who were engaged in a caretaking capacity. The wreck, lying on its beam ends, disintegrated in the rough seas as the heavy weather continued.
Casualties: 0

The *Bahamas Star* is berthed at Miami in October 1962. Seven years later she became the short-lived *La Janelle*. *Ian Shiffman*

LAKE MANITOBA (1901) Canadian Pacific Line, UK

9,674grt; 469ft (143.1m) lbp x 56ft (17.1m) beam
752 passengers in three classes
C. S. Swan & Hunter, Wallsend-on-Tyne (Yard No 263)
Triple-expansion steam reciprocating, twin screw
The passenger-cargo ship *Lake Manitoba* caught fire at Montreal on 26 August 1918 and, to prevent her from capsizing, she was scuttled at her berth. She was refloated that September but inspection of the damage showed her to be a constructive total loss. Abandoned to the underwriters, she was sold by them to Bishop Navigation Company, which had her rebuilt as the cargo vessel *Iver Heath*. Under this name she survived until 1924 when she was broken up at Bremen.
Casualties: not known

LAKE MICHIGAN (1901) Canadian Pacific Line, UK

9,240grt; 469ft (142.9m) lbp x 56ft (17.1m) beam
750 passengers in three classes
C. S. Swan & Hunter, Wallsend-on-Tyne (Yard No 264)
Triple-expansion steam reciprocating, twin screw
During a voyage from Liverpool and the River Clyde to St John, New Brunswick, on 16 April 1918, the passenger-cargo ship *Lake Michigan* was attacked by the German submarine U100. She was torpedoed and sunk 93 miles north-by-west of Eagle Island, County Mayo, on Ireland's west coast, in the position 55.30N, 11.52W.
Casualties: 1 (the Master)

LAKE SUPERIOR (1884) Elder Dempster Line, UK

4,562grt; 400ft (121.9m) lbp x 44ft (13.4m) beam
More than 270 passengers
J. & G. Thomson, Clydebank (Yard No 222)
Compound-expansion steam reciprocating, single screw
The passenger-cargo steamship *Lake Superior*, on passage from St John, Brunswick, to Liverpool, was wrecked outside the Canadian port on 31 March 1902. She was broken up where she lay.
Casualties: 0

LAKONIA (1929) ex-*Johan Van Oldenbarnevelt* (1963) Greek Line, Greece

20,314grt; 608ft (185.4m) loa x 75ft (22.8m) beam
1,210 passengers in a single class
Nederlandsche SB, Amsterdam (Yard No 194)
Motor-ship, twin screw

At the end of a career that had involved route service for both travellers and emigrants and wartime troopship duties, the former Dutch passenger liner *Johan Van Oldenbarnevelt* was converted into the cruise ship *Lakonia*. In this guise she left Southampton for her first cruise, on 19 December 1963. Three days later, when 200 miles from Madeira, in the position 35.00N, 15.15W, fire broke out in her barber shop and quickly spread throughout the ship. In spite of having more than sufficient lifeboats for all on board, the evacuation of the ship was fraught with difficulty, partly because the deck crew was inexperienced with the ship but also due to her poorly maintained davit gear, which denied the use of many boats, while others were launched only partially loaded. The survivors were picked up by the Argentine liner *Salta* and the cargo ships *Montcalm*, *Rio Grande* and *Mehdi*, which had rushed to the scene. The *Lakonia* was taken in tow for Gibraltar by the salvage tug *Herkules*, but on 29 December, when she was about 250 miles from her destination, she heeled over and sank in the position 35.56N, 10.00W.
Casualties: 128 (95 passengers and 33 crew)

The former sister of the *Marnix van Sint Aldegonde*, the Greek cruise ship *Lakonia* is seen at Southampton just prior to the tragic fire that terminated her career. *Mick Lindsay*

LAMORICIÈRE (1921) Compagnie Générale Transatlantique (French Line), France

4,713grt; 370ft (112.8m) lbp x 50ft (15.2m) beam
381 passengers
Swan Hunter & Wigham Richardson, Low Walker, Tyneside (Yard No 1106)
Steam turbines, triple screw

The Swan Hunter-built *Lamoricière* was employed on French Line's Mediterranean services. *Ian Rae*

The trans-Mediterranean passenger ship *Lamoricière* sailed form Algiers, bound for Marseilles, with 272 passengers and a crew of 100 on 6 January 1942. Shortly after leaving port she ran into a violent storm but initially went to the aid of the cargo ship *Jumieges*, which was in difficulty off the Balearic

Islands. By the next day it was the *Lamoricière* that was in trouble for, having been disabled in the extreme conditions, she was herself now in need of urgent assistance. Her engine room was flooded and all power lost, but not before distress calls had been transmitted. These were answered by the French steamships *Gouverneur General Chanzy* and *Gouverneur General de Gueydon*, and the destroyer *L'Impetueuse*, which located the helpless *Lamoricière* north of Minorca. The extreme weather prevented a rescue operation from being undertaken, however, and on 9 January the ship foundered three miles from shore before the weather had moderated sufficiently to permit an attempt. Many of her occupants went down with her. The 95 survivors who were picked up from the sea were landed at Barcelona two days after the sinking.
Casualties: 277

LANCASTRIA (1922) ex-*Tyrrhenia* (1924) Cunard Line, UK

16,243grt; 579ft (176.5m) loa x 70ft (21.3m) beam
1,785 passengers in three classes
William Beardmore, Dalmuir (Yard No 557)
Steam turbines, twin screw

Similar to the ships of Anchor Line's '*Cameronia*' class, the *Lancastria* sailed on the London to Southampton, Le Havre and New York service. *Real Photos*

The dramatic moment as the *Lancastria* sinks off St Nazaire, France, during the evacuation of British and French troops in Operation 'Aerial'. *Imperial War Museum (HU2795)*

Taken over as a wartime troopship, the *Lancastria* commenced auxiliary duties on 5 March 1940. Just three months later, when the fall of France was imminent, she was drafted to St Nazaire from Plymouth to assist in the Operation 'Aerial' evacuation of units of the British Expeditionary Force that had been pushed back by the advancing Germans and had made their way to France's Atlantic coast. After arriving in Charpentier Roads, outside the French port, on 17 June 1940, the *Lancastria* embarked a large number of troops together with a small party of civilians. The precise number of her occupants is not known for certain but, including the crew, it is variously reported as being either 5,310 or 5,506. As she was about to weigh anchor, the embarkation area came under attack from German bombers, and aircraft in the third wave hit the *Lancastria* with four bombs, one of which penetrated to her engine room and exploded there.

The stricken troopship assumed an immediate list and, in spite of great urgency in trying to launch the lifeboats, only two were successfully floated. After around twenty minutes, sinking bow-first, she rolled over onto her port side and capsized completely. Small craft that had hurried to the scene managed to rescue a number of survivors from the water and it is believed that others managed to make it ashore by their own efforts, but the loss of life was massive. Indeed, the *Lancastria* holds the dubious distinction of being the worst British merchant ship loss of the Second World War. The official figure for the number of survivors is 2,477, indicating a death toll in excess of 3,000. The Association of Lancastria Survivors holds the firm belief that as many as 9,000 persons had been aboard the *Lancastria* when she sank, suggesting that the casualty numbers have been grossly understated. The wreck, in the position 47.09N, 02.20E was broken up from September 1951 because it was an obstruction to navigation.
Casualties: More than 3,000, including 66 crew

LANFRANC (1907) Booth Line, UK

6,287grt; 433ft (132.0m) loa x 52ft (15.9m) beam
571 passengers in two classes
Caledon, Dundee (Yard No 189)
Triple-expansion steam reciprocating, twin screw
The *Lanfranc* was requisitioned by the Admiralty for the First World War service as a hospital ship, and in this capacity she was torpedoed without warning by the German submarine UB40 on 17 April 1917, 42 miles north-half-east of Le Havre, while she was returning to Southampton from the French port carrying 576 persons, of whom 234 were British wounded and 167 were injured German soldiers. There were also 52 medical staff and a crew of 123 men aboard. The *Lanfranc* sank in the position 49.56N, 00.20W. The survivors were picked up by escorting naval ships.
Casualties: 34 (14 British military personnel, 15 German military personnel and 5 crew)

The steamship *Lanfranc*, seen here in wartime hospital ship livery, was one of a class of three vessels built for Booth Line's service from Liverpool to Brazil. *World Ship Society*

LA PROVENCE (1906) Compagnie Générale Transatlantique (French Line), France

serving under the wartime name PROVENCE II
13,753grt; 627ft (191.0) loa x 64ft (19.5m) beam
1,354 passengers in three classes
Penhoët, St Nazaire (Yard No 44)
Triple-expansion steam reciprocating, twin screw
On the outbreak of the First World War, the *La Provence* was commissioned under the name *Provence II* as an auxiliary cruiser serving with the French Navy, her duties including troop carrying. During such a voyage from Toulon to Salonika (Thessaloniki), Greece, on 26 February 1916, with 1,700 troops in addition to her crew, she was torpedoed and sunk by the German submarine U35 65 miles south-west of Cape Matapan (Akra Tainaron). She sank rapidly off Cerigo Island and there were only 870 survivors. As France's second most serious mercantile disaster of the First World War, the loss of the *Provence II* ranks only behind that of the *Gallia*.
Casualties: 990 (according to some reports, there were 1,059 casualties)

The *La Provence* entered the transatlantic service from Le Havre to New York in April 1906. She was one of the three worst French losses of the First World War. *Real Photos*

L'ATLANTIQUE (1931) Cie Sud-Atlantique, France

42,512grt; 744ft (226.7m) loa x 92ft (28.1m) beam
1,156 passengers in three classes
Penhoët, St Nazaire (Yard No P6)
Steam turbines, quadruple screw
In January 1933 the passenger liner *L'Atlantique* sailed from her home port Bordeaux with a reduced crew bound for Le Havre for her annual dry-docking and overhaul. When she was approximately twenty miles from Guernsey, in the position 49.30N, 03.17W, an outbreak of fire was discovered in the passenger accommodation on E deck at 3.30am on 4 January. The speed with which the fire spread was alarming. Less than 5 hours after it had started, she was ablaze from stem to stern and down to the waterline and the crew had abandoned ship. Those that escaped were rescued by the ships that had responded to calls for assistance.

From this point an incredible episode unfolded, high in suspense and danger, as the derelict *L'Atlantique* drifted for the next two days before the tides and winds in the English Channel. At one point she crossed to the English coast and threatened to run aground somewhere between Portland Bill and the Isle of Wight. A group of salvage tugs, consisting of Smit vessels and eight units from the French Abeille fleet,

fought between themselves to secure the ship and claim salvage rights, while two French warships stood by ready to sink the liner should she become a menace to other shipping. Eventually, their differences settled, the combined tugs towed the *L'Atlantique* into Cherbourg's Gare Maritime where she remained, the centre of dispute over her fitness for reconstruction, for the next three years. Ultimately the courts found in favour of her owners, who had claimed her to be a constructive total loss and, upon settlement in March 1936, she was towed to Port Glasgow where she was broken up.
Casualties: 19

The *L'Atlantique* of Cie Sud-Atlantique, the largest passenger liner placed in South American service, sailed between Bordeaux and La Plata ports. *Tom Rayner collection*

The *L'Atlantique* is heavily ablaze in the English Channel on 5 January 1933. *Author's collection*

While the lawyers wrangled over her owners' insurance claim, the *L'Atlantique* remained laid up at Cherbourg as corpus delicti. *Maritime Photo Library*

LAURENTIAN (1872) ex-*Polynesian* (1893) Allan Line, UK

4,522grt; 400ft (121.9m) lbp x 42.5ft (12.95m) beam
1,036 passengers in two classes
Robert Steele, Cartsburn (Yard No 75)
Triple-expansion steam reciprocating, single screw
On 7 September 1909, while returning to Glasgow from Boston, the passenger steamship *Laurentian* became stranded in thick fog at Mistaken Point, Trepassey Bay,

Newfoundland, close to Cape Race. Her entire ship's company, including her forty passengers, was taken off safely in the ship's boats.
Casualties: 0

LAURENTIC (1909) ex-*Alberta* (1908) White Star Line, UK

14,892grt; 565ft (172.2m) loa x 67ft (20.4m) beam
1,660 passengers in three classes
Harland & Wolff, Belfast (Yard No 394)
Triple-expansion steam reciprocating, triple screw
After the outbreak of the First World War, the passenger liner *Laurentic* was first used as a troopship, later taken up by the Admiralty as an auxiliary cruiser. On 23 January 1917, while still under Navy control, she sailed from Liverpool bound for Halifax with a large consignment of gold bullion. Not long after her departure, the *Laurentic* struck two mines off Malin Head, County Donegal. She had left with a full complement of 475 and many of these men died of exposure after they were pitched into the bitterly cold sea when the *Laurentic* sank in less than an hour. The German submarine U80 was responsible for laying the minefield into which she had steamed. After the war, a daring Royal Navy salvage operation was launched to recover the *Laurentic*'s valuable cargo. By 1924 this had recovered the majority of the gold, some 3,186 bars, valued at £5 million. During August 1952 further salvage operations were undertaken and the remaining 22 gold bars were successfully located on the seabed.
Casualties: 354

The *Laurentic* was laid down as the *Alberta* for the Dominion Line, but passed to White Star ownership before she was launched. She entered the Liverpool to Montreal service and remained so employed until 1914 when she became a troopship. *Tom Rayner collection*

LAURENTIC (1927) Cunard White Star Line, UK

18,724grt; 603ft (183.8m) loa x 75ft (22.9m) beam
1,500 passengers in three classes
Harland & Wolff, Belfast (Yard No 470)
Triple-expansion steam reciprocating with LP steam turbine, triple screw
The passenger liner *Laurentic* had spent much of the time since August 1935 laid up after she had been involved in a collision in the River Mersey. Rescued from her idleness, she was converted into an armed merchant cruiser and entered service with the Royal Navy in October 1939. On 3 November 1940, while she was patrolling the Western Approaches, she went to the aid of the sinking Elders & Fyffes ship *Casanare* off the Bloody Foreland, County Donegal, but she was herself torpedoed and sunk by the same German submarine, the U99. Hit by three torpedoes, she sank rapidly in the position

53.55N, 14.30W. The Blue Funnel passenger-cargo ship *Patroclus* (qv), also serving as an auxiliary cruiser, went to the *Laurentic*'s aid, but while she was standing by to pick up the 368 survivors, 52 officers and 316 ratings, she became the third victim of the U99.
Casualties: 49

Prior to the outbreak of the Second World War, the passenger liner *Laurentic* had been laid up following a collision with Blue Star Line's *Napier Star* in the Irish Sea. Had it not been for the renewal of hostilities with Germany, she may well have been destined for breaking up. Here she is seen in the Mersey, the doctored bow wave suggesting a greater speed than she was in fact making. *Ian Allan Library*

LAVIA (1947) ex-*Flavian* (1986) ex-*Flavia* (1982) ex-*Media* (1961) Lavia Shipping SA, Panama

15,465grt; 557ft (169.8m) loa x 70ft (21.3m) beam
1,224 passengers in single class
John Brown & Co, Clydebank (Yard No 629)
Steam turbines, twin screw

Prior to becoming the *Lavia*, the former *Media* of Cunard Line's Liverpool to New York service became the *Flavia*. On the North Atlantic the *Media* and sister *Parthia* carried only a small number of First class passengers in a very high standard of accommodation. *Kenneth Wightman*

The ill-fated cruise ship *Lavia* laid up at Hong Kong. *Ian Shiffman*

The Cunard transatlantic liner *Media*, sold in 1961 for emigrant service between Italy and Australia, was adapted into a cruise ship in 1968. She was lost on 7 January 1989 while undergoing modernisation at Hong Kong under her latest name after almost three years of lay-up. Fire broke out aboard the *Lavia*, which neither her skeleton crew of nine men nor the 35 shipyard workmen aboard her were able to control. It rapidly engulfed the passenger accommodation and she was soon fiercely ablaze. She was towed from the harbour the following day and beached, but, top-heavy with water from the fire-fighting, she keeled over on to her port side and settled on the bottom, half-submerged. She was later pumped out and raised but, being beyond economic recovery, she was sold for breaking up at Kaohsiung, Taiwan, where she arrived under tow on 19 June 1989.
Casualties: 0

LEDA (1920) Bergen Line, Norway

2,520grt; 306ft (93.2m) lbp x 42ft (12.7m) beam
227 berthed and 74 deck passengers
Armstrong Whitworth, Low Walker, Tyneside
(Yard No 965)
Steam turbines, single screw
While in German hands, following the invasion of Norway, the ferry *Leda* was lost on 25 March 1945 during the evacuation of East Prussia while bound from Stettin (Szczecin) to Swinemünde. She was sunk by gunfire from Russian artillery batteries positioned at Gross Siegendorf, at the outlet of the River Oder. The *Leda* sank with her stern submerged in a depth of about 26 feet (8 metres) but her bow above water.
Casualties: 20

LEERDAM (1881) ex-*De Nederlander* (1882) Holland Amerika Line, The Netherlands

2,796grt; 322ft (98.1m) lbp x 40ft (12.2m) beam
436 passengers in two classes
Nederlandsche SB, Rotterdam (Yard No 108)
Compound-expansion steam reciprocating, single screw
The passenger steamship *Leerdam* was lost on 16 December 1889, after she was involved in a collision 30 miles north of the Noord Hinder light vessel.
Casualties: 0

LEINSTER (1897) City of Dublin Steam Packet Co, UK

2,646grt; 360ft (109.7m) lbp x 42ft (12.7m) beam
1,400 passengers
Laird, Birkenhead (Yard No 612)
Triple-expansion steam reciprocating, twin screw
The Irish Sea ferry *Leinster*, carrying 180 passengers, 22 Post Office sorters, 489 military personnel and a 77-man crew, was lost on 10 October 1918 when she was torpedoed without warning by the German submarine UB123 while bound from Dublin to Holyhead. The attack took place seven miles east-south-east of the Kish Bank light vessel, Dublin Bay, and resulted in heavy loss of life. At the time of the attack the weather was poor and the sea rough, so many of the passengers had taken to their berths for comfort. When they rushed on deck, there was great confusion and many of the lifeboats were launched in haste, insufficiently full and lowered unevenly, contributing to the death toll. The

survivors were picked up by a Royal Navy destroyer that had sped to the scene, but which arrived after the *Leinster* had foundered in the position 53.19N, 05.47W.

Casualties: 501 (The German U-boat records give the number killed as 530)

LENIN (1909) ex-*Simbirsk* (1923) Black Sea Shipping Co (Sovtorgflot), USSR

2,713grt; 311ft (94.8m) lbp x 42ft (12.7m) beam
Passenger numbers not known
Schichau, Danzig (Yard No 832)
Triple-expansion steam reciprocating, single screw

Built originally for the Russian Volunteer Fleet Association and registered at Vladivostok, the *Lenin* was switched to the Black Sea, based at Odessa, after she was absorbed into the Soviet Union's nationalised merchant fleet. She was lost on 11 August 1941 when she was mined off Sevastopol in the position 44.20N, 33.44E.

Casualties: not known

LEONARDO DA VINCI (1960) Italia Crociere Internationale, Italy

33,340grt; 767ft (233.9m) loa x 92ft (28.1m) beam
1,284 passengers in two classes
Ansaldo, Sestri Ponente, Genoa (Yard No 1550)
Steam turbines, twin screw

The replacement for the *Andrea Doria* was an equally stylish ship, the *Leonardo da Vinci*, seen here in the Panama Canal. After serving for much of her career on the Genoa and Naples to New York service, she transferred to full-time cruising. *Italia Line*

The cruise ship *Leonardo da Vinci* lists to starboard after the fire that destroyed her in July 1980. *Antonio Scrimali*

After adaptation from operation as a scheduled service passenger liner into a full-time cruise ship, the *Leonardo da Vinci* was laid up in September 1978, languishing at a berth in La Spezia with an uncertain future. While there, on 3 July 1980, a fire broke out in her chapel and quickly spread throughout the empty vessel, whose fire protection systems were not in operation. The fire continued unabated for four days. An attempt was made to tow the ship beyond the harbour breakwater to minimise the risk of pollution to nearby holiday beaches but, in the process, the *Leonardo da Vinci* sank in shallow water in the outer harbour with a 60-degree list to port. Controversy surrounded the gutted vessel for, while her condition realistically precluded economic repair, her insured value exceeded her scrap value by a significant margin. Despite this, during 1981 her charred, half-submerged hulk was raised and she was subsequently broken up for scrap a year later.

Casualties: 0

LEOPOLDVILLE (1929) Cie Maritime Belge, Belgium

11,509grt; 517ft (157.6m) loa x 62ft (18.9m) beam
360 passengers in two classes
John Cockerill, Hoboken (Yard No 623)
Quadruple-expansion steam reciprocating, twin screw

The twin-funnelled sister ships *Albertville* and *Leopoldville* entered the Antwerp to Matadi, Belgian Congo (Zaire), service in 1928 and 1929 respectively. The sinking of the *Leopoldville* was Belgium's worst ever shipping loss. *Bettina Rohbrecht*

After the fall of Belgium in May 1940, the British Ministry of War Transport took over the passenger-cargo ship *Leopoldville* as a troopship. While bound from Southampton to Cherbourg on 24 December 1944, carrying 2,235 American troops and her crew of 228 men, she was torpedoed by the German submarine U486 when only five miles from her destination. The torpedo exploded with an incredible force and the troopship's two after decks collapsed, trapping some of the men. Nevertheless, she remained afloat and evacuation of the ship was begun, but with little sense of urgency because it was not felt that she was in immediate danger of sinking. The destroyer HMS *Brilliant* came alongside the *Leopoldville* and 1,500 persons, troops and crew, were transhipped and taken to Cherbourg. About an hour later, while awaiting the destroyer's return to collect the remainder of the troopship's complement, her bulkheads suddenly gave way and the *Leopoldville* foundered within ten minutes in the position 49.45N, 01.34W. In the confusion, many of the crew abandoned ship, believing that they had been given the order to do so. However, this left undrilled and inexperienced soldiers to lower the remaining

lifeboats as best they could, delaying further evacuation. When small craft, sent out from the French coast, arrived on the scene it was too late to save many of those in the water, while others had gone down with the ship.
Casualties: 808 (802 troops and 6 crew)

LEROS (1968) ex-*Dimitra* (1997) ex-*Bihar* (1994) ex-*Ionian Sea* (1993) ex-*Ionian Fantasy* (1991) ex-*Yum* (1988) ex-*Canguro Bruno* (1982) Agios Gerasimos (GA Ferries), Greece

8,952grt; 415ft (126.4m) loa x 63ft (19.3m) beam
334 berthed and 366 deck passengers (as built)
Italcantieri, Castellammare (Yard No 648)
Motor-ship, twin screw
Fire broke out aboard the passenger ro-ro ferry *Leros* while she was lying idle at Piraeus on 14 December 1998. The fire was extinguished but left her extensively damaged and she was towed to Atalanti, where she was beached. Although she was later recovered and restored, returning to service with Dane Sea Line, she survived only two more years until broken up at Aliaga, Turkey, where she arrived for demolition on 26 March 2001.
Casualties: not known

The passenger-vehicle ferry *Leros* at Piraeus in 1999 in Dane Sea Line colours. *Frank Heine FERRIES*

LETITIA (1912) Anchor-Donaldson Line, UK

8,991grt; 470ft (143.5m) lbp x 56ft (17.3m) beam
1,300 passengers in two classes
Scott's, Greenock (Yard No 437)
Triple-expansion steam reciprocating, twin screw

The *Letitia* stranded at Chebucto Head in August 1917. *Imperial War Museum (Q61170)*

During the First World War the passenger-cargo liner *Letitia* was taken over for conversion into a hospital ship under Canadian control, a role she continued to perform until 1

August 1917 when she was lost on the coast of Nova Scotia. While bound from Liverpool to Quebec, repatriating wounded Canadians, she ran onto the rocks and was stranded at Portuguese Cove, Chebucto Head, near Halifax. She became a total wreck.
Casualties: 0

LIGURIA (1918) ex-*Melita* (1935) Lloyd Triestino, Italy

15,183grt; 546ft (166.4m) loa x 67ft (20.4m) beam
1,750 passengers in two classes (as a British ship)
Harland & Wolff, Belfast, sub-contracted to Barclay Curle, Whiteinch, Glasgow (Yard No 517)
Triple-expansion steam reciprocating with LP turbine, triple screw
The passenger liner *Liguria* had been in service as an Italian Government troopship since 1935 and, in this capacity, she was at Tobruk on 6 July 1940 when she was hit by an aerial torpedo launched by a British warplane. Seriously damaged, she was laid up, but during a later air raid on 22 January 1941 she was hit by a bomb, burned out and capsized. British salvage teams raised the *Liguria* in 1950 and she was towed to Savona for scrapping, arriving there on 31 August 1950.
Casualties: not known

LIMA (1907) Pacific Steam Navigation Co, UK

4,946grt; 401ft (122.3m) lbp x 52ft (15.9m) beam
283 passengers in two classes (her dormitories could accommodate 693 emigrants)
John Brown, Clydebank (Yard No 378)
Triple-expansion steam reciprocating, single screw
While bound from Liverpool to Callao, Peru, on 23 December 1909, the passenger steamer *Lima* was driven ashore on Huamblin Island, Magellan Strait, off the coast of Chile, in stormy weather. The position was 44.45S, 75.12W. The *Lima* was carrying 299 persons in total, of whom around 200 were passengers. Distress signals were fired and luckily, despite the remote location, they were seen by the steamship *Hatumet*, which came to her aid. Using a rope attached to the *Lima*'s stern, 205 persons were helped into two lifeboats that had been launched and they were then ferried to the *Hatumet*, which remained standing by. Among these survivors were 188 passengers, including all the women and children. Unfortunately, during the night six of the brave crewmen who had first attached the lifeline and who had toiled throughout the day with the rescue work were drowned when the rope became entangled, causing their boat to capsize. The *Hatumet* took the survivors to Ancud while the remaining 88 persons aboard the *Lima* were lifted off to safety the following day by a Chilean cruiser.
Casualties: 6 (all crew)

LIPARI (1922) Chargeurs Réunis, France

9,954grt; 478ft (145.7m) lbp x 59ft (18.0m) beam
225 passengers in three classes
Chantiers de la Loire, St Nazaire (Yard No 129)
Steam turbines, twin screw
The French passenger-cargo ship *Lipari* was sunk by shellfire while she was berthed in the harbour at Casablanca, when the port came under bombardment from Allied warships on 8 November 1942. She caught fire and broke in two. Earlier in

her career the *Lipari* had been stranded near Brest on 30 April 1923, but had been refloated a month later.
Casualties: not known

LISBOA (1910) Empreza Nacional de Navagacao à Vapor, Portugal

7,450grt; 433ft (131.9m) lbp x 54ft (16.5m) beam
1,328 passengers
D. & W. Henderson, Meadowside, Glasgow (Yard No 469)
Triple-expansion steam reciprocating, twin screw
The passenger-cargo ship *Lisboa* had only been on the Lisbon to Angola and Mozambique service for four months when she was wrecked on Soldiers Reef, near Paternoster, about 100 miles from Cape Town on the night of 23 October 1910. Radio messages requesting assistance were transmitted, in response to which the German ship *Adolf Woermann* and the British cruiser HMS *Hermes* proceeded to the scene. By then most of the passengers and crew aboard the *Lisboa* had made good their escape in the boats and had reached the nearby shore in safety. The exception was a group of persons who were drowned when the falls of their boat broke, tipping them into the water. Casualties: 7

LLANDAFF CASTLE (1926) Union-Castle Line, UK

10,786grt; 490ft (149.3m) loa x 61ft (18.6m) beam
410 passengers in two classes
Workman Clark, Belfast (Yard No 488)
Quadruple-expansion steam reciprocating, twin screw
The passenger-cargo ship *Llandaff Castle* was converted into a troopship in 1940. On 30 November 1942, while she was bound from Mombasa and Dar-es-Salaam to Durban following the Allied landings in Madagascar, carrying 150 passengers and 163 crew, she was torpedoed by the German submarine U177. Attacked about 100 miles south-east of Lourenço Marques (Maputo), she sank in the position 27.20S, 33.40E. It was said that when the U-boat surfaced and enquired of survivors in the sea as to the identity of their ship, a chorus responded with 'Hardship!'. Casualties: 3 (all crew)

The *Llandaff Castle* ran in consort with the *Llandovery Castle* on the round-Africa service from London. *David Reed*

LLANDOVERY CASTLE (1914) Union-Castle Line, UK

11,423grt; 517ft (157.6m) loa x 63ft (19.2m) beam
429 passengers in three classes
Barclay Curle, Whiteinch, Glasgow (Yard No 504)
Quadruple-expansion steam reciprocating, twin screw

After the outbreak of hostilities in August 1914, the new liner *Llandovery Castle* continued to make commercial sailings on the African services, although somewhat intermittently, until December 1915, when she was taken over for service as a troopship. Two years later she was converted into a hospital ship and attached to the Canadian forces. The *Llandovery Castle* was crossing from Halifax, Nova Scotia, to Liverpool on 27 June 1918, with 258 persons, of whom 94 were nurses or medical officers from the Canadian Medical Service, when the German submarine U86 torpedoed her without warning and sank her 116 miles south-west of Fastnet Rock. As in other cases of submarine attacks on hospital ships, the *Llandovery Castle* had been clearly marked and had been displaying a brightly illuminated Red Cross sign. She sank within ten minutes of the attack but her crew still managed to get all the ship's boats away. However, the U86 surfaced and turned her guns on the helpless lifeboats. By the time rescue arrived, only one boat, containing 24 persons, remained afloat. After the war, two of the submarine's officers, who were tried for war crimes by the German Supreme Court, were found guilty, but their punishment was limited to a four-year prison sentence.
Casualties: 234 (88 medical staff and 146 crew)

The *Llandovery Castle* entered the service from London to West and East Africa just before the outbreak of the First World War. *Real Photos*

LOMBARDIA (1920) ex-*Resolute* (1935) ex-*Brabantia* (1922) ex-*William O'Swald* (1916) Lloyd Triestino, Italy

20,006grt; 616ft (187.8m) loa x 72ft (21.9m) beam
103 passengers plus 4,420 troops
Deschimag AG Weser, Bremen (Yard No 193)
Triple-expansion steam reciprocating with LP turbine, triple screw

The *Lombardia* was originally the Hamburg Amerika transatlantic liner *Resolute*, shown here. *Ian Allan Library*

The German passenger liner *Resolute* was sold to the Italian Government in August 1935 for conversion into the troopship *Lombardia*, managed by Lloyd Triestino. She was struck by bombs during an air raid on Naples on 4 April 1943, which left her flooded and grounded. Exactly four months later, on 4 August 1943, the *Lombardia* was hit in a second strike. Set on fire, she burned out, heeled over and sank. Her wreck was raised in the winter of 1946-47, and on 1 June 1947 it was towed to La Spezia for breaking up.
Casualties: not known

LUCANIA (1893) Cunard Line, UK

12,950grt; 620ft (188.6m) loa x 65ft (19.9m) beam
2,000 passengers in three classes
Fairfield, Govan (Yard No 365)
Triple-expansion steam reciprocating, twin screw
The transatlantic passenger liner *Lucania* caught fire on 14 August 1909 while she was berthed at the Huskisson Dock, Liverpool. Though not completely gutted, the destruction within the ship was virtually complete, especially to her passenger accommodation, and she was declared unfit for the express mail service. There being no financial justification for repairing her, she was sold for breaking up. In spite of the fact that she had been ravaged by fire, she was able to proceed to the ship-breaker's yard for demolition under her own steam, achieving the remarkable speed, under the circumstances, of 17 knots.
Casualties: 0

The *Lucania*, seen here at Liverpool, was a holder of the Atlantic Blue Riband together with her sister ship *Campania*. The *Campania* was lost after conversion into one of the earliest aircraft carriers after she had been sold to the Admiralty.
Cunard Line

LUDWIG (1861) ex-*Hansa* (1883) Steinmann & Company, Belgium

3,987grt; 328.2ft (100m) lbp x 42ft (12.7m) beam
660 passengers in three classes
Caird, Greenock (Yard No 92)
Compound-expansion steam reciprocating, single screw
The passenger steamship *Ludwig* sailed from her home port of Antwerp, bound for Montreal, for the last time on 3 July 1883 with a complement of seventy persons, made up of 27 passengers and 43 crew. She was sighted passing Prawle Point, south-east of Plymouth, Devon, but thereafter was never heard of again.
Casualties: 70

LUSITANIA (1871) Elder Dempster Line, UK

3,912grt; 379ft (115.5m) lbp x 41ft (12.5m) beam
429 passengers in three classes
Laird, Birkenhead (Yard No 381)
Triple-expansion steam reciprocating, single screw
On 26 June 1901 the passenger steamer *Lusitania* ran onto the rocks three miles north of Cape Ballard, Newfoundland, while bound from Liverpool to Montreal. In her time she had served the Pacific Steam Navigation, Orient and Elder Dempster concerns, and had served on the Liverpool to South America via Cape Horn route, the Plymouth to Melbourne, Australia, route across the Indian Ocean, and the Liverpool to Halifax and St John, New Brunswick route.
Casualties: 0

LUSITANIA (1906) Empreza Nacional de Navagacao à Vapor, Portugal

5,557grt; 420ft (128.2m) lbp x 51ft (15.6m) beam
Passenger numbers not known
Raylton Dixon, Middlesbrough (Yard No 519)
Triple-expansion steam reciprocating, twin screw
While she was returning to Lisbon on 18 April 1911, the *Lusitania* was stranded in poor visibility on the Bellows Rocks, Cape of Good Hope, near the entrance to Table Bay. She was carrying almost 800 persons, of whom 450 were natives travelling to cocoa plantations on the Portuguese island of Sao Tome in the Gulf of Guinea. Another 200 were European passengers. The boats were lowered and the ship abandoned. One lifeboat capsized and, of its occupants, an officer and three passengers were drowned. Three other boats made it ashore at Cape Point while the remaining survivors were picked up by the warship *Forte* and the tug *Scotsman*. On 22 April, four days after the incident, the *Lusitania*, which appeared to be held fast on the rocks, was dislodged by the swell and foundered in deep water.
Casualties: 4

LUSITANIA (1907) Cunard Line, UK

31,550grt; 787ft (239.9m) loa x 87ft (26.5m) beam
2,165 passengers in three classes
John Brown, Clydebank (Yard No 367)
Steam turbines, quadruple screw
Like the earlier loss of the *Titanic*, the sinking by torpedo of the Cunard express transatlantic liner *Lusitania* has come to represent a milestone of huge consequence in both world and maritime affairs. It signified the point at which civilians became the legitimate targets of a conflict, and since when undefended ships could no longer go about their peaceful business safe from the risk of attack without warning.

Accompanied by threats of potentially hostile action, the *Lusitania* made her last departure from New York bound for Liverpool on 1 May 1915. She was carrying 1,959 people, among them 440 women and 129 children. Six days later, as she was approaching St George's Channel, south of Ireland, she was torpedoed without warning fifteen miles south of the Old Head of Kinsale by the German submarine U20. The *Lusitania* sank with alarming suddenness, barely fifteen minutes after the attack. Although her engines were stopped, she was still going ahead in the water, and this, coupled with her increasing list to starboard, hampered the efforts to launch the lifeboats. A flotilla of small craft, including local trawlers, hurried to the scene from the coast nearby but they were able to rescue fewer than forty per cent of those who had been aboard the *Lusitania*. Germany defended its actions by arguing that the *Lusitania* had been carrying a quantity of war materials, which may well have been the case, but this hardly justified the slaughter of more than 1,000 innocent victims who were given no opportunity to abandon ship before it was sunk. The loss of the *Lusitania* was the worst British maritime disaster of the First World War.

Casualties: 1,198, including 94 children and 291 female passengers

The Cunard Line's *Lusitania* is seen here on trials in the summer of 1907. She and her sister ship *Mauretania* were two of the most advanced passenger liners of their day, sweeping aside the opposition to take the transatlantic speed records. *Author's collection*

A graphic illustration of the *Lusitania* sinking, by one of Britain's most celebrated marine artists, Norman Wilkinson. The original caption conveys all the sentiments of the British public, as expressed through the popular press, at what was considered an appalling deed, but one that was to be replicated and far exceeded in later attacks in both World Wars. *Illustrated London News*

M

MADIANA (1877) ex-*Balmoral Castle* (1892) ex-*San Augustin* (1886) ex-*Balmoral Castle* (1882) Quebec Steamship Co, Canada

2,948grt; 344ft (105.1m) lbp x 39ft (12.0m) beam
250 passengers in three classes
Robert Napier, Govan (Yard No 356)
Compound-expansion steam reciprocating, single screw
The passenger-cargo steamer *Madiana* was wrecked ten miles north of Hamilton, Bermuda, on 10 February 1903. At the time she was conveying passengers from New York bound for Kingston, Jamaica. Earlier in her life, this ship had rammed and sunk the paddle ferry *Princess of Wales* while she had been running builder's trials for Barclay Curle on the Skelmorlie measured mile in the Firth of Clyde.
Casualties: not known

MADRID (1922) ex-*Sierra Nevada* (1925) Norddeutscher Lloyd, Germany

8,753grt; 439ft (133.8m) lbp x 56ft (17.1m) beam
732 passengers in three classes
Stettiner Vulcan, Stettin-Bredow (Yard No 666)
Triple-expansion, twin screw
During an Allied air raid on Ymuiden on 9 December 1941, the South Atlantic passenger-cargo ship *Madrid*, which was off Den Helder, was bombed and sunk.
Casualties: not known

MAGDALENA (1949) Royal Mail Line, UK

17,547grt; 570ft (173.8m) loa x 73ft (22.3m) beam
479 passengers in two classes
Harland & Wolff, Belfast (Yard No 1354)
Steam turbines, twin screw
While she was on the return leg of her maiden voyage to Argentina from London, on 25 April 1949, the passenger-cargo liner *Magdalena* ran hard aground on the Tehas Tijucas Rocks, between the Cagarras and Palmas Islands, a few miles south of Rio de Janeiro, when tidal currents took her off course. She was fast making water in Nos 1 and 3 holds and a tender was requested to take off her 350 passengers. The steamer *Goiazloide* responded to the call, taking the passengers and elements of the crew back to Rio, while much of her cargo of oranges and meat was transferred to barges to lighten her. An approaching cold front made it imperative to refloat her, but while this was achieved during the night of 25-26 April it was not before she had been badly buffeted in the rapidly deteriorating weather conditions.

Taken in tow by the tugs *Tritao*, *Triunfo*, *Saturno* and *Commandante Dorat*, the stricken ship was proceeding satisfactorily until, as she crossed the harbour bar at Rio de Janeiro, she was pounded heavily on the bottom, fracturing and buckling her sides at the aft end of No 3 hold. Within twenty minutes she had broken in two, aft of her bridge. Those members of her crew who were still aboard were rescued by two Brazilian destroyers and a flotilla of harbour craft. The *Magdalena*'s after part ran ashore on the sandy bottom at Ponta de Fora in Imbui Bay. The bow section, which was interfering with shipping, was detonated immediately to remove the menace. Consideration was given to salvaging the *Magdalena*'s stern section in the hope of saving her engines and refrigeration plant. It was partly refloated on 13 May 1949 but some two or so weeks later, on 2 June 1949, the underwriters accepted £50,000 for it on the condition that it was broken up where it was beached and sold for scrap at the best price obtainable. In the Court of Inquiry into the disaster that took place in London in September 1949, the *Magdalena*'s Master was found to have committed 'a grave dereliction of duty' in leaving the responsibility for his new vessel in the hands of junior officers as she navigated a narrow, unlit channel.

Casualties: 0

The Royal Mail passenger liner *Magdalena* running builder's trials in Belfast Lough in February 1949.
Ulster Folk & Transport Museum

The luckless *Magdalena* was another passenger ship lost on her maiden voyage. Her aft section is seen stranded at Ponta de Fora, near Rio de Janeiro. *Author's collection*

MAGELLAN (1897) ex-*Indus* (1903)
Messageries Maritimes, France

6,357grt; 446ft (135.9m) 50ft (15.2m) beam
200 passengers in three classes (as built)
Messageries Maritimes, La Ciotat (Yard No 75)
Triple-expansion steam reciprocating, twin screw

After the outbreak of the First World War, the French passenger ship *Magellan* continued to make commercial sailings to ensure continuation of the French mail service to the Far East. There was just a brief interruption from March to April 1915 when she undertook troop-carrying to the Dardanelles. Later, on a return voyage from Yokohama, bound for Marseilles with 736 persons, the *Magellan* was proceeding through the Mediterranean in convoy, escorted by HMS *Cyclamen*, when she was torpedoed and sunk by the German submarine U63 on 11 December 1916. She

foundered 10 miles south of the Pantellaria Islands, south-east of Sicily, within two hours of the attack. The survivors were picked up by the French torpedo-boat *Sagaie* and the *Magellan*'s fleet-mate *Sinaï*, which herself was torpedoed and sunk later the same day by the same U-boat. Two other ships in the convoy, the *Alcyon* and *Normandie*, together with three British trawlers, in turn picked up the *Sinaï*'s survivors.

Casualties: 36 (26 passengers and 10 crew)

Built originally for the service to the Far East, the renamed *Magellan* was transferred to the South American trade in 1904. In 1912 she reverted to the service from Marseilles to the Orient. *World Ship Society*

MAID OF KENT (1925) Southern Railway, UK

2,693grt; 329ft (100.4m) lbp x 45ft (13.7m) beam
1,400 passengers in two classes
William Denny, Dumbarton (Yard No 1174)
Steam turbines, twin screw

The cross-Channel ferry *Maid of Kent*, serving as Hospital Carrier No 21, was caught on the French side of the English Channel at the time of the fall of France, supporting the efforts to evacuate injured British troops back to the UK. After arriving empty from Newhaven on her third mercy crossing, she was bombed by German aircraft at Dieppe on 21 May 1940. Trapped within the Paris Basin along with fleet-mate *Brighton*, inside the port and unable to leave earlier because the lock gates had been jammed, she was struck by four bombs, one of which entered her engine room, starting fires that rapidly spread throughout the ship. She sank at her berth and the wreck was removed later by the Germans and scuttled out at sea.

Casualties: 43

The cross-Channel passenger ferry *Maid of Kent* was owned by the Southern Railway. *Chris Bancroft collection*

MAIN (1868) Anglo-American Steamship Co

3,087grt; 348ft (106.1m) lbp x 40ft (12.2m) beam
770 passengers in three classes
Caird, Greenock (Yard No 146)
Compound inverted steam engines, single screw
Acquired from Norddeutscher Lloyd in 1891, without a change of name, the passenger steamship *Main* was lost barely a year later when she was destroyed by fire on the Portuguese island of Fayal (Faial) in the Azores on 23 March 1892. The gutted ship was abandoned as a derelict.
Casualties: not known

MAIN (1900) Norddeutscher Lloyd, Germany

10,067grt; 520ft (158.5m) loa x 58ft (17.7m) beam
3,451 passengers in three classes
Blohm & Voss, Steinwerder, Hamburg (Yard No 138)
Quadruple-expansion steam reciprocating, twin screw
The passenger-cargo steamer *Main*, together with her sister ship *Rhein* and many other fleet-mates, was berthed at the Norddeutscher Lloyd pier at Hoboken, New Jersey, on 30 June 1900 when fire broke out. For the full account, see the entry for the *Saale*.

MAIPU (1951) Dodero Line, Argentina

11,515grt; 523ft (159.4m) loa x 64ft (19.6m) beam
753 passengers in two classes
De Schelde, Vissingen (Yard No 267)
Motor-ship, twin screw
On 4 November 1951 the passenger-cargo ship *Maipu* was bound for Hamburg from Buenos Aires and Amsterdam with 107 passengers plus her crew. Also aboard her were Dutch engineers from Flushing who were making final checks on the virtually new ship. At the same time, heading in the other direction, bound for Bremerhaven from New York, was the American troop transport *General M. L. Hersey*, carrying 3,000 troops. The two ships collided in thick fog in the position 53.54N, 07.52E, about three miles north of the Weser light vessel, the crash leaving the *Maipu* with a huge gash on her port side through which water rushed into her forward hold. Her pumps were unable to cope with the flood and it was soon evident that she was sinking. The troopship stood by the fatally weakened *Maipu* and took off her passengers and crew, all of whom were safely rescued. Three hours later she sank in about 75 feet, and the transport, whose hull had also been holed above the waterline, unable to help further, proceeded to Bremerhaven. At first, salvage experts believed the *Maipu* was completely beyond recovery as she had capsized as she sank. Although she was eventually raised by the Bugsier Salvage Co, it was only to be taken to the breaker's yard, barely six months after she had first entered service.
Casualties: 0

MAITAI (1892) ex-*Miowera* (1908) Union Steamship Co of New Zealand, UK

3,393grt; 345ft (105.2m) lbp x 43ft (12.9m) beam
360 passengers
C. S. Swan & Hunter, Wallsend-on-Tyne (Yard No 176)
Triple-expansion steam reciprocating, single screw
The passenger steamer *Maitai* served on the run from the United States to New Zealand. She was wrecked at South Reef, Avarua, on Rarotonga in the Cook Islands group, on 25 December 1916 while bound from San Francisco to Wellington. Casualties: not known

MALABAR (1925) Burns, Philip & Co, UK

4,512grt; 351ft (107.0m) lbp x 49ft (14.8m) beam
165 passengers
Barclay Curle, Whiteinch, Glasgow (Yard No 609)
Motor-ship, single screw
Having departed Melbourne for Sydney with passengers and cargo and a crew of 108, many of whom were Chinese and Malays, on her regular service to Singapore via Port Moresby, the passenger-cargo ship *Malabar* was stranded on the north side of Long Bay, some nine miles (fourteen kilometres) south of Port Jackson, in foggy conditions on 2 April 1931. The ship hit the rocks just inside the headland and immediately the engines were put full astern to try to free her. She was firmly wedged, however, so the engines were stopped and the boats lowered to evacuate the passengers and crew ashore. An attempt was then made by the trawler *Charlie Cam* to pull the *Malabar* off the rocks but to no avail. Salvage was also attempted with the tug *St Aristell*, but in the rising seas it was abandoned. The stricken vessel, which had begun to flood and submerge at the aft end, was pounded to pieces in the swell. Casualties: 0

Burns, Philip & Co's *Malabar* operated between Melbourne and Singapore, via Sydney. *World Ship Society*

MALAYSIA KITA (1951) ex-*Malaysia Baru* (1972) ex-*Princess Abeto* (1971) ex-*Pacifique* (1970) ex-*Vietnam* (1967) Fir Line, Panama

11,792grt; 532ft (162.1m) loa x 72ft (22.0m) beam
1,612 pilgrim passengers
Constructions Navales de La Ciotat (Yard No MC1)
Steam turbines, twin screw
While lying in the Eastern anchorage at the Singapore Roads on 11 May 1974, a fire of unknown cause broke out aboard the pilgrim ship *Malaysia Kita* and soon spread out of control. Her 52 crew members were taken off and the abandoned ship was towed out of the harbour with a view to beaching her off Tanjong Katong where the fire could be left to burn itself out. However, the ship sank on her port side in shallow water in the position 01.17N, 103.53E and was declared a constructive total loss. Her upper structure over the entire length of the hull was destroyed and her funnel had collapsed. The wreck was salvaged in June 1975 and taken to Kaohsiung, Taiwan, for scrapping.
Casualties: 0

The burned-out wreck of the *Malaysia Kita* during the salvage operation and secured at a berth in Singapore in June 1976, after she had been refloated. *Both Mick Lindsay*

MALAYSIA RAYA (1954) ex-*Empress Abeto* (1971) ex-*Laos* (1970) Fir Line, Panama

11,792grt; 532ft (162.1m) loa x 72ft (22.0m) beam
1,696 pilgrim passengers
Chantiers Navales de La Ciotat (Yard No 170)
Steam turbines, twin screw

Another former passenger liner converted for the pilgrim trade, the *Malaysia Raya* was lying at anchor off Port Kelang, Malaya, on 23 August 1976 when fire broke out aboard her and she was completely gutted. The wreck was beached on 27 August but was subsequently refloated. Fit only for demolition, the *Malaysia Raya* was sold to Taiwanese breakers and arrived at Kaohsiung on 27 April 1977.
Casualties: not known

Sister ship of the *Malaysia Kita*, the *Malaysia Raya*, here anchored at Singapore in March 1975, suffered the same fate. *Ian Shiffman*

MALDA (1922) British India Line, UK

9,066grt; 465ft (141.7m) lbp x 58ft (17.7m) beam
175 passengers
Barclay Curle, Whiteinch, Glasgow (Yard No 588)
Steam turbines, twin screw

While bound from Calcutta to Colombo on 6 April 1942, the passenger-cargo ship *Malda* was attacked by Japanese carrier aircraft when off Gopalpore, in the position 19.45N, 86.27E, and received considerable bomb damage. Subsequently she was finished off by shells from cruisers operating with the Japanese naval task force. At the time she was only carrying her crew of 179 men.
Casualties: 25

British India Line's *Malda*. *World Ship Society*

MALINES (1922) London & North Eastern Railway, UK

2,969grt; 321ft (97.7m) lbp x 43ft (13.2m) beam
373 passengers
Armstrong Whitworth, High Walker, Tyneside
(Yard No 972)
Steam turbines, twin screw

The LNER North Sea ferry *Malines*. *H. B. Christiansen Collection / Online Transport Archive*

The half-submerged *Malines* near Port Said in July 1942. Though salvaged, she was ultimately scrapped as a constructive total loss. *Imperial War Museum (A11886)*

While serving as a troop transport and convoy escort on 22 July 1942, the ferry *Malines* was hit by an aerial torpedo in the approaches to Port Said. The missile struck her on her starboard side, passed through her and exploded on the port side. Taken in tow by minesweepers, she was beached in shallow water, settling by the stern and coming to rest on the bottom, flooded to her main deck. The damage was severe. Raised on 21 December 1942, the *Malines* was moved to Alexandria for dry-docking the following March, after which she was returned to Port Said in November 1943. She was paid off as a constructive total loss on 16 April 1944 and, despite her condition, was towed back to the UK, an arduous and difficult business during which she was in constant danger of breaking up or foundering. After much expense and effort, the wreck arrived at Wallsend-on-Tyne on 7 November 1945 only to be adjudged as being beyond economic repair. She was broken up at Dunston from 24 April 1948.

Casualties: 7 (all crew)

MALOJA (1911) P&O Line, UK

12,431grt; 569ft (173.4m) loa x 62ft (18.9m) beam
770 passengers in two classes
Harland & Wolff, Belfast (Yard No 414)
Quadruple-expansion steam reciprocating, twin screw

P&O Line's 'M' class consisted of seven passenger vessels built for the London to Sydney route. The *Maloja*, the sixth unit, entered service in February 1912. *World Ship Society*

After the outbreak of the First World War, the *Maloja* continued about her scheduled commercial sailings. Accordingly, in February 1916 she set out from London bound for Bombay with 121 passengers and 335 crew. However, she struck a mine when about two miles south-west of Dover on 27 February and foundered after only a very brief period. The *Maloja*'s engines were reversed in order to slow her forward movement and stop her dead, as this would help with the lowering of the lifeboats, but as the ship's engine room was soon flooded, the engines, having been reversed, could not then be stopped altogether. Now moving in a sternwards direction at some eight or so knots with a 75-degree list, all attempts to launch the boats were fraught with danger and ultimately became virtually impossible. While the crew of the *Maloja* were struggling in this fashion, the Canadian ship *Empress of Fort William* attempted to come alongside to provide her survivors with a means of escape, but she too struck a mine and foundered.

Casualties: 122 (all from the *Maloja*)

MAMARI (1911) ex-*Mamilius* (1933) ex-*Zealandic* (1926) Shaw, Savill & Albion, UK

serving as the wartime dummy aircraft carrier
HMS HERMES
10,898grt; 478ft (145.5m) lbp x 63ft (19.2m) beam
1,006 passengers in two classes
Harland & Wolff, Belfast (Yard No 421)
Quadruple-expansion steam reciprocating, twin screw

Acquired by the Admiralty in 1939, the emigrant passenger ship *Mamari* was drastically modified externally to resemble the aircraft carrier HMS *Hermes* and stationed at Scapa Flow as a decoy. While proceeding to Chatham Dockyard on 3 June 1941, where she was to be converted into a wartime refrigerated cargo ship, the *Mamari* struck the wreck of the tanker *Ahamo* when thirty miles north of Wells, Norfolk, and was stranded in the position 53.23N, 01.00E. Seven days later, while still aground following the incident, she was torpedoed by an E-boat and abandoned as a total loss.

Casualties: not known

MANHATTAN (1932) United States Lines, USA

serving under the wartime name WAKEFIELD [AP-21]
24,289grt; 705ft (214.9m) loa x 86ft (26.3m) beam
1,239 passengers in three classes
New York Shipbuilding Corp, Camden, New Jersey
(Yard No 405)
Steam turbines, twin screw

Just prior to the United States' involvement in the Second World War, but no doubt in anticipation of such an outcome, the transatlantic passenger liner *Manhattan* was converted into a troop transport for the US Department of War Shipping. Renamed *Wakefield*, she was nearing the end of a voyage, in convoy, from Europe on 3 September 1942, repatriating 950 American nationals from the British Isles and Ireland, when a fire of undetermined cause was discovered on the starboard side of B deck in the stateroom accommodation. It spread so rapidly that within ten minutes the flames had reached A and C decks and could be seen around her forward funnel. The *Wakefield* was soon engulfed in smoke and, breaking off from the convoy, was turned away from the wind so that the smoke and flames were blown away from her. Escorting American warships, the cruiser USS *Brooklyn* and the destroyers USS *Mayo* and *Madison*, came alongside and, at great risk of the fire spreading to them, rescued all the passengers and crew, including some men in the water who had made good their escape through portholes. Having flooded her magazines, her commander, officers and fire-fighting parties then also abandoned the ship and she was left to burn uncontrollably for the next four days.

The Canadian tugs *Foundation Franklin* and *Foundation Aranmore* were also dispatched from Halifax, Nova Scotia, and Boston, Massachusetts, respectively, to go the *Wakefield*'s assistance. Surprisingly, when they reached the scene she was still afloat and, despite the ravages of the fire, still considered to be worth saving. At the time of the outbreak she had been about 200 miles from Halifax and 350 miles from Boston. It was decided, therefore, to attempt to tow her to Nova Scotia to beach her, a tow that proved to be both difficult, through the need to constantly play water on the tow ropes to prevent them from burning through, and hazardous, because of the suspected presence of German submarines in the area.

Nevertheless, the *Wakefield* was successfully delivered to Halifax where she was beached at McNabs Cove on 8 September and left while the fire subsided. As she was entering the Canadian port, her bow had struck the Naval Fuelling Pier, cutting it halfway through; luckily, none of the fuel pipes were ruptured. The fire aboard the *Wakefield* was finally extinguished on 12 September and two days later she was moved to Pier B, Halifax, where her decks were shored up with wooden beams prior to her being towed on to Boston, where she arrived in early October 1942. She was declared a constructive total loss, but the United States Navy decided, in spite of this, to buy her outright and rebuild her from the keel up as a purpose-designed troopship. She returned to service in April 1944 after the work had been completed at the Boston Navy Yard and remained active until May 1946, when she was laid up with the reserve fleet. After surviving another 19 years in this inactive state, the *Wakefield* was finally broken up from March 1965.

Casualties: 0

The *Wakefield* prior to the tow to Boston. A lengthy restoration culminated in her return to service as a dedicated troop transport, but she was never to sail again commercially. *Canadian Department of National Defence*

The United States Line's *Manhattan*, in a pre-war view off New York City in 1936. *Ian Allan Library*

The transport *Wakefield* (formerly the *Manhattan*) on fire in mid-Atlantic. *United States Coast Guard*

A close-up view showing some of the fire damage sustained by the *Wakefield*. *Canadian Department of National Defence*

MANILA MARU (1915) Osaka Shosen Kaisha, Japan

9,518grt; 475ft (144.8m) lbp x 61ft (18.6m) beam
167 passengers in two classes
Mitsubishi, Nagasaki (Yard No 244)
Triple-expansion steam reciprocating, twin screw

While serving as a hospital ship with the Japanese Navy, the passenger-cargo ship *Manila Maru* was sunk by the American submarine USS *Mingo*. The attack took place on 25 November 1944 about 120 miles west of Brunei, Borneo, in the position 05.30N, 113.21E.

Casualties: not known

The trans-Pacific passenger ship *Manila Maru*. *Mitsui-OSK Lines*

MANUKA (1903) Union Steamship Co of New Zealand, UK

4,534grt; 368ft (112.4m) lbp x 47ft (14.4m) beam
357 passengers
William Denny, Dumbarton (Yard No 689)
Triple-expansion steam reciprocating, twin screw

While bound from Melbourne to Wellington on 16 December 1929, the passenger-cargo ship *Manuka* ran ashore in dense fog at Long Point, near the Nuggets, some 67 miles south of Dunedin, Otago. Her decks burst and she was soon completely flooded. Lying broadside to the rocks, she gradually submerged, breaking up in the surf to become a total loss. Her complement of around 200, a combination of passengers and crew, all made it ashore safely. The *Manuka*'s cargo included a collection of British paintings valued at £25,000, all of which were lost.

Casualties: 0

MARCO POLO (1912) ex-*Gange* (1936) ex-*Presidente Wilson* (1930) ex-*General Diaz* (1920) ex-*Kaiser Franz Josef I* (1919) Adriatica Line, Italy

12,588grt; 500ft (152.4m) loa x 62ft (18.9m) beam
374 passengers in three classes
Cantieri Navale Triestino, Monfalcone (Yard No 20)
Quadruple-expansion steam reciprocating, twin screw
In September 1943, after the armistice between Italy and the Allies, the passenger-cargo liner *Marco Polo* was placed under the management of a German company, Mediterranean Reederei GmbH. On 12 May 1944, as German forces were retreating northwards in the face of the Allied advance through Italy, she was scuttled at La Spezia to block the harbour entrance and prevent access to the port. Her wreck was raised in 1949 and sold for breaking up.
Casualties: not known

The steamship *Kaiser Franz Josef I* was the largest passenger ship ever to operate under the Austrian national flag, her original owners being Unione Austriaca. Ceded to Italy after the First World War, she served three companies under four names on three different routes over the next 20 years. In the last of these, from 1937, she was Adriatica Line's *Marco Polo*, sailing between Venice and Alexandria. *World Ship Society*

MARECHAL LYAUTEY (1925) Cie de Navigation Paquet, France

8,256grt; 428ft (130.0m) lbp x 56ft (17.3m) beam
1,154 passengers in four classes
Forges et Chantiers de la Méditerranée, La Seyne (Yard No 1185)
Triple-expansion steam reciprocating, twin screw
The passenger steamship *Marechal Lyautey*, one of a class of four vessels, was engaged on the service from France to West Africa via the Canaries until the outbreak of the Second World War. She was at Marseilles at the time of the German retreat from southern France and, on 26 August 1944, together with a number of other French-flag ships, she was deliberately scuttled, in her case on the north side of the Bassin de la Pinede, in order to block the port and prevent its use by the advancing Allies.
Casualties: not known

MARIETTE PACHA (1925) Messageries Maritimes, France

12,239grt; 522ft (159.1m) loa x 62ft (18.9m) beam
949 passengers in four classes
Soc Provencal de Constructions Navales, La Ciotat (Yard No 150)
Triple-expansion steam reciprocating, twin screw
After serving as a troopship from September 1939 to June 1940, the passenger-cargo ship *Mariette Pacha* was employed making repatriation voyages from Beirut and Syria until September 1941. The following year she served as a guard ship at Sète, south-west of Montpellier, then was laid up at Port-de-Bouc in 1943. On 24 July 1944 the Germans ordered her to be taken around the headland to Marseilles, some twelve miles to the east, but when the crew refused and disembarked, a German crew was mustered to move the ship. Taken to the Jetée du Large, Quai Wilson, at the north end of the Bassin de la Madrague, she was deliberately scuttled there on 21 August 1944. Cut in two by explosives, she was beyond recovery and her wreck was demolished from 1948.
Casualties: not known

MARIPOSA (1883) Alaska Steamship Co, USA

3,158grt; 314ft (95.7m) lbp x 41ft (12.5m) beam
More than 324 passengers in three classes
William Cramp, Philadelphia (Yard No 233)
Triple-expansion steam reciprocating, single screw
Built for service in both the San Francisco to Honolulu and Tahiti trades, the *Mariposa* was sold to the Alaska Steamship Company in 1912. In their ownership she was lost on 19 November 1917 when she was stranded on Straits Island Reef, Sumner Strait, Alaska.
Casualties: not known

MARMARA (1956) Denizcilik Bankasi TAO (Turkish Maritime Lines), Turkey

6,042grt; 403ft (122.6m) loa x 56ft (16.9m) beam
590 passengers
AG 'Weser' Seebeckwerft, Bremerhaven (Yard No 789)
Motor-ship, single screw
While under refit at Halic, on the Golden Horn, near Istanbul, on 5 March 1972, the passenger-cargo ship *Marmara* caught fire and sank some eight hours after the outbreak started. Her wreck was raised in November 1972 but, declared a constructive total loss, she was sold for scrap and broken up locally beginning in 1974.
Casualties: not known

MARMORA (1903) P&O Line, UK

10,509grt; 546ft (166.4m) loa x 60ft (18.3m) beam
564 passengers in two classes
Harland & Wolff, Belfast (Yard No 350)
Quadruple-expansion steam reciprocating, twin screw

The *Marmora* made several voyages to Bombay before joining the London to Sydney service in March 1904. *Tom Rayner collection*

Taken over by the Admiralty in August 1914 for conversion to an auxiliary cruiser, the passenger-cargo ship *Marmora* served with the 10th Cruiser Squadron. In this role she engaged in the hunt for German raiders. She also escorted

convoys bound for the Indian Ocean. On 23 July 1918, while patrolling south of Ireland, she was torpedoed by the German submarine UB64 and sank rapidly in the position 50.24N, 08.48W. A prompt evacuation prevented a high casualty count, but there was loss of life among her crew of naval ratings caused by the exploding torpedo.
Casualties: 10

MARNIX VAN ST ALDEGONDE (1930)
Nederland Line, The Netherlands

19,355grt; 608ft (185.3m) loa x 74ft (22.6m) beam
771 passengers in four classes
Nederlandsche Schps Maats, Amsterdam (Yard No 195)
Motor-ship, twin screw
In September 1939 the passenger liner *Marnix van St Aldegonde* was laid up at Surabaya, but in 1940, after returning to Europe, she was converted into a troopship. On 6 November 1943 she was bound in convoy KMF25A from Liverpool to the Mediterranean with 2,924 troops in addition to her 311-man crew. When she was off the Algerian coast, in the position 37.12N, 06.16E, she was attacked by German aircraft, which hit her with torpedoes. The severely damaged ship was abandoned by all but a skeleton crew and was then taken in tow for Philippeville (Skikola) by naval ships and the American transport *Santa Elena* (qv), which sustained damage in the manoeuvres when she was in collision with the *Marnix van St Aldegonde*. The efforts to save the stricken troopship were in vain and she foundered the following day about 6 miles from Cape Bougaroin lighthouse.
Casualties: 0

The *Marnix van St Aldegonde*, sister ship of the *Johan Van Oldenbarnevelt*, which was destroyed by fire as the *Lakonia*, operated between Amsterdam and the Dutch East Indies.
Alex Duncan

The *Marnix van St Aldegonde* during Operation 'Torch' in November 1942, with a loaded landing craft heading for the beach-head. She was sunk a year later in this location.
Imperial War Museum (A12705A)

MARVALE (1907) ex-*Corsican* (1922)
Canadian Pacific Line, UK

11,438grt; 516ft (157.3m) loa x 61ft (18.7m) beam
1,506 passengers in three classes
Barclay Curle, Whiteinch, Glasgow (Yard No 467)
Triple-expansion steam reciprocating, twin screw
While the former Allan passenger-cargo liner *Marvale* was returning to Glasgow from Quebec on 21 May 1923, she struck Cape Freels Rock, St Shott's Bay, twenty miles west of Cape Race, in dense fog. Badly damaged and leaking, she was headed inshore in an attempt to beach her. About a mile off Cape Pine she began to sink, eventually going down on an even keel in nine fathoms of water. Thanks to good discipline, all 437 passengers and crew aboard her escaped in the boats without injury, landing at Trepassey Bay. They were later taken to Southampton aboard the *Melita*, another Canadian Pacific ship. Divers from the salvage vessels *Lord Strathcoma* and *Cabot* succeeded in recovering baggage, mail and the ship's safe, complete with log and manifests, although there was a narrow escape for some of them when part of the hull suddenly disintegrated. Salvage prospects for the *Marvale*, which were already poor, were dashed completely when the wreck broke up in stormy weather. Casualties: 0

MASHOBRA (1914) British India Line, UK

8,236grt; 449ft (136.9m) lbp x 58ft (17.7m) beam
129 berthed passengers plus deck passengers
Barclay Curle, Whiteinch, Glasgow (Yard No 505)
Triple-expansion steam reciprocating, twin screw
After a period of service as a troop transport on the outbreak of the First World War, the passenger liner *Mashobra* resumed commercial sailings on the London to Calcutta route. During a return voyage, to the UK, she was torpedoed by the Austrian submarine U29, 140 miles south-west of Cape Matapan (Akra Tainaron) on 15 April 1917. The order to abandon ship was given, but soon afterwards the submarine, which had surfaced following the torpedo attack, began shelling the already fatally damaged *Mashobra*, hastening her demise. She sank in the position 35.34N, 20.40E. The survivors were picked up by trawlers and taken to Malta, where they arrived on 16 April. Casualties: 8 (all engine room crew)

MASHOBRA (1920) British India Line, UK

8,324grt; 465ft (141.7m) loa x 58ft (17.7m) beam
130 berthed passengers in single class plus 2,375 deck passengers
Barclay Curle, Whiteinch, Glasgow (Yard No 577)
Triple-expansion steam reciprocating, twin screw
On the outbreak of the Second World War the *Mashobra* was taken over by the Fleet Air Arm as a depot ship and stationed at Scapa Flow. In May 1940 she was activated for participation in the operations against Narvik in Norway. After arriving off the Norwegian coast on 25 May 1940, she was bombed and badly damaged by German aircraft. Although still afloat, recovery for return to the UK was impossible in the circumstances so she was beached four days later at Gangsaas, near Halstad, where her guns and stores were removed. Prior to the British withdrawal at the end of the Norwegian campaign, the wrecked *Mashobra* was destroyed by naval units. Casualties: not known

With her sister ship *Manela*, the liner *Masbobra* was employed on the service from London to Calcutta, making calls at Tangier, Port Said, Aden, Colombo and Madras; Marseilles was added on the homeward run. The *Masbobra* is seen being evacuated near Narvik prior to her abandonment during the Norwegian campaign of May 1940. *Imperial War Museum (N218)*

MASSILIA (1920) Cie Sud-Atlantique, France

15,363grt; 600ft (182.9m) loa x 64ft (19.5m) beam
1,041 passengers in four classes
Forges et Chantiers de la Méditerranée, La Seyne
(Yard No 1061)
Triple-expansion steam reciprocating, quadruple screw
After taking members of the French Government from Bordeaux to Casablanca in June 1940, the passenger-cargo liner *Massilia* was laid up in the Mirabeau Basin, Marseilles, for the next four years. As they withdrew from southern France, German troops sank her in the North Pass on 22 August 1944 in order to block the harbour. Refloated after the war's end, the wreck was broken up from 1948.
Casualties: not known

The *Massilia* was the last vessel of a three-ship class that included the *Gallia*, torpedoed in the First World War with heavy loss of life. The other member of the trio was the *Lutetia*. They served on the route from Bordeaux to La Plata ports. *World Ship Society*

MATSUMAYE [MATSUMAE] MARU (1924) Department of Communications & Railways, Government of Japan

3,485grt; 350ft (106.7m) lbp x 52ft (15.9m) beam
990 passengers
Mitsubishi, Nagasaki (Yard No 396)
Steam turbines, twin screw

The ferry *Matsumaye Maru* was attacked and bombed by American carrier-based aircraft on 14 July 1945 as she was passing through the Tsugaru Strait, between Hokkaido and Honshu. She sank in the position 41.48N, 140.41E.
Casualties: not known

MAZATLAN (1965) ex-*Akershus* (1973) Government of Mexico (Caminos y Puentes Federales de Ingresos y Servicios Conexos)

5,012grt; 357ft (108.9m) loa x 57ft (17.3m) beam
224 passengers in two classes plus 576 on deck (as built)
Helsingor Vaerft, Elsinore (Yard No 373)
Motor-ship, twin screw
The ro-ro passenger ferry *Akershus* transferred to Mexican owners in 1973 for service between La Paz and Topolobampo in the Bay of California as the *Mazatlan*. While performing these duties she was lost on 20 August 1989, outward bound from La Paz with 301 passengers besides her crew, when she caught fire and had to be abandoned. She sank later the same day in the position 25.08N, 109.38W.
Casualties: 0

MECCA (1951) ex-*Gullfoss* (1974) Orri Navigation Lines, Saudi Arabia

3,858grt; 355ft (108.2m) loa x 48ft (14.6m) beam
209 passengers (as built)
Burmeister & Wain, Copenhagen (Yard No 702)
Motor-ship, single screw
Originally owned by an Icelandic company, the *Mecca* was lost on 18 December 1976 while bound from Mecca and Jeddah to Port Sudan carrying 1,105 pilgrims and a crew of 76. When she was eighteen miles out of Jeddah, heading in a southerly direction, a fire was discovered in unoccupied First-class cabins below the bridge. It rapidly spread out of control and the ship drifted on to the Ras Alsanda reef, fourteen miles south of Jeddah. Two days later the *Mecca* slipped off the reef, capsized and sank in deep water in the position 21.19N, 39.06E.
Casualties: 0

MECKLENBURG (1909) Zeeland Steamship Co, The Netherlands

2,885grt; 350ft (106.6m) lbp x 43ft (13.0m) beam
356 passengers in two classes
Fairfield, Govan (Yard No 463)
Triple-expansion steam reciprocating, twin screw
The North Sea passenger ferry *Mecklenburg* was sunk on 27 February 1916 when, near the Galloper light vessel, she hit a mine that had been laid by the German submarine UC7. At the time, she had been on a crossing from Tilbury to Vlissingen (Flushing) carrying passengers.
Casualties: not known

MEDINA (1911) P&O Line, UK

12,358grt; 570ft (173.7m) loa x 62ft (18.9m) beam
680 passengers in two classes
Caird, Greenock (Yard No 317)
Quadruple-expansion steam reciprocating, twin screw
The construction of the P&O liner *Medina* at the Caird

shipyard had immediately preceded that of fleet-mate *Ballarat* (qv). Coincidentally, she was sunk just three days after the *Ballarat* and in the same sea area. The loss of the *Medina* occurred on 28 April 1917 as she neared the end of a voyage from Sydney. She had already called at Plymouth and was heading for London when, three miles east-north-east of Start Point, she was attacked by the German submarine UB31. The torpedo struck the *Medina*'s starboard side, immediately flooding her engine room and leaving her dead in the water. Distress calls were transmitted and the passengers and crew swiftly mustered in readiness to abandon the ship. Within an hour of the attack she sank, going down in the position 50.15N, 03.30W, but by then she had been safely evacuated. Naval vessels took the lifeboats in tow to Dartmouth and Brixham.

Casualties: 6 (all engine room crew: 1 officer and 5 firemen)

The last vessel of P&O's 'M' class, the *Medina* had the distinction of being selected as the Royal Yacht for King George V and Queen Mary's tour of India in early 1912. *Tom Rayner collection*

MEDITERRANEAN SKY (1953) ex-*City of York* (1971) Karageorgis Lines, Greece

14,941grt; 541ft (164.8m) loa x 71ft (21.7m) beam
850 passengers
Vickers-Armstrongs, High Walker, Tyneside (Yard No 122)
Motor-ship, twin screw

The former Ellerman Lines passenger-cargo liner *City of York*, rebuilt as the *Mediterranean Sky*, is seen here at Brindisi on 30 July 1996. Her hull was originally painted bright yellow with her owners' name along the side. *Frank Heine FERRIES*

The remains of the *Mediterranean Sky* at Elefsina on 30 July 2005. *Frank Heine FERRIES*

The former Ellerman Lines passenger-cargo ship *City of York* was taken over in 1971 for conversion into the passenger-vehicle ferry *Mediterranean Sky* for the service from Ancona to Rhodes, and by the time she commenced sailings she was quite unrecognisable. By the late 1990s she was becoming increasingly inactive and entered a long lay-up at Eleusis in December 1999. On 26 November 2002 she developed an unexpected but extreme list. Assisted by a tug, she was being moved to the nearby shipyard, presumably for attention, when she grounded in shallow water close to the shore at Elefsina. Subsequently the list increased until she capsized onto her side and was abandoned as a total loss. It is not known whether she was still in Karageorgis ownership at the time of the incident.

Casualties: 0

MEIKONG (1871) Messageries Maritimes, France

3,370grt 370ft (112.8m) lbp x 39ft (11.9m) beam
300 deck passengers
Messageries Maritimes, La Ciotat (Yard No not known)
Compound-expansion steam reciprocating, single screw

While returning to Marseilles via the Suez Canal from Hong Kong on 17 June 1877, the passenger-cargo steamship *Meikong* was wrecked in fog at Cape Gardafui, Somalia. Battered by huge waves, she settled on her starboard side. An attempt to evacuate the ship using her lifeboats had to be abandoned when two of her deck crew were killed. Her passengers and remaining crew were later rescued by the British steamship *Glenatney* without further mishap. The *Meikong* broke in two and for a long time remained a danger to navigation, and was responsible for the loss of the transport ship *Aveyron*, which ran onto the submerged wreckage on 20 August 1884.

Casualties: 2 (both crew)

MEKNES (1913) ex-*Puerto Rico* (1929) Compagnie Générale Transatlantique (French Line), France

6,127grt; 413ft (125.9m) lbp x 51ft (15.5m) beam
550 passengers
Penhoët, Grand Quevilly, St Nazaire (Yard No not known)
Triple-expansion steam reciprocating with LP turbine, twin screw

After the fall of France in June 1940, the passenger-cargo steamship *Meknes*, already serving as a troopship, came under Vichy control and was utilised for the repatriation of French servicemen who wished to return home from the UK. In this capacity she left Southampton for Marseilles on 24 July 1940, carrying 1,300 naval officers and ratings in addition to her crew of 102 men. She was clearly marked with the French tricolor painted on her sides and was brightly illuminated. Despite this, she was attacked by the German E-boat S27, which intercepted her some 45 miles south-east of Portland Bill, in a position variously reported as either 50.04N, 02.15W or 50.15N, 02.10W. The naval vessel opened fire with machine-guns, in response to which the identity and nationality of the *Meknes* was signalled, and although she had not been commanded to stop she was immediately hove to. Other than having the desired effect of curtailing the attack, the E-boat ignored these actions, its only response being to launch a torpedo at the heavily loaded ship without any warning. The explosion caused the *Meknes* to sink within 10 minutes and with heavy loss of life. It is known that 898 survivors managed to reach the English coast, rescued by the British destroyers HMS *Drake*, *Wolverine*, *Sabre* and *Shikari*. Others may also have made it to the French side of the Channel, although this is doubtful because of the distance. Even so, this left a large number of French naval personnel and mercantile crew members unaccounted for.

Casualties: 422 (The figures stated here come from the French Lines Association archives and are largely supported by Lloyd's War Loss Records, compiled at the time of the sinking. However, other reports state that the *Meknes* had the lower number of 1,079 Navy personnel aboard her in addition to her crew of 102. Moreover, they give the lower figure of 383 as the number of persons listed as missing.)

The French passenger steamship *Meknes* spent her career until 1936 on the service from Bordeaux to Casablanca. She then inaugurated a new service from Le Havre to the Baltic.
Arnold Kludas

MELODY (1949) ex-*Phoenix* (1979) ex-*Djebel-Dira* (1970) Athens Marine Cruises, Greece

4,253grt; 371ft (113.2m) loa x 51ft (15.6m) beam
283 passengers in single class
Swan Hunter & Wigham Richardson, Low Walker, Tyneside (Yard No 1854)
Steam turbines, single screw

Two views of the wreck of the *Melody*, lying half-sunk at Atalanti Island, Piraeus, in July 1990.
Frank Heine FERRIES / Ian Shiffman

A former French-flag passenger-cargo ship, reconstructed as the cruise ship *Phoenix*, the *Melody*, as she became, was gutted by fire on 6 July 1990 at Keratsini. She was beached the following day at Atalanti Island and abandoned as a derelict, half-submerged with her stern under water. Some ten years earlier, in December 1980, the *Melody* had suffered severe storm damage while en route to Haifa, Israel, and had spent much of the intervening period laid up unrepaired.

Casualties: not known

MENDI (1905) British & African SN Co (Elder Dempster), UK

4,230grt; 370ft (112.8m) lbp x 46ft (14.0m) beam
170 passengers in two classes
Alexander Stephen, Glasgow (Yard No 407)
Triple expansion steam reciprocating, single screw

In January 1917 the passenger steamship *Mendi*, which had been taken over as a wartime troopship, joined a convoy with five other vessels, escorted by the cruiser HMS *Cornwall*, to transport Australian and South African troops from Cape Town to France. Among the *Mendi*'s troop complement were 806 officers and men of the South African Native Labour Contingent, which included of Zulu, Pondo, Swazi and Xhosa tribesmen. She also had a crew of 88. After putting into Plymouth on 20 February 1917, the convoy sailed east along the English Channel bound for Le Havre, the destination port.

Early on the following day, the convoy was passing south of the Isle of Wight in thick fog, the ships sounding their sirens but not permitted to show navigation lights. At a point some 12 miles off St Catherine's Point, the *Mendi* was in collision with the Royal Mail steamer *Darro*, another of the convoy ships. The bow of the *Darro* struck the *Mendi*'s starboard side, penetrating into the forward troop deck and causing numerous fatalities. The *Mendi* immediately assumed a severe list, hampering efforts to launch lifeboats, and within 20 minutes she rolled over and sank with many of the victims still trapped inside her. The *Darro* could not remain on the scene to render assistance because of the submarine threat and the risk that the lives of her troop passengers might be added to the already heavy casualties from the *Mendi*. By the time other rescue vessels arrived on the scene, they were only able to pick up 236 survivors.

Casualties: 658 (621 soldiers, 8 Army officers and 29 crew) Some reports state that the *Mendi* was carrying a total of 824 persons of whom 656 – 625 troops and 31 crew – lost their lives.

The steamship *Mendi* was employed on African routes for Elder Dempster. She is commemorated today by a South African Navy frigate that bears the name, as well as 'Mendi Day' each 21 February and the 'Order of Mendi', the highest award for bravery, bestowed upon deserving citizens by the President of South Africa. *World Ship Society*

MENDOZA (1920) Société Générale des Transports Maritimes à Vapeur (SGTM), France

8,199grt; 460ft (140.2m) lbp x 58ft (17.7m) beam
More than 248 passengers in four classes
Swan Hunter & Wigham Richardson, Low Walker, Tyneside (Yard No 1098)
Steam turbines, twin screw

The French passenger steamship *Mendoza* was captured by the armed merchant cruiser HMS *Asturias* in June 1940, following the German occupation of France, and placed under the control of the Ministry of War Transport, managed by Alfred Holt & Co (Blue Funnel Line). She was on passage from Mombasa to Durban on 1 November 1942, with 253 military and naval passengers plus a 153-strong crew, when she was torpedoed by the German submarine U178 about 100 miles to the west of Durban. She sank in the position 29.20S, 32.14E.
Casualties: ~30 (around 7 passengers and 23 crew)

MERIDA (1906) Ward Line, USA

6,207grt; 400ft (121.9m) lbp x 50ft (15.2m) beam
261 passengers in three classes
William Cramp, Philadelphia (Yard No 332)
Triple-expansion steam reciprocating, twin screw

The career of the coastwise passenger-cargo ship *Merida* was abruptly and prematurely ended when she was sunk in 12 May 1911 after colliding with the American steamship *Admiral Farragut* 55 miles east of Cape Charles, Virginia. The *Merida* was returning to New York from Vera Cruz, Mexico, and Havana, Cuba, carrying 197 passengers and 128 crew, all of whom were saved, besides a valuable cargo of silver and gold. Salvage operations in July 1933 recovered some of this bullion.
Casualties: 0

MERION (1902) American Line, USA

serving as the wartime dummy battle-cruiser HMS TIGER
11,612grt; 547ft (166.7m) loa x 59ft (18.0m) beam
1,850 passengers in two classes
John Brown, Clydebank (Yard No 345)
Triple-expansion steam reciprocating, twin screw

The American Line emigrant steamer *Merion* was sister of the *Haverford* on the Liverpool to Philadelphia service.
World Ship Society

The transatlantic liner *Merion* was lost in the First World War when she became a victim of the German submarine UB8 while deployed as a decoy for the battle-cruiser HMS *Tiger*. Taken up on the outbreak of war, the Admiralty had her modified for this unusual role and she was sent, together with other similarly altered vessels, to the Mediterranean as part of

a special naval decoy fleet. On 31 May 1915, still carrying her strange disguise, she was torpedoed and sunk in the Aegean Sea, off Strati Island, near Mudros, on the Island of Lemnos.
Casualties: not known

Adapted as the dummy battle-cruiser HMS *Tiger*, the *Merion* is unrecognisable. *Imperial War Museum (SP2350)*

METEOR (1904) Bergen Line, Norway

serving under the wartime name METEOR II (ex-Rostock)
3,718grt; 346ft (100.2m) lbp x 44ft (13.5m) beam
205 passengers
Blohm & Voss, Steinwerder, Hamburg (Yard No 170)
Triple-expansion steam reciprocating, twin screw

Built for the Hamburg Amerika Linie, the *Meteor* was acquired by the Bergen Line in 1921 after she had been surrendered to the UK as a First World War prize. After a successful career as a cruise ship that continued between the wars, the *Meteor* was seized at Bergen in April 1940 and pressed into service as a hospital ship based in the Baltic, still manned by her 70-strong Norwegian crew. On 9 March 1945 she was bombed by Russian aircraft, capsized and sank alongside the quay at Pillau (Baltiysk). In contravention of international law, the *Meteor* was being used as a military transport, although still painted in hospital ship livery, and she had around 230 German soldiers on board.
Casualties: 24, including 4 crew

The Bergen Line cruise yacht *Meteor* had been a Hamburg Amerika Line ship until she was surrendered to Great Britain after the First World War, transferring to her Norwegian owners in 1926. *Bjørn Pedersen*

MEXICAN (1882) Union-Castle Line, UK

4,661grt; 378ft (115.3m) lbp x 47ft (14.3m) beam
280 passengers in three classes
James Laing, Sunderland (Yard No 273)
Triple-expansion steam reciprocating, single screw

Originally built for the Union Line, the mail steamship *Mexican* was absorbed into the combined Union-Castle fleet after its formation on 1 March 1900, and it was intended that she should continue on the Cape run. These plans were short-lived, though, for on 5 April 1900, while she was bound for Southampton with 104 passengers, she sank about eighty miles north of Cape Town after colliding with the cattle steamship *Winkfield* in dense fog in the middle of the night. The *Winkfield* was hardly damaged, so the *Mexican*'s passengers and mail were transferred to her for return to Cape Town. Twelve hours after the collision the *Mexican* sank. Casualties: 0

MEXIQUE (1915) ex-*Lafayette* (1928) ex-*Ile de Cuba* (launch name, 27 May 1914) Compagnie Générale Transatlantique (French Line), France

12,220grt; 563ft (171.6m) loa x 64ft (19.5m) beam
1,250 passengers in four classes
Chantiers de Provence, Port du Bouc (Yard No 77)
4 x compound-expansion steam reciprocating with LP turbine, quadruple screw

During the months leading up to the Second World War, the aging passenger liner *Mexique*, which had been laid up in June 1939 prior to being sold for scrap, was reactivated, first for a series of mercy voyages, taking Jewish refugees to Mexico, then as a troopship from April 1940. She became a victim of a magnetic mine on 19 June 1940 while bound for Bordeaux at the end of a voyage from Oran, North Africa. She struck the mine in Le Verdon Roads, at the entrance to the River Garonne, and became a total loss. Her entire crew of 173 men was rescued. Casualties: 0

Launched as the *Ile de Cuba* for CGT's West Indies service, the decision was made before she was completed to operate her instead on the New York route from Bordeaux and she was renamed *Lafayette*. After the First World War, during which she served as a hospital ship, the *Lafayette* resumed her transatlantic schedules until 1924, when she was switched to the Central American service. Four years later she was renamed *Mexique*. World Ship Society

MIIKE MARU (1941) Nippon Yusen Kaisha, Japan

11,739grt; 535ft (163.1m) loa x 66ft (20.1m) beam
236 passengers in two classes (as designed)
Mitsubishi, Nagasaki (Yard No 760)
Motor-ship, twin screw

The passenger-cargo ship *Miike Maru* was still under construction when war broke out between Japan and the United States and Great Britain. She was therefore fitted out on completion as a troopship. She was sunk on 21 April 1944 by torpedoes fired by the American submarine USS *Trigger* when she was south-west of Yap, the island at the north-eastern point of the Caroline Islands Group, in the position 08.20N, 134.53E. Casualties: 18

MIKHAIL LERMONTOV (1972) Baltic Steamship Co (Sovtorgflot), USSR (under charter to CTC Lines)

19,872grt; 577ft (175.8m) loa x 77ft (23.6m) beam
700 passengers in single class
Mathias-Thesen Werft, Wismar (Yard No 129)
Motor-ship, twin screw

Intended for the service from Leningrad to Montreal, the *Mikhail Lermontov* in fact entered cruise service on her completion due to the collapse of the transatlantic passenger trade, making only occasional line voyages. By 1979 she was concentrated exclusively on cruising and during such a trip, on 16 February 1986, she met an untimely end after running onto rocks off Cape Jackson, New Zealand, only seven hours after leaving Picton. On board at the time were 408 passengers, mostly elderly Australians, and a 330-strong crew. The accident occurred as the ship was visiting New Zealand's fjord region, off Milford Sound. The weather was unsettled at the time and it was after dark when she struck the rocks in this notorious shipping graveyard. Rumours abounded that her Russian Master had ignored navigational advice from his New Zealand pilot. In fact, it was an error on the part of the pilot that led to the disaster, as the subsequent enquiry established beyond any shadow of a doubt. For some quite inexplicable reason the pilot, who was also booked aboard the ship as a passenger for a later part of the cruise, decided to take the *Mikhail Lermontov* between the lighthouse at Cape Jackson and the Cape itself, over an area clearly marked on charts as foul ground. At the time the ship's Master was not even present on the liner's bridge.

With four watertight compartments breached and the engine room bulkhead threatened, the ship developed an immediate list and was soon in a rapidly deteriorating predicament. An attempt was made to beach the ship, a standard move in these circumstances, but as a result accusations were later made that the passengers' well-being had been neglected and the ship given first priority; however, had it been successful, they would have benefited from the closer proximity of rescue and refuge. In the event this move was overtaken by other developments. Below decks a valiant and courageous battle was being fought to save the stricken ship as emergency crews struggled to shore up the bulkhead forward of the engine room. When these efforts failed and sea water flooded on to the electrical generation and distribution equipment, it short-circuited and all electrical power was lost. As the main engines depended on the electrical supply to keep running, once it was interrupted they too stopped. Without propulsion the *Mikhail Lermontov* could not be beached and, dead in the water, she commenced to founder.

When it was realised that the ship could not be saved, evacuation got under way. This operation was concluded just as the ship went down, having remained afloat for some two or three hours after striking the reef. She rolled over on her side, sinking bow-first. The position was 40.30S, 174.12E, just off Gannet Point at the southern end of Port Gore Bay. The survivors were picked up from lifeboats by a number of ships that had been alerted to the disaster, among them the LPG tanker *Tarihiko*, the inter-island diesel-electric train ferry *Arahura* and the naval patrol boat *Taupo*. All were taken to Wellington, some injured, but worse by far, after initial checks had been made it was feared that approximately twenty persons were missing. It was speculated that they were adrift somewhere in the entrance to the Cook Strait and a search was organised, continuing well beyond 10 hours after the ship had sunk. Ultimately, everyone, apart from one crew member who went down with the ship, was satisfactorily accounted for.

While the enquiry by the Marine Division of the New Zealand Ministry of Transport censured the pilot, the Soviet authorities also disciplined the cruise ship's Chief Navigator and Second Mate, both of whom had been on the bridge at the time of the fateful manoeuvre, in both cases for failing to challenge the pilot's navigational directions.
Casualties: 1

The *Mikhail Lermontov* was distinguished when, in June 1973, during a brief resurgence of line service, she became the first Russian-flag passenger vessel to be permitted to enter New York for 25 years. *Frank Heine FERRIES*

MILLENNIUM EXPRESS II (1967) ex-*Med* (2000) ex-*Memed Abashidze* (2000) ex-*Charm M* (1997) ex-*Viscountess M* (1995) ex-*Ionic Ferry* (1992) ex-*Dragon* (1986) Oxalis Investments (Access Ferries), Panama

6,141grt; 442ft (134.6m) loa x 72ft (21.9m) beam
511 berthed and 339 deck passengers (as built)
Chantiers de Bretagne, Prairie-au-Duc (Yard No 16108); completed by Dubigeon-Normandie, Nantes-Chantenay (Yard No 824)
Motor-ship, twin screw

Originally the P&O Ferries' *Dragon* of the Southampton to Le Havre service, the *Millennium Express II* is seen at Korinth on 7 July 2001. *Frank Heine FERRIES*

The former cross-Channel passenger ro-ro ferry *Millennium Express II*, engaged on similar duties in the Mediterranean, suffered an outbreak of fire in her engine room on 2 March 2002 in the position 37.21N, 21.01E. At the time she was on passage, without passengers, bound from Piraeus to Albania, where she was to commence a new service between Italy and Albania, following many previous career changes. The fire

spread from her machinery spaces and she had to be abandoned by her crew. The empty ship was taken in tow by the tug *Karapiperis 14* and anchored off Zante (Zakynthos) where the fire was extinguished and the water that had accumulated inside her was pumped out. Subsequent inspection revealed extensive fire damage and the *Millennium Express II* was declared a constructive total loss. She was broken up at Aliaga, Turkey, from 10 April 2003.
Casualties: 0

MINNEAPOLIS (1900) Atlantic Transport Line, UK

13,543grt; 616ft (187.8m) loa x 65ft (19.8m) beam
228 passengers in single class
Harland & Wolff, Belfast (Yard No 328)
Quadruple-expansion steam reciprocating, twin screw
The *Minneapolis*, serving as a troopship, was on a voyage from Marseilles to Alexandria in a light condition, carrying just her crew of 189 persons, when she was torpedoed by the German submarine U35 on 23 March 1916. The attack took place 195 miles east-half-north from Malta. An attempt to tow her to Valletta, where her survivors had been taken, was abandoned and, after remaining afloat for almost two days, the *Minneapolis* sank in the position 36.30N, 18.22E.
Casualties: 12

MINNEHAHA (1900) Atlantic Transport Line, UK

13,714grt; 616ft (187.8m) loa x 65ft (19.8m) beam
250 passengers in single class
Harland & Wolff, Belfast (Yard No 329)
Quadruple-expansion steam reciprocating, twin screw
On 7 September 1917 the liner *Minnehaha* was torpedoed and sunk by the German submarine U48 in a location ten miles to the south of the Baltimore lighthouse, County Cork, and some twelve miles south-east of the Fastnet Rock. She had not been engaged for wartime auxiliary duties and, at the time of the attack, was on a commercial voyage to New York carrying civilian passengers. The *Minnehaha* remained afloat for only a matter of minutes and, had she been carrying nearer to her full complement of passengers, the consequences could have been far more serious.
Casualties: 43

MINNETONKA (1902) Atlantic Transport Line, UK

13,528grt; 616ft (187.8m) loa x 65ft (19.8m) beam
250 passengers in single class
Harland & Wolff, Belfast (Yard No 339)
Quadruple-expansion steam reciprocating, twin screw

Atlantic Transport Line added four new ships, the *Minneapolis*, *Minnehaha*, *Minnetonka* (seen here) and *Minnewaska*, to its London to New York service between the years 1900 to 1909. All four ships were lost in the First World War. *World Ship Society*

Deployed as an armed auxiliary transport during the First World War, to guard convoys as well as carry troops, the liner *Minnetonka* was torpedoed on 30 January 1918 by the German submarine U64 as she was conveying the mails from Port Said to Marseilles. She sank forty miles east-north-east of Malta, in the position 36.12N, 14.55E. At the time the *Minnetonka* had been empty apart from her crew.
Casualties: 4

MINNEWASKA (1909) Atlantic Transport Line, UK

14,317grt; 616ft (187.8m) loa x 65ft (19.8m) beam
330 passengers in single class
Harland & Wolff, Belfast (Yard No 397)
Quadruple-expansion steam reciprocating, twin screw
The *Minnewaska* was converted into a troopship in 1915 and immediately took part in the conveyance of soldiers to the Dardanelles battle zone. As she was nearing Mudros on 29 November 1916, carrying 1,800 troops she had brought from Alexandria, she struck a floating mine about 1½ miles south-west of Dentero Point in Suda Bay. In an attempt to save her, the *Minnewaska* was run ashore, but so extreme was the damage caused by the mine that she was abandoned as a total loss. The wreck was broken up by an Italian firm from late 1918.
Casualties: 0

The fourth vessel of the 'Minneapolis' class, the *Minnewaska*, did not join her sisters until after a seven-year interval because the original *Minnewaska*, which would have entered service for Atlantic Transport Line in 1903, was sold to White Star while still under construction and renamed *Arabic*.
World Ship Society

MISSANABIE (1914) Canadian Pacific Line, UK

12,469grt; 520ft (158.5m) loa x 64ft (19.5m) beam
1,720 passengers in two classes
Barclay Curle, Whiteinch, Glasgow (Yard No 510)
Quadruple-expansion steam reciprocating, twin screw
The *Missanabie* entered service on the Liverpool to Nova Scotia and Montreal route in October 1914, just after the start of the First World War, and she continued throughout with her commercial schedules. She was bound from Liverpool to New York in ballast on 9 September 1918, her position approximately 52 miles east-south-east of Daunts Rock, near Cobh, County Cork, when the German submarine UB87 torpedoed and sank her.
Casualties: 45

The *Missanabie*, seen here, and *Metagama* entered the service from Liverpool to St John's, Newfoundland, and Montreal in the months immediately preceding the First World War.
World Ship Society

MIYAZAKI MARU (1909) Nippon Yusen Kaisha, Japan

7,892grt; 465ft (141.7m) lbp x 54ft (16.5m) beam
265 passengers in three classes
Kawasaki, Kobe (Yard No 292)
Triple-expansion steam reciprocating, twin screw
As the Japanese passenger-cargo steamship *Miyazaki Maru* was approaching the English Channel on 31 May 1917, bound for London from Yokohama with passengers, she was torpedoed by the German submarine U88. The attack occurred off Ushant, about 150 miles west of the Scilly Isles, and the *Miyazaki Maru* sank in the position 49.05N, 09.35W.
Casualties: not known

The *Miyazaki Maru* was one of a large group of passenger-cargo ships built for the Japan to Europe service. Her loss prompted her owners to move her sister ships to trans-Pacific routes for the next five years. *Nippon Yusen Kaisha*

MIZUHO MARU (1912) ex-*Infanta Isabel* (1927) Osaka Shosen Kaisha, Japan

8,506grt; 460ft (140.2m) lbp x 58ft (17.7m) beam
2,044 passengers in three classes (as a Spanish ship)
Russell, Port Glasgow (Yard No 633)
Quadruple-expansion steam reciprocating, twin screw
The passenger ship *Mizuho Maru* was taken over as a troop transport following the outbreak of war in the Pacific in December 1941. While operating in this role she was torpedoed by the American submarine USS *Redfish* off the north-west coast of Luzon on 21 September 1944. She sank in the position 18.38N, 120.43E. She was the former sister ship of the *Principe de Asturias* (qv), which stranded in March 1916. Casualties: not known

The passenger cargo steamship *Mizuho Maru* is seen in a painting dramatically portraying her final moments in September 1944. She was purchased from Cia Transoceanica, Spain, in August 1926 to serve on the Pacific route from Japan to the United States of America. *Mitsui-OSK Lines*

MOBY PRINCE (1968) ex-*Koningin Juliana* (1985)
Nav Archipelago Maddalenino SpA, Italy

6,187grt; 430ft (131.0m) loa x 67ft (20.5m) beam
574 berthed and 626 deck passengers (as built)
Cammell Laird, Birkenhead (Yard No 1331)
Motor-ship, twin screw

The *Moby Prince*, a former Dutch-flag North Sea ferry, was the victim of a freak accident on 10 April 1991, suffering heavy loss of life. While outward bound from Livorno for Olbia in thick fog carrying 144 persons, the *Moby Prince* collided with the oil tanker *Agip Abruzzo* at anchor in Livorno Roads, three miles outside the port. The impact ruptured the tanker's plating in the vicinity of her storage tanks, causing her cargo to leak. When the oil ignited with a huge explosion, both vessels were engulfed in flames. The *Moby Prince* was completely gutted, while the blaze aboard the *Agip Abruzzo* took 7 days to bring under control. There was just one survivor. Fit only for scrap, the hulk of the *Moby Prince*, having lain derelict for seven years, was broken up at Livorno from 22 July 1998.
Casualties: 143

Once the sleek Zeeland Steamship Company's ferry *Koningin Juliana*, the *Moby Prince*, painted more appropriately for Mediterranean service, displays Navarma's whale logo on her hull. This view was taken at Livorno on 21 July 1989.
Frank Heine FERRIES

The burned-out *Moby Prince* at Livorno three years later, on 22 July 1992. Her crumpled bow and completely incinerated hull testify to the extreme forces that overwhelmed her.
Frank Heine FERRIES

MOHAMED ALI EL-KABIR (1922) ex-*Teno* (1935)
Pharaonic Mail Line, Egypt

7,527grt; 423ft (128.9m) lbp x 56ft (17.1m) beam
More than 243 passengers
Scott's, Greenock (Yard No 517)
Steam turbines, twin screw

Originally in service under the Chilean flag, the Egyptian passenger ship *Mohamed Ali El-Kabir* was requisitioned as a British troopship in 1940. During a voyage from Avonmouth to Gibraltar carrying around 860 troops and military stores, on 7 August 1940, she was torpedoed by the German submarine U38. The attack took place 230 miles off the Bloody Foreland, on the west coast of Ireland, and the *Mohamed Ali El-Kabir* sank in the position 55.22N, 13.18W. Around 760 of her occupants survived.
Casualties: 96 (82 troops, her Master, 9 crew and 4 Royal Navy personnel)

MOHAWK (1926) Clyde-Mallory Lines, USA

5,896grt; 388ft (118.1m) lbp x 54ft (16.6m) beam
446 passengers in two classes
Newport News Shipbuilding & Drydock Co, Newport News, Virginia (Yard No 287)
Steam turbines, single screw

Photographed in dry dock at Newport News, the *Mohawk* was one of a number of similar American coastal passenger ships named after Indian tribes. *Northrop Grumman Shipbuilding*

Sister of the *Cherokee* (qv), the *Mohawk* was lost on 25 January 1935, the day after she had left New York southbound along the eastern seaboard, when she was in collision with the Norwegian freighter *Talisman* 4 miles off Sea Girt, New Jersey. A large hole was torn in the *Mohawk*'s side, extending

below the waterline, and as she flooded she developed a heavy list. Effort was made to beach her, but she sank in less than an hour in the position 40.02N, 73.52W. There had been difficulty in launching her boats because the davits were thick with ice. The 118 survivors, 38 passengers and 80 crew, were picked up by the *Algonquin*, a fleet-mate of the *Mohawk*, and the fruit ship *Limon*.
Casualties: 45 (15 passengers and 30 crew)

MOLDAVIA (1903) P&O Line, UK

9,505grt; 540ft (164.6m) loa x 58ft (17.7m) beam
514 passengers in two classes
Caird, Greenock (Yard No 301)
Triple-expansion steam reciprocating, twin screw
The liner *Moldavia* was requisitioned for conversion into an auxiliary cruiser for service with the Admiralty from 1915. After the United States' entry into the conflict in 1917, she also doubled as a troopship and was used for the transportation of American soldiers from England to France. On 23 May 1918, while bound for France on a return voyage from Halifax, she was torpedoed in the English Channel, south of Brighton, by the German submarine UB57. The majority of the troops she was carrying and her entire crew were safely transferred to escorting destroyers. The *Moldavia* sank in the position 50.24N, 00.26W.
Casualties: 57 (American troops)

The *Moldavia*, with her sister *Mongolia*, was employed on the route from London to Colombo, Melbourne and Sydney.
Tom Rayner collection

MONARCH OF BERMUDA (1931) Furness Withy, UK

22,424grt; 579ft (176.6m) loa x 76ft (23.3m) beam
830 passengers in single class
Vickers-Armstrongs, Newcastle-on-Tyne (Yard No 1)
Turbo-electric, quadruple screw
The former luxury passenger liner *Monarch of Bermuda* was undergoing her post-war refit in March 1947, prior to her return to commercial service, when she was almost completely destroyed by a fire that swept through her at her builder's yard on the River Tyne. The wreck was towed to dry dock at Rosyth for inspection, where it was found that, despite the ravages of the fire throughout the rest of the vessel, her turbo-electric machinery had suffered little damage. In spite of a shortage of steel at the time, the Ministry of Transport bought the wreck for reconstruction into the austerity standard Australian emigrant carrier *New Australia*, as there was a heavy demand for tonnage for this trade. The rebuilding contract, which was awarded to John I. Thornycroft at Southampton, involved the replacement of virtually 3,000 tons of steel in the ship's upper structure at a cost of almost £3 million. Work was carried out at berth 40 in

Southampton's Eastern Docks, and on 15 August 1950, under the management of Shaw, Savill & Albion, the *New Australia* made her maiden departure with emigrants bound for the Antipodes. Later, she became the Greek Line's *Arkadia*.
Casualties: 0

The *Monarch of Bermuda*, seen here, later joined by her sister ship *Queen of Bermuda*, took over on the New York to Hamilton 'cruise line' service after the loss of the *Bermuda*.
Tom Rayner collection

The scene on A deck aboard the gutted *Monarch of Bermuda*, in a photograph from 19 August 1947, reveals the damage wreaked by the fire that swept through her. Apart from destroyed decking and wooden fittings, the metalwork is twisted and buckled. *Ian Allan Library*

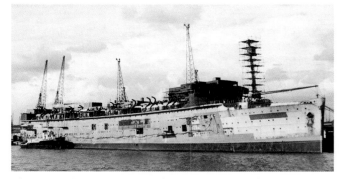

The *Monarch of Bermuda* under reconstruction by Thornycroft at Southampton prior to re-emergence as the austere emigrant-carrier *New Australia*.
Richard de Kerbrech collection

MONA'S QUEEN (1934) Isle of Man Steam Packet Co, UK

2,756grt; 336ft (102.9m) lbp x 48ft (14.7m) beam
2,400 passengers
Cammell Laird, Birkenhead (Yard No 998)
Steam turbines, twin screw

While engaged in the Operation 'Dynamo' evacuation of British Expeditionary Force troops, the *Mona's Queen* was returning to France from Dover, where she had earlier taken some 4,000 exhausted servicemen, when she struck a magnetic mine half a mile east of Dunkirk's pier-head on 29 May 1940. The violent explosion broke her in two and she sank almost immediately. Thirty-one members of her crew miraculously survived.

Casualties: 26 (plus one survivor who died later)

The Isle of Man passenger ferry *Mona's Queen* in the River Mersey. *Ian Allan Library*

Sinking off Dunkirk, the *Mona's Queen*, broken in two by a mine explosion, takes the plunge.
Imperial War Museum (HU1146)

MONGOLIA (1903) P&O Line, UK

9,505grt; 540ft (164.6m) loa x 58ft (17.7m) beam
520 passengers in two classes
Caird, Greenock (Yard No 302)
Triple-expansion steam reciprocating, twin screw

The *Mongolia*, which had been severely damaged by a fire in 1908, was not taken up for war service in 1914 but continued to make commercial voyages on the Australia route.
Tom Rayner collection

After the outbreak of the First World War the liner *Mongolia* continued to operate commercial schedules until 24 June 1917, when she ran onto a mine laid by the raider *Wolf* about seventeen miles west of Jaujira, fifty miles south-by-west of Bombay (Mumbai). The *Mongolia* was bound from London to Bombay, China and Sydney carrying passengers and mail, besides a quantity of cargo. She remained afloat for less than fifteen minutes, so powerful was the blast, but, despite having little time available to them, her officers and crew managed to get all the survivors of the explosion away in the boats, taking them to land nearby.

Casualties: 24 (4 passengers and 20 crew)

MONGOLIAN (1891) Canadian Pacific Line, UK

4,892grt; 400ft (121.9m) lbp x 45ft (13.7m) beam
1,180 passengers in three classes
D. & W. Henderson, Meadowside, Glasgow (Yard No 350)
Triple-expansion steam reciprocating, single screw

When the Allan Line was absorbed by Canadian Pacific in 1917, the liner *Mongolian*, together with other vessels of the Allan fleet, transferred on paper to their new ownership even though in practice they were engaged in war activities for the Admiralty. However, because the *Mongolian*, like her fleet-mate *Calgarian*, did not survive the war, she never made a commercial sailing for Canadian Pacific. She was torpedoed and sunk by the German submarine UC70 on 21 July 1918. The attack occurred during a voyage from Middlesbrough to London, when she was some five miles south-east of Filey Brig, Yorkshire. She sank in the position 54.10N, 08.58W.

Casualties: 36 (all crew)

MONTANA (1874) Guion Line, UK

4,321grt; 400ft (121.9m) lbp x 44ft (13.4m) beam
1,050 passengers in three classes
Palmers, Jarrow (Yard No 282)
Compound-expansion steam reciprocating, single screw

Sister-ship of the *Dakota* (qv), the passenger steamship *Montana* suffered a similar fate and in the same region when she was stranded near Anglesey on 14 March 1880. Found to be unfit for repair when she was refloated, she was taken to Sunderland for breaking up.

Casualties: 0

MONTE CERVANTES (1927) Hamburg Sud-Amerika Line, Germany

13,013grt; 524ft (159.7m) loa x 66ft (20.1m) beam
2,492 passengers in two classes
Blohm & Voss, Steinwerder, Hamburg (Yard No 478)
Motor-ship, twin screw

The motor passenger ship *Monte Cervantes* carried predominantly emigrant passengers in Steerage class. On 22 January 1930, just over two years after she first entered service, she struck uncharted, submerged rocks in the Beagle Channel, off Tierra del Fuego, during an extended voyage from Buenos Aires to Ushuaia, before returning to Hamburg. She had 1,517 passengers aboard her, in addition to her 300-strong crew, and the majority of this large complement was taken off by one of her 'Monte' class sisters. The holed ship, which had begun to sink, slipped from the rocks that were holding her and she was beached on the Eclaireur Reef in a bid to save her. She remained fast for two days, but on 24 January, with only a skeleton crew on board, she suddenly capsized and sank. All but one were rescued.

The *Monte Cervantes* remained in this situation, with her stern protruding above the surface, until 1951, when the Italian salvage company Savamar commenced work to raise her. She was refloated in July 1954 and patched up on the spot, but when she was taken in tow for Ushaia the *Monte Cervantes* sank in deep water.

Casualties: 1 (her Master)

MONTE OLIVIA (1925) Hamburg Sud-Amerika Line, Germany

13,750grt; 524ft (159.7m) loa x 65ft (19.8m) beam
2,528 passengers in two classes
Blohm & Voss, Steinwerder, Hamburg (Yard No 409)
Motor-ship, twin screw

Engaged in the transportation of evacuees and wounded from East Prussia and Silesia in early 1945, the passenger-cargo liner *Monte Olivia*, which had previously served as a naval support ship, an accommodation ship and, finally, a hospital ship, was destroyed during a US Air Force bombing raid on Kiel on 3 April 1945 after she had arrived there with refugees. Raised on 12 June 1946, her gutted and mangled wreck was scrapped from 1948.

Casualties: not known

The five-ship 'Monte' class of the Hamburg Sud-Amerika Line was introduced to the River Plate service between 1924 and 1931, each experiencing misfortune. One was wrecked in 1930, three were bombed and sunk during the Second World War, and the last was seized by the British as a war prize, only to fall victim to fire in 1954. This is the *Monte Olivia* near the Deutsche Werft shipyard, Hamburg.
Hamburg Sud-Amerika Line

MONTE PASCOAL (1931) Hamburg Sud-Amerika Line, Germany

13,870grt; 524ft (159.7m) loa x 65ft (19.8m) beam
2,408 passengers in two classes
Blohm & Voss, Steinwerder, Hamburg (Yard No 491)
Motor-ship, twin screw

The passenger liner *Monte Pascoal* served as an accommodation ship for the workers at the Wilhelmshaven naval dockyard from January 1940 until 3 February 1944, when she was bombed during an air raid on the port. She was completely gutted by fire and sank at her berth. Later, after she had been sealed, the *Monte Pascoal* was pumped out and refloated on 12 May 1944. However, no attempt was made to

restore the severely damaged vessel and the following May she was seized in this condition when the British army entered Wilhelmshaven. As she was assessed as being beyond economic recovery, she was loaded with materials used in the manufacture of chemical warfare weapons, towed out into the Skagerrak and deliberately sunk there on 31 December 1946.

Casualties: not known

The *Monte Pascoal*, packed with passengers, sails from Hamburg, probably at the time of her maiden departure for South America on 26 January 1931. *Hamburg Sud-Amerika Line*

MONTE SARMIENTO (1924) Hamburg Sud-Amerika Line, Germany

13,625grt; 524ft (159.7m) loa x 65ft (19.8m) beam
2,470 passengers in two classes
Blohm & Voss, Steinwerder, Hamburg (Yard No 407)
Motor-ship, twin screw

The *Monte Sarmiento* was taken over for service as an accommodation ship for naval crews after the outbreak of war and stationed, in this role, at Kiel. When Kiel came under attack during an Allied air raid on 26 February 1942, she was hit by bombs and sunk. The wreck was raised in 1943 and towed to Hamburg where it was broken up.

Casualties: not known

The first ship of Hamburg Sud-Amerika Line's 'Monte' class, the *Monte Sarmiento* is seen on 15 November 1924, the date of her maiden departure from Hamburg. *Hamburg Sud-Amerika Line*

MONTE UDALA (1948) Naviera Aznar SA, Spain

10,170grt; 487ft (148.5m) loa x 62ft (19.0m) beam
392 passengers in three classes
Cia Euskalduna, Oleveaga, Bilbao (Yard No 133)
Motor-ship, single screw

During a return voyage to Genoa from Buenos Aires on 8 September 1971, the passenger-cargo liner *Monte Udala* unexpectedly sprang a leak. Her engine room was soon flooded and the ship was in a very dangerous condition, sinking fast. Her passengers and crew abandoned her before she capsized and sank in the position 15.02S, 36.38W, 70 miles from Ilheus and some 250 miles south-east of Salvador, Brazil.

Casualties: 0

The Spanish motor passenger-cargo ship *Monte Udala* sailed on the Genoa to Buenos Aires service, via Barcelona, with a sister ship, the *Monte Urbasa*. *World Ship Society*

MONTEVIDEO MARU (1926) Osaka Shosen Kaisha, Japan

7,267grt; 449ft (131.1m) loa x 56ft (17.1m) beam
806 passengers in two classes
Mitsubishi, Nagasaki (Yard No 412)
Motor-ship, twin screw

The passenger-cargo ship *Montevideo Maru* was torpedoed and sunk with heavy loss of life by the American submarine USS *Sturgeon* on 1 July 1942 while she was bound from Rabaul to Hainan. The attack took place off the Baghador lighthouse, west of Luzon Island, in the position 18.37N, 119.29E, the ship sinking within eleven minutes. Nominally a transport at the time, the *Montevideo Maru* was in fact operating as one of the infamous 'Hell-ships', illegally conveying Allied prisoners of war to work camps. There was heavy loss of life among the Australian soldiers that were aboard her, not one of them surviving.

Casualties: 1,053 PoWs (Besides PoWs, the *Montevideo Maru* was also carrying 200 civilian prisoners – it is not clear whether these casualties were among the total of 1,053 recorded deaths or in addition to that number.)

The *Montevideo Maru*, seen at Cape Town with civilian passengers milling on deck, was lost as a 'Hell-ship' transporting Allied prisoners of war via Hainan Island, China, to Japan. *Alex Duncan*

MONTREAL (1896) ex *Halifax* (1905) ex *Minho* (1903) Compagnie Générale Transatlantique (French Line), France

3,377 grt; 346ft (105.4m) lbp x 44ft (13.4m) beam
800 passengers in single class
Robert Napier, Govan (Yard No 450)
Triple-expansion steam reciprocating, single screw

The passenger-cargo ship *Montreal*, originally built for Royal Mail Line, was bound from Le Havre to the West Indies on 24 March 1917 when she was torpedoed some 77 miles northeast of Cape Ortegal, in the Bay of Biscay, by the German submarine U46. The *Montreal* sank in the position 45.40N, 07.40W.

Casualties: 0

MONTROSE (1922) Canadian Pacific Line, UK

serving under the wartime name HMS FORFAR
16,402grt; 576ft (175.6m) loa x 70ft (21.3m) beam
1,810 passengers in two classes
Fairfield, Govan (Yard No 529)
Steam turbines, twin screw

The passenger liner *Montrose* was requisitioned to serve as the armed merchant cruiser HMS *Forfar* in November 1939. While she was patrolling 500 miles to the west of Ireland on 2 December 1940, she was torpedoed by the German submarine U99 and sank the following day in the position 54.23N, 20.11W. The destroyer HMS *Thames* picked up the 21 survivors, comprising three officers and 18 ratings.

Casualties: 173 (her commander, 36 officers and 136 ratings)

Although built for the Montreal service, the *Montrose* and her sisters *Montcalm* and *Montclare* spent much of the 1930s engaged on cruises. The *Montrose* is seen leaving Tilbury on a cruise in 1934. *Ian Allan Library*

MOOLTAN (1905) P&O Line, UK

9,621grt; 520ft (158.5m) lbp x 58ft (17.7m) beam
514 passengers in two classes
Caird, Greenock (Yard No 306)
Quadruple-expansion steam reciprocating, twin screw

The *Mooltan* was sailing through the Mediterranean on 26 July 1917, returning to London from Sydney with 554 persons and the mails, bound from Malta to Marseilles in a convoy escorted by the Japanese destroyers *Kusonoki* and *Ume*, when she was torpedoed without warning 53 miles north-north-west of Cape Serrat, Tunisia. Having taken aboard the survivors from the *Mooltan*, the escort ships attempted to ram the German submarine UC27, but they were unsuccessful and were compelled to break off to provide

protection for the remaining merchantmen in the convoy. Meanwhile, the doomed *Mooltan* sank in the position 37.56N, 08.34E.
Casualties: 2

The liner *Mooltan* operated on the service from England to Australia via the Mediterranean and Suez. *World Ship Society*

MORAVIAN (1864) Allan Line, UK

3,323grt; 389ft (118.7m) lbp x 40ft (12.0m) beam
330 passengers in two classes
Robert Steele, Cartsburn, Greenock (Yard No not known)
Compound-expansion steam reciprocating, single screw
On 30 December 1881, while bound for Liverpool from Montreal, the passenger-cargo ship *Moravian* was wrecked at Flat Island, off Cape Sable, near the coast of Nova Scotia.
Casualties: 0

MORRO CASTLE (1930) Ward Line, USA

11,520grt; 531ft (162.0m) loa x 70ft (21.4m) beam
530 passengers in two classes
Newport News Shipbuilding & Drydock Co, Newport News, Virginia (Yard No 337)
Turbo-electric, twin screw
Early on 9 September 1934, when the passenger ship *Morro Castle* was nearing the end of a return voyage from Havana carrying 341 passengers and 240 crew members, fire was discovered in the writing room on the port side of B deck. At the time she was eight miles off the New Jersey coast, about thirty miles south of Scotland Light. Attempts to fight the fire were largely ineffective and it soon spread to the main lounge, which was two decks high and extended the full width of the ship. To make matters worse, her captain had died during the voyage and she was under the acting command of her Chief Officer (William Warms), who appears to have had difficulty coping with the emergency that suddenly confronted him and he failed to make a number of vital decisions. The ship's fire doors were not closed. Nor was the forced ventilation shut off. There was a delay in sending out distress calls and the ship continued at full speed into the strong prevailing wind, driving the flames aft. When the ship was turned about, in an attempt to make for the New Jersey shore, the wind completed the destruction of the superstructure as it now fanned the fire in the other direction.

To add to the confusion, the entire ship was thrown into total darkness when the main electricity cable burned through. When all engine room power was lost soon afterwards, it was obvious that the *Morro Castle* was doomed.

Four other vessels, including the liners *President Cleveland* and *Monarch of Bermuda* and the *City of Savannah* and the *Andrea S. Luckenback*, went to the assistance of the blazing ship, between them rescuing a total of 162 of those who were on board. Many survivors were badly injured with burns and required urgent medical attention. Others attempted to swim what appeared to be the short distance to the nearby shore, but with mixed fortunes. An attempt to tow the *Morro Castle* to New York by the Coast Guard cutter *Tampa* was unsuccessful and she drifted ashore at Asbury Park, New Jersey, where the still-burning ship provided an extraordinary sight for thousands of spectators.

The wreck was later removed and taken to Gravesend Bay, New York, prior to inevitable breaking up at Baltimore. There has been speculation that the fire aboard the *Morro Castle* was an act of arson perpetrated by a known psychopath in her crew who, it was conjectured, was also responsible for the murder of her Master, Captain Robert Wilmott.
Casualties: 134 (94 passengers, including a death by pneumonia brought on by prolonged immersion, and 40 crew). These are the official figures, as quoted by Thomas Gallagher in the book *Fire At Sea*; higher and lower figures are recorded in other sources.

The *Morro Castle* and her sister ship *Oriente* maintained the Ward Line service from New York to Havana. She is seen in a pre-delivery shipyard photograph.
Northrop Grumman Shipbuilding

The gutted *Morro Castle*, beached at Asbury Park, New Jersey, briefly became a major sight-seeing attraction in September 1934. *Steamship Historical Society of America*

MOSEL (1873) Norddeutscher Lloyd, Germany

3,200grt; 365ft (111.3m) loa x 40ft (12.2m) beam
896 passengers in three classes
Caird, Greenock (Yard No 167)
Compound-expansion steam reciprocating, single screw
The transatlantic passenger steamship *Mosel* was wrecked in dense fog near the Lizard Rock on 9 August 1882 while outward bound with mainly emigrant passengers. Earlier in her career, on 11 December 1875, she had been the victim of a sabotage attempt when a bomb exploded alongside her while she was in dock at Bremerhaven preparing for departure. A passenger, who intended to leave the ship incognito at Southampton after setting a timing device to trigger the bomb in mid-ocean, had planned an insurance fraud, but the bomb exploded on the quayside as stevedores manhandled his package. The detonation killed 128 persons besides injuring many others and caused extensive damage both to the *Mosel* and the quayside buildings. The perpetrator, caught in his cabin, attempted to commit suicide by shooting himself and, though hospitalised still alive, he managed to complete the deed by deliberately aggravating his wounds.
Casualties: 0 (in the 1882 stranding)

The *Mosel*, which was stranded at the Lizard in 1882, had been the victim seven years earlier of an attempted marine insurance fraud, possibly among the first of its kind. Although they had no definite proof, the investigators firmly believed that the conspirator had been responsible for many other passenger ships lost at sea with all hands around that time.
Hapag-Lloyd

MOSELLE (1871) Royal Mail Line, UK

3,298grt; 358.2ft (109.2m) lbp x 41ft (12.5m) beam
More than 150 passengers in three classes
John Elder, Govan (Yard No 125)
Compound-expansion steam reciprocating, single screw
The passenger steamer *Moselle* struck the rocks near Colon, Panama, on 29 October 1891 while she was returning to Southampton from Limon, Costa Rica. She was not carrying passengers at the time but, at the mercy of the waves, she was reduced to a total wreck. Casualties: 0

MOSKVA (1867) ex-*Hammonia* (1878) Russian Volunteer Fleet, Russia

3,035grt; 340ft (103.6m) lbp x 40ft (12.2m) beam
678 passengers in three classes (as built)
Caird, Greenock (Yard No 135)
Inverted steam engines, single screw
The former Hamburg Amerika passenger steamer *Hammonia*, sister to the *Cimbria* (qv), was lost four years after she was sold to the Russian Volunteer Fleet for whom she was renamed *Moskva*. She was wrecked at Cape Gardafui, Gulf of Aden, on 9 July 1882, during a voyage from Odessa to Hankow. Casualties: 0

MOSSAMEDES (1895) ex-*Sumatra* (1915) Empreza Nacional de Navegacao, Portugal

4,615grt; 400ft (121.9m) lbp x 47ft (14.2m) beam
98 passengers in two classes (as built), but substantially increased – see below
Alexander Stephen, Linthouse, Glasgow (Yard No 359)
Triple-expansion steam reciprocating, single screw
The passenger accommodation aboard the passenger-cargo ship *Mossamedes* was increased considerably after she moved under the Portuguese flag. She sailed from Cape Town, bound for Lisbon, on 20 April 1923 with a total complement of 258, comprising passengers, including 29 women and 33 children, and a full crew. Four days out, the liner ran ashore in dense fog at False Cape Frio, South West Africa, when she was caught by strong currents. The position was 18.33S, 12.03E. She immediately began to break up in the rough seas and radioed for assistance until all power was lost when the engine room flooded. The British cargo ship *Port Victor* proceeded to the location only to discover on her arrival that the *Mossamedes* had been abandoned and there was no sign of life. The German steamer *Urundi* from Walvis Bay also arrived on the scene and the two vessels conducted a thorough search before proceeding to Cape Town.

The lifeboats from the *Mossamedes* had in fact made for Porto Alexandre. In the absence of any knowledge that help was close at hand, the critical situation had compelled those aboard to abandon ship. One of the boats had capsized on launching and its occupants drowned, while another, containing 24 persons, including two Englishmen, was lost and never heard of again. After a week at sea the remaining 227 survivors were picked up. The Portuguese gunboat *Salvador Correia* rescued 110 castaways, while the French gunboat *Cassiopée* picked up three more. They were all taken to Mossamedes, Angola. A further 84 persons were taken to Porto Alexandre by fishing boats.
Casualties: 31 (from the two lifeboats)

MOUNT TEMPLE (1901) Canadian Pacific Line, UK

9,792grt; 485ft (147.8m) lbp x 59ft (18.0m) beam
500 passengers
Armstrong Whitworth, Low Walker, Tyneside
(Yard No 709)
Triple-expansion steam reciprocating, twin screw
The former Elder Dempster passenger-cargo steamship *Mount Temple* was captured by the German commerce raider *Möwe* on 6 December 1916 during a voyage from Montreal to Brest and London. Her cargo, consisting of horses and other merchandise, was plundered before she was scuttled some 620 miles west-half-south of Fastnet Rock. Her survivors were taken prisoner. Earlier in her career, on 1 December 1907, she had run aground on West Ironbound Island, Lahave, Nova Scotia. The 600 persons aboard her then were got ashore by breeches buoy and were picked up the next day by the steamer *Laurier*, which took them to Halifax. The *Mount Temple* remained fast until 16 April 1908, when she was finally refloated to be fully restored to resume passenger sailings. Casualties: 3

MUNCHEN (1923) Norddeutscher Lloyd, Germany

13,483grt; 551ft (167.8m) loa x 65ft (19.8m) beam
1,079 passengers in three classes
Stettiner Vulcan, Stettin-Bredow (Yard No 669)
Triple-expansion steam reciprocating, twin screw

Shortly after docking at Norddeutscher Lloyd's New York pier on 11 February 1930, fire broke out in the *Munchen*'s cargo holds through the spontaneous combustion of a quantity of potassium nitrate. This, in turn, ignited large volumes of shellac, which formed the bulk of her cargo. Fortunately, the passengers had already disembarked, the last of them still clearing formalities in the custom hall, but, as the blaze spread, accompanied by numerous violent explosions, the entire pier had to be evacuated and officials and members of the *Munchen*'s crew were also compelled to leave the area. By the time the fire had been brought under control, the *Munchen* had sunk at her berth. It was then discovered that her partly submerged hull was resting on the river bed directly over the Hudson Tunnel, which provided a rail link between Manhattan and Hoboken, threatening to collapse it. All tunnel traffic was immediately suspended while engineers investigated the danger, but they were able to give the all-clear after only a few hours of interruption.

The *Munchen* herself was almost totally destroyed internally, apart from a small section at the forward end of the ship, and Lloyd's underwriters and salvage inspectors held the opinion that she was a total loss. However, after divers revealed that the hull below water level was intact and her engines reasonably unscathed, her owners registered their intentions to try to save her. The wrecked liner was refloated on 3 April 1930 and, following temporary repairs at Brooklyn, she departed for Bremen under her own steam on 12 May. After extensive rebuilding she re-emerged, eight months later, as the vastly different *General von Steuben*.
Casualties: 0

Sister ship of the *Stuttgart*, the transatlantic steamship *Munchen* is seen at New York after she had been raised from the river bed in April 1930. Evidence of the sinking can be seen in the marks along the side of her hull.
Steamship Historical Society of America

MUNSTER (1938) British & Irish Steam Packet Co (Coast Lines), Republic of Ireland

4,305grt; 353ft (107.6m) lbp x 50ft (15.3m) beam
425 passengers
Harland & Wolff, Belfast (Yard No 996)
Motor-ship, twin screw

The Irish Sea ferry *Munster* struck a mine while approaching the Bar light vessel on 7 February 1940 while bound from Belfast to Liverpool carrying more than 200 passengers besides her crew. The mine exploded slightly forward of her bridge, on the port side, causing fatal damage. She sank in the position 53.36N, 03.24W.
Casualties: 0

The British & Irish Steam Packet ferry *Munster* operated between Cork or Dublin and Liverpool with her sister ship *Leinster*. *World Ship Society*

N

NAGASAKI MARU (1922) Toa Kaiun Kaisha, Japan

5,272grt; 395ft (120.4m) lbp x 54ft (16.5m) beam
440 passengers
William Denny, Dumbarton (Yard No 1137)
Steam turbines, twin screw
Originally a Nippon Yusen Kaisha ship and styled along the lines of British railway ferries of the period, the passenger ferry *Nagasaki Maru* became a war loss on 13 May 1942 while serving as a transport, when she struck a Japanese mine off Nagasaki and sank in the position 33.00N, 129.40E.
Casualties: not known

NAPOLI (1899) ex-*Sannio* (1913) ex-*British Prince* (1905) Transoceanica Line, Italy

9,203grt; 470ft (143.3m) lbp x 57ft (17.3m) beam
2,270 passengers in two classes
Palmers, Jarrow (Yard No 742)
Triple-expansion steam reciprocating, twin screw
While bound for New York from Naples and Genoa in convoy, on 8 July 1918, the passenger-cargo ship *Napoli* was sunk following a collision off Porto Maurizio, before the convoy had proceeded very far from Genoa. The accident occurred in the tight formation of ships when the *Napoli* came into fatal contact with the Norwegian steamship *Otto Sverdrup*.
Casualties: not known

NARKUNDA (1920) P&O Line, UK

16,632grt; 606ft (184.7m) loa x 69ft (21.0m) beam
673 passengers in two classes
Harland & Wolff, Belfast (Yard No 471)
Quadruple-expansion steam reciprocating, twin screw

Under construction during the First World War, the *Narkunda* finally entered the London to Bombay service on 24 April 1920, making her first Sydney voyage three months later. Whereas her sister ship *Naldera* was disposed of for scrap in 1938, remarkably at the same time the *Narkunda* was given a new lease of life when she was converted to oil-firing. The *Naldera* was the last of 83 ships built by Caird of Greenock for the P&O company. *Alex Duncan*

In May 1940 the passenger liner *Narkunda* was taken over as a troopship. She participated in the invasion of North Africa in November 1942, during which she was sunk shortly after disembarking her troops at the Bougie (Bejaia) beachhead. As she was approaching the landing zone on 13 November, she had sustained damage when the Italian submarine *Platino* succeeded in hitting her with a torpedo, but had been able to continue. However, the following evening, as she made her departure for Algiers, she was attacked by German bombers and sunk in the position 36.49N, 05.01E.
Casualties: 31 (all crew)

NATAL (1881) Messageries Maritimes, France

4,088grt; 413ft (125.9m) lbp x 39ft (11.9m) beam
209 passengers in three classes
Messageries Maritimes, La Ciotat (Yard No 53)
Compound-expansion steam reciprocating, single screw
The passenger-cargo ship *Natal*, requisitioned by the French Government in the First World War to maintain essential postal services, later supported military operations, including the transportation of both troops and prisoners. In this latter capacity, after departing Marseilles in convoy bound for Madagascar with 503 passengers plus her crew, she was involved in a collision on 30 August 1917 with the *Malgache* of Cie Marseillaise de Madagascar, sailing under charter to SGTM. The incident occurred five miles south-south-east of Planier Island, the *Natal* being blacked-out because of the U-boat risk; the *Malgache*, however, which was sailing independently bound from Algeria to Marseilles, was showing her lights. The *Natal* sank in less than fifteen minutes and many of her occupants could not be saved.
Casualties: 105 (76 passengers, her Master and 28 crew)

NAVARINO (1956) ex-*Gripsholm* (1974) Karageorgis Cruises, Greece

22,725grt; 631ft (192.3m) loa x 82ft (24.9m) beam
842 passengers in two classes (as built)
Ansaldo, Sestri Ponente, Genoa (Yard No 1500)
Motor-ship, twin screw
While she was being moved from Piraeus to the Hellenic shipyard at Skaramanga for overhaul and repairs on 28 October 1981, in readiness for a transfer of ownership, a fire broke out off Eleusis in the former First class accommodation of the cruise ship *Navarino*. Whereas the fire caused some damage, the fire-fighting effort was responsible for far greater and more widespread havoc. Some cabin suites and public spaces were flooded and ruined, and the *Navarino* was left with a 7-degree list to port. The ship's intended new owners, AB Sally, refused to take delivery of her until all damages had been made good and the ship dry-docked for final inspection. The former was achieved by 26 November and the *Navarino* was then moved to No 2 floating dry dock for inspection and survey to confirm that all was once more in order. As the docking procedure was nearing completion, however, the dock suddenly listed and the luckless liner slipped off the keel blocks and took an immediate 20-degree list to starboard, causing heavy damage to the ship and the dock, the latter left partly submerged. The starboard bilge blocks were forced through both the dock's decking and the *Navarino*'s hull bottom. Many portholes on the liner were open, as were her watertight doors, and she rapidly filled with water, increasing

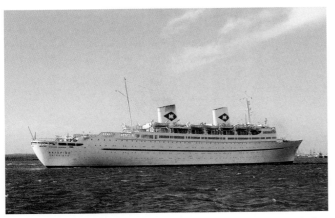

The cruise ship *Navarino*, the one-time *Gripsholm* of Swedish America Line, visiting Southampton in January 1979. *Mick Lindsay*

The *Navarino*, collapsed onto her starboard side in the flooded floating dock at Skaramanga, presented a challenging salvage situation. *Neptun Roda Baloget*

the list to 35 degrees, flooding the engine spaces and 66 per cent of the cabin accommodation up to A deck, and ruining all electrical installations and wiring. Two shipyard workers were severely injured in the accident. The *Navarino* was declared a constructive total loss.

AB Sally called off the deal to purchase her and, in her ungainly predicament, she presented a formidable challenge to salvage experts. The contract for this was awarded to a consortium of Neptun Transport & Marine Service (UK), Roda Baloget, and the locally based Nicolas E. Vernicos Shipping Co. Collectively, over a period of four months they successfully recovered both the former liner and the dry dock. The procedure first involved securing the *Navarino* within the dry dock, to prevent any further deterioration of the situation. This was achieved during early February 1982 with the aid of five steel stanchions erected between the ship and the cradling dock walls. Next, the vessel's stability was enhanced by closing the watertight doors and systematically pumping out compartments, patching them up and re-flooding them where necessary to bring her onto an even keel. The final phase of the salvage operation involved the discharge of water from within the ship by use of compressed air in order to restore her buoyancy.

By 13 March 1982 the *Navarino* was once more afloat, with only a 5-degree list, and three days later she was secured

alongside a quay in the shipyard. The salvage of the dry dock was satisfactorily achieved three days later, concluding the operation. The *Navarino*'s saga did not end here, though. She lingered at her berth for a year until purchased by Multiship Italia 1 for further duties. Renamed *Samantha*, she was towed to Naples for repairs in May 1983, later moved to Piraeus, where she arrived on 13 October 1984, gaining the new identity *Regent Sea* in the process (see the entry for *Sea – ex-Regent Sea –* in Appendix 3).
Casualties: 0

NAZARIO SAURO (1924) Lloyd Triestino, Italy

8,150grt; 447ft (136.2m) lbp x 52ft (15.9m) beam
450 passengers
Ansaldo, Sestri Ponente, Genoa (Yard No 248)
Steam turbines, twin screw
The passenger ship *Nazario Sauro* was trapped at Massowah (Massawa), Eritrea, when it fell to British forces in April 1941. On 6 April 1941, five days after Army units had entered Asmara, the colony's capital, the crew of the *Nazario Sauro* scuttled their ship at Nocra, on Dalac Island, to prevent it from falling into British hands. After the war, on 8 November 1949, the wreck was condemned in the London prize court and removed for breaking up.
Casualties: not known

NEKKA MARU (1935) Osaka Shosen Kaisha, Japan

6,784grt; 427ft (130.1m) lbp x 56ft (17.1m) beam
850 passengers
Mitsubishi, Nagasaki (Yard No 594)
Steam turbines, twin screw
While serving as a naval transport on 23 November 1943, the passenger-cargo ship *Nekka Maru* was torpedoed by the American submarine USS *Gudgeon* off Nantien, China. She sank in the position 28.43N, 122.07E.
Casualties: not known

NEPTUNIA (1920) ex-*Johan de Witt* (1948) Greek Line, Greece

10,519grt; 499ft (152.1m) loa x 59ft (18.1m) beam
787 passengers in two classes
Nederlandsche SB, Amsterdam (Yard No 150)
Triple-expansion steam reciprocating, twin screw

The *Neptunia*, photographed at Southampton, was the former Dutch passenger ship *Johan de Witt*. *Tom Rayner collection*

The transatlantic passenger-cargo liner *Neptunia* struck Daunts' Rock, at the entrance to Cobh Harbour, on 2 November 1957 and was beached in Whitegate Roads in a badly damaged condition. She was abandoned to the underwriters as a constructive total loss and on 2 March 1958, after her hull had been sealed, she was towed to Hendrik Ido Ambacht, in the Netherlands, by the Dutch tug *Gele Zee*. She arrived there on 7 March and was subsequently demolished for scrap.
Casualties: 0

NEPTUNIA (1932) Italia Line, Italy

19,475grt; 590ft (179.8m) loa x 76ft (23.2m) beam
1,532 passengers in three classes
Cantieri Riuniti dell'Adriatico, Monfalcone (Yard No 252)
Motor-ship, twin screw
In 1940 the passenger liner *Neptunia*, together with her sister *Oceania* (qv), was requisitioned to serve as a troop transport with the Italian Navy. On 18 September 1941 the sister ships, carrying a total number of troops estimated at 7,000, were sailing together in a large convoy bound from Taranto to Tripoli when they were both sunk by torpedoes fired by the British submarine HMS *Upholder*. The convoy had an escort of five destroyers, but when the convoy was about sixty miles from Tripoli the British warship managed to penetrate their defensive screen to launch her attack and came close to sinking a third former Italia Line passenger ship, the *Saturnia*, which was also in the convoy. The *Neptunia* was hit by two torpedoes and foundered shortly afterwards in the position 33.02N, 14.42E. The *Oceania* was hit by another of the *Upholder*'s torpedoes and severely disabled. She was taken in tow by two of the destroyers but later, after receiving two further hits, she too sank in the same vicinity. Casualty figures from the sinking of the *Neptunia* and her sister vary considerably from source to source, with some reports claiming that 5,000 men were drowned out of the total complement of soldiers and crew aboard the two ships. If correct, this would make their losses in combination the worst disaster involving Italian ships during the Second World War.
Casualties: 384 (from the *Neptunia* and *Oceania*, according to official Italian records)

The sister ships *Neptunia*, pictured here, and *Oceania* were ordered by and built for the Cosulich Line. In January 1937 they became Italia ships when Cosulich became the last unit to officially amalgamate with the Italia Flotta Riunite combine. The first three years of their careers were spent on the run from Trieste and Naples to Brazil, Uruguay and Argentina, but from February 1935 they were switched to the service from Genoa to Bombay and Shanghai via Suez.
M. Cicogna Collection, Trieste

NERISSA (1926) Furness Bermuda Line, UK

5,583grt; 349ft (106.4m) lbp x 54ft (16.5m) beam
229 passengers
W. Hamilton, Glen Yard, Glasgow (Yard No395)
Triple-expansion steam reciprocating, single screw
The passenger-cargo steamship *Nerissa* was torpedoed by the German submarine U552 on 30 April 1941, during a voyage from Halifax, Nova Scotia, and St John's, Newfoundland, to Liverpool with 175 passengers and 112 crew members. The attack took place about 200 miles west of Inishtrahull and she sank in the position 57.57N, 10.08W.
Casualties: 207 (124 passengers and 83 crew)

The *Nerissa* was employed with other Furness ships on the route from New York to Bermuda and the West Indies.
Ian Allan Library

NEURALIA (1912) British India Line, UK

9,082grt; 480ft (146.3m) lbp x 58ft (17.7m) beam
50 passengers and 1,050 troops
Barclay Curle, Whiteinch, Glasgow (Yard No 497)
Quadruple-expansion steam reciprocating, twin screw
On the outbreak of the Second World War, the *Neuralia*, a Ministry of Transport peacetime troopship, was taken over for full-time trooping. On 1 May 1945, while bound from Split, Yugoslavia, to Taranto, she stuck a mine off the coast of southern Italy, in the position 40.11N, 17.44E. At the time she was carrying 12 passengers and a crew of 265 men. The *Neuralia* was the last British passenger ship loss of the war.
Casualties: 4

The *Neuralia*, with her sister ship *Nevasa*, was employed on the India and East African services, in addition to which she was also engaged as a Ministry of Transport peacetime troopship. *J. G. Callis*

NEUSTRIA (1884) Fabre Line, France

2,926grt; 328ft (100.0m) lbp x 40ft (12.2m) beam
1,118 passengers
Claperade Frères, Rouen (Yard No not known)
Compound-expansion steam reciprocating, single screw
On 27 October 1908 the passenger steamship *Neustria* made her final departure from New York bound for Marseilles, but, after clearing the port, she was neither seen nor heard of again. No record has been found to indicate how many people were on board at the time of her disappearance, but the *Neustria* had a sizeable passenger capacity and her normal crew strength was 41.
Casualties: not known

NEWARK CASTLE (1902) Union-Castle Line, UK

6,253grt; 415ft (126.2m) lbp x 51ft (15.6m) beam
540 passengers in three classes
Barclay Curle, Whiteinch, Glasgow (Yard No 430)
Triple-expansion steam reciprocating, twin screw
During a voyage from Durban to Delagoa Bay and Mauritius on 12 March 1908, the 'Extra' passenger steamer *Newark Castle* was stranded in Richard's Bay, Zululand, 4 miles from Port Durnford, near the Umhlatuzi River. The weather was fine and the sea calm and the boats were lowered without difficulty, taking off the majority of the 46 passengers, many of whom were soldiers, and 69 crew members. A small crew contingent remained aboard the ship with her Master and they were later rescued by a South African tug. Meanwhile, the lifeboats, which were heading for Durban, were intercepted by the trawler *Elelyn* and picked up safely. One exception was a boat that had capsized in an attempt to reach the shore, from which three persons drowned. By this time the weather had deteriorated and the gusting conditions permitted the *Newark Castle* to drift free, but she ran aground on another sandbank seven miles away, where she became a total wreck.
Casualties: 3

The *Newark Castle* was another 'Extra' steamer of the *'Alnwick Castle'* type, running the emigrant service to South Africa. *David Reed*

NEWFOUNDLAND (1925) Furness Warren Line, UK

6,791grt; 423ft (128.9m) loa x 55ft (16.8m) beam
185 passengers in two classes
Vickers, Barrow-in-Furness (Yard No 617)
Quadruple-expansion steam reciprocating, twin screw

The passenger-cargo ship *Newfoundland* was taken over as a hospital ship at the onset of the Second World War. In this capacity she participated in the Allied landings at Salerno, Italy, in September 1943. After arriving from Bizerta, she anchored off the beaches where, on 13 September, she was bombed and set on fire by German aircraft. She burned out of control for two days until Allied warships were instructed to sink her with their guns. The wreck lay in the position 40.13N, 14.21E. At the time of the attack, the *Newfoundland* had been occupied by a total of 315 persons, of whom only two were medical cases.
Casualties: 21 (5 doctors, 6 nurses, 6 Army medical staff and 4 crew)

The *Newfoundland* was engaged in the service from Liverpool to St John's, Newfoundland, Halifax, Nova Scotia, and Boston with her sister ship *Nova Scotia*. *Real Photos*

NEW ORIENT PRINCESS (1968) ex-*Leader Prince* (1992) ex-*Gulangyu* (1988) ex-*New Gulangyu* (1984) ex-*Kong Olav V* (1984) Well Direction Maritime, Panama

4,843grt; 410ft (125.0m) loa x 63ft (19.3m) beam
950 passengers including 408 on deck
Cantieri Navali del Tirreno e Riuniti, Riva Trigoso, Genoa (Yard No 278)
Motor-ship, twin screw

The *New Orient Princess*, seen here as the *Gulangyu*, was originally the *Kong Olav V* of DFDS Seaways. *Frank Heine FERRIES*

After 15 years on the Copenhagen to Oslo route for DFDS, the former ro-ro passenger ferry *Kong Olav V* moved to the Far East where she was employed on various routes for a number of different owners. As the *New Orient Princess*, she was lost on 25 August 1983 when she caught fire off Hak Kok Tau,

Hong Kong, during a gambling cruise to 'nowhere'. Initially anchored to facilitate fire-fighting, she was subsequently beached on the appropriately named Junk Island. Assessed as being beyond economic recovery, she was broken up in China where demolition commenced in May 1994.
Casualties: not known

NEW YORK (1924) Eastern Steamship Lines, USA

4,989grt; 385ft (117.4m) lbp x 73ft (22.1m) beam
About 750 passengers in two classes
Bethlehem Shipbuilding Corp, Sparrows Point (Yard No 4219)
Steam turbines, twin screw
The American passenger ship *New York* was transferred to the Ministry of War Transport in 1942 and placed under the management of Coast Lines. On 25 September 1942 she was sailing in a North Atlantic convoy bound for the UK from New York and St John's, Newfoundland, carrying a total of 62 personnel. In the position 54.34N, 25.44W she was torpedoed and sunk by the German submarine U91.
Casualties: 59 (50 crew and 9 gunners)

NEW YORK (1927) Hamburg Amerika Line, Germany

23,337grt; 677ft (206.3m) loa x 72ft (21.9m) beam
960 passengers in three classes
Blohm & Voss, Steinwerder, Hamburg (Yard No 474)
Steam turbines, twin screw
After returning to Hamburg via Murmansk in late 1939, the passenger liner *New York* was taken over briefly as a naval support ship. Subsequently she was laid up as an accommodation ship based at Kiel, where she remained until January 1945, when she was reactivated for the evacuation operation ('Hannibal') rescuing refugees and military personnel from Germany's eastern territories. At the end of one of these mercy voyages, on 3 April 1945, she was at Kiel when US Air Force bombers raided the port. Struck by bombs, the *New York* capsized onto her port side on fire. Her wreck was refloated on 21 March 1949 and towed to Dalmuir on the Clyde for breaking up, arriving on 2 August 1949. Demolition was completed at Troon from January 1950.
Casualties: not known

The four liners of the 'Albert Ballin' class, introduced to the transatlantic service from 1923, fared badly during the Second World War. The *New York*, depicted here, and *Deutschland* were sunk in aerial attacks, while the other pair struck mines.
Author's collection

NGAN-KIN (1883) China Navigation Co (John Swire & Co), UK

2,732grt; 289ft (88.1m) lbp x 43ft (13.1m) beam
Passenger numbers not known
Scotts, Greenock (Yard No 227)
Compound expansion steam reciprocating, single screw
The passenger-cargo steamer *Ngan-Kin* stranded on Hirado Island in the River Yangtse, seven miles below Hankow (Hankau), at high water on 29 July 1933 while she was on passage from Shanghai to Hankow. Despite every effort at the following high tides, she could not be refloated and was abandoned to be broken up on the spot.
Casualties: 0

NIAGARA (1913) Canadian Australasian Line, UK

13,415grt; 543ft (165.5m) loa x 66ft (20.1m) beam
704 passengers in three classes
John Brown, Clydebank (Yard No 415)
Triple-expansion steam reciprocating with LP turbine, triple screw
The *Niagara* departed from Auckland on 17 June 1940 bound for the UK, via Suva, Honolulu and Vancouver, carrying only 53 passengers but with a valuable cargo of gold valued at £2.5 million. A day out, as she negotiated the Hauraki Gulf, off Whangarei, she struck a mine that had been laid by the German raider *Orion* some days earlier, which exploded adjacent to her No 2 hold. As her forepart flooded, the *Niagara* began to settle by the head, ultimately sinking in 75 fathoms, in the position 35.53S, 174.54E. Before she went down, calls for assistance were transmitted, in answer to which the Huddart Parker liner *Wanganella* and the coaster *Kapiti* responded, between them picking up all the passengers and the 201-man crew, who had taken to the boats. Salvage operations, initiated immediately after the loss of the *Niagara* and continuing until February 1942, then resumed post-war in 1953, were successful in recovering all the gold bullion.
Casualties: 0

The steamship *Niagara* was originally built for the Union Steamship Company of New Zealand for service on the route from Sydney to Vancouver via New Zealand. In 1932, in the face of growing American and Japanese competition on the route, the Union Steamship Co formed a consortium with Canadian Pacific, called the Canadian Australasian Line, for the continued operation of the *Niagara* with her larger fleet-mate *Aorangi*.
Ian Allan Library

NICOLAS PAQUET (1928) Cie de Navigation Pacquet, France

8,517grt; 426ft (130.5m) lbp x 57ft (17.3m) beam
1,100 passengers
Forges & Chantiers de la Méditerranée, La Seyne (Yard No 1195)
Triple-expansion steam reciprocating, twin screw

The passenger steamship *Nicolas Pacquet* was lost off the Algerian coast, four miles off Cape Spartic, about 1½ miles from Cape Spartel lighthouse on 6 July 1933 during a voyage from Marseilles to Casablanca. Casualties: not known

NIEUW ZEELAND (1928) Koninklijke Paketvaart Maatschappij, The Netherlands

11,069grt; 527ft (160.6m) loa x 62ft (18.9m) beam
155 passengers in single class
Rotterdamsche Droogdok Maatschappij, Rotterdam
(Yard No142)
Steam turbines, twin screw

In 1940 the Dutch passenger ships *Nieuw Zeeland* and *Nieuw Holland* were transferred to British control on behalf of the Dutch Government in exile and both became troopships. On 11 November, while returning to the United Kingdom, after she had disembarked troops for the North Africa landings, the *Nieuw Zeeland* was torpedoed off the African coast by the German submarine U407, and sank in the position 35.59N, 03.45W. At the time she was carrying thirteen passengers plus her crew of 243, most of whom survived.
Casualties: 15 (all crew)

The *Nieuw Zeeland*, with her sister liner *Nieuw Holland*, was engaged on the service from Java to Australia. This view shows the *Nieuw Zeeland* while serving as an Allied troopship in the Second World War. *Imperial War Museum (FE307)*

NIKKO MARU (1903) Nippon Yusen Kaisha, Japan

5,559grt; 428ft (130.5m) lbp x 49ft (14.9m) beam
219 passengers in three classes
Mitsubishi, Nagasaki (Yard No 148)
Triple-expansion steam reciprocating, single screw

The passenger-cargo ship *Nikko Maru* was operating as a troop transport when she was sunk in the Yellow Sea, in the position 36.46N, 123.36E, on 9 April 1945. She was torpedoed by the American submarine USS *Tirante*.
Casualties: not known

NISOS RODOS (1953) ex-*Renetta* (1977) ex-*Deutschland* (1972) Maleas Shipping Co, Greece

3,863grt; 377ft (114.9m) loa x 56ft (17.2m) beam
1,200 passengers
Kieler Howaldtswerke AG, Kiel (Yard No 980)
Motor-ship, twin screw

The ro-ro ferry *Nisos Rodos*, on passage from Rhodes to Piraeus with 100 passengers and 58 crew, suffered an engine fire following an explosion while off Amorgos on 25 May 1978. Calls for emergency assistance were immediately transmitted and the ship was fully evacuated, the survivors being taken to Piraeus. Further explosions aboard the stricken ferry followed as the fire intensified. She was taken in tow but, as she was refused entry into Piraeus, she was beached two days later in a listing condition at Legrena, near Lavrion (Laurium), 25 miles south-east of Athens. It was estimated that 95 per cent of the vessel had been gutted. Her hull structure was buckled and her decks were sagging, much metalwork having been melted by the intense heat. Later refloated, the *Nisos Rodos* was towed to Kynosaura, Salamis Island, where she was beached again on 12 July 1978. With little doubt that she was a constructive total loss, she was sold for scrapping, which commenced locally from October 1979.
Casualties: 0

Looking the worse for wear, the *Nisos Rodos* is moored at Piraeus in April 1978. *Frank Heine FERRIES*

NITTA MARU (1940) Nippon Yusen Kaisha, Japan

serving under the wartime name IJNS CHUYO
17,150grt; 590ft (179.8m) loa x 73ft (22.3m) beam
285 passengers in three classes
Mitsubishi, Nagasaki (Yard No 750)
Steam turbines, twin screw

In May 1942 the passenger liner *Nitta Maru*, only completed in March 1940, was taken in hand at the Kure naval shipyard for conversion into an escort aircraft carrier. She was commissioned that year, on 25 November, as the *Chuyo* and immediately entered the Pacific sea war. She was torpedoed and sunk by the American submarine USS *Sailfish* on 4 December 1943 in the position 32.37N, 143.39E, about 275 miles south-east of Honshu.
Casualties: 1,250

Many of the passenger liners under construction for Japanese companies in the 1930s were designed with a view to conversion to aircraft carriers in time of national emergency. Among the vessels included in this scheme were the Nippon Yusen Kaisha sisters *Nitta Maru*, *Kasuga Maru* and *Yawata Maru*, three new ships planned for the Yokohama to Hamburg service. Due to the outbreak of war in Europe the *Nitta Maru* instead entered the Yokohama to San Francisco service when she was completed in March 1940. *Nippon Yusen Kaisha*

The escort carrier *Chuyo* (ex-*Nitta Maru*) at anchor in a Japanese naval base. With a complete absence of deck structures, she and her sisters truly fit the description 'flat-tops'. *US National Archives*

NJASSA (1924) Deutsche-Ost Afrika Line, Germany

8,754 grt; 433ft (132.1m) lbp x 58ft (17.7m) beam
ca. 200-250 passengers in three classes
Blohm & Voss, Steinwerder, Hamburg (Yard No 399)
Steam turbines, single screw

The passenger-cargo ship *Njassa* was a Wilhelmshaven on 30 March 1945 where she was bombed and sunk by Allied warplanes. Her wreck was broken up. The *Njassa*'s sister-ships *Tanganjika* and *Usambara* (qv) were lost in similar fashion.
Casualties: not known

NORD AMERICA (1882) ex-*Nord America* ex *Stirling Castle* (1883) ex-*Stirling Castle* (launch name: 21 January 1882) La Veloce Line, Italy

4,920grt; 419ft (127.6m) lbp x 50ft (15.2m) beam
1,313 passengers in two classes
John Elder, Govan (Yard No 257)
Triple-expansion steam reciprocating, single screw

Unusually, after she was first transferred to the La Veloce, this passenger steamship carried both her new name and her former name, in the form *Nord America ex Stirling Castle*, each side of her bows. She was lost sixteen years later, while working the Palermo to New York route, when she was wrecked near Arzilla, Cape Spartel, Morocco, on 5 December 1910. Towed to Genoa, she was scrapped there in 1911.
Casualties: not known

NORGE (1881) ex-*Pieter de Coninck* (1889) Det Forenede D/S (Scandinavian American Line), Denmark

3,359grt; 340ft (103.6m) lbp x 41ft (12.5m) beam
1,100 passengers
Alexander Stephen, Linthouse, Glasgow (Yard No 252)
Compound-expansion steam reciprocating, single screw

The passenger steamship *Norge* made her final departure from Copenhagen on 22 June 1904 when she sailed for New York with 700 emigrant passengers and a crew of 80 or so. Six days later she struck the rocks near Rockall, 200 miles west of the Hebrides, and sank soon after getting herself free. There were only 129 survivors, making the disaster one of the worst in the pre-First World War period after those that involved the *Titanic* and *Empress of Ireland*. Those fortunate enough to be rescued from the few lifeboats that were launched were

picked up by the trawler *Silvia* (27 persons), the steamer *Cervona* (32 persons), and the steamer *Energie* (another 70).
Casualties: About 650

The ill-fated *Norge*, a Danish-flag emigrant carrier on the Atlantic run, was acquired by owners Scandinavian American Line in 1898 from the Thingvalla Line. *World Ship Society*

NORMANDIE (1935) Compagnie Générale Transatlantique (French Line), France

serving under the wartime name USS LAFAYETTE [AP-53]
83,423grt; 1,029ft (313.8m) loa x 118ft (35.9m) beam
1,972 passengers in three classes
Penhoët, St Nazaire (Yard No T6)
Turbo-electric, quadruple screw

Laid up at New York on the outbreak of the Second World War, the transatlantic record-breaking ocean liner *Normandie* was seized by the US War Shipping Administration in December 1941 when the United States entered the war. Essentially she was a Vichy French vessel and, therefore, a legitimate prize. Handed over to the US Navy, she was taken in hand immediately for conversion into the troop transport *Lafayette*, but, driven by an over-enthusiastic desire to get involved in taking on the enemy, it was undertaken in a hasty and ill-organised fashion. Stores and provisions for trooping activities, including highly inflammable life-jackets, were taken aboard even as structural alterations were still being carried out, hampering the workmen and creating a fire risk.

On 9 February 1942 that potential risk became a reality when some of the life-jackets stowed in the ship's First class restaurant were ignited by sparks from cutting torches that were being used to remove obstructive stanchions. An equally disorganised and uncoordinated fire-fighting effort ensued, exacerbated by incompatibility between shore hydrants and onboard hose connections, a mixture of French and American fittings, the resulting delays allowing the fire to get firmly established. Gallons of water were subsequently pumped into the great liner by appliances and fire-boats from the New York Fire Department, and after four hours the fire had been all but extinguished.

However, it was an extremely cold day and much of the water froze in the vessel's upper structure, making her top-heavy. Listing increasingly to port, the full extent of her instability was revealed as the tide rose in the River Hudson, lifting her off the bottom until, at 2.45am on 10 February, the *Lafayette* capsized onto her side, coming to rest half-submerged alongside her berth. The complicated salvage operation that followed was not concluded until September 1943 and involved the removal of all of the *Normandie*'s top

structure above her main Promenade deck in order to right her. The exercise had also cost a vast amount of money. By that time there was little to be gained from spending even more to renovate her for auxiliary use, especially as the war would probably be over before she could be made ready. After the war, her former owners showed no interest in taking her back for refurbishment for commercial service, also, no doubt, because the cost could not be justified. Consequently, the remains of this once proud and elegant ship were unceremoniously towed away for scrapping at New Jersey in October 1946, ending one of the shortest of careers.
Casualties: 1

In spite of the fire-prone reputations of pre-war French liners, the *Normandie* had numerous fire-prevention features incorporated into her design. These included fire-retardant paints, fireproof screens above the watertight bulkheads and an abundant supply of hydrants. *Maritime Photo Library*

The *Lafayette* (ex-*Normandie*) on fire at New York, the smoke from the blaze billowing over Manhattan island's skyscrapers. *US National Archives*

NORONIC (1913) Canada Steamship Line, Canada

6,905grt; 362ft (110.3m) lbp x 52ft (15.9m) beam
562 passengers
Western Drydock & Shipbuilding Co, Port Arthur, Ontario (Yard No 6)
Triple-expansion steam reciprocating, single screw

Disaster befell the Great Lakes excursion ship *Noronic* during a cruise to the St Lawrence Seaway. Fire was discovered aboard her during the night of 16-17 September 1949 when she was berthed at Pier 9, Toronto Docks. At the time there were 695 persons on board, 524 passengers and 171 crew, the majority asleep in their cabins. The outbreak was discovered in a linen cupboard on C deck; its cause was never determined, but it is thought to have been a smouldering cigarette, although arson was also suspected. The crew was ill-prepared to tackle the emergency, while the fire-fighting equipment was inadequate and badly maintained. Furthermore, the *Noronic*'s design and structure also embodied features that were potentially hazardous in such a situation: she was shallow draught with a high centre of gravity; the construction materials were light and mostly of a highly inflammable nature; there were no fire doors or bulkheads on any of the decks to prevent the lateral travel of a fire; she had insufficient stairways and exits, with many portholes covered wholly or partially by metal screens; and she did not have a public address system. For the passengers, the consequences of these shortcomings were exacerbated by the complete lack of direction signs to indicate emergency boat and fire stations and many were caught in their cabins or trapped in blazing corridors.

By the time the Toronto Fire Department arrived on the scene the fire was well established, having spread at an alarming rate, and much of their effort, apart from fighting the fire, was devoted to aiding passengers make their escape. The high number of human casualties ranks the tragedy as one of the worst experienced by the Canadian Merchant Marine. The precise number of deaths cannot be stated for certain because the owners had not kept accurate passenger lists. Completely gutted, the *Noronic* sank at her berth. After the wreck was raised, it was towed away for breaking up.
Casualties: 119 (This is the figure from the official report on the fire, but some accounts give a figure of 136.)

The *Noronic* and the similar *Hamonic* were distinctive Great Lakes excursion steamers, but widespread use of wood in their upper structures made them especially vulnerable to the ravages of fire. *Bowling Green State University*

A scene during the frantic evacuation of the blazing *Noronic* as passengers make their escape along the quayside.
Toronto Fire Department

The hulk of the *Noronic* sunk alongside Queen's Quay, Toronto, and a view of some of the fire damage within the ship, whose wooden superstructure was almost completely destroyed.
Both: Toronto Fire Department

NORSEMAN (1898) ex-*Brasilia* (1900) Dominion Line, UK

9,546grt; 516ft (157.3m) loa x 62ft (18.9m) beam
2,400 passengers in single class
Harland & Wolff, Belfast (Yard No 318)
Quadruple-expansion steam reciprocating, twin screw
During a voyage from Plymouth to Salonica, the passenger ship *Norseman*, taken over by the Admiralty for war service,

was torpedoed by the German submarine U39 on 22 January 1916 when she was off Gran Capo, in the Gulf of Salonica (Thessaloniki), having sailed from Liverpool on 1 January with a call en route at Plymouth. With various craft lashed alongside her to give her buoyancy, the stricken ship was taken in tow for Mudros and beached at Tuzla Point where she was abandoned. Beyond recovery, she was broken up on the spot by a firm of Italian ship-breakers commencing in 1920. Although all her human occupants were got off safely, around 400 mules and horses that were trapped in the holds perished. Their carcasses soon began to rot and, as the heat of the Mediterranean summer intensified, became a major health hazard, giving off an overpowering stench.
Casualties: 0

The *Norseman*, a former Hamburg Amerika Line passenger ship, was adapted for a North Atlantic cargo service with her passenger accommodation reduced to Steerage class only. Later she transferred to a London to Sydney route.
Maritime Photo Library

NORWAY (1962) ex-*France* (1979) Norwegian Cruise Line, Bahamas

76,049grt; 1,035ft (315.5m) loa x 111ft (33.7m) beam
2,370 passengers
Penhoët, St Nazaire (Yard No G19)
Steam turbines, twin screw
The last of the classic, pure transatlantic express passenger liners, the *France* was acquired for conversion into a unique cruise ship named *Norway* and placed, initially, on special itineraries in the Caribbean. Later, her cruise schedule took her further afield as she underwent a series of refurbishments that extended her passenger accommodation. Although concerns about her continuation in service were being raised, she remained active through the turn of the millennium until 25 May 2003 when she experienced a massive boiler explosion, caused by extensive fatigue cracking, while she was berthed at Miami between cruises. The explosion caused widespread damage in the engineering spaces and to the adjacent crew accommodation as superheated steam mixed with smoke, soot and debris swept with incredible force throughout the area. Besides the dead, there were many more crew members who were seriously injured. The disabled ship was towed back to Hamburg where she languished for two years until, in June 2005 under the name *Blue Lady*, she was towed around South Africa to the Far East, finally arriving at Alang where she was beached for breaking up on 15 August 2006. Even then, concerns about environmental damage, because of the vast quantities of asbestos inside her, delayed the inevitable.
Casualties: 8 (all crew)

The *Norway* (ex-*France*), for many years the longest passenger liner ever built, photographed while en route to Indian shipbreakers. Although referred to as the *Blue Lady*, she did not carry that name. *Ian Shiffman*

NORWEGIAN (1865) ex-*City of New York* (1884) Allan Line, UK

3,523grt; 375ft (114.4m) lbp x 40ft (12.1m) beam
500 passengers in two classes
Tod & McGregor, Glasgow (Yard No 132)
Compound-expansion steam reciprocating, single screw
Renamed *Norwegian*, this former Inman passenger steamer ran aground at Daunts Rock, Little Cod Bay, near the entrance to Queenstown (Cobh Harbour), Ireland, on 29 May 1903, while operating the Glasgow to Boston service. She sustained considerable damage. As it was uneconomical to repair her she was sold for breaking up in the Netherlands.
Casualties: 0

NOTTING HILL (1881) Twin Screw Line, UK

4,021grt; 420ft (128.0m) lbp x 45ft (13.7m) beam
840 passengers in two classes
Dobie, Govan (Yard No 109)
Compound-expansion steam reciprocating, twin screw
During her first season with her new owners, having been built originally for Hill & Nott of Liverpool, the transatlantic passenger-cargo steamship *Notting Hill* struck an iceberg in mid-Atlantic on 5 February 1884 while on passage from London to New York. Severely damaged, she was abandoned in the position 45.56N, 46.13W and later foundered.
Casualties: 0

NOVA SCOTIA (1926) Furness Warren Line, UK

6,796grt; 423ft (128.9m) loa x 55ft (16.8m) beam
185 passengers in two classes
Vickers, Barrow-in-Furness (Yard No 623)
Quadruple-expansion steam reciprocating, twin screw
The passenger-cargo ship *Nova Scotia* was lost on 28 November 1942 while serving as a troopship under the control of the Ministry of War Shipping. During a voyage from Aden to Durban carrying a full complement of 928 passengers and 127 crew, she was torpedoed off the African coast, near Lourenço Marques, by the German submarine U177. Her passengers comprised 12 service personnel, 6 non-military passengers and 780 Italian prisoners of war under the guard of 130 South African troops. She sank rapidly, in the

position 28.30S, 33.00E, and there was heavy loss of life. Casualties: 863 (14 of the service personnel and non-military passengers, 650 prisoners of war, 88 guards and 111 crew). In some accounts, the total casualties are reported to have been 768.

The *Nova Scotia* and her sister ship *Newfoundland* were replaced in 1947 by two slightly larger ships of the same names. *Furness Withy Group*

NUBIA (1895) P&O Line, UK

5,914grt; 430ft (131.1m) lbp x 49ft (15.0m) beam
152 passengers in two classes
Caird, Greenock (Yard No 276)
Triple-expansion steam reciprocating, single screw
The passenger-cargo steamship *Nubia*, which had also served as a government troopship and hospital ship at the time of the Boer War, was wrecked a short distance – about half a mile – north of Colombo Harbour, Ceylon (Sri Lanka), on 20 June 1915. At the time she was bound for Shanghai from Bombay.
Casualties: not known

Sister ship of the *Simla* and *Malta*, the *Nubia* operated on the Calcutta service but was also employed as a peacetime troopship. During the Boer War she served as both troopship and hospital ship. *Tom Rayner collection*

NUBIAN (1876) Union Line, UK

3,091grt; 369ft (109.4m) lbp x 39ft (11.8m) beam
200 passengers in two classes
Mitchell, Low Walker, Tyneside (Yard No 300)
Triple-expansion steam reciprocating, single screw
On 20 December 1892 the passenger-cargo ship *Nubian* became beached and sank on the southern shore of the River Tagus, at Lisbon, after striking rocks. At the time she was bound from Southampton to Cape Town. Beyond economic recovery, she was broken up.
Casualties: not known

OCEANA (1888) P&O Line, UK

6,610grt; 468ft (142.8m) lbp x 52ft (15.9m) beam
410 passengers in two classes
Harland & Wolff, Belfast (Yard No 201)
Triple-expansion steam reciprocating, single screw
On 16 March 1912, when outward bound in the English
Channel, the passenger steamship *Oceana* collided with the
sailing barque *Pisagua*, one of the celebrated 'Flying Ps' of the
Laeisz Line, inward bound from Mexillones for her home port
Hamburg .At the time the *Oceana* was still under the charge
of a Trinity House pilot. The accident occurred four miles off
Beachy Head, in darkness, although it was a clear night and it
was later conjectured that the *Pisagua*'s sails may have been
obscuring her navigation lights. Whatever the cause, the
Pisagua was not seen until it was too late and, despite last-
minute evasive action, the sailing vessel struck the *Oceana*'s
port side, careering along its length, ripping away the
lifeboats, mangling the davits and tearing an enormous gash
in her side that extended below the waterline.

The passenger ship's engines were immediately stopped,
the watertight doors closed and the pumps started while,
simultaneously, a detailed examination of the situation below
decks was ordered. Instructions were also given for the firing
of distress rockets while the remaining lifeboats were swung
out and occupied. In the general confusion, despite what
otherwise seems to have been a measured response to the
situation, one lifeboat was lowered prematurely, while the
ship was still under way, and it capsized as it hit the water,
spilling its occupants into the sea, some of whom perished.
The emergency boat followed, without accident, and picked
up the survivors from the sea.

Oceana was one of the 'Jubilee' class, commemorating the 50th
anniversary of Queen Victoria's ascendancy to the British
throne. She entered the London to Sydney service via Colombo
and Melbourne but later transferred to the Bombay service.
Tom Rayner collection

Shortly afterwards the cross-Channel steamer *Sussex*
arrived in response to the rockets and the *Oceana*'s
remaining passengers, together with part of her crew, were
transferred to her. The steamship *Queensgarth* also arrived
and stood by as the Newhaven tug *Alert* took the *Oceana* in
tow with the intention of getting her to Dover. As the coast

was neared, her list drastically increased and, just before it was
possible to beach her, she sank in shallow water just south of
Eastbourne with her masts showing. Meanwhile, the *Pisagua*,
whose stem was buckled and foretop mast completely
missing, had made Dover.

Apart from her passengers, the *Oceana* had been carrying
a valuable cargo of gold and silver specie, valued at three-
quarters of a million pounds, destined for Port Said and
Bombay. Divers of the Liverpool Salvage Association were
later able to recover all but £3,000 worth of the treasure. The
Oceana's wreck was blown up to clear it. The subsequent
court of enquiry exonerated the *Pisagua*, placing the blame
for the disaster with those who had been responsible for
navigating the *Oceana*. Casualties: 14

OCEANIA (1932) Italia Line, Italy

19,507grt; 589ft (179.5m) loa x 76ft (23.2m) beam
1,385 passengers in three classes
Cantieri Riuniti dell'Adriatico, Monfalcone (Yard No 253)
Motor-ship, quadruple screw
The passenger liner *Oceania* was a sister of the *Neptunia*.
Both were sunk on 18 September 1941. For the full account
of the sinking, see the *Neptunia*.

OCEANIC (1899) White Star Line, GB

17,274grt; 704ft (214.6m) loa x 68ft (20.7m) beam
1,710 passengers in three classes
Harland & Wolff, Belfast (Yard No 317)
Triple-expansion steam reciprocating, twin screw
On the outbreak of the First World War, the passenger liner
Oceanic was requisitioned for service as an armed merchant
cruiser and, after conversion, was attached to the 10th Cruiser
Squadron. Only a matter of weeks after she had been
commissioned, on 8 September 1914, she ran onto the Hoevdi
rocks, three miles south-east of Foula Island, in the Shetlands,
in dense fog and was left firmly wedged. Her entire
complement of 400 officers and men were rescued by the
trawler *Glenogil*. Three days later the *Oceanic* was declared
to be a constructive total loss and was broken up in situ, the
wreckage finally cleared in 1924. Casualties: 0

OCEANOS (1952) ex-*Eastern Princess* (1976) ex-*Ancona* (1974) ex-*Mykinai* (1971) ex-*Jean Laborde* (1970) Epirotiki Lines, Greece

7,554grt; 492ft (150.0m) loa x 64ft (19.6m) beam
499 passengers in three classes (as built)
Chantiers de la Gironde, Bordeaux (Yard No 225)
Motor-ship, twin screw
After scheduled passenger service from France to East Africa,
then between Singapore and Australia over a 15-year period,
the *Oceanos* was adapted for full-time cruising, an activity
that took her to South Africa from 1991 to work an itinerary
taking in ports along Africa's Indian Ocean coastline. On 3
August 1991, while on such a cruise bound from East London
to Durban, the *Oceanos* developed a leak in her engine room
that proved to be very serious. Soon after the discovery was
made, all power aboard the ship failed and she began to sink.
Distress calls had been transmitted and were responded to by
helicopters of the South African Air Force and the container
ship *Nedlloyd Mauritius*, which, between them, evacuated all

580 passengers and crew, although the last persons to be rescued were lifted off with only minutes to spare. The *Oceanos* foundered on 4 August in the position 32.06S, 29.06E.

Casualties: 0

The cruise ship *Oceanos* makes her final departure from Cape Town on the cruise that ended in calamity. Unlike many disasters that have unfolded in obscurity isolated on the open ocean, the loss of the *Oceanos* was recorded on video camera and featured prominently in TV documentaries.
Frank Heine FERRIES

OCEAN PRINCESS (1967) ex-*Italia* (1983) Argimar SA, Bahamas

8,469grt; 492ft (149.0m) loa x 70ft (21.3m) beam
550 passengers in single class
CN Felszegi, Muggia Riva Trigoso (Yard No 76)
Motor-ship, twin screw

The cruise ship *Ocean Princess* was on a cruise up the River Amazon on 1 March 1993 when she struck a submerged wreck and was beached in a flooded condition. Her passengers were evacuated and the ship was refloated on 20 March, but the damage was extensive, for her engine room and at least two of her accommodation decks had been submerged under water for almost three weeks. Although declared a constructive total loss, and despite the greater likelihood that she would be demolished, she was sold to Ellis Marine Co, Greece, with the intention that she should be repaired and reconditioned for further service. The *Ocean Princess* left Belém under tow for Piraeus on 15 March 1993 but remained laid up inactive at the Greek port for well over a year, still missing her lifeboats used in the evacuation and showing the scars of her ordeal. Her name at the bow was altered to *Sea Prince*, but alongside her bridge she still carried the name *Ocean Princess*. Ultimately she was indeed refurbished, returning to service as the *Sea Prince V* in 1995, later that year being renamed *Princesa Oceanica* before becoming the *Sapphire* in 1996.

Casualties: 0

Seen at Piraeus in July 1994, the fire-damaged *Ocean Princess*, laid up pending renovation, bears the name *Sea Prince* at her bow. Her lifeboat launchers are empty and in the deployed position, evidence of the rapid evacuation of the burning ship.
Frank Heine FERRIES

ODER (1874) Norddeutscher Lloyd, Germany

3,265grt; 351ft (107.0m) lbp x 40ft (12.2m) beam
896 passengers in three classes
Caird, Greenock (Yard No 177)
Compound-expansion steam reciprocating, single screw

Sister ship of the *Mosel* (qv), the passenger steamer *Oder* was wrecked on Socotra Island near the entrance to the Gulf of Aden on 30 May 1887 after she had been switched to her owners' Far East service via the Mediterranean and the Suez Canal.

Casualties: not known

Norddeutscher Lloyd's *Oder* served on the Bremen and Southampton to New York service. *Real Photos*

OHIO (1873) Alaska Steamship Co, USA

3,104grt; 360ft (109.7m) lbp x 42ft (12.8m) beam
951 passengers in two classes
William Cramp, Philadelphia (Yard No 181)
Triple-expansion steam reciprocating, single screw

The passenger steamship *Ohio* was lost on 20 November 1909 when she was stranded in the Findlay Channel, British Colombia, as she made her way up the inside passage through Hecate Strait to Ketchikan. In rough seas in the early hours of the morning she struck an uncharted rock and ripped open her hull for almost 100 feet. Her engines were reversed to pull her clear, but while heading for the shore in order to be beached, she sank in shallow water with only her masts and

funnel showing above the surface. It was all over in less than half an hour, yet of the 213 passengers she was carrying, 208 were rescued. Among those drowned was the ship's Purser, who returned for the contents of the ship's safe, and the radio operator, who stayed to the last with his set to continue transmitting distress calls. The remains of the *Ohio*'s wreck still lie on the shore where she came to grief.
Casualties: 5 (2 passengers and 3 crew)

OMRAH (1899) Orient Line, UK

8,291grt; 507ft (154.5m) loa x 56ft (17.1m) beam
823 passengers in three classes
Fairfield, Govan (Yard No 404)
Triple-expansion steam reciprocating, twin screw
The passenger liner *Omrah* was requisitioned as a troopship during the First World War and in this capacity, in the spring of 1918, she was part of a large seven-transport convoy, assembled to take units of the 52nd and 74th Army Divisions from Alexandria to Marseilles. On the return voyage, on 12 May 1918, the *Omrah* was torpedoed and sunk by an enemy submarine 40 miles south-west-by-south of Cape Spartivento, Sardinia. The *Omrah* was empty at the time, apart from her crew, carrying only the mails.
Casualties: 1

The *Omrah* entered the service from London to Melbourne and Sydney via the Suez Canal in February 1899. She had an exceptionally tall funnel. *Real Photos*

ONTARIO (1864) National Line, UK

3,325grt; 371ft (113.2m) lbp x 41ft (12.5m) beam
1,272 passengers in two classes
Palmers, Jarrow (Yard No 153)
Inverted steam engines, single screw
The steamship *Ontario* was intended as the third of a class of three ships for the transatlantic service, the others being the *Erin* (qv) and *Helvetia* (see Appendix 3). On completion she sailed on an initial voyage from her builder's yard on the River Tyne to deliver general cargo to Alexandria prior to being repositioned at Liverpool for her maiden voyage to New York. In the event she never made an Atlantic crossing, for on 16 October 1864, while steaming down the North Sea, she was wrecked on Happisburgh Sands, off the Norfolk coast. Her entire crew managed to reach the shore without loss of life. The *Ontario* probably had the briefest of careers of all the ships actually completed and sent to sea.
Casualties: 0

OP TEN NOORT (1926) Koninklijke Paketfaarht Maats, The Netherlands

serving under the wartime name HIKAWA MARU No 2
ex-Teno Maru
6,076grt; 438ft (129.4m) lbp x 55ft (16.8m) beam
182 berthed and 1,218 deck passengers
Nederlandsche SB, Amsterdam (Yard No 185)
Compound-expansion steam reciprocating, twin screw
While serving as a hospital ship, the passenger-cargo ship *Op Ten Noort* was captured by a Japanese submarine south-west of Bawean on 28 February 1942 and seized as a prize of war. After at least one 'Hell-ship' run with prisoners under her Dutch name, she served as the hospital ship *Teno Maru* for the Imperial Japanese Navy, being renamed *Hikawa Maru No 2* from 1944. Under this name she struck a mine on 17 August 1945 and sank in the position 35.44N, 135.31E. Some reports state that she was decommissioned in 1943 and became a war loss in October 1944.
Casualties: not known

ORAMA (1911) Orient Line, UK

12,927grt; 569ft (173.4m) loa x 64ft (19.5m) beam
1,080 passengers in three classes
John Brown, Clydebank (Yard No 403)
Triple-expansion steam reciprocating with LP turbine, triple screw
Converted into an armed merchant cruiser and engaged in convoy escort duties during the First World War, the *Orama* was escorting a large eastbound convoy across the Atlantic in company with eight American destroyers on 19 October 1917 when she was torpedoed by the submarine U62 off the southern coast of Ireland. She remained afloat for almost four hours, during which time her officers and men were safely transferred to the escorting destroyers. One of these, the USS *Conynham*, tried to ram and sink the German U-boat but the attempt failed. The *Orama* finally sank in the approximate position 48.00N, 09.20W.
Casualties: not known

The last of the six ships of the pre-First World War 'Otway' class, built for the London to Brisbane service, was the *Orama*, which, with the *Orvieto*, was a slightly larger development of the initial vessels of the group. *P&O*

ORAMA (1924) Orient Line, UK

19,840grt; 658ft (200.6m) loa x 75ft (22.9m) beam
1,836 passengers in two classes
Vickers, Barrow-in-Furness (Yard No 598)
Steam turbines, twin screw
In June 1940, six months after she was taken over as a troop transport, the liner *Orama* was attached to the task force assembled to convey units of the British Expeditionary Force

from Scapa Flow to Narvik during the Norwegian Campaign. The *Orama*'s task group included the destroyers HMS *Acasta* and *Ardent*, the aircraft carrier HMS *Glorious* and the naval tanker *Oil Pioneer*. On 8 June they came under attack from a squadron of German naval vessels, among them the battlecruisers *Scharnhorst* and *Gneisenau*, the heavy cruiser *Admiral Hipper* and a number of lighter craft. Between them, they sank all five British vessels. The *Orama* took the full force of the bombardment from the guns of the *Admiral Hipper*. She was also torpedoed, finally sinking in the position 67.44N, 03.52E. By then she was empty of troops, carrying only her crew of 299 men, and the survivors, rescued from the sea by the *Admiral Hipper*, became prisoners of war.

Casualties: 19

The five-ship class of post-First World War Orient liners, of which the second *Orama* was the first to be completed, suffered heavily during the Second World War. By the war's end only two still survived. The *Orama* had briefly and uniquely sported a cream-coloured hull, a hint of a change to come on later Orient Line ships. *Ian Allan Library*

ORANIA (1922) Royal Holland Lloyd, The Netherlands

9,763grt; 450ft (137.2m) lbp x 59ft (18.1m) beam
1,192 passengers
Workman Clark, Belfast (Yard No 379)
Steam turbines, twin screw

Sister ship of the *Flandria*, later French Line's *Bretagne*, under the Royal Holland Lloyd flag, the *Orania* and her consort served on the route from the Netherlands to the West Indies and Dutch colonies in South America. *World Ship Society*

On 19 December 1934, as the passenger-cargo ship *Orania* was entering Leixoes Harbour, Oporto, she was rammed amidships by the Portuguese steamship *Loanda*. Her passengers and crew were safely disembarked before she sank inside the harbour, lying half-submerged on her port-side beam ends, with her funnels under water. The wreck presented a considerable menace to navigation, and because it was obstructing the harbour entrance it denied access to all but the smallest vessels. Salvage operations began in the summer of 1935, but the wreck was not fully removed until 1936.

Casualties: 0

ORAVIA (1897) Pacific Steam Navigation Co, UK

5,321grt; 421ft (128.3m) lbp x 49ft (14.9m) beam
630 passengers in three classes
Harland & Wolff, Belfast (Yard No 310)
Triple-expansion steam reciprocating, twin screw
The passenger-cargo steamer *Oravia* was lost during a voyage from Liverpool to Callao, via Cape Horn, when she was wrecked on rocks at the entrance to Port Stanley in the Falkland Islands on 12 November 1912.

Casualties: not known

ORAZIO (1927) Italia Line, Italy

11,669grt; 506ft (154.2m) loa x 62ft (18.8m) beam
640 passengers in three classes
Cantieri ed Officine Meridionali, Baia (Yard No 14)
Motor-ship, twin screw
On 20 January 1940 the passenger-cargo liner *Orazio* left Genoa on a regular sailing for Valparaiso, South America, with a total complement of 645 passengers and crew. Her next port of call was scheduled to be Barcelona but, late on 21 January, distress calls were received from the ship, which had been stricken by fire 35 miles off Toulon, in the position 42.36N, 05.28E. French destroyers raced to the scene, discovering the *Orazio* to be a blazing inferno. The warships rescued 48 survivors between them while the passenger liners *Colombo* and *Conte Biancamano*, which had also hastily answered the calls for assistance, took on board 173 and 318 persons respectively. Rescue operations were severely hampered by strong winds, which also intensified the fire. The ship foundered three days later in the position 42.33N, 05.30E.

Casualties: 108

The *Orazio* operated on the Genoa to Valparaiso service via Marseilles, Barcelona, Trinidad, the Panama Canal and Callao, until January 1940 when she was destroyed by fire off the French coast. Her sister ship was the *Virgilio*. *World Ship Society*

ORCADES (1937) Orient Line, UK

23,456grt; 664ft (202.4m) loa x 82ft (25.0m) beam
1,068 passengers in two classes
Vickers-Armstrongs, Barrow-in-Furness (Yard No 712)
Steam turbines, twin screw

In October 1939 the passenger liner *Orcades* was requisitioned for war service as a troopship. Three years later, on 10 October 1942, she was bound in convoy for the UK from Cape Town with 712 passengers and 352 crew when she was hit by two torpedoes fired by the German submarine U172. The attack took place 300 miles west-south-west of the Cape of Good Hope. Despite a brave attempt by a volunteer crew of 55 men to get the severely damaged *Orcades* back to Cape Town, her steering gear failed. Three more torpedo hits sealed her fate and she had to be abandoned, eventually sinking in the position 31.51S, 14.40E. An accident while lowering the boats accounted for some of the casualties, but the remaining survivors were safely picked up by the Swedish steamship *Narwik*.

Casualties: 48 (18 passengers and 30 crew)

The sister liners *Orion* and *Orcades*, pictured, were introduced to Orient Line's Australian service in the mid-1930s. They marked a dramatic change to more modern styling in the Orient fleet, particularly with their Art Deco-design interiors. It was with this pair that Orient also introduced the 'biscuit' hull colouring, which was to become a distinguishing feature of all future Orient Line passenger ships. *Vickers-Armstrongs*

ORDU (1937) ex-*Copiapo* (1948) Denizcilik Bankasi, Turkey

7,279grt; 414ft (126.3m) lbp x 58ft (17.8m) beam
487 passengers
Nakskov SV, Nakskov, Lolland, Denmark (Yard No 82)
Motor-ship, single screw
The passenger-cargo ship *Ordu*, originally built to the account of Chilean owners, was lost on 13 October 1968 when she caught fire off Amasra, about thirty miles north-east of Zonguldak, Turkey, in the Black Sea. At the time she was bound from Istanbul to Hopa, near the border with Georgia. Beyond economic recovery, she was broken up at Halic, Turkey, from 30 March 1970.

Casualties: not known

OREGON (1883) Cunard Line, UK

7,375grt; 520ft (158.5m) loa x 54ft (16.5m) beam
1,472 passengers in two classes
John Elder, Govan (Yard No 274)
Compound-expansion steam reciprocating, single screw
The passenger steamship *Oregon* had been a transatlantic record-breaker under the ownership of the Guion Line prior to being sold to Cunard in June 1884. During a westbound

crossing, on 14 March 1886, carrying 641 passengers and a crew of 255, she was rammed and sunk by an unidentified American schooner 26 miles south-east of Fire Island, New York Bay. It was impossible to close the *Oregon*'s watertight doors due to congestion with coal dust, and with nothing to impede the rapid inflow of water she was soon flooded and foundered. Fortunately, the Norddeutscher Lloyd liner *Fulda* arrived in sufficient time to save all aboard as well as much of the *Oregon*'s cargo. It was speculated that the offending schooner had been the *Charles Morse*, which was lost with all hands around that time and in that vicinity.

Casualties: 0

ORFORD (1928) Orient Line, UK

19,941grt; 659ft (200.9m) loa x 75ft (22.9m) beam
1,700 passengers in two classes
Vickers-Armstrongs, Barrow-in-Furness (Yard No 627)
Steam turbines, twin screw
The liner *Orford* was requisitioned for trooping duties in September 1939, which she continued to perform until the following summer when she was drafted into the operation to evacuate the British Army from France. She was directed to Marseilles from Mombasa, having been on loan to the French Government for the transportation of colonial troops to France from Madagascar. Upon her arrival off Marseilles, on 1 June 1940, the *Orford* was caught in an air raid and was bombed and set on fire by German aircraft. She was beached but, left unattended, burned out completely. Her wreck was raised in 1947 and towed to Savona, Italy, for breaking-up.

Casualties: 14

The Orient Line passenger ship *Orford* was the penultimate ship of her class, her consorts in the London to Brisbane service being the *Orama*, *Oronsay*, *Otranto* and *Orontes*. *Real Photos*

ORIANA (1960) Hangzhou Songcheng Group, People's Republic of China

41,920grt; 804ft (245.1m) loa x 97ft (29.6m) beam
2,134 passengers in two classes (as built)
Vickers-Armstrongs, Barrow-in-Furness (Yard No 1061)
Steam turbines, twin screw
Twenty-six years spent on the Antipodes scheduled services and as a cruise ship for P&O-Orient Lines (later P&O) came to an end when the *Oriana* was sold to become a stationary tourist centre at Sakai, Beppu Bay, Kyushu, Japan. In 2001 she was sold to Chinese owners and moved to Pudong, Shanghai,

where, at considerable expense, she underwent a comprehensive refit for intended use as a permanently moored luxury liner 'theme park'. Moved from Shanghai to Xinghai Bay, Dalian, the venture was not successful as she did not attract sufficient visitors. With her future far from certain, the *Oriana* capsized in a typhoon on 16 June 2004 and became a total loss. After she had been raised, the wrecked ship was towed to Zhangjiagang, Jiangsu Province, on 12 May 2005 and demolition followed. Casualties: not known

With the *Canberra*, the *Oriana* was one of the two largest passenger liners placed on the Australia service from Southampton, later extended to a trans-Pacific service calling at Vancouver and San Francisco. After a spell as a dedicated cruise ship she was purchased as a static cultural and tourist attraction in Japan. Here she is seen at Shanghai on 18 May 2002, undergoing extensive refurbishment prior to the move to Dalian, where she was lost in a typhoon. *David L. Williams*

ORISSA (1895) Pacific Steam Navigation Co, UK

5,358grt; 421ft (128.3m) lbp x 48ft (14.6m) beam
630 passengers in three classes
Harland & Wolff, Belfast (Yard No 286)
Triple-expansion steam reciprocating, twin screw
On 25 June 1918 the passenger steamship *Orissa* was on passage from Liverpool to Philadelphia in a light condition when she was torpedoed by the German submarine UB73 west of Scotland, 21 miles west-south-west of Skerryvore Rock. She sank in the position 56.20N, 07.20W.
Casualties: 6 (all crew)

The liner *Orissa* was one of a class of three ships completed late in the 19th century, the others being the *Oravia* and *Oropesa* for the Pacific Steam Navigation's South America services from Liverpool. *World Ship Society*

ORIZABA (1886) Pacific Steam Navigation Co (managed by Orient Line), UK

6,298grt; 460ft (140.2m) lbp x 49ft (15.0m) beam
692 passengers in three classes
Barrow Shipbuilding Co, Barrow-in-Furness (Yard No 138)
Triple-expansion steam reciprocating, single screw

On completion the passenger-cargo steamer *Orizaba* was placed on the route to Australia under the management of Orient Line, this company and her owners operating a joint Orient-Pacific service. She remained so engaged until 16 February 1905 when she was wrecked in poor visibility on Garden Island, near Fremantle, Western Australia. She was nearing the end of an outward voyage from London to Sydney.
Casualties: not known

ORONSA (1906) Pacific Steam Navigation Co, UK

8,067grt; 465ft (141.7m) lbp x 56ft (17.1m) beam
1,080 passengers in three classes
Harland & Wolff, Belfast (Yard No 377)
Quadruple-expansion steam reciprocating, twin screw
The *Oronsa* was attacked by the German submarine U91 12 miles west of Bardsey Island, Wales, on 28 April 1918, while she was sailing in convoy bound for Liverpool from New York, having set out earlier from Talcahuano, Chile. The torpedo struck the *Oronsa* at the aft end, exploding with such force that it caused her boilers to blow up. The devastation from the combined explosions was extensive and, with such severe damage, she foundered in just ten minutes. Despite the speed with which she sank, all of her lifeboats were successfully launched in a disciplined and well-organised evacuation operation. Destroyers that were escorting the convoy picked up her survivors.
Casualties: 4 (all crew)

ORONSAY (1925) Orient Line, UK

20,043grt; 659ft (200.9m) loa x 75ft (22.9m) beam
1,836 passengers in two classes
John Brown, Clydebank (Yard No 500)
Steam turbines, twin screw

Due to the loss of three of its 'Orsova' class ships during the First World War, the Orient Line implemented a vigorous rebuilding programme between 1924 and 1929, which added five new 20,000grt vessels to its fleet. The second of these ships was the *Oronsay*, which spent fourteen years, from February 1925, operating on the run from London to Brisbane. *Ian Allan Library*

The liner *Oronsay* was requisitioned for service as a troopship in late 1939. She was sunk by the Italian submarine *Archimede* on 9 October 1942, while she was bound in convoy from Cape Town to Freetown carrying 130 passengers and a crew of 346. The *Archimede* torpedoed her when she was around 800 miles west-south-west of Monrovia, in the position 04.29N, 20.52W, destroying her engine and boiler rooms. Her occupants were ordered to abandon ship, but while the boats were being lowered a second torpedo was fired into the *Oronsay*. It was not long afterwards that

she foundered. Of the survivors, 288 were rescued by a British warship, while among others, who were picked up by the French sloop *Dumont D'Urville* and a French merchant vessel and taken to Dakar, were 63 who were interned as prisoners of war.
Casualties: 5

OROPESA (1895) Pacific Steam Navigation Co, UK

serving under the wartime name CHAMPAGNE
5,364grt; 421ft (128.3m) lbp x 48ft (14.9m) beam
630 passengers in three classes
Harland & Wolff, Belfast (Yard No 285)
Triple-expansion steam reciprocating, twin screw
Loaned to the French Navy from 1917, the British passenger liner *Oropesa* adopted the temporary name *Champagne*. She had served as an auxiliary cruiser with the 10th Cruiser Squadron since the outset of the war and she continued in this role while under French control, although her British crew of 305 officers and ratings was retained. On 9 October 1917, while the *Champagne* was patrolling in the Irish Sea some five miles to the west of the Calf of Man, she was torpedoed and sunk by the German submarine U96. After the first torpedo struck, the order was given to abandon ship and, despite the rough seas, which hampered the launching of the boats, they were all got away expeditiously. The collapsible boats presented more of a challenge as the strong winds made it difficult to get them over the side. During these operations the *Champagne* was hit by a second torpedo and a group of four ratings volunteered to man the forward gun to try to hold the submarine at bay while the evacuation proceeded. A third torpedo strike soon afterwards broke the ship in two and she went down rapidly, only one of the gun crew surviving. The lifeboats were either sailed or towed by trawlers to the Isle of Man.
Casualties: 56 (5 officers and 51 naval ratings)

OROPESA (1920) Pacific Steam Navigation Co, UK

14,118grt; 552ft (168.2m) loa x 66ft (20.1m) beam
632 passengers in three classes
Cammell Laird, Birkenhead (Yard No 835)
Steam turbines, twin screw

The second *Oropesa* was built for the service from Liverpool to Valparaiso but she also spent long periods under charter to the Royal Mail Line on the route from Hamburg to New York, and for six years she was laid up at Dartmouth. *Alex Duncan*

The passenger ship *Oropesa*, which served as a troopship during the Second World War, was torpedoed by the German submarine U96 on 16 January 1941, as she was bound for the United Kingdom from Mombasa with 39 passengers and a crew of 210. The attack took place 100 miles north-west of the Bloody Foreland, County Donegal, and after she had been hit by three torpedoes she sank in the position 56.28N, 12.00W.
Casualties: 113

ORYOKU MARU (1937) Osaka Shosen Kaisha, Japan

7,365grt; 426ft (129.8m) lbp x 57ft (17.4m) beam
805 passengers in three classes
Mitsubishi, Nagasaki (Yard No 681)
Steam turbines, twin screw
While serving as a wartime 'Hell-ship' transport, the *Oryoku Maru* was bombed and sunk on 15 December 1944 by American carrier-based aircraft while she was in Subic Bay off the Bataan Peninsula, Luzon Island, Philippines. She sank in the position 14.45N, 120.13E. She had been massively overloaded with a complement comprising 1,619 American prisoners of war, 700 civilians, 1,000 Japanese seamen, 100 crew and 30 Japanese guards, a total of 3,449. The number of prisoners that were killed in the aerial attack is shown below, but this is only half the story. Those Americans who had survived the bombing were transferred to two other transports, the *Enoura Maru* and *Brazil Maru*, and taken to Takao, Formosa, where on arrival the first-named was also bombed and sunk, killing a further 200. The *Brazil Maru*, now carrying all those prisoners that remained alive, continued on to Moji, Japan, where she arrived two weeks later, but in that time hundreds more died. Less than 500 of the remaining prisoners of war were disembarked, many of them destined to die in captivity ashore.
Casualties: 286 (all American PoWs)

The *Oryoku Maru* was engaged on the Osaka Shosen Kaisha service to Dairen from Osaka. Her sister ship *Kokuryu Maru* was virtually identical. *Mitsui-OSK Lines*

The *Oryoku Maru* under attack off the Bataan Peninsula, seen in a high-level aerial photograph. *US National Archives*

OSLOFJORD (1938) Norwegian Amerika Line, Norway

18,673grt; 590ft (179.8m) loa x 73ft (22.3m) beam
860 passengers in three classes
Deschimag AG Weser, Bremen (Yard No 932)
Motor-ship, twin screw

On the outbreak of the Second World War, the Norwegian liner *Oslofjord* was laid up at New York, where she remained until after the German occupation of Norway, when she came under British control. She was converted into a troopship at Halifax, Nova Scotia, in October 1940, but did not survive to provide service in this valuable wartime role. On 1 December, as she was ending the voyage to the UK following her conversion, bound for Newcastle following a call at Liverpool, she struck an aircraft-laid mine off the entrance to the River Tyne about half a mile from the T2 buoy. The *Oslofjord* was beached south of the Tyne Pier, near South Shields, but in stormy weather over the night of 21-22 December she broke her back. Her forward end capsized and she was abandoned as a constructive total loss.

Casualties: 1

Newest ship in the Norwegian Amerika Line fleet, the twin-funnelled *Oslofjord* had only completed two seasons in the North Atlantic service when the outbreak of war in Europe led to a termination of her commercial career. *Bjørn Pedersen*

OTRANTO (1909) Orient Line, UK

12,124grt; 554ft (168.9m) loa x 64ft (19.5m) beam
1,117 passengers in two classes
Workman Clark, Belfast (Yard No 278)
Quadruple-expansion steam reciprocating, twin screw

One of the last disasters to a passenger liner in the First World War, and one of the worst, involved the *Otranto*. Taken over at the beginning of the war for service as an auxiliary cruiser, the *Otranto* was later tasked with the combined duties of convoy escort and troop transport. In this role she was nearing Great Britain at the end of a passage from New York on 6 October 1918, carrying a large number of American troops as part of convoy HX50. Among the vessels that formed this substantial troop convoy together with the *Otranto* were the passenger ships *Saxon, Briton, Kashmir, Oriana, Scotian, Plassey, Oxfordshire, City of York, Orontes, La Lorraine, Teucer* and *Rhesus*. There were also three American destroyers providing the screen. Only one of these, however, the USS *Dorsey*, was under instructions to continue as far as the coast of Ireland, where British warships were expected to take over escort responsibilities through to the port of disembarkation. However, the British escorts were held up through bad weather, a problem the convoy itself had experienced from the outset, making it difficult to maintain formation in high seas and poor visibility.

As the ships approached the Irish Sea, the *Dorsey* turned about in accordance with her orders, leaving the convoy unescorted. At this point the Convoy Commodore, aboard the *Otranto*, appears to have lost his bearings. He ordered an alteration of course to port, to take the convoy, in his belief, away from the coast of Ireland, which he thought lay ahead, but the instruction was misunderstood aboard the *Kashmir*, the next ship in line lying off the *Otranto*'s port beam, and she was helmed, instead, to starboard. As the result of these manoeuvres the two ships were left heading towards each other on a collision course.

Despite warning signals and last-minute manoeuvres to avert a collision, the *Kashmir* smashed bow-on into the *Otranto*'s port side, between Nos 1 and 2 holds, almost cutting her in half. Panic immediately broke out among the American infantrymen, many of whom were deserters who had been drafted into Casual Companies for the crossing. With her stokehold and engine room compartments flooded, the ship began to settle rapidly, listing to port with her bow down. Matters worsened as the *Otranto* began to break apart, the impact of the *Kashmir* having weakened her entire structure. The forward bulkheads ruptured under the pressure of water, the boat deck collapsed, hurling many would-be evacuees into the stormy seas, and the lifeboats were pounded to splinters. The loose metalwork and wooden debris that was hurled about as the ship disintegrated inflicted hideous injuries on the men who were upon the open decks.

When land loomed into sight – the north coast of Islay, as it turned out, because the convoy had been off course – it was hoped that the helpless ship might drift ashore there and land her occupants before she completely broke in two. There were no means to summon help because the *Otranto*'s wireless transmitter had been swept away, and the other ships of the convoy, including the *Kashmir*, which had been only superficially damaged, had already disappeared ahead into the murk, unaware of the scenes of mayhem unfolding in their wake. Fortuitously, at this point the destroyer HMS *Mounsey*, one of the eight delayed convoy escorts expected from Lough Swilly, arrived on the scene, the only one of the expected vessels that had managed to battle through the appalling weather. Seeing the predicament of the stricken troopship, a rescue operation was immediately launched, but before a full evacuation of the remainder of the *Otranto*'s complement could be completed she had run ashore near Kilchiaran on Islay, where the violent seas smashed her to pieces. There were just 367 survivors.

Casualties: 431 (351 American servicemen and 80 crew)

One of six similar ships placed on the Australia run via Suez, the *Otranto* was lost in one of the most appalling sea disasters of the First World War. *P&O*

The *Otranto* again in wartime colours, serving as a troop transport and convoy escort. *Maritime Photo Library*

OTTAWA (1880) Dominion Line, UK

3,712grt; 359ft (109.4m) lbp x 40ft (12.2m) beam
1,480 passengers in three classes
Charles Connell, Scotstoun (Yard No 120)
Compound-expansion steam reciprocating, single screw
The passenger steamship *Ottawa*, the first unit of a class of three ships, was lost on the return leg of her maiden voyage to Quebec and Montreal. She had sailed outward-bound from Glasgow, where she had been built, and was returning to Liverpool on 22 November 1880 when she ran onto rocks at Cape La Roche, near Quebec, and was wrecked. All those aboard her were taken off safely.
Casualties: 0

OTWAY (1909) Orient Line, UK

12,077grt; 552ft (168.2m) loa x 63ft (19.2m) beam
1,100 passengers in two classes
Fairfield, Govan (Yard No 459)
Quadruple-expansion steam reciprocating, twin screw
The liner *Otway*, requisitioned by the Admiralty in December 1914, was commissioned for naval service as an auxiliary cruiser with the 10th Cruiser Squadron from 1915. She was sunk during a routine patrol north of the Hebrides on 22 July 1917, torpedoed by the German submarine UC49. She sank in the position 58.54N, 06.28W.
Casualties: 10 (naval ratings)

Working the Orient Line services to Australia, the liner *Otway* was a sister ship of the *Orsova*, *Osterley*, *Orvieto*, *Orama* and *Otranto*. The six-ship class represented an ambitious expansion of the company's fleet. *P&O*

OZAMIS CITY (1965) ex-*Iligan City* (1980) ex-*Fuji* (1978) William Lines, Philippines

2,865grt; 303ft (92.3m) loa x 44ft (13.3m) beam
1,346 passengers
Mitsubishi, Shimonoseki (Yard No 617)
Motor-ship, single screw
The ferry *Ozamis City* was stranded off Siquijor, Philippines, on 22 October 1990. She was subsequently salvaged and taken in tow for Cebu, where she arrived on 5 November of that year only to be driven ashore seven days later in typhoon 'Mike'. Declared a constructive total loss and considered fit only for scrap, the wreck was sent for breaking-up at Manila, commencing in November 1991.
Casualties: not known

PACIFIC (1849) Collins Line, USA

2,860grt; 282ft (86.0m) lbp x 45ft (13.7m) beam
280 passengers in two classes
Brown & Bell, New York (Yard No not known)
Side lever steam engines, paddles

The *Pacific* was a sister ship of the ill-fated *Arctic* (qv), which was lost after a collision in September 1854. In January 1856 the *Pacific* disappeared at sea while on a westbound voyage from Liverpool to New York. She had sailed from the Mersey on 23 January carrying, according to most accounts, 45 passengers and 141 crew. Fears for the overdue *Pacific* mounted and as the weeks passed with no news of her it was assumed that she had struck an iceberg and foundered. Whatever the cause of her loss, no trace of wreckage or any other object associated with the ship was found until 1991 when her wreck was discovered off the coast of Wales. The losses of the two sister ships contributed to the collapse of their owners.
Casualties: 186 (Some reports quote a total figure of 240 for the victims of the loss of the *Pacific*).

PALERMO (1899) ex-*Lazio* (1913) ex-*British Princess* (1905) Navigazione Generale Italiana, Italy

9,203grt; 470ft (143.3m) lbp x 56ft (17.1m) beam
2,270 passengers in two classes
Palmers, Jarrow (Yard No 741)
Triple-expansion steam reciprocating, twin screw

The Italian passenger steamship *Palermo* was returning to Genoa from New York, conveying horses and munitions for the Italian war effort, plus a small number of passengers besides her crew, when she was torpedoed and sunk off the east coast of Spain, about 25 miles from Cape San Sebastian, on 2 December 1916. The submarine responsible was the German boat U72. Salvage operations, to attempt to recover a large consignment of gold that it was believed had formed part of her cargo at the time of her loss, were undertaken in May 1956.
Casualties: 0

PALLAS ATHENA (1952) ex-*Carla Costa* (1992) ex-*Carla C* (1986) ex-*Flandre* (1968) Epirotiki Lines, Greece

19,942grt; 600ft (182.8m) loa x 80ft (24.5m) beam
754 passengers in single class
Chantiers de France, Dunkirk (Yard No 206)
Motor-ship, twin screw

This former transatlantic passenger liner was remodelled as a cruise ship in 1969 after she had been acquired by Costa Armatori. Five years later she was converted from steam turbine to diesel propulsion. Later, after she had transferred to Greek-flag owners as the *Pallas Athena*, she was engulfed by fire while at Piraeus between cruises on 24 March 1994 in an outbreak that started in one of her passenger cabins. Her passengers had already disembarked, which was just as well for she was soon ablaze along the length of her superstructure and down into the hull. Only the bow area escaped the worst of the fire. While still smouldering she was towed into deeper waters beyond the port, where she was declared a total loss despite remaining afloat on an even keel. She was broken up at Aliaga where she arrived on 25 December 1994.
Casualties: not known

The burned-out *Pallas Athena* (the former *Flandre*) in Piraeus Roads in July 1994. For an indication of her appearance prior to the fire, see the *Antilles* on page 24. *Frank Heine FERRIES*

PAMPA (1906) Société Générale des Transports Maritimes à Vapeur (SGTM), France

4,471grt; 408ft (124.4m) lbp x 47ft (14.3m) beam
171 passengers in three classes
London & Glasgow Shipbuilding Co, Glasgow (Yard No 325)
Triple-expansion steam reciprocating, twin screw

The French passenger ship *Pampa*, which served as a hospital ship during the First World War, was torpedoed and sunk by the German submarine UC22 in the Mediterranean on 27 August 1918. She was attacked 84 miles east of Valletta, while on passage from Marseilles and Bizerta to Salonica (Thessaloniki).
Casualties: 117

PAPANUI (1899) Australian business syndicate, formerly New Zealand Shipping Co, UK

6,582grt; 430ft (131.1m) lbp x 54ft (16.5m) beam
479 passengers in three classes
William Denny, Dumbarton (Yard No 602)
Triple-expansion steam reciprocating, single screw

The emigrant steamer *Papanui* caught fire in the South Atlantic on 5 September 1911 during a voyage bound for Fremantle via Cape Town carrying 364 emigrants. The outbreak, in bunker fuel stowed in Number 3 hold, was fought for six days without success, and because it had worsened significantly her Master was persuaded by a delegation of passengers and officers to make for Jamestown, St. Helena, passed three days earlier, to obtain assistance. Upon her arrival, on 11 September, the *Papanui* anchored in James Bay and lifeboats from shore assisted in the disembarkation of the passengers. Meanwhile, the still smouldering vessel remained unattended while her Master complained to the island's authorities that his officers and crew had mutinied. The following day, explosions shook the *Papanui* and flames could be seen from a huge fire amidships. Under orders from the authorities, the blazing ship was beached and abandoned. Completely burnt out, the wreck settled in the bay where it remains to this day.
Casualties: 0

PAPAROA (1899) New Zealand Shipping Co, UK

7,697grt; 430ft (131.1m) lbp x 54ft (16.5m) beam
479 passengers in three classes
William Denny, Dumbarton (Yard No 613)
Triple-expansion steam reciprocating, single screw
Sister ship of the emigrant steamer *Papanui*, the *Paparoa* met a similar fate to her consort and in the same area of the southern Atlantic Ocean while bound for Brisbane and New Zealand on 17 March 1926. When she was in the position 29.38S, 14.25E, near St. Helena, fire broke out in cargo hold No 3, and its contents of coal and insulation material were soon well ablaze. As the fire raged, the *Paparoa* developed a severe list and, with her pumps choked, it became necessary to abandon ship by the 33 persons aboard her, four colonial seamen, five stowaways and 24 members of the crew. Having radioed for assistance, she rendezvoused with the P&O steamer *Barrabool*, which stood by to assist with the evacuation and took aboard the survivors, who were landed at Cape Town. Later, the cruiser HMS *Birmingham* arrived on the scene and it is reported that members of her crew boarded the *Paparoa* in an attempt to extinguish the fire. When this failed, they opened her sea cocks to scuttle her, a risky exercise in the circumstances. Whatever the action taken, the blazing ship was reported last seen in position 28.26S, 13.42E, ablaze from stem to stern with flames roaring 100 feet into the air. Casualties: 0

PARANA (1908) Société Générale des Transports Maritimes à Vapeur (SGTM), France

6,248grt; 420ft (128.0m) lbp x 50ft (15.2m) beam
171 passengers in three classes
Forges et Chantiers de la Méditerranée, La Seyne (Yard No 1008)
Triple-expansion steam reciprocating, twin screw
The French passenger steamer *Parana* was torpedoed by the German submarine UC74 on 23 August 1917 during a voyage from Marseilles to Salonica (Thessaloniki) in convoy with the *Médie* and *Pampa* under the escort of three destroyers. The attack took place off the Greek coast, five miles north of Cape Fessa, Euboea, in the Doro Straits between Andros and Euboea. In an attempt to beach the crippled ship, she reached Karystos Bay but sank before she could be run ashore. Casualties: 7

PARIS (1921) Compagnie Générale Transatlantique (French Line), France

34,569grt; 764ft (233.0m) loa x 85ft (26.0m) beam
1,934 passengers in three classes
Penhoët, St Nazaire (Yard No 68)
Steam turbines, quadruple screw
A both serious and suspicious fire occurred aboard the transatlantic passenger liner *Paris* while she was berthed at Le Havre on 18 April 1939, for outbreaks were discovered, simultaneously, in the ship's bakery and on A deck. Sabotage was suspected as being the cause, although no responsible individual or organisation could be identified. The conflagration spread rapidly to the ship's First class saloon and the *Paris* was very soon engulfed in smoke and flames. She capsized at the quay, a total loss, on the following morning.

Art treasures, some from the Louvre, which had been loaded for New York, were mostly removed safely, although it was feared for a time that some modern paintings by Picasso and Renoir had been ruined. Fortunately, they were safely accounted for later. The wreck of the *Paris* was found to be obstructing the entrance to the Le Havre dry dock in which the giant *Normandie* was then berthed, and it was only possible for her to be released after the masts and funnels of the *Paris* had been cut away. Due to the outbreak of the Second World War just five months later, the wreck was not removed and it was damaged further, where it lay, in air attacks during June 1944. In December 1946 the *Paris* once more hit the headlines when the *Liberté*, which had broken free from her moorings in a gale, fouled the wreck, tore open her hull and sank on an even keel in the harbour. Casualties: not known

Laid down in 1913 and launched on 12 September 1916, the construction of the *Paris* was then suspended until after the First World War. She entered the French Line's front-line transatlantic service from June 1921. *L. L. von Münching*

After the fire, the capsized *Paris* lies alongside the Transat quay at Le Havre with the *Normandie* beyond, trapped in dry dock. *Author's collection*

PARTIZANKA (1927) ex-*City of Lisbon* (1947) ex-*Shawnee* (1947) Jugoslovenska JP, Yugoslavia

6,209grt; 409ft (120.3m) lbp x 62ft (19.0m) beam
754 passengers in two classes (as built)
Newport News Shipbuilding & Drydock Co, Newport News, Virginia (Yard No 307)
Steam turbines, twin screw
After World War Two service as hospital ships, the former Clyde-Mallory liners *Shawnee* and *Iroquois* were sold to become respectively, the *City of Lisbon* and the Turkish-flag *Ankara*. While the *Ankara* continued in operation, latterly as a cruise ship, until the early 1980s, her sister-ship survived for

barely two years. Saved from impending breaking-up, following a collision on 28 May 1947, the *City of Lisbon* was repaired and refitted at Rijeka with fairly basic accommodation. Renamed *Partizanka*, she carried emigrants to Australia and South America until she was destroyed by an explosion and fire while in drydock at Split, on the Adriatic, on 12 August 1949.
Casualties: not known

PATAGONIA (1869) Pacific Steam Navigation Co, UK

2,878grt; 353ft (107.6m) lbp x 41ft (12.5m) beam
520 passengers in three classes
Randolph Elder, Govan (Yard No 92)
Triple-expansion steam reciprocating, single screw
While outward bound on 2 October 1894, on the route from Liverpool to Valparaiso, Chile, the passenger steamer *Patagonia* was wrecked at Lingueral, seven miles north of Tome, near Talcahuano, Chile.
Casualties: not known

PATRA (1941) ex-*Kronprins Frederik* (1976) Arab Navigation Co, Egypt

3,895grt; 376ft (114.4m) loa x 50ft (15.2m) beam
311 passengers
Helsingørs Vaerft, Elsinore (Yard No 262)
Motor-ship, twin screw
The Red Sea ferry *Patra*, formerly the DFDS-owned *Kronprins Frederik*, was lost on 24 December 1976 when she was gutted by fire during a voyage from Jeddah to Suez carrying Muslim pilgrims. She sank some fifty miles from Jeddah in the position 21.56N, 38.28 E.
Casualties: 102

PATRIA (1894) Hamburg Amerika Line, Germany

7,118grt; 460ft (140.2m) lbp x 52ft (15.9m) beam
2,060 passengers in two classes
Stettiner Vulcan, Stettin-Bredow (Yard No 216)
Triple-expansion steam reciprocating, twin screw
The transatlantic emigrant steamship *Patria* was destroyed by fire in the English Channel on 15 November 1899, while she was bound for Hamburg. Her passengers and crew were taken off by the *Athenia*. Meanwhile, the *Patria* was taken in tow but she was stranded near Deal on 17 November and was later broken up.
Casualties: 0

PATRIA (1914) Messageries Maritimes, France

11,885grt; 512ft (156.1m) loa x 60ft (18.2m) beam
2,240 passengers in three classes
Forges et Chantiers de la Méditerranée, La Seyne (Yard No 1058)
Triple-expansion steam reciprocating, twin screw
On 15 August 1940 the British authorities took over the French passenger ship *Patria*, which had been laid up at Haifa since June of that year, placing her under the management of the British India Line. Earlier, her attempted departure to Beirut on 25 June, following the Armistice with Germany, had been obstructed. It was decided that she should be employed to transport illegal Jewish immigrants from Palestine to British colonies. The first such voyage was scheduled to take 1,904 illegal emigrants to Mauritius, and on 23 November they were embarked together with 116 Palestinian Police. The ship's departure was, however, indefinitely delayed and she remained at her moorings for two days, awaiting instructions. During this period her large complement of passengers remained aboard in far from ideal conditions.

Early on 25 November an explosion ripped open the *Patria*'s starboard side below the waterline, causing her to list and then, after only a brief interval, to capsize and sink. Numerous open portholes on the starboard side had contributed to the rapid flooding, allowing uninhibited ingress of water. Local harbour craft that rushed to the scene managed to rescue many of those who had been on board the *Patria*, but many were unaccounted for and presumed dead, although it is known that some had escaped ashore. The surviving refugees, less 25 who were taken to hospital, were held in detention centres. A commission of enquiry concluded that the *Patria* had been the victim of an act of sabotage and attributed the responsibility to subversive Jewish resistance groups, although the actual perpetrators of the atrocity were never identified. Underwriters advised against the salvage of the partially submerged ship as it had no further commercial value and it lay on its side, in about 6 fathoms, until 1952, when it was demolished and removed.
Casualties: 279 (This is the official British figure, but the French Lines Association archives estimate that there were nearer to 300 fatalities. Only 25 bodies were recovered.)

Though built for the Marseilles to New York service of Fabre Line, from 1932 the *Patria* (1914) was operated under charter by Messageries Maritimes between Marseilles and ports in the eastern Mediterranean until that company purchased her outright in January 1940. *World Ship Society*

PATROCLUS (1923) Blue Funnel Line, UK

11,314grt; 530ft (161.5m) loa x 62ft (18.9m) beam
150 passengers in single class
Scott's, Greenock (Yard No 518)
Steam turbines, twin screw
The *Patroclus* was commissioned as an armed merchant cruiser in January 1940 and spent the next ten months patrolling the Western Approaches. On 4 November 1940 she went to the aid of another armed merchant cruiser, the *Laurentic* (qv), which had been torpedoed off the west coast of Ireland, and took the survivors aboard. While she was rendering assistance in this fashion, the *Patroclus* was also torpedoed by the German submarine U99. The explosion destroyed her forepart such that it completely disintegrated and fell away into the sea. In spite of this, she did not

immediately sink, kept afloat for more than five hours by empty barrels stowed in her holds, which gave her additional buoyancy. In the event it took five more torpedoes to finish her off, and she finally sank in the position 53.43N, 14.41W. The survivors, including many who had been rescued from the *Laurentic*, a total of 34 officers and 230 ratings, were picked up the following morning by HMS *Achates* and another destroyer. Casualties: 76

The Blue Funnel steamship *Patroclus* berthed at Liverpool. *World Ship Society*

PAUL LECAT (1911) Messageries Maritimes, France

12,989grt; 529ft (161.0m) loa x 58ft (18.7m) beam
1,274 passengers in four classes
Constructions Navales, La Ciotat (Yard No 136)
Quadruple-expansion steam reciprocating, twin screw
While dry-docked at Marseilles on 30 December 1928, a fire broke out aboard the passenger-cargo liner *Paul Lecat* in her dining room, and by the time it had been extinguished by the fireboats *Joliette* and *Durance*, after burning for a day and a night, she was left extensively damaged. It proved to be difficult to extricate the ship from the dry dock as she was listing to starboard and her structure had been considerably weakened. A subsequent hull survey on 3 January 1929 confirmed that the liner was a constructive total loss, and on 24 April 1929 she was sold for breaking up at La Spezia, Italy. Casualties: 0

PEGASUS (1975) ex-*Sundancer* (1984) ex-*Svea Corona* (1984) Epirotiki Lines, Greece

12,576grt; 502ft (153.1m) loa x 72ft (22.0m) beam
810 passengers
Dubigeon-Normandie SA, Nantes (Yard No 141)
Motor-ship, twin screw
Under the name *Sundancer*, this former ro-ro ferry, converted into a cruise ship, had already sustained serious enough damage to be declared a constructive total loss, after she ran onto rocks near Vancouver Island on 30 June 1984. Towed to Piraeus after she had been refloated, she was repaired and re-emerged as the *Pegasus* for Black Sea and Mediterranean cruising. However, on 2 June 1991 she was severely damaged when fire broke out aboard her while she was at Venice just prior to making her departure under charter as an exhibition ship for Bosch electrical equipment. The charter was cancelled and she was again towed to Piraeus for repairs, where she remained idle until 1994, when she was sold for refit into the *Ionian Express* (qv) for return to cruise service. Casualties: 0

PEGU (1921) Henderson Line (British & Burmese Steam Nav Co), UK

8,084grt; 466ft (142.0m) lbp x 59ft (18.0m) beam
150 passengers in single class
William Denny, Dumbarton (Yard No 1140)
Triple-expansion steam reciprocating, single screw
The *Pegu*, replacement for an earlier ship of the same name, was lost early in the Second World War when she was stranded near the Beta Buoy in the Crosby Channel, River Mersey, on 24 November 1939. She broke in two and became a total loss. Casualties: not known

The Henderson Line steamship *Pegu* served on the route from Glasgow and Liverpool to Rangoon. *H. B. Christiansen Collection / Online Transport Archive*

PENNLAND (1922) ex-*Pittsburgh* (1926) Holland Amerika Line, The Netherlands

16,322grt; 601ft (183.2m) loa x 67ft (20.4m) beam
538 passengers in single class
Harland & Wolff, Belfast (Yard No 457)
Triple-expansion steam reciprocating with LP turbine, triple screw

The Dominion Line's *Pittsburgh* and *Regina* were constructed for the transatlantic service from Liverpool. From 1925 they were separated for four years, but were later reunited under the Red Star Line house flag as the *Pennland* and *Westernland*. They retained these names when they passed to Holland Amerika Line in June 1939. *Ian Allan Library*

After the fall of the Netherlands in May 1940, the passenger liner *Pennland* was placed under the control of the British Ministry of War Transport and converted into a troopship. On 25 April 1941, while she was bound from Alexandria to Athens to evacuate British and Australian soldiers as the campaign to save Greece reached its climax, she was bombed and sunk by German aircraft. Among the 100 or so troops she embarked were soldiers she had only shortly before transported to the Balkans to bolster the Allied resistance there. Hit by no fewer than eight bombs, one of which penetrated to the engine compartments and exploded there, with many more near misses, the *Pennland* did not survive for long, sinking in the position 37.10N, 23.50E. This places her to the north-east of Crete, not in the Gulf of Athens as some reports say. Lloyd's records state that she was sunk off Bela Pouli, near the San Giorgio Islands. The survivors from the troops and her 251-strong crew were picked up by the destroyer HMS *Griffin* and landed at Suda Bay, Crete, the next day.

Casualties: 4 (all engine room crew)

PENNSYLVANIA (1873) Pacific Mail Line, USA

3,300grt; 360ft (109.7m) lbp x 42ft (12.8m) beam
951 passengers in two classes (as built)
William Cramp, Philadelphia (Yard No 180)
Triple-expansion steam reciprocating, single screw
The *Pennsylvania*, the former pioneer transatlantic passenger ship of the American Line, caught fire on 12 November 1918 while in Iquique Bay, Chile, after she had been transferred to routes in the Pacific operating for the forerunners of the future Dollar Line and American President Line. She was completely destroyed.

Casualties: not known

PERICLES (1908) Aberdeen Line, UK

10,925grt; 518ft (157.9m) loa x 62ft (19.0m) beam
500 passengers in two classes
Harland & Wolff, Belfast (Yard No 392)
Quadruple-expansion steam reciprocating, twin screw
On 31 March 1910, while returning to London from Sydney and Brisbane, the passenger-cargo steamship *Pericles* ran onto an uncharted underwater reef six miles south of Cape Leeuwin, West Australia, some 150 miles south of Fremantle. Bottom damage, extending from the bow to midships, was so extreme that the ship immediately began to settle by the head. An attempt was made to beach her but this proved to be impossible once the engine room had flooded. The 300 passengers and crew thereupon abandoned ship and landed on the coast near Cape Leeuwin Light. Thankfully, the weather was fair and no lives were lost.

Casualties: 0

PERSIA (1900) P&O Line, UK

7,974grt; 500ft (152.4m) loa x 54ft (16.5m) beam
526 passengers in two classes and/or 2,500 troops
Caird, Greenock (Yard No 295)
Triple-expansion steam reciprocating, single screw

The *Persia* was the last unit of the 'India' class, a five-ship group of which only the *China* survived to be broken up.
Tom Rayner collection

While bound from London and Marseilles to Bombay, with a total complement of 501 persons, the P&O liner *Persia* was torpedoed and sunk on 30 December 1915 by the German submarine U38 in the position 34.10N, 26.00E, 71 miles

south-east-by-south of Cape Mátala (Akra Lithinon), Crete. The submarine attacked without warning, its torpedo striking the *Persia* forward on her port side, causing the boiler on that side of the ship to explode. She sank very quickly, giving little opportunity to fully evacuate the vessel, and some of her boats, still close by, were sucked under as she sank, drowning their occupants. The following day trawlers picked up the survivors from four boats, the only ones that had managed to get away safely, and they were taken to Alexandria.

Casualties: 334

PERUGIA (1901) Anchor Line, UK

4,348grt; 375ft (114.3m) loa x 47ft (14.3m) beam
1,400 passengers in single class
D. & W. Henderson, Glasgow (Yard No 422)
Triple-expansion steam reciprocating, single screw
The transatlantic emigrant steamer *Perugia* was sailing in ballast on 3 December 1916 when she was torpedoed in the Gulf of Genoa, north-west of Sardinia, by the German submarine U63. She sank in the position 42.54N, 07.39E. At the time she was in Royal Navy service as a 'Q' ship.

Casualties: not known

PIEMONTE (1918) ex-*Minnedosa* (1935) Lloyd Triestino, Italy

15,186grt; 546ft (166.4m) loa x 67ft (20.4m) beam
1,341 passengers in three classes (as a British ship)
Barclay Curle, Whiteinch, Glasgow (Yard No 518)
Triple-expansion steam reciprocating with LP turbine, triple screw
Acquired from Canadian Pacific for use as a troopship under the management of Lloyd Triestino, the passenger-cargo ship *Piemonte* continued with these duties after Italy declared war in June 1940. Hit by a torpedo on 17 November 1942, when she was two miles from Capo Rasocolmo, near Messina, Sicily, she was taken to Sparta where she was patched up. From there she made for Messina to obtain full repairs but, when these were not carried out, she was laid up. While at Messina, the *Piemonte* sustained slight damage during an air raid on 10 July 1943, but in a later raid, on 15 August 1943, she received several bomb hits and capsized, although it is also claimed that she was scuttled on that date. Her wreck was refloated in 1949 and, on 24 July of that year, it was towed to La Spezia to be broken up.

Casualties: not known

PIERRE LOTI (1913) ex-*Avyator* (1922) ex-*Emperor Nicolas I [Imperator Nikolai I]* (1917) Messageries Maritimes, France

serving under the wartime name SOUTHERN SEA
5,114grt; 381ft (116.2m) lbp x 52ft (15.8m) beam
200 passengers
John Brown, Clydebank (Yard No 420)
Triple-expansion steam reciprocating, twin screw
After orders had been given for her to be taken to Australia, the passenger-cargo ship *Pierre Loti* was sailed from Noumea to Sydney in October 1940, where she passed into the control of the Ministry of War Transport, managed by Blue Funnel Line under the name *Southern Sea*. Two years later, on 12 December 1942, she was stranded on the Laval Bank in the

estuary to the River Ogooué, Gabon, in the position 00.47N, 09.18E, due to a navigational error. An attempt was made to refloat her on 15 July 1943 but this was unsuccessful. Other efforts followed but these were equally fruitless and she was finally abandoned as a total loss on 4 November 1943. The wreck subsequently broke up in a storm. Her officers and men had in the meantime been taken to Lagos, Nigeria, aboard the steamer *Matang*, where they arrived on 29 August 1943. Casualties: 0

PIETER CORNELISZOON HOOFT (1925)
Nederland Line, The Netherlands

14,729grt; 549ft (167.3m) loa x 68ft (20.7m) beam
643 passengers in four classes
Chantiers de la Loire, St Nazaire (Yard No 256)
Motor-ship, twin screw
The passenger-cargo liner *Pieter Corneliszoon Hooft* was destroyed by fire at Amsterdam on 14 November 1932, barely eighteen months after a major rebuilding operation at the Rotterdam Drydock Co. Shortly after she had arrived in ballast from Batavia (Djakarta), fire broke out aboard the deserted ship – she had been fumigated with cyanide gas – in the First class cabin accommodation, immediately abaft the bridge. The cause was unknown but presumed to have been an electrical short-circuit. As the ship was soon uncontrollably ablaze from forward of midships to her stern, she was moved from the quayside to a compass buoy near Yssel Lake to eliminate the risk of the fire spreading. In this situation the *Pieter Corneliszoon Hooft* was virtually allowed to burn herself out and the huge flames lit up the port area during the night. Any chance of saving her diminished when her fuel oil tanks exploded. The gutted wreck eventually settled in 30 feet of water, listing to starboard with her plates buckled and her hull distorted. In this condition she was abandoned to the underwriters. The wreck was removed from Amsterdam Harbour in December and, after an examination at Ymuiden, was towed to Pernis (Hendrik Ido Ambacht) for breaking-up. Casualties: 0

PILSUDSKI (1935) Gdynia America Line, Poland

14,294grt; 526ft (160.3m) loa x 70ft (21.3m) beam
759 passengers in two classes
Cantieri Riuniti dell'Adriatico, Monfalcone (Yard No 1126)
Motor-ship, twin screw

The nicely proportioned Italian-built sister ships *Pilsudski* and *Batory* were placed on the Gdynia to New York service in the mid-1930s. This is the *Pilsudski*. *World Ship Society*

After the defeat of Poland, the liners *Pilsudski* and her sister *Batory* came under British control and were refitted as troopships. The *Pilsudski* was able to give only limited service because she struck a mine in the mouth of the River Humber on 26 November 1939, while she was bound from Newcastle to Australia. She sank in the position 53.15N, 00.30E. Casualties: 10 (all crew)

PIRIAPOLIS (1938) Cie Maritime Belge, Belgium

7,340grt; 459ft (139.9m) lbp x 61ft (18.6m) beam
194 passengers
John Cockerill, Hoboken (Yard No 655)
Motor-ship, single screw
As the passenger-cargo ship *Piriapolis* was returning to Antwerp from Buenos Aires in early June 1940, she was diverted first to La Pallice, then to French Channel ports to assist in the evacuation of British and French troops. While engaged in this operation, when she was some five miles from the Antifer Light on 11 June 1940, she was caught in a German air raid on Le Havre, and was bombed and sunk. Casualties: not known

PO (1911) ex-*Vienna* (1937) ex-*Wien* (1921)
Lloyd Triestino, Italy

7,367grt; 454ft (138.4m) loa x 53ft (16.2m) beam
300 passengers
Lloyd Austriaco, Trieste (Yard No 125)
Quadruple-expansion steam reciprocating, twin screw
After Italy's entry into the Second World War in June 1940, the passenger ship *Po* was taken up for service as a hospital ship. She was bombed by British aircraft off Valona (Vlore), Albania, on 14 March 1941 and again the following day, sinking about a mile offshore in the position 40.22N, 19.28E. Casualties: not known

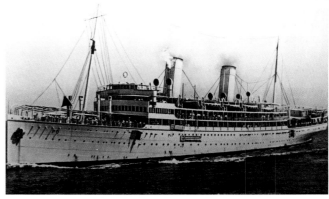

The Lloyd Triestino steamship *Po* was formerly the Lloyd Austriaco company's *Wien*, forfeited after the First World War, when Austria lost her Adriatic coastal boundary. She sailed in the Far East service, via Suez. *World Ship Society*

POLYNESIEN (1890) Messageries Maritimes, France

6,363grt; 482ft (146.9m) lbp x 49ft (14.9m) beam
586 passengers in four classes
Messageries Maritimes, La Ciotat (Yard No 68)
Triple-expansion steam reciprocating, single screw
The passenger steamship *Polynesien* was requisitioned in August 1914 by the French Government to maintain essential

postal services. Later she functioned as a troopship, and on 10 August 1918, while on passage from Marseilles and Bizerta to Salonica (Thessaloniki), she made a call at Malta to replenish her coal supplies. As she was passing through the safe channel near the entrance to Valletta Harbour she was either torpedoed or she struck an uncleared mine that had been laid in that vicinity. In either case, the German submarine held responsible was the UC22. The explosion holed her on the port side in way of her bunkers but she remained afloat. Assistance from tugs was summoned in a bid to get her into the harbour, but within an hour of them arriving on the scene, the *Polynesien* sank. The survivors, a total of 499 persons, were picked up and landed safely.

Casualties: 19, including 11 crew

Messageries Maritimes' *Polynesien* was one of a class of four ships placed in the France to Australia service through the Suez Canal. *World Ship Society*

POMERANIAN (1882) ex-*Grecian Monarch* (1887) Canadian Pacific Line, UK

4,365grt; 400ft (121.9m) loa x 43ft (13.1m) beam
1,100 passengers in three classes
Earle's, Hull (Yard No 241)
Compound-expansion steam reciprocating, single screw
The elderly passenger steamship *Pomeranian* was torpedoed and sunk on 15 April 1918, while on passage from London to St John, New Brunswick, by the German submarine UC77. The attack took place in the English Channel, in Lyme Bay, nine miles north-west-by-west-half-west of Portland Bill.

Casualties: 55

Allan Line purchased the *Pomeranian* from the Monarch Line in September 1887 and placed her on the service from London to Montreal. In 1893 she was severely damaged in a wild Atlantic storm, claiming 12 lives. *Maritime Photo Library*

POMMERANIA (1873) Hamburg Amerika Line, Germany

3,382grt; 361ft (110.0m) lbp x 40ft (12.2m) beam
770 passengers in three classes
Caird, Greenock (Yard No 175)
Compound-expansion steam reciprocating, single screw
After calling at Plymouth on 25 November 1878 at the end of an eastbound crossing from New York, the passenger steamship *Pommerania* proceeded up the Channel for her home port of Hamburg with 109 passengers and the US mails. She was also carrying a 111-man crew. When she was passing Folkestone at about midnight, she was struck on her starboard side by the iron barque *Moel Eilian*, losing four of her lifeboats in the collision. Distress signals were fired and the five remaining lifeboats were filled and launched, although one of these turned over and its occupants drowned. The *Pommerania* remained afloat for only about twenty minutes and unwisely, during this time, many of the remaining passengers, although instructed to stay on deck, returned below to collect their possessions and valuables. When the ship suddenly sank, they were taken down with her. With the exception of the ship's Master, picked up in fortuitous circumstances by the *City of Amsterdam*, the other survivors were rescued by the steamship *Glengarry*, which had answered the *Pommerania*'s distress signals. As for the *Moel Eilian*, she had been so critically damaged that she was unable to render any assistance. Instead, she made for Dover where she was later repaired.

Casualties: 48

The Hamburg Amerika Line transatlantic passenger ship *Pommerania* was lost in a collision off Folkestone. *Hapag-Lloyd*

PORTHOS (1914) Messageries Maritimes, France

12,692grt; 528ft (160.9m) loa x 61ft (18.6m) beam
1,598 passengers in four classes
Chantiers de la Gironde, Bordeaux (Yard No 153)
Triple-expansion steam reciprocating, twin screw
The *Porthos*, which had been requisitioned for auxiliary service in September 1939, was hit by shellfire on 24 September 1940 when the French naval base at Dakar, where she was laid up, came under bombardment from British warships. Set on fire and her holds flooded, she was recovered within days for continued operation. Two years later, on 7 November 1942, she arrived off Casablanca in a French convoy at the time of the Allied landings in North Africa. During fighting on the following day she was again hit

by shells and capsized alongside the quay; she remained there until November 1944, when salvage work commenced. Raised in the following May, before any repairs could be considered the *Porthos* sank again in 1946 when she was driven onto rocks during a gale. After she had been refloated for the second time, she was not considered fit for restoration for commercial service and was disposed of for breaking-up, the work lasting until January 1951.
Casualties: 26

The *Porthos* was a sister ship of the *Athos* and *Sphinx*. All served on the Marseilles to Far East route. *World Ship Society*

PORTUGAL (1886) Messageries Maritimes, France

5,358grt; 443ft (135.0m) lbp x 46ft (14.0m) beam
915 passengers in three classes
Messageries Maritimes, La Ciotat (Yard No 63)
Triple-expansion steam reciprocating, single screw
Chartered by the Russians – or possibly purchased outright – for service as a Black Sea hospital ship, the *Portugal* was sunk on 17 March 1916. While towing a line of boats containing wounded from the shore in Batum Roads she was torpedoed by the German submarine U33, despite the fact that she was clearly painted in hospital ship colours. At the time she had been dead in the water because of problems with the tow, making her an easy target. The torpedo struck her amidships and she broke in two, sinking very quickly.
Casualties: 90, including 45 medical staff

POSEIDON EXPRESS (1974) ex-*Provence* (189) Laurel Sea Transport NE, Greece

7,824grt; 467ft (142.3m) loa x 68ft (20.7m) beam
255 berthed and 1,033 deck passengers
Pieltra Ligure CN, Pietra Ligure (Yard No 13)
Motor-ship, twin screw
While entering Paros harbour in stormy weather on 19 April 1996, the ro-ro ferry *Poseidon Express* struck a reef while trying to avoid another ferry, the *Naias II* (also rendered *Naias Express*), whose mooring lines had parted, and she sank in shallow waters the following day after heeling over onto her port side. The stricken vessel was righted and refloated by 2 July 1996 and thereafter towed to Elefsina Bay, Eleusis, where she arrived six days later for decisions to be made on her future. It turned out that she had not sustained as extreme structural damage as first thought. Nevertheless, she was not repaired but remained laid up until late July 1999 when she arrived at Aliaga, Turkey, to be scrapped, bearing the temporary name *Bel Air*.
Casualties: not known

The *Poseidon Express* in Arkadia Lines colours is seen arriving at Piraeus in July 1994. Befitting her name, she seems to be moving at some speed as she enters the harbour confines. *Frank Heine FERRIES*

PRAGUE (1930) London & North Eastern Railway, UK

4,220grt; 351ft (106.9m) lbp x 50ft (15.3m) beam
1,500 passengers
John Brown, Clydebank (Yard No 528)
Steam turbines, twin screw
Following arduous war service, latterly as a hospital carrier, the ferry *Prague* was returned to the Harwich to Hook of Holland service on 14 November 1945 after only a minimal refit, in order to inaugurate the post-war service at the earliest opportunity. Subsequently, she was taken in hand for the full refit that she needed, but in the course of this, at Clydebank on 14 March 1948, she caught fire and was all but destroyed. The gutted vessel was broken up at Barrow-in-Furness commencing on 14 September 1948. Casualties: not known

Another LNER passenger ferry, this is the *Prague*, sister ship of the *Vienna* and *Amsterdam*. *Ian Allan Library*

PRESIDENT CLEVELAND (1921) ex-*Golden State* (1923) American President Line, USA

serving under the wartime name TASKER H. BLISS [AP-42]
14,123grt; 539ft (164.3m) loa x 72ft (21.9m) beam
560 passengers in two classes
Newport News Shipbuilding & Drydock Co, Newport News, Virginia (Yard No 256)
Steam turbines, twin screw
In June 1941 the *President Cleveland* became the United States Army transport *Tasker H. Bliss*, later transferring to the US Navy. She was one of many Allied passenger vessels, serving as wartime auxiliaries, which were lost during the landings that launched the Allied campaign in North Africa. When she was off Fedalah, Casablanca, on 12 November 1942 she was torpedoed by the German submarine U130, caught fire and sank in the position 33.40N, 07.35W.
Casualties: not known

PRESIDENT COOLIDGE (1931) American President Line, USA

21,936grt; 654ft (199.3m) loa x 81ft (24.7m) beam
990 passengers in four classes
Newport News Shipbuilding & Drydock Co, Newport
News, Virginia (Yard No 340)
Turbo-electric, twin screw

The turbo-electric passenger liners *President Coolidge* and *President Hoover* were the first large American-flag luxury liners built for the trans-Pacific service from San Francisco to China and Japan. They represented a major achievement for the Dollar Line, which had only been operating on the route since February 1924, but after 1938, when the company fell on leaner times, its fleet and services were reorganised by the American Government under the American President Line's banner. *American President Lines*

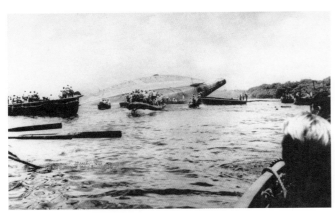

The *President Coolidge* sinking off Espiritu Santo in October 1942. By driving her onto a reef, her Master ensured that there was sufficient time to fully evacuate her before she sank in deep water. *American President Lines*

Following the entry of the United States into the Second World War, the passenger liner *President Coolidge* was converted into an army troop transport. While carrying 5,050 US troops, bound from Noumea, New Caledonia, to Luganville Bay, New Hebrides (Vanuatu), she struck an American mine in the approaches to the volcanic island of Espiritu Santo on 26 October 1942. The stricken troopship was beached on a reef, and apart from a slight list to port she remained, for a short while at least, on an even keel, permitting a rapid and disciplined evacuation, no mean feat with so many on board. As the list to port gradually worsened, many of her occupants

had to make their way on ropes down the side of the sloping hull, where they were picked up from the water and helped to reach the safety of nearby beaches. The operation was completed in good time for, by then, the *President Coolidge* was almost over onto her beam ends. It was hardly any time after the last person had abandoned ship when she slipped off the reef and sank in deep water. Since the war, the wreck of the *President Coolidge* has become a popular aqua-diving site and it was declared a protected underwater national park in 1984.
Casualties: 3 (an Army captain and 2 crew members)

PRESIDENT DAL PIAZ (1929) Compagnie Générale Transatlantique, France

serving under the wartime name AMALFI ex-Melfi
4,866grt; 363ft (110.6m) lbp x 53ft (16.1m) beam
392 passengers in three classes plus 300 deck passengers
Swan Hunter & Wigham Richardson, Low Walker, Tyneside
(Yard No 1294)
Steam turbines, twin screw

The *President Dal Piaz* was similar to the same company's *Carthage*, another passenger ship built by Swan Hunter on the Tyne. *Ian Rae*

The *President Dal Piaz* was scuttled at Cassis on 26 June 1944 under the name *Amalfi*. *L. L. von Münching*

The French Lines' passenger cargo steamer *President Dal Piaz* was seized by the Italian Government in July 1940 and renamed *Melfi* under which name she served as a dazzle-painted troopship. In 1943 she was returned to France but was seized by the Germans at Marseilles. On 15 February 1944, she was taken over by the Italians for the second time and renamed *Amalfi*. Together with a number of other passenger vessels, used to block ports and prevent their use by the advancing Allies, she was scuttled at Cassis, between Marseilles and La Ciotat, on 26 June 1944 and became a constructive total loss. Her ruined condition did not warrant reconstruction after the war and she was broken up.
Casualties: not known

PRESIDENT DOUMER (1933) Messageries Maritimes, France

11,898grt; 492ft (150.0m) loa x 64ft (19.5m) beam
903 passengers in four classes
Soc Provencale des Constructions Navals, La Ciotat
(Yard No 157)
Motor-ship, twin screw
The French Navy commandeered the passenger-cargo ship *President Doumer* in 1940 for service as a troopship, duties she commenced that April after conversion at Brest. However, on 29 May 1940, as the fall of France was becoming a distinct possibility, she was seized at Port Said and pressed into service as a British troopship under the management of the Bibby Line. Ninety-four members of her French crew remained with her. On 16 October 1942, carrying 63 passengers and 282 crew, she sailed from Freetown together with 35 other merchant ships and a naval escort, bound for the UK as convoy SL 125. From 27 October and over the next four days, as the convoy headed north of the Canaries, it came under sustained attack by eight German submarines. The *President Doumer* became the tenth victim, torpedoed and sunk on the evening of 30 October 1942 by U604 when north-east of Madeira, in the position 35.08N, 16.44W. Some of the survivors were lost when the Norwegian freighter *Alaska*, which had picked them up from the sea, was herself torpedoed and sunk a day later.
Casualties: 260 (all passengers and 197 crew)

At a time when most new Messageries Maritimes' vessels were emerging with the distinctive but unusual square funnels that were introduced in the inter-war years, for the *President Doumer* the designers unexpectedly reverted to a conventional style of funnel. She was engaged in the service from Marseilles to Madagascar and the Far East. *World Ship Society*

PRESIDENT HOOVER (1931) Dollar Line, USA

21,936grt; 654ft (199.3m) loa x 81ft (24.7m) beam
988 passengers in four classes

Newport News Shipbuilding & Drydock Co, Newport News, Virginia (Yard No 339)
Turbo-electric, twin screw

The *President Hoover* in Dollar Lines colours. Because of her loss in 1937 she did not form part of the newly constituted American President Lines fleet, unlike her sister *President Coolidge*, which had the dollar logo on her funnels replaced by a bald eagle emblem. *Ian Allan Library*

The *President Hoover* stranded on the Formosan island of Kashoto. In the first view, members of her passenger complement clamber ashore using rope lines. The second view shows the bleak, craggy volcanic rock where she came ashore. Both photographs were taken by her Second class Purser, Walter A. Lawrence. *Both: American President Lines*

Having been mistaken for a Japanese troop transport and attacked by a squadron of Chinese bomber aircraft at the mouth of the River Yangtse on 30 August 1937, the passenger liner *President Hoover*, which was actually on a mercy mission to Shanghai to evacuate American nationals, was lost just over three months later when engaged in a similar exercise. Her final voyage commenced on 22 November 1937. After calls at Yokohama and Kobe, she was bound for Manila when, on 10 December 1937, as she was passing along the east coast of Formosa (Taiwan), some 20 miles offshore, she ran onto a coral reef off the volcanic island of Kashoto (sometimes rendered Hoishoto and now known as Huoshao Dao or Lu Dao), in the position 22.50N, 121.25E. The night was foggy and drizzly, and strong currents had taken the ship off course. Apart from a skeleton party that remained aboard, her 650 or so passengers and the remainder of her 333-man crew abandoned ship.

The German cargo steamer *Preussen*, summoned by a radio call, stood by and assisted with the evacuation. Those rescued were all landed on the island and accommodated at Churyo (Chaikou) village for two days until other ships arrived to take them on to Manila, the passengers travelling aboard the *President McKinley*, the crew aboard the *President Pierce*. Many of the passengers, who included a number of dignitaries, regarded the whole episode as something of an adventure, although there were also some complaints about lost property and interference by boisterous and inebriated members of the crew. The *President Hoover* remained firmly wedged on the reef. Various attempts were made to salvage her but she was finally given up as lost in June 1938. The wreck was sold to Japanese ship-breakers and scrapped on the spot. There were suggestions that she had maintained a course close inshore to avoid another attack by Chinese warplanes. Casualties: 0

PRESIDENT LINCOLN (1907) ex-*Scotian* (launch name, 8 October 1903) Hamburg Amerika Line, Germany

18,168grt; 616ft (187.8m) loa x 68ft (20.7m) beam
3,350 passengers in three classes
Harland & Wolff, Belfast (Yard No 353)
Quadruple-expansion steam reciprocating, twin screw
Ordered and launched for the Furness Leyland Line, these owners withdrew from the building contract while she was fitting out and she was laid up incomplete from October 1903 until purchased by the Hamburg Amerika Line as the *President Lincoln*. Interned at New York in August 1914, the American Government seized her in April 1917 and she was pressed into service as a troop transport under the control of the US War Shipping Administration. On 31 May 1918, while returning empty to America from France, having brought a contingent of American troops to Europe, the *President Lincoln* was torpedoed by the submarine U90 and sank in the position 47.57N, 15.11W.
Casualties: 26 (all crew)

The Hamburg Amerika Line passenger steamship *President Lincoln* spent seven years on the Atlantic run for her original owners, retaining her name after she was pressed into US Government service as a troop transport from 1917.
Alex Duncan

PRESIDENT MADISON (1920) ex-*Bay State* (1923) Admiral Mail Line, USA

14,187grt; 535ft (163.1m) loa x 72ft (22.0m) beam
560 passengers in two classes

New York Shipbuilding Corp, Camden, New Jersey
(Yard No 251)
Steam turbines, twin screw
On 24 March 1933 the passenger-cargo ship *President Madison* was in Seattle at the Todd Drydock Company's yard undergoing side-plating repairs. This involved the removal of existing plating just 7 feet above the waterline on her starboard side, temporarily leaving a gaping hole. During the night the *President Madison* developed a sudden list and keeled over against the quay. The cause was not determined, but was suspected as having been the result of uneven filling or discharge of her ballast tanks. As the list brought the hole in her side down to water level, the sea rushed into the *President Madison*, completing the act of capsizing her. She came to rest, half submerged, with her superstructure resting against the pier and her hull settled on the bottom. For many of those on board, 150 workmen and watch crew, there was a scramble to save themselves and get off the ship before she went under.

In the event there were some remarkable escapes. Two Chinese crewmen had the presence of mind to get out through a porthole on the starboard side just as it was breaking the surface and they safely swam ashore. Another crewman, an engine room storekeeper, slept through the night unaware of the ship's predicament and woke to find himself in darkness with the deck canted crazily. He was later rescued, but two other men, who were similarly trapped, were less lucky. The accident left the *President Madison*'s accommodation, machinery and refrigeration spaces flooded throughout, and after she was righted it was necessary to replace furnishings, woodwork and wiring as well as her main engines and generators. Repairs lasted a full eight months, but although she was returned to service she was not fully utilised from that time. In 1939 she was sold to a Philippines-based company and renamed *President Quezon* (qv).
Casualties: 2

The flooded *President Madison* lists to starboard with her masts and king posts buckled alongside the pier at Seattle where she was undergoing a refit. *Frank Braynard*

PRESIDENT PIERCE (1921) ex-*Hawkeye State* (1923) American President Line, USA

serving under the wartime name HUGH L. SCOTT [AP-43]
12,579grt; 535ft (163.1m) loa x 72ft (21.9m) beam
561 passengers in two classes
Bethlehem Shipbuilding Corp, Sparrows Point, Maryland
(Yard No 4180)
Steam turbines, twin screw

In July 1941 the *President Pierce* was taken over for military service with the United States Army under the name *Hugh L. Scott*, transferring to the US Navy the following August. While anchored off Fedalah, near Casablanca, on 12 November 1942, she was torpedoed, like her sister ship *President Cleveland* (qv), by the German submarine U130, which had penetrated a minefield and a destroyer screen in order to carry out its attacks. The former *President Pierce* sank in the position 33.40N, 07.35W. She was one of five American naval transports to be lost during the Allied landings in North Africa.
Casualties: not known

PRESIDENT QUEZON (1921) ex-*President Madison* (1939) ex-*Bay State* (1923) Philippine Mail Line, Philippines

14,187grt; 535ft (163.1m) loa x 72ft (22.0m) beam
560 passengers in two classes (as built)
New York Shipbuilding Corp, Camden, New Jersey (Yard No 251)
Steam turbines, twin screw

Six years after the *President Madison* (qv) had returned to service in November 1933, following her capsizing incident at Seattle that March, she was sold to Philippine owners and renamed *President Quezon*. On the first run for her new owners she ran aground in high seas and a severe storm, tearing open her hull on a sunken reef at Tanega Shima, eighty miles (125 kilometres) south of Kagoshima on the Japanese island of Kyushu. The date was 27 January 1940. Water poured into the engine room, stopping the engines and leaving the ship without power, quite helpless. She was carrying only 12 passengers in addition to her crew of 114, and they were all assisted to evacuate the sinking ship by Japanese vessels that had proceeded to the scene. All the survivors were taken to Kobe, 63 of them aboard the motor ship *Ukishima* [*Ukisima*] *Maru*. The *President Quezon* foundered in the position 30.16N, 130.57E, but the wreck was later raised and scrapped in Japan.
Casualties: 1 (a ship's cook)

PREUSSEN (1926) Brauenlich Reederei, Germany

2,529grt; 313ft (95.4m) lbp x 38ft (11.7m)
1,200 unberthed passengers
Stettiner Oderwerke, Stettin-Grabow (Yard No 725)
Motor-ship, twin screw

The *Preussen* operated the Seedienst Ostpreussen passenger service along Germany's Baltic coastline, from Kiel, Lübeck, Travemünde and Swinemünde to Pillau, along with the *Tanneberg* (qv) and *Hansestadt Danzig* (2,431 grt), the latter vessel her smaller near-sister ship, owned by Norddeutscher Lloyd. The service was established to overcome transportation problems affecting Germans isolated in Silesia and East Prussia that arose following the extension of Polish borders to the Baltic by a corridor after the First World War, cutting the area off from the rest of Germany. The three ships, serving as wartime minesweepers, were sunk together on 9 July 1941 while sailing in convoy in the Baltic, bound from Finland to Swinemünde. When they came under attack from Russian warships, evasive action took them into a minefield off the south-east coast of Sweden, near the island of Oland, where each struck a mine and sank. The position was 56.12N, 16.17E
Casualties: not known for any of the three ships

PRIAMURYE (1960) ex-*Vladivostok* (1968) Far Eastern Shipping Co (Sovtorgflot), USSR

4,871grt; 401ft (122.2m) loa x 53ft (16.0m) beam
333 passengers in single class
Mathias-Thesen Werft, Wismar (Yard No not known)
Motor-ship, twin screw

Built for scheduled passenger services, by the time of her loss on 18 May 1988 the *Priamurye* was engaged as a cruise ship and, as such, was berthed at Osaka, Japan, when fire broke out aboard her in the middle of the night. At that time the majority of her 295 passengers and 129 crew were asleep, oblivious to the danger. For some unknown reason, the city's Fire Service was not alerted until almost an hour had passed, by which time the fire had spread out of control and intensified. By this time those aboard, now aware of the fire threat, were trying to get off the ship and many broke windows and jumped into the sea to escape. Even after the local fire brigade had arrived at the dockside, there were further delays in fighting the fire because of language differences between the Soviet ship's personnel and the Japanese firemen. The result was that the *Priamurye* was beyond restoration by the time the fire had been extinguished. She was broken up at Kaohsiung, Taiwan, arriving there under tow in October 1988.
Casualties: 11

PRIDE OF AL SALAM 95 (1972) ex-*Pride of Ailsa* (1996) ex-*Pride of Sandwich* (1992) ex-*Free Enterprise VI* (1987) Al Salam Shipping & Trading, Panama

15,503grt; 457ft (139.4m) loa x 72ft (22.5m) beam
68 berthed and 1,132 deck passengers (as built)
IHC 'Gusto' NV, Schiedam (Yard No 881)
Motor-ship, triple screw

The *Pride of Al Salam 95* at Suez on 15 May 1998. Her built-up superstructure would have given her a high centre of gravity, making her less stable. Note the long drop to the water's surface from the main lifeboat cluster, while the forward lifeboat seems to be in an inaccessible position.
Frank Heine FERRIES

Two years prior to becoming a P&O Ferries ship, the *Free Enterprise VI* and her sister ship had been lengthened, widened and raised by an additional deck by Schichau-Unterweser, Bremerhaven, a treatment that other, similar ferries had received. The result was that they were top-heavy and, with a raised centre of gravity, inclined to be less stable. Following changes to the compartmentation rules for European ro-ro ferries following the *Estonia* disaster, she was sold on to become the *Pride of Al Salam 95*, engaged in the pilgrim service across the Red Sea. On 17 October 2005 she was in collision with the bulk carrier *Pearl of Jebel* off Port Tewfik, at the southern entrance of the Suez Canal, while bound from Jeddah to Port Suez with 1,300 pilgrims returning from Mecca. With her hull torn open and the engine room flooding, she sank rapidly but, fortunately, not before all aboard her had been rescued. Casualties: 1 (heart attack)

PRINCE GEORGE (1910), Canadian National Line, Canada

3,372grt; 307ft (93.5m) lbp x 42ft (12.9m) beam
250 passengers in two classes
Swan Hunter & Wigham Richardson, Wallsend-on-Tyne (Yard No 859)
Triple-expansion steam reciprocating, twin screw
Constructed for the Grand Trunk Pacific Development Company to a typical North American design with rounded superstructure at the forward end and wooden wheelhouse, the *Prince George* was placed in the American north-west service between Oregon, Washington state, British Columbia and Alaska, working out of Vancouver. The Grand Trunk Pacific Railway was absorbed by Canadian National Railways in 1923.

On the morning of 22 September 1945, within minutes of arriving at Ketchikan, Alaska, fire started in her engine room and rapidly spread through the ship. The fire alarms alerted the passengers, only eight on this trip, who, together with 38 of her crew members, were swiftly disembarked. Local fire-fighters soon arrived on the scene to fight the blaze but their efforts were in vain and when it became apparent that there was a risk of the fire spreading to the quay and dockside installations, orders were given to have the *Prince George* removed. The last of her crew, some 50 men, who had remained aboard assisting the efforts to extinguish the fire, were evacuated by the Coast Guard cutter *Annapolis* while tugs towed the *Prince George* away and attempted to beach her on Pennock Island. However, the rising tide refloated her, so the tugs reconnected and dragged her onto rocks between Gravina and Pennock, effectively abandoning her to a fiery grave. Inspection of the wreck after the fire had burned out revealed that two of her funnels had collapsed while the third was canted over at an angle; her masts were gone and her ribs exposed along the length of the hull. She was partially sunk and listing to port. With no hope of recovery, she was raised and broken up at Seattle in 1950. Casualties: 1

The passenger ferry *Prince George*, destined for service on the west coast of America and Canada, leaves the River Tyne where she was built. In the background on the far bank of the river the ruins of Tynemouth Priory can be seen. *Ian Rae*

The *Prince George* on fire at Ketchikan on 22 September 1945. *Ketchikan Museums*

PRINCE GEORGE (1948) Fairport Investments, Canada

5,825grt; 350ft (106.7m) loa x 52ft (15.9m) beam
368 passengers
Yarrows, Esquimault (Yard No 105)
Uniflow steam reciprocating, twin screw
The former Canadian National Railways ferry *Prince George* was gutted by fire on 14 October 1995 while she was berthed alongside the quay at Britannia Beach, some thirty miles north of Vancouver, where she had lain idle for eight years following brief service as a floating hotel during Expo '86. Plans to adapt her into a floating restaurant had not materialised. The fire, which had broken out in the area of her forward lounge, soon spread unabated, it proving difficult to fight such a blaze in her remote location. By the time the fire had been extinguished, the *Prince George* was badly burned along the entire length of her superstructure and down into the hull immediately beneath. Condemned for demolition, as she was being towed away to breakers in China on 25 October 1996 she sank in the Unimak Pass, in the position 53.58N, 166.30W. Casualties: not known

The *Prince George* of Canadian National Lines (the marine division of Canadian National Railways) passes under the Lions Gate Bridge at Vancouver in June 1983. *Frank Heine FERRIES*

PRINCE LEOPOLD (1930) Belgian Marine Administration, Belgium

2,950grt; 360ft loa (105.8m lbp) x 46ft (14.1m) beam
1,400 passengers
Cockerill, Hoboken (Yard No 639)
Steam turbines, twin screw

The North Sea ferry *Prince Leopold* was taken over in September 1940 for war service with the Royal Navy as an Infantry Landing Ship and participated in the landings at Dieppe, Sicily and Salerno. While engaged in this capacity during Operation 'Neptune', the naval component of the invasion of Normandy, making crossings from Southampton to the beachheads with reinforcements, she was torpedoed by the German submarine U621 on 29 July 1944 when twenty miles south-east of the Isle of Wight. Taken in tow, with the frigate HMS *Chelmer* standing by, she capsized and sank later that day less than six miles from the Nab Tower, in the position 50.27N, 00.56W. Wreck dispersal operations were commenced that November because she lay near the main shipping lane. Casualties: not known

The Belgian Marine passenger ferry *Prince Leopold* served with the Royal Navy as an Infantry Landing Ship during many of the amphibious landings of the Second World War until she was lost carrying reinforcements to France after D-Day.
World Ship Society

PRINCE PHILIPPE (1940) Belgian Marine Administration, Belgium

2,938grt; 370ft (112.8m) loa x 49ft (15.0m) beam
1,800 passengers (as designed)
Cockerill, Hoboken (Yard No 687)
Motor-ship, twin screw

The passenger ferry *Prince Philippe*, last of the '*Prince Baudouin*' class, never entered commercial service across the Dover Strait as she was completed after the outbreak of war and was lost while commissioned as an Infantry Landing Ship.
Imperial War Museum (FL7080)

Another Belgian ferry taken over for wartime service as an Infantry Landing Ship, the *Prince Philippe* never in fact entered commercial service for she escaped from Belgium on 17 May 1940 when almost complete and was commissioned as HMS *Prince Philippe* on 14 June 1941. Based initially at Inverary on Loch Fyne, she was moved south to Liverpool just sixteen days later. After leaving the River Mersey on 14 July to calibrate her direction-finding equipment, she was in

collision with the CAM ship *Empire Wave* in the Firth of Clyde. The accident occurred in thick fog north-east of Larne, the impact so great that the *Prince Philippe* sank the following day in the position 55.05N, 05.24W with the loss of many of her crew. There were 29 survivors. Casualties: 171

PRINCESS IRENE (1914) Canadian Pacific Line, UK

5,934grt; 395ft (120.4m) loa x 54ft (16.5m) beam
240 berthed and 1,260 deck passengers (as designed)
William Denny, Dumbarton (Yard No 1006)
Steam turbines, twin screw

Intended for her owners' coastal passenger services in British Columbia with a sister ship *Princess Margaret*, neither the *Princess Irene* nor her consort were operated commercially by Canadian Pacific. Taken over incomplete by the Admiralty for auxiliary service as minelayers in the First World War, the *Princess Margaret* was never returned while the *Princess Irene* was lost in tragic circumstances on 27 May 1915. While she was undergoing repairs at Sheerness dockyard, Kent, she blew up. Late that morning, two huge columns of flame were seen to shoot upwards from the *Princess Irene*, immediately followed by a tremendous explosion that shook the surrounding area. The mines being stowed aboard her had somehow detonated. Her entire complement of 270 officers and ratings was aboard at the time, together with 78 dockyard personnel, and many were killed. Her remains were later removed.
Casualties: 130 (53 crew and 77 workmen) These figures have been drawn from Lloyd's and CPR records. Alternatives to these are given in some sources.

PRINCESS KATHLEEN (1925) Canadian Pacific Line, UK

5,908grt; 350ft (106.7m) lbp x 60ft (18.3m) beam
234 berthed and 1,266 deck passengers
John Brown, Clydebank (Yard No 504)
Steam turbines, twin screw

After troopship duties during the Second World War, the *Princess Kathleen* returned to her owners' Vancouver-Seattle-Victoria service, later transferring to the Alaska route. On 7 September 1952, while bound from Vancouver to Skagway with some 300 passengers, she was stranded in a gale at Lena Point, about thirty miles north of Juneau, Alaska. As the tide rose her stern was swamped, pulling her down until she slipped off the reef and sank in deep water.
Casualties: 0

Canadian Pacific introduced a series of large three-funnelled passenger ferries on its British Columbia coastal services between 1925 and 1930. Two earlier ships of this configuration, completed during the First World War, never undertook commercial sailings for the company. This is the *Princess Kathleen*, which entered service in January 1925.
World Ship Society

PRINCESS LOUISE (1921) Bank of San Pedro, USA

4,032grt; 317ft (96.7m) lbp x 48ft (14.7m) beam
1,000 passengers (as built)
Wallace, North Vancouver (Yard No 108)
Triple-expansion steam reciprocating, single screw

After she had been withdrawn from passenger service in 1963, the former Canadian Pacific ferry *Princess Louise* was used as a hotel-cum-restaurant at the British Columbia Ferries terminal at Tsawwassen, moving to Los Angeles for the same purpose in 1966. More recently she was moved again, to San Pedro, California, where, on 30 October 1989, she capsized while lying at the Southwest Marine Inc Shipyard. It was speculated that the cause was the loss of plates on her water ballast tank, causing her to flood. After she had been refloated on 30 May 1990, the intention had been to scuttle her off Catalina Island, but while under tow, on 20 June 1990, she sank before reaching that destination after taking in water sixteen miles south-west of Point Firmin.
Casualties: not known

PRINCESS MARGUERITE (1925) Canadian Pacific Railway, UK

5,875grt; 350ft (106.7m) lbp x 60ft (18.3m) beam
234 berthed and 1,266 deck passengers
John Brown, Clydebank (Yard No 505)
Steam turbines, twin screw

Princess Marguerite was sister of the *Princess Kathleen*.
Gowen Sutton & Co

The *Princess Marguerite* on fire off Port Said on 17 August 1942. *British Columbia Provincial Archives*

Sister ship of the *Princess Kathleen*, the *Princess Marguerite* was lost during the Second World War, torpedoed by the German submarine U83 north of Port Said on 17 August 1942. The *Princess Marguerite* was bound from Port Said to Famagusta, Cyprus, carrying around 1,000 troops when she was attacked. The explosion of the torpedo ignited the oil in her fuel tanks, and fire spread rapidly, engulfing the

ammunition in her magazine, which also detonated. She sank inside an hour in the position 32.03N, 32.47E. The survivors were picked up by the escorting destroyer, HMS *Hero*.
Casualties: 49

PRINCESS OF THE ORIENT (1974) ex-*Sun Flower Satsuma* (1993) ex-*Sun Flower 11* (1991) Sulpicio Lines, Philippines

13,614grt; 642ft (195.8m) loa x 79ft (24.0m) beam
1,218 passengers
Kurushima Dock Co, Onishi (Yard No 775)
Motor-ship, twin screw

After 19 years' service on Japanese domestic routes, this ro-ro passenger ferry transferred to similar duties between the islands of the Philippines archipelago. On 18 September 1998, while on passage from Manila to Cebu City carrying a total of 458 persons, the *Princess of the Orient* was caught in typhoon 'Vicki'. Overwhelmed by the weather, she sank near Fortune Island at the entrance of Manila Bay.
Casualties: 99

PRINCESS OF THE STARS (1984) ex-*Ferry Lilac* (2004) Sulpicio Lines, Philippines

23,824grt; 633ft (192.9m) loa x 97ft (29.4m) beam
1,992 passengers
Ishikawajima-Harima, Aioi (Yard No 2904)
Motor-ship, twin screw

The ill-fated *Princess of the Stars* was the subject of the worst maritime disaster to occur since the start of the new millennium. *Sulpicio Lines*

The *Princess of the Stars* capsized off Romblon island on 23 June 2008, with just part of her bow section above water. The aperture in her hull is the bow thruster. *Reuters – Romeo Ranoco*

One of the worst shipping disasters of the past quarter of a century and the most recent to be recorded in these pages was the loss of the inter-island ferry *Princess of the Stars* on 22 June 2008. While bound from Manila to Cebu City, she capsized in typhoon 'Fengshen' off the coast of San Fernando, Romblon island, about two miles west of Sibuyan island, Sibuyan Sea, in the central Philippines. Distress signals were

sent out when the ship's engines stalled, but by the time rescue craft could reach the scene the *Princess of the Stars* had turned over. Some bodies were found in the sea but the majority of her complement had been trapped inside the hull, which gradually, though not completely, submerged. Typically, there was uncertainty as to the precise number of persons aboard the ship, but Sulpicio Lines belatedly released figures of 751 manifested passengers and a crew of 111, the vast majority of whom perished. Some 48 persons or thereabouts survived the incident. However, none of these numbers can be relied upon as being accurate. It is a testimony to the fury of a tropical storm that such a large vessel should fall its victim, raising questions as to whether vessels designed for relatively sheltered waters should put to sea in such extreme weather conditions, particularly when the outcome could be as grave as it was in this case. As something of a landmark incident, it focussed attention on the appalling safety record of the owners of the *Princess of the Stars*, resulting in their operating licence being revoked.
Casualties: ~814

PRINCESS OF THE WORLD (1972) ex *Marimo* (1996) Sulpicio Lines, Philippines

9,627 grt; 545ft (166.0m) loa x 79ft (24.1m) beam
833 passengers
Setoda Shipbuilding Co, Setoda (Yard No 246)
Motor-ship, twin screw
The former Japanese ro-ro passenger/vehicle ferry *Princess of the World* was destroyed by fire off Dalunguin Point, Zamboanga, at the extreme western tip of the island of Mindanao, in the Philippines, on 7 July 2005. It was reported that the outbreak, which originated in the main engine intake manifold, occurred while the ship was berthed alongside the Timex Wharf at Zamboanga, so she was presumably towed clear after all her passengers and crew had been evacuated. The fire spread throughout the ship and it was completely gutted. By the time it had burnt itself out the *Princess of the World* was fit only for scrapping. Casualties: 0

PRINCESS SISSY (1949) ex-*Elektra* (1974) ex-*Mediterranean II* (1964) ex-*Sidi Okba* (1964) Solemare Shipping Co (Sol Lines), Panama

5,327grt; 372ft (113.4m) loa x 51ft (15.6m) beam
478 passengers in single class
J. Samuel White, Cowes, Isle of Wight (Yard No 1943)
Steam turbines, single screw
Built originally as a passenger-cargo ship for French owners SGTM to work scheduled passenger services, the *Princess Sissy* passed to Typaldos Lines, Greece, in 1964, and under the name *Elektra* was adapted to run Mediterranean cruises. On 7 January 1976, during a cruise from Genoa with 361 passengers and 115 crew, she grounded thirty miles from Split, Yugoslavia, between the islands of Korcula and Hvar, in the position 43.05N, 16.35E. All passengers and 78 of the crew were evacuated aboard the *San Giorgio* and taken to Trieste. The remainder of the crew remained aboard the *Princess Sissy* in a bid to save her, but, completely wrecked, she was declared a constructive total loss. Refloated on 5 April 1976 and towed to Split, she remained laid up there for four years until she was sold for breaking-up locally, commencing on 26 May 1980. Casualties: 0

The cruise passenger ship *Princess Sissy* photographed at Valletta, Malta. *Michael Cassar*

PRINCESS VICTORIA (1947) British Transport Commission, UK

2,694grt; 310ft (94.5m) lbp x 48ft (14.6m) beam
1,500 passengers
William Denny, Dumbarton (Yard No 1399)
Motor-ship, twin screw
The worst British shipping disaster of the 1950s involved the ro-ro passenger ferry *Princess Victoria*, built originally for the London, Midland & Scottish Railway. On 31 January 1953 she was bound from Stranraer to Larne in extremely inclement weather with 127 passengers and 49 crew. Off the mouth of Loch Ryan just before 10.00 she radioed for assistance, advising that she was hove-to and not under control. The destroyer HMS *Contest* immediately put out from Greenock, expecting to arrive on the scene by early afternoon, but less than an hour later the heavy seas stove in the doors at the aft end of the *Princess Victoria*'s car deck, flooding the ship and causing her to list to starboard. By 14.00, with no sign of the *Contest*, which had also found difficulty in making headway in the extreme conditions, the *Princess Victoria* advised that she was virtually on her beam ends with her engine room flooded and was being abandoned. That was her last message for she sank soon afterwards approximately five miles north of Mew Island lighthouse, Belfast. The delayed *Contest* and other ships picked up the 42 survivors.
Casualties: 134

The worst British shipping disaster following the Second World War was the loss of the *Princess Victoria* when she foundered near Belfast in January 1953. *H. B. Christiansen Collection / Online Transport Archive*

PRINCIPE DE ASTURIAS (1914) Pinillos, Izquierdo & Cia, Spain

8,371grt; 460ft (140.2m) lbp x 58ft (17.7m) beam
2,044 passengers
Russell, Port Glasgow (Yard No 663)
Quadruple-expansion steam reciprocating, twin screw
The loss of the passenger-cargo liner *Principe de Asturias* on 5 March 1916 was the worst maritime tragedy ever suffered by the Spanish merchant marine. After leaving Las Palmas, outward bound from Barcelona to Buenos Aires with 395 passengers and 193 crew, she ran into dense fog off the Brazilian coast near Sao Sebastiano, south of Santos. In the early hours of the morning she slammed into the rocks three miles off Ponta Boi. The violence of the impact opened a huge hole underwater and the sea water flooding into her caused the boilers to explode, breaking the ship in two. Almost immediately she capsized and foundered, sinking in deep water. It was impossible in such a brief interlude to implement any organised evacuation, and as a consequence the loss of life was very heavy. The French steamship *Vega* picked up 57 passengers and 86 members of the crew, the only survivors. The *Principe de Asturias* had been hugging the coast, increasing the risk of an accident, to avoid the attention of blockading British warships because there were a number of German citizens among her complement.
Casualties: 445 (This figure is drawn from Lloyd's records, but other sources give the number of fatalities as 415.)

PRINCIPESSA JOLANDA (1907) Lloyd Italiano, Italy

9,210grt; 485ft (147.8m) lbp x 55ft (16.9m) beam
About 1,700 passengers in two classes (as designed)
Esercizio Bacini, Riva Trigoso (Yard No not known)
Quadruple-expansion steam reciprocating, twin screw
Few ships could have had a shorter life than the luckless *Principessa Jolanda* (also rendered *Principessa Iolanda*), constructed as the first of a pair; her sister ship, the *Principessa Mafalda* (qv), was laid down in 1906. The launch of the *Principessa Jolanda* was scheduled for 21 September 1907 and at the allotted time she entered the water, complete with her superstructure, her funnels in place and her masts already stepped. To the horror of the crowd that had turned out to wish her well, she developed an immediate list to port, which increased steadily until she capsized onto her port side and sank with only a small part of her hull to be seen above water. It was inferred that a fire on the sliding ways had led to the accident but other, more serious, factors must have had a bearing, especially given the short duration of her passage to the water. Most untypically, the builders' involvement with the submerged ship concluded with the arrangements for her demolition.
Casualties: 0

PRINCIPESSA MAFALDA (1908) Navigazione Generale Italiana, Italy

9,210grt; 485ft (147.9m) lbp x 55ft (16.9m) beam
1,700 passengers
Esercizio Bacini, Riva Trigoso (Yard No 42)
Quadruple-expansion steam reciprocating, twin screw
The passenger steamship *Principessa Mafalda* was the sister ship of the *Principessa Jolanda* (qv), which, having capsized

disastrously following her launch in September 1907, never even entered commercial service. Twenty years later, on 25 October 1927, disaster also overtook the *Principessa Mafalda* off the Brazilian coast while she was heading, outward-bound, from Genoa for Rio de Janeiro and Buenos Aires. On the previous round trip she had experienced problems with her port engine and, although a thorough overhaul had been carried out at Genoa between voyages, it continued to give trouble. As she was nearing Bahia, Brazil, on the fateful day, the port propeller shaft fractured, wrecking the shaft casing. Water immediately flooded into the boiler room, causing the boilers to explode.

There was immediate alarm among her 971 passengers, who included a particularly sensitive group of 110 Syrians. Initially, they were all calmed by assurances that nothing worse had happened than a mechanical breakdown, but it soon became apparent that the ship was in a far graver predicament as she steamed in circles and settled lower and lower in the water. As realisation spread among the passengers that in reality the circumstances were more acute than they had been advised, panic was sparked to such an extent that crewmen who would have been better engaged in helping to save the ship had to be diverted to controlling the passengers. Before any organised evacuation could be set in motion, fighting broke out between passengers trying to get into the lifeboats, and one or two boats that were launched in haste only capsized as soon as they reached the water. Other passengers were jumping into the sea, only to expose themselves to another menace, for the waters were infested with sharks.

Fortunately, the Blue Star cargo vessel *Empire Star* had only passed the *Principessa Mafalda* a short while before the mishap and she turned back in answer to the liner's distress call. A rescue operation from the *Empire Star* was immediately mounted and in this she was joined by other ships as they arrived on the scene: the French ships *Formose* and *Mosella*, the British ships *Rossetti*, *Avelona*, another Blue Star ship, and *King Frederick*, and the Dutch cargo steamer *Alhena*. The *Principessa Mafalda* capsized and sank some four hours after the propeller shaft had failed, in the position 16.48S, 37.41W. By that time 659 of the passengers had been saved. The ship had also been carrying a crew of 288 men, of whom 242 survived, but among those who perished were eight officers and the ship's Master, who had been involved in supervising the evacuation to the very last.
Casualties: 358 (312 passengers and 46 crew, including her Master)

Sister ship of the *Principessa Jolanda*, which capsized and was lost during her launch, the *Principessa Mafalda* was lost in the worst Italian shipping disaster between the two world wars. Her normal service was on the Italy to South America route.
World Ship Society

PRINCIPE UMBERTO (1909) Navigazione Generale Italiana, Italy

7,929grt; 476ft (145.1m) lbp x 53ft (16.2m) beam
1,423 passengers in three classes
Cantieri Navali Riuniti, Palermo (Yard No 13)
Quadruple-expansion steam reciprocating, twin screw

On 8 June 1916, while proceeding across the lower Adriatic in company with two other troopships and an escorting destroyer, the *Principe Umberto* was sunk when the convoy came under attack from two Austrian submarines 15 miles south-west of Linguetta. Of the two, the U5 fired the torpedo that sunk the *Principe Umberto*. At the time she was carrying a large contingent of soldiers bound for Mudros, many of whom were drowned when the *Principe Umberto* sank in the position 40.19N, 19.10E, the badly damaged vessel having remained afloat for only a very brief time. The sinking of the *Principe Umberto* was the worst passenger shipping loss of the First World War and Italy's worst ever maritime disaster. Casualties: 1,750

PRINSENDAM (1973) Holland Amerika Line, The Netherlands

8,566grt; 437ft (130.2m) loa x 63ft (19.1m) beam
375 passengers in a single class
De Merwede, Hardinxveld (Yard No 606)
Motor-ship, twin screw

Fire broke out aboard the cruise ship *Prinsendam* during an extended positioning cruise from Vancouver to Singapore on 4 October 1980. A fuel oil line in her engine room ruptured, releasing diesel fuel, which ignited when it came into contact with hot pipes. The engine compartments were promptly sealed and flooded with carbon dioxide gas, following which there was a delay while the fumes dissipated before its effect could be investigated. When this was possible, it was discovered that the fire had not been extinguished and in fact was intensifying. Moreover, the flames had caused damage to the electrical system, denying power from the generator that supplied the ship's pumps, so that it was impossible to fight the outbreak by this method. At the time, the *Prinsendam* was in the Gulf of Alaska, in the position 57.38N, 140.25W, with 320 passengers on board, mostly elderly Americans, and 190 crew.

The ship sent out radio messages requesting help, in response to which United States Coast Guard cutters were dispatched to the scene, while the nearby supertanker *Williamsburgh*, which had helicopter landing facilities, was also alerted. Initially, the rescue services attempted to airlift the passengers and crew, who had by now taken to the boats, directly ashore, at Yakutat, Alaska, but once the *Williamsburgh* arrived on the scene she was used as an immense refuge centre, later transferring survivors to Valdes. The *Williamsburgh* rescued 370 and the cutter *Boutwell* took 87 survivors to Sitka, while a further 62 persons had been landed at Yakutat in the early stages of the operation. The *Prinsendam* was taken in tow by the ocean-going tug *Commodore Straits* in an attempt to get her to Portland, Oregon, but as the days progressed the liner's condition deteriorated. She had assumed a list to starboard, which steadily worsened until on 11 October the tug cut her free and she foundered eighty miles west of Sitka in the position 55.53N, 136.27W. Casualties: 0

The Holland Amerika Line cruise ship *Prinsendam*.
Ian Shiffman

The *Prinsendam* listing heavily to port in stormy seas during rescue operations in the Gulf of Alaska in October 1980. At the time she had been on a month-long voyage from Vancouver to Singapore. *US Coast Guard*

PRINSES ASTRID (1931) Belgian Marine Administration, Belgium

2,950grt; 360ft loa (105.8m) lbp x 46ft (14.1m) beam
1,400 passengers
Cockerill, Hoboken (Yard No 638)
Steam turbines, twin screw

Having survived the Second World War, in which she served as an Infantry Landing Ship, the ferry *Prinses Astrid* succumbed to a mine on 1 June 1949 when she was bound from Ostend to Dover with 218 passengers and a crew of 65. While proceeding through a narrow channel into Dunkirk, some four miles west of the port, she hit the mine, the force of the explosion opening up her side. The *Prinses Astrid* was run onto a sandbank, allowing sufficient time for a full evacuation, but the vessel itself broke in two, a total loss. The survivors were picked by the steamship *Cap Hadid*. The channel had been swept by the Royal Navy in 1946 and declared safe by the International Mine Clearance Board. It was suspected that the mine had either drifted in from the open sea or had been buried in a sandbank and had been washed free by the combined effects of tides and waves. Casualties: 5 (all crew)

PRINSES JULIANA (1909) Zeeland Steamship Co, The Netherlands

2,885grt; 350ft (106.6m) lbp x 43ft (13.0m) beam
356 passengers in two classes
Fairfield, Govan (Yard No 461)
Triple-expansion steam reciprocating, twin screw
The North Sea passenger ship *Prinses Juliana* struck a submarine-laid mine on 1 February 1916 close to the Sunk light vessel. She was beached near Felixstowe but became a total loss.
Casualties: not known

PRINSES JULIANA (1920) Zeeland Steamship Co, The Netherlands

2,908grt; 350ft (106.8m) lbp x 43ft (13.0m) beam
800 passengers
Royal Schelde, Vlissingen (Yard No 171)
Triple-expansion steam reciprocating, twin screw
While en route between the Hook of Holland and Scheveningen on 12 May 1940, at the height of the refugee and troop evacuation operation following the German invasion of the Low Countries, the *Prinses Juliana*, employed as a troopship, was bombed one kilometre north of the North Pier at the Hook of Holland. The order to abandon ship was given and all her lifeboats launched. The *Prinses Juliana* was beached in the position 51.59N, 04.06E, but broke in two and became a total loss. The destroyer HMS *Wild Swan* stood by to take off those survivors who had remained aboard the ship.
Casualties: not known

The *Prinses Juliana*, a Zeeland Steamship Company passenger ferry, was lost during Second World War evacuation operations. *World Ship Society*

PRINS FREDERIK (1882) Nederland Line, The Netherlands

2,997grt; 350ft (106.7m) lbp x 39ft (11.9m) beam
Passenger numbers not known
John Elder, Govan (Yard No 260)
Compound-expansion steam reciprocating, single screw
On 25 June 1890, in thick fog, the *Prins Frederik* was in collision with the steamship *Marpessa* at the western entrance to the English Channel and sank as the result. She had been bound from Holland to Java carrying 170 persons, some of whom were troops, the majority of whom got away safely. Her wreck, which has never been found, is of great interest to treasure hunters for she was carrying 400 thousand silver coins for army pay.
Casualties: 7 (all soldiers)

PRINZ AUGUST WILHELM (1903) Hamburg Amerika Line, Germany

4,733grt; 370ft (113.0m) lbp x 45ft (13.8m) beam
818 passengers in two classes
Flensburger, Flensburg (Yard No 217)
Quadruple-expansion steam reciprocating, single screw
The passenger steamship *Prinz August Wilhelm*, primarily an emigrant carrier, was burned and scuttled by her crew at Puerto, Colombia, on 22 April 1918. The action was taken because it was feared that the blockaded ship was about to be seized by the Colombian Government.
Casualties: 0

PRINZESSIN VICTORIA LUISE (1901) Hamburg Amerika Line, Germany

4,419grt; 407ft (124.2m) lbp x 47ft (14.4m) beam
200 passengers
Blohm & Voss, Steinwerder, Hamburg (Yard No 144)
Quadruple-expansion steam reciprocating, twin screw
The *Prinzessin Victoria Luise* was a sleek, white, clipper-bowed passenger vessel. She entered service as a cruising yacht but in her short life she also undertook occasional voyages to New York from Hamburg and Plymouth. On 16 December 1906, during a Caribbean cruise, she ran aground at Plum Point, near Kingston, Jamaica. She remained fast and, after a seaquake on 14 January 1907, became a constructive total loss. The explanation given for her loss was that an earlier quake, some two weeks prior to the stranding, had raised the ocean floor, rendering all navigational charts of the area unreliable.
Casualties: not known

The *Prinzessin Victoria Luise* made cruises to the North Cape, the Mediterranean and Black Sea, switching to the West Indies out of New York each winter. *Arnold Kludas*

PROVIDENCE (1920) Messageries Maritimes, France

11,996grt; 512ft (156.0m) loa x 58ft (18.2m) beam
2,240 passengers in three classes
Forges et Chantiers de la Méditerranée, La Seyne (Yard No 1066)
Triple-expansion steam reciprocating, twin screw
After brief service with the Allies, followed by repatriation voyages for French and Syrian servicemen in 1941 and service for the German occupation authority after January

1943, the passenger-cargo liner *Providence*, sister ship of the *Patria* (qv), was laid up at Berre, on the north-east shore of the 'étang' of the same name, beyond Port de Bouc and Lavera. On 5 March 1944 she was driven ashore and sank there after her anchor chains broke in a bad storm. Salvaged on 15 November of that year, she was transferred to Oran for reconstruction, in the course of which considerable changes were made to her accommodation, thereafter providing for many fewer passengers. The *Providence* returned to her owners' Mediterranean service after the Second World War, continuing until 24 October 1951, when she was sold for breaking-up at La Spezia.

Casualties: 0

QUEBEC (1896) ex-*Ebro* (1905) Compagnie Générale Transatlantique (French Line), France

3,342grt; 345ft (105.4m) lbp x 44ft (13.4m) beam
800 passengers in single class
Robert Napier, Govan (Yard No 451)
Triple-expansion steam reciprocating engines, single screw

Acquired from Royal Mail, with a sister *Minho* renamed *Halifax*, later *Montreal* (qv), the *Quebec* and her sister were both lost during the First World War. The *Quebec* struck a mine in the mouth of the River Gironde, off Chassiron, on 24 January 1917 while returning to Bordeaux from San Juan, Puerto Rico. The minefield had been laid in the estuary by the German submarine UC21.

Casualties: 4

QUEEN OF THE NORTH (1969) ex-*Queen of Surrey* (1980) ex-*Stena Danica* (1974) British Columbia Ferry Services Inc, Canada

8,889grt; 410ft (125.0m) loa x 65ft (19.7m) beam
1,541 passengers
Weser Seebeck, Bremerhaven (Yard No 934)
Motor-ship, twin screw

The former Baltic ro-ro passenger/vehicle ferry *Queen of the North*, on passage from Prince Rupert to Port Hardy, foundered off the coast of British Columbia on 22 March 2006. She struck submerged rocks while proceeding in rough seas and sank in the position 53.19N, 129.13W. Although she went down rapidly, an almost complete evacuation was achieved.

Casualties: 2

The *Queen of the North* of BC Ferries approaches the Lions Gate Bridge, Vancouver, in April 1982. *Frank Heine FERRIES*

QUETTA (1881) British India Line, UK

3,484grt; 380ft (115.8m) lbp x 40ft (12.3m) beam
108 passengers in two classes (this figure does not equate to her complement at time of incident)
William Denny, Dumbarton (Yard No 243)
Compound-expansion steam reciprocating, single screw

While bound from Brisbane and Cooktown to London on 28 February 1890, with a complement of 171 passengers and 121 crew (some reports give the total number as 282), the passenger steamer *Quetta*, a graceful, schooner-rigged vessel, struck an uncharted rock off Mount Adolphus Island in the Torres Straits, Queensland. She struck the rock with such force that the underwater hull plating on her port side was ripped away from the bow to midships, exposing the engine room to the elements. In these circumstances the ship settled rapidly precluding any organised life-saving operation. The situation was worsened by the outbreak of panic among the Lascar crew members. Although the loss of life was heavy, the 149 survivors, a surprisingly high number in the circumstances, were either picked up by the cargo ship *Albatross* or succeeded in getting ashore in boats at Somerset, Cape York.

Casualties: 133 (passengers and crew)

RAFFAELLO (1965) Islamic Republic of Iran Navy

45,933grt; 904ft (275.5m) loa x 99ft (30.2m) beam
1,775 passengers in three classes (as built)
Cantieri Riuniti dell'Adriatico, Trieste (Yard No 1864)
Steam turbines, twin screw

The last great transatlantic liner to be built for the Italia Line was sold to Iran in December 1976 for use as a naval accommodation ship based at Bushire in the Arabian Gulf. During the Iran-Iraq conflict, the *Raffaello* was hit by guided missiles fired by Iraqi warplanes during an air attack on Bushire on 21 November 1982. Set on fire aft, the blaze spread throughout the former liner and she was scuttled offshore to prevent the fire from spreading. By the next day the fire had been extinguished but by then the *Raffaello* was a complete write-off.

Casualties: not known

One of the final pair of giant liners built for Italia Line's transatlantic scheduled service, the *Raffaello* was the most recent war loss of a passenger ship, sunk off Bushire during the Iran-Iraq War. *Ian Shiffman*

RAJPUTANA (1925) P&O Line, UK

16,644grt; 568ft (173.1m) loa x 71ft (21.6m) beam
595 passengers in two classes
Harland & Wolff, Greenock (Yard No 661)
Quadruple-expansion steam reciprocating, twin screw

Sister ship of the celebrated *Rawalpindi* and two other ships of that class, the *Rajputana* maintained the service from London to Bombay between the wars. *Real Photos*

When the liner *Rajputana* was requisitioned for duties as an armed merchant cruiser in December 1939, like her sister ships *Ranpura*, *Rawalpindi* and *Ranchi* she had her second funnel removed as part of the conversion. She was deployed escorting Atlantic convoys, and while so engaged on 13 April 1941 she was torpedoed west of Ireland by the German submarine U108. Over a period of two hours she was hit twice, but remained afloat long enough to enable most of those aboard her to evacuate safely. Rescue ships, guided to the scene by Allied patrol aircraft, took aboard the survivors. The *Rajputana* sank stern-first in the position 64.50N, 27.25W, four hours after she was first torpedoed.
Casualties: 41 (6 officers and 35 ratings)

The *Rajputana* seen in her wartime livery as an armed merchant cruiser. *H. B. Christiansen Collection / Online Transport Archive*

RAKUYO MARU (1921) Nippon Yusen Kaisha, Japan

9,419grt; 460ft (140.2m) lbp x 60ft (18.3m) beam
711 passengers in three classes
Mitsubishi, Nagasaki (Yard No 342)
Steam turbines, twin screw
The passenger-cargo ship *Rakuyo Maru*, engaged as one of the infamous 'Hell-ships', left Singapore on 4 September 1944 bound in convoy for Kobe with 1,318 prisoners of war, together with the *Kachidoki Maru* (see Appendix 2). She was torpedoed and sunk en route, on 12 September 1944, by the American submarine USS *Sealion II* when she was about 100 miles north-east of the Paracel Islands, South China Sea, in the position 18.42N, 114.30E. Escorting Japanese destroyers rescued a number of surviving British and Australian prisoners, while others were picked up by American submarines.
Casualties: 1,179 (PoW casualties – crew losses unknown)

The steamship *Rakuyo Maru*, with four consorts, the *Anyo Maru*, *Bokuyo Maru* and *Ginyo Maru*, operated on the service from Japan to ports on the west coast of South America, via the United States. The quartet was introduced by Toyo Kisen Kaisha in the years before and after the First World War and was absorbed into the Nippon Yusen Kaisha fleet when the two companies merged in 1926. *Nippon Yusen Kaisha*

RANGITANE (1929) New Zealand Shipping Co, UK

16,712grt; 553ft (168.5m) loa x 70ft (21.3m) beam
595 passengers in three classes
John Brown, Clydebank (Yard No 522)
Motor-ship, twin screw
While the *Rangitane* was on passage from Auckland to the UK via the Panama Canal on 27 November 1940, with a total complement of 312 passengers and crew, she was intercepted by the German raiders *Komet* and *Orion* when she was some 320 miles north of East Cape, New Zealand. Without warning she was shelled by the two German auxiliaries and left dead in the water, ablaze and badly damaged. She was at risk of sinking suddenly and the danger also existed that the raiders would renew their assault. In spite of these circumstances an orderly abandonment of the survivors was carried out and, once they were in the boats, the *Rangitane* was finished off with a torpedo, sinking in the position 36.58S, 175.22W. The *Rangitane*'s survivors were taken aboard the *Komet* and *Orion*, and held captive for several weeks until, on 21 December 1940, they were landed on the island of Emirau, in the Bismarck Archipelago, where they joined a substantial group of other prisoners, more than 500 in total. Rescued subsequently, these captives had been taken, collectively, from other victim ships by the raiders *Komet* and *Orion*, together with two others, the *Kulmerland* and *Narvik*.
Casualties: 16 (6 passengers and 10 crew)

The New Zealand Line placed three twin-funnelled motor-ships, the *Rangitiki*, *Rangitata* and *Rangitane*, on the Southampton to Wellington service in 1929. This is the ill-fated *Rangitane*. *Trevor Bell*

RASA SAYANG (1956) ex-*Golden Moon* (1980) ex-*Rasa Sayang* (1978) ex-*De Grasse* (1973) ex-*Bergensfjord* (1971) Aphrodite Maritime Co, Greece

18,739grt; 578ft (176.2m) loa x 72ft (22.0m) beam
878 passengers in two classes (as built)
Swan Hunter & Wigham Richardson, Wallsend-on-Tyne (Yard No 1849)
Motor-ship, twin screw
While undergoing repairs at Perama on 27 August 1980, in preparation for a return to commercial service after a period of lay-up, fire broke out in the engine room of the converted cruise ship *Rasa Sayang* and, in spite of all efforts to contain it, the blaze spread throughout the entire vessel. Fifty shipyard workers who were on board at the time, one of whom had, it was believed, started the fire with a welder's torch, were rescued by firemen. To minimise the risk of explosion damage within the port, the *Rasa Sayang* was towed to Kynosoura, about five miles west of Piraeus, where she was run aground

and left to burn herself out. However, before the fire was fully extinguished the *Rasa Sayang* rolled over onto her starboard side to rest, almost completely submerged, in shallow water, a total loss.

Casualties: 0

The *Rasa Sayang*, originally Norwegian America Line's transatlantic passenger liner *Bergensfjord*, anchored at Singapore. *Ian Shiffman*

The half-submerged wreck of the *Rasa Sayang* at Eleusis. *Antonio Scrimali*

RAVENNA (1901) Soc de Navigazione a Vapore Italia, Italy

4,252grt; 363ft (110.6m) lbp x 43ft (13.1m) beam
1,362 passengers
Odero, Foce, Genoa (Yard No 195)
Triple-expansion steam reciprocating, single screw
While returning to Genoa from Buenos Aires on 4 April 1917, the Italian passenger steamship *Ravenna* was torpedoed and sunk by the German submarine *U52* when she was 2 miles off Cape Mele in the Gulf of Genoa. She sank in the position 44.00N, 08.28E.

Casualties: not known

RAWALPINDI (1925) P&O Line, UK

16,697grt; 570ft (173.7m) loa x 71ft (21.6m) beam
600 passengers in two classes
Harland & Wolff, Greenock (Yard No 660)
Quadruple-expansion steam reciprocating, twin screw
The passenger liner *Rawalpindi*, like her three sister ships, was taken over as an armed merchant cruiser in October 1939. During the conversion for naval service, her second funnel was removed. On 23 November 1939 she was patrolling between Iceland and the Faroes when she sighted the German battlecruisers *Scharnhorst* and *Gneisenau* returning to Germany from a commerce raiding sortie in the Atlantic. Because the *Rawalpindi* was hopelessly outmatched, an attempt was made to escape under cover of

a smoke screen into a nearby fog bank, but her retreat was cut off by the *Scharnhorst*. After their warning shots had been ignored, the battlecruisers directed their fire onto the helpless *Rawalpindi* and after only five salvos her guns had been silenced, her bridge and wireless room destroyed and she was on fire amidships. The reason why the German warships did not finish her off there and then – for she was completely at their mercy – was that they had sighted approaching British naval units. They ceased firing and rapidly fled the scene, but not before they had taken prisoner 26 ratings, the occupants of two of three lifeboats that had been lowered in a lull during the action. The eleven survivors in the third boat were rescued by the armed cruiser *Chitral*, herself another P&O liner that had been converted into an AMC. The blazing *Rawalpindi* finally foundered in the position 63.40N, 12.31W, after she had drifted empty and abandoned for three hours.

Casualties: 266 (comprising her Captain, 39 officers and 226 naval ratings)

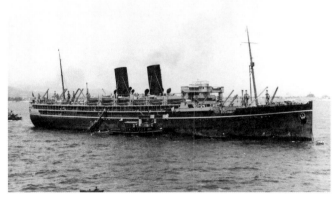

The *Rawalpindi* was one of a class of four ships introduced to the London, Bombay and Far East service in 1925-26, the others being the *Ranchi*, *Ranpura* and *Rajputana*. *Tom Rayner collection*

This famous painting of the *Rawalpindi* by Norman Wilkinson shows the action with the battlecruisers *Gneisenau* and *Scharnhorst*. *P&O*

REGENCY (1952) ex-*Apollon XI* (1981) ex-*Achilleus* (1969) ex-*Semiramis II* (1969) ex-*Orpheus* (1969) ex-*Irish Coast* (1968) Nav Intercontinental SA,

4,811grt; 340ft (103.5m) loa x 52ft (15.8m) beam
340 berthed passengers
Harland & Wolff, Belfast (Yard No 1461)
Motor-ship, twin screw

The former Irish Sea ferry *Irish Coast*, which went through a sequence of name changes following retirement from those duties in 1968, was lost on 11 October 1989 as the *Regency*, following a second career as a Mediterranean cruise ship. She was in collision with the *Caranan* at Batangas, south of Manila, in the Verde Pass, and abandoned aground there, only to become a complete wreck. Partially demolished where she lay, the remains of the hull were towed to Navotas, Manila Bay, for breaking-up to be completed. Casualties: not known

REGINA ELENA (1907) Navigazione Generale Italiana, Italy

7,940grt; 476ft (145.1m) lbp x 53ft (16.2m) beam
1,424 passengers in three classes
Cantieri Liguria Anconitani, Ancona (Yard No 19)
Quadruple-expansion steam reciprocating, twin screw
The Italian passenger steamer *Regina Elena* was torpedoed and sunk on 4 January 1918 by the German submarine UC20 off Tripoli while she was bound from Massowah in East Africa to the Libyan port. Casualties: not known

RELIANCE (1920) ex-*Limburgia* (1922) ex-*Johan Heinrich Burchard* (1920) Hamburg Amerika Line, Germany

19,618grt; 618ft (187.4m) loa x 72ft (21.9m) beam
819 passengers in two classes
Tecklenborg, Geestemünde (Yard No 256)
Triple-expansion steam reciprocating with LP turbine, triple screw

The *Reliance* had a career of some variety, commencing as the centre of a reparations dispute at the end of the First World War and followed by 15 years' service on various routes for three different owners. Her longest period of uninterrupted service was nine years from 1926, with the Hamburg Amerika Line, serving on the North Atlantic run with her sister ship *Resolute*. *Ian Allan Library*

While berthed at Hamburg on 7 August 1938, a fire of unknown cause was discovered aboard the passenger liner *Reliance* in a room on one of the middle decks that was used as a store for fancy-dress decorations and costumes. The fire spread rapidly, causing such severe damage to her superstructure that from the exterior it was possible to see well inside the ship. To prevent her from capsizing she was deliberately scuttled, but even as she settled on the harbour bottom she assumed a quite severe list. It seems that the raging inferno inside her had impaired her stability and when the difficult operation of refloating her was undertaken she had to be carefully trimmed with sand ballast to keep her on an even keel. Several persons, both crew and firemen, were injured in the calamity while trying to bring the blaze under

control. After a dry-dock inspection at the Blohm & Voss shipyard, which revealed that the vessel was beyond recovery, the charred wreck of the *Reliance* was broken up from April 1940.
Casualties: 1 (a night watchman who was unaccounted for)

REMUERA (1911) New Zealand Shipping Co, UK

11,276grt; 502ft (153.0m) loa x 62ft (18.9m) beam
530 passengers in three classes
William Denny, Dumbarton (Yard No 929)
Triple-expansion steam reciprocating, twin screw
On 26 August 1940, as she was returning from Wellington via the Panama Canal to the UK, the *Remuera* was attacked by German torpedo bombers off Rattray Head, on the Scottish north-east coast. There were no passengers aboard her at the time, only her 94-strong crew. The *Remuera* sank in the position 57.50N, 01.54W.
Casualties: 0

REPUBLIC (1903) ex-*Columbus* (1903) White Star Line, UK

15,378grt; 585ft (178.3m) loa x 68ft (20.6m) beam
2,200 passengers in three classes
Harland & Wolff, Belfast (Yard No 345)
Quadruple-expansion steam reciprocating, twin screw
In all the annals of the sea, the loss of the passenger liner *Republic* by collision on 23 January 1909 will be remembered as the first occasion on which wireless telegraphy was used to summon aid to a ship in distress. She was bound from New York to Genoa and Alexandria with 250 First class passengers, 211 Steerage and a crew of around 300 when, early on the fatal day, she became enshrouded in thick fog near Martha's Vineyard, about twenty miles south of Nantucket Island. Inward-bound from Naples in the same vicinity was the Italian emigrant ship *Florida*, carrying 830 passengers. By the time the ships were in sight of each other it was already too late to avoid an impact. The *Florida* crashed bow-on into the *Republic*'s port side, holing her in way of the engine room. This rapidly flooded, causing a severe list to develop, and, when all engine power was lost, the ship was plunged into darkness.

The White Star Line's *Republic* was involved in the first maritime disaster where radio was used to summon help after the Italian emigrant ship *Florida* had collided with her. *Richard de Kerbrech collection*

The wireless office had escaped serious damage and the distress call CQD, translated literally as 'Come, Quickly, Danger' but whose official meaning was 'All ships to the rescue – great danger', was sent out just before the power supply was interrupted and relayed by shore stations that intercepted it. Several ships responded, among them the White Star liner *Baltic*, the French Line's *La Lorraine*, the *New York* of the American Line and the Anchor liner *Furnessia*, the furthest of them having intercepted the message some 175 miles from the scene.

Although the first thirty feet of the *Florida*'s bows had been violently contracted, she was not apparently in immediate danger of sinking and the *Republic*'s passengers and crew were initially transferred to her. After the arrival of the other ships, they were taken aboard the *Baltic* while the *Florida*'s occupants were prudently transhipped to the *La Lorraine* as a precaution. An attempt was made to tow the *Republic* to port by the US Coast Guard cutters *Gresham* and *Seneca*, but before they had proceeded far she foundered. The *Florida* made New York under her own steam and was repaired at the Morse Drydockyard, Brooklyn, later becoming the *Cavour* (qv).
Casualties: 4

REWA (1906) British India Line, UK

7,308grt; 456ft (139.0m) lbp x 56ft (17.1m) beam
165 passengers
William Denny & Bros, Dumbarton (Yard No 762)
Steam turbines, triple screw
The *Rewa* was taken over as a hospital ship during the First World War and she maintained this auxiliary service throughout the conflict. On 4 January 1918 she was nearing the end of a voyage to Avonmouth from Salonica (Thessaloniki), carrying military casualties that she had picked up at Malta and Gibraltar, when she was attacked in the Bristol Channel, nineteen miles from Hartland Point, by the German submarine U55. The fact that she was prominently displaying clear identification of her status and was brightly illuminated did not deter the assault. Her total complement comprised 279 wounded and 80 medical staff, plus her crew of 207. The torpedo struck the *Rewa* amidships on her port side, causing an immediate list and making the launching of lifeboats difficult. Even so, fourteen of her boats were safely got away, taking the majority of the personnel on board, the evacuation helped by excellent discipline and good organisation. The *Rewa* sank in the position 50.55N, 04.49W. Once waterborne, the boats were kept together and flares were used to attract the attention of rescue vessels. Two trawlers and a tanker arrived on the scene early the following day and took the survivors to safety ashore.
Casualties: 4 (all crew)

The sister steamships *Rewa*, illustrated, and *Robilla* were engaged in the service from London to India. *Alex Duncan*

REX (1932) Italia Line, Italy

51,062grt; 880ft (268.2m) loa x 97ft (29.6m) beam
2,258 passengers in four classes
Ansaldo, Sestri Ponente, Genoa (Yard No 296)
Steam turbines, quadruple screw
When war broke out between Italy and Great Britain and France, the transatlantic express liner *Rex* was laid up, first at Pola then, from August 1940, at Trieste. The *Rex* was not involved in the war effort because her large size made her vulnerable to air attack, and even after Italy had capitulated and the Germans had seized her on 9 September 1943 she remained idle. A year later, on 5 September 1944, while she was being moved to what was thought to be a safer location, she ran aground near Semedella, in Capodistria Bay (Koper, Slovenia), south of Trieste. The giant ship, quite unmanoeuvrable and hopelessly exposed, made an easy target, and when she was discovered there by Royal Air Force Beaufighter aircraft, they attacked her with rockets. It was assumed that, hugging the coast, she was heading towards Trieste, not away, to be scuttled there to block the harbour entrance, an action that had to be prevented. The assault continued into the next day, by which time the *Rex* had been hit by a total of 123 rockets. The first attack left her on fire along her entire length, and by the time the second was over she had rolled over onto her port side, sinking in shallow water, close inshore. The wreck was demolished on the spot by Yugoslav interests beginning in August 1947, the final remains being cleared by explosives in June 1958.
Casualties: not known

The transatlantic express liner *Rex*, originally conceived by the Navigazione Generale Italiana Company, was the largest passenger liner to fly the Italian flag and Italy's only holder of the Atlantic Blue Riband, taking the honours westbound in August 1933 with an average speed of 28.92 knots. She was also the largest Italian merchant ship sunk in the Second World War. *Author's collection*

Ablaze and capsized onto her port side, the *Rex* is seen while under attack from RAF aircraft in September 1944.
L. L. von Münching

RHONE (1865) Royal Mail Line, UK

2,738grt; 310ft (94.5m) lbp x 40ft (12.2m) beam
313 passengers
Millwall Ironworks, Millwall (Yard No not known)
Compound-expansion steam reciprocating, single screw

The Royal Mail Line suffered a disaster of unprecedented magnitude on 29 October 1867 when, during a hurricane, it lost three of its ships and had three others severely damaged. The misfortune occurred while the vessels were anchored off St Thomas, one of the Virgin Islands in the West Indies. They were the screw steamships *Rhone*, *Solent*, *Tyne*, *Wye* and *Derwent*, together with the old paddler *Conway*, the *Rhone* being the latest addition to the Royal Mail fleet. With the hurricane fast approaching the anchorage, steam was raised on the *Rhone*, the intention being to ride out the storm while still secured by anchor in the deeper but still relatively sheltered water off Peter Island. This proved to be a successful move, at least until there was a lull in the weather, at which time it was decided to raise anchor and head for the open sea. The manoeuvre had been almost completed when the hurricane struck again with renewed vigour, casting the *Rhone* onto the rocks off Salt Island, where she broke up and sank. There had been 145 persons aboard her, 16 of whom were passengers. Of these, only 22 survived, all but one of them members of the crew.

The *Wye* succeeded in getting out of the crowded harbour only to be smashed onto the rocks of Buck Island, where she became a total wreck. From aboard her there were only 28 survivors, but the loss of life could have been greater; fortunately, she was not carrying passengers at the time, only her 69-strong crew. As for the other ships, the *Derwent* and *Conway* were both dragged from their moorings, the former becoming a total loss, the latter receiving extensive damage. The *Solent* and *Tyne* survived the catastrophe but lost their masts and all standing rigging together with the majority of their deck gear. In all, sixty vessels had been anchored at or near St Thomas on the day that this fearsome hurricane struck the area, and all but two were lost or received damage to some extent.

Casualties: 164 (123 from the *Rhone* and 41 from the *Wye*)

RIO DE JANEIRO MARU (1930) Osaka Shosen Kaisha, Japan

9,627grt; 461ft (140.5m) lbp x 62ft (18.9m) beam
1,136 passengers in two classes
Mitsubishi, Nagasaki (Yard No 457)
Motor-ship, twin screw

The *Rio de Janeiro Maru*, sister ship of the *Buenos Aires Maru*, operated a round-the-world service via South America.
Alex Duncan

The passenger-cargo ship *Rio de Janeiro Maru* was converted into a submarine tender late in 1941 for service with the Imperial Japanese Navy. She was attacked near Truk, in the Caroline Islands, on 17 February 1944 by bombers from US aircraft carriers and sank in the position 07.20N, 151.53E.

Casualties: not known

RIO DE LA PLATA (1950) Empresa Lineas Maritimas Argentinas, Argentina

11,317grt; 550ft (167.5m) loa x 66ft (20.0m) beam
372 passengers in single class
Ansaldo, Sestri Ponente, Genoa (Yard No 890)
Motor-ship, twin screw

On 19 November 1964, while undergoing a refit at a dockyard on Demarchi Island, Buenos Aires, the *Rio de la Plata* caught fire. The outbreak was started by an acetylene torch that was being used in a hold. She was completely burned out and subsequently declared a constructive total loss. The badly listing wreck remained in its situation until 1968 when it was finally broken up locally.

Casualties: 0

RIVIERA (1951) ex-*Varna* (1979) ex-*Ocean Monarch* (1967) Dolphin (Hellas) Shipping, Greece

13,581grt; 516ft (157.3m) loa x 72ft (22.0m) beam
600 passengers in single class
Vickers-Armstrongs, Newcastle-upon-Tyne (Yard No 119)
Steam turbines, twin screw

Sent to Perama for a refit as a precursor to re-entering cruise operations from Venice, the former passenger-cargo liner *Riviera* was engulfed by fire during the night of 28 May 1981. The refurbishment work had dragged on since its commencement in 1979, hindered by her owners' financial problems. Shortly before the outbreak of fire it had been announced that the ship was due to return to service that season under the name *Reina del Mar*, a change of identity that, in the event, never happened. The fire had started in her boiler room and spread to the engine room. By morning her entire interior was completely destroyed and the superstructure had caved inwards. The listing ship's chains were cut and she was towed to an anchorage south of Kynosoura peninsula, only to go aground on Salamina Island. A salvage tug attempted to refloat the still burning ship and tow her offshore, but on 1 June she capsized onto her starboard side and sank about half a mile offshore.

Casualties: 0

ROBERT LEY (1939) Deutsche Arbeitsfront, Germany (managed by Hamburg Amerika Line)

27,288grt; 669ft (203.9m) loa x 79ft (24.1m) beam
1,774 passengers in single class
Howaldtswerke, Hamburg (Yard No 754)
Diesel-electric, twin screw

Following the outbreak of war in Europe in September 1939, the government cruise ship *Robert Ley* was converted into a hospital ship, later serving as a naval accommodation ship stationed first at Gotenhafen (Gdynia), then at Pillau (Baltiysk). During the evacuation of Germany's eastern territories in early 1945, Operation 'Hannibal', the *Robert Ley* made a westbound voyage that took her as far as Hamburg,

where she arrived on 24 March 1945. That night, prior to the disembarkation of the vessel, the port was subjected to one of the heaviest Allied air raids of the war, during the course of which she was hit and set on fire. Completely burned out, many of the refugees who were still aboard her lost their lives. In 1947 the wrecked liner was towed to the United Kingdom for breaking-up, arriving at Inverkeithing on 6 June.
Casualties: not known

Although some 20 purpose-built cruise ships were planned for the 'Kraft durch Freude' (Strength Through Joy) movement, in the event only two were constructed, the second of these commemorating the director of the Deutsche Arbeitsfront organisation, Dr Robert Ley. The cruise ship *Robert Ley* entered service in April 1939 but had completed only a few cruises before the outbreak of war diverted her to less frivolous activities. *Author's collection*

The bombed and burned-out wreck of the *Robert Ley* was towed to Inverkeithing for breaking-up, where she ended her days alongside the British battleship HMS *Rodney*. *L. L. von Münching*

ROHILLA (1906) British India Line, UK

7,409grt; 460ft (140.3m) lbp x 56ft (17.2m) beam
165 passengers
Harland & Wolff, Belfast (Yard No 381)
Quadruple-expansion steam reciprocating, twin screw

British India Line's *Rohilla*, seen as the Boer War transport No 5. *Ian Allan Library*

The passenger-cargo steamship *Rohilla*, sister of the *Rewa* (qv), was taken over as a hospital ship on the outbreak of the First World War. On 30 October 1914 she ran onto the rocks south of Whitby, at Saltwick Nab, while on passage from Leith to Dunkirk in a gale. The Whitby, Redcar and Upgang lifeboats went to her aid but, because of the conditions, they were prevented at first from taking off any of the 229 persons aboard her. Ultimately, 146 were rescued, including the *Rohilla*'s entire complement of nurses, but the remainder perished in the rough seas.
Casualties: 83

ROHILLA MARU (1880) ex-*Rohilla* (1900)
Toyo Kisen Kaisha, Japan

3,501grt; 400ft (121.9m) loa x 40ft (12.3m) beam
184 passengers in two classes
Caird, Greenock (Yard No 217)
Compound-expansion steam reciprocating, single screw
On 7 July 1905 the former P&O passenger-cargo steamship *Rohilla Maru* was wrecked on the Manaita Rock, at Ujina in the Inland Sea, Japan.
Casualties: not known

ROHNA (1926) British India Line, UK

8,602grt; 461ft (140.5m) lbp x 61ft (18.6m) beam
161 berthed passengers in three classes plus
3,851 deck passengers
Hawthorn Leslie, Hebburn-on-Tyne (Yard No 542)
Quadruple-expansion steam reciprocating, twin screw

One of the worst British losses of the Second World War, British India Line's *Rohna* was the first passenger ship, possibly the first merchant ship to be sunk by a missile. Prior to the war she had served on the Far East service with her sister, the *Rajula*. *P&O*

The passenger-cargo liner *Rohna*, which had been converted into a troopship, was one of the first merchant ships to fall victim to a form of guided missile, in her case a glider bomb launched by a German warplane. She was lost on 26 November 1943 while bound from Oran to India in convoy. Loaded to capacity, she was carrying a total of 2,232 persons, of whom around 2,000 were Allied troops, the majority American, and 195 were members of her crew. Off Djidjelli, Algeria, the convoy came under attack from German aircraft, and the *Rohna* was struck amidships on her port side by the projectile, its explosion causing extensive damage. Fires were started and the aft end of the ship was soon engulfed in flames. It was impossible to launch any of the port-side boats and many of those from the starboard side capsized through overcrowding, the result being heavy loss of life. Fourteen British troops who had been aboard the *Rohna* were among the 1,083 survivors. She sank by the stern after an hour and a half in the position 36.56N, 05.20E, her engines and boilers breaking free and bursting through the hull plating as she went under.

Casualties: 1,149 (1,029 American troops and 120 crew) Other reports state that the *Rohna*'s complement on her final voyage was 2,195, of whom 1,170 persons were casualties, including 1,050 troops and 120 crew.

ROMA (1926) Italia Line, Italy

serving under the wartime name AQUILA
32,583grt; 759ft (231.3m) loa x 82ft (25.0m) beam
1,675 passengers in three classes
Ansaldo, Sestri Ponente, Genoa (Yard No 277)
Steam turbines, quadruple screw

Laid up at Naples in June 1940, the passenger liner *Roma* was taken over by the Italian Navy in July 1941 for conversion into an aircraft carrier. Renamed *Aquila* in February 1942, she was subjected to the most extreme alterations that left her quite unrecognisable. A new raked bow, a cruiser stern and anti-torpedo bulges were fitted to her hull, an offset island superstructure was erected on the flight deck, and her original turbine engines were replaced by a new set, originally intended for cruisers. Progress with the reconstruction was slow and by the time of the Italian capitulation on 8 September 1943 was still not fully complete. The Germans seized her, but although she was virtually ready for sea trials no further work on her was carried out, besides which shipyard workers had sabotaged vital onboard installations. Apart from that she had not received a complement of aircraft.

On 20 June 1944, and again on 6 January 1945, the *Aquila* was bombed during air raids on Genoa. On 20 April 1945 Italian one-man torpedoes sank her at her moorings to prevent the Germans from scuttling her as a blockship in the entrance to Genoa harbour. The wreck was refloated in 1946 and towed to La Spezia three years later, when consideration was given to completing the carrier conversion. However, in the wake of the Second World War there was no appetite for committing that sort of expenditure and the nature of her alterations made it impossible for her to be re-converted into a liner, so she was broken up locally from 1951.

Casualties: not known

Prior to 1939 the *Roma* had served on the Genoa to New York run with her near sister *Augustus*, first for Navigazione Generale Italiana and, from 1932, for Italia Line. *Real Photos*

The Italian aircraft carrier *Aquila*, the former *Roma*, at Genoa. She was never completed and saw no war service. *Imperial War Museum (C5319)*

ROMANTIKA (1939) ex-*Romanza* (1991) ex-*Aurelia* (1970) ex-*Beaverbrae* (1954) ex-*Huascaran* (1947) New Paradise Cruises Ltd, Cyprus

9,511grt; 469ft (148.6m) loa x 60ft (18.4m) beam
900 passengers
Blohm & Voss, Steinwerder, Hamburg (Yard No 518)
Diesel-electric, single screw

Taken as a war reparation, the former Hamburg Amerika Line passenger-cargo ship *Huascaran* was converted into an austerity emigrant carrier with 775 berths for the Canadian Pacific Line. Sold on to Italian owners for similar employment, she was later adapted into a cruise ship, exploiting the large amount of passenger accommodation with which she had been fitted. In this capacity the *Romantika* was destroyed in a fire that broke out on 4 October 1997 during a cruise to Israel and Egypt when she was south-west of Cyprus, in the position 33.47N, 32.52E, returning from Port Said. Her complement of 487 passengers and crew were transferred to the cruise ship *Princesa Victoria*. She was beached at Limassol, in Akrotiri Bay, the next day. It took four days to extinguish the fire and the severely damaged *Romantika* was abandoned as a total loss. Casualties: 0

The Chandris cruise ship *Romantika* at Piraeus. *Ian Shiffman*

ROTORUA (1910) New Zealand Line, UK

11,130grt; 502ft (153.0m) loa x 62ft (18.9m) beam
534 passengers in three classes
William Denny, Dumbarton (Yard No 915)
Triple-expansion steam reciprocating, triple screw

The liner *Rotorua* was returning from Wellington, New Zealand, on 22 March 1917, when she was torpedoed without warning and sunk by the German submarine UC17, 24 miles east of Start Point, in the position 50.18N, 02.56W.

Casualties: 1

ROTORUA (1911) ex-*Shropshire* (1923) Federal Steam Navigation Co, UK

10,890grt; 544ft (165.8m) loa x 61ft (18.6m) beam
671 passengers in three classes
John Brown, Clydebank (Yard No 400)
Quadruple-expansion steam reciprocating, twin screw

The replacement passenger-cargo ship *Rotorua* operated as a troopship from September 1939. She was sunk on 11 December 1940 while returning to Avonmouth from Lyttelton, New Zealand, and Halifax, Nova Scotia, torpedoed by the German submarine U96 in the position 58.56N, 11.20W, about 110 miles west of St Kilda, Scotland. At the time the *Rotorua* was carrying 150 persons, of whom 27 were service passengers, one was a Chinese prisoner and the remainder were her crew of 122 men. Two of the survivors were taken prisoner.
Casualties: 21 (3 service personnel, her Master and 17 crew)

The New Zealand Line acquired a replacement *Rotorua* in 1922 when they took over the former Federal Line's *Shropshire*, which had been laid up following a serious fire. She was fully rebuilt and converted to oil-firing before she made her first voyage from Southampton to Wellington in March 1923, joining sister *Remuera*. *H. B. Christiansen Collection / Online Transport Archive*

ROYAL EDWARD (1908) ex-*Cairo* (1910) Royal Line, UK

11,117grt; 545ft (166.1m) loa x 60ft (18.3m) beam
1,000 passengers in two classes
Fairfield, Glasgow (Yard No 450)
Steam turbines, triple screw

The sinking of the troopship *Royal Edward* in August 1915 was only exceeded in its gravity by the loss of the *Lusitania* just three months earlier and by the same means. She is seen here as the *Cairo*, one of a pair of passenger ships built originally to the account of the Egyptian Mail Steamship Company for an express service between Alexandria and Marseilles. *Tom Rayner collection*

Among the worst British shipping disasters of the First World War was the sinking of the liner *Royal Edward* on 13 August 1915 while she was serving as a troopship supporting the Gallipoli campaign. The German submarine UB14 torpedoed her six miles west of the island of Kandeliusa, in the Aegean Sea, in the position 36.31N, 26.51E. The *Royal Edward* had been bound from Avonmouth to Mudros via Alexandria and was carrying 1,366 troops and a 220-man crew. She sank rapidly by the stern and, despite the efforts of the hospital ship *Soudan*, two French destroyers and a number of trawlers, which arrived on the scene to render assistance, only 651 survivors were rescued.
Casualties: 935 (803 troops and 132 crew)

ROYAL PACIFIC (1965) ex-*Empress* (1991) ex-*Empress of Australia* (1985) Anchor of the Seas Ltd, Bahamas

13,176grt; 445ft (135.6m) loa x 70ft (21.3m) beam
623 passengers
Cockatoo Docks & Engineering Co, Sydney (Yard No 220)
Motor-ship, twin screw

Following service on the Sydney to Hobart and Burnie route, the *Empress of Australia* moved to the Mediterranean for continued scheduled passenger service before undergoing a thorough conversion into the cruise ship *Empress*. Later, as the *Royal Pacific*, she was in collision with the Taiwanese factory trawler *Terfu* during a 'gambling' cruise from Singapore on 23 August 1992. The accident occurred when she was twelve miles off Port Dickson, in the Strait of Malacca. Struck and holed on her port side, she sank in the position 02.27N, 101.36E.
Casualties: 9

ROYAL PACIFIC (1967) ex-*Riviera* (2004) ex-*D. Juan* (2000) ex-*Crown Del Mar* (1994) ex-*Las Palmas de Gran Canaria* (1988) King Crown International, Taiwan (Panama flag)

8,983 grt; 429ft (130.6m) loa x 63ft (19.2m) beam
500 berthed and 250 deck passengers (as built)
Union Naval de Levante, Valencia (Yard No 94)
Motor-ship, twin screw

The *Royal Pacific* (1967) spent the first twenty-one years of her career as the Spanish-flag *Las Palmas de Gran Canaria*, seen here in April 1973. *Kenneth Wightman*

Built originally as a ro-ro passenger ferry, the *Royal Pacific* had been engaged in full-time cruise service from around the turn of the millennium, latterly operated in the form of casino cruises out of Kaohsiung, Taiwan. She caught fire in Kaohsiung harbour on 29 June 2005 while undergoing repairs. The fire-fighters pumped large volumes of water into the vessel to extinguish the blaze and as a result she capsized the next day with her starboard side under water. The fire was suspected as having been started by an electrical short circuit in her engine room. The *Royal Pacific* was broken up in situ, bringing her diverse 38 year career to an end.
Casualties: 0

RUTH ALEXANDER (1913) ex-*Callao* (1922) ex-*Sierra Cordoba* (1917) Dollar Line, USA

8,226grt; 439ft (133.8m) lbp x 56ft (17.1m) beam
739 passengers in three classes (as built)
Stettiner Vulcan, Stettin-Bredow (Yard No 329)
Triple-expansion steam reciprocating, twin screw
The first American passenger ship to be lost in the Second World War was the *Ruth Alexander*, which was bombed and sunk by Japanese aircraft on 31 December 1941 off the north-west coast of Borneo, in the position 01.00N, 119.10W. At the time she had been on passage from Manila to Balik Papan.
Casualties: 1 (a crew member)

RUY BARBOSA (1913) ex-*Caxias* (1924) ex-*Bahia Laura* (1917) Brazilian Government

9,791grt; 491ft (149.7m) lbp x 59ft (18.0m) beam
2,700 passengers in two classes (as built)
Bremer Vulkan, Vegesack (Yard No 562)
Triple-expansion steam reciprocating, twin screw
While returning to Brazil from Hamburg on 31 July 1934, the passenger steamship *Ruy Barbosa*, a former German vessel whose passenger accommodation was largely allocated to emigrant travellers, was wrecked at Mindello, seven miles north of Leixoes, Oporto, in Portugal.
Casualties: not known

S

SAALE (1886) Norddeutscher Lloyd, Germany

5,381grt; 438ft (133.5m) lbp x 48ft (14.6m) beam
1,240 passengers
Fairfield, Govan (Yard No 312)
Triple-expansion steam reciprocating, single screw
When fire broke out at the Norddeutscher Lloyd's pier at Hoboken on 30 June 1900, the passenger-cargo ship *Saale* was the worst affected of the passenger ships present. The fire started in the pier buildings due to spontaneous combustion in bales of cotton. This in turn set light to a quantity of barrels of whisky. The fire spread to the ships alongside the quays while tugs tried frantically to tow them clear. In spite of their heroic actions, the tugmen's efforts were largely in vain. So rapid was the passage of the conflagration that the entire pier complex was ablaze within minutes and, to prevent the fire spreading to the Hamburg Amerika wharves alongside, the officials there agreed to the demolition of the pier by explosives to create a fire gap.

The *Saale*, which was completely gutted, was cut adrift and sank on Communipaw Flats. The intense heat destroyed her upper decks. Apart from the *Kaiser Wilhelm der Grosse*, which escaped intact, the other liners present, the *Bremen* and *Main*, also sustained severe damage. An explosion on the former, which at the time had a party of women and children visitors aboard, worsened her state of devastation. Both ships, badly burned, were eventually towed upstream where they ran aground. It was estimated subsequently that more than $2 million worth of damage was caused by the fire. In spite of the extent of the destruction, all three ships were later raised and repaired. The *Bremen* and *Main* were returned to their transatlantic passenger-carrying schedules, surviving until 1929 and 1925 respectively. The *Saale* was rebuilt as the freighter *J. L. Luckenbach* and continued in service until 1924.
Casualties: 109 on the *Saale*, 68 on the *Main* and 12 on the *Bremen*

The Norddeutscher Lloyd steamship *Saale* on fire off New Jersey on 30 June 1900. *World Ship Society*

SAGAING (1925) Henderson Line, UK

7,994grt; 454ft (138.4m) lbp x 61ft (18.6m) beam
150 passengers in single class
William Denny, Dumbarton (Yard No 1167)
Triple-expansion steam reciprocating, single screw

The passenger-cargo ship *Sagaing* was at Trincomalee, Ceylon (Sri Lanka), on 9 April 1942, in the process of disembarkation, when she was bombed by Japanese aircraft and set on fire. Her passengers, as well as the majority of her 138-man crew, were safely evacuated ashore. Towed from the dockside and beached, the *Sagaing* was later refloated, only to be declared a constructive total loss. Rather than lose use of her entirely, it was decided that, with all structure above her main deck removed, she could be utilised as a makeshift pier, and for this purpose she was deliberately scuttled in August 1943, with her truncated hull placed keel-down in a specially dredged mud berth.

Casualties: 2 (both crew)

ST DAVID (1932) Fishguard & Rosslare Railways & Harbours Co, UK

2,702grt; 327ft (99.7m) lbp x 47ft (14.2m) beam
1,050 passengers
Cammell Laird, Birkenhead (Yard No 982)
Steam turbines, twin screw

The Irish Sea ferry *St David* was taken over as a hospital carrier in September 1939 and in this capacity she was in the thick of the action during the evacuation of Dunkirk. She was also present during the later landings at Sicily, Salerno and Anzio. During the latter operation, while working a shuttle between the beachheads and the ports of Naples and Bari carrying wounded, she was attacked by German aircraft, bombed and sunk on 24 January 1944. She sank within five minutes in the position 41.10N, 12.21E, between 20 and 25 miles out to sea from the invasion beachhead, allowing little time for escape.

Casualties: 57

The Fishguard & Rosslare Irish Sea passenger ferry *St David* is seen here as a hospital carrier alongside the east pier at Dunkirk surrounded by smoke at the height of the evacuation operation on 29 May 1940. She survived this onslaught only to be lost during the Anzio landings in January 1944.
Imperial War Museum (HU73187)

ST LOUIS (1895) ex-*Louisville* (1920) ex-*St Louis* (1917) American Line, USA

11,629grt; 554ft (168.8m) loa x 63ft (19.2m) beam
1,340 passengers in three classes
William Cramp, Philadelphia (Yard No 277)
Quadruple-expansion steam reciprocating, twin screw

Following auxiliary service in the First World War, the passenger-cargo liner *St Louis* was sent to Hoboken, New Jersey, for a refit prior to return to commercial service, during

the course of which, on 8 December 1920, she was burned out. To prevent her from capsizing and leaving a complicated salvage recovery operation, she was deliberately scuttled. After she had been refloated, the *St Louis* remained tied up inactive at New York for almost four years. Purchased by the Anderson Overseas Corporation, some consideration was given to restoring her as a dedicated cruise ship, but the cost for the extensive work involved was prohibitive. Finally, after she had been sold to Genoese ship-breakers, she left New York on 20 May 1924 in tow of the *Zwarte Zee* bound for Italy and demolition.

Casualties: not known

The American Line passenger ship *St Louis*, sister of the *St Paul*, saw troop transport service during the First World War as the USS *Louisville*, during which employment she sported two very distinct camouflage colour schemes. *US National Archives*

ST LOUIS (1929) Hamburg Amerika Line, Germany

16,732grt; 574ft (174.9m) loa x 73ft (22.3m) beam
973 passengers in three classes
Bremer Vulkan, Vegesack (Yard No 670)
Motor-ship, twin screw

The German motor-ship *St Louis*, which entered service on the North Atlantic route in March 1929, was in the headlines in the summer of 1939 when she was involved in a diplomatically sensitive mission conveying 900 Jewish refugees to Havana, Cuba. The full story has been chronicled in the book and film *Voyage of the Damned*. *World Ship Society*

In January 1940 the passenger liner *St Louis* became a naval accommodation ship based at Kiel. Three years later, on 30 August 1944, she was bombed and severely damaged during an air raid on the port. The partly burned-out liner was beached and abandoned until 1946, when she was refloated. She was then towed to Hamburg where, secured at the Altona landing stage, she provided temporary hotel accommodation for the port's homeless. The *St Louis* was judged to be

unworthy of restoration and, once her humanitarian role was concluded, she departed Hamburg in tow for Bremerhaven, where she arrived on 15 April 1950 for breaking-up.
Casualties: not known

ST PAUL (1895) American Line, USA

serving under the wartime name KNOXVILLE
11,629grt; 554ft (168.8m) loa x 63ft (19.2m) beam
1,370 passengers in three classes, reduced to two classes
in 1913
William Cramp, Philadelphia (Yard No 278)
Quadruple-expansion steam reciprocating, twin screw

American Line's *St Paul*, sister of the *St Louis*.
Richard de Kerbrech

The USS *Knoxville*, the former *St Paul*, is seen capsized onto her starboard side between the New York piers while fitting out as an armed transport. The cause of the incident remained a mystery, but conspiracy theorists said it was linked to an incident in the Solent that occurred ten years earlier to the day, when she rammed and sank the British cruiser HMS *Gladiator*.
Author's collection

As she was approaching her pier at New York on 25 April 1918, following the completion of her conversion from a passenger ship to a troopship, the transatlantic passenger-cargo liner *St Paul*, renamed *Knoxville*, suddenly developed a list to port, which increased alarmingly and caused her masts to snap off as they caught against structures on the quayside. The ship came to rest on her port side, half submerged, with her funnels almost jammed against the pier. A complicated salvage operation ensued, which necessitated the removal of the liner's funnels and other fittings on her upper deck. She was eventually righted, by the Merritt, Chapman & Scott salvage organisation, using a line of A-shaped levers, 21 in all, erected on her hull and connected to steam winches ashore, a system later used by the same concern to raise the *Lafayette* (ex-*Normandie* – qv). The *St*

Paul was eventually restored at considerable expense, returning to service on the American Line's New York to Cherbourg and Southampton route under her original name in March 1920; however, just three years later she was laid up, then sold for breaking-up. No wholly satisfactory explanation was ever given for this unexpected accident.
Casualties: not known

SALAZIE (1883) Messageries Maritimes, France

4,255grt; 413ft (125.9m) lbp x 41ft (12.5m) beam
209 passengers in three classes
Messageries Maritimes, La Ciotat (Yard No 56)
Compound-expansion steam reciprocating, single screw
On 24 November 1912 the passenger steamship *Salazie* was caught in an intense cyclone 100 miles from Diego Suarez and was driven ashore on the Nosykomba Reefs, north of Vohemar, Madagascar. Her passengers and crew had to survive for three days in primitive shelter until they were rescued by the steamer *L'Eugene Grosos* of the Cie Havraise Peninsulaire. The *Salazie* broke up on the coastline where she had come to rest and became a total wreck, later sold for breaking-up in situ.
Casualties: 1 (an officer)

SALEM EXPRESS (1966) ex-*Al Tahra* (1988) ex-*Lord Sinai* (1984) ex-*Nuits Saint Georges* (1982) ex-*Fred Scamaroni* (1980) Samatour Shipping Co, Egypt

4,771grt; 377ft (115.0m) loa x 58ft (17.8m) beam
1,420 passengers
Chantiers de la Méditerranée, La Seyne (Yard No 1367)
Motor-ship, twin screw
During a voyage in stormy weather crossing the Red Sea on 4 December 1991 with 644 persons on board, mainly Egyptian passengers, the passenger ferry *Salem Express* struck a coral reef and sank. She was bound from Jeddah to Safaga and Suez when the accident occurred, some six miles out from Safaga, in what were known to be shark-infested waters. Whether any of the high death toll was attributed to this additional hazard is not known. Of her total complement, 180 were rescued.
Casualties: 464

SALIER (1875) Norddeutscher Lloyd, Germany

3,098grt; 354ft (107.6m) lbp x 39ft (11.9m) beam
942 passengers in two classes
Earle's, Hull (Yard No 185)
Compound-expansion steam reciprocating, single screw
During a voyage from Bremen to La Plata, soon after leaving La Coruna, the passenger steamship *Salier* ran onto the rocks north of Cape Corrubedo, south of Cape Finisterre, near the entrance to Arosa Bay on 8 December 1896. Struggling through storm-force winds and heavy seas, she had been forced inshore towards the treacherous shoals in that region.
Casualties: 279 (passengers and crew, including her Master)

The *Salier* commenced her career in the transatlantic service, but was later switched to the Bremen to South America route. *Arnold Kludas*

SALLY ALBATROSS (1980) ex-*Viking Saga* (1986)
P/R Sally Albatross Rederi, Finland

14,330grt (25,611grt from 1992); 476ft (145.2m) loa x 84ft (25.5m) beam (521ft (158.9m) loa from 1992)
2,000 passengers (as first built)
Wartsila, Turku (Yard No 1247); rebuilt by Finnyards, Rauma (Yard No 309)
Motor-ship, twin screw

The Finnish-flag Baltic ro-ro ferry *Sally Albatross*. Her original machinery and cut-down hull were salvaged for the construction of a replacement vessel of the same name. *Mike Lennon*

The fire-damaged *Sally Albatross* prior to the commencement of the reconstruction work. *Mike Lennon*

The Baltic ro-ro passenger ferry *Sally Albatross* was extensively damaged in a fire that broke out aboard her on 9 January 1990 while she was undergoing repairs at the Finnboda Varf yard at Stockholm. She was declared a constructive total loss, but on the basis that her owners could retain her hull and original machinery for reconstruction as a new ferry. The gutted ship arrived at Mäntyluoto under tow from Stockholm on 27 June 1990, and entered the Rauma Repola O/Y shipyard to have her charred superstructure removed down to the lower vehicle deck level. Three months later she was towed to Naantali where the remaining hull was cut down and dismantled further to form the foundation of the reincarnated vessel of the same name, which was to be constructed by Finnyards at Rauma.

Two years later a new, somewhat larger *Sally Albatross* entered service, but this vessel, a dedicated cruise ship from the outset, was not lucky either. On 2 March 1994 she was grounded in icy conditions during a day cruise from Helsinki and began to flood, taking on a 13-degree list that rapidly increased to 25 degrees, until finally she settled in 35 feet or so of water. There were no casualties from her 1,101 passengers and 158 crew. The question was, should she too be abandoned as a total loss and scrapped or be salvaged and repaired? In the event she was recovered at a cost of $36 million, but her owners felt that the second *Sally Albatross* was fatefully unlucky, like her predecessor, so immediately disposed of her. She became the *Leeward*, later changing her name a number of times, and today (2009) she remains in service.

Casualties: not known

The *Sally Albatross*, the second ship of the name but with the same hull and engines, was also an unlucky vessel. She was seriously damaged after becoming stranded in icy conditions in March 1994. *Mike Lennon*

SALSETTE (1909) P&O Line, UK

5,842grt; 440ft (134.1m) loa x 53ft (16.2m) beam
220 passengers in two classes
Caird, Greenock (Yard No 314)
Quadruple-expansion steam reciprocating, twin screw
The passenger-cargo ship *Salsette* continued to operate the commercial service from London to Sydney via Bombay, Colombo and Melbourne throughout 1916 and 1917. Outward-bound from Tilbury with civilian passengers and mails on 20 July 1917, she was torpedoed by the German submarine UB40 in the English Channel, fifteen miles southwest of Portland Bill. Struck forward on her starboard side, the detonation destroyed many lifeboats and killed crew

members in that area. Although the *Salsette* remained afloat for only five minutes, all her remaining lifeboats were launched and she was abandoned in an orderly fashion. The survivors were taken to Weymouth.

Casualties: 15 (all crew)

Constructed for the Tilbury to Aden and Bombay service, the *Salsette* was one of the earliest ships in the P&O fleet to have a white hull and buff funnels. *Tom Rayner collection*

SALTA (1911) Société Générale des Transports Maritimes à Vapeur (SGTM), France

7,284grt; 449ft (136.9m) loa x 53ft (16.2m) beam
219 passengers in three classes
Forges et Chantiers de la Méditerranée, La Seyne
(Yard No 1048)
Triple-expansion steam reciprocating, twin screw

The French passenger ship *Salta*, serving as a British hospital ship, having been transferred to the Admiralty for this purpose, was bound from Southampton to Le Havre on 10 April 1917 when she struck a mine half a mile north of the Whistle Buoy, in the Le Havre Roads. She sank in the position 49.32N, 00.02W. There were no wounded servicemen aboard her, her function at the time being the carriage of hospital stores, but she did have RAMC personnel on board as well as her crew, many of whom were killed. It was reported that the *Salta* had strayed into a minefield laid by friendly forces. However, some sources suggest that the mine that the *Salta* struck had been laid by a submarine, presumably German.

Casualties: 86

The French steamship *Salta*, seen here as a First World War hospital ship, normally operated between Marseilles and South America. *World Ship Society*

SAMAINA (1962) ex-*Mary Poppins* (1976) ex-*Gosta Berling* (1975) ex-*Escapade* (1967) ex-*Gosta Berling* (1967) ex-*Nils Holgersson* (1967) Samaina Shipping Co (Arkadia Lines SA), Greece

3,783grt; 361ft (110.0m) loa x 50ft (15.3m) beam
900 passengers
Hanseatische, Hamburg (Yard No 18)
Motor-ship, twin screw

The ro-ro passenger-cargo ferry *Samaina* was in collision with the Greek Navy fast attack craft *Anthipoploiarhos Kostakos* on 4 November 1996 off the island of Samos. The naval vessel sank with the loss of four lives. The damaged *Samaina* was taken to Eleusis where she was laid up, remaining idle and unrepaired for the next five years while liability claims were heard in the Greek courts. Although the Master and officers of the *Samaina* were cleared of any responsibility in an official enquiry, the *Samaina* was arrested as surety for the compensation sought by relatives of the dead naval crewmen. The saga concluded with a ruling that blamed both parties equally for the incident and led to the sale of the *Samaina* to Indian ship-breakers. She arrived at Alang on 21 July 2000 for the commencement of demolition.

Casualties: 0 (from the *Samaina*)

The ferry *Samaina* is seen at Piraeus in July 1990. Beyond her starboard bow is an unidentified former Sealink ferry. *Frank Heine FERRIES*

SANTA ANA (1965) ex-*Stena Nordica* (1973) Consolidada de Ferrys CA, Venezuela

2,607grt; 262ft (79.8m) loa x 53ft (16.2m) beam
935 passengers
Chantiers de la Seine Maritime, Le Trait (Yard No 173)
Motor-ship, twin screw

While bound from Puerto la Cruz to the offshore island of Punta de Piedras, both Venezuela, on 7 May 1980, fire broke out in the engine room of the passenger ro-ro ferry *Santa Ana* 4 hours after she had left port. In addition to her crew, she was carrying 115 passengers. The crew were unable to extinguish the fire, which rapidly spread beyond its source, and they abandoned ship to be picked up by another ferry, the *Cacica Isabel*, which also took the *Santa Ana* in tow. The blazing ferry was beached at Punta Charagato, at the northern end of Isla de Cubagua, in the position 10.51N, 64.10W. There she was completely gutted, her metalwork collapsed and distorted by the intense heat, and abandoned as a total loss. The partially submerged wreck was still there more than fifteen years later. Casualties: 0

The wreck of the burned-out *Santa Ana* at Isla de Cubagua on 24 January 1996. Her partially open clam-shell bow door, more pronounced in the second view, somehow adds to the sense of desolation. *Both Frank Heine FERRIES*

SANTA BARBARA (1929) Grace Line, USA

serving under the wartime name McCAWLEY [AP-10]
8,156grt; 486ft (142.0m) lbp x 64ft (19.5m) beam
157 passengers in single class
Furness, Haverton Hill (Yard No 105)
Motor-ship, twin screw

The passenger-cargo steamship *Santa Barbara* was requisitioned by the American Government in July 1940 for service as an armed transport under the name *McCawley*. As such, she fell the victim of a Japanese aircraft-launched torpedo in the Blanche Channel, Rendova Island, in the Solomon Islands group, on 30 June 1942. The ship was abandoned but remained afloat, though down in the water, only to be torpedoed again, in error, and sunk by an American PT boat.
Casualties: 15

SANTA CLARA (1930) Grace Line, USA

serving under the wartime name SUSAN B. ANTHONY [AP-72]
8,183grt; 483ft (147.2m) lbp x 63ft (19.2m) beam
150 passengers
New York Shipbuilding Corp, Camden, New Jersey (Yard No 387)
Turbo-electric, twin screw

When she was converted into a Second World War armed transport, the passenger-cargo liner *Santa Clara* was renamed *Susan B. Anthony*. While serving in this capacity, she was sunk on 7 June 1944 during Operation 'Overlord', the invasion of Normandy. The *Susan B. Anthony* was carrying a large contingent of troops, brought from the Bristol Channel,

when, in the approaches to the beachheads, she struck a mine off the French coast in the position 49.33N, 00.47W. Everyone aboard her was taken off safely by landing craft. Her wreck was cleared after the war. Casualties: 0

The Grace Line turbo-electric liner *Santa Clara*, which served on the route from New York to South America, is here seen as the armed transport *Susan B. Anthony*, photographed on 13 May 1943 at the Norfolk Navy Yard. *US National Archives*

SANTA ELENA (1933) Grace Line, USA

9,135grt; 484ft (147.5m) lbp x 72ft (21.9m) beam
290 passengers
Federal Shipbuilding & Drydock Co, Kearny, New Jersey (Yard No 124)
Steam turbines, twin screw

The passenger-cargo ship *Santa Elena*, which had been converted into a troop transport, sailed in convoy from Liverpool for Naples in November 1943 with 1,889 Canadian troops, 44 guardsmen, 101 nurses and a crew of 133. On 6 November, when she was off Bougie (Bejaia), Algeria, in the position 37.12N, 06.16E, having rendered assistance to the already stricken *Marnix Van Sint Aldegonde* (qv), she was attacked herself by German aircraft, torpedoed and sunk. The survivors were taken off her by another American troop transport, the former Matson passenger liner *Monterey*.
Casualties: 4 (all crew)

SANTA LUCIA (1933) Grace Line, USA

serving under the wartime name LEEDSTOWN [AP-73]
9,135grt; 484ft (147.5m) lbp x 72ft (21.9m) beam
290 passengers
Federal Shipbuilding & Drydock Co, Kearny, New Jersey (Yard No 123)
Steam turbines, twin screw

The passenger-cargo ship *Santa Lucia* was requisitioned for war service in 1942 as the troop transport *Leedstown*. She became the first American passenger ship loss of the Operation 'Torch' Allied landings in North Africa, sunk off Cape Matifou, Algiers, on 9 November 1942 after she had arrived off the beachhead the previous day carrying a total of 1,043 personnel, 505 troops and her crew of 538 men. Having first been hit by an aircraft-launched torpedo, she was then severely damaged by the explosions of three 'near miss' bombs as the aerial bombardment continued. Although protected by a screen of gunboats, the German submarine U331 was able to finish her off on 9 November when three out of a four-torpedo salvo fired at the *Leedstown* scored hits. Incredibly, all those who were aboard her survived.
Casualties: 0

SANT ANNA (1910) Fabre Line, France

9,350grt; 470ft (143.3m) lbp x 56ft (17.1m) beam
1,970 passengers in three classes
Forges et Chantiers de la Méditerranée, La Seyne
(Yard No not known)
Triple-expansion steam reciprocating, twin screw
The French passenger steamship *Sant Anna*, serving as a troopship, was torpedoed and sunk by the German submarine UC54 during a voyage from Marseilles to Malta on 11 May 1918. She sank south of Pantelleria with heavy loss of life.
Casualties: 638

SANTO DOMINGO (1877) ex-*Dublin Castle* (1883) Cia Trasatlantica Española, Spain

2,911grt; 344ft (105.1m) lbp x 38ft (11.7m) beam
250 passengers in three classes (as built)
Robert Napier, Govan (Yard No 361)
Compound-expansion steam reciprocating, single screw
A former Castle Line mail steamer, the *Santo Domingo* went ashore and was wrecked off the Isle of Pines, near Cienfuegos, Cuba, on 12 July 1898, during a voyage from Spain to the West Indies.
Casualties: not known

SANTOS MARU (1925) Osaka Shosen Kaisha, Japan

serving under the wartime name MANJU MARU
7,267grt; 430ft (131.1m) lbp x 56ft (17.1m) beam
808 passengers
Mitsubishi, Nagasaki (Yard No 410)
Motor-ship, twin screw
In December 1941 the passenger-cargo ship *Santos Maru* was requisitioned for service as a submarine tender. It is not clear whether she was renamed *Manju Maru* at this date or by her owners before the outbreak of war and prior to being 'called up'. (Lloyd's records her loss under the name *Santos Maru* while the Miramar database attributes the change of her name to Osaka Shosen Kaisha.) She was torpedoed and sunk by the United States submarine USS *Atule* on 25 November 1944, in the position 20.12N, 121.51E, approximately fifty miles south-west of Basco on the island of Bataan, Luzon Island.
Casualties: not known

The *Santos Maru* operated between Japan and the east coast of South America via South Africa and the Indian Ocean until the outbreak of war in the Pacific. *Alex Duncan*

SARAY STAR (1967) ex-*European Star* (1994) ex-*Ciudad de Compostela* (1992) Libton Shipping Inc, Malta

9,777grt; 429ft (130.8m) loa x 63ft (19.3m) beam
716 passengers
Soc Espanola de Construccion Navale, Bilbao
(Yard No 123)
Motor-ship, twin screw
The ro-ro passenger-cargo ferry *Saray Star* suffered an outbreak of fire in her galley on 10 June 1994 when she was approximately 28 miles north of Cephalonia, in the position 38.42N, 19.50E, while on passage from Piraeus to Venice. The fire spread throughout the accommodation areas to engulf the entire ship and a full evacuation of passengers and crew took place. After burning uncontrollably for three days, the *Saray Star* sank in the position 38.48N, 20.09E.
Casualties: 0

Seen as the *European Star* at Brindisi in July 1992, from 1994 this distinctive ro-ro passenger ship became the *Saray Star*. Her lines were reminiscent of certain American passenger ships of the 1940s and 1950s period. *Frank Heine FERRIES*

SARDEGNA (1923) ex-*Sierra Ventana* (1935) Lloyd Triestino, Italy

11,452grt; 511ft (155.7m) loa x 61ft (18.6m) beam
1,113 passengers in three classes (as built)
Bremer Vulkan, Vegesack (Yard No 610)
Triple-expansion steam reciprocating, twin screw

The former Hamburg Sud-Amerika liner *Sierra Ventana* passed to the Italia Line in 1935. Renamed *Sardegna*, she made commercial voyages to South America as well as trooping voyages to Tripoli. In 1937 she was sold to Lloyd Triestino. *World Ship Society*

On 29 December 1940, while bound from Bari with Italian troops destined for Valona (Vlore), Albania, the passenger ship *Sardegna* was torpedoed off the Albanian coast by the Greek submarine *Proteus*. She sank in the position 40.31N, 19.02E. The survivors were picked up by escorting vessels, one of which, the torpedo boat *Antares*, rammed and sank the *Proteus*. Casualties: not known

SATRUSTEGUI (1948) ex-*Exploradeur Iradier* (1952) Cia Trasatlantica Española, Spain

6,615grt; 401ft (122.2m) loa x 55ft (16.8m) beam
236 passengers
Union Naval de Levante, Valencia (Yard No 42)
Motor-ship, single screw
While dry-docked at Barcelona undergoing repairs on 30 June 1973, the passenger-cargo ship *Satrustegui* caught fire. Completely gutted, her wreck was sold for breaking-up and she arrived at Castellon on 1 February 1974 for work to commence.
Casualties: not known

SAUDI (1956) Mogul Line, India

5,973grt; 426ft (129.8m) loa x 57ft (17.4m) beam
999 deck passengers
Lithgows, Port Glasgow (Yard No 1089)
Triple-expansion steam reciprocating, single screw
The passenger-cargo ship *Saudi*, bound from Aqaba, Jordan, to Cochin without passengers, was overwhelmed by severe weather on 25 June 1973 after her cargo shifted. She sank off Cape Guardafui, Somalia, in the position 11.55N, 51.25E, with such speed that there was no time to launch the boats and every one of the 98 persons aboard her, including three wives, had to jump into the sea.
Casualties: 39 (all crew)

SAVAS (1940) Denizbank Denizyollari Isletmesi Müdürlügü, Turkey

serving under the wartime name DARESSALAM
6,133grt; 386ft (117.6m) lbp x 53ft (16.0m) beam
610 passengers in four classes (as designed)
Blohm & Voss, Steinwerder, Hamburg (Yard No 522)
Triple-expansion steam reciprocating, twin screw
The *Savas*, like her sister *Egemen* (qv), was still under construction in Germany at the start of the Second World War. Taken over by the German authorities, neither of them saw commercial service for the owners who had ordered them. The *Savas* was used as an accommodation ship and target ship in the Baltic. She was sunk the same day as her sister, bombed by Allied aircraft on 3 May 1945 at Kiel. Left much as a hulk for the next eight years, although she still provided basic hotel and restaurant accommodation for the homeless of Hamburg, she was finally towed to Grays, Essex, for breaking up in 1953.
Casualties: not known

SAVOIE (1906) ex-*Kraljica Marija* (1940) ex-*Araguaya* (1930) French Government, managed by the Compagnie Générale Transatlantique (French Line)

10,196grt; 532ft (162.1m) loa x 61ft (18.6m) beam
365 passengers in single class (as a British ship)
Workman Clark, Belfast (Yard No 230)
Quadruple-expansion steam reciprocating, twin screw

The Yugoslav passenger ship *Kraljica Marija* was sold to the French Government in 1940, placed under the management of CGT (French Line) and rechristened *Savoie* for service to South American ports. On 8 November 1942, at the time of the North African landings, the *Savoie* was anchored in the harbour at Casablanca when she was hit by gunfire and sunk. Refloated subsequently, her wreck was towed outside the harbour and beached. It was later broken up where it lay. It is not certain whether the name *Savoie* was a temporary wartime name or a permanent name that would have been retained had commercial operations not been interrupted by the war.
Casualties: not known

SCANDINAVIA (1927) ex-*Stella Polaris* (2006) Petro-Fast A/B, Sweden

5,105grt; 416ft (126.8m) loa x 51ft (15.5m) beam
200 passengers
Gotaverken, Gothenburg (Yard No 400)
Motor-ship, twin screw
The sleek cruise yacht *Stella Polaris*, which had been moored in Japan as a floating hotel since 1970, was reactivated in 2006 with a view to conversion into a hotel-restaurant ship permanently moored in Stockholm. Renamed *Scandinavia*, she was taken in tow for Shanghai, China, where the renovation work and repairs were to be carried out prior to her return to Sweden, but when the tow was heading away from Japan towards the Chinese mainland on 1 September 2006, she foundered in the position 33.27N, 135.43E, south of the Inland Sea, in Wakayama prefecture, between Honshu and Shikoku. The *Scandinavia* had started to list earlier and had been taken into port at Kushimoto for attention, but when it was thought she was no longer taking water the tow had been resumed.
Casualties: 0

The graceful *Scandinavia* was lost at a time when, despite her age, she was about to undergo renovation, possibly for a static role. She was originally the classic Swedish cruise yacht *Stella Polaris*, as seen here at Southampton in June 1963 with the tug *Brambles*. *Kenneth Wightman*

SCANDINAVIAN SEA (1970) ex-*Blenheim* (1981) DFDS Seacruises Ltd, Bahamas

10,736grt; 490ft (149.4m) loa x 66ft (20.0m) beam
580 berthed and 527 deck passengers
Upper Clyde Shipbuilders, Clydebank (Yard No 744)
Motor-ship, twin screw

The *Scandinavian Sea*, formerly a Fred Olsen Lines vessel, was almost destroyed by fire on 9 March 1984. During a day cruise from Port Canaveral, to which port she was returning, a fire broke out due to an electrical fault. She managed to dock and all her occupants, 946 passengers and 202 crew, were evacuated. The fire, however, raged out of control and was not extinguished until two days later. It destroyed 30 per cent of the vessel, primarily the central area abaft of her bridge over five of her eight decks. Declared a constructive total loss, she was sold 'as is' to Greek interests only to be resold to an American buyer and renamed *Venus Venturer*. Subsequently she was sold again and rebuilt as the *Discovery I* (qv), sailing from Valencia on 7 October 1986 to Port Everglades, from where she was to commence a programme of one-day gambling cruises.
Casualties: 0

The *Scandinavian Sea*, a former Fred Olsen passenger/vehicle ferry, was converted into a cruise ship for service in the Gulf of Mexico. *Mike Lennon*

SCANDINAVIAN STAR (1971) ex-*Island Fiesta* (1984) ex-*Stena Baltica* (1984) ex-*Massalia* (1984) Scandinavian World Cruises (Stena Group), Bahamas

10,513grt; 466ft (142.1m) loa x 72ft (21.9m) beam
810 passengers
Dubigeon-Normandie, Nantes (Yard No 124)
Motor-ship, twin screw
After thirteen years on Mediterranean scheduled-service routes, the *Scandinavian Star* was fitted out for day excursions in the region of Mexico. Six years later, while under charter to the Da-No Line bound from Oslo to Frederikshavn, she caught fire in the Skagerrak shortly after leaving Oslo on 7 April 1990. While still on fire, she was towed to Lysekil and later, after it had abated, to Copenhagen for a detailed examination. Despite the extent of the damage, repair was considered and the *Scandinavian Star* was towed to Hull on 11 August for the clearance of hull debris and to permit an assessment of her suitability for repair. This contract was switched to CLC Marine Services, Southampton, to where she was transferred on 10 September 1990, but in the interim she was renamed *Candi*. After long deliberations, she was finally repaired, though not to her original standard, and returned to service as the *Regal Voyager* in 1994. Found among the victims recovered from the ship was the body of a known arsonist, and it was suspected that the *Scandinavian Star* had been the target of an arson attack. While she lay idle at Southampton as the *Candi*, her port side was painted black and used as a backdrop for the BBC Television series *House of Elliot*.
Casualties: 158 (Some reports give a figure of 176 casualties, but this is not substantiated.)

The gutted *Scandinavian Star* tied up at Southampton's berth 49 in the Eastern Docks, her name truncated to *Candi*. *David Reed*

SCHARNHORST (1935) Norddeutscher Lloyd, Germany

serving under wartime name IJNS SHINYO [JINYO]
18,184grt; 652ft (198.7m) loa x 74ft (22.6m) beam
293 passengers in two classes
Deschimag AG Weser, Bremen (Yard No 891)
Turbo-electric, twin screw
Laid up in Japan in September 1939, following the outbreak of war in Europe, the passenger liner *Scharnhorst* was sold by her owners to the Imperial Japanese Navy in February 1942. They had her converted into an aircraft carrier at Kure and she was commissioned as the *Shinyo* on 15 December 1943. The *Shinyo* was torpedoed on 17 November 1944, 140 miles north-east of Shanghai, by the American submarine USS *Spadefish*. Her fuel tanks exploded, causing a massive fire, and she sank in the position 33.02N, 123.33E.
Casualties: most of her crew of 942 officers and ratings

The *Scharnhorst*, together with sister ship *Gneisenau*, maintained Norddeutscher Lloyd's Far East service from Bremen. Taken under an Axis agreement and reconstructed as an escort carrier, the conversion plans may well have been shared because for a while the *Gneisenau* was also earmarked for adaptation into an aircraft carrier. *World Ship Society*

SCHILLER (1872) Adler Line, Germany

3,421grt; 381ft (116.0m) loa x 40ft (12.2m) beam
990 passengers in three classes
Robert Napier, Govan (Yard No 323)
Compound-expansion steam reciprocating, single screw
Ten days after leaving New York for Hamburg on 27 April 1875, the passenger steamship *Schiller* ran onto the rocks off the Scilly Isles. She was carrying 254 passengers and 101 crew.

She had been nearing the end of her Atlantic crossing, and had run into thick fog in the approaches to the English Channel. Unable to take observations, she had run off course and within half a mile of the Bishop Rock lighthouse, whose fog signals had not been heard. She crashed bow-first onto the Retarrier Ledges on the night of 7 May. The weather was freshening and the rough seas turned her broadside on so that, with waves breaking over her, she could not be made to respond to the helm and it was impossible to extricate the doomed vessel. In the worsening conditions the *Schiller* could not be safely abandoned and the one boat launched in a bid to get people off capsized immediately it was floated. Some of her boats were washed away, while another two were destroyed when the ship's funnel collapsed on them. Many of the *Schiller*'s complement took refuge in a deck house, but they were swept to a watery grave when it was washed overboard. Distress signals were fired but not seen, and help did not arrive until the next day, when the weather had abated somewhat. By then only 43 remained alive. They were picked up and landed at St Mary's by the steamer *Lady of the Isles*. Many of the victims were buried in mass graves at Old Town. Apart from her passengers, the *Schiller*, which was pounded to pieces in the wild seas, had also been conveying some $300,000 worth of US gold specie. Within a year most had been recovered although it is rumoured that the construction of a row of houses at Hugh Town, known as Schiller Row, was financed by money salvaged from the wreck.

Casualties: 312

The Adler Line was absorbed by Hamburg Amerika very soon after the *Schiller* was wrecked on the Scilly Isles. Her fleet-mates all made the transition to the new owners. *Hapag-Lloyd*

SCHWERIN (1926) Deutsche Reichsbahn, Germany

3,133grt; 334ft (101.8m) lbp x 59ft (18.0m) beam
800 passengers
Schichau, Elbing (Yard No 1170)
Triple-expansion steam reciprocating, twin screw
The Baltic train ferry *Schwerin* was bombed at Rostock on 20 February 1944, severely damaged and abandoned as a hulk. At the end of the Second World War she was apparently either allocated to or seized by the USSR, but because of the extent of her damage she was almost certainly scrapped as she was unfit for restoration.

Casualties: not known

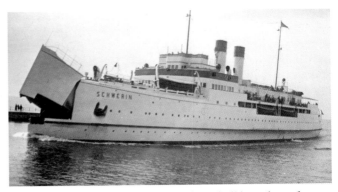

An early example of a ferry with a clam-shell bow door, the railway ferry *Schwerin* is about to dock. She maintained the Warnemünde to Gedser service. *Arnold Kludas*

SCOTIA (1921) London, Midland & Scottish Railway, UK

3,454grt; 392ft loa (116.0m lbp) x 45ft (13.8m) beam
300 berthed and 1,200 deck passengers
William Denny, Dumbarton (Yard No 1037)
Steam turbines, twin screw
While serving as an auxiliary transport during the evacuation of servicemen from the Dunkirk beaches, the Irish Sea ferry *Scotia* was bombed and sunk by German aircraft on 1 June 1940. At the time of the attack she was on her second round trip of the operation, having earlier landed 3,000 British soldiers at Dover. The *Scotia* departed from the French port late in the morning bound for Sheerness with around 2,000 French troops, but when she was about two hours out into the English Channel a wave of enemy aircraft swooped low over her, hitting her with several bombs, one dropping down her funnel and exploding deep within her. She immediately heeled over to starboard, bow down, until her forward funnel and foremast were completely submerged. The destroyer HMS *Esk* went to the aid of those aboard her and managed to rescue the majority, either picked up from the water or by transhipment when she was brought close alongside the sinking *Scotia*'s boat deck. Others who had clambered down the *Scotia*'s side to the port bilge keel, were dragged to the *Esk* using ropes.

Casualties: between 200 and 300 troops plus 28 crew

The LMS Irish Sea ferry *Scotia*, with sister ships *Cambria* and *Hibernia*, worked the Holyhead to Kingstown (Dublin) service. *Ambrose Greenway*

SCOTLAND (1865) National Line, UK

3,803grt; 375ft (114.3m) lbp x 42ft (12.8m) beam
Passenger numbers no known
Palmer Bros, Jarrow (Yard No 155)
Inverted steam reciprocating engines, single screw
The transatlantic passenger steamship *Scotland* collided with the barquentine *Kate Dyer* off Fire Island, New York Bay, on 1 December 1866. The severely damaged *Scotland* was driven ashore where she subsequently broke up. All the occupants of both ships were safely rescued. Casualties: 0

SCOTSMAN (1894) Dominion Line, UK

7,101grt; 470ft (143.5m) lbp x 49ft (15.0m) beam
More than 230 passengers in three classes
Harland & Wolff, Belfast (Yard No 289)
Triple-expansion steam reciprocating, twin screw
The passenger-cargo steamer *Scotsman* was wrecked at Chateau Bay in the Straits of Belle Isle on 22 September 1899 while she was headed, inward-bound, from Liverpool for Montreal. She was carrying, besides her crew, some 200 passengers. Casualties: 13

SEA BREEZE I (1958) ex-*Starship Royale* (1989) ex-*Royale* (1989) ex-*Federico C* (1983) Ulysses Cruises Inc (Dolphin Cruise Line), Panama

15,483grt; 606ft (184.7m) loa x 79ft (24.0m) beam
1,259 passengers
Ansaldo, Sestri-Ponente, Genoa (Yard No 1516)
Steam turbines, twin screw
Built for the scheduled service run from Italy to South America, the *Federico C* became a full-time cruise ship in 1983. As the *Sea Breeze I*, she foundered on 17 December 2000, following engine failure and subsequent flooding, in the position 37.36N, 71.20W, east of Cape Charles, some 250 miles to the east of the entrance to Chesapeake Bay. At the time she was not carrying passengers, and the 34 members of crew that were aboard her were rescued by the US Coast Guard. Casualties: not known

The cruise ship *Sea Breeze I* spent 25 years on the Italy to South America service, two renamings earlier, as the *Federico C*. *Ian Shiffman*

SEA DIAMOND (1986) ex-*Birka Princess* (2006) Louis Cruise Lines

22,712grt; 469ft (143.0m) loa x 81ft (24.7m) beam
1,394 berthed and 106 deck passengers (as built)
Valmet O/Y Helsingin Telakka, Helsinki (Yard No 321)
Motor-ship, twin screw

The cruise ship *Sea Diamond*, built originally as a ro-ro ferry with cruise-standard accommodation, was on a cruise in Greek waters on 5 April 2007 when she was stranded on rocks at the entrance of Santorini harbour, Thira, north of Crete. At the time she had a complement of 1,154 passengers and 391 crew. A day later she slipped off the rocks and sank in deep water, in the position 36.25N, 25.27E. Consideration was given to making an attempt to refloat her and getting her to the safety of port in Crete, but abandonment was considered the higher priority, which was just as well as things turned out, and an almost complete, incident-free evacuation proved possible where she had stranded. Casualties: 2

Seen here as the *Birka Princess*, the loss of the *Sea Diamond*, as she became, in April 2007 was a narrowly averted major disaster. Luckily, virtually all of her passengers, including some school parties on an educational cruise, were taken off before she foundered in deep water. *Mike Lennon*

SEATTLE MARU (1909) Osaka Shosen Kaisha, Japan

6,182grt; 419ft (127.7m) lbp x 49ft (14.9m) beam
176 passengers
Kawasaki, Kobe (Yard No 298)
Triple-expansion steam reciprocating, twin screw
The passenger-cargo ship *Seattle Maru* was torpedoed on 16 July 1944 by the American submarine USS *Piranha* 100 miles north-west of Luzon, Philippine Islands. She sank in the position 19.26N, 120.18E.
Casualties: not known

SEAWISE UNIVERSITY (1940) ex-*Elizabeth* (1970) ex-*Queen Elizabeth* (1969) CY Tung Group (Seawise Foundations Ltd), Hong Kong

83,673grt; 1,031ft (314.1m) loa x 119ft (36.2m) beam
2,285 passengers in three classes (as built)
John Brown, Clydebank (Yard No 552)
Steam turbines, quadruple screw
Sold to new owners in late 1970, the former Cunard transatlantic express liner *Queen Elizabeth* sailed to Hong Kong from the United States, where she arrived on 16 July 1971, to undergo a major overhaul and refurbishment to become the floating university and cruise ship *Seawise University*. This work was nearing completion on 9 January 1972 when the owners entertained a party of 200 or so people on board, mostly company officials and employees, to celebrate the ship's imminent renaissance. Fire broke out during the festivities and rapidly spread throughout the ship, penetrating five of her eleven decks while more than 80 per

cent of her superstructure was ablaze. Those aboard her hastily abandoned ship, some of them being picked up from the water, and there were only fourteen cases of serious injury. Fire-fighting was conducted exclusively from launches of the Hong Kong Marine and Police Departments, but as numerous internal explosions shook the vessel she assumed an extreme list and fire-fighting was suspended due to the danger of the ship capsizing. Ultimately, it was abandoned altogether and, as anticipated, the flooded *Seawise University* heeled over onto her starboard side to settle on the seabed in shallow water.

It seems that through the extreme speed with which the fire took a grip on her, there had been no opportunity to seal the watertight doors. The devastation was so extensive that all her decks had collapsed and it was evident from her port side, still visible above the water, that the shell had fallen in likewise. The Marine Court of Inquiry stated that the *Seawise University* was so badly gutted that little useful information would be obtained from a detailed physical examination of her interiors. Evidence given at the Inquiry revealed that the fire had started on A deck and that, prior to this outbreak, fourteen other small fires had been extinguished aboard her. Sabotage was suspected as the cause, as the fire had erupted in several locations simultaneously. Though there was no definite proof, it was put down to rivalry between the various factions of Chinese workers. The once great ship was ignominiously broken up where she lay, in the aptly named Junk Bay, by a Japanese demolition company.

Casualties: 0

Vying with the *Normandie* for the crown of greatest ever passenger liner, Cunard Line's *Queen Elizabeth* was taken up for conversion into the educational cruise ship *Seawise University* shortly after the end of her transatlantic career. Here she is seen at Cape Town en route to Hong Kong for conversion. *Ian Shiffman*

Ablaze from end to end, almost certainly the victim of sabotage, the conversion into the *Seawise University* had been all but complete when she was gutted by fire. *Author's collection*

The rusting and collapsed wreck of the *Seawise University* lay off Hong Kong for two years before removal got under way. *Ian Shiffman*

SENECA (1894) ex-*Cuba* (1925) ex-*Powhattan* (1920) ex-*Rawlins* (1902) ex-*Resolute* (1900) ex-*Yorktown* (1898) Clyde Line, USA

2,963grt; 328ft (94.5m) lbp x 40ft (12.2m) beam
Passenger numbers not known
Delaware River, Chester, Pennsylvania (Yard No 273)
Triple-expansion steam reciprocating, single screw
The American coastwise passenger ship *Seneca* was destroyed by fire on 30 December 1927 in Fletcher's dry dock, Hoboken, when a furious conflagration was caused by a spark igniting a film of petroleum floating on the River Hudson. The fire destroyed the Lackawanna Rail Road pier, the buildings and piers of two adjacent industrial plants and eight barges moored alongside their wharves. It spread to the *Seneca*, trapped in dry dock, and almost engulfed the nearby steamships *Indian Arrow* and *W. J. Hanna*. The Hudson River ferry *Hendrick Hudson* likewise narrowly escaped a similar fate. The *Seneca* was burned down to the waterline. Her entire superstructure and wooden decks were destroyed, the shell plating buckled, and her main engines, which were submerged as the flooded ship listed and sank, were ruined. In all, the fire caused US$1.5 million worth of damage.
Casualties: 0

SHANGHAI MARU (1923) Toa Kaiun Kaisha, Japan

5,293grt; 395ft (120.4m) lbp x 54ft (16.5m) beam
440 passengers
William Denny, Dumbarton (Yard No 1138)
Steam turbines, twin screw
The passenger-cargo ship *Shanghai Maru*, built originally for Nippon Yusen Kaisha, was lost on 30 October 1943 following a collision with the cargo ship *Sakito Maru* in the position 31.55N, 123.10E, about 75 miles north of Shanghai.
Casualties: not known

SHOHO [SYOHO] MARU (1923) Department of Communications & Railways, Government of Japan

3,460grt; 350ft (106.7m) lbp x 52ft (15.9m) beam
985 passengers
Uraga Dock Co, Uraga (Yard No 200)
Steam turbines, twin screw
While serving as a wartime transport, the passenger ferry *Shoho Maru* was bombed by US carrier-based aircraft in Rikuoka Bay, Japan, on 14 July 1945. She sank in the position 40.51N, 140.47E, near Noshiro. Casualties: not known

SHOKEI MARU (1923) Department of Communications & Railways, Government of Japan

3,619grt; 360ft (109.7m) lbp x 46ft (14.0m) beam
878 passengers
Mitsubishi, Kobe (Yard No 97)
Steam turbines, twin screw

The passenger ferry *Shokei Maru* struck a mine and sank in the Korea Strait on 30 July 1945. Believed to be beyond recovery, it appears that she was salvaged and returned to service after the Second World War, remaining active until June 1961, when she was disposed of for breaking-up at Hakodate.
Casualties: not known

SHROPSHIRE (1926) Bibby Line, UK

serving under the wartime name HMS SALOPIAN
10,549grt; 502ft (153.0m) loa x 60ft (18.3m) beam
275 passengers in single class
Fairfield, Govan (Yard No 619)
Motor-ship, twin screw

The passenger-cargo ship *Shropshire* was commandeered by the Admiralty on the outbreak of the Second World War and was commissioned as the armed merchant cruiser HMS *Salopian* in October 1939. She was torpedoed and sunk on 13 May 1941, some 400 miles south-east of Cape Farewell, Greenland, in the position 59.04N, 38.15W, the attack having been made by the German submarine U98. Apparently the submarine missed with three torpedoes before she finally hit the target with another two. The *Salopian* remained afloat long enough for a full evacuation of her 278 occupants to be safely completed.
Casualties: 0

The Bibby passenger ship *Shropshire*, lost as HMS *Salopian*.
World Ship Society

SICILIA (1923) ex-*Coblenz* (1935) Lloyd Triestino, Italy

9,646grt; 479ft (146.0m) loa x 57ft (17.4m) beam
438 passengers
Deschimag AG Weser, Bremen (Yard No 326)
Steam turbines, twin screw

The passenger-cargo ship *Sicilia* was taken over as a naval hospital ship following Italy's entry into the Second World War. She was destroyed during an Allied air raid while berthed at Naples on 5 April 1943. Demolition of the wreck, which was raised after the war, was completed by the end of March 1949.
Casualties: not known

SIDI-BEL-ABBÈS (1929) Société Générale de Transports Maritimes à Vapeur (SGTM), France

4,392grt; 368ft (112.2m) lbp x 50ft (15.3m) beam
436 passengers in four classes
Swan Hunter & Wigham Richardson, Low Walker, Tyneside (Yard No 1358)
Steam turbines, twin screw

The French passenger steamship *Sidi-Bel-Abbès* was taken over as a troopship in the Second World War under British management. On 20 April 1943 she was torpedoed by the German submarine U565 while carrying around 1,100 Senegalese troops from Oran to Casablanca. She sank ten miles north of the Habibas Islands, near Oran, in the position 35.59N, 01.25W. The survivors, 520 in number, were picked up by British naval escorts.
Casualties: About 610

One of three SGTM passenger ships ordered by the French concern from Tyneside shipbuilders Swan Hunter & Wigham Richardson, this is the *Sidi-Bel-Abbès*. The other two were the *Campana* and *Provence*. *World Ship Society*

SIERRA CORDOBA (1924) Norddeutscher Lloyd, Germany

11,492grt; 511ft (155.7m) loa x 62ft (18.8m) beam
2,065 passengers in three classes or 1,000 in single class when cruising
Bremer Vulkan, Vegesack (Yard No 611)
Triple-expansion steam reciprocating, twin screw

The *Sierra Cordoba*, which had operated during the four years immediately prior to the war as a government cruise ship, saw wartime service from 1940 as a naval accommodation ship at Kiel. Taken as a British war prize in May 1945, she caught fire at Hamburg on 13 January 1946 and was completely burned out. Two years later, the *Sierra Cordoba*'s charred hulk, carrying ammunition that was to be dumped in the North Sea, was taken in tow for the River Clyde where she was to be broken up, but she broke adrift in stormy seas on 17 January 1948 and was lost, presumed sunk. The small number of men who were aboard her were rescued by the trawler *Astrid*. In fact, when relocated on 2 March 1948, she was found in an uncleared minefield off Esbjerg at Hvide Sande, in the position 55.51N, 07.35E, where she had stranded in shallow water, lying on her side, partially submerged. While salvors deliberated on how best to extricate the gutted hulk from its situation, it went adrift a second time that June, a danger to navigation in the area. Last observed eighteen miles west of Ringkobing Fjord and considered to be beyond salvage, she subsequently sank, leaving no further trace.
Casualties: 3 (in the fire of 1946)

The *Sierra Cordoba* was destroyed by fire, then lost in a minefield while en route to Great Britain for breaking-up. *Author's collection*

SIMLA (1894) P&O Line, UK

5,884grt; 430ft (131.1m) lbp x 49ft (14.9m) beam
152 passengers in two classes
Caird, Greenock (Yard No 275)
Triple-expansion steam reciprocating, single screw
The *Simla* was one of a number of passenger liners fitted with troop accommodation spaces for occasional voyages chartered to the British Government during peacetime, but from the outbreak of the First World War this became her full-time employment. While bound from Marseilles to Alexandria via Malta on 2 April 1916 she was torpedoed and sunk by the German submarine U39. The attack took place 45 miles north-west-half-west from Gozo lighthouse in the Maltese Islands group, and she sank in the position 36.25N, 13.12E.
Casualties: 10 (all crew)

The *Simla*, which was introduced with sister ships *Nubia* and *Malta* to the London to Calcutta service, was also used as a troopship because of her substantial troop capacity. *Tom Rayner collection*

SIMON BOLIVAR (1927) Royal Netherlands SS Co, The Netherlands

8,309grt; 420ft (128.0m) lbp x 59ft (18.0m) beam
215 passengers
Rotterdamsche Droogdok, Rotterdam (Yard No 138)
Quadruple-expansion steam reciprocating, single screw
When outward-bound from Holland to Paramaribo, Surinam, on 18 November 1939, with a complement of approximately 400 passengers and crew, the passenger-cargo ship *Simon Bolivar* stuck two mines off Harwich, one on either side of

her hull, the second detonating a quarter of an hour after the first. The explosions caused massive damage, destroying many of the lifeboats and toppling her masts. She immediately began to settle by the stern, making it difficult to launch the remaining boats. Although she was close to port, her plight was such that she urgently needed assistance, but it could not be summoned because the explosions had destroyed her radio equipment. Fortunately, other vessels did reach the scene and were able to evacuate the survivors before the *Simon Bolivar* sank, going under in the position 51.49N, 01.41E.
Casualties: 84

The Dutch passenger ship *Simon Bolivar* was engaged in the service from Amsterdam to the West Indies. *L. L. von Münching*

SINAIA (1924) Fabre Line, France

8,567grt; 439ft (133.8m) lbp x 56ft (17.1m) beam
554 passengers
Barclay Curle, Whiteinch, Glasgow (Yard No 583)
Triple-expansion steam reciprocating, twin screw
On the outbreak of the Second World War, the passenger ship *Sinaia* was laid up in her home port of Marseilles where she was seized by the Germans in November 1942. From 1943 she served in the Mediterranean as an Axis hospital ship. She was scuttled at Marseilles on 22 August 1944 by retreating German army units. The *Sinaia* was refloated on 9 December 1946 and her wreck moved to the Leon Gourret quay in 1953. However, after evaluation she was not considered worth reconditioning and was declared a total loss. Breaking up commenced soon afterwards.
Casualties: not known

SINDIBAD I (1965) ex-*Al Kamar III* (1988) ex-*Sindibad* (1982) ex-*Espresso Rosso* (1982) ex-*Canguro Rosso* (1978) Khaled Ali Foula, Egypt

4,156grt; 415ft (126.4m) loa x 63ft (19.3m) beam
377 berthed and 336 deck passengers
Navalmeccanica, Castellammare (Yard No 638)
Motor-ship, twin screw
The ro-ro passenger ferry *Sindibad I* caught fire while she was lying at Suez on 20 December 1992. She was towed out into the roadstead where fire-fighting continued, but after the fire had been extinguished she was declared a total loss and the wreck was disposed of for scrap.
Casualties: not known

SIQUEIRA CAMPOS (1907) ex-*Cantuaria Guimaraes* (1931) ex-*Curvello* (1927) ex-*Gertrud Woermann* (1917) Lloyd Brasileiro, Brazil

6,456grt; 415ft (126.7m) lbp x 51ft (15.5m) beam
191 passengers in three classes
Reiherstiegwerft, Hamburg (Yard No 421)
Triple-expansion steam reciprocating, twin screw
Acquired for service on the Santos to Hamburg route, these duties were suspended during the Second World War and the passenger-cargo ship *Siqueira Campos* was confined to Brazilian coastal operations. On 25 August 1943, while bound for Pernambuco (Recife) to Ceara (Fortaleza), she was in collision with her fleet-mate *Cuyaba* four miles off Caponga. The *Siqueira Campos* was beached some forty miles south of Ceara and was soon awash, a total loss. The *Cuyaba* also went ashore at Mucuripe but was later refloated and repaired, and subsequently enjoyed many more years of service.
Casualties: not known

SIRIO (1883) Navigazione Generale Italiana, Italy

4,141grt; 380ft (115.8m) lbp x 42ft (12.8m) beam
1,320 passengers in three classes
Robert Napier, Govan (Yard No 385)
Triple-expansion steam reciprocating, single screw

The NGI steamer *Sirio* was one of a pair, with the *Orione*, placed on the Italy to South America service.
M. Cicogna collection, Trieste

The *Sirio* in August 1906, sunk in shallow water off Cape Palos, near Cathagena. *M. Cicogna collection, Trieste*

On 4 August 1906, when the passenger steamship *Sirio* was bound from Genoa to Montevideo and Buenos Aires, she ran onto the rocks at Bajos on the Hormigas Islands, Cape Palos, as she was negotiating the inside passage to the Spanish port of Carthagena. She began to sink immediately and panic broke out among those aboard her, a large complement comprising 695 passengers and a 127-man crew. In the general mayhem and violent scramble for the boats, many were unable to escape, and when the *Sirio* developed a severe list to starboard and sank stern-first she took many of her complement with her.
Casualties: 442

SIRITARA OCEAN QUEEN (1964) ex-*Ocean Princess* (2006) ex-*Olviara* (2004) ex-*Nandini* (2003) ex-*Silver Star* (2003) ex-*Royal Dream* (1998) ex-*Odessa Song* (1997) ex-*Bashkiria* (1992) Siritara Enterprise Co, Thailand

6,092grt; 401ft (122.2m) loa x 53ft (16.0m) beam
334 passengers (as built)
Mathias-Thesen Werft, Wismar (Yard No 190)
Motor-ship, twin screw
Another of the former '*Mikhail Kalinin*' class of nineteen short sea passenger ships built for the Soviet Union between 1958 and 1964, the *Bashkiria* went through numerous name changes before she became the Thai-flag cruise ship *Siritara Ocean Queen*. Her career under this name was short-lived, for she capsized while berthed at Bangkok when the Chao Phraya River flooded on 10 October 2006.
Casualties: not known

The *Siritara Ocean Queen* was the former Russian passenger ship *Bashkiria*, here seen undergoing conversion and facelift before commencing her new cruise ship role.
Frank Heine FERRIES

SKAUBRYN (1951) Greek Line, Greece

9,786grt; 458ft (139.7m) loa x 57ft (17.4m) beam
1,221 passengers
Oresundsvarvet, Landskrona (Yard No 107)
Motor-ship, single screw
On one of her voyages to the Antipodes as an emigrant ship, the *Skaubryn* caught fire in the Indian Ocean on 31 March 1958, in the position 10.30N, 59.30E, after an engine room explosion caused by an oil spill occurred during the repair of a diesel motor. Her complement, 904 migrants and 176 private passengers, in addition to the crew, abandoned ship and were picked up by the *City of Sydney* assisted by the Polish ship *Malgorzata Fornalska*, which towed lifeboats containing 200 persons alongside the British ship. The *City of Sydney* took the survivors to Aden where they were transferred to the *Roma*, another emigrant vessel. The *Skaubryn* was taken in tow for Djibouti by the frigate HMS *Loch Fada* and the Dutch tug *Cycloop*, but foundered on 6 April 1958 in the position 12.05N, 50.33E.
Casualties: 1 (passenger, heart failure)

SLAMAT (1924) Rotterdam Lloyd, The Netherlands

11,636grt; 530ft (161.5m) loa x 62ft (18.9m) beam
420 passengers in three classes
De Schelde, Vlissingen (Yard No 176)
Steam turbines, twin screw

The Dutch passenger ship *Slamat* became a British troopship after the fall of the Netherlands in May 1940, and as such was employed during the evacuation of British troops from Crete to Nauplia on the Greek mainland. She was bombed by German dive bombers in the Gulf of Nauplia, Peloponnesus, on 27 April 1941, while she was carrying around 900 men, a combination of troops and her crew. The *Slamat* sank in the position 37.01N, 23.10E while her survivors were picked up from the sea by the destroyers HMS *Diamond* and *Wryneck*. Unfortunately, in the continuing air attacks both British warships were also sunk with further loss of life from among those whose had been aboard the *Slamat*.

Casualties: ~843 (193 when the *Slamat* was sunk and about 650 when HMS *Diamond* and *Wryneck* were sunk). Besides these fatalities, a further 253 lives were lost from the officers and ratings of the naval vessels.

The Cunard emigrant ship *Slavonia* was acquired with sister ship *Pannonia*, both laid down for British India, while she was still on the stocks. The pair operated the Trieste to New York service. The second view shows her on the rocks.
Both H. B. Christiansen Collection / Online Transport Archive

The Dutch passenger ship *Slamat* was engaged in the service from Rotterdam to Batavia (Djakarta) via the Suez Canal.
Royal Schelde

SLAVONIA (1903) ex-*Yamuna* (1904) Cunard Line, UK

10,606grt; 526ft (160.3m) loa x 60ft (18.1m) beam
2,099 passengers
James Laing, Sunderland (Yard No 600)
Triple-expansion steam reciprocating, twin screw

Five years after entering the emigrant trade from Fiume and Trieste to New York, on 10 June 1909 the *Slavonia* ran ashore near Velos at the south-west of the island of Flores, in the Azores, during a return voyage to the Mediterranean. She radioed for assistance and her calls were answered by the Hamburg Amerika Line steamers *Batavia* and *Prinzess Irene*, which between them took off the 373 passengers and 225 crew members. The *Slavonia* was not so fortunate. She could not be removed from the ledge onto which she had become stranded and was written off as a total loss.

Casualties: 0

SOBRAON (1900) P&O Line, UK

7,382grt; 450ft (137.2m) lbp x 54ft (16.5m) beam
171 passengers in two classes plus troops
Caird, Greenock (Yard No 293)
Triple-expansion steam reciprocating, twin screw

The *Sobraon* and her sisters *Assaye* and *Plassy* were commissioned to fulfil trooping requirements for the British Government, and when not so engaged they were to fill in on other services. On only her third voyage, the *Sobraon* was stranded on Tung Ying Island, north-east of Foochow, at night in dense fog on 24 April 1901 while bound from Shanghai to London.

Casualties: not known

SOL OLYMPIA II (1966) ex-*Santa Cruz de Tenerife* (1985) Sol Mediterranean Lines, Cyprus

7,236grt; 429ft (130.8m) loa x 63ft (19.3m) beam
500 passengers
Soc Española de Construcciones Navale, Bilbao
(Yard No 122)
Motor-ship, twin screw

The ro-ro passenger ferry *Sol Olympia II* was destroyed by fire on 6 June 1986 while she was undergoing repairs in the floating dry dock at Eleusis Shipyards, Greece. The fire started in the crew accommodation from where it rapidly spread. It raged for two days during which time fire-fighting was particularly difficult because of her situation. Declared a constructive total loss, after removal from the dry dock, which appears not to have been seriously damaged, she was sold to Turkish ship-breakers at Aliaga where she arrived on 26 September 1987.

Casualties: not known

The gutted *Sol Olympia II* at Elefsina on 11 September 1987. *Frank Heine FERRIES*

SONTAY (1907) Messageries Maritimes, France

7,247grt; 447ft (136.2m) loa x 52ft (15.9m) beam
239 passengers in two classes
Messageries Maritimes, La Ciotat (Yard No 133)
Triple-expansion steam reciprocating, twin screw

The passenger steamer *Sontay* was on passage from Milo, Salonica (Thessaloniki), to Marseilles on 16 April 1917 with a complement of some 500 or more persons, of whom 325 were soldiers and around 100 were naval ratings heading home on leave, the remainder being her crew of 81. She was being escorted by the gunboats *Moqueuse* and *Capricieuse*. Between Sardinia and Sicily, in the position 35.02N, 16.28E, she was torpedoed by the German submarine U33 and sank in just five minutes. In this brief space of time it was inevitable that a full abandonment could not be completed, but there is no doubt that the death toll would have been far higher than it was but for the disciplined and prompt manner in which the evacuation was carried out.

Casualties: 49 (45 military personnel and 4 crew). This is the official French figure; however, the number of survivors is also stated to be 350, which does not correlate with the number of persons the *Sontay* was said to have been carrying.

SOPHIA (1953) ex-*Sova Birgitta* (1965) Constantine S. Efthymiadis, Greece

8,945grt; 496ft (151.3m) loa x 62ft (19.0m) beam
Passenger numbers not known
Kockums MV A/B, Malmo (Yard No 361)
Motor-ship, single screw

Built originally as an oil tanker, the *Sophia* was converted into a ro-ro ferry in 1966 for service between the Greek islands. On 17 May 1976 she sprang a leak while berthed at Keratsini, between Perama and Piraeus. She developed a severe list, which increased as more water flooded into her, and, concerned that she would capsize and block the navigable channel, it was decided that the *Sophia* should be towed to a beach some 20 metres from her pier. Left resting on the

bottom, with a 60-degree list, she gradually sank deeper and deeper into the seabed and was declared a total loss.

Casualties: not known

The Greek passenger ferry *Sophia* was another oil-tanker conversion, like the *Heleanna*. *Michael Cassar*

The *Sophia* seen capsized onto her port side at Piraeus in October 1986. *Frank Heine FERRIES*

SOUNION (1936) ex-*Cammell Laird* (1970) ex-*Royal Ulsterman* (1968) Med-Link Lines Shipping Co, Cyprus

3,290grt; 340ft (99.9m) lbp x 48ft (14.5m) beam
750 passengers (as built)
Harland & Wolff, Belfast (Yard No 963)
Motor-ship, twin screw

Formerly a Coast Lines Group ferry employed on Irish Sea routes, the *Sounion* was lost on 3 March 1973 in an incident that was suspected as having been an act of either terrorism or sabotage. While engaged on a round-trip cruise from Cyprus, she was docked at Beirut when, shortly before her scheduled departure for Haifa, she was rocked by a huge explosion that was thought, at first, to have originated in her boiler room. It tore a large hole in her stern and the flooded *Sounion* soon sank stern-downwards alongside the quay in 30 feet of water. All of her 254 passengers were safely evacuated. Later, on 17 April, she was refloated, and it was only then that the more likely cause of the disaster was revealed for, beneath the sunken hull, human remains were found clad in frogmen-type diving suits. The wrecked ship was towed away and broken up at Perama, where she arrived on 10 September 1973.

Casualties: 2 (both crew members)

SOUTHLAND (1900) ex-*Vaderland* (1915)
White Star Line, UK

12,018grt; 580ft (176.8m) loa x 60ft (18.3m) beam
1,362 passengers in three classes
John Brown, Clydebank (Yard No 341)
Quadruple-expansion steam reciprocating, twin screw
After the outbreak of the First World War the liner *Vaderland* was transferred from Red Star Line and renamed *Southland*. A short time later, in 1915, she was requisitioned for troop carrying. While engaged in these duties, bound from Liverpool to Philadelphia on 14 June 1917, the *Southland* was sunk some 140 miles north-west of Tory Island, in the position 56.01N, 12.14W, when the German submarine U70 fired two torpedoes into her.
Casualties: 4 (all crew)

SPHINX (1914) Messageries Maritimes, France

serving under the wartime name SUBIACO
11,375grt; 503ft (153.3m) loa x 60ft (18.3m) beam
384 passengers in three classes
Chantiers de la Loire, St Nazaire (Yard No 215)
Triple-expansion steam reciprocating, twin screw
The passenger-cargo ship *Sphinx* became a French Navy hospital ship in December 1939 and supported the Allied campaign in Norway. From July the following year through to September 1941 she was employed in treating and repatriating sick and injured French servicemen, from Liverpool (evacuees from Dunkirk), from Oran after the British bombardment of French warships at Mers el Kebir, and from Syria, making repeated voyages to Marseilles and Toulon. Derequisitioned on 18 May 1943, she was seized by the occupying authorities seven days later and taken to Genoa where, on 19 August, she was commandeered by the Italians, who renamed her *Subiaco*. She was sunk at Genoa on 5 January 1944, bombed and burned out in an American air raid. Refloated after the war, she was broken up where she lay from 28 November 1945.
Casualties: not known

Messageries Maritimes had three ships building for the Marseilles to Far East service immediately prior to the First World War. Only the *Porthos* and *Athos* commenced commercial operations before the war, while the third ship, the *Sphinx*, was taken over by the French Navy on completion.
World Ship Society

STAMPALIA (1909) ex-*Oceania* (1912)
La Veloce Line, Italy

8,999grt; 476ft (145.3m) lbp x 55ft (16.8m) beam
2,500 passengers in two classes
Cantieri Navali Riuniti, La Spezia (Yard No 48)
Triple-expansion steam reciprocating, twin screw
The Italian emigrant carrier *Stampalia* was bound from Genoa for Liverpool and New York when the German submarine UB47 torpedoed her on 18 August 1916 as she was rounding Cape Matapan (Akra Tainaron) to enter the Ionian Sea. She sank in the position 36.40N, 22.10E.
Casualties: not known

STATENDAM (1917) Holland Amerika Line, The Netherlands

serving under the wartime name JUSTICIA
32,234grt; 776ft (236.5m) loa x 86ft (26.2m) beam
3,430 passengers in three classes (as designed)
Harland & Wolff, Belfast (Yard No 436)
Triple-expansion steam reciprocating with LP steam turbine, triple screw
Launched on 9 July 1914, all work on the Dutch passenger liner *Statendam* was halted on the outbreak of war and she lay incomplete for the next three years. She was requisitioned for completion as a troopship in 1917 following negotiations between her intended owners and the British Government. Placed under the management of the White Star Line, she was renamed *Justicia*. On 19 July 1918 she was bound in convoy from Liverpool to New York when she was torpedoed by the German submarine UB64 as the convoy passed twenty miles north-north-west of the Skerryvore Rock. Escorting warships drove off the enemy submarine and the *Justicia* was taken in tow for Lough Swilly by tugs. However, the assault was resumed the next day by other submarines and the UB124 hit her with two more torpedoes, making a total of five, sealing her fate. The *Justicia* sank stern-first at midday on 20 July, in the position 55.38N, 07.39W. Escorting warships, among them HMS *Marne*, *Millbrook* and *Pigeon*, picked up the survivors. They also succeeded in sinking the UB124.
Casualties: 16 (all engine room crew)

Holland Amerika ordered the *Statendam* for its transatlantic express service prior to the First World War. Still incomplete when she was taken over by the British Government for conversion into a troopship, she was renamed *Justicia*, perhaps denoting an intention to place her under Cunard Line control, but when she entered service, in April 1917, it was under the management of White Star Line. This rare view shows her making her maiden arrival at New York with White Star Line's *Adriatic* in attendance.
Richard de Kerbrech (Mystic Seaport Museum)

Another view of the *Justicia*, the former *Statendam*.
In her short life she was also painted in dazzle colouring.
Imperial War Museum (Q61171)

STATENDAM (1929) Holland Amerika Line, The Netherlands

29,511grt; 698ft (212.7m) loa x 81ft (24.7m) beam
1,654 passengers in four classes
Harland & Wolff, Belfast (Yard No 612)
Steam turbines, twin screw

Until the advent of the *Nieuw Amsterdam* in March 1938, the *Statendam* (1929) was the flagship of the Holland Amerika Line and its largest ship, sailing in the premier service between Rotterdam and New York. *L. L. von Münching*

The *Statendam* on fire at the Wilhelminakade, Rotterdam, in May 1940. *Author's collection*

These detailed views give an indication of the extent of the damage caused to the *Statendam* by shellfire and bombs and the fire they ignited. *Both: L .L. von Münching*

In December 1939 the passenger liner *Statendam* was laid up at Rotterdam, where it was believed that she would remain safe under the protection of Dutch neutrality. However, when Germany invaded the Netherlands in May 1940 the *Statendam* was trapped in the docks at Rotterdam, tied up alongside at the Wilhelminakade. On 11 May, as the fighting reached the docks area, she was caught in the crossfire of ground forces, together with fleet-mates *Veendam* and *Boschdyk*. She was also bombed by German aircraft and caught fire; over the next three days she was completely burned out. In August 1940 the wrecked liner, quite beyond recovery, was towed to Hendrik Ido Ambacht and broken up; a complete waste, for she could have proved extremely valuable to the occupying forces.
Casualties: not known

STATE OF FLORIDA (1875) ex-*Queen Margaret* (1880) State Line, UK

3,155grt; 372ft (113.3m) lbp x 38ft (11.7m) beam
570 passengers in three classes
London & Glasgow Shipbuilding Co, Govan
(Yard No 181)
Compound-expansion steam reciprocating, single screw

The Glasgow-registered passenger steamship *State of Florida* was returning to her home port from New York on 18 April 1884 with 89 passengers and 78 crew. Approaching her in Miramichi Bay, New Brunswick, on a collision course, was the small wooden barque *Ponema*, on passage from Liverpool to Chatham in ballast. The two vessels collided in the position 49.00N, 36.10W, about 1,200 miles west of Ireland. It was apparently a fine, clear night, yet the ships seem not to have been aware of each other until virtually the moment of impact. The *Ponema* crashed into the *State of Florida*'s starboard side, demolishing four lifeboats as she careered off into the night. Her bows were completely shattered and she foundered almost instantaneously, certainly before any of her boats could be lowered. Only her Master and two sailors were saved. Aboard the *State of Florida* the remaining four lifeboats were launched safely enough, although one of these later capsized, spilling its occupants into the sea. The Norwegian barque *Theresa* picked up the survivors, 47 persons all told, 44 from the *State of Florida* and the three from the *Ponema*.
Casualties: 135 (123 from the *State of Florida*, 12 from the *Ponema*)

STEUBEN (1922) ex-*General von Steuben* (1938) ex-*Munchen* (1930) Norddeutscher Lloyd, Germany

14,690grt; 551ft (167.9m) loa x 65ft (19.8m) beam
484 passengers in single class
Stettiner Vulcan, Stettin-Bredow (Yard No 669)
Triple-expansion steam reciprocating with LP turbine, twin screw

After almost four years of idleness, based at Kiel as a German Navy accommodation ship, the former government cruise ship *Steuben* put to sea as a transport in the Baltic in the summer of 1944. Initially, she conveyed troops to the ever-closer eastern battle front and wounded servicemen on the return voyages back to Kiel. From early 1945 she joined the Operation 'Hannibal' armada assembled to evacuate civilians and military personnel from East Prussia and Silesia. Her final voyage commenced on 9 February 1945 when she left Pillau (Baltiysk) bound for Kiel with 2,500 wounded and 2,000 refugees, together with her 450-strong crew. Shortly before midnight on the following day, when she was off Stolpmünde (Ustka) in the position 54.41N, 16.51E, she was torpedoed by the Russian submarine S13, the boat that had sunk the *Wilhelm Gustloff* (qv) eleven days earlier. Hit by two torpedoes, the *Steuben* sank rapidly and, in spite of efforts from escorting naval vessels, there was heavy loss of life.
Casualties: About 3,000

Following full restoration after the major fire aboard her in New York in February 1930, the *Munchen* spent much of the 1930s as the white-hulled cruise ship *General von Steuben*, her name being shorted to *Steuben* in 1938. Even before she joined the ranks of the 'KdF' cruise fleet, she spent much of the time cruising. *Real Photos*

STOCKHOLM (1939) Swedish America Line, Sweden

29,000grt; 675ft (205.6m) loa x 63ft (25.4m) beam
1,350 passengers in three classes or 640 in single class when cruising (as designed)
Cantieri Riuniti dell'Adriatico, Monfalcone, Trieste (Yard No not known)
Motor-ship, triple screw

Scheduled to enter the Stockholm to New York service in March 1939, the dual-purpose transatlantic liner and cruise ship *Stockholm*, one of the first passenger vessels of this configuration, was nearing completion on 19 December 1938 when fire broke out aboard her at the builders' yard. Caused by an electrical short-circuit, it soon had a firm grip on the entire vessel, the flames being fanned by a strong wind. Fire-fighting was made difficult by the clouds of dense acrid smoke that belched from the blazing ship. The *Stockholm* eventually heeled over and capsized at the fitting-out quay

and a survey declared her fit only for scrap. Her engines, however, were salvaged and installed in a replica ship, bearing the same name (qv), which was constructed to replace her.
Casualties: not known

Swedish America Line's dual-role passenger liner and cruise ship *Stockholm* had her accommodation spaces laid out specially to facilitate rapid transition between roles. She caught fire when almost complete and is seen ablaze and listing at Monfalcone on 19 December 1938. *Cantieri Riuniti dell'Adriatico*

STOCKHOLM (1941) Swedish America Line, Sweden

serving under the wartime name SABAUDIA
29,307grt; 675ft (205.7m) loa x 83ft (25.3m) beam
1,350 passengers in three classes or 640 passengers in single class when cruising (as designed)
Cantieri Riuniti dell'Adriatico, Monfalcone, Trieste (Yard No 1203)
Motor-ship, triple screw

The replacement *Stockholm* (see the *Stockholm* above) was finally completed in October 1941, only to find herself blockaded by the war that had broken out during her delayed construction. Her owners, Swedish America Line, being unable to take delivery of the vessel, sold her to the Italian Government, which placed her under the management of the Italia Line with the intention of using her as a troop transport. She was renamed *Sabaudia* on 6 December 1941. Her movements between then and September 1943, when the war with Italy came to an end, are unclear. It has been claimed that the *Sabaudia* made a limited number of trooping voyages, but there is no evidence to support this. The fact that she had still not received a full complement of lifeboats by 1944 suggests otherwise. In fact, although she was partially converted into a troopship, she remained inactive, laid up at Trieste throughout, until the Germans commandeered her for use, briefly, as a barracks ship. Later she was towed to a supposedly safer anchorage at Vallone de Zaule, north of Muggia, but she was discovered there by RAF warplanes on 6 July 1944, bombed and set on fire. The drifting and blazing ship eventually ran aground, listing over to starboard and partially sunk on her beam ends. Further air raids in early 1945 only served to worsen the damage. The gutted wreck, lying in disputed Adriatic waters since the war's end, was finally refloated in 1947 and taken to the San Rocco shipyard at Muggia for breaking-up. The career of the *Stockholm/Sabaudia* had been brief and unproductive, but her main engines were salvaged and installed in new vessels then under construction.
Casualties: not known

The replacement *Stockholm*, launched on 10 March 1940, ran trials in October 1941 wearing Swedish America Line colours, but she was not delivered to her owners, even though Sweden was a neutral country, because of war risks, but also because the transatlantic service had been suspended.
Cantieri Riuniti dell'Adriatico

As the Italian troopship *Sabaudia*, the *Stockholm* is seen in the shipyard at Monfalcone. Though some conversion work was carried out, she was never used. Her hull and funnel also appear to have been repainted. *Aldo Fraccaroli*

The wrecked *Sabaudia* at Vallone di Zaule. *Alex Duncan*

STRATHALLAN (1938) P&O Line, UK

23,722grt; 664ft (202.4m) loa x 82ft (25.0m) beam
1,011 passengers in two classes
Vickers-Armstrongs, Barrow-in-Furness (Yard No 723)
Steam turbines, twin screw

Eighteen months after first entering service, the *Strathallan* was requisitioned for service as a Second World War troopship. Her loss, in late 1942, was another instance of the many passenger ships sunk at or around the time of the Allied landings in North Africa. She had sailed in convoy from Glasgow on 11 December 1942, carrying a total of 5,122

persons, including 4,408 reinforcement troops, 248 nurses and a crew of 431. Ten days later, when she was about forty miles north of Oran (Ouahran), in the position 36.52N, 00.34W, she was torpedoed by the German submarine U562. Fires that started in her engine room spread to a cargo hold containing ammunition, causing huge explosions. The ship was immediately and rapidly abandoned because of the risk of more explosions as the fire raced through the lower decks towards other ammunition stores. The survivors were picked up safely by other ships, some of which ventured close to the stricken *Strathallan*'s stern, despite the evident danger, in order to expedite the evacuation. The ship itself was taken in tow by a salvage tug but sank on the morning of 22 December 1942 in the position 30.01N, 00.33W, only twelve miles from port.
Casualties: 11 (5 troops and 6 crew)

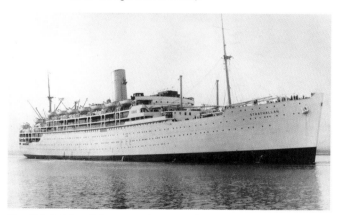

The third ship of the second group of P&O's 'White Sisters', introduced to the London to Sydney service in the 1930s, was the *Strathallan*. *P&O*

The *Strathallan* ablaze after she had been torpedoed north of Oran on 21 December 1942. *P&O*

STROMMA REX (1948) ex-*Prince Philippe* (1973) Stromma Belgium NV, Belgium

3,701grt; 373ft (113.7m) loa x 49ft (14.9m) beam
1,638 passengers
Cockerill, Hoboken (Yard No 727)
Motor-ship, twin screw

After 25 years on the cross-Channel service between Ostend and Dover, the *Prince Philippe* was transferred to the Baltic under the name *Stromma Rex* to operate the regular ferry service between Norrkoping, Sweden and Mariehamn, on the Aland Islands, Finland. On 2 September 1973, as she was approaching Mariehamm with 156 passengers, there was an explosion in her engine room followed by a fire. Despite the loss of power and the already spreading fire, her Master managed to berth the ship to permit all passengers and crew to safely disembark. The *Stromma Rex* was not so fortunate, however, and by the time the blaze had abated, after eight hours, she was gutted throughout. Declared a constructive total loss, she was sold to breakers at Ystad where demolition commenced in October 1973.

Casualties: 0

The former Belgian cross-Channel ferry *Prince Philippe* is seen at Ostend in April 1973 after she had been adapted as the *Stromma Rex* for Baltic service after her days on the Dover route were ended. *John Edgington*

STUTTGART (1923) Deutsche Arbeitsfront, Germany (managed by Norddeutscher Lloyd)

13,387grt; 551ft (167.9) loa x 65ft (19.8m) beam
990 passengers in single class
Stettiner Vulcan, Stettin-Bredow (Yard No 670)
Triple-expansion steam reciprocating, twin screw

The state cruise ship *Stuttgart* was transferred to the German Navy in late 1939 and converted into a hospital ship, based in the Baltic. During the first Allied air raid on the port of Gotenhafen (Gdynia), on 9 October 1943, she was bombed and set on fire by American warplanes. At the time she had a large number of wounded servicemen being treated in her wards, only very few of whom could be rescued as the fire spread rapidly out of control. Blazing from end to end, the wrecked ship was towed outside the harbour and sunk by gunfire with the bodies of the victims still on board.

Casualties: 80-100

Formerly employed on the North Atlantic service from Bremerhaven to New York, the *Stuttgart* was transferred to the Deutsche Arbeitsfront in 1938 and used full-time on 'KdF' workers' cruises, although she remained under the management of her original owners, Norddeutscher Lloyd. *B. & A. Feilden*

SUEVIC (1901) White Star Line, UK

12,531grt; 565ft (172.2m) loa x 63ft (19.3m) beam
400 passengers in single class
Harland & Wolff, Belfast (Yard No 333)
Quadruple-expansion steam reciprocating, twin screw

The passenger-cargo liner *Suevic* was stranded on Stag Rock near the Lizard when homeward-bound from Melbourne on 17 March 1907. She was due to call at Plymouth and London to disembark her 382 passengers before returning to Liverpool, her home port. In the foggy conditions in the Channel approaches, the distance to the shore was misjudged. Unwisely, depth soundings were not taken and the ship was already upon the rocks before any corrective action was taken. The engines were put astern but the firmly wedged *Suevic* could not be budged. Lifeboats from all the stations along the coast went to the ship's assistance. They took off the passengers and 74 members of the crew, landing them at Cadgwith and Coverack, from where they were ferried to Helston.

The salvage steamers *Ranger* and *Linnet* of the Liverpool & Glasgow Salvage Association were dispatched to the scene to organise the offloading of the *Suevic*'s cargo and to undertake the refloating of the vessel if this was possible. However, the bow section was firmly held and had sustained severe bottom damage through the motion caused by the Atlantic swell. Had the stern section not been in reasonably sound condition it is likely that the *Suevic* would have been abandoned as a total loss there and then. As it was, the salvors decided to cut the vessel in two using explosives, at a point between her bridge structure and second mast. Gelignite had to be used as the use of oxy-acetylene was then unknown. This accomplished, the bow was left to break up while the 400-foot (121.9m) after section, which contained the engines, boilers and virtually all of the passenger accommodation, was towed to Southampton for rebuilding.

A new 212-foot (64.6m) bow section was constructed at the Belfast shipyard of Harland & Wolff and towed around the coast by the tugs *Blazer* and *Pathfinder*, arriving at Southampton on 25 October 1907. The surgery was then completed by the connection of the two sections in dry dock, a technique already proven when a similar reconstruction of the Royal Mail ship *Lochmona* was undertaken after she broke in two in the entrance to the River Mersey. The *Suevic* returned to service, as good as new, in January 1908. She enjoyed a long life from this date, serving as a troopship in the First World War and ending her days as a whaling mother-ship.

Casualties: 0

The White Star's *Suevic*, with sister ship *Runic*, maintained her owners' Australia service via Cape Town. It was on the homeward leg of one of these voyages that she was impaled on Stag Rock, near the Lizard peninsula. *M. R. M. Cooper*

Following a salvage operation, in which her bow section was abandoned, the *Suevic* was rebuilt at Southampton and saw 20 more years' passenger service.
Richard de Kerbrech collection / Gibsons

SUN VISTA (1963) ex-*Meridian* (1997) ex-*Galileo* (1989) ex-*Galileo Galilei* (1984) Metro Holdings, Bahamas

30,440grt; 702ft (213.9m) loa x 94ft (28.6m) beam
1,428 passengers
Cantieri Riuniti dell'Adriatico, Monfalcone
(Yard No 1862)
Steam turbines, twin screw

The Lloyd Triestino passenger liner *Galileo Galilei* was converted into a full-time cruise ship, and by 1997 was trading under the name *Sun Vista*. On 20 May 1999, while she was off Penang, Malaysia, bound for Singapore during a cruising in waters off South East Asia with 1,104 passengers, fire broke out in her engine room. All passengers and crew were evacuated in orderly fashion before the *Sun Vista* sank in the position 04.36N, 99.52E.
Casualties: 0

The cruise ship *Sun Vista*, formerly the Lloyd Triestino passenger liner *Galileo Galilei*, arrives at Singapore.
Ian Shiffman

SUPERFERRY 7 (1980) ex-*Wilines Mabuhay 2* (1996) ex-*Naminoue Ferry* (1996) W. G. & A. Jebsens, Philippines

4,886grt; 461ft (140.5m) loa x 67ft (20.5m) beam
Passenger numbers not known
Towa, Shimonoseki (Yard No 525)
Motor-ship, twin screw

The ro-ro passenger ship *Superferry 7* was in Manila's north harbour on 26 March 1993 when she caught fire. All her 1,600 passengers had disembarked prior to the outbreak. Her accommodation was completely gutted and the hulk was towed to an anchorage where it was abandoned half-submerged. It was raised late in 1997, after four years of being flooded in this situation, by which time she was unfit for any kind of restoration and was broken up by the salvors on the spot.
Casualties: not known

SUPERFERRY 9 (1986) ex-*Wilines Mabuhay 5* (1996) ex-*Ariake* (1995) Aboitiz Transport System, Philippines

7,269 grt; 464ft (141.5m) loa x 76ft (23.0m) beam
passenger numbers not known
Usuki Tekkosho, Saiki (yard no. 1328)
Motor-ship, single screw

After passing through the Basilan Strait, bound from General Santos City, in the south of the Philippines archipelago, to Iloilo, on Panay Island, in the early hours of 5 September 2009, the ro-ro passenger ferry *Superferry 9* began to list severely. She was some ten miles west of Bonga Point, Siocon Bay, to the northwest of Zamboanga, Mindanao. The cause was unknown although the ship had reported generator problems and it was speculated that she had a hole in her side. Aboard her were a total of 968 persons, 851 passengers and 117 crew. Distress calls were transmitted and an evacuation started using rafts but many of the frightened passengers were reluctant to leave the ship. The *Superferry 9* sank some six hours after the emergency began. The rescue ships that had arrived on the scene while she was still on the surface were initially able to pick up some 870 persons; 258 of them aboard the passenger ship *Ocean Integrity*, 441 aboard the rescue vessel *Myriad*, a fleet-mate of the *Superferry 9*, and 171 aboard the Philippines Navy gunboat 116. Subsequently, a further 87 persons were found safe. In May 2009, the *Superferry 9* had been involved in another incident when her engines failed off Camiguin province, leaving 900 passengers stranded.
Casualties: 9 fatalities plus 2 unaccounted for. This assumes that the manifested complement is correct as well as the figures for survivors, as communicated by the various rescue vessels.

SUPERFERRY 14 (1981) ex-*White Sanpo 2* (2000) W. G. & A. Jebsens, Philippines

10,181grt; 510ft (155.6m loa) x 77ft (23.6m) beam
508 berthed and 542 deck passengers
Hayashikane, Shimonoseki (Yard No 1240)
Motor-ship, twin screw

The passenger/vehicle ferry *Superferry 14* caught fire following an explosion when she was off Corregidor, at the entrance to Manila Bay, on 27 February 2004. She had just left

Manila bound overnight to Bacolod, on the north-west coast of Negros Island, with 744 passengers and 155 crew. The fire spread rapidly, necessitating a prompt evacuation of the ship. The *Superferry 14* was grounded and partially sank while the unchecked fire completely gutted her. Although it was reported that the explosion had been in her engine room, it was also suggested that it had been caused deliberately by terrorist action, though as far as is known this was never confirmed.
Casualties: ~119

SUWA MARU (1914) Nippon Yusen Kaisha, Japan

10,672grt; 521ft (158.8m) loa x 62ft (18.9m) beam
511 passengers in three classes
Mitsubishi, Nagasaki (Yard No 236)
Triple-expansion steam reciprocating, twin screw
The passenger-cargo ship *Suwa Maru*, employed as a Japanese wartime troop transport, was torpedoed south-west of Wake Island on 28 March 1943 by the American submarine USS *Tunny*. She was run aground on Wake Island in a damaged condition, the hope being that she might be refloated later and repaired. This was not to be, however, for on 5 April two other US submarines, the *Seadragon* and *Finback*, finished her off. Her wreck lay in the position 19.13N, 166.34E.
Casualties: not known

Apart from a short period between 1917 and 1922, when they were placed in the trans-Pacific service, the five vessels of the class that included Nippon Yusen Kaisha's *Suwa Maru* operated between Japan and Europe through the Suez Canal. *World Ship Society*

SVANETIA (1937) Black Sea Shipping Co (Sovtorgflot), USSR

4,125grt; 331ft (100.7m) x 48ft (14.6m) beam
244 passengers
Helsingors Vaerft, Elsinore (Yard No 244)
Motor-ship, twin screw
The elegant, modern passenger-cargo ship *Svanetia* was employed on the Odessa to Alexandria run via Istanbul. While serving as a troopship, she was caught at Sevastopol on 17 April 1942 during an air raid by German warplanes and bombed and sunk.
Casualties: not known

T

TABORA (1912) Deutsche Ost-Africa Line, Germany

8,022grt; 449ft (136.9m) lbp x 54ft (16.6m) beam
316 passengers in three classes
Blohm & Voss, Steinwerder, Hamburg (Yard No 211)
Quadruple-expansion steam reciprocating, twin screw
While lying at Dar-es-Salaam on 23 March 1916, the German passenger steamship *Tabora* was shelled and sunk by the British warships HMS *Hyacinth*, *Vengeance* and *Challenger*.
Casualties: not known

The German liner *Tabora* operated between Hamburg and East African ports. *H. B. Christiansen Collection / Online Transport Archive*

TACOMA MARU (1909) Osaka Shosen Kaisha, Japan

6,178grt; 419ft (127.7m) lbp x 49ft (14.9m) beam
179 passengers in two classes
Kawasaki, Kobe (Yard No 297)
Triple-expansion steam reciprocating, twin screw
The passenger-cargo ship *Tacoma Maru* was torpedoed by the American submarine USS *Hake* on 1 February 1944 off the island of Halmahera in the Moluccas Group. She sank in the position 01.30N, 128.58E.
Casualties: not known

The *Tacoma Maru*, seen here, was one of the pioneer vessels of Osaka Shosen Kaisha on the trans-Pacific route between Osaka and Tacoma, Washington, which she maintained with her sister ships *Chicago Maru* and *Seattle Maru*. *Mitsui-OSK Lines*

TACORA (1872) Pacific Steam Navigation Co, UK

3,525grt; 375ft (114.3m) lbp x 41ft (12.5m) beam
485 passengers in three classes
John Elder, Govan (Yard No 147)
Compound-expansion steam reciprocating, single screw
The new, clipper-bowed passenger steamship *Tacora* was wrecked near Cape Santa Maria, Montevideo, Uruguay, on 28 October 1872, 24 days after leaving Liverpool on her maiden voyage to Valparaiso, Chile.
Casualties: 13

TAHITI (1904) ex-*Port Kingston* (1904)
Union Steamship Co of New Zealand, UK

7,898grt; 460ft (140.2m) lbp x 55ft (16.9m) beam
515 passengers
Alexander Stephen, Linthouse, Glasgow (Yard No 403)
Triple-expansion steam reciprocating, twin screw
On 16 August 1930, while the passenger steamship *Tahiti* was bound for San Francisco from Wellington, New Zealand, with 128 passengers, a crew of 148 and the mails, she lost her starboard propeller when some 450 miles from Raratonga. The problem was more serious than simply a shed propeller for the propeller shaft had also fractured just forward of the stern tube and the broken portion had punctured the hull and damaged the bulkhead. Water began to flood into the *Tahiti* through the shaft and she was soon in a perilous condition. Distress calls were sent out but it was not until late that day that the Norwegian cargo vessel *Penybryn* reached the scene. Fortunately, the *Tahiti* was faring better than had been expected and, because the weather was fine and there was no immediate danger of her sinking, the *Penybryn* stood by through the night. The following morning the Matson Line passenger ship *Ventura* also arrived to assist, and the *Tahiti*'s passengers, crew and mail were transhipped to her. The *Tahiti* sank stern-first during the evening of 17 August 1930 in the position 26.27S, 166.05W.
Casualties: 0

TAINUI (1908) Shaw, Savill & Albion, UK

serving under the wartime name EMPIRE TRADER
9,957grt; 477ft (145.4m) lbp x 61ft (18.6m) beam
414 passengers in three classes
Workman Clark, Belfast (Yard No 277)
Triple-expansion steam reciprocating, twin screw

The Shaw Savill passenger-cargo ship *Tainui*.
Richard de Kerbrech collection

The passenger-cargo ship *Tainui*, which had in fact been sold to ship-breakers, passed into Government ownership in 1940 and was renamed *Empire Trader*. Her former owners, Shaw Savill Line, retained the management of the ship. While she was crossing to New York from Newport and Belfast on 21 February 1943 in convoy ON166, the *Empire Trader* was torpedoed by the German submarine U92 in the position 48.25N, 30.10W. All 106 survivors were picked up from lifeboats by the Convoy Rescue Ship *Stockport*, which was itself torpedoed two days later. Meanwhile, the *Empire Trader* was escorted in the direction of the Azores by HMCS *Dauphin*, but on the orders of the Admiralty, because the main convoy required the escort's attentions, she was shelled and sunk by the corvette in the position 48.27N, 29.47W.
Casualties: 0

TAIYO MARU (1911) ex-*Cap Finisterre* (1920)
Nippon Yusen Kaisha, Japan

14,457grt; 591ft (180.1m) loa x 65ft (19.8m) beam
344 passengers in single class
Blohm & Voss, Steinwerder, Hamburg (Yard No 208)
Quadruple-expansion steam reciprocating, twin screw
On 8 May 1942 the passenger-cargo liner *Taiyo Maru*, which had been taken over by the Japanese Government after war broke out in the Pacific, was bound for South East Asian ports with a large complement of more than 1,000 persons, including her 300-strong crew. The passengers comprised around 700 industrialists, engineers and mechanics from the Mitsui organisation, who were tasked with setting up manufacturing facilities using native labour forces in the countries that Japan had conquered. When the *Taiyo Maru* was south-west of the island of Kyushu, in the position 30.45N, 127.40E, she was torpedoed by the submarine USS *Grenadier* and sank with heavy loss of life.
Casualties: ~780

The Hamburg-Sud Amerika liner *Cap Finisterre* was ceded to the Japanese as a First World War reparation after spending a brief interlude as an American-flag troopship. Toyo Kisen Kaisha placed her in the Pacific service from Yokohama to San Francisco, renaming her *Taiyo Maru*. In 1926 she passed to Nippon Yusen Kaisha when the two companies merged.
Real Photos

TAKACHIHO [TAKATIHO] MARU (1934)
Osaka Shosen Kaisha, Japan

8,154grt; 473ft (144.2m) loa x 59ft (18.0m) beam
785 passengers
Mitsubishi, Nagasaki (Yard No 533)
Steam turbines, twin screw

From late 1941 the passenger-cargo ship *Takachiho Maru* was diverted to war activities with the Japanese military forces, continuing in this capacity until 19 March 1943 when she was torpedoed and sunk by the American submarine USS *Kingfish*. The attack took place about 150 miles east of Foochow, in the position 25.50N, 122.30E.
Casualties: not known

TAKLIWA (1924) British India Line, UK

7,936grt; 466ft (142.0m) loa x 60ft (18.4m) beam
136 berthed and 3,302 deck passengers
Barclay Curle, Whiteinch, Glasgow (Yard No 601)
Triple-expansion steam reciprocating, twin screw
The passenger-cargo steamer *Takliwa*, which provided accommodation for a large number of native passengers on Far East and Indian Ocean routes, was stranded at Parsons Point, Great Nicobar Islands, in the Andaman Sea, west of Thailand, on 14 October 1945, and was subsequently burned out and destroyed. She had been en route from Hong Kong to Madras at the time. Casualties: not known

TALAMBA (1924) British India Line, UK

8,018grt; 466ft (142.0m) loa x 60ft (18.3m) beam
128 berthed and 2,777 deck passengers
Hawthorn Leslie, Hebburn-on-Tyne (Yard No 533)
Triple-expansion steam reciprocating, twin screw
During the Second World War the *Talamba* served as a hospital ship. Late in the evening of 10 July 1943, while employed in this capacity during Operation 'Husky', the Allied landings at Sicily, she was bombed and sunk three miles off Avola, Sicily. Besides her crew of 168, the *Talamba* had embarked 400 or so wounded servicemen just prior to the attack. Her status was clearly evident as she was brightly illuminated and was painted in hospital ship livery, but this did not deter the German aircraft from attacking her. She foundered early on the following day in the position 36.55N, 15.14E. The wounded and the majority of her crew were rescued by other ships. Casualties: 5 (all crew)

The *Talamba* was sister ship to the *Tairea* and *Takliwa*, which maintained British India Line's service from India to South Africa. They were small ships to have three funnels.
World Ship Society

TALTHYBIUS (1912) Blue Funnel Line, UK

serving under the wartime name TARUYASU MARU
10,224grt; 518ft (157.9m) loa x 60ft (18.3m) beam
600 passengers in single class
Scott's, Greenock (Yard No 436)
Triple-expansion steam reciprocating, twin screw

The passenger-cargo liner *Talthybius* was captured by the Japanese in a damaged and waterlogged condition at Singapore in February 1942. Raised and repaired, she was placed in service as the *Taruyasu Maru*. On 30 June 1945 she struck a mine off Toyama in the position 37.07N, 137.04E and sank. After the war the British salvaged her and she was sent to Hong Kong for repairs, arriving on 23 November 1948. Patched up and renamed *Empire Evenlode* for the voyage home, she was sent to the scrapyard at Briton Ferry, Glamorgan, on her arrival in September 1949. Although renamed and returned to the UK, the former *Talthybius* had no further commercial value, did not return to the service of her owners, and was effectively a war loss under the Japanese flag.
Casualties: not known (when mined)

TAMPOMAS II (1971) ex-*Great Emerald* (1980) ex-*Emerald* (1980) ex-*Central No 6* (1975) PT Pelayaran Nasional, Indonesia

6,139grt; 422ft (128.6m) loa x 75ft (22.7m) beam
718 passengers
Mitsubishi, Shimonoseki (Yard No 689)
Motor-ship, twin screw
The worst Indonesian shipping disaster involved the ro-ro ferry *Tampomas II*, which caught fire in the Java Sea on 27 January 1981 while bound from Jakarta to Ujung Pandang, Sulawesi, with 1,054 manifested passengers and a crew of 82. The outbreak, which originated on the car deck, occurred off the south-east coast of Kalimantan, off the Masalembo Islands, when the ship was two days out. The fire spread rapidly, followed by explosions. The weather was poor with heavy monsoon rain and rough seas, which hampered the rescue efforts, and many of the passengers, in a state of panic, jumped over the side without waiting for a formal abandonment in the lifeboats. Rescue craft tried to assist the evacuation of some 500 passengers who were trapped at the stern, but because of the sea state they were unable to approach closer than 200 metres. The *Tampomas II* was suddenly rocked by another explosion and sank rapidly, taking those still aboard with her. It was reported that 753 persons had survived the disaster, including 70 of the crew, but the true extent of the disaster will never be known for many passengers had boarded without tickets and were not, therefore, reflected in the manifested number. It can be seen that the total of the rescued, together with the number of those who had perished, according to the official counts, does not tally with the number of persons she was said to have been carrying.
Casualties: 431 (official figure)

TANGANJIKA (1922) Hamburg Amerika Line, Germany

8,540grt; 449ft (136.9m) lbp x 58ft (17.7m) beam
250 passengers
Blohm & Voss, Steinwerder, Hamburg (Yard No 459)
Steam turbines, single screw
The passenger-cargo ship *Tanganjika* was at Wilhelmshaven on 4 November 1943 when the port was subjected to an Allied air raid. She was bombed, set on fire and sunk. The wreck was salvaged and broken up after the war.
Casualties: not known

TANGO MARU (1905) Nippon Yusen Kaisha, Japan

7,475grt; 456ft (139.0m) lbp x 52ft (15.9m) beam
274 passengers in three classes
Mitsubishi, Nagasaki (Yard No 156)
Triple-expansion steam reciprocating, twin screw
The passenger steamship *Tango Maru* was lost in the East China Sea on 19 September 1943, but although she was engaged as a military auxiliary, the circumstances had nothing to do with the war. She was wrecked at Naze, Amamioshima, but it is not known whether the cause was adverse weather or navigational error. The records at Lloyd's advise that she was sunk on 13 November 1943 through unspecified 'war causes', but this is incorrect. Another Japanese vessel by the name of *Tango Maru*, a cargo ship utilised as a transport, was sunk on 25 February 1944 (see Appendix 2) and the two ships may have been confused.
Casualties: not known

TANNENBERG (1935) Hamburg Amerika Line, Germany

5,504grt; 398ft (121.3m) loa x 51ft (15.6m) beam
753 berthed and 1,175 deck passengers
Stettiner Oderwerke, Stettin-Grabow (Yard No 780)
Steam turbines, twin screw
The *Tannenberg* was an elegant passenger ship engaged in the pre-war Seedienst Ostpreussen service. Of her 753 berthed passengers, the majority were accommodated in a type of Steerage class or 'Wanderkojen', probably in dormitory berths. For details of her loss, see the *Preussen*.

The smart white Baltic passenger ship *Tannenberg* of the 'Seedienst Ostpreussen' was owned by Hamburg Amerika Line. *Arnold Kludas*

TANTALLON CASTLE (1894) Union-Castle Line, UK

5,636grt; 440ft (134.2m) lbp x 51ft (15.4m) beam
490 passengers in three classes
Fairfield, Govan (Yard No 373)
Quadruple-expansion steam reciprocating, single screw
The passenger-cargo steamer *Tantallon Castle*, the first Union-Castle vessel to have quadruple-expansion steam engines installed, was wrecked after she ran aground in fog on Robben Island, at the entrance to Table Bay. The accident occurred on 7 May 1901 as she was nearing the end of an outward voyage to Cape Town from Southampton. Within a few days the ship had been reduced to no more than a pile of wreckage, with material strewn about the nearby beaches.
Casualties: not known

TARSUS (1931) ex-*Harry Lee* (1948) ex-*Exochorda* (1940) Turkish State Maritime, Turkey

9,359grt; 475ft loa (138.1m lbp) x 62ft (18.8m) beam
465 passengers
New York Shipbuilding Corp, Camden, New Jersey (Yard No 395)
Steam turbines, single screw
On 14 December 1960, while anchored near Istinye in the Bosphorus, the passenger-cargo ship *Tarsus* was gutted by fire in the most unfortunate circumstances. The Yugoslav tanker *Peter Zoranic*, bound from Tuapse, south of Novorossiysk, in the Black Sea, to Hamburg with a cargo of benzene and petrol, was in collision in the Bosphorus with the Greek tanker *World Harmony*, which was heading for Novorossiysk in ballast. Locked together by the impact of the collision, the blazing tankers drifted onto the *Tarsus*, on which customs clearance activities had been in progress, setting her alight as well. All three ships were completely burned out. Many of those who survived the disaster had severe burn injuries.
Casualties: 52

The Turkish State Maritime passenger ship *Tarsus* was the only survivor of American Export Line's pre-war 'Four Aces' class. Her accommodation was expanded significantly for the Istanbul to New York service. *World Ship Society*

TARTAR (1883) Canadian Pacific Line, UK

4,425grt; 377ft (114.7m) lbp x 47ft (14.3m) beam
280 passengers in three classes
Aiken & Mansel, Whiteinch, Glasgow (Yard No 116)
Triple-expansion steam reciprocating, single screw
The passenger steamship *Tartar* was acquired from the Union Line by Canadian Pacific for employment on the trans-Pacific service and she sailed to Vancouver from Southampton via Cape Horn. She also made six voyages to Skagway with prospectors at the time of the Klondike gold-rush. On 17 October 1907 she was in collision with the Canadian Pacific coastal steamer *Charmer* and was beached at English Bay, British Columbia. Beyond economic recovery, the *Tartar* was subsequently sold for breaking-up at Osaka, where she arrived in March 1908. Casualties: 0

TASMANIA (1884) P&O Line, UK

4,488grt; 400ft (122.0m) lbp x 45ft (13.8m) beam
151 passengers in two classes
Caird, Greenock (Yard No 237)
Compound-expansion steam reciprocating, single screw
While she was returning to London from Bombay via the Mediterranean, with a call scheduled at Marseilles, the passenger-cargo steamer *Tasmania* was wrecked off the coast of Corsica on 17 March 1887. In the early hours of the morning she struck the Monachi Rocks, off Point Roccapina, with considerable force, leaving her forepart, from the bow to the mizzen mast, submerged. The 120 passengers and 161 crew sought refuge at the ship's after end while evacuation of the ship was organised. In the heavy seas, eight boats were smashed or swamped, but by daybreak the majority of the women and children passengers had been safely got away. The remainder of the *Tasmania*'s occupants were rescued during the morning of 18 March by the yacht *Norseman* and the French steamship *Perseverant*. Those who were killed, all officers and crew, were washed overboard and drowned while supervising the launching of boats.
Casualties: 34 (all crew, including the Master and First Officer)

The *Tasmania* was lead ship of a class of four, the others being the *Chusan*, *Coromandel* and *Bengal*. Designed for P&O's India service, they could also act as relief ships on the Australia route, while rapid conversion into troopships or auxiliary cruisers was also catered for in their specification.
Tom Rayner collection

TATSUTA [TATUTA] MARU (1930) Nippon Yusen Kaisha, Japan

16,975grt; 583ft (177.7m) loa x 72ft (21.9m) beam
820 passengers in three classes
Mitsubishi, Nagasaki (Yard No 451)
Motor-ship, quadruple screw
In 1941 the passenger liner *Tatsuta Maru* was taken over by the Japanese Navy for trooping duties. In this capacity she was torpedoed and sunk by the US submarine *Tarpon* on 8 February 1943, in the position 33.45N, 140.25E, about fifty miles south-east of Mikura Jima, off the eastern coast of Honshu.
Casualties: not known

Sister ship to the *Asama Maru*, the *Tatsuta Maru* operated with her consort on the service from Yokohama to San Francisco.
Nippon Yusen Kaisha

TEL AVIV (1909) ex-*Martha Washington* (1934) Cosulich Line, Italy

8,347grt; 459ft (140.2m) lbp x 56ft (17.1m) beam
1,373 passengers in two classes
Russell, Port Glasgow (Yard No 589)
Triple-expansion steam reciprocating, twin screw
Fire broke out in the passenger accommodation of the passenger-cargo ship *Tel Aviv* on 27 March 1934 while she was docked at Trieste. The damage, which was estimated to exceed 1 million lire, affected many of the Second-class cabins, her main hall and the bridge and navigation areas. Some decks were completely gutted and many plates and beams were buckled or had fallen in. The *Tel Aviv* was taken to the Sant'Andrea dry dock for repairs to be carried out, but instead she was scrapped locally by Cantieri Riuniti dell'Adriatico, as reconstruction was not financially practicable.
Casualties: not known

TERUKUNI MARU (1930) Nippon Yusen Kaisha, Japan

11,930grt; 527ft (160.6m) loa x 64ft (19.5m) beam
249 passengers in three classes
Mitsubishi, Nagasaki (Yard No 467)
Motor-ship, twin screw
On 21 November 1939, as the Japanese passenger-cargo ship *Terukuni Maru* was nearing the end of a Europe-bound voyage, she struck a mine in the mouth of the River Thames, 1½ miles from the Sunk lightship. The explosion opened up Nos 2 and 3 holds and she sank inside an hour in the position 51.50N, 01.30E. Eight lifeboats were launched, permitting all of the 206 persons she was carrying to escape, among them 28 passengers. The *Terukuni Maru* became Japan's first passenger ship casualty of the Second World War, even though it was more than two years before Japan became involved in the conflict.
Casualties: 0

The *Terukuni Maru* operated on the service from Yokohama to London, Rotterdam and Hamburg. Her sister ship on the route was the *Yasukuni Maru*, and both were Second World War losses, but in quite different circumstances. *Bettina Rohbrecht*

TEVERE (1912) ex-*Gablonz* (1921) Lloyd Triestino, Italy

8,448grt; 452ft (137.8m) lbp x 56ft (17.1m) beam
240 passengers
Cantieri San Rocco, San Rocco, Trieste (Yard No 21)
Quadruple-expansion steam reciprocating, twin screw
The passenger-cargo ship *Tevere* was taken over as an Italian Navy hospital ship in 1940. On 21 April 1941, while undergoing repairs to mine damage sustained on 22 February 1941 in the approaches to Tripoli, she was bombed during an air raid on the Libyan port. This essentially sealed her fate, for she was never fully repaired and on 20 January 1943 she was scuttled by withdrawing Italian forces to deny access to the port to the Allies. Not refloated until 16 January 1950, she was towed to Savona for scrapping on 6 May of that year.
Casualties: not known

The three Lloyd Austriaco sister ships *Helouan*, *Gablonz* and *Wien* passed into Lloyd Triestino ownership after the First World War. The *Gablonz*, renamed *Tevere*, was operated in the service from Italy to the Far East. *World Ship Society*

TEXAS (1872) Dominion Line, UK

2,818grt; 325ft (99.1m) lbp x 36ft (11.0m) beam
680 passengers in two classes
A. McMillan, Dumbarton (Yard No 171)
Compound-expansion steam reciprocating, single screw
While bound for Montreal from Avonmouth on 4 June 1894, the passenger steamship *Texas* was wrecked at St Shotts, near Cape Race.
Casualties: 0

THE FIESTA (1957) ex-*Sun Ambassador* (1991) ex-*Veracruz 1* (1990) ex-*Veracruz Primero* (1983) ex-*Freeport* (1976) ex-*Carnivale* (1975) ex-*Theodor Herzl* (1969) Festival Shipping & Tourist Enterprises, Greece

6,193grt; 488ft (148.7m) loa x 65ft (19.72m) beam
960 passengers
Deutsche Werft, Finkenwerder (Yard No 697)
Steam turbines, twin screw

The cruise ship *The Fiesta*, a converted scheduled-service passenger-cargo liner, was lost on 14 October 1991. She caught fire in a shipyard at Drapetzona, Piraeus, while undergoing a facelift and overhaul, and capsized at her berth as a result of becoming top heavy from water poured into her by fire-fighters. Severely damaged and beyond economic recovery, her wreck had been removed for disposal by March 1992.
Casualties: not known

THEOPHILE GAUTIER (1926) Messageries Maritimes, France

8,194grt; 445ft (135.6m) loa x 56ft (17.1m) beam
280 passengers
Chantiers de France, Dunkirk (Yard No 132)
Motor-ship, twin screw
The French motor-passenger ship *Theophile Gautier* came under the control of the Vichy régime following the Armistice agreed between France and Germany in June 1940. After departing from Piraeus, she remained at Beirut from 16 September 1940 to 11 June 1941 when, exposed to aerial bombardment as the British campaign in Syria pushed towards the Mediterranean coast, she sailed again for Thessaloniki, Greece, by then an Axis safe haven, where she arrived unharmed on 19 June. Clearly, she was viewed as an enemy vessel and thus a legitimate target when the British submarine HMS *Talisman* encountered her in the Aegean Sea on 4 October 1941, sailing in a convoy escorted by Italian torpedo-boats bound for Marseilles with 5 military passengers and a crew of 105 men. Torpedoes were fired at the *Theophile Gautier* as she was passing Euboea Island and she sank soon after in the position 37.50N, 24.25E.
Casualties: 18 (2 soldiers and 16 crew)

The *Theophile Gautier* was the first French-built passenger motor-ship. She ran a circular line service in the Mediterranean, which was extended in 1937 to take her into the Black Sea. *World Ship Society*

THEOSKEPASTI (1962) ex-*Isla de Coche* (1986) ex-*Nordia* (1974) Pyrgi Chios Shipping Co, Greece

3,749grt; 322ft (98.0m) loa x 61ft (18.6m) beam
1,140 passengers
Wartsila Sandviken, Helsinki (Yard No 370)
Motor-ship, twin screw
The ro-ro passenger ferry *Theoskepasti* caught fire on 24 October 1987 when she was in St George Harbour, Piraeus, undergoing repairs. It was a major outbreak and the vessel was soon engulfed in flames, the fire raging for six days and completely gutting her. In this condition she was towed out of the port and beached close to Atalanti Island, between Piraeus and Salamis, on 30 October. She was subsequently refloated but, declared a constructive total loss, she was beached for a second time, at Eleusis, on 13 November 1987 to await breaking-up. Casualties: 0

The ro-ro ferry *Theoskepasti* heads to sea from Rafina in September 1987, her stern door wide open in the ramp position. *Frank Heine FERRIES*

THERMOPYLAE (1891) Aberdeen Line, UK

3,711grt; 362ft (110.4m) lbp x 44ft (13.5m) beam
695 passengers in two classes
Hall Russell, Aberdeen (Yard No 264)
Triple-expansion steam reciprocating, single screw
The *Thermopylae*, an elegant green-hulled, clipper-bowed passenger-cargo ship that served on the UK to Australia route via the Cape of Good Hope, became a total loss on 13 September 1899 after running onto the rocks at Green Point, Cape Town. Casualties: 0

THESSALONIKI (1890) ex-*City of Vienna* (1913) National Greek Line, Greece

4,672grt; 412ft (125.6m) lbp x 47ft (14.2m) beam
1,900 passengers in single class
Workman Clark, Belfast (Yard No 59)
Triple-expansion steam reciprocating, single screw
While bound from Patras, Greece, to New York on 5 January 1916, the emigrant steamer *Thessaloniki* ran into difficulties in bad weather and was abandoned at sea 350 miles east of Sandy Hook. She subsequently foundered, but all aboard her, passengers and crew, were safely rescued. Casualties: 0

THE VIKING (1888) ex-*Atrato* (1913) Viking Cruising Co (part of the Blue Star group), UK

serving under the wartime name VIKNOR
5,386 grt; 421ft (128.4m) lbp x 50ft (15.2m) beam
279 passengers in three classes (as built)
Robert Napier, Govan (Yard No 410)
Triple-expansion steam reciprocating, single screw
The yacht-like cruise ship *The Viking*, built originally for Royal Mail Line, was commandeered by the Admiralty in December 1914 and converted into an Armed Merchant Cruiser attached to the 10th Cruiser Squadron, serving under the name *Viknor*. She was lost on 13 January 1915, in very rough weather off Tory Island, Ulster, foundering with all hands. It was concluded that she had struck a German mine that had only recently been laid in that vicinity but which lookouts had not seen in the inclement conditions. Only a short time earlier she had been in radio contact with the station at Malin Head. Wreckage and dead bodies washed up on the north coast of Ireland for some days after the sinking.
Casualties: 296 (her Master, 22 officers and 273 naval ratings)
NB. Among the *Viknor*'s ratings were 25 seamen from the Newfoundland Division of the Royal Naval Reserve who are commemorated on the Beaumont Hamel Memorial in northern France, at the site of the Battle of the Somme.

TILAWA (1924) British India Line, UK

10,006grt; 471ft (143.6m) loa x 59ft (18.0m) beam
136 berthed and 3,156 deck passengers
Hawthorn Leslie, Hebburn-on-Tyne (Yard No 530)
Quadruple-expansion steam reciprocating, single screw
On 23 November 1942, while she was bound from Bombay to Mombasa and Durban with 732 native passengers, the passenger-cargo ship *Tilawa* was attacked by the Japanese submarine I29. The first torpedo did not cause critical damage but it precipitated panic among the native passengers as they fought desperately to get off the ship. The boats were rushed and in the general pandemonium that followed many accidents were caused and many lives lost. Some were crushed by falling boats that were lowered incorrectly, others were drowned when overcrowded boats capsized. The *Tilawa*'s crew members, numbering 226, were gradually able to assert their authority and restore order to permit a more disciplined abandonment. Subsequently, when it became apparent that the *Tilawa* was not immediately going to sink, the lifeboats and rafts with their occupants were gathered close around the ship with a view to reboarding her. At this point, however, the Japanese submarine fired a second torpedo into the *Tilawa*. She rolled over and rapidly disappeared beneath the surface, sinking in the position 07.35N, 61.06E.
Casualties: 280 (252 native passengers and 28 crew)

The British India steamships *Talma* and *Tilawa*, shown in the photograph, maintained the service from Calcutta to Japan. Apart from higher grades of accommodation, they also offered berths for 1,000 Asiatic passengers in Steerage class. *P&O*

TITANIC (1912) White Star Line, UK

46,329grt; 883ft (269.1m) loa x 93ft (28.2m) beam
2,603 passengers in three classes
Harland & Wolff, Belfast (Yard No 401)
Triple-expansion steam reciprocating with LP steam turbine, triple screw

So much has already been written about the sinking of the transatlantic passenger liner *Titanic* on her maiden voyage that the following account will be largely confined to the basic facts of the incident.

The *Titanic*, the epitome of Edwardian grandeur afloat, sailed from Southampton on 10 April 1912 bound for New York via Cherbourg and Queenstown. On board were 1,308 passengers in three classes and 898 officers and crewmen, a total of 2,206 persons. Four days out, the *Titanic* was steaming at full speed in spite of warnings that ice lay in her path, and when a lookout spotted an iceberg directly ahead at approximately midnight, it proved impossible to avoid it. As it scraped along the liner's starboard side it opened her up like a tin-opener, leaving a gash more than 300 feet long below the waterline that extended through six watertight compartments. It is unlikely that even a modern ship could survive with such damage and certainly not the so-called 'unsinkable' *Titanic*, with her less sophisticated three-compartment standard of watertight subdivision.

Once it became apparent that the great ship was doomed, her occupants were alerted and the lifeboats prepared for an evacuation, but it was only then that the awful realisation dawned upon the impotent victims, that there was insufficient room for all. The lifeboat capacity was adequate for only 1,178 persons maximum. Other ships were alerted to the *Titanic*'s grave situation and rescue now depended upon them, but it was calculated that the ship would already have sunk below the icy surface before even the nearest could reach the scene. Confirming those dire predictions, when the *Carpathia* arrived early on 15 April the *Titanic* had already foundered and barely a third of her complement had survived the ordeal of that harrowing and terrible night in mid-ocean.

Like the later, wartime loss of the *Lusitania*, the *Titanic* disaster may be viewed retrospectively as pivotal, influencing much that followed in terms of attitudes and legislation, albeit positive rather than negative in her case. It prompted the inauguration of the international Safety of Life at Sea (SOLAS) conference, which, in turn, introduced the statutory requirement to provide adequate lifeboats for all. But, indirectly, it also acted as a catalyst for improvements to the overall shipboard provision for and treatment of passengers in all classes. Perhaps the most disturbing feature of the *Titanic* tragedy, apart from the inadequate provision of lifeboats, was the disparity of treatment of passengers according to their status when it came to saving lives. The tradition of the time, if a ship had cause to be abandoned on the ocean, was 'women and children first'. That was not the case on the *Titanic*, however, where considerable discrimination seems to have been practised, and a more accurate description would have been 'wealthiest passengers first, regardless of sex or age'. The breakdown of the numbers of survivors by class attests to this. Of the total passengers that were saved, 41 per cent were from First-class compared with only 36 per cent from Third-class or Steerage, but those figures do not account for the fact that there were far more passengers in the latter category. If a comparison is made between the numbers saved as a percentage of those carried for each class, the disparity is shown to have been much worse, for it was 63 per cent of all First-class passengers in contrast to just 38 per cent of all Steerage passengers. Perhaps the most damning figures are those for the different numbers of rescued women and children, 97 per cent for First-class, 87 per cent for Second-class but just 47 per cent for Steerage.

Contrary to popular myth, the sinking of the *Titanic* is not now the worst maritime disaster ever to have occurred, either in peacetime or wartime. Yet it continues to attract a disproportionate and enduring curiosity that may well be explained by two of the issues central to that particular disaster: first, the folly of believing that human ingenuity could overcome the forces of nature, and second, the lack of regard for the sanctity of life irrespective of race or social standing. Regrettably, in a religious dimension, there are still those at large in the world today who still embrace the latter attitude.

Casualties: 1,503 (1,293 passengers and 210 crew)

A builders' trials photograph of the *Titanic* dating from March 1912. *Harland & Wolff*

A rather romanticised impression of the sinking of the *Titanic*, in common with the majority of the artist's renderings of the disaster. Loss of engine power would have thrown the ship into darkness and, in the middle of the ocean at night, little of the ship would have been discernible. *Author's collection*

TJIKARANG (1\922) Royal Interocean Lines, The Netherlands

9,505grt; 483ft (147.2m) lbp x 60ft (18.3m) beam
12 berthed and 1,920 deck passengers
Nederlandsche Schps Maats, Amsterdam (Yard No 153)
Triple-expansion steam reciprocating, twin screw
On 2 March 1942, at the time of the fall of the Dutch East Indies, the passenger-cargo ship *Tjikarang*, which had predominantly unberthed, deck accommodation, was scuttled at Sourabaya, Java, to prevent her capture and use by the Japanese. Lying in the position 07.11S, 112.43E, the wreck remained there until after the war when it was removed for demolition.
Casualties: not known

The steamship *Tjikarang* operated between the Dutch East Indies and ports on the Chinese mainland, carrying mainly deck passengers. *World Ship Society*

TJINEGARA (1931) Royal Interocean Lines, The Netherlands

9,227grt; 440ft (134.1m) lbp x 62ft (18.9m) beam
160 berthed and 1,600 deck passengers
Nederlandsche Schps Maats, Amsterdam (Yard No 205)
Motor-ship, single screw
During a voyage from Brisbane, Australia, to Noumea, New Caledonia, on 26 July 1942, the passenger-cargo ship *Tjinegara* was torpedoed and sunk by an unidentified Japanese submarine in the position 23.10S, 165.00E. The *Tjinegara* was only about eighty miles from her destination – and safety – when she was attacked.
Casualties: 0

TJISAROEA (1926) Royal Interocean Lines, The Netherlands

serving under the wartime name CHIHAYA MARU
7,089grt; 420ft (128.0m) lbp x 55ft (16.8m) beam
117 berthed and 1,093 deck passengers
Nederlandsche Schps Maats, Amsterdam (Yard No 179)
Steam turbines, single screw
Captured by Japanese forces south of the Lombok Islands in the Indian Ocean on 4 March 1942, while bound from Tandjong Priok and Cochin to Fremantle, the passenger-cargo ship *Tjisaroea* was condemned by the Yokosuka Prize Court on 29 August 1942 and pressed into Japanese service as the *Chihaya Maru*. In this guise she was torpedoed 300 miles east of the Ryukyu Islands on 2 November 1943 by the American submarine USS *Seahorse* and sank in the position 28.37N, 134.47E.
Casualties: not known

TONGARIRO (1901) New Zealand Shipping Co, UK

8,895grt; 457ft (139.3m) lbp x 58ft (17.7m) beam
170 passengers
Hawthorn Leslie, Hebburn-on-Tyne (Yard No 358)
Triple-expansion steam reciprocating, twin screw
On 30 August 1916, towards the end of a voyage from London via Newport News, Virginia, to Wellington, the passenger-cargo steamer *Tongariro* ran onto the Bull Rock, off Portland Island, Hawkes Bay, New Zealand, and became a complete wreck.
Casualties: not known

TOSCANA (1900) Cia Transoceanica, Italy

4,252grt; 363ft (110.6m) lbp x 43ft (13.3m) beam
1,362 passengers in two classes
Odero, Sestri Ponente (Yard No 194)
Triple-expansion steam reciprocating, single screw
The small Italian passenger ship *Toscana* operated with a sister, the *Ravenna*, on routes from Italy to South America, with occasional voyages to New York. She sank on 5 February 1918 following a collision off Porto Maurizio, between Nice and Genoa on Italy's north-west coast, some 25 miles (40 kilometres) from the French/Italian border.
Casualties: not known

TOYA MARU (1947) Ministry of Railways, Government of Japan

4,337grt; 373ft (113.4m) x 52ft (15.9m) beam
1,128 passengers in three classes
Mitsubishi, Kobe (Yard No 816)
Steam turbines, twin screw
While bound from Aomori, northern Honshu, across the Tsugaru Strait to Hakodate, Hokkaido, on 26 September 1954, the ro-ro train ferry *Toya Maru*, carrying around 990 persons, dragged her anchors in a typhoon and capsized with alarming suddenness, which gave little opportunity for those aboard her to evacuate. The ship was driven ashore outside Hakodate where it became a complete wreck. Salvaged later, it was broken up in Japan commencing in January 1956. The sinking of the *Toya Maru* ranks, with the *Estonia*, *Dona Paz*, *Kiang Ya* and *Princess of the Stars*, as one of the worst passenger ferry disasters. The number of survivors was reported as being just 196. Two other Japanese Railway ferries were lost on the same day, the *Kitami Maru* and *Seikan Maru No 11*. Up to the time of the disastrous loss of the *Toya Maru*, Japanese ro-ro ferries did not have stern doors fitted as it was considered they would inhibit the outflow of water from a flooded vehicle deck, a policy that was subsequently changed.
Casualties: 794 (Some reports give a figure of 1,155 or 1,172 casualties, but this does not accord with her complement although it was reported that there were a greater number of victims because many had managed to get aboard un-ticketed, if so, evasion of the boarding controls on a massive scale.)

The loss of the railway steamer *Toya Maru* in 1954 was Japan's worst post-war shipping disaster and its worst peacetime disaster ever. *World Ship Society*

TRANSBALT (1899) ex-*Riga* (1918) ex-*Belgravia* (1905) Sovtorgflot, USSR

11,439grt; 516ft (157.3m) loa x 62ft (18.9m) beam
300 passengers in single class
Blohm & Voss, Steinwerder, Hamburg (Yard No 133)
Quadruple-expansion steam reciprocating, twin screw

The ageing passenger-cargo ship *Transbalt* was the victim of mistaken identity when she was torpedoed and sunk by the American submarine USS *Spadefish* on 13 June 1945. She was returning to Vladivostok from Port Townsend and Seattle, under the management of the Russian Red Cross, and was at the western end of the La Perouse Channel when the submarine sighted her, misidentifying her as a Japanese ship. She sank in the position 45.42N, 140.41E, south of Sakhalin Island, but Japanese ships picked up all 99 members of her crew.
Casualties: 0

The *Belgravia* was one of the five vessels of Hamburg Amerika Line's 'B' class of steamers. In May 1905 she was sold to the Russian Navy and renamed *Riga*, only to return to commercial passenger-carrying duties the following year. After the First World War, with her name changed to *Transbalt* from 1919, she spent three years as a hospital ship before resuming passenger and cargo sailings for the Soviet state shipping line.
World Ship Society

TRANSILVANIA (1938) Navrom (Romanian State Maritime Service), Romania

6,672grt; 433ft (128.6m) loa x 58ft (17.7m) beam
420 passengers in single class
Burmeister & Wain, Copenhagen (Yard No 633)
Motor-ship, twin screw

The *Transilvania*, with her sister ship *Basarabia*, which transferred to the Soviet Union as the *Ukraina* in 1948, was built originally for Serviciul Maritim Romania for the Constantza to Alexandria service via Istanbul. On 23 September 1979, while she was awaiting repairs at Galatz (Galati) on the River Danube, the *Transilvania* capsized while being moved from her berth, a manoeuvre that had been intended to avoid her grounding. Declared a constructive total loss following salvage, she was broken up.
Casualties: not known

TRANSYLVANIA (1914) Anchor Line, UK

14,315grt; 567ft (172.8m) loa x 66ft (20.1m) beam
2,420 passengers in three classes
Scott's, Greenock (Yard No 451)
Steam turbines, twin screw

The passenger-cargo liner *Transylvania* was taken up for troop-carrying in May 1915 in support of the Balkans campaign, continuing with these duties over the next two years. On 3 May 1917 she left Marseilles bound for Alexandria accompanied by the Japanese destroyers *Matsu* and *Sakaki*, carrying a full complement of 200 military officers and 2,800 soldiers in addition to her crew. A day later, as the convoy was crossing the Gulf of Genoa, some 2½ miles south of Cape Vado, the *Transylvania* was torpedoed by the German submarine U63, hit on her port side in the engine compartments. The *Matsu* immediately manoeuvred close alongside the stricken troopship in readiness to take off her occupants while her course was altered to head for the nearby coast in the hope that she could be beached. However, she was struck by a second torpedo that had narrowly missed the *Matsu*, possibly the intended target, and sank soon after in the position 44.15N, 08.30E. Between them, the Japanese destroyers picked up many survivors.
Casualties: 414 (her Master, 402 troops and 11 merchant seamen)

A pre-First World War view of Anchor Line's *Transylvania*.
Tom Rayner collection

The Cunard Line ordered the *Transylvania* and her sister ship *Tuscania* for a joint Mediterranean to New York service with Anchor Line. In the event they passed into Anchor Line ownership, sailing instead on the Glasgow to New York route. The *Transylvania* is seen here as a troopship at Alexandria in June 1915, embarking 3,000 troops bound for Gallipoli.
Jim Payne (Through Their Eyes)

TRANSYLVANIA (1925) Anchor Line, UK

16,923grt; 552ft (168.2m) loa x 70ft (21.3m) beam
1,342 passengers in three classes
Fairfield, Govan (Yard No 600)
Steam turbines, twin screw
Taken over as an armed merchant cruiser in October 1939, the *Transylvania* was torpedoed by the German submarine U56 off Malin Head, while she was patrolling north of Ireland on 10 August 1940. Due to the rough seas her lifeboats could not be lowered, and rescue of around 300 members of her naval crew depended on trawlers that came to the stricken vessel's aid. They were subsequently landed on Ireland's west coast. The *Transylvania* was taken in tow in a bid to save her but she foundered before reaching port, sinking in the position 55.50N, 08.03W.
Casualties: 48

The *Transylvania* of 1925 was engaged with sister ship *Caledonia* on the Anchor Line Glasgow to New York service. Their first and third funnels were dummies. *Ian Allan Library*

TSINGTAO MARU (1930) ex-*Choshun [Shoshun] Maru* (1934) Dairen Kisen Kaisha, Japan

4,017grt; 360ft (109.7m) lbp x 46ft (14.0m) beam
Passenger numbers not known
Mitsubishi, Kobe (Yard No 205)
Steam turbines, twin screw
On 18 October 1944 the passenger-cargo ferry *Tsingtao Maru* was with her sister ship *Hoten Maru* (qv), approximately forty miles north of Luzon Island, Philippines, when they were attacked and bombed by US carrier-based aircraft. They sank in the position 18.54N, 121.51E.
Casualties: not known

TSUGARU MARU (1924) Department of Communications & Railways, Government of Japan

3,484grt; 350ft (106.7m) lbp x 52ft (15.9m) beam
1,200 passengers
Mitsubishi, Nagasaki (Yard No 395)
Steam turbines, twin screw
The passenger ferry *Tsugaru Maru* was lost on 14 July 1945 when US carrier-based aircraft bombed her off the Tsugaru Strait, separating Hokkaido from Honshu. She sank in the position 41.17N, 140.32E.
Casualties: not known

TUBANTIA (1914) Royal Holland Lloyd, The Netherlands

13,911grt; 560ft (170.7m) loa x 65ft (19.8m) beam
1,520 passengers in four classes
Alexander Stephen, Glasgow (Yard No 455)
Quadruple-expansion steam reciprocating, twin screw
On 16 March 1916, while bound from Amsterdam to Buenos Aires with 82 passengers and a crew of 296, the *Tubantia* was torpedoed and sunk by the German submarine UB13. The attack took place in thick fog some 4 miles from the Noordhinder lightship, and at the time the Dutch passenger vessel was about to anchor because of the poor visibility. The torpedo penetrated amidships, wrecking the engine room, and the *Tubantia* sank four or so hours later but not before Dutch torpedo boats had taken off all on board. Throughout the 1920s the wreck of the *Tubantia*, lying in the position 51.46N, 02.45E, was the subject of earnest salvage operations prompted by the belief that concealed within cheeses that had formed the bulk of her cargo was £2 million worth of smuggled gold.
Casualties: 0

The *Tubantia* sailed between Amsterdam and River Plate ports with her sister ship *Gelria*. *L. L. von Münching*

TURAKINA (1902) New Zealand Shipping Co, UK

9,920grt; 473ft (144.2m) lbp x 59ft (18.0m) beam
195 passengers in three classes
Hawthorn Leslie, Hebburn-on-Tyne (Yard No 382)
Triple-expansion steam reciprocating, twin screw
The passenger-cargo ship *Turakina* was sunk by torpedo 120 miles west-south-west of Bishop Rock, in the position 48.30N, 08.34W, while sailing empty from London to New York on 13 August 1917. Her attacker was the German submarine U86.
Casualties: 2

The steamship *Turakina* operated between the United Kingdom and New Zealand. *World Ship Society*

TURKMENIA (1961) Far Eastern Shipping Co, (Sovtorgflot), USSR

4,720grt; 401ft (122.2m) x 52ft (15.9m) beam
333 passengers in single class
Mathias-Thesen Werft, Wismar (Yard No 112)
Motor-ship, twin screw
During a youth cruise in the western Pacific on 12 November 1986, carrying hundreds of students, the 'Mikhail Kalinin' class passenger ship *Turkmenia* (also rendered as *Turkmeniya*) suffered an outbreak of fire. She was towed back to Vladivostok where no attempt was made to repair her because the cost could not be justified. Instead she was retired and hulked as a storage vessel. The *Turkmenia*'s normal route, when not engaged on cruises, had been from Vladivostok to Yokohama, Kobe and Hong Kong.
Casualties: not known

TUSCANIA (1915) Anchor Line, UK

14,348grt; 576ft (175.6m) loa x 66ft (20.1m) beam
2,417 passengers in three classes
Alexander Stephen, Linthouse, Glasgow (Yard No 459)
Steam turbines, twin screw
On 5 February 1918 the liner *Tuscania* was returning to Liverpool at the end of a transatlantic voyage from New York carrying 2,235 persons, of whom 2,030 were American Army officers and troops. When she was seven miles north of the Rathlin Island lighthouse she was torpedoed and sunk by the German submarine UB77 in the position 55.37N, 06.26W.
Casualties: 166 (122 American servicemen and 44 crew)

Sister ship to the *Transylvania*, which commenced service with the Cunard Line, the *Tuscania* of 1915 was an Anchor Line ship from the start. *World Ship Society*

UKISHIMA [UKISIMA] MARU (1937) Osaka Shosen Kaisha, Japan

4,730grt; 356ft (108.4m) lbp x 52ft (15.7m) beam
841 passengers in four classes
Mitsui, Tamano (Yard No 225)
Motor-ship, single screw
The passenger-cargo ship *Ukishima Maru*, one of a pair with the *Naminoue Maru*, was distinctive for a relatively modern motor-vessel in having a counter stern. She suffered an enormous explosion in Maizuru Bay, Japan, on 24 August 1945, ten days after the Japanese surrender. The explosion has been attributed to a mine, although there is some doubt about this. She sank in the position 35.30N, 135.22E. At the time of the incident her function was a naval transport vessel and she was carrying a large complement of 4-5,000 Korean forced-labourers from a military industrial facility at Aomori, taking them from Maizuru to Busan (Pusan), Korea. There was heavy loss of life. The governments of Korea, both North and South, regard the sinking of the *Ukishima Maru* as a war crime, perpetrated deliberately by the Japanese military, and have filed compensation claims through the Kyoto District court, which have been partially successful. The claimants have submitted evidence that, prior to the detonation, the majority of Japanese personnel had left the ship and that large quantities of explosives had been secreted aboard the ship prior to her departure. (In Talbot Booth's *Merchant Ships* her name is rendered incorrectly as *Ukushima* [*Ukusima*] *Maru*).
Casualties: 549 (524 Koreans and 25 Japanese)

UKRAINA (1928) Black Sea Shipping Co (Sovtorgflot), USSR

4,727grt; 354ft (17.9m) loa x 51ft (15.6m) beam
450 passengers in single class
Baltic Shipbuilding & Engineering Works, Leningrad
(Yard No not known)
Motor-ship, twin screw
The passenger ship *Ukraina*, fourth of her class, was at Novorossiysk on 2 July 1942 when she was bombed by German aircraft and sunk together with many other civilian ships in the port. One of the heaviest air raids at that time, some 54 Junkers Ju-88 aircraft were involved. It is reported that the wreck of the *Ukraina* was raised in 1947 and utilised in some capacity in 1950, but it is not known what or for how long. She certainly did not return to passenger service and doubtless was scrapped soon after.
Casualties: not known

ULSTER PRINCE (1930) Belfast Steamship Co, UK

3,791grt; 359ft (109.4m) loa x 46ft (14.1m) beam
500 passengers
Harland & Wolff, Belfast (Yard No 697)
Motor-ship, twin screw
While serving with the Royal Navy as a wartime Stores &

Ammunition Carrier during the evacuation of Greece, the Irish Sea ferry *Ulster Prince* ran aground off Nauplia on 25 April 1941. She had just returned from Suda Bay, Crete, to where she had been expected to transport some 2,000 troops. In this predicament, caught out in the open, she made an easy target for attack from the air, and later the same day she was bombed by German aircraft. Fires broke out fore and aft and it was not long before she was ablaze along her entire length. The inferno raged for more than a day and left her a total loss.

Casualties: not known

Among the first diesel-powered passenger ferries, all built by Harland & Wolff, were the trio of twin-funnelled ships that included the *Ulster Prince*. They were completed for the Belfast Steamship Company's Belfast to Liverpool service. *B. & A. Feilden*

ULSTER QUEEN (1929) Belfast Steamship Co, UK

3,791grt; 359ft (109.4m) loa x 46ft (14.1m) beam
500 passengers
Harland & Wolff, Belfast (Yard No 696)
Motor-ship, twin screw

The *Ulster Queen* anchored at Belfast. *H. B. Christiansen Collection / Online Transport Archive*

After the outbreak of the Second World War the ferry *Ulster Queen* was earmarked for requisition for war duties, but on 28 February 1940, while still working on the Belfast to Liverpool route, she ran ashore at Maughold Head, Isle of Man, in a gale. The LMS steamer *Duke of Lancaster* took off her 88 passengers while efforts were made to free her, but she became impaled on a rock and was left lying high and dry at low water, but flooding when the tide was full. Initially abandoned as a complete loss, the urgent demand for shipping for the war effort prompted that salvage should be undertaken and, after considerable work, she was refloated on 25 March. Four days later she was dry-docked at Belfast for repairs to begin.

The Admiralty acquired her on 15 August and ordered her

to be converted into an Anti-Aircraft Ship, and she was finally commissioned in this capacity as HMS *Ulster Queen* on 26 July 1941. From that point she saw out the war largely unscathed, later adapted further as a Fighter Direction Ship. Due to the extensive modifications required both for her recovery and to fulfil naval work, she never returned to her owners' commercial service. Instead, when she paid off on 22 March 1946 she was laid up in reserve until late 1950, when she was taken to Antwerp for breaking-up.

Casualties: 0

The second view of the *Ulster Queen* shows her stranded at Maughold Head on 28 February 1940. Threatened with abandonment as a constructive total loss, war needs dictated that she should be recovered, the work, which included conversion into an anti-aircraft ship, lasting until late July 1941. *H. B. Christiansen Collection / Online Transport Archive*

ULTONIA (1898) Cunard Line, GB;

8,845grt; 513ft (156.4m) loa x 57ft (17.4m) beam
2,100 steerage passengers
C. S. Swan & Hunter, Wallsend-on-Tyne (Yard No 228)
Triple-expansion steam reciprocating, twin screw
Originally a livestock carrier, the *Ultonia* was modified in 1903 to carry a large number of Hungarian emigrants on the Fiume to New York route, after Cunard had secured the contract for this trade. On 27 June 1917, as she was returning to London from New York, the *Ultonia* was torpedoed by the German submarine U53 about 190 miles south-west of Fastnet, and sank in the position 48.25N, 11.23W.

Casualties: 1

Transferred from the Liverpool to Boston service to the route from Trieste to New York, the *Ultonia* exploited the Italian emigrant trade that was then at its height. *Real Photos*

ULYSSES (1913) Blue Funnel Line, UK

14,499grt; 580ft (176.8m) loa x 68ft (20.7m) beam
250 passengers in single class

Workman Clark, Belfast (Yard No 319)
Triple-expansion steam reciprocating, twin screw
The *Ulysses* was bound from Sydney to Liverpool, via the Panama Canal and Halifax, on 11 April 1942 when she was torpedoed by the German submarine U160. The attack took place as she was passing the North Carolina coastline, off Palm Beach, and she sank in the position 34.23N, 75.35W.
Casualties: 0

The *Ulysses*, the last vessel of the Blue Funnel's seven-ship 'Aeneas' class, was built for the service from Glasgow and Liverpool to Brisbane. *Alex Duncan*

UMBRIA (1912) ex-*Bahia Blanca* (1935)
Italian Government (managed by Italia Line)

9,349grt; 491ft (149.7m) lbp x 59ft (18.0m) beam
2,408 passengers
Reiberstiegwerft, Hamburg (Yard No 444)
Triple-expansion steam reciprocating, twin screw
After spending five years as an Italian Government troopship, with occasional route voyages to the Far East, the passenger-cargo ship *Umbria* was scuttled by her crew off Port Sudan on 12 June 1940 during a voyage from Genoa to Rangoon. Italy had declared war on Great Britain two days earlier and the action was taken to prevent the ship from falling into British hands. The wreck lay in the position 19.38N, 37.17E and remained there until it was broken up for scrap at a later date.
Casualties: not known

UNION (1867) Norddeutscher Lloyd, Germany

2,873grt; 337ft (102.7m) loa x 40ft (12.2m) beam
About 650 passengers
Caird, Greenock (Yard No 133)
Inverted steam reciprocating engines, single screw
The transatlantic passenger steamship *Union*, a sister ship of the *Deutschland* (qv), operated on the Bremen and Southampton to New York service. She became a casualty on 28 November 1870 when she was wrecked off the Scottish coast, at Rattray Head, Aberdeenshire.
Casualties: 0

URAL MARU (1929) Osaka Shosen Kaisha, Japan

6,374grt; 405ft (123.5m) lbp x 55ft (16.8m) beam
773 passengers
Mitsubishi, Nagasaki (Yard No 452)
Steam turbines, twin screw
The passenger-cargo ship *Ural Maru* was torpedoed and sunk about 150 miles west of Masinlok, the Philippines, on 27

September 1944 by the American submarine USS *Flasher*. She was carrying an estimated 2,350 persons and sank with very heavy loss of life in the position 15.45N, 117.19E.
Casualties: About 2,000

The loss of the OSK passenger-cargo ship *Ural Maru* in the Second World War ranks as one of the worst involving a Japanese merchant vessel. *Mitsui-OSK Lines*

URUGUAY (1913) ex-*Infanta Isabel de Borbon* (1931)
Cia Trasatlantica Española, Spain

10,348grt; 500ft (152.4m) loa x 61ft (18.7m) beam
2,125 passengers in four classes
William Denny, Dumbarton (Yard No 969)
Triple-expansion steam reciprocating, twin screw
Like her sister, the *Argentina*, the *Uruguay* was a victim of the Spanish Civil War, bombed and sunk in a Nationalist air attack on Barcelona on 23 January 1939. She was raised on 25 July 1939 and sold for breaking-up, the work carried out locally from 1940.
Casualties: not known

USAMBARA (1922) Deutsche Ost-Afrika Line, Germany

8,690grt; 433ft (132.0m) lbp x 58ft (17.7m) beam
250 passengers
Blohm & Voss, Steinwerder, Hamburg (Yard No 397)
Steam turbines, single screw
The passenger-cargo ship *Usambara* was severely damaged during an Allied air raid on Stettin (Szczecin) on 11 April 1944. Partially repaired, she was in use as a barracks ship when she was bombed and completely destroyed during a subsequent air attack on 20 March 1945.
Casualties: not known

USARAMO (1920) Deutsche Ost-Afrika Line, Germany

7,775grt; 418ft (127.4m) lbp x 56ft (17.1m) beam
250 passengers
Blohm & Voss, Steinwerder, Hamburg (Yard No 387)
Steam turbines, single screw
The passenger-cargo ship *Usaramo* was at Vigo, Spain, on the outbreak of the Second World War. After she had successfully made it along the coast to western France in October 1940, she was taken over for the German Navy by the occupying forces but within days was made available to the Italians as a submarine depot ship based at Bordeaux. She was deliberately sunk by the Germans in the River Gironde, off Lagrange, on 25 August 1944. After the end of hostilities, her wreck was salvaged and sold for scrapping.
Casualties: not known

The three sister ships *Usaramo*, *Ussukuma* and *Wangoni* were engaged in a round-Africa service via Cape Town. This is the *Usaramo*, which was scuttled by her crew not to avoid capture as a prize but as an obstruction to hinder the Allied advance through southern France. *World Ship Society*

USSUKUMA (1920) Deutsche Ost-Afrika Line, Germany

7,834grt; 418ft (127.4m) lbp x 56ft (17.1m) beam
250 passengers
Blohm & Voss, Steinwerder, Hamburg (Yard No 389)
Steam turbines, single screw
After she had been stopped by the cruiser HMS *Ajax* on 6 December 1939, the passenger-cargo ship *Ussukuma* was scuttled by her crew off Bahia, Brazil, self-destruction being preferred to capture of the vessel for use by the enemy. Casualties: 0

UTOPIA (1874) Anchor Line, UK

2,731grt; 350ft (106.7m) lbp x 35ft (10.7m) beam
640 passengers
Robert Duncan, Port Glasgow (Yard No 67)
Triple-expansion steam reciprocating, single screw
The emigrant steamer *Utopia*, bound from Naples for New York with 821 passengers, three of them stowaways, and a crew of 59, entered the Bay of Gibraltar on 17 March 1891. Already there, riding at anchor, was the British Mediterranean Fleet. In the dark and stormy conditions the *Utopia* misjudged the clearance as she crossed ahead of the battleship HMS *Anson*. The battleship's underwater ram bow sliced into the *Utopia*'s side, opening a hole near her stern that was 26 feet long by 15 feet wide. The bulkheads were ripped away, as were the engines and mountings as the ram penetrated deep into the steamship, and as a consequence within five minutes she was settling stern-first.

Naval pinnaces from the anchored ships sped to the scene to render assistance and much heroism was displayed by the sailors in their efforts to rescue the terrified emigrants. Nevertheless there were many victims. In the course of the rescue two sailors from the *Immortalitie* were also drowned when their boat was smashed. The *Utopia*'s wreck, lying in shallow water with its funnel and masts protruding clear of the surface, constituted a menace to navigation so, utilising a wooden coffer-dam, she was raised and removed on 8 July 1891. She was then towed to the River Clyde where she was laid up until late April 1900, when she was sold for breaking-up at Dordrecht, commencing that September.
Casualties: 564 (538 emigrants and 26 crew)

VALBANERA (1906) Pinillos, Izquierdo & Cia, Spain

5,099grt; 400ft (121.8m) lbp x 48ft (14.6m) beam
More than 1,000 passengers
Charles Connell, Scotstoun (Yard No 309)
Triple-expansion steam reciprocating, single screw
The Spanish passenger-cargo steamer *Valbanera* was lost on 9 September 1919 when she foundered in a storm five miles east of the Rebecca Shoals lighthouse while bound from Santiago de Cuba to Havana. Her entire complement of passengers and crew perished. Casualties: 488

VALPARAISO (1873) Pacific Steam Navigation Co, UK

3,575grt; 379ft (115.6m) lbp x 42ft (12.7m) beam
966 passengers in three classes
John Elder, Govan (Yard No 160)
Compound-expansion steam reciprocating, single screw
Similar to the *Tacora* (qv), which was lost on her maiden voyage to Chile in 1872, the passenger steamship *Valparaiso* was lost on 28 February 1887 when she was wrecked in Vigo Bay, Spain, while outward bound for Chile from Liverpool. Casualties: 0

VALPARAISO (1890) *ex-Gera* (1908) Lloyd del Pacifico, Italy

4,930grt; 430ft (131.1m) lbp x 47ft (14.3m) beam
1,988 passengers in three classes
Fairfield, Glasgow (Yard No 353)
Triple-expansion steam reciprocating, single screw
The passenger-cargo ship *Valparaiso* was making her way through the Mediterranean on 14 October 1917 when she was torpedoed and sunk by the German submarine UB48 near Marsa Susah (Apollonia), Libya, about 150 miles north-east of Benghazi. Her wreck lies in the position 33.24N, 21.58E. Casualties: 0

VANDYCK (1911) Lamport & Holt Co, UK

10,328grt; 511ft (155.7m) loa x 60ft (18.5m) beam
610 passengers in three classes
Workman Clark, Belfast (Yard No 301)
Quadruple-expansion steam reciprocating, twin screw
The *Vandyck* fell victim of the German commerce raider *Karlsruhe* while she was bound from Buenos Aires to New York on 26 October 1914. Intercepted off the coast of Brazil, 690 miles west-by-south of the St Paul Rocks, in the position 01.14S, 40.40W, she was arrested following a brief chase. Her occupants, including more than 200 passengers, were transferred to the *Asuncion*, a vessel that the *Karlsruhe* had captured earlier, and were taken aboard her to Para (Belém), where they arrived on 1 November. Meanwhile the *Vandyck*'s cargo was looted, including a consignment of 1,000 tons of frozen meat. The *Vandyck* was subsequently sunk by explosive charges off Maranhao on 27 October 1914. Casualties: 0

The first *Vandyck* operated between New York and South America. *Alex Duncan*

VANDYCK (1921) Lamport & Holt Co, UK

13,241grt; 535ft (163.1m) loa x 64ft (19.5m) beam
680 passengers in three classes
Workman Clark, Belfast (Yard No 359)
Steam turbines, twin screw

A full-time cruise ship since the early 1930s, the *Vandyck* was taken over in October 1939 and converted into a troopship. Later she was deployed as an armed boarding vessel, attached to the Royal Navy, as part of the task force assembled for the Norwegian offensive in the summer of 1940. While she was off the Norwegian coast, west of Narvik, sailing in convoy on 10 June 1940, she was bombed and sunk by German dive-bombers. Of her complement of 168 officers and ratings, 161 survivors of the attack were captured and became prisoners of war.

Casualties: 7 (2 officers and 5 ratings)

The second *Vandyck* served in partnership with her sister *Voltaire* on the run from New York to La Plata ports until 1930. Both ships were then laid up, but their careers resumed from 1932 when they undertook a full-time cruising service. *World Ship Society*

VASILISSA SOPHIA (1917) National Steam Navigation Co, Greece

serving under the wartime name LEASOWE CASTLE
9,737grt; 488ft (148.7m) loa x 58ft (17.7m) beam
2,110 passengers in three classes (as designed)
Cammell Laird, Birkenhead (Yard No 806)
Quadruple-expansion steam reciprocating, twin screw

The Greek liner *Vasilissa Sophia* was under construction at Birkenhead when the Controller of War Shipping commandeered her under the Liner Requisition Scheme and ordered her completion as a troopship. She was placed under the management of the Union-Castle Line and given the name

Leasowe Castle in accordance with that company's system of nomenclature, although it never, in fact, owned her. Had she survived the war she would, no doubt, have reverted to her original owners, but in the event she never undertook any commercial voyages. On 26 May 1918 the *Leasowe Castle* was sailing in convoy from Egypt to Marseilles when she was torpedoed and sunk 104 miles north-north-west of Alexandria by the German submarine UB51. She sank in the position 31.30N, 27.56E. The *Leasowe Castle* was carrying in excess of 3,000 troops besides her crew, the majority of whom were rescued.

Casualties: 101 (92 troops, her Master and 8 crew)

Ordered for the transatlantic service of Greek Line, the *Vasilissa Sophia* was employed in the First World War, under Union-Castle management, as the troopship *Leasowe Castle*. *David Reed*

VATERLAND (1943) Hamburg Amerika Line, Germany

41,000grt; 827ft (252.1m) loa x 98ft (29.9m) beam
1,322 passengers in three classes (as designed)
Blohm & Voss, Steinwerder, Hamburg (Yard No 523)
Turbo-electric, twin screw

Hamburg Amerika Line had an ambitious plan in the late 1930s to introduce three large new turbo-electric liners on the Hamburg, Southampton and Cherbourg to New York route. Though launched without a name, it is understood that the first ship, and the only one to be started, was to be christened *Vaterland*. *Blohm & Voss*

One of three planned new transatlantic express liners, the *Vaterland* (it is understood that this was her presumed name but that it was not bestowed upon her when she was launched without ceremony on 24 August 1940 to clear the launching ways) was laid up incomplete in Kuhwerder Harbour, Hamburg, where she was utilised as a floating store. During the heavy air raids on Hamburg of 25 July 1943 she was hit by several bombs that blew out her decks and she was completely gutted when the wooden material stored aboard caught fire. The wreck of the *Vaterland* was surrendered in May 1945 but, being fit only for scrap, was demolished in a local breakers' yard during 1948. Casualties: not known

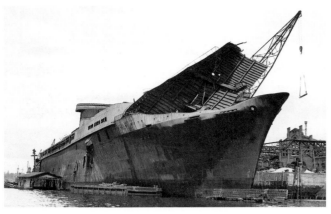

Heavily damaged during the bombing of Hamburg, the *Vaterland* was fit only for scrap at the war's end. *Imperial War Museum (A29698)*

VEENDAM (1873) ex-*Baltic* (1873-1898)
Holland Amerika Line, The Netherlands

4,036grt; 437ft (133.2m) loa x 41ft (12.4m) beam
1,010 passengers in three classes
Harland & Wolff, Belfast (Yard No 75)
Triple-expansion steam reciprocating, single screw
Having been a transatlantic speed-record-holder under the White Star flag, the passenger steamship *Baltic* was sold to Holland Amerika in 1888 and renamed *Veendam*. She was lost in mid-Atlantic after striking a submerged derelict on 6 February 1898 while on passage from Rotterdam to New York. She foundered the next day in the position 49.19N, 19.47W.
Casualties: 0

VEGA (1938) Bergen Line, Norway

serving under the possible wartime name WEGA
7,287grt; 425ft (126.5m lbp) x 58ft (17.7m) beam
465 passengers in two classes
Cantieri Riuniti dell'Adriatico, San Marco
(Yard No 1205)
Motor-ship, twin screw
The *Vega*, which worked the Bergen and Stavanger to Newcastle route with her fleet-mate *Venus*, was laid up in September 1939 only to be captured by the invading German army at Stanghelle in the Osterfjorden, near Bergen, on 9 April 1940. However, she was returned to her owners and continued in lay-up until 18 March 1941 when the Kriegsmarine seized her. They had her rebuilt as a target ship at Bergen and it is believed, though not confirmed, that she was renamed *Wega*. From March 1942 she was used as an accommodation ship at Travemünde. During a voyage from East Prussia to Lübeck with refugees on 4 May 1945, she was bombed and sunk off Staberhuk, Fehmarn Islands, by Russian warplanes. She caught fire, was beached and completely burned out. There she remained, lying half-submerged on her port side, for the next three years. Sold on an 'as is, where lies' basis in October 1948, she was cut into three sections. The middle section, containing her engines, was lifted and towed to the Howaldtswerke shipyard at Kiel, where it was broken up after the engines had been removed. The bow and stern sections of the *Vega* were broken up in situ.
Casualties: 1

Built for the Bergen to Newcastle service, the passenger ferry *Vega* was a larger and, with her angled bow, more rakish version of Bergen Line's earlier *Venus*. *Bjørn Pedersen*

VENEZIA (1907) Fabre Line, France (under charter to Compagnie Générale Transatlantique)

6,707grt; 457ft (139.3m) lbp x 51ft (15.6m) beam
1,880 passengers in two classes
Swan Hunter & Wigham Richardson, Low Walker, Tyneside
(Yard No 772)
Triple-expansion steam reciprocating, twin screw
While engaged in a charter voyage, bound from Havana, Cuba, and Vera Cruz, Mexico, to St Nazaire and Le Havre, on 14 October 1919, the passenger-cargo ship *Venezia* was destroyed by fire. She sank in the position 43.32N, 45.04W.
Casualties: not known

VENEZUELA (1898) La Veloce Line, Italy

3,474grt; 359ft (109.5m) lbp x 42ft (12.7m) beam
888 passengers in two classes
Odero, Sestri Ponente, Genoa (Yard No 179)
Triple-expansion steam reciprocating, single screw
The clipper-bowed emigrant passenger steamship *Venezuela*, which served the Italy to Central America route, was wrecked at Carmel, near Marseilles, on 21 February 1909.
Casualties: not known

VENEZUELA (1905) ex-*Brasile* (1912) Compagnie Générale Transatlantique (French Line), France

5,026grt; 394ft (120.2m) lbp x 48ft (14.6m) beam
1,108 passengers in three classes
Liguri Anconitani, Ancona (Yard No 8)
Triple-expansion steam reciprocating, twin screw
The passenger steamer *Venezuela* was lost off the coast of Morocco, near Casablanca, on 7 March 1920. After a number of months, during which she could not be freed, the wreck broke in two and was abandoned. It was demolished on the spot from 1921.
Casualties: not known

VENEZUELA (1924) ex-*Empress of Australia* (1956) ex-*De Grasse* (1953) Sicula Oceanica (SIOSA), Italy

18,769grt; 614ft (187.2m) loa x 71ft (21.8m) beam
1,480 passengers in three classes
Cammell Laird, Birkenhead (Yard No 886)
Steam turbines, twin screw
Just two years after the *Empress of Australia* had joined the SIOSA fleet as the *Venezuela*, undergoing a dramatic

refurbishment that included the addition of a modern raked bow extension, she stranded on the rocks off Cannes Harbour in a flooded condition on 16 March 1962. Earlier she had struck a bank about a quarter of a mile south of the Moines Beacon. The strong Mistral wind pivoted the vessel so that she ended up over the rocky ridge for her entire length, her starboard side facing the shore. In this situation she settled on the bottom, flooded up to her main deck. With the aid of a salvage team and the tugs *Neri Francesco*, *Forte* and *Casteldoria*, she was pumped out and refloated on 16 April. An inspection followed, after which she was granted a seaworthiness certificate by the Registro Italiano Navale, then towed to Genoa for dry-docking. A more detailed examination with full access to the underwater hull revealed that the *Venezuela* had in fact been extensively damaged on her bottom and was beyond economic recovery. She was therefore sold for breaking up at La Spezia, beginning in August 1962.

Casualties: 0

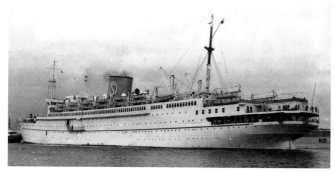

Originally French Line's *De Grasse* and briefly the *Empress of Australia*, as a replacement for Canadian Pacific's burned-out *Empress of Canada*, the third phase of her career was as the *Venezuela* of SIOSA, sailing to South America from Italy. *Richard de Kerbrech collection*

VENUS (1931) Bergen Line, Norway

5,407grt; 399ft (121.5m) lbp x 54ft (16.5m) beam
456 passengers in three classes
Helsingor Vaerft, Elsinore (Yard No 198)
Motor-ship, twin screw

Laid up at Stanghelle with her consort, the *Vega*, in September 1939, the *Venus* was requisitioned by the Germans on 16 March 1940 and used in the Baltic until returned to her owners on 16 October that year. Later, when the Kriegsmarine commandeered her on 8 May 1941, she was rebuilt at the Neptunwerft shipyard, Rostock, as a target vessel with her entire interior fittings removed. On 20 March 1945 she was bombed and sunk in shallow waters at Hamburg by Allied aircraft. At the war's end she was declared a constructive total loss, but with long waiting times for new tonnage, the decision was made to recover and repair the *Venus*. After she had been raised, she was towed to her builders' yard at Elsinore, arriving on 29 September 1945. There followed an extensive amount of work to restore her, and she did not resume the North Sea passenger service until 12 May 1948. Thereafter, she continued with scheduled-service crossings and off-peak cruises until she was sold for breaking-up, arriving at Faslane, Scotland, on 19 October 1968.

Casualties: not known

The *Venus* represented a major development in the Bergen Line fleet engaged in the Newcastle service. Though severely war-damaged, she survived to return to ferry operations substantially rebuilt. She also ran an annual programme of cruises to the Atlantic isles. *Kenneth Wightman*

VERGINA CITY (1967) ex-*Ivory Maru* (1992)
Venture Shipping Ltd, Panama

3,164grt; 293ft (89.4m) loa x 44ft (13.4m) beam
1,661 passengers
Uraga Dock, Uraga (Yard No 894)
Motor-ship, twin screw

VERGINA TREASURE (1967) ex-*Cobalt Maru* (1992)
Noble House Shipping Co, Panama

3,159grt; 293ft (89.3m) loa x 44ft (13.4m) beam
1,676 passengers
Mitsubishi, Kobe (Yard No 973)
Motor-ship, twin screw

The sister-ferries *Vergina City* and *Vergina Treasure* were destroyed simultaneously in fires that broke out aboard them at Eleusis, Greece, on 27 July 1995 while they were undergoing refits and repairs. The damage to both vessels was considerable. Their gutted wrecks, beyond economic restoration, were sold to Turkish ship-breakers and they arrived in tow at Aliaga for demolition in October 1995. The full circumstances of these incidents is not known – whether, for instance, the fire spread across from one vessel to the other if they were lying close alongside each other. If not, such a remarkable coincidence or unique occurrence might well raise the question as to whether another factor such as arson was perhaps also involved.

Casualties: not known for either ship

VERONA (1908) Navigazione Generale Italiana, Italy

8,886grt; 482ft (146.9m) lbp x 58ft (17.7m) beam
2,564 passengers in two classes
Workman Clark, Belfast (Yard No 271)
Triple-expansion steam reciprocating, twin screw

The Italian passenger steamship *Verona*, bound to an unknown destination from Genoa with troops, had just departed from Messina on 11 May 1918 when she was torpedoed and sunk near Punta Pellaro (Peloro), on the Strait of Messina, Italy, by the German submarine UC52. She sank in the position 37.04N, 16.19E. The sinking of the *Verona* was the second worst Italian shipping loss of the First World War.

Casualties: 880

VESTRIS (1912) Lamport & Holt, UK

10,494grt; 511ft (155.6m) loa x 61ft (18.5m) beam
610 passengers in three classes
Workman Clark, Belfast (Yard No 303)
Quadruple-expansion steam reciprocating, twin screw

The passenger-cargo liner *Vestris* foundered in controversial circumstances on 12 November 1928, about 350 miles from the entrance to the Chesapeake River. She had departed from New York two days earlier with 325 persons, 128 of them passengers, bound for Buenos Aires, intending to make calls en route at Barbados, Rio de Janeiro, Santos and Montevideo. Although the voyage began in fine conditions, the *Vestris* ran into dirty weather in the Atlantic and was soon feeling the full effects of a severe and deep depression. Water began to enter the ship through the starboard ash discharge ejector, by way of a coal chute door at the aft end, and through a sanitary discharge. This caused her to list and increasing difficulty was experienced in getting her to respond to the helm. After two exceptionally large waves hit the ship, her cargo and bunker coal shifted, aggravating her already tender condition. Her Master had the ship lie hove-to for a period, but this did not improve the situation.

The *Vestris* was a vessel of the shelter deck type, requiring her lower weather deck to be soundly battened down prior to sailing in order to preserve its watertight integrity in extreme conditions. On this occasion, however, this had not been carried out properly with the result that the *Vestris* was soon in a critical state. The deteriorating situation required important decisions to be made and implemented with haste regarding the well-being of her occupants, but for some reason the Captain delayed sending out distress calls and giving the order to abandon ship. Finally, on the morning of 12 November, after 24 hours in which the ship's predicament had steadily worsened, it was decided that the *Vestris* should be vacated, and it was only at this time that SOS signals were transmitted. Altogether 58 ships were alerted.

Meanwhile, the women and children passengers aboard the *Vestris* were put into boats on the ship's port side, although these were still not launched because the Captain believed that rescue ships would arrive on the scene before the *Vestris* foundered. Consequently, they were left hanging in the falls for some time, to the discomfort of those waiting inside, before two were finally lowered, only for one of them to be swamped soon after it was waterborne. Of the ship's other port-side boats, one that was not released from the falls went down with the ship together with another that had remained in the chocks throughout. A fifth port-side lifeboat had its falls cut, only to be crushed against the ship's side. The result of these misfortunes was that 29 women and all of the 12 child passengers lost their lives in the disaster. Most of the male passengers and members of the Barbadian crew left the ship in boats from the starboard side and fared considerably better. Some also jumped into the sea while others clambered over the davits and lowered themselves down the falls into the water. The survivors were picked up by the Norddeutscher Lloyd passenger liner *Berlin*, the cargo ships *Myriam* and *American Shipper*, and the American battleship USS *Wyoming*. The *Vestris* ultimately sank in the position 37.35N, 71.08W. The tragedy raised numerous questions over the seaworthiness of shelter deck vessels and the general handling of emergencies. Casualties: 111 (68 passengers and 43 crew, including her Master)

The *Vestris* was a sister ship of the *Vandyck* of 1911 and the *Vauban*, all three engaged on the service linking North and South America. *World Ship Society*

VICEROY OF INDIA (1929) P&O Line, UK

19,627grt; 612ft (186.5m) loa x 76ft (23.2m) beam
673 passengers in two classes
Alexander Stephen, Linthouse, Glasgow (Yard No 519)
Turbo-electric, twin screw

Converted into a troopship in November 1940, the passenger liner and cruise ship *Viceroy of India* was lost during the North Africa landings in November 1942. After she had disembarked her troops at Algiers, she set sail on 11 November bound for Gibraltar and the United Kingdom. When she was 35 miles from Oran she was torpedoed by the German submarine U407 and sank in the position 36.24N, 00.35W, turning over as she went down, her bows briefly pointing skywards. Despite the fact that she was no longer carrying troops, she still had her full crew complement aboard, a total of 432 persons, plus 22 passengers. Fortunately, the majority of them survived the sinking and were picked up by the destroyer HMS *Boadicea*. Casualties: 4

The first large British turbo-electric passenger liner, the *Viceroy of India* entered the London to Bombay service in February 1929 and remained so employed until September 1939, though she was also known for her annual programmes of luxury cruises. She is seen entering Tilbury Docks, possibly for the first time. *Ian Allan Library*

The *Viceroy of India* sinks after being torpedoed off North Africa on 11 November 1942. *Imperial War Museum (HU62985)*

VICTORIA (1931) Lloyd Triestino, Italy

13,062grt; 540ft (164.6m) loa x 68ft (20.7m) beam
600 passengers in four classes
Cantieri Riuniti dell'Adriatico, San Marco (Yard No 782)
Motor-ship, quadruple screw

In 1940 the passenger motor-ship *Victoria* was taken over and converted into a troop transport attached to the Italian Navy. As such she was lost on 24 January 1942, sunk by torpedoes dropped by British aircraft in the position 33.40N, 17.45E, as she was passing through the Gulf of Sirte (Sidri), Libya. At the time the *Victoria* had been bound from Taranto to Tripoli.

Casualties: not known

The twin-funnelled *Victoria* was a nicely proportioned liner and the fastest diesel-powered ship in the world until the advent of the Dutch-flag *Oranje* in 1939. Her career began on the run from Trieste to Alexandria, but from October 1936 she switched to the Bombay service from Genoa with an extension to Shanghai. *Ian Allan Library*

VIGO (1922) Hamburg Sud-Amerika Line, Germany

7,418grt; 413ft (125.9m) lbp x 55ft (16.1m) beam
870 passengers in two classes
Howaldtswerke, Kiel (Yard No 606)
Triple-expansion steam reciprocating, single screw

The passenger-cargo ship *Vigo* was adapted as a mine destructor vessel (probably the equivalent of a British auxiliary minesweeper) after she was requisitioned in 1939 for wartime service with the German Navy, and as such she was designated initially as 'Sperrbrecher X', changed to 'Sperrbrecher 10' in 1940. Ironically, or so it would seem, she struck a mine on 6 March 1944 in the position 53.49N, 06.32E, placing the incident near the Friesian Islands, to the west of the mouth of the River Ems. The stricken vessel made it as far as a point to the north of the Ems entrance before sinking on 7 March in the position 53.59N, 07.09E.

Casualties: 1

The passenger-cargo ship *Vigo*, with her sisters *Espana* and *La Coruna*, operated between Hamburg and La Plata ports.
Hamburg Sud-Amerika Line

VIKING PRINCESS (1950) ex-*Riviera Prima* (1964) ex-*Lavoisier* (1962) A/S Sigline (Berge Sigval Bergensen), Norway

12,812grt; 537ft (163.6m) loa x 64ft (19.6m) beam
326 passengers in two classes
Chantiers de la Loire, St Nazaire (Yard No 341)
Motor-ship, twin screw

The former French passenger-cargo liner *Lavoisier* was sold for conversion into a cruise ship, adopting the name *Viking Princess* for service on Caribbean itineraries. During a cruise on 8 April 1966, when she was between Cuba and Haiti in the position 19.27N, 74.18W, fire broke out in the ship's engine room and swiftly spread out of control. The passengers and crew were ordered to abandon ship and were picked up by the *Cap Norte*, the *Navigator* and the *Chunking Victory*. The *Navigator*, a Liberian-flagged ship, took the *Viking Princess* in tow to Port Royal, Jamaica, but, beyond economic recovery, the wreck was sold for breaking-up at Bilbao, Spain, where it arrived on 14 July 1966.

Casualties: 2 (both passengers, the result of heart failure)

The cruise ship *Viking Princess* was originally the Chargeurs Réunis route service passenger-cargo liner *Lavoisier*.
World Ship Society

VILLE DE BRUGES (1922) ex-*President Harding* (1940) ex-*President Taft* (1922) ex-*Lone Star State* (1922) Soc Maritime Anversoise, Belgium

13,869grt; 535ft (163.1m) loa x 72ft (21.9m) beam
625 passengers in two classes (as an American ship)
New York Shipbuilding Corp, Camden, New Jersey (Yard No 255)
Steam turbines, twin screw

While she was making her departure from Antwerp, bound for New York, on 14 May 1940, the *Ville de Bruges* was sunk by German bombers in the mouth of the River Scheldt, some ten miles from her home port. She was carrying 34 refugees and a crew of 117. The blazing ship was beached and abandoned in the position 51.19N, 04.16E, and remained there until 1952 when the wreckage was removed.

Casualties: 3 (all crew)

VILLE DE LA CIOTAT (1892) Messageries Maritimes, France

6,378grt; 485ft (147.8m) lbp x 49ft (14.9m) beam
352 passengers in three classes
Messageries Maritimes, La Ciotat (Yard No 70)
Triple-expansion steam reciprocating, single screw

Requisitioned at Saigon on 21 June 1915 to collect Russian troops from Vladivostok, this command was later rescinded, and while she was coaling en route, at Moji, Japan, on 8 July, the *Ville de la Ciotat* was earmarked instead to run troop and prisoner transportation voyages in the Mediterranean. While returning to Marseilles from Shanghai and Yokohama on 24 December 1915 with 135 passengers and a crew of 181, the *Ville de la Ciotat* was torpedoed and sunk east of Crete, 105 miles south-west of Cape Matapan (Akra Tainaron), by what was claimed to be an Austrian submarine but which was in fact the German U34. The position was 35.01N, 21.26E. The survivors were taken to Malta, many of them aboard the British ship *Meroe*.

Casualties: 82 (34 passengers and 48 crew)

VILLE DE ST NAZAIRE (1870) Compagnie Générale Transatlantique (French Line), France

2,623grt; 285ft (86.9m) lbp x 41ft (12.5m) beam
Passenger numbers not known
Chantiers de l'Ocean, Bordeaux (Yard No not known)
Compound-expansion steam reciprocating, twin screw
The passenger ship *Ville de St Nazaire* was a pioneering example of a twin-screw steamer. She sailed from New York on 6 March 1897 bound for the West Indies with a complement of 83 persons, 9 of whom were passengers. Two days out, off Cape Hatteras, North Carolina, the ship ran into a hurricane. She had been taking water through a minor leak since leaving port, and this caused no particular concern at first; it was for this reason that the *Ville de St Nazaire* had continued with her passage. As the weather deteriorated, however, the leak worsened and the order was finally given to abandon ship on the evening of 8 March. A number of boats got away but only two of these were picked up. The first was intercepted by the American schooner *Hilda* on 15 March, but only four out of its original 38 occupants were still alive. The other boat was picked up by the steamship *Yanariva*; this contained 14 survivors. No news was ever received about the remaining 31 persons from the *Ville de St Nazaire*.

Casualties: 65

VILLE DE VERDUN (1917) Cie Havraise Péninsulaire de Nav à Vapeur, France

4,576grt; 350ft (106.8m) lbp x 51ft (15.6m) beam
318 passengers
North of Ireland Shipbuilding Co, Londonderry
(Yard No 68)
Triple-expansion steam reciprocating, single screw
The circumstances behind the construction of this small passenger vessel, particularly by an obscure shipbuilder in Northern Ireland, are not known, but the fact that it was during wartime may have some bearing. Suffice to say that the *Ville de Verdun* did not survive for long and may never have entered commercial service for she was torpedoed and sunk by the German submarine U34 on 6 February 1918 while she was bound from Dakar to Marseilles. The attack occurred off Guardamar, Spain, some seventy miles north-east of Cap Bougaroni (Bougaroun), Algeria, in the position 38.03N, 00.36W.

Casualties: not known

VILLE DU HAVRE (1866) ex-*Napoleon III* (1873) Compagnie Générale Transatlantique (French Line), France

5,065grt; 413ft (128.50m) lbp x 46ft (14.1m) beam
320 passengers in three classes
Thames Iron Works, Blackwall (Yard No not known)
Compound-expansion inverted steam reciprocating, single screw
As she was returning to Le Havre on a voyage from New York, the passenger steamship *Ville du Havre*, carrying 313 passengers, was in collision with the British iron clipper ship *Loch Earn* in the approaches to the English Channel after dark on 22 November 1873. Besides causing much other damage, two of her masts were toppled as the two ships smashed together, and as they fell to the deck many people were crushed. This and the sudden crisis that confronted the rudely awoken passengers caused many of them to panic. In these circumstances it was difficult to launch those lifeboats that remained intact. The *Ville du Havre* was in a dire state and there was evidently little time available for saving life. The *Loch Earn* lay dead in the water near the crippled passenger vessel and her Master organised a rescue effort from his ship that enabled 61 passengers and 26 crew members to reach safety. A higher number of survivors may have been evacuated had time permitted, but the *Ville du Havre* foundered only twelve minutes after the collision. The following day the survivors were transferred to the American steamship *Tremontain* and taken to Cardiff, while the *Loch Earn* continued on her voyage in spite of the extreme damage she too had sustained. However, six days later she too sank, but all members of her crew safely abandoned her and were picked up.

Casualties: 266

Built as the *Napoleon III*, the *Ville du Havre* was one of several early French Line transatlantic passenger ships that were converted from paddle to screw propulsion.
Cie Générale Transatlantique (French Line)

VIMINALE (1925) Italia Line, Italy

8,657grt; 467ft (142.5m) lbp x 57ft (17.4m) beam
226 passengers in two classes
Cantieri San Rocco, San Rocco, Trieste (Yard No 59)
Motor-ship, twin screw
Requisitioned in October 1940 for service as a troopship, the passenger-cargo motor-ship *Viminale* was seriously damaged at Palermo on 3 January 1943 by a Chariot XVI human torpedo driven by a British frogman (Sub-Lt R. G. Dove RN). Taken in tow for Taranto, on 21 January, the *Viminale* was between Messina and Taranto, in the position 38.34N, 15.45E,

when she was struck by a torpedo fired by the British submarine HMS *Unbending*. To prevent her from sinking, she was run aground at Cape Salvo, Melito. She was refloated seven days later but returned to Messina. Six months later, on 25 September 1943, during a second attempt to tow her to a shipyard on the Italian mainland, the *Viminale* was sunk by a combination of aircraft bombs and gunfire from surface ships, going down in the position 38.44N, 15.50E, approximately twelve miles south-west of Cape Vaticano.
Casualties: not known

VIRGILIO (1927) Italia Line, Italy

11,718grt; 506ft (154.2m) loa x 62ft (18.9m) beam
640 passengers in three classes
Cantieri Officine Meridionali, Baia (Yard No 15)
Motor-ship, twin screw
First taken up in June 1940 as a troopship, the passenger-cargo liner *Virgilio* was employed as a naval hospital ship from March 1941 until September 1943, when Italy sued for peace. She struck a magnetic mine off Tripoli in January 1943 and was taken to La Spezia for repairs, resuming operations that May. The Germans seized her at La Spezia in September 1943 and she was moved to the French naval base of Toulon. Three months later, on 6 December 1943, the *Virgilio* was severely damaged by bombs and torpedoes during an air raid on the port. At the end of June 1944, as the Germans were retreating from the area, the wrecked and un-repaired *Virgilio* was deliberately blown up to block the naval base and delay the Allied advance. Declared unfit for salvage after the war, the wreck was broken up locally.
Casualties: not known

VITTORIA (1883) ex-*Tamaulipas* (1887)
La Veloce Line, Italy

4,290grt; 440ft (134.1m) loa x 44ft (13.4m) beam
990 passengers in three classes
Robert Napier, Govan (Yard No 388)
Compound-expansion steam reciprocating, single screw
The passenger-cargo ship *Vittoria*, built originally for Cia Mexicana Trasatlantica, was acquired by La Veloce and placed on the Genoa to Buenos Aires service. She was badly damaged by fire and beached at Alicante, Spain, on 11 January 1899. Her wreck was subsequently towed back to Genoa where it was broken up for scrap.
Casualties: 0

VOLTAIRE (1923) Lamport & Holt Co, UK

13,248grt; 535ft (163.1m) loa x 64ft (19.5m) beam
680 passengers in three classes
Workman Clark, Belfast (Yard No 360)
Quadruple-expansion steam reciprocating, twin screw
The passenger-cargo ship *Voltaire* was sunk by a German raider. On 4 April 1941 she was intercepted by the auxiliary cruiser *Thor* when she was some 700 miles west-south-west of the Cape Verde Islands. The *Voltaire*, which had also been commissioned as an armed merchant cruiser, was on passage from Trinidad to Freetown, Gambia. As the ships began to exchange fire, the *Voltaire* put up a determined resistance but her lighter, less powerful armament was no match and after an hour of intense action she was ablaze and, with her

steering gear jammed, completely unmanoeuvrable. She sank around half an hour later in the position 14.25N, 40.40W, after her survivors, her Commander, 21 officers and 175 naval ratings, had abandoned ship. They were picked up by the *Thor* only to be held as prisoners of war until the end of hostilities in 1945.
Casualties: 75 (13 officers and 62 ratings)

The *Voltaire*, sister of the second *Vandyck*, is seen anchored in the River Mersey. Both were lost in the Second World War.
Ian Allan Library

VOLTURNO (1902) Canadian Northern Steamship Co, Canada (under charter to Uranium Steamship Co)

3,602grt; 340ft (103.6m) lbp x 43ft (13.1m) beam
1,024 passengers
Fairfield, Govan (Yard No 448)
Triple-expansion steam reciprocating, twin screw
The transatlantic emigrant steamship *Volturno* was bound from Rotterdam to New York when fire broke out in the forward cargo hold on 9 October 1913 when she was in the position 48.25N, 34.33W. On board her were 657 persons, 564 of them passengers who were mainly peasants of Polish, Romanian and Serbian origin. She was also conveying a full cargo of barium oxide, peat moss, rags and straw bottle covers, and it was in this highly inflammable mixture that the fire originated, followed soon after by a violent explosion that wrecked the forward part of the ship, jamming the steering gear and severing the engine room telegraph. Distress calls were sent out from the stricken ship and were answered by the Cunarder *Carmania*, which, in turn, relayed the message to other vessels in the vicinity. This brought a total of eight ships to the scene in response, including the Atlantic Transport Line's *Minneapolis*, Hamburg Amerika Line's *Grosser Kurfurst* and the *Kroonland* of Red Star. However, none of these was able to render assistance due to the mountainous seas that had added to the *Volturno*'s perilous situation. An attempt was made to launch some of her lifeboats but four immediately capsized while two others, successfully floated, were lost with their occupants. The arrival of the tanker *Narragansett* brought some relief as she was able to calm the seas to some extent by pouring a quantity of oil onto the turbulent water. This enabled the remaining passengers and crew to be taken off the *Volturno* on the following day. Her abandoned, burning hulk drifted for six more days after the rescue, until a boat's crew from the Dutch ship *Charlois* boarded her and scuttled her by opening the sea cocks. The position was 48.49N, 34.39W.
Casualties: 136 (103 passengers and 33 crew)

Though she only measured 3,600 gross tons, the steamer *Volturno* had capacity for 1,000 emigrants. The accommodation was cramped and basic and, realistically, was typical of the conditions that the majority of transatlantic passengers in the late 19th and early 20th centuries experienced. In the modern era, it parallels the overcrowding that seems to be the 'norm' on Philippino and Indonesian inter-island ferries.
LL von Münching

The *Volturno* ablaze in mid-Atlantic in October 1913.
National Maritime Museum

WAESLAND (1867) ex-*Russia* (1880) American Line, USA

4,752grt; 435ft (135.6m) lbp x 43ft (13.1m) beam
1,100 passengers in two classes (as a Red Star vessel)
J. & G. Thomson, Govan (Yard No 93)
Triple-expansion steam reciprocating, single screw
Built as the Cunard Line's first screw-propelled transatlantic passenger steamship and its last ship to have a clipper bow and figurehead, the *Russia* was sold to Red Star and renamed *Waesland*, continuing to work in the North Atlantic trade between Antwerp and New York after she had been rebuilt, lengthened and re-engined. From 1895 she switched to the Liverpool to Philadelphia route following transfer to the American Line. On 7 March 1902 she was sunk off Anglesey after colliding with the Houston Line steamship *Harmonides*.
Casualties: 2

The Red Star packet steamer *Waesland*, originally Cunard Line's *Russia*. *World Ship Society*

WAHEHE (1922) Woermann Line, Germany

serving under the wartime name EMPIRE CITIZEN
4,709grt; 361ft (110.0m) lbp x 50ft (15.2m) beam
250 passengers
Reiherstiegwerft, Hamburg (Yard No 518)
Quadruple-expansion steam reciprocating, single screw
The *Empire Citizen*, the captured German passenger-cargo ship *Wahehe*, seized by British warships off Vigo on 21 February 1940 before her crew could scuttle her, was on passage from Liverpool to Rangoon on 2 February 1941 when she was torpedoed in the North Atlantic by the German submarine U107. Apart from her crew of 71 men, she also had 12 passengers aboard. She sank in the position 58.12N, 23.22W.
Casualties: 78 (all the passengers and 66 crew)

WAHINE (1966) Union Steamship Co of New Zealand, UK

9,205grt; 489ft (149.0m) loa x 73ft (22.1m) beam
924 passengers
Fairfield, Govan (Yard No 830)
Turbo-electric, twin screw

The Union Steamship Company had introduced some striking new tonnage after the Second World War on its North/South Island and trans-Tasman services, among them the *Hinemoa*, *Tofua* and *Maori*. The latest addition, in June 1966, was the striking turbo-electric-powered *Wahine*. *Author's collection*

Overwhelmed by hurricane-force cyclonic winds, the *Wahine* is seen stranded on Barrett's Reef on 10 April 1968. *Wellington Evening Post*

On 10 April 1968 the New Zealand inter-island ferry *Wahine* was heading from Port Lyttelton to Wellington carrying 727 passengers. The conditions off the east coast of New Zealand's South Island were rough as a cold front was moving north. At the same time a tropical storm was approaching from the Tasman Sea and the two weather systems met over the Cook Strait just as the *Wahine* was nearing Barretts Reef, south of the entrance to Wellington Harbour. In the severe cyclone that followed, hurricane-force winds of up to 130 miles per hour tore through the strait, whipping up mountainous waves and driving the *Wahine* onto the shoals. Although she dropped anchors, these were dragged when the rising tide and the violent seas lifted her off after half an hour. She lost her starboard propeller and was badly holed, one hole in particular, on her starboard side, being subsequently measured in an underwater examination as 20 feet by 6 feet. As it was situated immediately beneath her main generators, it permitted water to flood the engine room and all power was lost.

At the mercy of the elements, great effort was made to control the ship's drift and try to navigate her into Wellington Harbour through Chaffers Passage. The tug *Tapuhi* was sent to assist, but in the conditions could do very little. A line passed to her parted immediately and the tug could not approach near enough to take off any of the passengers. At this point, despite her damage and the loss of power, it was felt that the *Wahine* could ride out the storm, but just after midday she developed a severe list to starboard. Without power for the pumps, the ship's fate was sealed and the order to abandon ship was given. It was speculated that the

movement of 68 vehicles stowed on the car deck had contributed to the sudden and acute list. Unfortunately, the inclination meant that only the starboard-side lifeboats could be lowered. Nevertheless, aided by the New Zealand Rail train ferry *Aramoana* and the tugs *Tapuhi* and *Taioma*, the majority of the *Wahine*'s occupants were ferried ashore at Seatoun beach. About 200 persons who leapt into the water but could not be picked up were swept across the harbour to the eastern shore. A number of them were drowned or killed when they were dashed against the rocks, their bodies washing up on the shoreline. By mid-afternoon the *Wahine* had capsized onto her side at the western side of the main entrance channel to Wellington.

It was only over the following two days that the full extent of the disaster was revealed. There was uncertainty at first as to the precise number of passengers the *Wahine* had been carrying. The records indicated that 605 tickets had been issued at Lyttelton, but crew members reported that there had also been stowaways on board. Wellington police issued a complete and final list on 12 April. It stated that, in fact, there had been 823 persons in total aboard the ferry, 727 passengers and 96 crew. Of these there were 771 survivors, among them 101 persons who were detained in hospital with severe injuries. That May, the *Wahine*'s owners were advised that she was a constructive total loss and the underwriters accepted the claim on the hull. She was not salvaged as the operation would have been too expensive; instead, the wreck was dismantled as it lay and gradually removed.
Casualties: 52

WARATAH (1908) Blue Anchor Line, UK

9,339grt; 465ft (141.7m) lbp x 59ft (18.1m) beam
850 passengers in two classes
Barclay Curle, Whiteinch, Glasgow (Yard No 472)
Quadruple-expansion steam reciprocating, twin screw
The passenger-cargo ship *Waratah* put into Durban to coal and load cargo on 25 July 1909 on her second return voyage from Sydney to London via Cape Town. Additional passengers also embarked so that when she left for Cape Town on the following day she had a total of 211 persons on board, 92 passengers and 119 crew. One day out from Durban on the coastwise passage, she passed the cargo vessel *Clan Macintyre*, also bound for England, and the two ships exchanged signals in the position 31.36S, 29.58E. This was the last that was seen of the *Waratah*. Initially there was no undue anxiety for the *Waratah* and her occupants, as it was assumed that she had been slowed down by heavy weather in the area, although the ship could not be contacted to confirm this as she was not carrying wireless equipment.

When there was no sign of her by 31 July, the tug *T.E. Fuller* and the naval cruisers *Forte*, *Pandora* and *Hermes* were dispatched from Cape Town to seek her, but when they returned after a week they had no news of the missing vessel. A more extensive search was then arranged by the owners and underwriters, supported by the Australian Government. The Union-Castle cargo ship *Sabine* was chartered to scour the southern oceans, but by the time she re-entered Cape Town on 7 December 1909, after three months at sea, she had found nothing to indicate the lost ship's whereabouts or the cause of her disappearance. A week later the *Waratah* was officially posted as missing by Lloyd's of London. A further three-month search was made from February 1910 by the steamship *Wakefield*, but when her quest also failed to shed any light on the mystery, the *Waratah*'s total loss was reluctantly accepted.

Casualties: 211

Built for the 'Branch Line' service from London to Adelaide, Melbourne and Sydney via Cape Town, the *Waratah* was the final addition to the Blue Anchor Line fleet. *P&O*

WARILDA (1914) Adelaide Steamship Co, UK

7,713grt; 428ft (130.5m) loa x 56ft (17.1m) beam
430 passengers in three classes
William Beardmore, Dalmuir (Yard No 505)
Quadruple-expansion steam reciprocating, twin screw

The Australian coastwise passenger ship *Warilda* served as an Admiralty hospital ship during the First World War. In this capacity, while sailing from Le Havre to Southampton with 700 wounded servicemen on 3 August 1918, she fell the victim to a torpedo fired by the German submarine UC49. Although the attack was made in murky conditions, the *Warilda* was conspicuously marked and she would not have been the first hospital ship that was sunk in disregard of the Geneva Convention rather than because of misidentification. Interestingly, the German sinking report described her as an armed ambulance transport conveying casualties! Fortunately, the *Warilda* remained afloat for around two hours, permitting the evacuation of the majority of those aboard her, a total of 678 survivors. She sank in the position 50.11N, 00.13W, 32 miles south-south-west of the Owers light vessel.

Casualties: 123

Designed for the Australian coastal services, the *Warilda* was taken over on completion as a hospital ship and did not survive the First World War to take up the duties for which she had been ordered. *Alex Duncan*

WARWICK CASTLE (1931) Union-Castle Line, UK

20,107grt; 677ft (206.3m) loa x 75ft (22.9m) beam
699 passengers in three classes
Harland & Wolff, Belfast (Yard No 840)
Motor-ship, twin screw

The *Warwick Castle* served as a troopship during the Second World War. On 14 November 1942, as she was bound from Gibraltar to the River Clyde, returning from French North Africa after landing troops of the Operation 'Torch' invasion force, she was torpedoed by the German submarine U413. She was carrying 165 passengers besides her crew of 263. The attack took place 200 miles off the coast of Portugal and she sank in the position 39.16N, 13.25W.

Casualties: 63, including her Master

In what amounted to a revolutionary change of policy in new construction for its fleet, Union-Castle Line ordered three large motor-ships for its express service to the Cape from Southampton. Last of the trio to enter service was the *Warwick Castle*. In 1938 the three liners were rebuilt, having more powerful engines installed while their original twin funnels were replaced with a single, more modern one.
World Ship Society

W. A. SCHOLTEN (1874) Holland Amerika Line, The Netherlands

2,589grt; 351ft (107.0m) lbp x 38ft (11.6m) beam
650 passengers in two classes
Robert Napier, Govan (Yard No 327)
Compound-expansion steam reciprocating, single screw

The transatlantic passenger steamship *W. A. Scholten* was involved in a collision with the British collier *Rosa Mary* in the English Channel on 19 November 1887. At the time she was bound from Rotterdam to New York with 156 passengers and 54 crew. The collision occurred about four miles east of Dover in hazy weather, the *W. A. Scholten* running into the anchored collier, which was hove-to waiting for clearer conditions before getting under way. The *W.A. Scholten* had a large hole torn in her port bow through which she made water fast. She sank bow-first within thirty minutes of the crash, listing heavily to port as she went under. The list prevented the launching of many of the lifeboats and only two were got clear in the short time available. The survivors, many of them in the water supported by lifebelts, were rescued by the British cargo steamship *Ebro*.

Casualties: 132 (including her Master)

WATUSSI (1928) Woermann Line, Germany

9,552grt; 468ft (142.6m) lbp x 60ft (18.3m) beam
300 passengers
Blohm & Voss, Steinwerder, Hamburg (Yard No 481)
Steam turbines, single screw

While she was on passage from Zanzibar and Mozambique to Hamburg on 2 December 1939, the passenger-cargo ship *Watussi* was spotted by an Allied aeroplane as she was steaming along fifty miles south of Cape Agulhas, the southernmost tip of South Africa. The plane radioed for a warship to intercept the German liner, but the officers and crew of the *Watussi*, having also picked up the call, decided instead to scuttle the ship to prevent her capture. Casualties: 0

WILHELM GUSTLOFF (1938) Deutsche Arbeitsfront, Germany (managed by Hamburg Sud-Amerika Line)

25,484grt; 684ft (208.5m) loa x 77ft (23.5m) beam
1,465 passengers in single class
Blohm & Voss, Steinwerder, Hamburg (Yard No 511)
Motor-ship, twin screw

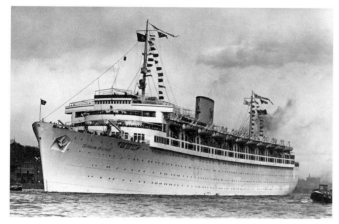

The *Wilhelm Gustloff* was the first purpose-built cruise ship to be completed for the workers' cruises run by the Kraft durch Freude ('Strength Through Joy') association, one of the Nazi Government's more savoury propaganda diversions. She was named after a petty Nazi party official assassinated in Switzerland in February 1936. Intending to immortalise him, little could it have been realised that later events would make it a name never to be forgotten. *Blohm & Voss*

An artist's impression of the *Wilhelm Gustloff*'s last moments. *Author's collection*

The greatest loss of life in a single maritime disaster is attributed to the government cruise ship *Wilhelm Gustloff* during the closing stages of the Second World War. After wartime service, first as a hospital ship, then as a static naval accommodation ship at Gotenhafen (Gdynia), she was reactivated in January 1945 under Operation 'Hannibal', the evacuation of East Prussia and Upper Silesia, a mercy mission necessitated by the rapid advance of the Red Army into Poland. On 30 January 1945 the *Wilhelm Gustloff* set out from Gotenhafen bound for the Bay of Lübeck with a massive complement of civilian refugees, U-boat personnel and her crew, estimated to number between 6,000 and 8,000 in total.

Owing to the desperate circumstances of her departure, in which the compilation of an accurate passenger manifest was not a matter of great interest, together with the Nazi policy of concealing unwelcome news and the subsequent destruction of wartime records, her exact complement is not known. Inevitably, different sources quote widely varying numbers. Lloyd's records state that there were 5,000 refugees plus 3,700 U-boat personnel aboard her, besides her mixed naval/mercantile crew. The Bundesarchivs state that she was carrying a total complement of 6,100 persons. Based on word-of-mouth testaments, a measure of documentation and the personal recollections of survivors, these figures can only give an indication of the huge number that was aboard the ship on that fateful day.

What is certain is that there was massive loss of life when she was sunk, torpedoed by the Russian submarine S13 when she was north of Stolpmünde in Danzig Bay, in the position 55.28N, 17.31E. Hit by a perfect spread of three torpedoes, she sank within 45 minutes. She had been sailing in convoy and many of the accompanying vessels rushed to her aid, among them the heavy cruiser *Admiral Hipper*, the naval escorts *Löwe*, T36, TF19, TS2, M341 and V1703, as well as the Norddeutscher Lloyd passenger steamer *Gottingen*. Despite their efforts, there were only 904 survivors according to official German records. The wreck of the *Wilhelm Gustloff*, in three sections, lies on the seabed to this day in the position 55.07N, 17.42E.
Casualties: From 5,196 to more than 6,896. Heinz Schoen, the ship's Purser and a survivor of the sinking, and probably the best authority on both the *Wilhelm Gustloff*'s sinking and the entire 'Hannibal' Operation, states that, according to his information, she was carrying a total of 6,600 persons, of whom 5,348 lost their lives.

WIND SONG (1987) Windstar Cruises, Bahamas

5,703grt; 440ft (134.0m) loa x 52ft (15.8m) beam
159 passengers
Nouvelle Havre, Le Havre (Yard No 270)
Diesel-electric, single screw

Unique in this publication, the *Wind Song* was the only modern sail-and-engine-powered cruise ship to be overtaken by disaster. She sailed under the Bahamas flag. *Ian Shiffman*

The sail cruise ship *Wind Song*, one of a number of such vessels commissioned in response to a demand for a more gentle form of cruising, caught fire off Tahaa, French Polynesia, on 1 December 2002. The fire started in her engine room and spread to the rest of the ship. Her 127 passengers, together with 17 of her 92 crew members, were safely evacuated, while the remainder of the crew stayed aboard in an effort to extinguish the fire. In this they were assisted by French naval vessels that arrived on the scene. The *Wind Song*, which was severely damaged, was towed to Papeete, on Tahiti, for examination and a repair assessment. However, as she was found to be beyond economic recovery, the decision was made to scuttle the wreck. This took place on 23 January 2003, despite the intervention of environmental campaigners who objected to the plan, and she was sunk in the position 17.45S, 149.48W. Casualties: 0

WINDSOR CASTLE (1922) Union-Castle Line, UK

19,141grt; 686ft (209.1m) loa x 75ft (22.9m) beam
604 passengers in three classes
John Brown, Clydebank (Yard No 456c)
Steam turbines, twin screw
Following the outbreak of hostilities with Germany in September 1939, the passenger liner *Windsor Castle* was requisitioned for conversion into a troopship. She was lost on 23 March 1943 when German aircraft torpedoed her 110 miles north-west of Algiers. At the time the *Windsor Castle* was sailing in a convoy bound from Greenock to the Middle East via the Cape of Good Hope, and had aboard her 2,699 troops together with her 290-man crew. She remained afloat for thirteen hours after the attack, allowing adequate time for other convoy ships and escorts to take off her entire complement. According to her Master, the attack took place in the position 37.27N, 00.54E, but Lloyd's and other sources record the position as 37.28N, 01.10E. The *Windsor Castle* finally sank by the stern, while the rescue vessels were still gathered around her. Casualties: 1 (a crew member)

The *Windsor Castle* and *Arundel Castle* were the first new express liners placed on the South African mail service after the First World War. Completed with four funnels, a refit and modernisation in 1937 reduced the number to two while other refinements included a raked bow that added 25 feet (7.6 metres) to their length. *British & Commonwealth Shipping*

The *Windsor Castle* sinking north-west of Algiers on 23 March 1943. *British & Commonwealth Shipping*

WINSTON CHURCHILL (1967) Det Forenede Dampskibs-Selskabs (DFDS), Denmark

8,657grt; 462ft (140.7m) loa x 67ft (20.5m) beam
590 passengers
Cantieri Navale del Tirreno e Riuniti, Riva Trigoso (Yard No 277)
Motor-ship, twin screw
The stylish North Sea ro-ro ferry *Winston Churchill*, a development of the earlier *England* owned by the same company, was increasingly employed on cruises as her career advanced. She suffered a serious fire in her engine room while she was lying at Esbjerg, Denmark, on 3 April 1996. Extensive damage throughout the ship resulted in her being declared a constructive total loss. Despite this, she was sold to Emerald Empress Holding Ltd, a Florida-based shipowner, and this concern had her moved to Stavanger, Norway, to undergo repairs with a view to returning her to cruise operations from Miami, Florida, offering itineraries in the Gulf of Mexico area. The intention was to rename her *Mayan Empress*, registered in St Vincent. Fully restored at great cost, her new owners defaulted on payment, forcing the shipyard, Westcon, to seize the ship. However, another buyer could not be found and she remained at the shipyard for almost seven years until the end of 2003 when she was sold for breaking-up at Alang, arriving there on 24 January 2004.
Casualties: not known

The elegant DFDS passenger/vehicle ferry *Winston Churchill* was a larger and better-appointed development of the *England* of 1964. She had a long and uneventful career until she suffered a major engine room fire in 1996. She operated on various services from Esbjerg, including to Harwich, Newcastle and the Faeroe islands. She is seen here at Travemünde in September 1989. *Frank Heine FERRIES*

WOOSUNG (1918) China Navigation Co (J. Swire & Sons), UK

serving under the wartime name REIZAN MARU
3,426grt; 320ft (97.5m) lbp x 46ft (14.1m) beam
Passenger numbers not known
Taikoo, Hong Kong (Yard No 166)
Triple-expansion steam reciprocating, twin screw
The large coastal passenger ship *Woosung*, essentially an estuary craft, worked the Lower Yangtse service from Shanghai to Hankow. She was seized by the Japanese in 1941 and pressed into their service, renamed *Reizan Maru* in 1942. On 18 January 1945 she struck a mine in the River Yangtse and sank in the position 39.11N, 115.07E.
Casualties: not known

WORCESTERSHIRE (1904) Bibby Line, UK

7,160grt; 452ft (137.7m) lbp x 54ft (16.5m) beam
200 passengers in single class
Harland & Wolff, Belfast (Yard No 359)
Quadruple expansion steam reciprocating, twin screw
While bound from Rangoon to London and Liverpool on 17 February 1917, the liner *Worcestershire* struck a mine between ten and twelve miles south-west of the Colombo breakwater, Ceylon (Sri Lanka), and sank as a result of the damage she sustained.
Casualties: 2

WORLD DISCOVERER (1974) ex-*Bewa Discoverer* (launch name, 8 December 1973) Adventurer Cruises, Singapore

3,724grt; 287ft (87.5m) loa x 50ft (15.1m) beam
137 passengers
Schichau-Unterweser, Bremerhaven (Yard No 2250)
Motor-ship, twin screw
Reflecting another recent trend in cruise holidays – the desire to venture to remote, 'wilderness' places, often with extremes of climate – the small cruise ship *World Discoverer* was one of a small number of such vessels constructed to work these types of itinerary. There are obvious dangers when vessels carrying passengers are so far removed from the means of rescue and assistance at times of emergency, and there has been much debate as to how best such 'adventure' or 'explorer' cruises should be managed in order to reduce the risks.

Although her passenger capacity is the lowest of the ships described in this dictionary, the *World Discoverer* has been included here because she is an example of a passenger ship deployed on this type of cruise. She came to grief on 30 April 2000 when she was stranded in the Sandfly Passage, about 25 miles north of Honiara, Solomon Islands. She immediately developed a list of 20 degrees and was beached to avoid her sinking. Her 99 passengers and all her crew were safely evacuated. A salvage operation lasting between one and two months was anticipated, with the prospect of the vessel being fully recovered, but hostility from the local population, who also ransacked the stricken *World Discoverer*, forced the withdrawal of the salvage team. Although she had been pumped out and righted, she was abandoned to her fate.
Casualties: 0

Another adventure cruise ship, the *Explorer* was previously the *Lindblad Explorer* as shown here. She was similar in size to the *World Discoverer*. *Ian Shiffman*

As a postscript to the *World Discoverer* account, a more recent incident involving an 'adventure' cruise ship was the foundering of the Explorer Shipping Corp's 1969-built 2,346 gross ton, 239 feet (72.9m) overall *Explorer* on 23 November 2007 – a ship whose size and complement fall outside the scope of both the dictionary section and Appendices in this book. In her case she sank off King George Island, South Shetland Islands, Antarctica, after striking an iceberg, but fortunately there was no loss of life, rescue vessels having reached the ship in good time. However, it is of interest to look at this location on a map to see how far the ship was from recognised shipping lanes and cruise areas.

The adventure cruise ship *World Discoverer* photographed at Portsmouth on 5 May 1989. *Chris Bancroft*

**YAMATO MARU (1915) ex-*Guiseppe Verdi* (1928)
Nippon Yusen Kaisha, Japan**

9,760grt; 505ft (153.9m) lbp x 59ft (18.0m) beam
916 passengers
Esercizio Bacini, Riva Trigoso (Yard No 65)
Quadruple-expansion steam reciprocating, twin screw
While serving as a troop transport, carrying 1,092 military
passengers and crew, the passenger-cargo ship *Yamato Maru*
was torpedoed and sunk by the American submarine USS
Snook on 13 September 1943. The attack took place 200
miles south-east of Shanghai, in the position 30.06N, 123.33E.
Casualties: 27

**YARMOUTH CASTLE (1932) ex-*Evangeline* (1964)
Yarmouth Cruise Lines, USA**

5,043grt; 378ft (115.2m) x 65ft (19.8m) beam
350 passengers
William Cramp, Philadelphia (Yard No not known)
Steam turbines, twin screw

The coastal passenger ship *Evangeline*, seen in an unidentified
port, became the cruise ship *Yarmouth Castle* in 1964.
World Ship Society

The former *Evangeline*, which had served for almost thirty
years, discounting war service, on coastal routes along the
American eastern seaboard, was sold for cruise operation late
in her life and renamed *Yarmouth Castle* in 1964. During a
cruise to Nassau from Miami on 13 November 1965 with 371
passengers – more than her certificated number – and a crew
of 175, fire broke out aboard. It had started in one of the
passenger cabins and rapidly spread. In many respects it was
reminiscent of the *Morro Castle* tragedy, although the
behaviour of the officers aboard that vessel was exemplary
compared with that of the Master and senior crew of the
Yarmouth Castle, who failed both to coordinate any effort in
fighting the fire or to supervise an orderly muster of the
passengers ready for evacuation. Matters were made worse
because of a failure to send out distress calls in good time,
something that was prevented altogether when the radio
shack was consumed by the flames, together with the bridge
and many of the lifeboats. Panicking passengers added to the
mayhem and confusion. Luckily, two ships that had spotted

the burning *Yarmouth Castle* came to her assistance and 458
persons were evacuated aboard the *Bahama Star* and the
cargo ship *Finnpulp*. The blazing *Yarmouth Castle* rolled
over and sank approximately thirteen miles from Great
Stirrup Bay, less than six hours after the emergency had
begun.
Casualties: 88

YARRA (1883) Messageries Maritimes, France

4,142grt; 416ft (126.8m) lbp x 41ft (12.5m) beam
209 passengers in three classes
Messageries Maritimes, La Ciotat (Yard No 58)
Triple-expansion steam reciprocating, single screw
The passenger steamship *Yarra* continued to make
commercial voyages after the outbreak of the First World War,
maintaining the French postal services. She was torpedoed
and sunk, in the eastern Mediterranean north-west of Cape
Sidero, on 29 May 1917, by the German submarine UC74. The
Yarra had been in convoy with the *Oceanien* and *Empereur
Nicholas II*, escorted by the destroyer *Arbalete* and two
gunboats, the *Dedaigneuse* and the British HMS *Lily*. She had
been bound for Marseilles from Port Said and Madagascar
carrying the Egyptian mails and 690 persons, many of them
native passengers. Hit in the stokehold, the *Yarra* sank within
ten minutes.
Casualties: 56, including 7 Arab stokers

YASAKA MARU (1914) Nippon Yusen Kaisha, Japan

10,932grt; 523ft (159.4m) loa x 63ft (19.2m) beam
512 passengers in three classes
Kawasaki, Kobe (Yard No 369)
Triple-expansion steam reciprocating, twin screw
On 21 December 1915, while she was bound for Yokohama
on the return voyage from the River Tees and London, the
Yasaka Maru was torpedoed and sunk by the German
submarine U38 in the position 31.53N, 31.10E, north of
Damietta, some sixty miles from Port Said.
Casualties: 0

The *Yasaka Maru* was the last unit of a five-ship class built for
the Japan to Europe service. *Nippon Yusen Kaisha*

YASUKUNI MARU (1930) Nippon Yusen Kaisha, Japan

11,930grt; 527ft (160.6m) loa x 64ft (19.5m) beam
249 passengers in three classes
Mitsubishi, Nagasaki (Yard No 468)
Motor-ship, twin screw

On 31 January 1944, when she was north-west of the island of Truk, in the position 09.15N, 147.13E, the passenger-cargo ship *Yasukuni Maru* was torpedoed and sunk by the American submarine USS *Trigger*.
Casualties: not known

Sister of the *Terukuni Maru*, this is the *Yasukuni Maru*, probably photographed on the River Thames.
H. B. Christiansen Collection / Online Transport Archive

YAWATA MARU (1940) Nippon Yusen Kaisha, Japan

serving under the wartime name IJNS UNYO
17,128grt; 590ft (179.8m) loa x 73ft (22.3m) beam
285 passengers in three classes
Mitsubishi, Nagasaki (Yard No 751)
Steam turbines, twin screw
The passenger-cargo liner *Yawata Maru*, like her sisters *Nitta Maru* and *Kasuga Maru* (qv), was taken over for conversion by her builders into an escort carrier, in her case in January 1942. She re-emerged on 31 May 1942 as the *Unyo*, after an extraordinarily fast turn-round for such an elaborate modification (a similar conversion to Union-Castle's *Pretoria Castle* took more than a year). On 16 September 1944 she was torpedoed and sunk by the American submarine USS *Barb* in the South China Sea, 220 miles south-east of Hong Kong, in the position 19.18N, 116.26E.
Casualties: About 240

Built for the Yokohama to Hamburg service, the *Yawata Maru* instead entered the service to San Francisco because of the outbreak of war in Europe. *Nippon Yusen Kaisha*

YOMA (1928) Henderson Line, UK

8,139grt; 460ft (140.2m) lbp x 61ft (18.6m) beam
150 passengers in single class
William Denny, Dumbarton (Yard No 1206)
Quadruple-expansion steam reciprocating, single screw

On 17 June 1943 the passenger-cargo ship *Yoma* was sailing in convoy, bound for Port Said with 1,670 troops and her crew of 175 men, when the German submarine U81 torpedoed her off Benghazi, in the position 33.03N, 22.04E. She sank rapidly, but escorts and other convoy ships managed to pick up 1,361 survivors.
Casualties: 484 (451 troops, her Master and 32 crew)

The *Yoma* was one of a group of similar ships built for the Glasgow and Liverpool to Rangoon service via the Suez Canal. The others were the *Amarapoora*, *Kemmendine*, *Pegu* and *Sagaing*. They suffered heavily in the Second World War, four of the five being sunk. *H. B. Christiansen Collection / Online Transport Archive*

YONGALA (1903) Adelaide Steamship Co, Australia

3,664grt; 350ft (106.7m) lbp x 45ft (13.8m) beam
240 passengers in two classes
Armstrong Whitworth, Low Walker, Tyneside
(Yard No 736)
Triple-expansion steam reciprocating, single screw
The Australian coastwise passenger cargo steamer *Yongala* disappeared during a hurricane on 23 March 1911 and was lost with her entire complement. It was assumed that she had foundered off the Queensland coast, some ten miles off Cape Bowling Green.
Casualties: 142

YORKSHIRE (1920) Bibby Line, UK

10,184grt; 499ft (152.1m) loa x 58ft (17.7m) beam
305 passengers in single class
Harland & Wolff, Belfast (Yard No 509)
Steam turbines, twin screw

The turbine steamer *Yorkshire* was a one-off ship, built for the Liverpool to Rangoon service, which she entered in September 1920. *Alex Duncan*

The passenger steamship *Yorkshire*, carrying 118 passengers and 160 crew, fell victim to a torpedo fired by the German submarine U37 while she was bound for Liverpool on 17

October 1939. The attack took place some 700 miles out into the Atlantic, north-west of Cape Finisterre, in the position 44.52N, 14.31W. The survivors were rescued by the American cargo ship *Independence Hall*, which had arrived on the scene in response to distress calls, and they were landed at Bordeaux on 20 October.

Casualties: 58

YOSHINO [YOSINO] MARU (1907) ex-*Kleist* (1921) Nippon Yusen Kaisha, Japan

8,959grt; 464ft (141.3m) lbp x 57ft (17.5m) beam
1,908 passengers in three classes (as built)
Schichau, Danzig (Yard No 775)
Quadruple-expansion steam reciprocating, twin screw
On 31 July 1944, while serving as a Japanese naval transport, the *Yoshino Maru* was torpedoed and sunk by the American submarines USS *Steelhead* and *Parche* off the west coast of Dalupiri, in the Philippines Islands, while bound from Kaohsiung to Manila. The position was 19.10N, 120.58E, about twenty miles north of Luzon.

Casualties: not known

YUKON (1899) ex-*Colon* (1923) ex-*Mexico* (1906) Alaska Steamship Co, USA

5,747grt; 360ft (109.7m) lbp x 50ft (15.2m) beam
304 passengers
William Cramp, Philadelphia (Yard No 295)
Triple-expansion steam reciprocating, twin screw
After spending many years on the north-west Pacific coast service from Seattle to British Columbia, the Yukon and Alaska, as well as employment as a the Second World War auxiliary, the passenger steamship *Yukon* ran aground in Johnstone Bay, Prince William Sound, Alaska, on 4 February 1946, while she was returning to Seattle from Seward. She was abandoned to become a total wreck.

Casualties: 32

Built originally for the Ward Line for service from New York to Cuba, the *Yukon* was transferred to the United States' west coast after she was acquired by the Alaska Steamship Company in 1923. This wartime photograph was taken from a Canadian forces aircraft. *World Ship Society*

Z

ZAANDAM (1939) Holland Amerika Line, The Netherlands

10,909grt; 501ft (152.7m) loa x 64ft (19.5m) beam
160 passengers in single class
Wilton Fijenoord, Schiedam (Yard No 663)
Motor-ship, twin screw
The passenger-cargo ship *Zaandam* was placed under the control of the British Ministry of War Transport from May 1940, but was later transferred to the US War Shipping Administration for auxiliary service in the Pacific and Far Eastern theatres. She left Cape Town, bound for New York, on 21 October 1942, her total complement of 299 persons comprising 130 crew and 169 passengers. The latter group included the survivors from four American ships that had been sunk previously, the freighters *Examelia*, *Coloradan* and *Chickasaw City*, and the oil tanker *Swiftsure*. On 2 November, when she was some 300 miles off the coast of Brazil, north-east of Cape San Roque, the *Zaandam* was hit twice by torpedoes fired by the German submarine U174 and sank within ten minutes. As the explosions had destroyed the lifeboats on her port side, only those on the starboard side could be launched.

The ship had gone down in the position 01.25S, 36.22W, and for the survivors who had made it into the boats there followed an epic struggle for survival. For three of them it was to become the second longest trial of human endurance on the open ocean throughout all of the Second World War, lasting 83 days. The first group of survivors, a total of 106 men in two lifeboats, were picked up five days after the sinking by the American tanker *Gulf State* and taken to Port of Spain, Trinidad. A second party, numbering 60, landed on a remote part of the Brazilian coast on 10 November, their presence there notified to the British consul in Rio de Janeiro by the chief of police at Barreirinhas, after some of the officers had ridden there on horseback to advise him of their whereabouts.

The remaining five survivors, cast adrift on a flimsy raft onto which they had clambered, depended on others coming to their rescue for they had no means by which they could steer a course. Their only means of sustenance was rainwater and the occasional fish or seabird that they were able to snare. When two Americans among them (George Beasley and James Maddox) perished on the 66th and 77th days of the ordeal, their number was reduced to three. The remaining castaways, two Dutchmen (Cornelis Van der Slot and Nicko Hoogendam) and an American (Basil Izzi) were finally picked up by a United States Navy patrol craft on 24 January 1943, in the position 09.14N, 58.45W. By that date they had drifted almost 2,000 miles, existing on the leanest of rations – only what they had been able to secure by their own guile. Without doubt it was a tribute to their fortitude of spirit and determination to survive.

Casualties: 130, including 69 of the rescued crew members from other victim ships

The *Zaandam*, seen here, and *Noordam* entered the service from Rotterdam to New York in the months preceding the Second World War, completing only a small number of round voyages before hostilities interrupted their schedules.
LL von Münching

ZAMZAM (1909) ex-*British Exhibitor* (1933) ex-*Leicestershire* (1931) Soc Misr de Navigation Maritime, Egypt

8,299grt; 467ft (142.3m) lbp x 54ft (16.5m) beam
229 passengers in single class (as built)
Harland & Wolff, Belfast (Yard No 403)
Quadruple-expansion steam reciprocating, twin screw
The Egyptian passenger ship *Zamzam* sailed from Hoboken, New Jersey, in March 1941 bound for Alexandria, Egypt, via Trinidad, Brazil, Cape Town and Mombasa. She was carrying 201 passengers, of whom 142 were American citizens. Among her number were 144 missionaries and 33 children. She also had a crew of around 120 men. After leaving Pernambuco (Recife) on 9 April 1941, the ship followed a zig-zag course as she headed for South Africa and was blacked out at night for safety. Early on 17 April 1941 the *Zamzam* was shelled without warning by the German raider *Atlantis* (also known as *Tamesis*). On discovering the nature of her passengers, principally neutral Americans, all aboard her, including some who were injured, were evacuated to the *Atlantis*. The crippled *Zamzam* was then finished off with time bombs and she sank in the position 27.41S, 08.08W. All but three of her survivors were transferred to the Norddeutscher Lloyd cargo ship *Dresden*, which held them for 33 days before landing them at St Jean de Luz, France, near the Spanish border, where they were interned. It is known that of the three passengers, all severely wounded, who remained aboard the *Atlantis*, at least one died of his injuries.
Casualties: ~1

ZENITH (1956) ex-*Fairy Princess* (1995) ex-*Faith Power* (1994) ex-*Corinthia* (1993) ex-*Neptunia* (1987) ex-*Duke of Argyll* (1975) Galaxy Shipholding SA, Panama

4,841grt; 376ft (114.6m) loa x 57ft (17.5m) beam
1,500 passengers (as built)
Harland & Wolff, Belfast (Yard No 1541)
Steam turbines, twin screw
The former Heysham to Belfast ferry *Duke of Argyll* underwent a sequence of career and name changes after she was retired from Irish Sea service in 1975. She was in Chinese

waters under the name *Zenith* when she suffered an engine room fire on 31 October 1995 while she was lying at Hong Kong shortly after arriving there from elsewhere in China. The fire engulfed the ship, spreading to the accommodation areas, and she sank in shallow waters in the harbour, partially submerged with most of the burned-out hulk above the surface. Her blistered hull was listing to port while she was down more towards her stern end. In this condition she was fit only for scrap and, on 31 March 1996, after she had been refloated, she was towed to Zhongshan and broken up.
Casualties: not known

The *Duke of Argyll*, a former Sealink ferry, operated as the *Corinthia* between 1987 and 1993, here seen at Patras in August 1990. Later, as the *Zenith*, she was gutted by fire at Hong Kong.
Frank Heine FERRIES

ZIETEN (1902) Norddeutscher Lloyd, Germany

serving under the wartime name TUNGUE
8,043grt; 449ft (136.9m) lbp x 55ft (16.8m) beam
1,900 passengers in three classes
Schichau, Danzig (Yard No 692)
Triple-expansion steam reciprocating, twin screw
The passenger steamship *Zieten* was interned at Mozambique on 5 August 1914 and remained there until March 1916, when the Portuguese Government requisitioned her for auxiliary service. Under the new name *Tungue* she was torpedoed and sunk by the German submarine UB51 on 27 November 1917 some 120 miles north of Port Said, in the eastern Mediterranean, while she was bound from Karachi to Milo Island, Greece.
Casualties: not known

ZUIDERDAM (1944) Holland Amerika Line, The Netherlands

12,150grt; 518ft (157.9m) loa x 66ft (20.1m) beam
152 passengers in single class
Wilton Fijenoord, Schiedam (Yard No 672)
Motor-ship, twin screw
In May 1940, when the Netherlands was overrun by the Germans, the passenger-cargo ship *Zuiderdam* was incomplete, lying in the shipyard at Schiedam. She immediately became a target of the Dutch Resistance to prevent the Germans from gaining any use of her. Despite the sabotage attempts, the occupying forces were able to ensure that construction progressed and she was floated in her construction dock in the spring of 1941. On 28 August of that year, still incomplete, she was targeted in a British air raid on

Schiedam. She caught fire, burned out and capsized. Refloated on 25 July 1942, the *Zuiderdam* was laid up at Rotterdam. Two years later she was towed to Maasluis in the Nieuwe Waterweg, where she was scuttled on 22 September 1944, at the time of the German withdrawal, in order to block access to the port of Rotterdam. The *Zuiderdam* was raised on 13 November 1946 but, assessed as being beyond economic recovery, she was sold for breaking-up at Ghent in April 1948. Casualties: not known, either in the bombing raid or when scuttled

Sister ship to the *Westerdam*, the *Zuiderdam* was less lucky than her consort, for she did not survive the ravages of the Second World War, thanks to the determined efforts of the Dutch Resistance. *LL von Münching*

LOSSES OF PASSENGER SHIPS BELOW 2,500 GROSS TONS WITH MORE THAN 100 CASUALTIES

NB. Length dimensions may be either overall or between perpendicular

NAME	YEAR BUILT	FORMER NAMES	OWNER	BUILDER	YARD No	GRT	LENGTH ft (m)	LOSS				
								Date	Place/Position	Cause	Casualties	Survivors
AMAZON	1851		Royal Mail Line, UK	R.&H. Green, Blackwall	289	2,256	300 (91.4)	4/1/1852	110 miles west-southwest of Scilly Isles	Fire	104	59
ANGLIA	1900		London & North Western Railway, UK	William Denny, Dumbarton	619	1,862	329 (100.3)	17/11/1915	1 mile east of Folkestone Gate, Kent (51.02N, 01.19E)	Mine	134	250+
ANGLO.SAXON	1856	ex Saxon	Allan Line, UK	William Denny, Dumbarton	56	1,673	283 (86.3)	27/4/1863	Clam Cove, 4.5 miles north of Cape Race	Stranded	237	208
ANNIBAL BENEVOLO	1905	ex Commandante Alvim (1931) ex Ray Barbosa (1923) ex Jupiter (1917)	Lloyd Brasileiro, Brazil	Reiherstiegwerft, Hamburg	415	1,905	269 (82.0)	16/8/1942	Off coast of Brazil (11.41S, 37.21W)	Torpedoed by U507	159	4
ARDENA	1915	ex HMS Peony (1919)	Navigation Const. Toyias, Greece	A. McMillan, Dumbarton	462	1,092	267 (81.4)	27/9/1943	Off Argostoli (Argostolion), Cephalonia	Mine	~280
AUSTRIA	1857		Hamburg Amerika Line, Germany	Caird, Greenock	55	2,383	320 (97.5)	13/9/1858	Mid-Atlantic	Fire	471	67
BARON GAUTSCH	1908		Lloyd Austriaco, Austria	Gourlay, Dundee	229	2,069	270 (82.3)	13/8/1914	7 miles north of Brioni Islands, Adriatic Sea	Mine	177	159
BERLIN	1894		Great Eastern Railway, UK	Earle's, Hull	379	1,775	302 (92.2)	21/2/1907	Off North Pier, Hook of Holland, Netherlands	Stranded	144	15
BLENHEIM	1923		A/S Ganger Rolf, Norway	Nylands Voerksted, Kristiania	268	1,807	255 (77.8)	22/4/1941	Southeast of Repvagreset, Porsangerfjord, Norway	Fire & Explosion	138	?
BORUSSIA	1854		Dominion Line, UK	Caird, Greenock	38	2,349	292 (89.0)	02/12/1879	Atlantic Ocean	Foundered	169	15
CABO MACHICHACO	1882	ex Benisaf (1886)	Ybarra & Cia, Spain	Schlesinger Davis, Wallsend-on-Tyne	121	1,689		03/11/1893	Santander, Spain	Fire & Explosion	500	?
CAMBRIA	1869		Anchor Line, UK	R. Duncan, Port Glasgow	39	2,141	325 (99.1m)	19/10/1870	Near Inishtrahull Island, 10 miles from Donegal	Stranded	169	1
CAMORTA	1880		British India Line, UK	A.& J. Inglis, Pointhouse, Glasgow	160	2,119	285 (86.9)	6/5/1902	Baragua Flats, Irrawaddy (Ayeyarwady) River, Burma	Foundered	739	0
CARIBOU	1925		Newfoundland Government, Canada	New Waterway SB Co, Schiedam	130	2,223	266 (81.1)	14/10/1942	Cabot Strait (47.19N, 59.29W)	Torpedoed by U69	136	101
CEBU CITY	1972		Williams Lines Inc, Philippines	Niigata Engineering Co, Niigata	1085	2,452	324 (98.8)	1/12/1994	Manila Bay (14.33N, 120.41E)	Collision with Kota Suria	~145	?
CENTRAL.AMERICA	1852		G. Law & Co, USA	William H. Webb, New York	?	2,141	278 (84.7)	11/9/1857	Off Atlantic coast of United States	Foundered	427	151
CITY OF BOSTON	1864		Inman Line, UK	Tod & MacGregor, Meadowside, Glasgow	131	2,278	332 (101.2)	28/1/1870	Atlantic Ocean	Missing	177	0
CITY OF GLASGOW	1850		Inman Line, UK	Tod & MacGregor, Meadowside, Glasgow	57	1,610	237 (72.2)	17/3/1854	Atlantic Ocean	Missing	480	0
CORREGIDOR	1911	ex Engadine (1933)	Fernandez Hermanos Inc, Philippines	William Denny, Dumbarton	955	1,881	316 (96.3)	17/12/1941	Near Manila Bay (14.30N, 120.45E)	Mine	~500	?

NAME	YEAR BUILT	FORMER NAMES	OWNER	BUILDER	YARD No	GRT	LENGTH ft (m)	LOSS			Casualties	Survivors
								Date	Place/Position	Cause		
CRESTED EAGLE	1925		General Steam Navigation Co, UK	J. Samuel White, Cowes, Isle of Wight	1621	1,110	300 (91.4)	29/5/1940	Off Dunkirk (German aircraft)	Bombs	300+	~300
DAIJIN MARU	1900		Osaka Shosen Kaisha, Japan	Kawasaki, Kobe	16	1,576	244 (74.3)	2/2/1916	Off Chelang Point, 80 miles from Swatow	Collision with Linan	160	21
DANIEL STEINMAN	1875	ex Khedive (1877)	White Cross Line	Cockerill, Hoboken	190	1,785	278 (84.6)	3/4/1884	Broad Breaker, Sambro Island, Halifax, Nova Scotia	Foundered	124	~9
DONA JOSEFINA	1968	ex Kamishibo Maru (1980)	Carlos A Gothong Lines, Philippines	Mitsubishi, Shimonoseki	663	1,067	235 (71.6)	24/4/1986	Visayan Sea, off Sacay Point, Leyte	Foundered	194	220
DONIZETTI	1928		Tirrenia Soc. Anon. di Nav, Italy	Cantieri Navale Triestino, Monfalcone	195	2,428	294 (89.6)	23/9/1943	Southwest of Rhodes	Gunfire from HMS Eclipse and Fury	1,800	0
DON JUAN	1971		Negros Navigation Co, Philippines	Niigata Engineering Co, Niigata	1031	2,311	314 (95.7)	22/4/1980	Off Mindoro, Philippines (12.51N, 121.54E)	Collision with Tacloban City	121+	896
DRESDEN [as LOUVAIN]	1897		Great Eastern Railway, UK	Earle's, Hull	410	1,830	302 (92.1)	20/1/1918	Kelos Strait, Aegean (37.38N, 24.10E)	Torpedoed by UC22	224	?
EASTLAND	1903		Eastland Navigation Co, USA	Jenks Shipbuilding, Port Huron	25	1,961	265 (80.8)	24/7/1915	Chicago River, Chicago	Capsized	844	~1,690
GENERAL CHANZY	1892	ex Biarritz (launch name)	Cie Générale Transatlantique (French Line), France	Penhöet, St. Nazaire	?	2,299	341 (103.9)	10/2/1910	Off Point Llosa, northwest Minorca	Stranded & boiler explosion	159	1
GIANG BEE	1908	ex Reijniersz (1939)	Heap Eng. Moh Steamship Co, UK	Stoomb. Maats. Fijenoord, Rotterdam	220	1,697	270 (82.4)	13/2/1942	In the Bangka Strait between the islands of Bangka and Belitung	Bombs (Japanese aircraft)	223	22+
HSIN WAH	1921		China Merchants Steam Navigation Co, UK	Napier & Miller, Old Kilpatrick	236	1,940	270 (82.3)	16/1/1929	Off Waglan Island, China	Stranded	401	28
HSIN YU	1889	ex Li Yu (1895) ex Hsin Yu (1894)	China Merchants Steam Navigation Co, UK	Napier, Shanks & Bell, Yoker	47	1,377	250 (76.2)	22/4/1916	Off south coast of Chusan Island, China	Collision with Hai Yung	1,000	?
HUNGARIAN	1859		Allan Line, UK	William Denny, Dumbarton	70	2,187	298 (90.8)	20/2/1860	Cape Sable, Nova Scotia	Foundered	237	0
KIANG KWAN	1876		China Merchants Steam Navigation Co, UK	A.&J. Inglis, Pointhouse, Glasgow	126	1,647	230 (70.1)	25/4/1918	Off Hankow (Hankou - now Wuhan), China	Collision with Chutsai	500	?
KJOBENHAVN	1918	ex Regina (1943)	Det Forenede Dampskibs Selskab (DFDS), Denmark	Helsingors Vaerft, Elsinore	155	1,668	270 (82.1)	11/6/1948	4 miles S of Aalborg Bay lightship, 15 miles off coast of Jutland	Mine	141	261
KOW SHING	1883		Indo-China Steam Navigation Co, UK	Barrow Shipbuilding Co, Barrow-in-Furness	104	2,134	250 (76.2)	20/7/1894	Asian Strait, Korea	Torpedo & gunfire (Japanese warships)	~1,550	45
LA SEYNE	1870	ex Etoile du Chili (1876)	Messageries Maritimes, France	La Seyne	?	2,379	312 (95.1)	14/11/1909	Near Pulo Sauh, Rheo Straits, Singapore	Collision with Onda	101	61
LE JOOLA	1990		Government of Republic of Senegal	Germersheim Schiffswerft, Germersheim	847	2,087	261 (79.5)	26/9/2002	Off Gambia, West Africa	Capsized	970	~80
LIBAN	1882		Fraissinet Cie, France	Robert Napier, Govan	383	2,308	300 (91.5)	7/6/1903	Off Ile Marie, near Marseilles	Collision with Insulaire	~100	140+
NIL	1864		Messageries Maritimes, France	La Seyne	?	1,040		20/3/1874	Near Izo, Inland Sea, Japan	Stranded	142	43
PAGANINI	1928		Tirrenia SpA, Italy	Cantieri Navali Triestino, Monfalcone	194	2,427	294 (89.6)	28/6/1940	12 miles off Durazzo (41.27N, 19.11E)	Fire & Explosion	220	~700
PORTLAND	1891		Portland Steam Packet Co, USA	New England Shipbuilding Co, Bath, Maine	?	2,284	291 (88.7)	27/11/1898	Off Cape Ann, Truro, Massachusetts	Foundered	192	0

NAME	YEAR BUILT	FORMER NAMES	OWNER	BUILDER	YARD No	GRT	LENGTH ft (m)	LOSS				
								Date	Place/Position	Cause	Casualties	Survivors
PRESIDENT	1840		British & American Steam Navigation Co, UK	Curling & Young	?	1,863	275 (83.8)	*11/3/1841*	Atlantic Ocean	Missing	136	0
PRINCESS SOPHIA	1912		Canadian Pacific Railway, UK	Bow, McLachlan, Paisley, Glasgow	272	2,320	245 (74.7)	25/10/1918	Vanderbilt Reef, Lynn Channel, Alaska	Stranded	346	0
SANTA ISABEL	1916		Cia. Transatlantica, Spain	Sociedad Española de Construccion Navale, Matagorda	43	2,488	291 (88.7)	2/1/1921	Salvora island, Arosa Bay, Spain	Stranded	210	56
SARDINIAN	1888	ex *Paolo V* (1902) ex *Gulf of Corcorado* (1899)	Ellerman Lines, UK	Hawthorn, Leslie, Hebburn-on-Tyne	280	2,492	310 (94.5)	25/11/1908	Riscoli Rocks, Malta	Fire & beached	121	31+
SAVE	1951		Cia Nacional de Navegacao, Portugal	Grangemouth Dockyard, Grangemouth	494	2,037	259 (78.9)	9/7/1961	10 miles south of Quelemane, Mozambique	Fire, stranded & explosions	259	290
SENOPATI NUSANTARA	1969	ex *Kurushima I* (1996) ex *Naruto Maru* (1996)	PT Prima Vista, Indonesia	Taguma Zosen KK, Innoshima	75	2,178	253 (77.2)	29/12/1906	24 miles off Jepara, Mandalika Island, Java	Foundered	394+	245
SHIUN [SIUN] MARU	1947		Japanese National Railways	Harima, Aioi	370	1,449		11/5/1955	Off Takamatsu, Seto Inland Sea	Collision with *Uko Maru*	168	?
SIR HARVEY ADAMSON	1914		British India Line, UK	A.&J. Inglis, Pointhouse, Glasgow	306	1,030	220 (67.0)	*17/4/1947*	Off coast of Burma - last seen 13.13N, 97.36E	Missing	269	0
STELLA	1890		London & South Western Railway, UK	J.&G. Thomson, Clydebank	252	1,059	253 (77.1)	30/3/1899	Black Rock, off Casquets, Channel Islands	Foundered	112	105
SULTANA	1863	USA	J. Lithoberry, Cincinnati, Ohio		?	1,719		23/04/1865	Tagleman's Landing, near Memphis, Mississippi River	Explosion & fire (sabotage?)	1,653	741
TEUTON	1869	ex *Glenartney* (1873)	Union Line, UK	William Denny, Dumbarton	135	2,313	350 (106.7)	30/8/1881	4 miles off Quoin Point, Cape Agulhas	Foundered	236	36
TUCK YUE	1887	ex *Obio* (1907) ex *Obio No 1* (1905) ex *Obio* (1905) ex *Australind* (1904)	China Commercial Steam Navigation Co, UK	Blackwood & Gordon, Port Glasgow	212	1,019	225 (68.5)	28/11/1913	Near Port Arthur	Stranded	174	22
VALENCIA	1882		Pacific Coast Steamship Co, USA	William Cramp, Philadelphia	228	1,598		22/1/1906	Off Cloose, California	Foundered	120	34
VYNER BROOKE	1928		Sarawak Steamship Co, UK	Ramage & Ferguson, Leith	264	1,670	241 (73.4)	12/2/1942	15 miles north of Muntok, Banka Strait	Bombs (Japanese aircraft)	125	122

Dates in *italics* = date last seen

OTHER SIGNIFICANT LOSSES INVOLVING SMALLER LAKE, RIVER AND ESTUARY PASSENGER VESSELS:

NAME	YEAR BUILT	FORMER NAMES	OWNER	BUILDER	YARD No	GRT	LENGTH ft (m)	LOSS Date	Place/Position	Cause	Casualties	Survivors
BUKOBA	1979		Tanzania Railways Corpn.	Fulton, Ruisbroek	116	800	195 (59.5)	21/5/1996	Lake Victoria, Tanzania	Capsized	500+	132
EBISU [YEBISHU] MARU	1935		Kobe Sanbashi KK, Japan	Kasado Dockyard, Suitakeminami		424	162 (49.2m)	29/10/1946	Off Chinnampo (Nampo), Korea	Struck wreck & broke in three	497	?
GENERAL SLOCUM	1891		Knickerbocker Steamboat Co, USA	Devine & Burtis, Brooklyn, New York	?	1,284	236 (71.9)	15/6/1904	East River, New York	Fire	957	251
G.P. GRIFFITH	1847			D. Stebbins, Maumee, Ohio	?	587	193 (58.8)	17/6/1850	Off mouth of Chagrin River, 20 miles east of Cleveland	Fire	ca 320	ca 35
LADY ELGIN	1851		Hubbard & Co, USA	Bidwell & Banta, Buffalo	?	1,000	300 (91.4)	7/9/1860	Off Winnetka, Illinois, on Lake Michigan	Collision with *Augusta*	297	113
PRINCESS ALICE	1865	ex *Bute* (1870)	London Steamboat Co, UK	Caird, Greenock	123	251	219 (66.8)	3/9/1878	Gallions Reach, River Thames, London	Collision with *Bywell Castle*	640	200+
RAMDAS	1936		Indian Cooperative Navigation & Trading Co, UK	Swan Hunter & Wigham Richardson, Low Walker, Tyneside	1494	406	171 (52.1)	17/7/1947	South of Bombay (Mumbai), (18.51N, 72.52E)	Capsized	625	?
WAVERLEY	1889		London, Midland & Scottish Railway, UK	A&J Inglis, Pointhouse, Glasgow	257	537	235 (71.6)	29/5/1940	Off Dunkirk	Bombs (German aircraft)	~350	250+

Based upon the testimonies of survivors, this graphic illustration shows the sinking of the *Amazon*, an early victim of fire at sea. *Illustrated London News*

One of the worst disasters of the mid-19th century, when powered propulsion of ocean-going vessels was still in its infancy, the loss of the *Austria* remains the worst maritime tragedy attributed to an outbreak of fire. *Hapag-Lloyd*

The Lloyd Austriaco's *Baron Gautsch* was a mine victim early in the First World War. She is seen here, on the right, with the *Prinz Hohenlohe* to the left. *LL von Münching*

Many of the early American-flag passenger steamships were engaged in east-to-west-coast voyages at the time of the California gold-rush. The *Central America* was employed in this service at the time of her loss in September 1857 dramatically depicted in this painting. *Author's collection*

274   Passenger Ship Disasters

The one-time cross-Channel ferry *Engadine* was lost in the Philippines under the name *Corregidor*.
Chris Bancroft collection

One of the largest paddle steamers to operate on the River Thames and the estuary, together with fleet-mate *Royal Eagle*, was the excursion steamer *Crested Eagle*. A novel feature was her telescopic funnel, which could be lowered to give her clearance under London's bridges. *J. Samuel White*

Tirrenia Line's passenger-cargo ship *Donizetti* was sunk while serving as a troop transport. Her passenger accommodation was limited to only a small number of berths.
M. Cicogna collection, Trieste

The worst ever disaster on the Great Lakes involved the passenger steamer *Eastland*, which ran both regular services across Lake Michigan to South Haven and excursion trips from Chicago. *Eastland Disaster Historical Society*

Often heavily overloaded and known as a 'tender' ship, the *Eastland* capsized at her pier near Clark Street Bridge, in the Chicago River, on 24 July 1915 as she was departing on a chartered picnic cruise for employees of Western Electric. She had some 2,500 passengers on board.
Eastland Disaster Historical Society

French Line's *General Chanzy*, lost in February 1910 on the coast of Minorca. *Author's collection*

An artist's impression of the Allan Line's *Hungarian* sinking in extraordinarily wild seas. *H. B. Christiansen Collection / Online Transport Archive*

The Canadian Pacific coastal steamship *Princess Sophia* was built for the Alaska route as well as the Vancouver to Victoria night service. *Library & Archives of Canada*

The *Princess Sophia* stranded on Vanderbilt Reef, Alaska, on 24 October 1918. *Library & Archives of Canada*

Ellerman Lines' *Sardinia*, which was stranded off Malta, operated a pilgrim service to Mecca via Alexandria, carrying passengers on deck. *Real Photos*

The British India Line passenger vessel *Sir Harvey Adamson* ran a coastal service from Rangoon to Tavoy and Mergui. *British India Line*

The London & South Western Railway's passenger steamer *Stella* was lost on the Casquets Rocks while bound for Guernsey on a scheduled passage from Southampton. At the time she was full of Easter holidaymakers on a day round-trip. *World Ship Society*

Ablaze following the explosion aboard her, this impression of the incident shows smoke pouring from the side-wheel river steamer *Sultana* while hundreds of Union soldiers, being repatriated as the American Civil War drew to a close, struggled in the water. It was the heaviest loss of life associated with a disaster to a river passenger vessel. *Author's collection*

The *Teuton* was acquired from the Glen Line for the Southampton to Cape Town service. Soon after the order had been given to abandon her on 30 August 1881, her second and third bulkheads gave way with catastrophic suddenness, and within seconds she was sinking vertically. Only those who had boarded the first lifeboat survived. *British & Commonwealth Shipping*

Bearing a celebrated name, perpetuated today by her 60-year-old namesake which is still making an annual programme of coastal cruises, the *Waverley* of 1889 was one of the most popular of the Clyde paddle steamers. *Maritime Photo Library*

APPENDIX 2

LOSSES TO WARTIME TRANSPORTS (CARGO-PASSENGER OR NON-PASSENGER) WITH MORE THAN 250 CASUALTIES

Passenger Categories (CAT):   CAS = Casualties (Hospital Ship), NFL = Native Forced Labour, POW = Prisoners-of-War, REF = Refugees, TRP = Troops

NB. Length dimensions may be either overall or between perpendiculars

NAME	YEAR BUILT	CAT.	FORMER NAMES	OWNER	BUILDER	YARD NO	GRT	LENGTH ft (m)	LOSS			Casualties	Survivors
									Date	Place/Position	Cause		
ADEN MARU	1919	TRP		Ono Shoji Gomei Kaisha, Japan	Kawasaki Dockyard, Kobe	459	5,824	385 (117.3)	6/5/1944	Celebes Sea (02.43N, 124.07E)	Torpedoed by USS *Gurnard*	App. 9,000 with *Tajima* and *Tensbinzan Marus*	0
ANDREA GRITTI	1939	TRP		Soc. Italiano di Armamento (Sidarma), Italy	Cantieri Riuniti dell'Adriatico, Montfalcone	1231	6,338	440 (134.1)	3/9/1941	60 miles east of Augusta, Sicily (37.33N, 16.26E)	Bombs & Torpedo (British aircraft)	347	?
ANDROS	1910	REF	ex *Ascensione* (1926) ex *Catania* (1923)	Deutsche Levante Linie (HAPAG), Germany	AG 'Neptun', Rostock	300	2,996	321 (97.8)	12/5/1945	At Swinemünde	Bombs (Allied aircraft)	570	?
ARISAN MARU	1944	POW		Mitsui Sempaku KK, Japan	Mitsui, Tamano	376	6,886	450 (137.0)	24/10/1944	Bashi Strait, 200 miles north west of Luzon	Torpedoed by USS *Snook*	1,792	8
BAHIA LAURA	1918	TRP	ex *Rabenfels* (1938) ex *Slavic Prince* (1926)	Hamburg Sud-Amerika Line, Germany	Palmers, Hebburn-on-Tyne	865	8,561	448 (136.7)	30/8/1941	West of Seloen Island, Norway (70.35N, 21.45E)	Torpedoed by HMS *Trident*	ca. 450	1,289 (with *Donau*)
BENALBANACH	1940	TRP		Ben Line, UK	Charles Connell, Scotstoun	429	7,153	436 (135.0)	6/1/1943	East of Algiers (37.07N, 04.38E)	Torpedo (German aircraft)	410	ca. 50
BENJAMIN CONTEE	1942	POW		US War Shipping Administration, USA	Delta Shipbuilding Co, New Orleans	6	7,175	442 (134.6)	16/8/1943	Off Bone, Algeria	Torpedo (German aircraft)	264	1,536+
BREMERHAVEN	1921	CAS	ex *Reventazon* (1936)	Union' Handelsu. Schiff GmbH, Germany	Workman Clark, Belfast	369	5,394	400 (122.0)	31/10/1944	In Danzig (Gdansk) Bay (55.04N, 18.25E)	Bombs (Russian aircraft)	410	?
CAP GUIR	1927	REF	ex *Almazora* (1936)	Gerance d'Armement, France	R. Duncan, Port Glasgow	376	1,536	272 (82.9)	16/4/1945	Off Oland, Baltic Sea	Torpedo (aircraft)	774	?
DONAU	1939	TRP		Flensburger Dampf. Harald Schulte & Co, Germany	Neptunwerft, Rostock	476	2,931	332 (101.2)	30/8/1941	West of Seloen Island, Norway (70.35N, 21.45E)	Torpedoed by HMS *Trident*	ca. 1,250	1,289 (with *Babia Laura*)
EIFEL	1924	REF	ex *Rheingold* (1929)	Rabien & Stadtlander, Germany	Schichau, Elbing	1132	1,429	238 (72.4)	17/2/1945	25 miles off Libau	Bombs	785	?
ENOURA MARU	1944	POW		Nippon Yusen Kaisha, Japan	Mitsubishi, Kobe	677	6,968	450 (137.3)	9 & 21/1/1945	At buoy no.9 & wharf no. 14, Takao, Formosa (Taiwan)	Bombs (US carrier aircraft)	316	~754
GOTTINGEN	1944	REF		Norddeutscher Lloyd, Germany	Flenderwerft, Lübeck-Siems	345	6,267		23/2/1945	Southwest of Libau, Baltic Sea (56.18N, 20.16E)	Torpedoed by Russian submarine	1,000	?
GOYA	1942	REF		A/S J. Ludwig Möwinckels Rederi, Norway	Akers Mek. Verksted, Oslo	479	5,230	430 (131.1)	16/4/1945	North of Rixhoft, Baltic Sea (55.13N, 18.20E)	Torpedoed by L3	~6,800	?
HENRY R. MALLORY [as MALLORY]	1916	TRP		Clyde-Mallory Lines, USA	Newport News Shipbuilding & Drydock Co, Newport News, Virginia	193	6,063	424 (129.3)	7/2/1943	Mid-Atlantic: approx 650 miles northwest of Ireland (55.18N, 26.29W)	Torpedoed by U402	272	225
HOFUKU MARU [aka HOHUKU, HOFOKU & TOYOFUKU MARU]	1918	POW		Kokusai Kisen KK, Japan	Kawasaki Dockyard, Kobe	423	5,857	385 (117.3)	21/9/1944	West coast of Luzon (15.25N, 199.50E)	Bombs (US carrier aircraft)	~1,047	ca. 250
IKOMA MARU	1925	POW		Nippon Yusen Kaisha, Japan	Yokohama Dockyard, Yokohama	131	3,156	353 (107.5)	21/1/1944	200 miles north of New Guinea	Torpedoed by USS *Seahorse*	461	~191

NAME	YEAR BUILT	CAT.	FORMER NAMES	OWNER	BUILDER	YARD NO	GRT	LENGTH ft (m)	Date	Place/Position	Cause	Casualties	Survivors
JUNYO [ZYUNYO] MARU	1913	POW & NFL	ex Sureway (1926) ex Hartmore (1921) ex Hartland Point (1920) ex Ardgorm (1917)	Baba Shoji KK (Sanyo Sho), Japan	R. Duncan, Port Glasgow	324	5,131	405 (123.4)	18/9/1944	Off Indrapura, Strait of Malacca (02.53S, 101.11E)	Torpedoed by HMS Tradewind	5,620	ca. 900
KARLSRUHE	1906	REF		Hamburg Amerika Line, Germany	Seebeck, Geestemünde	228	897	218 (66.3)	13/4/1945	Off Hela, Baltic Sea	Bombs	970	?
KOKAI MARU	1939	POW		Shimetani Kisen Kaisha, Japan	Hakodate Dockyard, Hakodate	109	3,871	340 (103.7)	21/2/1944	30 miles west of New Hanover, Admiralty Islands (02.30S, 150.15E)	Bombs (US aircraft)	~420	?
KOSHU [KOSYU] MARU	1937	POW	ex Taisho Maru (1940)	Chosen Yusen KK, Japan	Uraga Dockyard, Uraga	421	2,612	295 (89.9)	4/8/1944	90 miles southwest of Cape Mandhar, Celebes (03.59S, 117.54E)	Torpedoed by USS Ray	1,540	513
KOWA MARU	1940	POW		Sanko Kisen KK, Japan	Nakata, Osaka	?	1,106	212 (64.5)	21/2/1944	30 miles west of New Hanover, Admiralty Islands (02.30S, 150.15E)	Bombs (US aircraft)	ca. 350	0
LISBON MARU	1920	POW		Nippon Yusen Kaisha, Japan	Yokohama Dockyard, Yokohama	70	7,038	445 (135.6)	1/10/1942	100 miles off Ningpo (29.57N, 122.56E)	Torpedoed by USS Grouper	842	974
MEMEL	1925	REF	ex Reval (1934)	Mathies Co, Germany	Flenderwerft, Lübeck-Siems	130	1,102	221 (67.3)	31/1/1945	Off Swinemünde	Mine	600	300
MOERO	1937	CAS & REF		Cie. Maritime Belge, Belgium	Flensburger, Flensburg	435	6,111	427 (130.0)	22/9/1944	Southeast of Gotland, 60 miles southwest of Ventspils, Latvia (57.26N, 20.18E)	Bombs (Russian aircraft)	655	618
NEUWERK	1912	REF	ex Ostsee (1939) ex Palanga (1935) ex Bugsee (1929) ex Newtownards (1927)	K. Westendorf, Germany	Crown, Monkwearmouth	145	857	200 (60.8)	10/4/1945	Off Hela, Baltic Sea	Torpedo	956	?
NORDSTERN	1939	REF	ex Minna (1940) ex Minos (1940)	D.G. Neptun, Germany	Unterweser, Lehe	270	1,127	235 (71.6)	6/10/1944	60 miles southwest of Memel (Klaipeda), Lithuania	Torpedoed by Russian submarine	~450	?
PALATIA	1928	POW	ex Khusan (1941) ex Palatia (1940)	Hamburg Amerika Line, Germany	H. Koch, Lübeck	273	3,979	374 (114.0)	21/10/1942	Near Sangnvaar lighthouse, off Lindesnes, Norway	Torpedo (British aircraft)	954	180
PANANIS [as SHINYO MARU]	1894	POW	ex Chang Teh (1937) ex Tung Tuck (1937) ex Cedana (1924) ex Clan Mackay (1913)	China Hellenic Lines, UK	Naval Construction & Armaments, Barrow-in-Furness	229	2,634	312 (95.1)	7/9/1944	Sulu Sea, Phillipines (08.11N, 122.40E)	Torpedoed by USS Paddle	667	~83
PAUL HAMILTON	1942	TRP		US War Shipping Administration, USA	North Carolina Shipbuilding Co, Wilmington, North Carolina	36	7,177	442 (134.6)	20/4/1944	Off Cape Bengut, Algeria (37.02N, 03.41E)	Torpedo (German aircraft) and explosion	580	0
PRESIDENT HARRISON [as KACHIDOKI MARU ex KAKKO MARU]	1921	POW	ex Wolverine State (1923)	American President Lines, USA	New York Shipbuilding Corp, Camden, New Jersey	248	10,533	516 (157.3)	12/9/1944	50 miles east of Hainan (19.18N, 111.53E)	Torpedoed by USS Pampanito	488	ca. 410
RIGEL	1924	POW		Bergen Line (Det Bergenske D/S), Norway	Burmeister & Wain, Copenhagen	326	3,828	368 (112.2)	27/11/1944	Off Tjotta, near Helgeland	Bombs (British aircraft)	2,306	415
RYUSEI MARU	1911	POW & NFL	ex Mabubay II (1938) ex Havo (1935) ex Bra-Kar (1916)	Matsumoto Masaichi, Japan	Tyne Iron Shipbuilding Co, Willington Quay, Tyneside	177	4,797	385 (117.3)	25/2/1944	150 miles northwest of Kudat, North Borneo (07.55S, 115.15E)	Torpedoed by USS Rasher	4,998	?

NAME	YEAR BUILT	CAT.	FORMER NAMES	OWNER	BUILDER	YARD NO	GRT	LENGTH ft (m)	LOSS			Casualties	Survivors
									Date	Place/Position	Cause		
SCILLIN	1903	POW	ex Scillin Secondo (1937) ex Giuliana Pagan (1935) ex Nicole Le Borgne (1934) ex Menting (1924) ex H.M. Pellatt (1920)	Fratelli Bianchi Soc. Di Nav, Italy	Russell, Port Glasgow	511	1,579	248 (73.1)	13/11/1942	9 miles north of Kuriat, Tunisia	Gunfire & torpedoed by HMS Sahib	739	?
SEBASTIANO VENIER	1940	POW		Soc. Italiano di Armamento (Sidarma), Italy	Cantieri Riuniti dell'Adriatico, Monfalcone	1233	6,310	452 (137.6)	9/12/1941	5 miles south of Navarino and wrecked at Cape Methoni	Torpedoed by HMS Porpoise	320	1,800
SINFRA	1929	TRP	ex Sandhamn (1939) ex Fernglen (1934)	Cyprien Fabre Line, France	Akers Mek. Verksted, Oslo	434	4,470	385 (117.4)	19/10/1943	Suda Bay, Crete	Bombs (British aircraft)	2,098	566
SUEZ MARU [aka Prison Ship PS45]	1919	POW		Kurihayashi Shosen Kaisha, Japan	Uraga Dock Co, Uraga	150	4,646	360 (109.7)	29/11/1943	Northeast of the Kangean Islands, Java (06.22 S, 116.35 E)	Torpedoed by USS Bonefish	548	? (0 PoWs)
TAIHEI MARU	1928	TRP		Daido Kaiun Kaisha, Japan	Mitsui, Tamano	146	6,285	413 (126.0)	9/7/1944	Approx. 150 miles east of Sakhalin (51.19N, 155.43E)	Torpedoed by USS Sunfish	956	ca. 1,044
TAJIMA [TAZIMA] MARU	1916	TRP		Nippon Yusen Kaisha, Japan	Kawasaki Dockyard, Kobe	380	6,995	445 (135.6)	6/5/1944	50 miles northwest of Menado, Celebes (02.24N, 124.07E)	Torpedoed by USS Gurnard	Approx. 9,000 with Aden and Tenshinzan Marus	0
TAMAHOKO MARU [aka TAMABOKO & TAMABOKU MARU]	1919	POW	ex Yone Maru (1930)	Kaiyo Kisen Kaisha (Chugai Shosen), Japan	Harima Dockyard, Aioi	11	6,780	425 (129.5)	24/6/1944	Off Shimodo, Nagasaki Bay, Japan (32.24N, 129.38E)	Torpedoed by USS Tang	560	212
TENSHINZAN MARU	1944	TRP		Mitsui Sempaku KK, Japan	Mitsui, Tamano	353	6,886	450 (137.0)	6/5/1944	50 miles northwest of Menado, Celebes (02.24N, 124.07E)	Torpedoed by USS Gurnard	Approx. 9,000 with Aden and Tajima Marus	0
THIELBEK	1940	POW		Knohr & Burchard, Germany	Lübecker, Lübeck	382	2,815	345 (105.0)	3/5/1945	Bay of Lübeck	Bombs (British aircraft)	2,414	ca. 50
TOENJOEK [as TANGO MARU]	1926	POW	ex Rendsburg (1940)	Nederlandsche Indische Co, The Netherlands	Vulcan-Werke, Hamburg	639	6,200	450 (137.2)	25/2/1944	150 miles northwest of Kudat, North Borneo (07.46S, 115.09E)	Torpedoed by USS Rasher	3,000	ca. 500
TOYAMA MARU	1915	TRP		Ono Shoji Gomei Kaisha, Japan	Mitsubishi, Nagasaki	243	7,089	462 (140.8)	29/6/1944	Off Okinawa Island (27.47N, 129.05E)	Torpedoed by USS Sturgeon	5,400	ca. 600
TSUSHIMA [TUSIMA] MARU	1914	REF		Nippon Yusen Kaisha, Japan	Russell, Port Glasgow	666	6,754	444 (135.4)	22/8/1944	Near the island of Akusekijima, Kokara group, southern Ryukyu Islands (29.33N, 129.30E)	Torpedoed by USS Bowfin	1,508 including 767 children	59
YOSHIDA [YOSIDA] MARU No 1	1919	TRP		Yamashita Kisen Kaisha, Japan	Asano Dockyard, Asano	8	5,425	400 (121.9)	26/4/1944	Off W coast of Luzon Island, Philippines (18.06N, 119.40E)	Torpedoed by USS Jack	3,000	0

The majority of the ship losses in this table occurred either as part of the infamous Japanese 'HellShip' transportation practices or during Operation 'Hannibal', the evacuation of Germany's eastern territories.

The Sidarma cargo ship *Andrea Gritti* was lost while carrying Italian troops. *M. Cicogna collection, Trieste*

Originally owned by Prince Lines as the *Slavic Prince*, the *Bahia Laura* was lost with the Flensburger Dampf cargo ship *Donau*, while both were carrying German troops to Norway. *WZ-Bilddienst*

The Danish cargo ship *Goya*, with her sister *Molda*, was seized by the German authorities following the occupation of Denmark. The *Goya* was lost with almost 7,000 refugees in one of the worst wartime disasters, ensuring that this otherwise ordinary vessel would be forever remembered. *Arnold Kludas*

The cargo ship *Hofuku Maru*, photographed in the Panama Canal on 11 September 1937. She was sunk while serving as a 'Hell-ship', carrying Allied prisoners of war.
US Naval Historical Center

The Clyde-Mallory Line steamer *Henry R. Mallory* had only 35 small passenger cabins providing accommodation for a maximum of 75 passengers, but as a Second World War troop transport she carried a far larger complement. Her loss in February 1943 with 272 casualties was only exceeded by that of the *Dorchester* as an American-flag victim of the war at sea. *Northrop Grumman Shipbuilding*

The *Ikoma Maru* was categorised as a passenger-cargo ship, having limited cabin space. She too was engaged as a prisoner of war transport. *Nippon Yusen Kaisha*

The cargo ship *Lisbon Maru* was sunk while transporting Allied prisoners of war to Moji via Hong Kong and Shanghai.
Nippon Yusen Kaisha

Sold to the USSR in 1941 and renamed *Khasan*, the cargo ship *Palatia* was recovered under her original name after war broke out between Russia and Germany in 1941. She was lost while transporting German troops to Norway. *World Ship Society*

The former American President Lines' *President Harrison* was sunk as the *Kachidoki Maru* after she had been captured by the Japanese. She is seen arriving in the Philippines from Shanghai before the outbreak of the Pacific War, carrying the US 4th Marine Regiment. *US Marine Corps*

The worst shipping disaster involving a Norwegian ship was the sinking of the cargo ship *Rigel*, while in German hands, in November 1944. At the time she was heavily overloaded with prisoners of war. *Bjørn Pedersen*

The Sidarma cargo ship *Sebastiano Venier* is seen fitting out. She was torpedoed while she was transporting Italian troops. *M. Cicogna collection, Trieste*

One of the worst atrocities of the Pacific War occurred when the cargo ship *Suez Maru*, on passage to Java with Allied prisoners of war, was torpedoed and sunk. In the wake of the sinking, the Captain of the escorting minesweeper ordered his crew to machine-gun hundreds of prisoners who had survived but were struggling in the sea. Photographs of the *Suez Maru* are very few and indistinct. *Allan Jones*

From a different perspective, an equally harrowing loss of the Pacific War was that of the *Tsushima* [*Tusima*] *Maru*, torpedoed and sunk while ferrying refugees from Okinawa to the Japanese main islands. The majority of the refugees were schoolchildren, 767 of whom were killed. The disaster remains the worst ever at sea involving child victims.
Author's collection

APPENDIX 3

PASSENGER VESSELS LOST EN ROUTE TO THE BREAKERS

NB. Length dimensions may be either overall or between perpendiculars

NAME	YEAR BUILT	FORMER NAMES	OWNER	BUILDER	YARD NO	GRT	LENGTH ft (m)	LOSS		
								Date	Place/Position	Cause
AEGAEON	1911	ex *Princess Alice* (1949)	Typaldos Lines, Greece	Swan Hunter & Wigham Richardson, Wallsend-on-Tyne	883	3,099	290 (88.4)	2/12/1966	At Civitavecchia, Italy	Stranded in tow
AMBULOMBO	1935	ex *Affan Oceana* (1966) ex *Ambulombo* (1965) ex *Manoora* (1961)	PT Perusahaan Pelajaram 'Arafat', Indonesia	Alexander Stephen, Linthouse, Glasgow	540	11,111	482 (146.9)	18/11/1972	Off Luzon, Philippines (18.19N, 120.34E)	Foundered in tow
BONAIRE STAR	1957	ex *Babama Star* (1975) ex *New Babama Star* (1972) ex *Miami* (1968) ex *Jerusalem* (1966)		Deutsche Werft, Finkenwerder, Hamburg	717	9,920	488 (148.7)	3/10/1979	Southeast of Hawaii (18.30N, 154.17W)	Foundered in tow
BRITANIS [as BELOFIN I]	1932	ex *Lurline* (1970) ex *Matsonia* (1963) ex *Monterey* (1956)	Belfin AG, Panama (Chandris Lines, Greece)	Bethlehem Shipbuilding Corp, Quincy, Massachusetts	1441	24,346	641 (195.5)	21/10/2000	50 miles west of Cape Town	Foundered in tow
CARIBIA	1949	ex *Columbia* (1968), ex *Caronia* (1968)	Universal Line, Panama	John Brown, Clydebank	635	25,794	715 (217.9)	12/8/1974	Near Apra Harbour, Guam	Stranded in tow
COLONIAL [as BISCO 9]	1908	ex *Assyria* (1929) ex *Ypiranga* (1921)	Companhia Colonial, Portugal	Krupp Germania, Kiel	134	8,309	449 (136.7)	16-17/9/1950	3.5 miles north of Davaar Island, near Campbeltown, Firth of Clyde	Broke tow and stranded
CONSTITUTION	1951	ex *Oceanic Constitution* (1982) ex *Constitution* (1974)	Unspecified owners, USA	Bethlehem Shipbuilding Corp, Quincy, Massachusetts	1619	20,199	682 (208.0)	17/11/1997	770 miles north of Honolulu	Foundered in tow
COPA CASINO	1951	ex *Pride of Galveston* (1993) ex *Pride of Mississippi* (1991) ex *Atlas* (1988) ex *Waterman* (1972) ex *Ryndam* (1968)	USA	Wilton-Fijenoord, Schiedam	732	15,015	503 (153.4)	16/3/2003	Off the Dominican Republic	Foundered in tow
FILIPINAS SAUDI I	1939	ex *Saudi Phil I* (1980) ex *Regina Magna* (1977) ex *Bremen* (1972) ex *Pasteur* (1959)	Philsimport International, Hong Kong	Penhöet, St. Nazaire	R8	23,801	697 (212.4)	9/6/1980	Indian Ocean, approx. 650 miles east of Somalia (07.35N, 60.12E)	Cut loose from tow and foundered
HELVETIA	1864		National Line, UK	Palmers, Jarrow	154	4,588	419 (127.7)	4/1894	Off Cape Finisterre	Abandoned and foundered
MAHENO	1905		Union Steamship Co of New Zealand, UK	William Denny, Dumbarton	746	5,323	400 (122.0)	7-9/7/1935	60 miles southeast of Sandy Cape; on Ocean Beach, Frazer Island, Queensland	Broke tow and stranded
SEA	1957	ex *Regent Sea* (1997) ex *Samantha* (1984) ex *Navarino* (1983) ex *Gripsholm* (1974)	Lujo Cruises SA, Bahamas	Ansaldo, Sestri Ponente, Genoa	1500	23,292	631 (192.3)	12/7/2001	South of Port Elizabeth, South Africa (35.21S, 26.13E)	Foundered in tow
SUN	1964	ex *Canyon Ranch at Sea* (2001) ex *Regent Sun* (1998) ex *Royal Odyssey* (1988) ex *Doric* (1982) ex *Hanseatic* (1973) ex *Shalom* (1967)	Germany	Chantiers de L'Atlantique, St. Nazaire	Z21	17,891	628 (191.4)	25/7/2001	120 miles off Cape St. Francis, South Africa	Foundered in tow
UGANDA [as TRITON]	1952		British India Line, UK	Barclay Curle, Whiteinch, Glasgow	720	16,907	539 (164.4)	22/8/1986	Chichin, near Kaohsiung, Taiwan	Driven ashore in typhoon

Aground at Civitavecchia, the Typaldos Lines' *Aegaeon*, the former *Princess Alice* of Canadian Pacific, stranded while under tow to La Spezia for breaking-up. *H. B. Christiansen Collection / Online Transport Archive*

The Chandris liner and cruise ship *Britanis*, bearing the temporary name *Belofin I*, foundered off Cape Town while bound for the breakers' yard. *Ian Shiffman*

The *Caribia*, the one–time Cunard 'Green Goddess' *Caronia*, broke free from her tow to Kaohsiung and ended up stranded on the coast of Guam where she gradually broke up, as these dramatic pictures testify. *United States Navy*

One of the two striking passenger liners introduced by American Export Lines in the 1950s for the New York to Mediterranean service, the *Constitution* foundered while under tow to the scrapyard in Taiwan some fifty years later. *American Export Lines*

The *Filipinas Saudi I* started her career as the Cie Sud-Atlantique's *Pasteur*, later becoming the *Bremen* of Norddeutscher Lloyd. Here she is seen in another phase of her long life, as Chandris Line's *Regina Magna* during a cruise to Stockholm. *Richard de Kerbrech*

Another passenger ship lost en route to the breakers' yard was the *Sea*, formerly the *Regent Sea*. Earlier still, she was the *Navarino* (see Dictionary entry), and before that the Swedish America Line's *Gripsholm*. The *Sea* is seen here at Tampa, Florida, in May 1999. *Frank Heine FERRIES*

The British India schools cruise ship *Uganda* is seen in a photograph taken before her participation in the Falklands War as a hospital ship. *Richard de Kerbrech*

Sold for breaking up under the name *Triton*, the former *Uganda* cheated the cutter's torch when she was stranded in shallow waters near Kaohsiung, Taiwan, and broke in two. Her half-submerged wreck is seen in this photograph dating from some time after late 1989. *Frank Heine FERRIES*

BIBLIOGRAPHY AND SOURCES

Books

Barnaby, Kenneth C. *Some Ship Disasters and Their Causes*
(Hutchinson, 1967)

Bonsor, Noel R. P. *North Atlantic Seaway*
(T. Stephenson, 1955)
South Atlantic Seaway (Brookside Publications, 1983)

Braynard, Frank O. *Lives of the Liners*
(Cornell Maritime Press, 1947)

Felton, Mark *Slaughter At Sea*
(Pen & Sword Books, 2007)

Hocking, Charles *Dictionary of Disasters at Sea During the Age of Steam, 1824-1962*
(Lloyd's Register of Shipping,1969)

Hooke, Norman *Modern Shipping Disasters, 1963-1987*
(Lloyd's of London Press, 1989)

Isherwood, John H. 'Steamers of the Past' (*Journal of Commerce & Shipping Telegraph*, 1966) – also articles under the same title from *Sea Breezes*, 1949-1980s

Jones, Allan *The Suez Maru Atrocity – Justice Denied*
(privately published, 2002)

Jordan, Roger *The World's Merchant Fleets, 1939*
(Chatham Publishing, 2006)

Kadar, Wayne Louis *Great Lakes Passenger Ship Disasters*
(Avery Color Studios, 2005)

de Kerbrech, Richard P. *Ships of the White Star Line*
(Ian Allan Publishing, 2009)

Kerr, George F. *Business in Great Waters*
(Faber & Faber, 1951)

Kludas, Arnold *Great Passenger Ships of the World*
Volumes 1-6
(Patrick Stephens, 1975-1986)
Great Passenger Ships of the World Today
(Patrick Stephens, 1992)

Ledwith, F. *Ships That Go Bump in the Night*
(United Kingdom Mutual/Lloyd's, 1975)

Lenton, H. T. & Colledge, J. J. *Warships of World War II*
(Ian Allan, 1973)

Michno, Gregory F. *Death on the Hellships*
(United States Naval Institute Press, 2001)

Padfield, Peter *An Agony of Collisions*
(Hodder & Stoughton, 1966)

Rushbrook, Frank *Fire Aboard*
(The Technical Press, 1961)

Seabrook, William C. *In The War at Sea*
(1946)

Smith, Eugene W. *Passenger Ships of the World, Past and Present*
(George H. Dean, 1963)

Talbot-Booth *Merchant Ships* – various years
(Sampson, Low, Marston & Co)

Watson, Milton H. *Disasters at Sea*
(Patrick Stephens, 1987 & 1995)

White, John Baker *Sabotage is Suspected*
(Evans Brothers, 1957)

Williams, David L. *Wartime Disasters at Sea*
(Patrick Stephens, 1997)

Williams, David L. & de Kerbrech, Richard P. *Damned by Destiny*
(Teredo Books, 1982)

Winser, John de S. *Short Sea: Long War*
(World Ship Society, 1997)

Wise, James E. Jr & Baron, Scott *Soldiers Lost at Sea*
(United States Naval Institute Press, 2004)

Other documents

'British Merchant Shipping (Losses), World War I' – reprint of the document originally published by HMSO in 1919
(New Zealand Ship & Marine Society, 1966)

'British Merchant Shipping (Losses), World War II' – reprint of the document originally published by HMSO in 1947 (New Zealand Ship & Marine Society)

'British Vessels Lost at Sea, 1939-1945' – reprint of the reference books originally published by HMSO in 1947
(Patrick Stephens, 1980)

'FERRIES, das Fährschiffahrtsmagazin' produced by Deutscher Fährschiffahrtsverein e.V.

'Lloyd's List 250th Anniversary Special Supplement, 1973-1984' (Lloyd's of London Press, 1984)

'Lloyd's Maritime Atlas' (Lloyd's of London Press/ J. D. Potter Ltd, 1987)

'Lloyd's Registers of Ships' and 'Mercantile Navy Lists' – various years (Lloyd's Register of Shipping)

'Lloyd's War Losses: the First World War' – facsimile reprint of 'Casualties to Shipping Through Enemy Causes, 1914-1918' (Lloyd's of London Press, 1990)

'Lloyd's War Losses: the Second World War' – facsimile reprint (Lloyd's of London Press, 1989-1993)
Board of Trade Enquiries into Wrecks, 1876-1972

Lloyd's Loss Books (1837-1913), Lloyd's Casualty Books (1914-1982) and Lloyd's Weekly Casualty Reports (1920-present)

'ShipPax Guides' published by ShipPax Information, Halmstad, Sweden

Magazine articles and papers

'Ferries In Peril' by Dag Pike (*New Scientist*, August 1985)

'Ferry Transport: The Realm of Responsibility for Ferry Disasters in Developing Nations' by Catherine T. Lawson & Roberta E. Weisbrod (*Journal of Public Transportation*, 2005)

'The IMO Passenger Ship Safety Initiative' by Jack Westwood-Booth (*Seaways*, March 2007)

'Improving Passenger Ship Safety – A New Set of Proposed Measures' (European Commission Directorate General for Energy and Transport, 2002)

'Safety of Large Passenger Vessels' by Allan Graveson of Nautilus UK – paper presented at the International Federation of ShipMasters' Associations AGA, May 2007 (also reported under the title 'Wake-Up Calls on Cruiseship Safety' in the *NUMAST Telegraph*, June 2007)

'Stockholm Agreement – Past, Present & Future (Part I)' by Professor Dracos Vassalos & Professor Apostolos Papanikolaou

Casualty accounts from *Safety At Sea* magazine (Industrial & Marine Publications/Lloyd's Register Fairplay)

Also various articles from *Marine News*, *Navy News*, *Sea Breezes*, *Ships Monthly*, *Soviet Shipping*, *Steamboat Bill*, *This England* and the *United States Naval Institute Proceedings*

Websites

www.clydesite.co.uk/clydebuilt
www.frenchlines.com/index_en.php
www.lostliners.com
www.maib.gov.uk (Marine Accident Investigation Board)
www.miramarshipindex.org.nz
www.safetyatsea.net
www.shippax.se
www.theshipslist.com
www.uboat.net/wwi/ships_hit/
www.ubootwaffe.net/ops/shipindex.cgi

ACKNOWLEDGEMENTS

I would like to record my appreciation to the following individuals and organisations without whose assistance the realisation of this book would have been difficult, if not impossible, to achieve:
Chris Bancroft, the late Frank Braynard, Klas Brogren, Michael Cassar, Nereo Castelli, Mario Cicogna, the late Alex Duncan, John Edgington, the late Major Aldo Fraccaroli, Leo van Ginderen, Ambrose Greenway, David Hutchings, Allan Jones, Knut Klippenberg, Mike Lennon, Mick Lindsay, Bill Miller, Jim Payne, Bjørn Pedersen, Ian Rae, the late Tom Rayner, David Reed, Bettina Rohbrecht, Luca Ruffato, the late Antonio Scrimali, Ian Shiffman, Geir Svendsen, Steven Tacey, Peter Tschursch, Adrian Vicary, L. L. von Münching and Edward Wilson.
American President Lines
Association French Lines (Mélinda Guettier and Cécille Cailleteau)
Bowling Green State University, USA (Robert W. Graham)
British & Commonwealth Shipping
British Columbia Provincial Archives
Canadian Dept. of National Defence
Eastland Disaster Historical Society (Ted Wachholz)
Fleet Air Arm Museum (Susan Dearing)
Fred Olsen (Steinar Nyborg)
Furness Withy Group
Guildhall Library, City of London (home of the Lloyd's records collections)
Hamburg Sud-Amerika Linie
Hapag-Lloyd AG (Peter Maass)
Illustrated London News
Imperial War Museum (Ian Proctor)
Kawasaki Heavy Industries
Ketchikan Museums, Alaska (Richard Van Cleave)
Library & Archives of Canada (Bronwen Masemann)
Lloyds Register – Fairplay (Philip Simons)
Mariners Museum
Maritiem Museum, Rotterdam (Elisa Schouten and Pieter Jan Klapwijk)
Merseyside Maritime Museum
Mitsubishi Heavy Industries
Mitsui-OSK Lines (Yasushi Kikuchi)
National Archives of Scotland
National Maritime Museum
Nippon Yusen Kaisha (Captain Toshio Nozaki)

Northrop Grumman Shipbuilding Corporation (Mike Dillard)
Online Transport Archive (Peter Waller and Martin Jenkins)
P & O Line
Princess Cruises
Public Record Office/National Archives, Kew, London
Reuters (Kim Lee)
Smit International
Southampton Central Library
Southern Newspapers
Steamship Historical Society of America
Toronto Fire Department
Ulster Folk & Transport Museum, Cultra, Northern Ireland (Alan McCartney)
United States Coast Guard
United States National Archives, Washington, DC
US Naval Historical Center
United States Naval Institute, Annapolis, Maryland
United States Navy
University of Washington (Nancy Hines)
Wellington Evening Post
World Ship Society (in Australia: John Bone and Glen Stuart; in Canada: Skip Gilham, Glen Smith and Gordon Turner; in the United States: Andy Kilk)
Wilhelmshaven Zeitung

Special mention should be made of the help received from two correspondents who most generously made so many of their black & white and colour images freely available to me, namely Arnold Kludas and Frank Heine, and, in the latter case, the benefit of his extensive knowledge of ferry-type vessels. Also my special thanks to Mark Dickinson, the General Secretary of Nautilus International, who kindly agreed to write the Foreword.

Finally, and in particular, I would like to single out two persons who were especially helpful to me during the course of this project. First, my good friend and writing partner Richard de Kerbrech, who not only found lots of useful photographs for the book and made his extensive personal library available to me for research, but who also gave me a great deal of personal support when serious problems arose while I was compiling the contents – thank you, Dick. Second, I would like to mention Tony Smith of the World Ship Society Photo Library, who never once complained about my endless lists of picture subjects and who, with few exceptions, was able to find and supply everything I asked for.

The *Dunbar Castle* sank near the Strait of Dover in January 1940 after striking a magnetic mine. *British & Commonwealth Shipping*